"If you plan to visit Micronesia, read this book first. Having spent a year on a small coral island in the Marshall Islands, I can attest to the accuracy of this handbook. . . . "
—Michael Gee, GREAT EXPEDITIONS, Canada

"Stanley especially points out spots off the beaten track for the adventurous visitor. How about a trip to the outer islands on a field trip ship in the Marshalls? A walk around Fefan Island in the Truk Lagoon? A speedboat to and snorkel in Kayangel, Belau's northernmost atoll? Stanley's done it all, and gives you tips on how to see the most in Micronesia while spending the least."
—Giff Johnson, MARSHALL ISLANDS JOURNAL, Majuro

"In addition to being an unequalled guide to low-budget, non-imperialistic travel, Stanley's book includes more accurate and complete historical and political background than any other guidebook. Highly recommended if you want to visit the region—in person or in fantasy."
—Charles Scheiner, BELAU UPDATE, New York

"The book is worth reading for its historical perspective alone, for the author is unafraid to approach such "delicate issues" as nuclear testing and "culture clash"— topics one would not normally find in Fielding's or Birnbaum's."
—Walter Boggs, RAPA NUI JOURNAL, California

"Remarkably informative, fair-minded, sensible, and readable . . . Stanley's comments on the United States' 40-year administration are especially pungent and thought-provoking."
—Robert Langdon, THE JOURNAL OF THE POLYNESIAN SOCIETY

"The history, social outlook and personal reflections in this work make it much more than a mere travel book. Every library in Micronesia should have a copy for reference purposes, and individuals who live or plan to travel in Micronesia ought to buy a personal copy. Highly recommended."
—Mark C. Goniwiecha, PACIFIC SUNDAY NEWS, Agana, Guam

". . . a book designed for the mutual benefit of travelers and their island hosts."
—Carol O'Connor, GUAM & MICRONESIA GLIMPSES, Guam

"A companion to the previously published South Pacific Handbook, this title will enthrall you whether you have the wanderlust or not."
—Joseph Kula, THE PROVINCE, Vancouver, B.C., Canada

For the tropic stars did flame for us, just as the travel books had promised. The nights were amethyst clear and cool. Eddies of warm air, loaded with earth scents and jungle dreams from islands beyond sight enmeshed us and were gone again. The swing of the old ship was so quiet, she seemed to be poised moveless while the stars themselves were rocking to the croon of the bow-wave, back and forth above her mastheads, as we lay tranced with watching.

—Sir Arthur Grimble,
A Pattern of Islands

MICRONESIA
HANDBOOK

GUIDE TO THE CAROLINE, GILBERT, MARIANA, AND MARSHALL ISLANDS

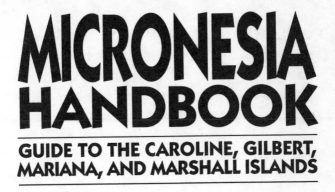

DIANA LASICH HARPER

MICRONESIA
HANDBOOK

GUIDE TO THE CAROLINE, GILBERT, MARIANA, AND MARSHALL ISLANDS

DAVID STANLEY

MOON
PUBLICATIONS INC.

MICRONESIA HANDBOOK: GUIDE TO THE CAROLINE, GILBERT, MARIANA, AND MARSHALL ISLANDS

Please send all comments, corrections, additions, amendments, and critiques to:

**DAVID STANLEY
c/o MOON PUBLICATIONS
722 WALL STREET
CHICO, CA 95928 USA**

Published by
Moon Publications Inc.
722 Wall Street
Chico, California 95928 USA
tel. (916) 345-5473

Printed by
Colorcraft Ltd., Hong Kong

PRINTING HISTORY

First Edition
Nov. 1985
Reprinted
March 1987
Second Edition
May 1989
Reprinted
April 1991
Third Edition
Sept. 1992

Library of Congress Cataloging in Publication Data

Stanley, David.
  Micronesia Handbook: guide to the Caroline, Gilbert, Mariana, and Marshall Islands/David Stanley.
      p. cm.
  Includes bibliographical references (p. 323) and index.
  ISBN 0-918373-80-8 : $11.95
  1. Micronesia—Guidebooks. I. Title.
DU500.S834 1992
919.6504—dc20
                          92-13894
                          CIP

Printed in Hong Kong

Cover photo: Belau's Rock Islands, courtesy of Gerald A. Heslinga

MICRONESIA HANDBOOK is a companion volume to the SOUTH PACIFIC HANDBOOK by David Stanley. MIKRONESIEN-HANDBUCH ,a German translation of this book, is published by Verlag Gisela E. Walther, Oppenheimerstr. 26, 2800 Bremen 44, Germany.

Although the publishers have made every effort to ensure that the information was correct at the time of going to press, the publishers do not assume and hereby disclaim any liability to any party for any loss or damage caused by errors, omissions, or any potential travel disruption due to labor or financial difficulty, whether such errors or omissions result from negligence, accident, or any other cause.

WARNING: Nothing in this book is intended to be used for navigation. Mariners are advised to consult official sailing directions and nautical charts.

CONTENTS

INTRODUCTION 1
The Land 2
Flora and Fauna 11
HIstory 16
Economy 31
The People 38
Accommodations and Food 41
Practicalities 43
Getting There and Around 52

REPUBLIC OF   M S I
THE MARSHALL ISLANDS 64
Introduction 64
Majuro and the Ratak Chain 76
The Ralik Chain 86

FEDERATED STATES
OF MICRONESIA   M I C 95
Introduction 95
State of Kosrae 101
State of Pohnpei 110
State of Chuuk 132
State of Yap 151

REPUBLIC OF BELAU . P A L . . . 167
Introduction 167
Koror 181
Other Islands 191

TERRITORY OF GUAM 200
Introduction 200
Sights of Guam 225

COMMONWEALTH OF
THE NORTHERN MARIANAS 230
Introduction 230
Saipan 241
Other Islands 252

REPUBLIC OF NAURU 260
Introduction 260
Sights of Nauru 269

REPUBLIC OF KIRIBATI 273
Introduction 273
Tarawa 288
Other Islands of Tungaru 295
The Phoenix Islands 303
The Line Islands 305

AMERICAN POSSESSIONS 309

APPENDIX 320
BOOKLIST 323
GLOSSARY 333
ALTERNATIVE PLACE NAMES . . . 336
INDEX 337

LIST OF MAPS

Abaiang	295	Koror	182
Abemama	298	Kosrae	104
Agana	212	Kwajalein	87
Air Micronesia Routes	53	Lelu Harbor, Around	106
Allied Response, The	21	Lelu Ruins	103
Angaur	197	Majuro	76
Arno	83	Maloelap	84
Bairiki	292	Marianas, The	231
Banaba	301	Marshall Islands, The	66
Belau Group, The	192	Micronesia	2
Belau, Republic of	198	Midway	310
Betio	290	Nan Madol Ruins	119
Bikenibeu	294	Nauru	265
Butaritari and Makin	297	Pacific Air Routes	54
Central Pacific, The	315	Palmyra	316
Christmas Island	306	Peleliu	195
Chuuk Lagoon	148	Pohnpei	113
Chuuk, State of	133	Puluwat	150
Colonia	161	Rota	256
Discovery and Settlement of the Pacific	18	Saipan and Tinian	242
D-U-D	79	Saipan, West Coast of	245
Enewetak	91	San Jose	252
Exclusive Economic Zones	34	Songsong	257
Fanning	305	Tabiteuea	300
Federated States of Micronesia	97	Tamuning to Tumon Bay	214
Guam	227	Tarawa	288
Jaluit	86	Tol	146
Japanese Challenge, The	20	Tonoas	144
Johnston	313	Tungaru	296
Kanton	304	Ulithi	164
Kayangel	194	Wake	311
Kiribati, Republic of	276	Weno	136
Kolonia	122	Weno, Central	138
Kolonia, Vicinity of	115	Woleai	165
		Yap Proper (Wa'ab)	156

MAP SYMBOLS

ROADS	FALLS		WATER
HIKING TRAILS	MOUNTAIN		
RAILROAD	CITY / TOWN		REEF
	POINT OF INTEREST		

LIST OF CHARTS

Belau Referenda, The 171
Capsule Kiribati Vocabulary 308
Chuuk Lagoon at a Glance, The . . 149
Chuuk's Climate 132
Federated States at a Glance 96
Guam's Climate 201
Kiribati at a Glance 275
Koror's Climate 168
Kosrae's Climate 102
Majuro's Climate 65
Marianas at a Glance 231

Marshalls at a Glance, The 65
Micronesian Postal Codes 44
Micronesian Time 43
Nauru's Climate 261
Oceania at a Glance 27
Pohnpei's Climate 111
Safety Rules of Diving 8
Saipan's Climate 232
Tarawa's Climate 274
Yap's Climate 151

ABBREVIATIONS

A$—Australian dollars
a/c—air conditioned
C—centigrade
d—double
EEZ—Exclusive
   Economic Zone
FSM—Federated States
   of Micronesia
km—kilometer
kph—kilometers per hour
LST—landing ship, tank
min.—minutes
mph—miles per hour
MV—motor vessel
no.—number
NZ—New Zealand
OW—one way

PNG—Papua New Guinea
pop.—population
pp—per person
RT—round trip
s—single
SPF—South Pacific Forum
t—triple
tel.—telephone
T.T.—Trust Territory
TTPI—Trust Territory of
   the Pacific Islands
U.S.—United States
US$—U.S. dollars
WW I—World War One
WW II—World War Two
YHA—Youth Hostel
   Association

ACKNOWLEDGEMENTS

Thanks to all the people at Moon Publications who contributed to this book: cartographers Bob Race and Brian Bardwell, designers Anne Hikido and Dave Hurst, indexer Anne-Marie Nicoara, editors Taran March, Asha Johnson, and Mark Arends.

Gordon Ohliger's drawings set the theme for each chapter: the 1946 "Baker" blast on Bikini Atoll (page 64), a reef heron enjoying the mangroves (page 95), Bird Island, Saipan (page 230), phosphate mining on Nauru Island (page 260), and a pair of Laysan albatrosses "skypointing" during a mating display on Midway Atoll (page 309), and Guam's Pacific Star Hotel (page 200). On page 167 Gordy employed the Belau storyboard technique to tell the tale of a magical breadfruit tree which gave forth fish in abundance through a broken limb in its hollow trunk. The villagers eventually became jealous of the old woman who owned the tree and chopped it down, hoping to obtain the abundance of fish for themselves. Instead, the sea surged up through the trunk and flooded the island, drowning all but the old woman. Later she gave birth to four children, who founded the villages of Aimeliik, Koror, Melekeok, and Ngeremlengui.

Many of the antique engravings included in this book were taken from M.G.L. Domeny de Rienzi's classic three-volume work *Oceanie ou Cinquième Partie du Monde* (Paris: Firmin Didot Freres, 1836).

I'm most grateful to Jack D. Haden of Australia who agreed to share his 12 years of experience in Nauru and Kiribati by thoroughly revising those chapters. As these were the only countries I didn't get to on my recent research trip (I have been to both on previous trips), Jack's help was invaluable. Similarly anthropologist Glenn H. Alcalay kindly read the Marshall Islands chapter and offered many useful suggestions.

Special thanks to Alphonse Ganang who got up very early one Sunday morning to drive the author from Maap to Yap Airport, to Masanori Inabi for his help in retrieving keys I stupidly locked in a rental car on a remote Rota beach, to Lynne and Mark Michael for information on Rota, to Nancy Vander Velde for information on corals, to Tjalling Terpstra of Amber Travel Agency, Amsterdam, Adrian Young of Air Nauru, and Thomas J. Goresch of Air Micronesia for help in updating Micronesian air routes, to Ingrid Schilsky for reading and correcting the Kiribati chapter, to Larry L. Morgan of the Office of Territorial and International Affairs, Washington, for current information on regional political development, to Margaret Argue of the South Pacific Peoples Foundation of Canada for a big box of resources, to Bill Weir for getting my computer operational, and to Ria for joining me on the trip and providing the support I needed to continue updating this book.

Thanks too to the following readers who took the trouble to write us letters about their trips: Dr. Brigitta Bayer, James Scott Bellevue, Dr. Eckhard Biechele, Jed Brown, John Connell, Randy Dyer, Regula Feitknecht, Phil Gottling, Pat Kennelly, Judy Kennon, Dale Langlois, Massimo Piras, Sir Hugh Reid, Dr. Hans Rohrer, T. Rohlen, Bernd Sauter, Charles Scheiner, Sigrid Shayer, Tahanga, Biteti Tentoa, Robert David Thompson, William S. Wakefield, Dr. James O. Whittaker, Sandra J. Whittaker, Susanne Wienhold-Meding, Mag. Martin Zausner, and Dr. Waltraud Zausner. You can have your name included here next edition for the price of a postage stamp.

**Attention Hotel Keepers,
Tour Operators, Divemasters:**

The best way to keep your listing in *Micronesia Handbook* up-to-date is to send us current information about your business. There's never any charge or obligation for a mention. Thanks to the following island tourism workers and government officials who *did* write in: Silbester N. Alfonso, Bud Bendix, Jim Clark, J.B. Collier, Romana Lynn Cruz, Carol Curtis, Lt. Commander Gregory A. Edman, Anne Fairlie, Marilou C. Fantonalgo, Patricia L. Feore, Al Ganang, Val Gavriloff, Gabrielle Hunt, Lawrence C. Janss, Jane Jennison-Williams, Leif Jonassen, Lorraine R. Jones, Walter Kamm, Bette Kirchner, Johnny P. Kishigawa, Marilyn S. Kitsu, John Meno, Cita Morei, Kaoti Onorio, Kachutosy O. Paulus, Carolyn K. Petersen, Ginger S. Porter, Reive Robb, Elieser Rospel, Cecilia Lizama Salvatore, Alistair Sands, Mary Jane Schramm, Revé Shapard, Roger G. Stillwell, Kireata Taaram, Iaram Tabureka, Sam W. Terry, Kararaua Tonana, Emily Topia, and Gus Whitcomb.

While out researching my books I find it cheaper to pay my own way, and nothing in this book is designed to repay favors from hotels, tour operators, or airlines. I prefer to arrive unexpected and uninvited, and to experience things as they really are. On the road I seldom identify myself to anyone. The companies and organizations included in this book are there for information purposes only and a mention in no way implies an endorsement.

IS THIS BOOK OUT OF DATE?

Travel writing is like trying to take a picture out the window of a bus: time frustrates the best of intentions. Things change fast—you'll understand how hard it is for us to keep up-to-date. So if something in *Micronesia Handbook* looks out-of-date, please let us hear about it. Did anything lead you astray or inconvenience you? In retrospect, what sort of information would have made your trip easier? Please share your discoveries with us. Everything will be carefully field-checked, but your lead could help us zero in on a fascinating aspect which might otherwise be overlooked.

Please be as precise and accurate as you can. Notes made on the scene are far better than later recollections. Write comments into your copy of *Micronesia Handbook* as you go along, then send us a summary when you get home. If this book helped you out, please help us make it even better. Address your letters to:

David Stanley,
c/o Moon Publications Inc.
722 Wall Street
Chico, CA 95928 USA

PREFACE

TOURISM IN MICRONESIA

Though Micronesia has yet to be fully "discovered" by the promoters of packaged consumer tourism, Guam and Saipan already figure alongside such fleshpots as Bali, Thailand, and Hawaii in the tourism markets of Tokyo, Nagoya, and Osaka. Belau is a hot new destination about to be opened to Japanese mass tourism and Pohnpei already has a big new Japanese scuba-diving operation that needs only a couple of luxury hotels nearby to become really profitable.

All this activity dates back to 1962 when the U.S. government lifted its requirement of a security clearance to visit Micronesia. Pan American Airways inaugurated direct flights from Tokyo to Guam in 1967, the same year Continental Airlines got together with local business interests to create a new joint venture, Continental Air Micronesia, which began service from Honolulu to Saipan in 1968.

Airstrips were gradually upgraded in all the district centers of the old Trust Territory of the Pacific Islands and by 1970 Air Mike's Island Hopper was calling at Majuro, Kwajalein, Pohnpei, and Chuuk (Truk) between Honolulu and Guam; feeder services flew on to Saipan, Yap, and Koror. Kosrae only became part of Continental's world in 1986 when a jet runway was dredged up from the lagoon.

To facilitate tourist movements on its services Continental built the first big hotels in Micronesia, the Truk Continental (1970), the Guam Hilton (1970), Koror's Hotel Nikko (1971), and the Saipan Hyatt Regency (1974). For various reasons Majuro, Pohnpei, and Yap never got the big hotels originally planned for them and there are still no large international tourist resorts on those islands.

It's not widely known that Guam is now the second-most-important tourist destination in the Pacific islands (after Hawaii), with three times as many tourists a year as Fiji and five times as many as Tahiti. Saipan, with much better beaches than Guam and no military bases, isn't far behind. On Guam tourism has surpassed military spending as a source of income for the territory and now tourism even conflicts with military use—the government of Guam is demanding that more of the 30% of the island's surface presently held by the military be released for airport expansion and other civilian use.

On Guam the big hotels have long been restricted to the Tumon Bay strip but with three additional high-rise hotels presently under construction at Tumon (a Holiday Inn, a Hyatt Regency, and a Hotel Nikko) hotel development has been pushed closer to downtown Agana. The 403-room Palace Hotel opened on Oca Point in 1991, just across Agana Bay from the city, and the soaring Onward Agana Beach Hotel is going up nearby. All these hotels would close within a week if Japanese tour companies stopped sending their packaged planeloads south.

The Japanese are big on golf and there are now a half dozen sprawling golf courses on 541-square-km Guam. Quite a chunk of Saipan's 123 square km is eaten up by its three courses and little 85-square-km Rota is threatened by at least two projected golf courses, including one with 54 holes! These facilities are too expensive for most local golfers and when they're combined with the military reservations, housing developments, shopping malls, roads, parking areas, and mountainous island interiors, there isn't a lot of land left over. Things are really heating up on Saipan and Guam, with day-long traffic jams along the west coast highways of both islands. The population of Saipan doubled in the 1970s and again in the 1980s.

When the Marianas Covenant was signed by President Ford in 1976 a provision was included to prevent outsiders from purchasing land during the first 25 years of the Commonwealth of the Northern Mariana Islands. This has prevented land speculation by Americans but has had little effect on Japanese corporations which obtain long-term leases on choice properties or buy land outright through Chamorro fronts. The west coast of Saipan is now one big Japanese-owned hotel after another.

Neighboring Tinian is threatened by gambling casino development. In 1989, 86% of the inhabitants of Tinian voted in favor of casinos after a well-financed campaign by developers, promising free medical care, electricity, and water; monthly royalties; scholarships for students; business development for locals; etc. At least five big casinos are to go up on the hillside east of San Jose village if gambling development goes ahead.

On Koror both the big resort hotels are Japanese-owned, and Japanese money is pouring into Belau tourism in increasing quantities. As on Guam and Saipan, the packaged tourists arrive on Japanese planes, ride in Japanese buses, stay at Japanese-owned hotels, eat Japanese food, buy Japanese duty-free goods, and prepay most of their expenses to Japanese companies in Japan itself. With very few exceptions the lucrative scuba-diving business is run by Americans and Japanese.

There are many cliches and misconceptions about tourism. It's said that tourism promotes world peace by facilitating contact between peoples, but it's unlikely tourists to the Mariana Islands meet many local people at all, as their hotel management is likely to be Asian and the service staff Filipino. At Chuuk tourists quickly disappear into the Truk Continental Hotel or onto live-aboard dive boats and are never seen in the local town. For such visitors the litter and poverty they behold from the bus window on the way to the hotel forms their image of the local community.

Tourism is said to be an "industry without smokestacks," but on small ocean islands the effect must be measured in terms of social pollution. Mass tourism soon destroys the spontaneity and charm of local populations, which is why travel guidebook writers are always pushing on into new, uncharted territory. Tourism puts heavy burdens on local infrastructures and causes overcrowding on roads, on beaches, and elsewhere. Rents, food costs, and store prices are soon driven up. In the Northern Marianas, Filipinas who came expecting decent jobs are forced to serve as prostitutes because they don't have the money to leave.

A tourist might think tourism helps preserve local cultures, but tourism promoters take from local cultures only what they can readily exploit. For example, the traditional dances of the Carolinian residents of Saipan are never seen at the nightly dinner shows in the big hotels because Japanese tourists expect to see Tahitian-style *tamure* dancing, so that's what they get! Polynesia may be on the opposite side of the Pacific from Saipan but it's enough that it looks "native" and sells. Similarly, most of the "handicrafts" sold on Guam and Saipan are mass-produced in the Philippines. This cultural exploitation is less evident in the Marshall Islands, the Federated States of Micronesia, and Belau, where most of the craft items sold are authentic.

Yet it is true that tourism is one of the few channels for economic development open to small tropical islands. In Micronesia, American education and television and decades of government handouts have created consumer attitudes which cannot be ignored. The imported products in the supermarkets and on the roads cost money and Micronesians must find a way to get it. With the end of the Cold War, American military requirements in Micronesia are declining fast and U.S. government subsidies to local governments are sure to follow suit.

Tourism seems to be an easy way of making money. Local governments earn income by imposing a hotel tax that is added to the room rates (10% in much of Micronesia) and airport taxes collected from tourists help cover the rising costs of keeping the terminals open. Tourist passengers make air transportation a viable business in the islands and without tourism many air routes used by local people would be canceled, and service sharply reduced on the rest.

Tourism also provides local governments with an incentive to protect their marine environments and for the coral reefs of Guam and the Northern Marianas, which once faced practices such as dynamite and bleach fishing, this is good news. In Belau the need to preserve the country's brilliant reefs was an effective argument against the construction of Japanese oil-storage facilities and American military bases.

In Micronesia today tourist development is concentrated in areas near the airports. Very few tourists ever leave Majuro, Weno (Moen), Yap Proper, or Koror. In Yap State travelers wishing to go beyond Yap Proper require special permission from the governor! Tourism is almost undeveloped in Kiribati (a forgotten corner of Micronesia) due to poor air service. It's not hard to "get lost" in Micronesia.

To date, tourist development in Micronesia (and in much of the third world) has been left to big corporations. Needless to say, local island people interested in becoming tourism entrepreneurs have difficulty competing with the computer-driven technology of Japanese and American corporations—they need help. Surprisingly (or perhaps not so surprisingly) such help is often not forthcoming from the local government agencies responsible for tourism development. For example, the Marianas Visitors Bureau and Guam Visitors Bureau don't even include many locally owned accommodations in their official lists, despite the government financing they receive! For small businesses or individuals the membership fees collected by these bureaus are prohibitive, while to the hotel chains it's petty cash, and only members are included in the lists.

This lack of support is repeated by Continental Airlines, which does nothing at all to promote Micronesia. They leave it to American scuba-tour operators and Japanese packagers to sell their seats and of course none of those passengers have the slightest opportunity of staying at a locally owned hotel.

There are exceptions, of course. At the Bechiyal Cultural Center on the north coast of Yap Proper, visitors sleep on a mat in the guest cottage or traditional men's house, or simply pitch a tent on the beach. Local meals are provided by the neighboring family and the whole operation is managed by the villagers themselves. The tourist office on Yap is almost alone in Micronesia in its willingness to make arrangements for visitors to stay with local families as paying guests. Thanks to enlightened leadership Japanese packaged tourism has thus far been kept out of Yap, and local people provide most of the services for the much smaller number of visitors.

The visitors bureau in Chuuk also arranges accommodation with outer-island families upon request and in the Marshalls the Ministry of Interior and Outer Island Affairs will do the same. Island councils on most of the outer atolls of Kiribati run small thatched guesthouses. In Belau there are several local guesthouses on Peleliu and Angaur, which wouldn't exist if they had to compete with large hotels. Falos Beach Resort at Chuuk and the Ngaraard Traditional Resort on Belau's Babeldaop also deserve recognition.

Another option for tourism development is the joint venture where a local community provides the land and labor and an outsider contributes the capital and expertise. Examples of this are The Pathways on Yap and The Village on Pohnpei. Both are built from local materials and provide income for local residents, but they remain under direct American management, which misses the point of letting the islanders run their tourism themselves.

The need for successful models to follow is clear. Several years ago on Pohnpei a resident Micronesian Japanese family set up a small resort built of local materials on a tiny lagoon islet near the famous ruins of Nan Madol. Joy Island now has many imitators on Pohnpei, including Black Coral Island, Fantasy Island, Rainbow Island, etc. At all these, visitors forgo electricity and sophisticated plumbing for the joys of nature, at the right price. Micronesia would be a much nicer region to visit if there were 1,000 Joy Islands and Bechiyals spread clear across the Pacific, plus simple guesthouses and "lodging with the people" programs in the towns. And that's partly what this book is all about.

GORDY OHLIGER

INTRODUCTION

Micronesia. Although many people have never heard of it, this vast cultural region includes thousands of lush tropical islands scattered between Hawaii and the Philippines. The name means "little islands," and two islands the size of Guam—the largest land mass in Micronesia—could fit comfortably inside the boundaries of greater Los Angeles.

While Tahiti and Fiji are household words, most Americans are completely unaware of this enormous area administered by their government since 1945. Until the early 1960s, civilians required a security clearance to travel to most of Micronesia, and several militarized islands and 30% of Guam are *still* officially off-limits. In Honolulu so little information is available on the region you'll begin to wonder if it really exists.

The U.S. is only the latest of six colonial powers to control Micronesia. Spain, Germany, and Japan were forced out in wars, while Britain and Australia left voluntarily. Of the seven political entities covered in this book, two are independent, two are U.S. territories, two are "freely associated" with the U.S., and one is still officially a trust territory. All of the American-associated areas (except Guam) originally fell under the Trust Territory of the Pacific Islands, a trust granted by the United Nations in 1947. What America has done with this simple third-world region over the past four decades is intriguing.

You have in your hands the original travel guidebook to the "American Lake." For the traveler, Micronesia is almost virgin territory —one of the last real frontiers on earth. The mysterious ruins of Pohnpei and Kosrae rival those of Easter Island; Star Wars technology develops in the Marshalls, as tradition-oriented Yap revolves around stone money; Belau and Chuuk rank among the world's premier scuba locales; nouveau riche Japanese cavort on Guam and Saipan; and Kiribati seems lost in time.

Countless unspoiled places exist here, and at some you'll never meet another visitor. Even so, access is relatively easy, hotels and rental cars are available in all the towns, and the people are very friendly. English is understood throughout, and you don't even have to change money: the only currencies used are American and Australian. The variety of travel experiences available will please beachcomber and island-hopper alike.

To fully understand the "micro" in Micronesia, however, you must leave the towns where American influence is strongest and visit the outer islands. This takes time and energy, but the payoff is unquestionably worth the effort. As the late 20th century closes in on the old Micronesia, traditional ways are disappearing fast under a flood of federal dollars and Japanese investment capital. The modern world has penetrated even the most remote atolls—the time to go is now.

THE LAND

Micronesia consists of four great archipelagos: the Marshalls, Gilberts, Carolines, and Marianas. These include thousands of coconut-covered islands sprinkled over

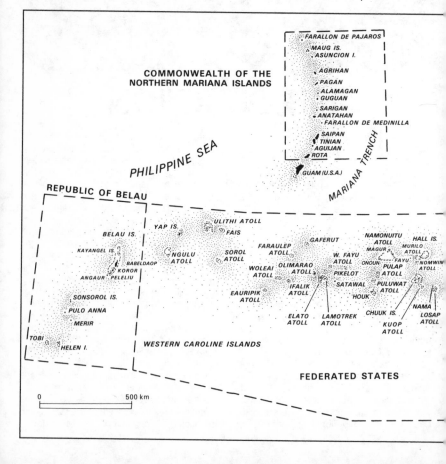

11,649,000 square km of the central Pacific, largely north of the equator. The islands, some 125 of which are inhabited, have a total land area of just 3,227 square km, only a little bigger than Rhode Island. The largest volcanic islands are Guam (541 square km), Babeldaop (396 square km), and Pohnpei (334 square km), while Agrihan is the highest (965 meters). Lagoon area included, Kwajalein is the world's largest atoll (2,173 square km), while in land area Christmas Island (388 square km) is the biggest of the coral islands. Many more are of the one-tree, shipwrecked-sailor variety.

Every island is different. Some are high islands with volcanic peaks, others low islands of sand and coral. All of the Marshalls and Gilberts are coral atolls or islands. In the Northern Marianas, Micronesia's only active volcanoes erupt. Nauru and Banaba are uplifted atolls. The Caroline Islands include both volcanic and coral types. Kosrae, Pohnpei, and Chuuk are high volcanic islands. Guam and Belau are exposed peaks of an undersea ridge stretching between Japan and New Guinea, volcanic in origin but partly capped with limestone. Yap is an uplifted section of the Asian continental shelf. This surprising

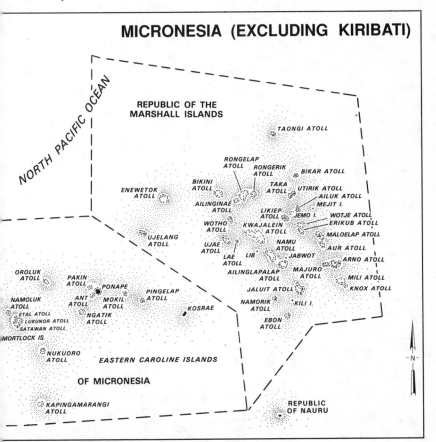

MICRONESIA (EXCLUDING KIRIBATI)

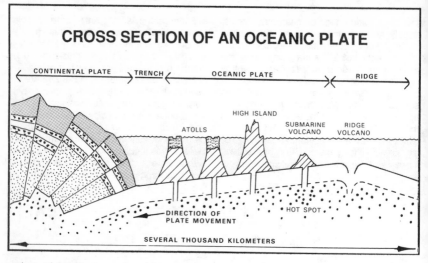

CROSS SECTION OF AN OCEANIC PLATE

CONTINENTAL PLATE | TRENCH | OCEANIC PLATE | RIDGE

HIGH ISLAND

ATOLLS

SUBMARINE VOLCANO

RIDGE VOLCANO

DIRECTION OF PLATE MOVEMENT

HOT SPOT

SEVERAL THOUSAND KILOMETERS

variety of landforms makes Micronesia a geologist's paradise.

Tectonic Plates

The westernmost islands of Micronesia flank some of the deepest waters on earth. The 11-km-deep Marianas Trench is the western edge of the vast Pacific Plate, the only one of earth's six plates that doesn't bear a continent. As this plate gets wedged under the Philippine Plate just east of the Marianas, volcanoes erupt along this section of the circum-Pacific Ring of Fire. The clashing plates have uplifted parts of Guam, Rota, Tinian, and Saipan from the sea. The Andesite Line, which marks the boundary between the Pacific and Philippine plates, follows these deep ocean canyons along the east side of the Northern Marianas, Yap, and Belau. East of this line, only volcanic and coral islands exist.

Shades Of Darwin

In 1952 scientists at Enewetak in the Marshalls managed to drill through to volcanic rock (at 1,290 meters deep) for the first time on any Pacific atoll, thus reconfirming Darwin's Theory of Atoll Formation. The famous formulator of the theory of evolution surmised that atolls form as high volcanic islands sub-

side into lagoons. The original island's fringing reef grows into a barrier reef as the volcanic portion sinks. When the last volcanic material finally disappears below sea level, the coral rim of the reef/atoll remains to indicate how big the island once was.

Of course, all this takes place over millions of years, but deep down below any atoll is the old volcanic core, as the researchers at Enewetak found. Darwin's theory is well illustrated at Chuuk, where a group of high volcanic islands remains inside the rim of Chuuk's barrier reef; these islands are still sinking imperceptibly. Return to Chuuk in 25 million years and all you'll find will be a coral atoll like Majuro or Kwajalein.

Hot Spots

High or low, all of the islands have a volcanic origin best explained by the Conveyor Belt Theory. A crack or "hot spot" opens in the seafloor and volcanic material escapes upward. A submarine volcano builds up slowly until the lava finally breaks the surface, becoming a volcanic island. The Pacific Plate moves northwest approximately 10 centimeters a year; thus, over geologic eons a volcano disconnects from the hot spot or crack from which it emerged. As the old volcanoes move on, new ones appear to the southeast, and the older islands are carried away from the cleft in the earth's crust from which they were born.

The island then begins to sink under its own weight, perhaps only one centimeter a century, and erosion cuts into the volcano—by this time extinct. In the warm, clear waters a living coral reef begins to grow along the shore. As the island subsides, the reef continues to grow upward. In this way a lagoon forms between the reef and the shoreline of the slowly sinking island. This barrier reef marks the old margin of the original island.

The process is helped along by rising and falling ocean levels during the various ice ages, which could expose more than 50 meters of volcanic and coral material to weathering. Rainwater causes a chemical reaction which converts the porous limestone into compacted dolomite, giving the reef a much denser base. Eventually, as the volcanic portion of the island sinks completely into the lagoon, the atoll reef is the volcanic island's only remnant.

As the hot spot moves southeast, in an opposite direction to the sliding Pacific Plate (and shifting magnetic pole of the earth), the process is repeated, time and again, until whole chains of islands ride the blue Pacific. In the Marshall, Gilbert, and Line islands this northwest-southeast orientation is clearly visible; the Carolines are more scattered, yet the tendency, from Namonuito to Kapingamarangi or Kosrae, is still discernible. In every case, the islands at the southeast end of the chains are the youngest. This rule also applies in the South Pacific.

Life Of An Atoll

A circular or horseshoe-shaped coral reef bearing a necklace of sandy, slender islets *(motus)* of debris thrown up by storms, surf, and wind is known as an atoll. Atolls can be up to 100 km across, but the width of dry land is usually only 200-400 meters from inner to outer beach. The central lagoon can measure anywhere from one to 50 km in diameter; huge Kwajalein Atoll has a width of 129 km. Entirely landlocked lagoons are rare; passages through the barrier reef are usually found on the leeward side. Most atolls are no higher than four to six meters.

A raised or elevated atoll is one that has been pushed up by some trauma of nature to become a coral platform rising as much as 60 meters above sea level. Raised atolls are often known for their huge sea caves and steep oceanside cliffs. A good example of this type is 21-square-km Nauru.

Where the volcanic island remains there's often a deep passage between the barrier reef and shore; the reef forms a natural breakwater which shelters good anchorages. Soil derived from coral is extremely poor in nutrients, while volcanic soil is known for its fertility. Dark-colored beaches are formed from volcanic material; the white beaches of travel brochures are entirely coral based.

Palmyra Atoll as it looked in 1935, before wartime dredging transformed the island's classic coral structure

The black beaches are cooler and easier on the eyes, enabling plantlife to grow closer, giving patches of shade; the white beaches are generally safer for swimming as visibility is better.

Now a new danger faces the atolls of Oceania in the greenhouse effect, a gradual warming of earth's environment due to fossil fuel combustion and the widespread clearing of forests. In the past 20 years the concentration of carbon dioxide in the atmosphere has increased 25%. As infrared radiation from the sun is absorbed by the gas, the trapped heat threatens to melt mountain glaciers and polar ice caps. Even more, seawater expands as it warms up and water levels could rise by one meter in 50 years, three meters by the year 2100. Not only will this reduce the growing area for food crops but rising sea levels will mean the intrusion of more salt water into the groundwater, especially if accompanied by droughts. In time entire populations could be forced to evacuate, and whole countries like the Marshall Islands and Kiribati could be flooded. The construction of seawalls to keep out the rising seas will cost billions. The greenhouse effect may also lead to a dramatic increase in typhoons. Researchers at Hawaii's East-West Center have called for a "Law of the Atmosphere," similar to the existing Law of the Sea, to coordinate international efforts to face this imminent challenge.

CORAL REEFS

To understand how a basalt volcano becomes a limestone atoll, it's necessary to know a little about the growth of coral. Worldwide, coral reefs cover some 200,000 square km between 35° north and 32° south latitudes. A reef is created by the accumulation of millions of tiny calcareous skeletons left by generations of microscopic animals called polyps. Though the skeleton is usually white, the living polyps are of many different colors. Only the top few centimeters of coral contain living polyps.

They thrive in clear, salty water where the temperature never drops below 18° C. They must also have some base not over 50 meters below the water's surface on which to form. The coral colony grows slowly upward on the consolidated base of its ancestors until it reaches the low-tide mark, after which development extends outward on the edges of the reef. Sunlight is critical for coral growth. Colonies grow more quickly on the ocean side due to clearer water and a greater abundance of food. A strong, healthy reef can grow four to five cm a year. Fresh or cloudy water inhibits coral growth, which is why villages and ports all across the Pacific are located at the reef-free mouths of rivers.

Polyps extract calcium carbonate from the water and deposit it in their skeletons. All reef-building corals also contain limy encrustations of microscopic algae within their cells. The algae, like all green plants, obtain their energy from the sun, and contribute this energy to the growth of the reef's skeleton. As a result, corals behave (and look) more like plants than animals, competing for sunlight just as terrestrial plants do. Many polyps are also carnivorous, and supplement their energy by capturing tiny planktonic animals and organic particles at night with minute stinging tentacles. A piece of coral is a colony composed of large numbers of polyps.

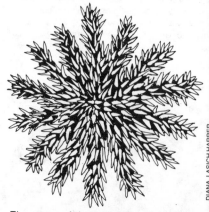

The crown-of-thorns starfish (Acanthaster planci) feeds on living coral, leaving only a chalky skeleton.

DIANA LASICH HARPER

staghorn fire coral *(Millepora alcicornis)*

acropora

CORALS OF THE PACIFIC

table coral

mushroom coral
(Fungia fungites)

elkhorn fire coral
(Millepora platyphylla)

honeycomb coral *(Favia matthaii)*

brain coral *(Meandrina)*

DIANA LASICH HARPER

10 SAFETY RULES OF DIVING

1. The most important rule in scuba diving is to *breathe continuously.* If you establish this rule, you won't forget and hold your breath, and overexpansion will never occur.
2. *Come up slowly.* This allows the gas dissolved in your body under pressure to come out of solution safely. This also prevents vertigo from fast ascents.
3. *Never escape to the surface.* Panic is the diver's worst enemy.
4. *Stop, think, then act.* Always maintain control.
5. *Pace yourself.* Know your limitations. A diver should always be able to rest and relax in the water. Proper use of the buoyancy vest will allow you to rest on the surface and maintain control under water. A diver who becomes fatigued in the water is a danger to himself and his buddy.
6. *Plan your dive.* Know your starting point, your diving area, and your exit areas. *Dive your plan.*
7. *Never dive with a cold.*
8. *Never exceed the safe sport diving limits of 30 meters.*
9. All equipment must be equipped with *quick releases.*
10. *Wear adequate protective clothing against sun and coral.*

Coral Types

Corals belong to a broad group of stinging creatures which includes polyps, soft corals, stony corals, sea anemones, sea fans, and jellyfish. Only those types with hard skeletons and a single hollow cavity within the body are considered true corals. Stony corals such as brain, table, staghorn, and mushroom corals have external skeletons and are important reef builders. Soft corals, black corals, and sea fans have internal skeletons. The fire corals are recognized by their smooth, velvety surface and yellowish brown color. The stinging toxins of this last group can easily penetrate human skin and cause swelling and painful burning that can last up to an hour. The many varieties of soft, colorful anemones gently waving in the current might seem inviting to touch, but beware! Many are also poisonous.

The corals, like most other forms of life in the Pacific, colonized the ocean from the fertile seas of Southeast Asia. Thus the number of species declines as you move east: the Western Caroline Islands have three times as many varieties of coral as Hawaii. Over 600 species of coral make their home in the Pacific, compared to only 48 in the Caribbean. The diversity of coral colors and forms is endlessly amazing. This is our most unspoiled environment, a world of almost indescribable beauty.

Exploring A Reef

Until you've explored a good coral reef, you haven't experienced one of the greatest joys of nature. While one cannot walk through pristine forests because there are no paths, it's quite possible to swim over untouched reefs—the most densely populated living space on earth. Dive shops throughout the region offer scuba diving, and snorkeling gear is sold in large stores, so do get into the clear, warm waters around you. Be careful, however, and know the dangers. Practice snorkeling in the shallow water; don't head into deep water until you're sure you've got the hang of it. Breathe easily; don't hyperventilate.

When snorkeling on a fringing reef, beware of deadly currents and undertows in channels which drain tidal flows. Observe the direction the water is flowing before you swim into it. If you feel yourself being dragged out to sea through a reef passage, try swimming across the current rather than against it. If you can't resist the pull at all, it may be better to let yourself be carried out. Wait till the current diminishes, then swim along the outer reef face until you find somewhere to come back in. Or use your energy to attract the attention of someone onshore. Most beach drownings occur in such situations, so try not to panic.

Snorkeling is usually best at one of the twice-daily high tides, and swimming along the outer edge or drop-off of a reef is thrilling for the variety of fish and corals. Attempt it only on a very calm day, and even then it's best to have someone stand onshore or on the reef's edge (at low tide) to watch for occasional big waves, which can take you by surprise and smash you into the rocks. Also, beware of unperceived currents outside the reef—you may not get a second chance.

A far better idea is to limit your snorkeling to the protected inner reef and leave the open waters to the scuba diver. Many of the professional scuba operators listed in this book offer resort courses for beginning divers. They know their waters and are able to show you the most amazing things in perfect safety. Micronesia offers the finest wreck diving (at Chuuk) and reef diving (at Belau) in the world. The main constraint is financial: snorkeling is free, while scuba diving becomes expensive.

Conservation

Coral reefs are one of the most fragile and complex ecosystems on earth, providing food and shelter for countless species of fish, crustacea (shrimps, crabs, and lobsters), mollusks (shells), and other animals. Hard corals grow only about 10 to 25 mm a year and it can take 7,000 to 10,000 years for a coral reef to form. Though corals look solid they're easily broken, and by standing on them, breaking off pieces, or carelessly dropping anchor you can destroy in a few minutes what took so long to form. Once a piece of coral breaks off it dies and it may be years before the coral reestablishes itself and even longer before the broken piece is replaced. Sometimes the damage is permanent; when this happens over a wide area the diversity of marinelife declines dramatically.

We recommend that you not remove coral, seashells, plantlife, or marine animals from the sea. In a small way, you are upsetting the delicate balance of nature, and coral is much more beautiful underwater anyway! This is a particular problem along shorelines frequented by large numbers of tourists, who can strip a reef in very little time. If you'd like a souve-

nir, content yourself with what you find on the beach. Also think twice about purchasing jewelry or souvenirs made from coral or seashells. Genuine traditional handicrafts which incorporate shells are one thing, but by purchasing unmounted seashells or mass-produced coral curios you are contributing to the destruction of the marine environment.

There's an urgent need for much stricter government regulation of the seas and in many places (such as Guam and the Northern Marianas) coral reefs are already protected by law. Exhortations such as the one above have only limited impact. As consumerism spreads, once-remote areas become subject to the familiar problems of pollution and overexploitation. The garbage is visibly piling up on many shores. As a visitor, don't hesitate to practice your conservationist attitudes and leave a clean wake.

CLIMATE

Temperatures are uniformly high year-round, and rainfall is well distributed. The Gilbert and Line islands get less rainfall from July to Nov., while the Marshalls, Carolines, and Marianas are somewhat drier and less humid from Dec. through April—the best times to come. The Northern Marianas enjoy Micronesia's most pleasant climate, with lower temperatures and moderate rainfall. Kosrae and Pohnpei, however, are among the rainiest places on earth; you're sure to enjoy a little rain if you stay longer than a few days. The Gilberts are much drier than the Marshalls and Carolines, and can even experience drought.

For terrestrial travelers the rainy season is almost as easy as the dry, as the rains are usually brief and heavy, instantly cooling the air and nurturing the thick vegetation. Much of it falls at night. For skin divers, however, the rainy season is slightly less favorable as rivers flush more sediment into the lagoons, though the waters tend to be still at this time, allowing diving at places inaccessible during the windier dry season. The smaller visitor levels during the wet also compensate for the higher precipitation and the presence of more mosquitos.

The northeast tradewinds blow steadily west across much of Micronesia in winter (Dec. through March), changing to calms, easterlies, or southeast trades in summer. Throughout Micronesia winds out of the west bring rain. The tradewinds are caused by hot air rising near the equator, then flowing toward the poles at high altitude. Cooler air drawn toward the vacuum is deflected to the west by the rotation of the earth. Micronesia's proximity to the equator explains the seasonal shift in the winds, as the intertropical convergence zone between the northeast and southeast trades (or doldrum zone— where the most heated air is rising) moves north of the islands in summer. The tradewinds cool the islands and offer clear sailing for mariners, making winter the most favorable season to visit.

A tropical cyclone or typhoon (hurricane) forms when thunderstorms release heat and the hot air rises. Cooler air rushes in toward the low pressure area created, spinning around the eye counterclockwise in the Northern Hemisphere, clockwise in the Southern Hemisphere. The main typhoon season in Micronesia is the rainy season, May through Dec., although typhoons can occur in any month. These storms are usually generated in the east and move west. Thus typhoons are far less common in the Marshalls than farther west. A typhoon would only temporarily inconvenience a visitor staying at a hotel and the days immediately following a typhoon are clear and dry.

Micronesia enjoys the cleanest air on earth—air that hasn't blown over a continent for weeks. To view the night stars in the warm, windless sky is like witnessing creation anew.

FLORA AND FAUNA

The variety of species encountered in the Pacific islands declines as you move away from the Asian mainland. Island birdlife is more abundant than land-based fauna, but still reflects the decline in variety from west to east. The flora too reflects this phenomenon. Although some plant species may have spread by means of floating seeds or fruit, wind and birds were probably more effective. The microscopic spores of ferns, for example, can be carried vast distances by the wind.

Flying foxes and insect-eating bats were the only mammals to reach Micronesia without the aid of man. Ancient navigators introduced wild pigs, dogs, and chickens; they also brought along rats and mice. Jesuit missionaries introduced the water buffalo or carabao to Guam in the 17th century.

Birdwatching is a highly recommended pursuit for the serious Pacific traveler; you'll find it opens unexpected doors. Good field guides are few (ask at local bookstores, museums, and cultural centers), but a determined interest will bring you in contact with fascinating people and lead to great adventures. The best time to observe forest birds is in the very early morning—they move around a lot less in the heat of the day.

Micronesia's high islands support a great variety of plantlife, while the low islands are restricted to a few hardy species such as breadfruit, cassava (tapioca), pandanus, and coconuts. On the atolls taro must be cultivated in deep organic pits.

As in the Malaysian region, mangrove swamps are common along high-island coastal lagoons. The cable roots of the saltwater-tolerant mangroves anchor in the shallow upper layer of oxygenated mud, avoiding the layers of hydrogen sulfide below. The tree provides shade for tiny organisms dwelling in the tidal mudflats—a place for birds to nest and for fish or shellfish to feed and spawn.

The mangroves filter and purify water flowing from land to sea and perform the same task as land-building coral colonies along the reefs: as sediments are trapped between the roots, the trees extend farther into the lagoon, creating a unique natural environment. The past decade has seen widespread destruction of the mangroves.

MARINELIFE

Micronesia's richest store of life is found in the silent underwater world of the lagoon and pelagic fishes, including angelfish, bonito, butterflyfish, eels, groupers, harpfish, jacks, mahi mahi, mullets, parrotfish, sharks, soldierfish, stingrays, surgeonfish, swordfish, trumpetfish, tuna, and countless more. It's believed that most Pacific marine organisms evolved in the triangular area bounded by New Guinea, the Philippines, and the Malay Peninsula. This "Cradle of Indo-Pacific Marinelife" includes a wide variety of habitats and has remained stable through several geological ages. From this cradle the rest of the Pacific was colonized.

Dolphins

While most people use the terms dolphin and porpoise interchangeably, a porpoise lacks the dolphin's beak (although many dolphins are also beakless). There are 62 species of dolphins, and only six species of porpoises. Dolphins leap from the water and many legends tell of their saving humans, especially children, from drowning (the most famous concerns Telemachus, son of Odysseus). In the eastern Pacific dolphins are often found in the vicinity of schools of tuna and many drown in purse seine nets set by humans.

Sharks

The danger from sharks has been greatly exaggerated. Of some 300 different species, only 28 are known to have attacked humans. Most dangerous are the white, tiger, hammerhead, and blue sharks. Fortunately, all these inhabit deep water, far from the coasts. Sometimes, however, attracted by wastes thrown overboard, they follow ships into port and create serious problems. An average of only 50 shark attacks a year occur worldwide so, considering the number of people who swim in the sea, your chances of being involved are pretty slim.

Sharks are not so dangerous where food is abundant, but they can be very nasty far offshore. You're always safer if you keep your head underwater (with a mask and snorkel), and don't panic if you see a shark—you might attract it. Even if you do, they're usually only curious, so look it straight in the eye, and slowly back off. Sharks are attracted by shiny objects (a knife or jewelry), bright colors (especially yellow and red), urinating, spearfishing, and splashing. Divers should ease themselves into the water. Sharks have poor eyesight and often mistake the white palms and soles of a bather's hands and feet for small fish.

SAVE THE WHALES

The cetaceans (whales, dolphins, and porpoises) are divided into two suborders: the Mysticeti (baleen whales) and the Odontoceti (toothed whales, narwhals, and dolphins). The baleen whales (including all in the chart except the sperm whale) have a series of plates in the roof of the mouth which are used to strain plankton, krill, and fish from the water. Dolphins and porpoises use their teeth to catch squid or fish. In 1982, the International Whaling Commission voted to end commercial whaling around the world on 1 Jan. 1986. Japan, Norway, and Iceland objected to the ban and continued to whale in the face of world opinion. Jacques Cousteau put it this way: "The only creatures on earth that have bigger—and maybe better—brains than humans are the cetacea, the whales and dolphins. Perhaps they could one day tell us something important, but it is unlikely that we will hear it. Because we are coldly, efficiently, and economically killing them off."

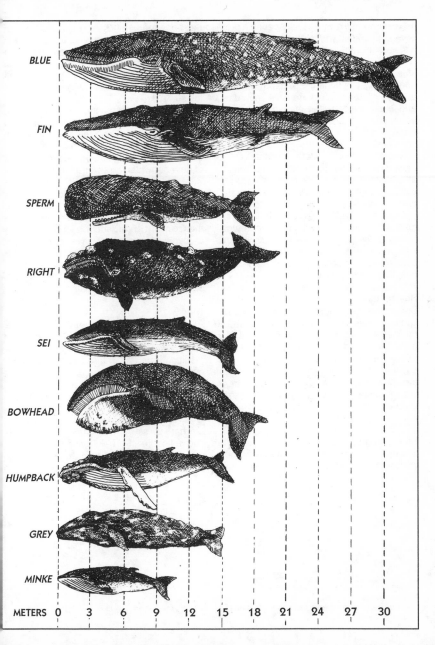

BLUE

FIN

SPERM

RIGHT

SEI

BOWHEAD

HUMPBACK

GREY

MINKE

METERS   0   3   6   9   12   15   18   21   24   27   30

Never swim alone if you suspect the presence of sharks. If you see one, get out of the water calmly and quickly, and go elsewhere (unless you're with someone knowledgeable, such as a local divemaster). Sharks normally stay outside the reef, but ask local advice. White beaches are safer than dark, and clear water safer than murky. Avoid swimming in places where sewage or edible wastes enter the water, or fish have just been cleaned.

Recent studies indicate that sharks, like most other creatures, are territorial. Thus an attack could be a shark's way of warning someone to get out of his backyard. Over half the victims of these incidents are not eaten, but merely wounded. Perhaps we underestimate the shark. Let common sense be your guide, not blind fear or carelessness. As one local resident put it, sharks are not dangerous at all in comparison with the man-eating hospitals of Micronesia.

Barracudas

Swimmers need not fear an attack by barracuda. In these lush tropical waters where marinelife abounds, barracudas can find a lot more tasty food. Most cases of barracuda attack are provoked: a spearfisherman shoots one in the tail, another is attracted by the spearfisherman's catch, a third is simply startled by chance. Still, if you see a barracuda, it's wise to swim away from it; in turn, it will usually swim away from you.

Sea Urchins

Sea urchins (living pincushions) are common in tropical waters. The black variety is the most dangerous: their long sharp quills can go right through a snorkeler's fins. Even the small ones, which you can easily pick up in your hand, can pinch you if you're careless. Sea urchins are found on rocky shores and reefs, never on clear, sandy beaches where the surf rolls in.

Most sea urchins are not poisonous, though quill punctures are painful and can become infected if not treated. The pain is caused by an injected protein which you can eliminate by holding the injured area in a pail of very hot water for about 15 minutes. This will coagulate the protein, eliminating the pain for good. If you can't heat water, soak the area in vinegar or urine for 15 minutes. Remove the quills if possible, but since they're made of calcium they'll decompose in a couple of weeks anyway—not much of a consolation as you limp along in the meantime. In some places sea urchins are a favorite delicacy: the orange or yellow meat is delicious with lemon and salt.

Others

Although jellyfish, stonefish, crown-of-thorns starfish, cone shells, eels, and poisonous sea snakes are hazardous, injuries resulting from any of these are rare. Gently apply methylated spirit, alcohol, or urine (but not water, kerosene, or gasoline) to areas stung by jellyfish. Harmless sea cucumbers (bêche-de-mer) punctuate the lagoon shallows. Stonefish also rest on the bottom and are hard to see due to camouflaging; their dorsal fins inject a painful, often lethal poison which burns like fire in the blood if you happen to step on one. Treat the wound by

The relatively harmless blacktip reef shark (Carcharhinus melanopterus) *may be seen in shallow lagoon water.*

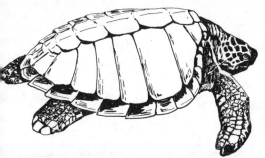

The Pacific ridley turtle (Lepidochelys olivacea) is one of the rarest of the seven species of sea turtles. Pacific ridleys eat crustaceans, fish eggs, and some vegetation.

the Western Carolines. Six of the seven species of sea turtles are facing extinction due to overhunting and harvesting of eggs. For this reason, importing any turtle product is prohibited in most countries. Geckos and skinks are small lizards often seen on the islands. The skink hunts insects by day; its tail breaks off if you catch it, but a new one quickly grows. The gecko is nocturnal and has no eyelids. Adhesive toe pads enable it to pass along vertical surfaces, and it changes color to avoid detection. Unlike the skink, which avoids humans, geckos often live in people's homes where they eat insects attracted by electric lights. Its loud ticking call may be a territorial warning to other geckos.

submerging it, along with an opposite foot or hand, in water as hot as you can stand for 30 minutes (the opposite extremity prevents scalding due to numbness). If a hospital or clinic is nearby, go there immediately. Fortunately stonefish are not common.

Never pick up a live cone shell; some varieties have a deadly stinger dart coming out from the pointed end which can reach any part of the shell's outer surface. Eels hide in reef crevices by day; most are dangerous only if you inadvertently poke your hand or foot in at them. Of course, never tempt fate by approaching them.

Although the meter-long monitor lizard looks fearsome, it's no threat to humans. The adaptable monitor can climb trees, dig holes, run quickly on land, and catch fish swimming in the lagoon. It'll eat almost anything it can catch, from insects to snails, smaller lizards, rats, crabs, birds, and bird eggs. Belau has boas, tree snakes, and water snakes, while the bird-eating brown tree snake has been introduced to Guam. None are venomous. This, and the lack of leeches, poisonous plants, and dangerous wild animals, makes Micronesia a paradise for hikers. The main terrestrial hazards are dogs and mosquitos.

REPTILES

Saltwater crocodiles, an endangered species, frequent the mangrove swamps of

LOUISE FOOTE

the mysterious ruins of Nan Madol

an old engraving of the latte stones of Tinian

HISTORY

The Micronesians

Austronesian-speaking Micronesian peoples entered the Pacific from Southeast Asia over 3,000 years ago. The first islands they located were the Marianas, followed by the Western Carolines. From this base they settled the Eastern Caroline, Tungaru, and Marshall islands. Trading beads uncovered at Yap prove that some contact was maintained with Southeast Asia as late as 200 B.C. In the westernmost atolls of Micronesia, an Indonesian-style loom is still used to make hibiscus-fiber skirts.

The first Micronesians lived from fishing and agriculture, using pottery and tools made from stone, shell, and bone. They cultivated breadfruit, taro, pandanus, coconuts, cassava, and (on the volcanic islands) yams. Pigs, chickens, and dogs were kept for food, but the surrounding sea yielded the most important source of protein. A matrilineal society, the husband and children be-

came members of the wife's landholding matrilineage. (Patrilineal Yap was an exception.) From chiefly clans came the ruling male chiefs. The paramount chiefs of Belau, the Marshalls, Pohnpei, and Yap are still influential figures.

The Micronesians were great voyagers who sailed their huge outrigger canoes between the Carolines and the Marianas. To navigate they read signs from the sun, stars, currents, swells, winds, clouds, and birds. Yap was an important trading center, in regular contact with Belau and the islands to the east. Annual expeditions brought tribute from the Yapese eastern outer islands to Ulithi and Yap. Old stories in the Carolines tell of a great empire, of which we unfortunately know little today. The magnificent ruins of Kosrae and Pohnpei, the stone money of Yap, the latte or taga stones of Guam, Rota, and Tinian, and the basalt monoliths and terraces of Babeldaop add to the mystery.

Magellan

Balboa was the first European to sight the Pacific, but Magellan was the first to sail upon it. Magellan proved that one could sail across this ocean and eventually find known territory again. In the late 15th century the Portuguese gained exclusive control of the trade route around the tip of Africa to the spice islands of Indonesia, forcing the Spaniards to find another route to the riches of the East. Thus the King of Spain outfitted Magellan with five ships for one of the greatest single journeys in history.

In Sept. 1519, this fleet crossed the bar of the Guadalquivir and sailed south across the Atlantic toward South America. On 21 Oct. a cape was sighted, and then they came upon a bay-like opening. Two ships investigating the channel discovered that the flood tide was stronger than the ebb, indicating a passage. What followed was Magellan's remarkable 38-day voyage through the strait now bearing his name, though he lost two ships to the tempestuous weather.

At last, on 28 Nov. 1520, the three surviving ships passed Cabo Deseado and entered the greatest of oceans. The ships sailed northwest for months across this unimaginably vast sea. Worms reduced their biscuits to powder, and the crew had to hold their noses as they drank the water. The hides that kept the rigging from chafing on the yards were eaten after being softened by being dragged overboard for four days. Sawdust was also eaten, and rats went for half a ducat each.

The ships finally sighted land on 24 Jan. 1521, and 11 days later came upon people in swift outrigger canoes. Guam and Micronesia had been discovered by Europeans! Then the islanders (Chamorros) stole Magellan's skiff. In vengeance, he took 40 armed men ashore, burned 50 houses and boats, killed seven men, and recovered his skiff. By 9 March his fleet had arrived northeast of the Moluccas (Maluku, Indonesia), at Samar in the Philippines. Magellan converted the Rajah of Cebu and 3,000 of his subjects to Christianity. Later, while leading an expedition against the neighboring island of Mactan to subdue its unruly chief for Christianity, the meddlesome explorer was struck down and killed by infuriated islanders. One ship sailed on alone across the Indian Ocean, around the Cape of Good Hope, and north through the Atlantic, reaching Seville, Spain, in Sept. 1522. These survivors were the first men to circumnavigate the globe. One hundred seventy men had perished on this passage, surely one of the most significant navigations of all time.

Colonial Intervention

Spain occupied the Marianas in 1668 as a support base for their galleons trading the silver of Mexico for the tea, silk, and spices of the Philippines. Little attention was paid to the Carolines or Marshalls until 1864, when the first resident German trader set up shop in the Marshalls, followed in 1869 by a post on Yap. The Germans established a protectorate over the Marshalls in 1878 and attempted to extend this to all of the Caroline and Marshall islands in 1885. The Spanish protested that they had already claimed the area in 1874 and asked the Pope to mediate the dispute. He ruled in favor of the Spanish, although the Germans were given trading rights and permitted to annex the Marshalls.

Meanwhile, British whalers and traders from Australia had been active in the Carolines and Marshalls since the 1830s, joined by Americans around 1850. These newcomers brought strife and disease to the islands, decimating the population. Chuuk was spared due to the fearsome reputation of its

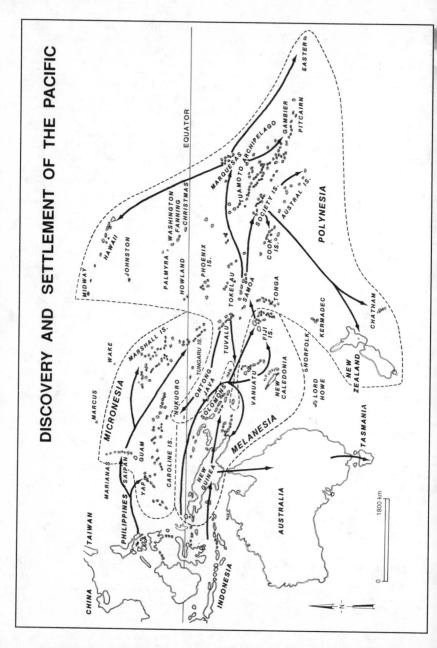

DISCOVERY AND SETTLEMENT OF THE PACIFIC

warriors, who frightened off intruders. Protestant missionaries had established themselves on Pohnpei and Kosrae by 1852, bringing with them a degree of order. The British established a protectorate over the Gilberts in 1892.

In 1898 the Spanish-American War shattered Spain's colonial empire, and the United States took advantage of the occasion to annex Guam and the Philippines. The Spanish had little choice other than to sell the Carolines and Northern Marianas to the Germans in 1899 for 25 million pesetas. The only surviving sign of the Spanish presence today, besides an old wall on Pohnpei, is Catholicism, which is still embraced by over half the people of Micronesia.

The Germans set about organizing the lucrative copra trade. To force the islanders to make copra for sale, they established a poll tax in 1910; those who couldn't pay were required to work on road construction. The Pohnpeians revolted against this high-handed behavior and killed the German governor. A German warship soon arrived, and the rebel leaders were executed and buried in a mass grave. The Micronesian view of the German period is best summed up in the story of a Belauan folk character named Binklang, based on the archetypical authoritarian, Herr Winkler.

The Japanese Period

By agreement with the British, the Japanese took the Northern Marianas, the Carolines, and the Marshalls from the Germans without a fight in Sept. and Oct. 1914, about the only part the Japanese played in WW I. Japanese traders had long been calling at the islands, so the change had little immediate impact on the Micronesians. Nauru and the German colonies in the South Pacific (Samoa and New Guinea) were seized by Australia and New Zealand.

After the war the Japanese government was appointed to administer the former German territories north of the equator under a League of Nations mandate binding them to an agreement not to forward "the establishment of fortifications or military and naval bases." In 1922 the neutralization of this part of the Pacific was further guaranteed by a treaty between the U.S. and Japan. In 1935, however, Japan withdrew from the League of Nations and began building large military bases on some of the islands. Finally, they annexed Nanyo Gunto (their name for Micronesia) outright. The headquarters of the Japanese South Seas Government or Nanyochokan was at Koror.

The Nanyo Kohatsu K.K. (South Seas Development Co., Ltd.) was founded in 1921 by Japanese big business interests. Sugar mills were built in the Marianas, while bauxite and phosphate mining was carried out in Belau. Commercial fishing, trochus shell production, and agriculture were also developed. So many trees were cut for construction that by 1936 there was a shortage of timber. After 1931 Japanese citizens were allowed to purchase or lease Micronesian land and large tracts passed into their hands by dubious means.

The number of Japanese colonists skyrocketed from 3,671 in 1920 to 84,476 in 1940, two-thirds of the total population. Most were concentrated in Belau and the Northern Marianas. The Japanese ran their part of the Pacific strictly as a colony, with little consideration for the Micronesians. Three classes of people evolved: the Japanese at the top, the Koreans and Okinawans in the middle, and the Micronesians or *toming* at the bottom. Most government jobs were reserved for Japanese; Koreans and Okinawans provided much of the labor for industry.

The Micronesians continued to live by subsistence agriculture or making copra, spectators on the sidelines of Japanese development. Interisland travel by canoe was banned and the authority of the traditional chiefs undermined. Nearly all economic activities in Micronesia before the war were based on immigration by Japanese who worked for the benefit of the mother country, thus it's not appropriate to compare the development during these years with the much quieter American period which would follow.

THE PACIFIC WAR

Both world wars had a profound effect on the Pacific. The first eliminated Germany from Micronesia, New Guinea, and Samoa, and gave Japan the central Pacific. The second expelled Japan, and brought the U.S. to the doorstep of Asia.

In 1942 the Japanese used their military bases in Belau to attack the Philippines and Indonesia; Chuuk was a springboard for their assault on the Solomons and New Guinea. With the Japanese conquest of Guam, Nauru, and Tungaru the whole of Micronesia was under one rule for the first time in history. For the Micronesians the war years were ones of forced labor, famine, and fear. They watched as their islands were ravaged by foreign armies; 5,000 Micronesians died. By 1945 all Japanese soldiers and civilians in Micronesia had either been killed, committed suicide, or been repatriated to Japan.

The Rising Sun

Japan had hoped to become the dominant power in Asia and the Pacific by establishing a "Greater East Asia Co-prosperity Sphere."

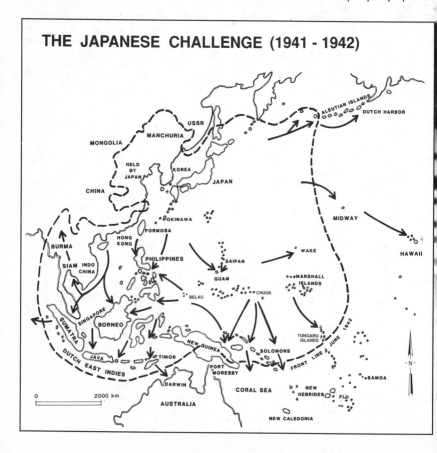

THE JAPANESE CHALLENGE (1941 - 1942)

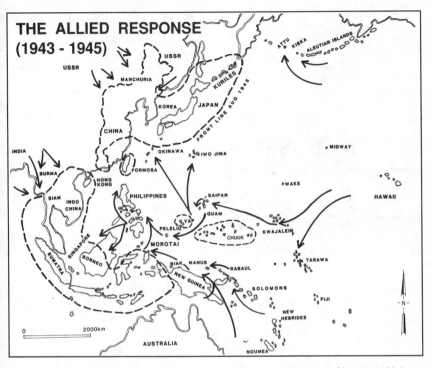

THE ALLIED RESPONSE (1943 - 1945)

The Japanese high command, attentive to the early successes of Nazi-fascist barbarism in Europe, decided the best way to achieve their ends was through force. In July 1941, after Japanese troops occupied French Indochina, the American, British, and Dutch governments declared an iron and oil embargo against Japan. When it became evident to the Japanese high command that they would have to fight or fizzle, they prepared their forces for war.

Their initial plan—to shatter the American fleet, create a large defensive perimeter, and cut off aid to opponents in China—was accomplished quickly. Although the surprise attack on Pearl Harbor on 7 Dec. 1941 was a disaster for the Japanese, as their bombs hit obsolete battleships and missed the new aircraft carriers, it did prevent the U.S. Navy from interfering with the occupation of South-

east Asia. Hong Kong, Shanghai, Malaya, Singapore, the Dutch East Indies, Burma, and the Philippines had all fallen to the Japanese by April 1942. China was cut off, the defensive perimeter complete, and the myth of European colonial invincibility shattered.

Then came the Doolittle bombing raid on Tokyo on 18 April, when the Japanese decided the perimeter would have to be wider for the homeland to be completely secure. They occupied Tulagi in the Solomon Islands in May, and started building an airbase on Guadalcanal. Landings took place throughout New Guinea, and a Japanese fleet advanced toward Port Moresby. En route it was intercepted by Allied naval units, and although the ensuing Battle of the Coral Sea—an air battle between navies which never sighted each other—has since been judged a draw, the Japanese invasion fleet turned

Admiral Isoroku Yamamotu planned the attacks on Pearl Harbor and Midway. He remained commander in chief of the Japanese combined fleet until a Betty bomber in which he was a passenger was shot down over Bougainville in the North Solomon Islands by American P-38s on 18 April 1943.

back. Less than a month later on 4 June, another Japanese invasion fleet became locked in the Battle of Midway: four Japanese carriers, with their planes and elite crews, were sunk by American aircraft. Japan had lost its naval superiority in the Pacific.

The Setting Sun

From July to Nov. 1942, Australian and Japanese armies fought back and forth across New Guinea's Kokoda Trail near Port Moresby. Simultaneously, Japanese soldiers struggled in the Solomons to recapture Guadalcanal from the Americans. By the end of 1942 the Japanese had lost both campaigns. A number of indecisive naval engagements accompanied the jungle war in the Solomons, but the sum total resulted in the fall of Japanese aerial superiority. The spring and early summer of 1943 saw a stalemate, while the

U.S. was rebuilding its strength for the next phase: recovery of the Philippines.

In the wide Pacific, the advantage is with the side on the offensive, as the Japanese learned when they tried to *defend* a vastly scattered front against overpowering mobile naval units. The Allied strategy was to approach the Philippines from two directions, with the U.S. and Australian armies fighting their way up through New Guinea and the U.S. Navy thrusting across the central Pacific. By mid-1943 troops under General Douglas A. MacArthur and Admiral Halsey had begun the long campaign in the Solomons (New Georgia, Bougainville) and New Guinea (Salamaua, Lae, Finschhafen, Madang). Large Japanese armies were bogged down in China and elsewhere, enabling the Allies to concentrate their forces at the weak points, neutralizing and bypassing entrenched strongholds (Rabaul, Chuuk, etc.) where the price of conquest would have been too great.

The central Pacific naval offensive under Admiral Chester W. Nimitz began in Nov. 1943, with landings at Tarawa and Butaritari in Tungaru. Casualties were high, but amphibious techniques were perfected. In Feb. 1944, Kwajalein and Enewetak were captured; Chuuk was bombed and neutralized. By this time U.S. carrier forces were strong enough to overcome most opposition.

The Philippines And Beyond

The New Guinea campaign continued, with Aitape and Hollandia (Jayapura) taken in April 1944, and Biak falling after a stiff fight in May. Landings on Saipan in the Marianas, which would provide the Americans with advanced bases for the bombing of the Japanese home islands, were scheduled for June. To prevent this, the Japanese Navy engaged the Allies in the Battle of the Philippine Sea, losing three carriers and 480 planes, and leaving the Philippines wide open to attack. Tinian and Guam were then taken by the Americans.

By July 1944, Japanese weakness was clearly evident, and U.S. submarines began to take a crippling toll on their merchant shipping. In Sept., the New Guinea and central Pacific offensives converged when Morotai (near Ternate) and Peleliu (Belau) were captured, providing springboards for the Philippines campaign. The Philippines could easily have been bypassed at this point and many lives saved—the Japanese were determined to hold the Philippines to defend their Indonesian-based oil supplies. But Gen. MacArthur had promised to return.

The American landings at Leyte in the Philippines in Oct. led to the largest naval battle of all time, the Battle of the Leyte Gulf, in which the U.S. attained clear naval superiority in the Pacific. The Japanese lost 24 major warships, including all their remaining carriers, compared to a U.S. loss of only six smaller ships. Kamikaze-piloted planes were used in this battle for the first time. In Jan. 1945, the Americans landed at Lingayen on Luzon, and by early March the remaining Japanese had been driven into the mountains, where they would hold out until the end of the war. Manila was completely destroyed due to a fanatical Japanese defense.

The next stage in the war was to be the invasion of Japan itself. The first of a damaging series of incendiary bombings of Japanese cities by Tinian-based B-29s occurred on 24 Nov. 1944. On the night of 9-10 March 1945 over 80,000 civilians burned as Tokyo went up in flames. General Curtis Le May, who directed the bombing, commented in 1978: "Killing Japanese didn't bother me very much at the time. It was getting the war over that bothered me. So I wasn't particularly worried about how many people we killed in getting the job done. I suppose if I had lost the war, I would have been tried as a war criminal. Fortunately we were on the winning side."

To gain advanced air bases able to provide fighter cover for the bombers, U.S. Marines landed at Iwo Jima on 19 February 1945. Although it took five bitter weeks, they finally cleared the island of defenders. Early 1945 also saw the belated British reconquest of Burma and the reopening of the road to China. In April, U.S. forces invaded Okinawa

aviator's grave, Japanese Cemetery, Peleliu

to secure an advanced naval base, but dug-in Japanese defensive positions and kamikaze attacks exacted serious casualties. Over 160,000 Okinawan civilians were cut down by U.S. fire or forced to commit suicide by Japanese troops.

Holocaust And Evaluation

Japan was already a defeated nation when, on 6 Aug. 1945 at 0815 Hiroshima time, the world entered the atomic age. Heat from the blast tore the skins off the victims and melted their eyeballs. Rescue workers found the city's rivers clogged with bodies of those who had tried to find relief from their burns. Thousands more died over the next few weeks. The final toll at Hiroshima and Nagasaki reached almost a quarter million. To this day the survivors, the *hibakusha,* lead broken, twisted lives with little aid or recognition, tormented by radiation-related diseases. This tragedy presented the Japanese imperial leadership with a face-saving opportunity to surrender.

Half a million Japanese soldiers and civilians had died in this senseless war far from their shores. Even today many Japanese are unable to come to terms with this tragedy,

Task Force 38.3 enters the Ulithi lagoon in line ahead, returning from strikes in the Philippines, 11 Dec. 1944

professing that they died for world peace! Of the 50,000 Micronesians, 10% were killed as foreign armies fought back and forth across the islands in a brutal struggle the islanders could only lose. The prewar infrastructures and economies were obliterated. Bitter memories of the war are still vivid in the minds of the older people, who associate the destruction with the prewar Japanese militarization of the area. The war made the North Pacific an "American Lake" and the U.S. presence is still strongly felt across the region.

THE POSTWAR PERIOD

Strategic Trust

In the Cairo Declaration of 1 Dec. 1943, Churchill and Roosevelt announced that after the war, Japan would be stripped of all the islands it had obtained in 1914. Soon after the Japanese surrender the U.S. Navy called for the annexation of Micronesia as a spoil of war, but the Truman Administration, sensitive to being branded colonialist, settled instead for a United Nations trusteeship. In 1947, the U.N. granted the former Japanese possessions in Micronesia to the U.S. as a trust territory under the United Nations Trusteeship Council, one of 11 established around the world at the time.

The Trust Territory of the Pacific Islands (TTPI) was the last of the 11 to attain self-government, and the only one designated a "strategic" trust, meaning the U.S. could establish military bases and conduct nuclear tests. Originally administered by the U.S. Navy, in 1951 control passed to the Dept. of the Interior, although the Northern Marianas remained under naval rule until 1962. At first Micronesia was administered from Honolulu, but in 1954 the Office of the High Commissioner shifted to Guam, and in 1962 the trust territory headquarters moved to Saipan. There were six districts: Marshall Islands, Ponape (Pohnpei), Truk (Chuuk), Yap, Palau (Belau), and Northern Marianas. The final decision-making power remained in Washington.

Military Use

Immediately after WW II, General MacArthur proposed an "offshore island perimeter" to defend American interests in the Far East. After the withdrawal from Vietnam in 1973, U.S. strategists resurrected plans for a chain of island-based military installations facing the Pacific Rim from Japan to the Indian

Ocean. Micronesia offered a wide defensive perimeter for the protection of Hawaii and the West Coast, weapons-testing sites, and bases from which to project American power across the Pacific.

Belau and the Northern Marianas seemed to fit into the system like jigsaw pieces, taking pressure off heavily militarized Guam and offering fallback positions should the U.S. have to abandon its facilities in the Philippines. The Pentagon succeeded in obtaining leases over much of the Northern Marianas in 1976. In a close 1983 vote, a compact which would deliver the Kwajalein missile range to the U.S. for 30 years and terminate all claims for compensation by the victims of nuclear testing was approved in the Marshalls.

The Belauans, resisting U.S. pressure, voted repeatedly to keep nuclear weapons and military bases off their islands, though the U.S. negotiators made it clear to Belauan representatives that unless they agreed by formal treaty to cede a third of their territory for military use over the next 50 years, they would not get the hundreds of millions of dollars offered. In 1979 the Republic of Belau became the first constitutionally nuclear-free zone in the world by a 92% referendum vote. The Federated States were considered of less strategic value, with no military bases planned.

Currently, with the Cold War over and conventional military deployments winding down worldwide, the emphasis is shifting to high-tech weapons systems and rapid deployment forces able to intervene in localized conflicts. East-West confrontations are being replaced by old fashioned North-South bullying. There have been no signs the U.S. intends to give up its sophisticated missile-testing facilities on Kwajalein nor the big bases on Guam, but major new bases in other parts of Micronesia now seem unlikely.

The American Role In Micronesia

From the start official U.S. policy was to preserve Micronesia for strategic use, while denying military access to foreign powers. The welfare of inhabitants was considered only in relation to this primary purpose. Article six of the U.N. Trusteeship Agreement bound the U.S. to "promote the economic advancement and self-sufficiency of the inhabitants." Instead, two decades of neglect were followed by two decades of handouts, undermining the self-sufficiency of the Micronesians and all but destroying their fisheries and agriculture.

In the early years of American administration, little was done to promote self-government, and only elementary education was available. Facilities remaining from the Japanese period were left to crumble. Vast sums of money were spent on a nuclear-testing program in the Marshalls from 1946 to 1958, but so little administrative and economic support was provided to the rest of Micronesia that economic output fell far below levels attained under the Germans and Japanese.

Then in the early 1960s independence fever swept the third world and it looked like the U.S. might lose control of its strategically located trust territory. In 1961 a visiting United Nations mission leveled heavy criticism at Washington for its "benign neglect." In response, President Kennedy appointed a commission headed by economist Anthony M. Solomon to explore means of strengthening the American hold on the region. The now-famous Solomon Report recommended agricultural development, capital improvements, and new health and welfare programs. The economic development proposals, which might have made the islands self-supporting, were never implemented. Instead, government

funds were pumped into administration, education, and health care, spawning a checkbook bureaucracy.

In 1963 President Kennedy issued National Security Action Memorandum 145, setting forth as policy "the movement of Micronesia into a permanent relationship with the United States within our political framework." To accomplish this, the Micronesians were to be further lured away from their traditional culture and made economically dependent on U.S. government subsidies. U.S. assistance to the TTPI jumped from $6.1 million in 1962 to $17 million in 1963, $67.3 million in 1971, and $138.7 million in 1979. Despite the flood of money essential services (water, electricity, communications, sanitation) remained as bad as ever. It seemed most of the money went into government salaries for people who performed no specific task. From the start politics in Micronesia was based mostly on family ties and the immediate benefits politicians could deliver to voters.

After 1966 large numbers of Peace Corps volunteers began arriving to teach English, spread American attitudes, and speed social change. At its high point, 900 volunteers were at work on less than 100 inhabited islands (today there are only about 60 Peace Corps volunteers in the Marshall Islands and the Federated States of Micronesia). Some volunteers openly sided with the Micronesians, providing legal advice on how to defend their rights, and protests from the Pentagon led the Nixon administration to phase out Peace Corps legal services.

An American-oriented curriculum was used in the schools and all the brightest students were sent to study in the States. Beginning in 1974, color television, an important part of the Americanization program, was introduced throughout Micronesia. Although never a profitable undertaking, TV was run by private business to avoid regulation and public scrutiny. State Department subsidies made the stations viable. Television has cut back sharply on other recreational activities and tends to substitute consumerism for local cultures.

Political Development

The U.S. exported its political structures to Micronesia as a way of supplanting traditional chiefs less malleable than American-educated politicians, dependent on Uncle Sam for their paychecks. However, when the first Congress of Micronesia met on Saipan in 1965, American officials were taken aback by the political sophistication and solidarity displayed by the Micronesian legislators. In 1966 this Congress asked President Johnson to appoint a status commission to expedite the transfer of political control from the American officials on Saipan to elected Micronesian leaders. Negotiations toward a new status began in 1969. In 1971 the Micronesians rejected an offer of commonwealth status, which would have allowed the U.S. government to exercise eminent domain over areas it needed for military use.

Frustrated U.S. officials fell back on a "divide and conquer" strategy, fragmenting Micronesia into four separate entities to foreclose the independence option. The CIA was brought in to spy on the Micronesian leaders (see front page, the *Washington Post,* 2 Dec. 1976). In 1975 the U.S. sliced off the Northern Marianas to form the Commonwealth of the Northern Marianas, a permanent American possession with large tracts of land leased by the military. In May 1977, President Carter announced that the U.S. would terminate the trusteeship in 1981 and ordered U.S. officials to speed up negotiations.

Free Association

Despite the withdrawal of the Marianas delegates, a draft constitution for a "Federated States of Micronesia" was prepared. On 12 July 1978 a plebiscite was held throughout the trust territory. Voters in the Marshalls and Belau (the most strategically significant areas) rejected the constitution and elected to separate from the other districts, forming political entities of their own. This reflected an awareness of their stronger bargaining position and an unwillingness to share future benefits. A few months later the Congress of Micronesia was dissolved, and the four central districts (Kosrae,

OCEANIA AT A GLANCE

Land areas and sea areas (the ocean area included within the 200-nautical mile Exclusive Economic Zone, or EEZ, of each country) are expressed in square kilometers. The Political Status category denotes the year in which the country became independent, or in which the territory or province fell under colonial rule by the power named. The sea areas (and various other figures) were taken from South Pacific Economies: Statistical Summary, published by the South Pacific Commission, Noumea.

COUNTRY	POPULATION	LAND AREA	SEA AREA	CAPITAL	POLITICAL STATUS	CURRENCY	AIRPORT TAX
Tahiti-Polynesia	188,814	3,543	5,030,000	Papeete	France1842	CFP	none
Pitcairn Islands	59	47	800,000	Adamstown	Britain 1838	NZ$	none
Easter Island	2,100	166	355,000	Hanga Roa	Chile 1888	*peso*	US$12.50
Galapagos	4,410	7,877	857,000	Baquerizo	Ecuador 1832	*sucre*	none
Cook Islands	17,177	240	1,830,000	Avarua	N.Z. 1901	NZ$	NZ$20
Niue	3,000	259	390,000	Alofi	N.Z. 1900	NZ$	NZ$10
Kingdom of Tonga	100,230	691	700,000	Nuku'alofa	ind. 1970	*pa'anga*	T$5
American Samoa	32,297	201	390,000	Utulei	U.S. 1900	US$	none
Western Samoa	157,349	2,842	120,000	Apia	ind. 1962	*tala*	WS$20
Tokelau	1,690	12	290,000	Fakaofo	N.Z. 1925	*tala*	none
Wallis and Futuna	14,000	274	300,000	Mata Utu	France 1887	CFP	none
Tuvalu	8,229	25	900,000	Funafuti	ind. 1978	A$	A$10
TOTAL POLYNESIA	**529,355**	**16,177**	**11,962,000**				
Fiji	714,548	18,272	1,290,000	Suva	ind.1970	F$	F$10
New Caledonia	145,368	18,576	1,740,000	Noumea	France 1853	CFP	none
Vanuatu	149,739	12,189	680,000	Vila	Ind. 1980	*vatu*	v.1500
Solomon Islands	285,796	27,556	1,340,000	Honiara	ind. 1978	SI$	SI$20
Papua New Guinea	3,060,600	462,243	3,120,000	Moresby	ind. 1975	*kina*	K15
Irian Jaya	1,173,875	421,981	324,000	Jayapura	Indonesia 1962	*rupiah*	US$5
TOTAL MELANESIA	**5,529,926**	**960,817**	**8,494,000**				
Nauru	8,902	21	320,000	Yaren	ind. 1968	A$	A$10
Kiribati	72,298	810	3,550,000	Bairiki	ind. 1979	A$	A$5
Marshall Islands	43,380	181	2,131,000	Majuro	ind. 1986	US$	US$10
Federated States of Micronesia	98,071	701	2,978,000	Pohnpei	ind. 1986	US$	US$5
Belau	15,122	488	629,000	Koror	U.S. 1945	US$	US$10
Guam	133,152	541	218,000	Agana	U.S. 1898	US$	none
Northern Marianas	43,345	478	1,823,000	Saipan	U.S. 1945	US$	none
TOTAL MICRONESIA	**414,270**	**3,220**	**11,649,000**				
TOTAL OCEANIA	**6,473,551**	**980,214**	**32,105,000**				

Pohnpei, Chuuk, and Yap) banded together, proclaiming the FSM constitution on 10 May 1979. The Marshall Islands also attained self-government in 1979, and in 1980 Belau became a self-governing republic.

In 1983 voters in Marshall Islands and the FSM approved compacts of free association with the U.S., but in Belau the compact has been defeated in seven referenda due to U.S. insistence on the right to establish military bases in the islands. Because of this the Belau compact must obtain at least 75% of the vote to override the republic's nuclear-free constitution (probably impossible to achieve) and the situation there remains stalemated. Belau must still choose between accepting the nuclear-weapons compact, U.S. commonwealth status, or independence, though with the need for new military bases receding, it's possible that the U.S. may generously agree to a nuclear-free compact, which would be approved immediately.

The 15-year compacts grant two independent entities—the Republic of the Marshall Islands and the Federated States of Micronesia—full control over their internal and external affairs. In exchange for billions of dollars in financial support, the U.S. retained the right to use the islands for military purposes for 15 years. (The stalled Belau compact grants the U.S. military rights for 50 years.) The U.S. has veto power over any Micronesian action in conflict with this right. Only the people of the Northern Marianas are U.S. citizens, although the others have the right of free entry to the States.

In 1986 the U.N. Trusteeship Council approved the termination of the U.S. trusteeship in Marshall Islands, the Federated States of Micronesia, and the Northern Marianas, and—though the status of Belau remained unresolved—the U.S. declared the trusteeship terminated in the three in Oct. 1986. Late in 1990 the Soviet Union withdrew its previous objections to these moves, and in Dec. 1990 the U.N. Security Council voted 14-to-1 (with Cuba dissenting) to dissolve the Trust Territory in the three entities mentioned above. In 1991 the TTPI headquarters was moved from Saipan to Koror (Belau).

On 17 Sept. 1991 the Federated States of Micronesia and the Marshall Islands were admitted to the United Nations, and despite the continuing dependence on Washington many countries have recognized these two states as independent and have opened imposing embassies on Majuro and Pohnpei. Belau remains a Trust Territory and the Northern Marianas has become a permanent possession of the U.S. (Micronesian diplomatic representatives overseas are listed in the Appendix.)

M.G.L. DOMENY DE RIENZI

The Future

How will history judge the American administration of Micronesia? The Spanish came to spread their religion and succeeded, often by murderous means. The paternal Germans taught the Micronesians the value of hard work and economic efficiency, lessons easily forgotten. The Japanese developed the islands by opening the floodgates to uncontrolled Asian immigration and militarization. Had they not started a disastrous war, Micronesia today would be as Japanese as Okinawa or Hokkaido.

The American approach to Micronesia was subtle and effective. While appearing benevolent, they instilled economic and political dependency to serve their military ends. On the other hand, the U.S. protected Micronesian land rights. During the Japanese period most of the land was alienated by Japanese settlers who soon outnumbered the native Micronesians. Under the TTPI most of this land went back to its original owners.

Today the U.S. seems almost in a hurry to get rid of Micronesia and save the $100 million a year it spends on aid to the islands. For the first time the U.S. is acknowledging that independence is an option for Belau after all! The Japanese are eagerly waiting on the sidelines but the Micronesians are not raring to have them after wartime experiences of Japanese brutality and exploitation.

International Relations

The U.S. government agency presently responsible for administering Belau, coordinating the relationship with Guam and the Northern Marianas, and overseeing the provision of federal funds and programs for the Marshall Islands and the FSM is the **Office of Territorial and International Affairs** under the Secretary of the Interior (Washington, DC 20240 U.S.A.).

The Federated States of Micronesia, Kiribati, Marshall Islands, and Nauru are members of the **South Pacific Forum** (GPO Box 856, Suva, Fiji Islands), a regional grouping concerned with economic development, trade, communications, fisheries, environmental protection, etc., established in 1971.

(The Republic of Belau has observer status.) At their annual meetings, the heads of government of the 15 SPF countries express their joint political views. Meetings held in Micronesia include the 1976 meeting on Nauru, the 1980 and 1989 meetings on Tarawa, and the 1991 meeting on Pohnpei. The 1993 meeting will again be on Nauru. At the 1985 Forum meeting the South Pacific Nuclear Free Zone treaty was signed. The 1989 meeting condemned driftnet fishing and set up a mechanism to monitor the greenhouse effect.

The **South Pacific Forum Fisheries Agency** (Box 629, Honiara, Solomon Islands), formed in 1979, coordinates the fisheries policies of the 16 member states (including all 15 SPF members and Belau) and negotiates licensing agreements with foreign countries. In 1988 the Federated States of Micronesia and Marshall Islands became parties to the **South Pacific Regional Trade and Economic Cooperation Agreement** (SPARTECA), which allows certain island products duty-free entry to Australia and New Zealand; Kiribati and Nauru also belong.

All of the countries included in this book belong to the **South Pacific Commission** (Box D5, Noumea Cedex, New Caledonia). The SPC was established in 1947 by the postwar colonial powers, Australia, France, the Netherlands, New Zealand, the United Kingdom, and the U.S. (the Netherlands withdrew in 1962). As the insular territories attained self-government they were admitted to membership, and in Oct. each year delegates from the 27 member governments meet at a **South Pacific Conference** to discuss the Commission's program and budget. The SPC promotes regional economic and social development through annual conferences, research, and technical assistance, and is strictly nonpolitical. Fields of activity include food, marine resources, environment management, rural development, community health, education, and statistical studies.

The main nonprofit, nongovernmental organization active in the region is the **Micronesia Institute** (1275 K St. NW, Suite 360, Washington, DC 20005-4006 U.S.A.; tel.

202-842-1140), particularly in the fields of health, education, entrepreneurship, private-sector economic development, and cultural and historical preservation. The **School of the Pacific Islands** (125 West Thousand Oaks Blvd., Thousand Oaks, CA 91360-4412 U.S.A.; tel. 805-497-7691) is a non-profit corporation which funds educational projects throughout Micronesia. The **Foun-** **dation for the Peoples of the South Pacific** (Box 85710, San Diego, CA 92186 U.S.A.; tel. 619-279-9820) has a project in Kiribati. Both these groups are financed indirectly by the U.S. government and large corporations as a public relations ploy to enhance the image of the United States, a role they share with the Peace Corps and military "Civic Action Teams" such as the Seabees.

DAVID STANLEY

loading cargo at Kolonia, Pohnpei

ECONOMY

Micronesia's greatest resource is its strategic position between the world's two largest economies, the U.S. and Japan. In 1984, for the first time in history, the U.S. did more business with Asian nations than with those in Europe. The military importance assigned to Micronesia by the Pentagon reflects the increasing economic importance of Asia to American banks and corporations. To defend these interests, since 1962 the U.S. has carried out a systematic program to bind Micronesia to America—politically, socially, and economically. American aid to the region, overwhelmingly the largest source of income, has been intended to achieve this goal.

Regional differences are great, with the Marshall Islands and the FSM having a per-capita gross domestic product of under $2,000 a year, Belau about $4,000 a year, and Guam and the Northern Marianas both over $15,000 a year. In Kiribati the GDP is less than $1,000 per capita. About two-thirds of the population of the Marshall Islands and Belau live in urban areas, while only about a third of the people of the FSM and Kiribati are in urban areas. By the same standards Guam and the Northern Marianas are almost totally urbanized.

Dependency

In 1961 imports to Micronesia led exports by two to one; by 1975 this had increased to 15 to one. In 1984 the U.S. provided $124 million in aid to the Trust Territory of the Pacific Islands, more than it spent in Guam and American Samoa combined. Most American aid goes to private consumption rather than public investment. Large numbers of Micronesians continue to flock to the towns to lead a life-style supported by U.S. tax money alone. The average government worker makes eight times as much as a villager and the gap between officials earning $30,000 a year and the majority making $1.35 an hour is huge.

Traditionally, Micronesians placed a higher value on the distribution of surpluses than on the accumulation of wealth. Now U.S. policy has created a large bureaucracy dependent on U.S. subsidies. What local revenue there is comes largely from taxes on the salaries of government employees and goods sold to them. Private business is limited mostly to companies selling consumer goods and services to government employees and tourists.

New needs have been created on the power of the U.S. tax dollar alone. The Micronesians depend on Washington for the very food they eat—in many places the taro patches are abandoned, the breadfruit is unharvested, and fish proliferate in the lagoons. Rice, the current staple, would flourish in Pohnpei's ideal conditions, but it's cheaper to import. Imported foods of poor nutritional value have created new health problems. The massive capital-improvements programs and administrative complexes do nothing to foster economic self-sufficiency; rather, they create even more dependency. Many are infrastructure improvements primarily designed to support official or military operations. Although the cost of providing electricity runs into the millions, much of it is consumed by government itself.

The influx of U.S. government money not only creates dependency, it also inflates local labor costs to the point where Micronesia cannot compete with other tropical islands for export-oriented foreign investment. High government pay scales hamper private business. The services provided may be admirable in themselves, but without an economic base to support them they guarantee that the associated states will always be dominated by the United States.

Over the next 15 years the associated states are required to spend 40% of their compact subsidies on capital improvements such as roads, airports, harbors, sewers, water-supply systems, government buildings, etc. Whether the new facilities will be maintained or simply left to crumble once completed remains to be seen. The fact that nearly all government construction contracts go to Japanese or Korean rather than local firms gives a good indication of what is to come, however.

All Japanese aid is tied to specific projects, with Japanese companies doing all of the work. Much Japanese aid to Micronesia is linked to fishing-rights negotiations, and assistance is stopped to countries that cause problems for Japanese fishing companies. The sole purpose of this checkbook diplomacy is to make countries amenable to Japanese business penetration and to mute criticism of the environmental destruction Japanese corporations wreak.

Health And Welfare

Certainly no one would argue with providing proper medical care, but despite the impressive facilities, the quality of treatment is low. It's not unusual to be told at one of the big showplace hospitals that all the doctors are at a "meeting" or have left for the day. Devastating cholera and tuberculosis epidemics swept Micronesia in the 1980s. Leprosy is still rampant on several islands. Proper sewers and water systems are not in place. Large numbers of people fall victim to diseases that have been eradicated almost everywhere else. What health care does exist is geared toward curing disease rather than preventing it. No emphasis is placed on family planning, thereby contributing to the population explosion. Cigarette smoking is almost universal. As usual, U.S. aid does things—good and bad—*to* people rather than helping them to do it *for themselves.*

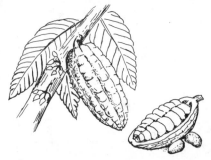

LOUISE FOOTE

Cocoa and chocolate are made from the seed of the cacao tree.

Education

New schools have been built and Micronesians attend U.S. colleges, but most of the graduates come home with arts degrees that prepare them for government service and little else. Although graduates in business and public administration abound, Micronesian doctors and dentists are rare. There's a serious problem of overeducation, as hundreds of students return from U.S. colleges to look for jobs that don't exist. To date the educational effort has been low quality, and few technical skills are imparted. The Micronesian Occupational College (MOC) at Koror offers some vocational training, and the Community College of Micronesia at Pohnpei handles

Apart from the coconut tree, the pandanus shrub is one of the most widespread and useful plants in the Pacific. Among other things, the islanders use the thorny leaves of the pandanus, or screw pine, for weaving mats, baskets, and fans. The seeds are strung into necklaces. The fibrous fruit makes brushes for decorating tapa cloth and can be eaten. The aerial roots can be made into fish traps.

DIANA LASICH HARPER

teacher training. A school of nursing operates at Majuro. However, practical technical and agricultural education has largely been left to Jesuit institutions, such as the Pohnpei Agricultural and Trade School (PATS) on Pohnpei. Mostly, American education has taught the Micronesians to be chronic consumers of U.S. tax money.

Law Of The Sea

This law has changed the face of Micronesia. States traditionally exercised sovereignty over a three-mile belt of territorial sea along their shores. The high seas beyond these limits could be freely used by anyone. Then on 28 Sept. 1945 President Harry Truman declared U.S. sovereignty over the natural resources of the adjacent continental shelf. U.S. fishing boats soon became involved in an acrimonious dispute with several South American countries over their rich anchovy fishing grounds, and in 1952 Chile, Ecuador, and Peru declared a 200-nautical-mile Exclusive Economic Zone (EEZ) along their shores. In 1958 the United Nations convened a Conference on the Law of the Sea at Geneva which accepted national control over continental shelves up to 200 meters deep. Agreement could not be reached on extended territorial sea limits.

National claims multiplied so much that in 1974 another U.N. conference was convened, leading to the signing of the Law of the Sea convention at Jamaica in 1982 by 159 states and other entities. This complex agreement of 200 pages, nine annexes, and 320 articles extended national control over 40% of the world's oceans. The territorial sea was increased to 12 nautical miles and the continental shelf ambiguously defined as extending 200 nautical miles offshore. States were given full control over all resources, living or nonliving, within this belt. To date only 47 states have ratified the convention, still 13 short of the 60 required for it to come into effect. Largely due to other nations' objections to provisions for the strict regulation of undersea mining, the only industrialized country to sign so far is Iceland.

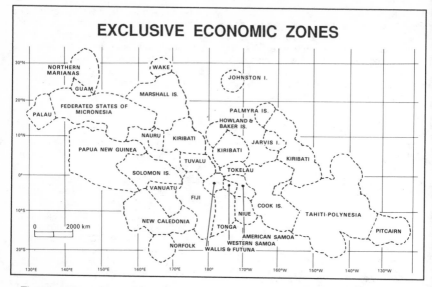

EXCLUSIVE ECONOMIC ZONES

Though still not international law, many aspects of the Law of the Sea have become accepted in practice. The EEZs mainly affect fisheries and seabed mineral exploitation; freedom of navigation within the zones is guaranteed. The Law of the Sea increased immensely the territory of oceanic states, giving them real political weight for the first time. The land area of the seven political entities covered in this book comes to only 3,227 square km, while their EEZs total 11,649,000 square km!

Fisheries

Tuna is the second-most-important fishing industry in the world (after shrimp and prawns), and 66% of the world's catch is taken in the Pacific. The western Pacific, where most of the islands are located, is twice as productive as the eastern, with fish worth over a billion dollars extracted annually. Although tuna is one of the few renewable resources the Micronesian islanders have, for many years the U.S. government (at the behest of the tuna industry) attempted to deny them any benefit from it by claiming that the fish were "migratory"; thus American

purse seiners were not subject to licensing fees for fishing within the 200-nautical-mile EEZs. Unlicensed American fishing for tuna in the Solomons and Kiribati was seen as systematic poaching, raising the specter of citizens of one of the richest nations on earth stealing from two of the poorest.

In 1985, when Kiribati signed a fishing agreement with the Soviet Union, the U.S. finally got the message. In 1987 the U.S. government agreed to a US$60-million aid package, which included licensing fees for American tuna boats to work the EEZs of the 16 member states of the South Pacific Forum Fisheries Agency (including Belau, the Federated States of Micronesia, Kiribati, Marshall Islands, and Nauru) for five years. The settlement, small potatoes for the U.S. but big money to the islanders, was seen as an inexpensive way of forestalling "Soviet advances" in the Central Pacific. In 1990 the question of whether island governments would be allowed to control their valuable tuna resources seemed settled when the U.S. Congress voted overwhelmingly to impose management on tuna stocks in the U.S. EEZ. The "migratory" fish finally had owners.

M.G.L. DOMENY DE RIENZI

The Forum Fisheries Agency, which negotiated the Tuna Treaty, now handles all fishing agreements between FFA member states and the U.S., Korea, Japan, and Taiwan. Japan has resisted signing multilateral fisheries agreements, preferring to deal with the Pacific countries individually. As a means of buying influence, fisheries development in Micronesia has been sponsored mainly by Japan rather than the U.S., with Japanese-built freezer plants established throughout the region. The Tuna Treaty now provides U.S. assistance to FFA countries in creating fishing industries of their own.

The bitter irony of local fish being sent to Japan to be canned, then sold back to islanders at high prices, is all too real. To protect American jobs, U.S. Customs regulations prohibit foreign fishing boats from unloading on U.S. territory, yet at the same time place high taxes on tuna *unless* it's canned on U.S. soil. This has deprived the Pacific peoples of the processing profits from their biggest natural resource. Now the U.S. has given the Marshalls, Marianas, FSM, and Belau as a group the option of supplying up to 10% of

the U.S. canned tuna market without being affected by these regulations. But problems such as the lack of sufficient freshwater supplies and a worldwide tuna glut make a cannery in Micronesia unlikely at the moment—the cannery at Belau closed in 1982. Some fishing boats do transfer their catches to refrigerated freighters at Tinian, but there are no shore facilities there.

Most of the tuna fished from the Pacific islands region is taken by around 110 purse seiners, 32 of them Japanese and 65 affiliated with the American Tunaboat Association. Longline vessels are used to supply the Japanese sashimi market. Some Pacific countries have established small pole-and-line fishing industries, but the capital-intensive, high-tech purse seiner operations carried out by the Americans and Japanese are still beyond their means. For the foreseeable future, licensing fees will be the island governments' only share of this resource. Meanwhile fisheries researchers in Belau have been successful in breeding giant clams. The clams, which produce meat faster than any terrestrial animal, could become the basis of a major seafood industry serving the $100-million-a-year Asian clam-meat market.

Until recently, purse seiner operations led to the drowning of tens of thousands of dolphins a year in tuna nets. Herds of dolphins tend to swim above schools of yellowfin tuna in the eastern Pacific; thus unscrupulous fishermen would deliberately set their nets around the marine mammals, crushing or suffocating them. In 1990, after a tuna boycott spearheaded by the Earth Island Institute (300 Broadway, Suite 28, San Francisco, CA 94133 U.S.A.), H.J. Heinz (StarKist) and other American tuna packers announced that they would can only tuna caught using dolphin-safe fishing methods. Neither longline nor pole-and-line tuna fishing involves killing dolphins, nor do dolphins associate with tuna in the western Pacific. Because Micronesia has always been a dolphin-safe tuna fishing area, the number of U.S. boats operating here suddenly increased when the canneries stopped buying tuna caught off Central and South America.

Unfortunately canneries in Italy, Japan, and some other countries continue to accept tuna from dolphin-killing Mexican and South American vessels without reservations. If you care about marine mammals, look for the distinctive "dolphin-safe" label before buying any tuna at all. Earth Island Institute has also lobbied successfully to halt the use of "seal bomb" explosives to herd dolphins (and the tuna below them) into fishing nets.

Another devastating fishing practice, the use of driftnets up to 65 km long and 15 meters deep, only began in the early 1980s. By the end of the decade 1,500 Japanese, Taiwanese, and Korean fishing boats were setting 30,000 km of these nets across the Pacific each night. These plastic "walls of death" indiscriminately capture and kill everything that bumps into them, from whole schools of tuna or salmon, to dolphins, seals, whales, blue sharks, sea turtles, and many other endangered species. Thousands of seabirds are entangled as they dive for fish in the nets. Driftnets are extremely wasteful as up to 40% of the catch is lost as the nets are hauled in and an equally large proportion has to be discarded because the fish are too

scarred by the net. Lost or abandoned "ghost nets" continue their gruesome harvest until they sink from the weight of corpses caught in them. This practice, which makes any sort of fisheries management impossible, was strongly condemned by the South Pacific Forum at its 1989 meeting on Tarawa, and driftnet fishing boats were banned from the 29.4 million square km of ocean included in the EEZs of the 15 member states. This act was mostly symbolic, as driftnetters operate only in international waters and don't pay licensing fees to anyone. In Dec. 1989 the United Nations General Assembly passed a resolution calling for a moratorium on driftnetting in international waters after 30 June 1992, and in 1990 the U.S. Congress passed a bill prohibiting the import of any fish caught with driftnets beginning in July 1992. Under mounting international pressure, Japan agreed in 1991 to end its driftnet fishing by the U.N. deadline. Right from the start Japan had prohibited driftnet fishing by Japanese vessels within 1,600 km of its own shores!

Manufacturing

The production of goods for export to the U.S., Australia, and New Zealand offers the best possibility for the development of light manufacturing. As insular possessions, the Marshall Islands, the FSM, and the Northern Marianas may export their products to the U.S. free of quotas, but not duties. Some 26 Asian-owned garment factories are now functioning on Saipan, and in 1989 a similar factory opened on Yap. Most of the work force is imported from Asia and the factories on Saipan have severely strained the local infrastructure. Micronesians have shown themselves unwilling to perform this type of exacting factory work for low wages; thus the real value of these endeavors is far less than one might assume from statistics. Local governments do earn additional tax revenues on the factories, however.

The South Pacific Regional Trade and Economic Cooperation Agreement (SPARTECA) allows the duty-free entry of most goods manufactured in the member states of the South Pacific Forum (FSM, Kiribati, Marshall Islands, and Nauru) to Australia and New Zealand, provided they have 50% local content.

Tourism

Guam is the major tourist center of Micronesia, with over 750,000 (mostly Japanese) visitors a year. Saipan comes next with more than 400,000 (also Japanese); the American-associated states altogether get about 50,000, with Belau alone accounting for about half of these. While only seven percent of tourists visiting Guam are Americans, the U.S. provides 62% of visitors to the Federated States of Micronesia. In 1985 the FSM got 5,111 tourists, 3,174 of them from the U.S. and 1,020 from Japan.

Tourism to Guam and Saipan does not bring the benefits the numbers might imply, since the Japanese arrive on Japanese planes, stay at Japanese-owned hotels, eat Japanese food, ride Japanese tour buses, and buy Japanese-made products at duty-free prices—mostly prepaid in Japan, preventing local operators from getting much of the action. Belau is now opening up to the same kind of operation.

Tourism officials on Yap say they don't want high-pressure, high-rise tourist hotels owned by Japanese corporations, but that they might welcome smaller, low-key beach hotels constructed of local materials by investors willing to work with Yapese partners who supply the land and labor. Small locally owned hotels provide much of the lodging in the Marshall Islands and the FSM. Tourism to Kiribati is insignificant.

LOUISE FOOTE

THE PEOPLE

The Micronesians are a mixed race, with strong Polynesian strains. They also absorbed the blood of many tribes during their stay in the Philippines over 3,000 years ago. Clearly recognizable, they are copper-skinned, thin-lipped, and have comparatively short, slight builds and straight black hair. Their societies were highly organized; the clans were led by hereditary chiefs who were most powerful in the Marshalls and Tungaru. Except in Yap and Tungaru, descent was largely matrilineal. Generally speaking, there were no priests or sacred places (Nan Madol was an exception). Micronesian mythology had a strong element of hero worship, and they tattooed their bodies using burnt breadfruit gum.

Contemporary Life
Micronesia is one of the most densely populated areas on earth, with a population growth rate of over three percent. More than half the inhabitants are under age 15, and the population will double by the end of the century. Many Micronesians reside in Guam, Hawaii, and California, where the employment opportunities are better.

The period 1960-1979 saw a shocking, eightfold increase in the suicide rate among young Micronesian males. In the 15-25 age group the rate is 250 incidences per 100,000—20 times higher than in the United States. Alcoholism is also a serious problem. Culture change in Micronesia is farthest advanced in the Marianas, where Spanish and American influence was strongest. The large numbers of police one sees in the towns of Micronesia reflect the lack of social control by village elders; on the outer islands relatively few police are present.

Language
Micronesians speak Austronesian languages different from those of Polynesia. Eleven major languages are spoken: Chamorro and Belauan are classified as Indonesian, while Yapese, Ulithian, Chuukese, Pohnpeian, Kosraean, Nauruan, Gilbertese, and Marshallese are Micronesian, and Kapingamarangi is Polynesian. Contemporary Chamorro is a mixture of the original tongue and Spanish. A continuous linguistic chain extends across Micronesia, with islanders from nearby islands able to understand one an-

other. The farther apart the islands, the less comprehension there is, until people from opposite ends of the region cannot understand one another at all.

If you'd like to take lessons in a local language during your stay, ask the Peace Corps office to suggest a tutor.

Religion

Missionaries of every Christian denomination under the sun are active in Micronesia. Some, such as the clean-cut young Mormon "elders" with their white shirts and ties, are highly visible, but the Assemblies of God, Baha'is, Baptists, Catholics, Evangelicals, Jehovah's Witnesses, Lutherans, Methodists, Pentecostals, Presbyterians, and Seventh-Day Adventists are all present. One group, Youth With A Mission, has programs on Guam and Saipan which are open to visitors (see the "Volunteers" section in the "Guam" and "Northern Marianas" chapters for details).

Some fundamentalist missions play a role in spreading American values and are dominated by foreign personnel, ideas, and money. A few of the conservative groups portray God as an affluent American and encourage Micronesians to wait for their reward in heaven, while "liberation theologists" tackle the worldly causes of social injustice. While the former stress passages in the Bible which call for obedience to authority and resignation to dependency, the latter try to apply the Bible to daily life and preach self-reliance. (Of course, these are generalizations intended only to stimulate thought.)

An example of how religious groups can be manipulated for political ends appeared in Kiribati in 1985 when the Kiribati Government signed a licensing agreement with the Soviet fishing company Sovryflot for purely commercial reasons (see "Economy" in the "Kiribati" chapter for details). This seemed to challenge American hegemony in the region, so Australian right-wingers got the Roman Catholic Bishop of Tarawa to issue a pamphlet titled "The Great Russian Bear," which was intended to undermine local government policy by inciting anticommunist hysteria.

Arts And Crafts

Dance and song are the supreme artforms in Micronesia; the plastic arts are poor, especially compared to Polynesia and Melanesia. In times past the Micronesian artist was lim-

woman weaving, Yap: She is using the simple back-strap loom which in the Pacific is found only in the Caroline Islands. Only narrow material can be woven on this type of loom.

ited by a lack of resources. Life itself was often a struggle, so there was less free time to devote to art than in other Pacific cultures. In place of sculpture and painting the emphasis was on functional, utilitarian crafts, with some geometric ornamentation. Showing their Asian origins, Micronesian designs and colors, known for extreme fineness and lightness, are more subdued than the Polynesian ones.

Most of the traditional handicrafts one sees today are practical items the people once used in their everyday lives, such as personal adornments, mats, baskets, and fans. Some of the finest Micronesian weaving is done in the Marshalls where pandanus and coconut fiber are plentiful. In the outer islands of the Carolines the backstrap loom, of Indonesian ancestry, is still used to weave wraparound *lava lava* skirts of banana and hibiscus fiber.

Breadfruit is the wood most often carved (especially for model and actual canoes), although coconut, ironwood, and hibiscus woods are also used. In Belau, a great revival of hardwood carving took place this century. The finely carved war clubs of the South Pacific are not common in Micronesia, where men fought with sling and spear. Warriors in the Gilberts carried shark-tooth-edged swords and wore woven body armor. The only masks known in Micronesia were those of the Mortlocks.

Except in the Marianas, the handicrafts sold in Micronesia are all authentic handmade products; they're easily distinguished from the mass-produced Filipino items sold to Japanese tourists on Guam and Saipan. Considering the time that goes into Micronesian handicrafts, prices are low (don't bargain). Many of the handicraft outlets are softsell, low-profit ventures.

When making purchases, beware of objects made from turtle shell, which are prohibited entry into the U.S. and many other countries under endangered species acts. Unfortunately, over the past 20 years Japan has imported the skins of over two million sea turtles, including over 1.2 million hawksbill turtles, 438,000 green turtles, and 492,000 olive ridley turtles. Japan continues to trade in the shells of these noble creatures to make handbags, belts, high heels, eyeglass frames, cigarette lighters, and combs, though in 1991 Japan agreed to ban hawksbill turtle imports beginning in Jan. 1993, after strong pressure from the United States.

ACCOMMODATIONS AND FOOD

Rooms

Moderately priced hotels can be found in most of the towns and only Guam and Saipan have Waikiki-style hotel rows. Prices range from $15 s all the way up to $375 d. If your hotel can't provide running water, electricity, air conditioning, or something similar because of a typhoon or otherwise, ask for a price reduction. You'll often get 10% off. Many deluxe hotels and car rental agencies have a special "corporate" or "business" rate they give to government employees, the military, Peace Corps volunteers, businesspeople, etc. A business card or plausible story should net you the discount. There's a serious accommodation shortage throughout the Federated States of Micronesia and occasionally every hotel room is full.

There aren't many hotels on the outer islands, but in the Marshalls and Federated States island mayors or chiefs will help you find a place to stay. Most atolls in Kiribati (except Tarawa and Abemama) have Island Council rest houses where you can sleep for around A$5-15 pp a night. Radio ahead to let them know you're coming. Elementary school teachers in remote areas are often very hospitable and may offer to put you up. Always try to find some tangible way to show your appreciation, such as paying for the groceries or giving a gift. It wouldn't hurt to offer cash payment if a stranger helps you when you're in a jam. Once you get home, don't forget to mail prints of any photos you've taken.

Camping

A tent will save the budget traveler a lot of money and prove very convenient to fall back on. It's rarely difficult to find people willing to let you camp on their land, and since most land is privately owned it's important always to ask permission of someone like a village mayor or chief first; they're usually agreeable. Ensure this same hospitality for the next traveler by not leaving a mess.

On the main islands it's not safe to leave your tent unattended; you must dismantle it daily and ask your host to store it for you, then reerect it at night. As yet the only regular

Breadfruit (Artocarpus communis) *grows on tall trees with large green leaves. From Indonesia ancient voyagers carried it to all of Polynesia. "Breadfruit Bligh" was returning from Tahiti with a thousand potted trees to provide food for slaves in Jamaica when the famous mutiny occurred. Propagated from root suckers, this seedless plant provides shade as well as food. A well-watered tree can produce as many as 1,000 breadfruits a year. Joseph Banks, the botanist on Capt. Cook's first voyage, wrote: "If a man should in the course of his lifetime plant 10 trees, which if well done might take the labour of an hour or thereabouts, he would completely fulfill his duty to his own as well as future generations."*

DIANA LASICH HARPER

campgrounds are on Guam and the facilities at these are minimal. On the outer islands, however, there should be no problem: in fact, when you ask for a camping spot, you'll often be invited to stay in the family's house—an offer that can be difficult to refuse.

FOOD

All the towns have reasonable restaurants serving island/American/Chinese/Japanese cuisine from $3 to $8. Sometimes they're surprisingly good. Grilled tuna and reef fish are delectable. The Japanese left Micronesians with an enduring taste for white rice, to which the Americans added white sugar, bread, and beer. Rice is still the staple, and on the outer islands you'll find a fare of rice, breadfruit, taro, lagoon fish, and sashimi (raw fish), plus the more prosaic canned mackerel and Spam.

Breadfruit grows on trees (remember Captain Bligh?). Taro is an elephant-eared plant cultivated in freshwater swamps. Although yams are considered a prestige food, they're not as nutritious as breadfruit and taro. Yams can grow up to three meters long and weigh hundreds of kilograms.

Papaya (pawpaw) is nourishing: a third of a cup contains as much vitamin C as 18 apples. To ripen a green papaya overnight, puncture it a few times with a knife. Don't overeat papaya—unless you *need* an effective laxative. Atoll dwellers especially rely on the coconut for food. The tree reaches maturity in eight years, then produces about 50 nuts a year for 60 years.

Many islanders eat sashimi, but know what you're doing before you join them—their stomachs may be stronger than yours. It's safer to eat well-cooked food, and don't forget to peel your own fruit. If you feel you simply must refuse food offered you by the locals be as polite about it as you can.

Islanders in the towns now eat mostly imported foods. Sometimes even infants are fed junk food, leading to a myriad of health problems. Surprisingly, American-made groceries and canned foods are often cheaper in Micronesia than in Hawaii or the U.S. mainland due to the low markups added by local stores. If you're going to the outer islands, take as many edibles with you as possible. Imported foods are always more expensive there than in the main towns and often staples such as bread are not available.

Keep in mind that virtually every food plant you see growing on the islands was planted by someone. Even fishing floats or sea shells washed up on a beach, or fish in the lagoon near someone's home, may be considered private property.

PRACTICALITIES

Visas

Entry to Micronesia is easy. No visa is required to visit the Marshalls, Federated States, Belau, and Northern Marianas for a stay of up to 30 days. If you're leaving on the next connecting flight, you won't need a visa for Nauru either. Entry requirements to Kiribati are more complicated (turn to the Kiribati chapter for details). Almost everyone other than Americans and Canadians should have a U.S. visa to enter Guam—obtain one in your home country. Citizens of many countries may enter Guam visa-free for varying periods, however, and the Guam chapter in this book provides details.

U.S. citizens can enter the Marshalls, Federated States, Belau, Guam, and Northern Marianas without a passport, but proper identification (voter's registration card, notarized copy of birth certificate, etc.) is required. A driver's license or social security card is not good enough. Everyone else must have a passport which should be valid six months ahead (Americans do need one for Nauru and Kiribati).

All Micronesian countries require a ticket to leave. If you arrive without one, you may be required to purchase one on the spot or be refused entry. You may also be required to prove that you have "sufficient funds." U.S. citizens don't require an onward ticket to enter Guam or the Northern Marianas.

Money, Measurements, And Mail

American currency (US$) is used throughout Micronesia, except in Kiribati and Nauru where Australian dollars (A$) circulate. In this book prices are quoted in US$ in US$ areas and A$ in the A$ areas, unless otherwise noted. At last report US$1=A$1.30 approximately. Some of the oldest and filthiest U.S. bank notes you'll ever see circulate in the western Pacific.

Credit cards are accepted at the large hotels and by car rental agencies in the U.S. dollar areas, but cash is easier at restaurants, shops, etc. To avoid wasting time hassling at banks for cash advances, it's best to bring enough traveler's checks to cover all your out-of-pocket expenses, and then some. Post offices in the U.S. currency areas cash U.S. postal money orders, a good way to have money sent from the States.

Make sure your traveler's checks are expressed in U.S. dollars; other currencies may be difficult or impossible to exchange. U.S. dollar traveler's checks are readily accepted as cash at hotels and large stores throughout the US$ part of Micronesia. Traveler's checks in other currencies can only be changed at major banks and are then subject to US$3 commission plus a US$5 postage charge. To report stolen American Express traveler's checks call 801-964-6665 collect (on Guam, tel. 472-8884).

MICRONESIAN TIME

Standard Time

	Hours from GMT	Time at 1200 GMT*
California	- 8	0400
Hawaii, Christmas I.	- 10	0200
Kwajalein	- 12	2400
International Dateline		Sunday
		Monday
Majuro, Kosrae	+ 12	2400
Tarawa, Nauru	+ 12	2400
Pohnpei	+ 11	2300
Truk, Yap	+ 10	2200
Guam, Saipan	+ 10	2200
Belau, Japan	+ 9	2100
Philippines	+ 8	2000
Hong Kong	+ 8	2000

*GMT is Greenwich Mean Time, the time at London, England. California adopts Daylight Saving Time from May to October.

If you'll be visiting Kiribati or Nauru, have your bank order a few Australian-dollar traveler's checks. A small stack of U.S. one dollar bills for minor· expenses is always handy when traveling. If you loan money to a Micronesian, look upon it as a gift. If you insist upon being repaid you'll only make an enemy without collecting anything.

Tipping is becoming more widespread, though as yet it's a way of life only on Guam. The serving staff in restaurants which cater mostly to foreign businesspeople or tourists expect to be tipped, but those in places patronized mostly by Micronesians do not. If you tip in these, the waiter or waitress will be slightly embarrassed and you'll be looked upon as a dumb tourist.

The electric current throughout the American portion of Micronesia is 110 volts, 60 cycles, with standard American outlets. In Kiribati it's 240 volts, 50 cycles, with Australian outlets.

To call direct to a phone number in Micronesia from the U.S., dial the international access code 011, then the country code, then the number. For the Northern Mariana Islands dial the country code 670 plus the regular seven-digit number, for Guam 671 plus seven digits. For the Marshalls dial 692-9 for Majuro or 692-8 for Ebeye, plus four digits in each case. For the Federated States of Micronesia dial 691-370 for Kosrae, 691-320 for Pohnpei, 691-330 for Chuuk, 691-350 for Yap, all plus four digits. For the Republic of Belau dial 680-9-488 plus four digits. Other regional country codes are 674 (Nauru), 686 (Tarawa), and 967 (Midway). Long-distance calls are relayed via COMSAT satellite stations.

Regular U.S. postal rates apply throughout Micronesia (except in Kiribati and Nauru). Always use airmail when posting a letter; surface mail takes months to arrive. Mail leaves Micronesia much faster than it arrives. All the countries included in this book issue their own postage stamps (except Guam and the Northern Marianas, which use U.S. stamps). These stamps, available at local post offices, are good investments and make excellent souvenirs.

All mail is delivered to post office boxes. In this book we've listed the box numbers and postal codes of most businesses. Micronesian post offices will hold general delivery mail. If you're mailing a letter to Micronesia from outside the U.S., include "via U.S.A." in the address and be sure to use the correct five-digit zip code. Here's a list of Micronesian postal codes:

MICRONESIAN POSTAL CODES

Agana, GU 96910
Tamuning, GU 96911
Dededo, GU 96912
Barrigada, GU 96913
Yona, GU 96914
Santa Rita, GU 96915
Merizo, GU 96916
Inarajan, GU 96917
Umatac, GU 96918
Agana Heights, GU 96919
Guam Main Facility (GMF) 96921
Asan, GU 96922
Mangilao, GU 96923
Chalan Pago, GU 96924
Piti, GU 96925
Sinajana, GU 96926
Maite, GU 96927
Agat, GU 96928
Yigo, GU 96929
Talofofo, GU 96930
Box numbers, Tamuning, GU 96931

Koror, PW 96940

Pohnpei, FM 96941
Chuuk, FM 96942
Yap, FM 96943
Kosrae, FM 96944

Saipan, MP 96950
Rota, MP 96951
Tinian, MP 96952

Majuro, MH 96960
Jaluit, MH 96961
Ebeye, MH 96970

HEALTH

Micronesia's a healthy place. The sea and air are clear and usually pollution-free. The humidity nourishes the skin and the local fruit is brimming with vitamins. If you take a few precautions you'll never have a sick day. The information provided below is intended to make you knowledgeable, not fearful. You can always see a doctor at government hospitals in the towns, but although the cost of medical attention is low, so is the quality. If you fall seriously ill get a flight home as soon as possible. On the outer islands, clinics deal only in basics.

The sale of travel insurance is big business, but the value of the policies themselves varies. If your health insurance policy at home covers you while you're traveling abroad, it's probably enough. If you do opt for the security of travel insurance look for a policy which covers theft or loss of luggage and emergency medical evacuations. If you'll be involved in any "dangerous activities" such as scuba diving, read the fine print to make sure your policy is valid.

Don't go from winter weather into the steaming tropics without a rest before and after. Scuba diving on departure day can give you a severe case of the bends. Avoid jet lag by setting your watch to local time at your destination as soon as you board the flight. Airplane cabins have low humidity, so drink lots of juice and don't overeat in-flight. It's also best to forego coffee as it will only keep you awake. Alcohol helps dehydrate you. If you start feeling seasick aboard ship stare at the horizon, which is always steady, and stop thinking about it. Motion sickness pills are available.

Frequently the feeling of thirst is false and only due to mucous membrane dryness. Gargling or taking two or three gulps of warm water should be enough. Other means to keep moisture in the body are to have a hot drink like tea or black coffee, or any kind of slightly salted or sour drink in small quantities. Salt in fresh lime juice is remarkably refreshing.

The tap water is often unsafe to drink (check locally). If the tap water is contaminated, local ice will be too. Avoid brushing your teeth with water unfit to drink. Wash or

Elephantiasis and leprosy are endemic to Micronesia.

M.G.L. DUMONT DE RIENZI

peel fruit and vegetables if you can. Cooked food is less subject to contamination than raw.

Sunburn

Though you may think a tan will make you *look* healthier and more attractive, it's very damaging to the skin, which becomes dry, rigid, and prematurely old and wrinkled, especially on the face. And a burn from the sun greatly increases your risk of getting skin cancer. Begin with short exposures to the sun, perhaps half an hour, followed by an equal time in the shade. Drink plenty of liquids to keep your pores open. Avoid the sun from 1000 to 1500. Clouds and beach umbrellas will not protect you fully. While snorkeling, wear a T-shirt to protect your back and beware of reflected sunlight. Sunbathing is the main cause of cataracts to the eyes, so wear sunglasses and a wide-brimmed hat.

Use a sunscreen lotion containing PABA rather than coconut oil (don't forget your nose, lips, forehead, neck, hands, and feet). Sunscreens protect you from ultraviolet rays (a leading cause of cancer), while oils magnify the sun's effect. A 29- or 30-factor sunscreen such as Presun 29 or Sundown 30 will provide adequate protection. Take care, however, as PABA can stain clothing and bedding. Apply the lotion before going to the beach to avoid being burned on the way, and reapply periodically to replace sunscreen washed away by perspiration. After sunbathing take a tepid shower rather than a hot one that would wash away your natural skin oils. Stay moist and use a vitamin E evening cream to preserve the suppleness of your skin. Calamine ointment soothes skin already burned, as does coconut oil and ice. Pharmacists recommend Solarcaine to soothe burned skin. A vinegar solution reduces peeling and aspirin relieves some of the pain and skin itching. Vitamin A and calcium counteract overdoses of vitamin D received from the sun. The fairer your skin the more essential it is to take care.

As earth's ozone layer is depleted due to the commercial use of chlorofluorocarbons (CFCs) and other factors, the need to protect oneself from ultraviolet radiation is becoming ever more urgent. In 1990 the U.S. Center for Disease Control in Atlanta reported that deaths from skin cancer increased 26% between 1973 and 1985. Previously the cancers didn't develop until age 50 or 60 but now much younger people are being affected.

Ailments

Cuts and scratches infect easily and take a long time to heal. Prevent infection from coral cuts by washing with soap and fresh water, then rubbing vinegar or alcohol (whiskey will do) into the wounds—painful but effective. Coral cuts can become inflamed if you enter salt water again, thus potentially spoiling your trip. All cuts turn septic quickly in the tropics, so try to keep them clean and covered.

For bites, burns, and cuts, an antiseptic spray such as Solarcaine or an antibiotic cream speeds healing and helps prevent infection. Pure aloe vera is good for sunburn, scratches, and even coral cuts. Not everyone is affected by insect bites in the same way. Some people are practically immune to insects, while traveling companions experiencing exactly the same conditions are soon covered with bites. You'll soon know which type you are.

Prickly heat, an intensely irritating rash, is caused by wearing heavy, inappropriate clothing. When the glands are blocked and the sweat is unable to evaporate, the skin becomes soggy, and small, red blisters appear. Synthetic fabrics like nylon are especially bad in this regard. Take a cold shower, apply calamine lotion, dust with talcum powder, and take off those clothes! Until things improve avoid alcohol, tea, coffee, and any physical activity which makes you sweat. If you're sweating profusely, increase your intake of salt slightly to avoid fatigue, but not without concurrently drinking more water.

Use antidiarrheal medications like Imodium or Lomotil sparingly: rather than taking drugs to plug yourself up, drink plenty of unsweetened liquids like green coconuts or fresh fruit juice to help flush yourself out. Egg yolk mixed with nutmeg helps diarrhea, or have a rice and tea day. Avoid dairy products.

Most cases of diarrhea are self-limited and require only simple replacement of fluids and salts lost in diarrheal stools. If the diarrhea is persistent or you experience high fever, drowsiness, jaundice, or blood in the stool, stop traveling, rest, and consider attending a clinic. For constipation eat pineapple or any peeled fruit.

Toxic Fish

Over 400 species of tropical reef fish, including wrasses, snappers, groupers, barracudas, jacks, moray eels, surgeonfish, and shellfish, are known to cause seafood poisoning (ciguatera). There's no way to tell if a fish will cause ciguatera: a species can be poisonous on one side of the island but not on the other.

Several years ago scientists determined that a one-celled dinoflagellate called *Gambierdiscus toxicus* was the cause. Normally these algae are found only in the ocean depths, but when a reef is disturbed by natural or human causes they can multiply dramatically in a lagoon. The dinoflagellate are consumed by tiny herbivorous fish and the toxin passes up through the food chain to larger fish where it becomes concentrated in the head and guts. The toxins have no effect on the fish that feed on them.

There's no treatment except to relieve the symptoms (tingling, prickling, itching, nausea, vomiting, erratic heartbeat, joint and muscle pains), which usually subside in a few days. Induce vomiting and take castor oil as a laxative if you're unlucky. Symptoms can recur for up to a year, and victims can be made allergic to all seafood. Avoid biointoxication by cleaning fish as soon as they're caught, discarding the head and organs, and taking special care with oversized fish. Whether the fish is consumed cooked or raw has no bearing on this problem. Local residents know from experience which species may be eaten.

Vaccinations And Diseases

Malaria is nonexistent, but cholera outbreaks occurred in Chuuk and Kiribati during the 1980s. Many immunization centers refuse to administer the cholera vaccination because it's only 50% effective for six months and bad reactions are common. Cholera is acquired via contaminated food or drink, so in the rare instance that you visit an area where the disease is currently present, eat only cooked food, peel your own fruit, and drink canned, bottled, or boiled beverages, or coconut juice from the shell.

Tetanus, diphtheria, typhoid fever, polio, and immune globulin shots are not required, but they're a good idea if you're going to out-of-the-way places. Tetanus and diphtheria vaccinations are given together and a booster is required every 10 years. Typhoid fever boosters are required every three years, polio every five years. Immune globulin (IG) isn't 100% effective against hepatitis A, but it does increase your general resistance to infections. IG prophylaxis must be repeated every five months. A yellow fever vaccination is required only if you've been in an infected area (South America or Central Africa) within the previous six days.

Infectious hepatitis A is a liver ailment transmitted person to person or through unboiled water, uncooked vegetables, or other foods contaminated during handling. You'll know you've been infected when your eyeballs and urine turn deep orange. Time and rest are the only cure. Viral hepatitis B is spread through sexual or blood contact.

Dengue fever is a mosquito-transmitted disease: signs are headaches, sore throat, pain in the joints, fever, rash, and nausea. It can last anywhere from five to 15 days, and although you can relieve the symptoms somewhat, the only real cure is to stay in bed and wait it out. It's painful, but dengue fever usually kills only infants. No vaccine exists, so just avoid getting bitten.

Horrible, disfiguring diseases such as leprosy and elephantiasis are hard to catch, so it's unlikely you'll be visited by one of these nightmares of the flesh. Over a dozen cases of AIDS have been reported at Guam and Saipan. Be aware of gonorrhea at Majuro, Pohnpei, and Koror.

INFORMATION

Regional tourist information offices and diplomatic posts are listed in an appendix at the end of this book. William H. Stewart, Economic Service Counsel, has designed an intriguing series of tourist maps, packed with interesting anecdotes on Belau, Guam, Kosrae, Pohnpei, Saipan, and Chuuk. These and a standard selection of tourist brochures are available from these offices. Also see the categories "Periodicals" and "Booksellers and Publishers" in the "Booklist."

Peace Corps volunteers are always good sources of information, and you'll find them in the most unlikely corners of Marshall Islands and the Federated States.

WHAT TO TAKE

Packing

Assemble everything you simply must take and cannot live without—then cut the pile in half. If you're still left with more than will fit into a medium-size suitcase or backpack, continue eliminating. Now put it all into your bag.

If the total (bag and contents) weighs over 16 kilograms, you'll sacrifice much of your mobility. If you can keep it down to 10 kilograms, you're traveling light. Categorize and pack all your things into plastic bags or stuff sacks for convenience and protection from moisture. In addition to your suitcase or pack, you'll want a day pack or flight bag. When checking in for flights carry anything which can't be replaced in your hand luggage.

Your Luggage

A medium-size backpack with a lightweight internal frame is best. Big external-frame packs are fine for mountain climbing, but are very inconvenient on public transportation and tend to jam conveyor belts at airports. Make sure your pack carries the weight on your hips, has a cushion for spine support, and doesn't pull backwards. The pack should strap snugly to your body but also allow ventilation to your back. It should be made of a water-resistant material such as nylon and have a Fastex buckle. The best packs have a zippered compartment in back where you can tuck in the straps and hip belt before turning your pack over to an airline or bus.

Look for a pack with double, two-way zipper compartments and pockets, which you can lock with miniature padlocks. It might not *stop* a thief, but it could be deterrent enough to make him look for another mark. A 60-cm length of lightweight chain and another padlock will allow you to fasten your pack to something. Keep valuables locked in your bag, out of sight.

Camping Equipment And Clothing

A small nylon tent guarantees you a place to sleep every night. It must be mosquito- and waterproof. Get one with a tent fly. It's usually too hot to get into a sleeping bag in the tropics, so you could leave that item at home. A youth hostel sleeping sheet is ideal—all YHA handbooks give instructions on how to make your own. You don't really need to carry a bulky foam pad as the ground is seldom cold.

A mosquito net could come in handy if you'll be visiting remote areas, and Long Road Travel Supplies (Box 638, Alameda, CA 94501 U.S.A.; tel. 510-865-3066) sells an excellent freestanding indoor net for $49 plus postage.

For clothes take loose-fitting cotton washables, light in color and weight. Synthetic fabrics are hot and sticky, and most of the things you wear at home will be too heavy for the tropics. If in doubt bring the minimum with you and buy local garb once you've arrived. Coin-operated laundromats are found all across Micronesia, so you don't need to take a lot of clothes. Be prepared for the humidity.

Micronesians dress informally for both business and social occasions, but it's important to know that the dress code in the islands is strict. Wearing short skirts, halter tops, bathing costumes, and other brief attire in public places is considered offensive. Women should wear clothing that covers the knees. On outer islands especially, women should wear a knee-length dress or wrap a meter-long piece of cloth around their thighs. Shorts are frowned on for women but usually okay for men. Men will want a clean shirt for evenings, but only Mormon missionaries wear ties. Topless or nude sunbathing can be done only with care in isolated, uninhabited areas.

Take comfortable shoes which have been broken in. Running shoes and rubber thongs (zories) are very handy and can be purchased locally. Scuba divers' rubber booties are lightweight and perfect for both crossing rivers and reef walking, though an old pair of sneakers may be just as good. The checklists provided will help you assemble your gear. All the listed items combined weigh well over 16 kilograms, so eliminate what doesn't suit you:

    pack with internal frame
    day pack or airline bag
    nylon tent and fly
    tent-patching tape
    mosquito net
    YH sleeping sheet
    sun hat
    essential clothing only
    bathing suit
    hiking boots
    rubber thongs
    rubber booties
    mask and snorkel

Accessories

Look in the ads in photographic magazines for the best deals on mail-order miniature 35mm cameras and film, or buy one at a discount shop in any large city. Run a roll of film through your camera to be sure it's in good working order. Register valuable cameras or electronic equipment with Customs before you leave home, or at least carry the original bill of sale, so there won't be any argument about where you bought the items when you return.

The compacts are very convenient for traveling though they're mostly useful for close-up shots; landscapes will seem spread out and far away. A wide-angle lens gives excellent depth of field but hold the camera upright to avoid converging verticals. A polarizing filter prevents reflections from glass windows. Avoid overexposure at midday by reducing the exposure half a stop. It's usually too bright to take good pictures here between 1000 and 1600.

Keep your camera in a plastic bag during rain and while traveling in motorized canoes, etc. Protect camera and film from direct sunlight and never leave them in a hot place like on a car floor or in a glove compartment. Load film in the shade and check that the takeup spool revolves when winding on. When packing, protect your camera against vibration. To protect against airport X-ray monitors, carry both camera and film in lead bags. Color print film is usually available in the American-associated states, but in Nauru and Kiribati the supply is unreliable, so take all you'll need. Color slide film is expensive everywhere and hard to find. When purchasing film in Micronesia take care to check the expiration date.

Bring a clip-on book light and extra batteries if you want to read at night. A mask and snorkel are essential equipment, though these can usually be purchased upon arrival. You'll be missing half of Micronesia's beauty without them. Scuba divers should bring their own regulator, buoyancy compensator, and tank pressure gauge (tanks, backpacks, and weight belts can usually be rented locally). Throughout this book we provide the frequencies of local AM and FM radio stations, should you choose to bring along a radio.

    camera and five rolls of film
    compass
    pocket flashlight
    extra batteries
    candle
    pocket/alarm calculator
    pocket watch
    inflatable neck pillow
    soft wax ear plugs
    sunglasses
    padlock and lightweight chain
    collapsible umbrella
    twine for a clothesline
    powdered laundry soap
    sink plug (one that fits all)
    mini-towel
    sewing kit
    mini-scissors
    nail clippers
    fishing line for sewing gear
    plastic cup
    can and bottle opener
    corkscrew
    penknife
    spoon
    water bottle
    matches
    tea bags
    dried fruits
    nuts
    crackers
    plastic bags
    gifts

Toiletries And Medical Kit

Since everyone has his/her own medical requirements, and brand names vary from country to country, there's no point going into detail here. Note, however, that even the

basics (such as aspirin) are unavailable on some outer islands, so be prepared. Bring medicated powder for prickly heat rash or sunburns. Charcoal tablets are useful for diarrhea and poisoning as they absorb the irritants. Bring an adequate supply of any personal medications, plus your prescriptions (in generic terminology).

High humidity causes curly hair to swell and bush, straight hair to droop. If it's curly, have it cut short or keep it long in a ponytail or bun. A good cut is essential with short hair. Water-based makeup is best, as the heat and humidity cause oil glands to work overtime. See "Health" above for more ideas.

    soap in a plastic container
    soft toothbrush
    toothpaste
    stick deodorant
    shampoo
    comb and brush
    skin creams
    makeup
    tampons or napkins
    white toilet paper
    multiple vitamins and minerals
    Cutter's insect repellent
    PABA sunscreen
    ChapStick
    a motion sickness remedy
    contraceptives
    iodine
    water purification pills
    delousing powder
    a diarrhea remedy
    Tiger Balm
    a cold remedy
    Alka-Seltzer
    aspirin
    antihistamine
    antifungal
    Calmitol ointment
    antibiotic ointment
    painkiller
    antiseptic cream
    disinfectant
    simple dressings
    Band-Aids

Money And Documents

Any post office will have a passport application. Carry your valuables in a money belt worn around your waist or neck under your clothing; most camping goods stores have these. If you plan to remain in one place for long, you can store your valuables in a safety-deposit box at the local bank for a nominal charge. If you have a car at home, bring along the insurance receipt so you don't have to pay insurance again every time you rent a car. Ask your agent about this. Some credit cards also include auto insurance.

Make several photocopies of the information page of your passport, and your personal identification, driver's license, scuba certification card, credit cards, airline tickets, receipts for purchase of traveler's checks, etc.—you should be able to get them all on one page. A brief medical history with your blood type, allergies, chronic or special health problems, eyeglass and medical prescriptions, etc. might also come in handy. Put these inside plastic bags to protect them from moisture and carry the lists in different places, leaving one at home.

How much money you'll need depends on your life-style, but time is also a factor. The longer you stay, the cheaper it gets. Suppose you have to lay out US$1,250 on airfare and have US$50 a day leftover for expenses. If you stay 15 days, you'll average US$134 a day ($50 times 15 plus $1,250, divided by 15). If you stay 30 days, the per-day cost drops to US$92 a day ($50 times 30 plus $1,250, divided by 30). If you stay 60 days it'll cost only US$71 a day, and just US$54 a day if you stay a year.

passport
vaccination certificates
airline tickets
scuba certification card
driver's license
traveler's checks
credit card
some U.S. cash
photocopies of documents
money belt
address book
notebook
envelopes
extra ballpoints

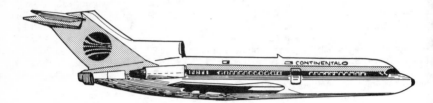

GETTING THERE AND AROUND

Continental Air Micronesia
The main regional carrier is **Continental Air Micronesia** or "Air Mike" (Box 8778, Tamuning, GU 96911 USA; tel. 671-646-0220), which has been offering convenient, reliable air service across the region since 1968. Their services are integrated into Continental Airlines's extensive worldwide system, so booking is usually no problem. If you live in the U.S. Mainland, Hawaii, or Alaska you can call Continental toll-free at (800) 231-0856 or (800) 525-0280 for current information on these services. When you get through to the airline, ask for the international desk. In Canada call their ticket offices in Toronto (tel. 416-690-7756) or Vancouver (tel. 604-222-2442).

There are several different types of fares: regular, seven-day advance purchase, family, student, and senior citizen (over age 62). For the family fare, the head of the family pays full fare, the spouse gets a third off, and accompanying children are charged less again. All must travel together. Sometimes Continental's operators don't mention the cheapest fares, so *be persistent*. If the first

clerk you get isn't knowledgeable, try again later—many agents answer their phones. This line gets busy, so call on a weekend or late at night. Otherwise visit any Continental Airlines office, or your travel agent, whose computers will have up-to-the-minute information on any of the flights mentioned below.

Although Continental Air Micronesia does offer nonstop flights from Honolulu to Guam, the most popular routing among readers of this book is the Boeing 727 Island Hopper service Honolulu-Majuro-Kwajalein-Kosrae-Pohnpei-Chuuk-Guam, with four flights a week in each direction. Not all flights call at Kosrae. In Guam you can change to other Continental Air Micronesia flights continuing to Yap, Koror, or Saipan. If you know you're going to do this, buy a through ticket to your turnaround point—usually cheaper than buying a separate ticket in Guam.

Continental doesn't engage in the gray-market discounting of tickets by bucket shops, thus their tickets are refundable, stopovers are allowed, reservations can be changed, and the tickets are valid for one year. Micronesians often complain about

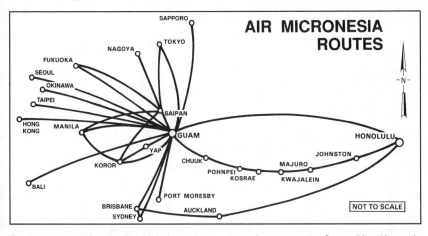

AIR MICRONESIA ROUTES

SAPPORO
TOKYO
NAGOYA
FUKUOKA
SEOUL
OKINAWA
TAIPEI
SAIPAN
HONG KONG
MANILA
GUAM
HONOLULU
YAP
JOHNSTON
KOROR
CHUUK
MAJURO
POHNPEI
KOSRAE
KWAJALEIN
BALI
PORT MORESBY
BRISBANE
AUCKLAND
SYDNEY

NOT TO SCALE

Continental Air Micronesia's high fares but the fact that there's only one regional airline is a boon for visitors who want to stop on a lot of islands on a single ticket. In the South Pacific, for example, one must change carriers several times to visit as many places and the total price would work out to be much higher. (All fares below, unless otherwise stated, are one way.)

A through ticket over the entire route Honolulu-Majuro-Kwajalein-Kosrae-Pohnpei-Chuuk-Guam-Yap-Koror will run US$795. If you only go Honolulu-Majuro-Kwajalein-Kosrae-Pohnpei-Chuuk-Guam, it's US$630. From Los Angeles or San Francisco the Island Hopper costs US$773 to Guam, US$1,026 to Koror.

Continental Air Micronesia's nonstop fares are cheaper, so you'll only want to pay the higher Island Hopper fare in one direction. Guam-Honolulu direct is US$476, Guam-California direct US$708.

The sidetrip Guam-Saipan-Tinian-Rota-Guam cannot be included in the Island Hopper, but this return ticket is easily purchased once inside Micronesia for about US$101 total. Some of Continental Air Micronesia's off-peak night flights out of Guam to Chuuk, Pohnpei, Yap, and Koror are sold at half price on a point-to-point basis—useful if a cheap flight has dropped you on Guam. If purchased separately Guam-Yap-Koror is US$320; Guam-Saipan is US$66.

One irony of Air Mike's fare structure (and something Micronesians can get pretty hot under the collar about) is the high cost of terminating at Majuro or points in the Federated States of Micronesia as opposed to Guam. For example, Honolulu-Majuro is US$565; Honolulu-Pohnpei, $551; Honolulu-Chuuk, $553; compared to US$476 for the much longer distance from Honolulu to Guam. Thus even if you only want to visit Majuro or a single island in the FSM, it may work out slightly cheaper to go via Guam!

Something else to ask about is the Circle Micronesia Fare, which gives you four stops between California and Koror for US$1,487 roundtrip, or US$1,144 roundtrip from Honolulu to Koror with four stops. Additional stops are US$50 each. Different fare levels apply if you only go as far as Guam or Saipan. The ticket must be purchased seven days in advance, is good for 10 days to six months, and all travel must be roundtrip. You'll be charged another US$50 to have the ticket reissued, so be sure to have all your stops written in from the start. Only the first flight has to be booked at the moment of purchase—all others can be left open or changed at no cost. Cancellation charges may apply if you want to delay your trip or refund the ticket.

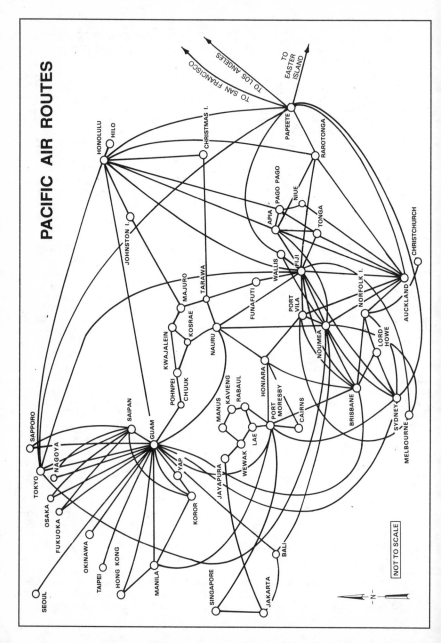

PACIFIC AIR ROUTES

Similarly, a Visit Micronesia Fare is offered from cities in Asia, Australia, or New Zealand, which allows travel to Yap, Koror, and the Northern Marianas via Guam at reduced rates.

Of course, Continental Airlines also has flights all across the U.S. mainland and they'll be happy to quote you through fare. It's sometimes possible to save money by flying from the U.S. to Hawaii on a special discount fare, then picking up Continental Air Micronesia there. Check the Sunday travel section of any large daily paper for cheap flights to Honolulu. This option is probably worth considering only if you want to include Hawaii in your trip anyway. You're often forced to spend a night in Honolulu or on Guam between connecting flights and always at your own expense.

You don't get an assigned seat number if you join a flight anywhere between Honolulu and Guam—just sit anywhere you like. Flying times are six hours from Honolulu to Majuro or California, 7½ hours from Honolulu to Guam nonstop, and around two hours on most flights within Micronesia itself. The Island Hopper takes almost 16 hours from Honolulu to Guam, so take it only if you want to stop somewhere!

Continental Air Micronesia's reliability is high, with over 75% of their flights leaving within five minutes of schedule, over 95% no more than one hour late. Complaints about lost baggage are rare. The service on Continental Air Micronesia flights is much friendlier and more personalized than on U.S. domestic Continental Airlines services—Micronesia's charm rubs off easily.

For years, 41,000-employee Continental Airlines has tottered on the edge of bankruptcy, and just as this book was going to press it was announced that Continental had sold Air Micronesia to a consortium of Micronesian and American investors for US$290 million. Though the deal had still to be approved by a U.S. bankruptcy court, it's unlikely the new owners will make drastic changes in Air Mike's highly successful (and profitable) operations, and most of the information above should still be valid.

Air Nauru

Air Nauru (80 Collins St., Melbourne, Victoria 3000, Australia; tel. 03-653-5709; fax 61-3-654-7376), flag carrier of the tiny, phosphate-rich Republic of Nauru, provides service between Micronesia and the South Pacific at reasonable rates. Most Air Nauru fares are calculated point to point via Nauru. To work out a route, combine any two of these one-way economy fares out of Nauru itself: Auckland (A$444), Chuuk (A$330), Guam (A$227), Honiara (A$140), Kosrae (A$176), Manila (A$340), Melbourne (A$380), Nandi (A$198), Noumea (A$211), Pohnpei (A$238), Suva (A$198), Sydney (A$335), Tarawa (A$103), Yap (A$443). The Air Nauru fare between Guam and Manila is US$246.

On 3 July 1991 Air Nauru inaugurated a new weekly service Nauru-Kosrae-Pohnpei-Chuuk-Yap-Guam and return, breaking Continental's monopoly on FSM routes. Stopovers are allowed, but again the individual interisland fares are tallied: Nauru-Kosrae A$176, Kosrae-Pohnpei US$92, Pohnpei-Chuuk US$115, Chuuk-Yap US$130, Yap-Guam US$130. Thus a return ticket Nauru-Guam with four stops in the FSM will run about A$870, or A$770 if Chuuk is the turnaround point. As the flight operates only once a week that's the minimum stay on each island.

In Jan. 1992 Air Nauru launched a weekly Honolulu-Christmas-Tarawa-Nauru service using Air Tungaru's landing rights in Hawaii. Fares are Honolulu-Christmas US$299, Honolulu-Tarawa US$403. Turn to the Christmas Island section in the book for more information.

Although the exchange rate is currently about US$1=A$1.30, if you buy your ticket in a U.S. dollar area you'll probably be charged the same figure, but in U.S. currency rather than Australian! All the above services operate at least once a week.

In the past Air Nauru has had a reputation for canceling flights on a moment's notice and bumping confirmed passengers to make room for local VIPs, but things are said to have improved since the airline's restructuring in 1991. They fly modern Boeing 737 aircraft and have a good safety record. One difficulty is obtaining reliable information—most travel agents won't touch them due to past service vagaries. Also keep in mind the compulsory A$10 airport departure tax that everyone (even through passengers continuing on the same aircraft!) must pay at Nauru.

Here are a few Air Nauru offices: Shop 4, 336 Sussex St., Sydney, NSW 2000, Australia (tel 283-2988); Sheraton Mall, 105 Symonds St., Auckland, New Zealand (tel. 796-979); Ratu Sakuna House, MacArthur St., Suva, Fiji Islands (tel. 679-312-377); Ground Floor, Pacific Star Building, Makati Ave. at Gil Puyat Ave., Makati, Metro Manila, Philippines (tel. 819-7241); Pacific Star Hotel, Box 6097, Tamuning, GU 96911 U.S.A. (tel. 671-649-7107). For information in the U.S., the best procedure is simply to call their Guam office or fax Melbourne. A late report indicates that to cut costs a few of the above offices may soon close and that other airlines may be appointed as Air Nauru general sales agents. If this seems to be the case, check with Air New Zealand or Qantas.

Air Marshall Islands

Air Marshall Islands (Box 1319, Majuro, MH 96960; tel. 692-9-3733) can also take you directly from Micronesia to the South Pacific, but for a much higher price. One-way fares out of Majuro on their weekly flight Majuro-Tarawa-Funafuti-Fiji run US$170 to Tarawa, US$409 to Funafuti, US$510 to Fiji. Fares from Tarawa are A$340 to Funafuti, A$653 to Fiji, or A$340 from Funafuti to Fiji. There are also 23-day excursion fares: US$709 RT between Fiji and Majuro, A$976 RT between Fiji and Tarawa, US$284 RT between Majuro and Tarawa.

AMI doesn't allow free stopovers on their through tickets, so if you want to stop at both Tarawa and Funafuti between Majuro and Fiji you must pay US$933 instead of the usual US$510 direct fare! It would cost half as much to fly Majuro-Tarawa on Air Marshall Islands, then Tarawa-Nauru-Fiji on Air Nauru. Air Nauru has an office on Majuro, but doesn't operate flights from there at the moment (this could change). For more information on Air Marshall Islands, including flights from Honolulu to Majuro, turn to the Marshall Islands chapter.

From Australia/New Zealand

Continental Air Micronesia has service between Brisbane/Sydney and Guam three times a week. For Koror you could fly to Manila and change to Continental's Manila-Koror flight. There are also nonstop Continental flights to Guam from Denpasar (Bali) and Port Moresby (PNG). Continental has ticket offices in many Australian and New Zealand cities, including Sydney (tel. 02-249-0222) and Auckland (tel. 09-795686).

Once again, a cheaper way to go would be on **Air Nauru** out of Sydney or Auckland to Tarawa, Kosrae, Pohnpei, Chuuk, or Guam (see above). From Guam, much of Micronesia is accessible on the half-price, off-peak Continental Air Micronesia night flights mentioned above.

From Europe

No direct flights connect Europe to Micronesia. The easiest access would be a cheap flight from Europe to California, Honolulu, or Manila, where you would join one of the Island Hopper routes described above and travel around the world. Prices quoted by European travel agents for a Continental through ticket from San Francisco or Los Angeles to Manila with all the stops vary considerably but could be in the neighborhood of US$1,150. Add the price of cheap Europe-California and Manila-Europe nonstops and you should able to do it all for slightly over US$2,000.

For the Continental portion of your ticket, go to a large professional travel agency specializing in business travel. Since Continental doesn't discount its Micronesia tickets there's no reason to go to a bucket shop, though you should shop around for discounted nonstop flights to the gateways. Of course it would be cheaper and easier for Europeans to wait to buy their Continental ticket in California, but U.S. "ticket-to-leave" requirements are an obstacle. If you know a reliable travel agent in the States you might consider mail-ordering your Continental ticket through them and paying by credit card.

Continental does have ticket offices in some Western European cities, including Athens (tel. 1-32-55061), Barcelona (tel. 4122986), Britain (tel. 0293-776464), Brussels (tel. 2-640-30-34), Copenhagen (tel. 33-137277), Frankfurt (tel. 757475), Lisbon (tel. 779961-4), Madrid (tel. 532-7410), Milan (tel. 2-7492872), Oslo (tel. 02-837800), Paris (tel. 42253181), Rome (tel. 64746634), Rotterdam (tel. 10-437-9911), Stockholm (tel. 08-240080), Vienna (tel. 5878057), and Zürich (tel. 01-8110-688). Those are the people to call first.

European travel agencies specializing in round-the-world travel via Micronesia include **Reisbureau Amber**, Da Costastraat 77, 1053 ZG Amsterdam, Holland (tel. 31-20-685-1155); **Malibu Travel**, Damrak 30, 1012 LJ Amsterdam; **Trailfinders**, 42-50 Earls Court Rd., Kensington, London W8 6EJ, England (tel. 071-938- 3366); and **Globetrotter Travel Service**, Rennweg 35, 8001 Zürich, Switzerland (tel. 01-211-7780).

The numerous flights between Guam/Saipan and Japan (about US$350) are described in the Guam and Northern Marianas chapters of this book. The Manila-Guam route is served by both Continental Air Micronesia (US$286) and Air Nauru (US$246). Continental also offers Manila-Koror. A Continental ticket Manila-Koror-Yap-Guam costs about US$416. Manila-Koror-Yap-Koror-Manila will be US$628.

Special Situations

Airline tickets are sometimes refundable only in the place of purchase, so ask about this before you invest in a ticket you may not use. Nearly every Pacific island requires that you have an onward ticket as a condition for entry, thus careful planning is in order. A travel agent may be able to help you, provided he/she knows where Micronesia is!

Always reconfirm your onward reservations after arriving on an island. Failure to do so at least 72 hours prior to departure could result in the cancellation of your complete remaining itinerary, and you might arrive at the airport to find the plane fully booked. Since 1987 most Air Mike offices have been computerized, so reconfirmation is done in minutes. When planning your trip allow a minimum two-hour stopover between connecting flights, although with airport delays on the increase even this might not be enough.

If your flight is delayed over four hours, the airline should give you a meal voucher. You must ask for this—the clerks may not offer. If the flight is canceled due to mechanical problems with the aircraft, the airline will cover your hotel bill and meals. If they reschedule the flight on short notice for reasons of their own, or you're bumped off an overbooked flight, they should also pay. They may not feel obligated to pay, however, if the delay is due to weather conditions, a strike by another company, national emergencies, etc. But don't expect anything at all from small commuter airlines.

To compensate for no-shows, most airlines overbook their flights. To avoid being bumped, check in early and go to the departure area well before flight time. In some airports flights are not called over the public address system, so keep your eyes open. Overbooked airlines often offer meals, rooms, and even cash to volunteers willing to relinquish their seats. Finally, don't lose your boarding pass or you may be turned back at the gate and required to buy a new ticket.

Baggage

Continental Air Micronesia allows two pieces of checked baggage plus a carryon on their big DC-10s and 727s, but the smaller commuter airlines may limit you to as little as 14 kilograms. If you'll be changing aircraft at a busy gateway city, think twice before checking your baggage straight through to your final destination. It's a nuisance but it's safer to collect it at the transfer point and check it in again. Stow anything which could conceivably be considered a weapon (scissors, penknife, toy gun, etc.) in your checked luggage. U.S. Customs now employs cute little dogs able to detect even the tiniest quantity of drugs.

Tag your bag with name, address, and phone number inside and out. Unless you want to risk having your luggage travel in the opposite direction, get into the habit of removing used baggage tags. As you're checking in, look to see if the three-letter city code on your baggage tag and the one on your boarding pass are the same. If your baggage is damaged or doesn't come out on arrival at your destination, future claims for compensation will be compromised unless you inform the airline officials *immediately* and have them fill out a report.

Airlines usually reimburse out-of-pocket expenses if your baggage is lost or delayed over 24 hours—the amount varies from US$25 to $50. Your chances of getting the cash are better if you're polite but firm. Keep receipts for any money you're forced to spend to replace missing articles. Claims for lost luggage can take weeks to process. Keep in touch with the airline to show your concern; also, hang onto your baggage tag until the matter is resolved. If you feel you did not receive the attention you deserved, write the airline an objective letter outlining the case. Get the names of the employees you're dealing with, so you can mention them in the letter.

ORGANIZED TOURS

Scuba Tours

Many experienced divers consider Micronesia the world's ultimate diving destination. Chuuk, Guam, Belau, and Pohnpei offer totally different diving experiences. You can save money by booking scuba diving directly with the island dive shops listed under "Sports and Recreation" in the individual chapters of this book. Write or call ahead or just wait to talk to them once you get there.

But unless you've got lots of time and are philosophical about disappointments, you'll probably want to go on an organized scuba tour. The list of companies offering such trips is long and growing, which says something about their popularity. In addition to the regular phone numbers given below, most have

toll-free numbers which you can obtain by calling (800) 555-1212.

Most of the prices quoted below are pp, double occupancy. To upgrade to a single room is about US$50 extra per night. When booking your tour ask if meals, regulator, pressure and depth gauges, mask, snorkel, fins, etc. are provided. Of course, diver certification is mandatory. Unless otherwise stated, airfare is *not* included. Prices aren't cheap, but the convenience of having all your arrangements made for you by a company able to pull weight with island suppliers is sometimes worth it.

Mike Musto's **Trip-N-Tour** (846 Williamston St., Suite 202, Vista, CA 92084 U.S.A.; tel. 619-724-0788) is the only scuba tour company which deals exclusively with Micronesia. Mike offers 16 different dive packages to Micronesia, including US$493-653 for a week at Chuuk, US$558-942 for a week at Belau, or US$1,087-1,688 for two weeks at Chuuk and Belau. Pohnpei, Yap, Guam, Saipan, Tinian, and Rota packages are also available.

Sea Safaris (3770 Highland Ave., Suite. 102, Manhattan Beach, CA 90266 U.S.A.; tel. 310-546-2464) is similar with 12-night Chuuk/Pohnpei safaris (US$1,395), 13-night

PACIFIC PHOSPHATE COMPANY MINING AGREEMENT

7c

REPUBLIC OF NAURU 1905

Chuuk/Belau safaris (US$1,750), and 18-night Chuuk/Belau/Pohnpei/Yap safaris (US$2,195). Airfare is extra. These trips include two tanks a day; three tanks are available at an additional charge.

Poseidon Ventures (359 San Miguel Dr., Newport Beach, CA 92660 U.S.A.; tel. 714-644-5344; or 505 N. Belt, Suite 675, Houston, TX 77060 U.S.A.; tel. 713-820-3483) offers monthly 11-night "Blue Diving Tours" to Chuuk and Belau for US$1,316. The price includes nine days of two-tank diving, hotels, taxes, and transfers (most meals extra). A three-night Pohnpei extension with two days of diving is US$350.

Tropical Adventures (111 Second Ave. N, Seattle, WA 98109 U.S.A.; tel. 206-441-3483) occasionally has specials that slice $100 or more off regular scuba package prices, so call them up to compare. Tropical's president, Bob Goddess, claims he's always accessible by phone. Over 5,000 divers a year book through this company, which has been in business since 1973.

Innerspace Adventures (13393 Sorrento Dr., Largo, FL 34644 U.S.A.; tel. 813-595-5296) has been operating scuba trips to Micronesia since 1971, longer than any other wholesaler. Innerspace's president, Tom Jacobus, specializes in offbeat dive sites, such as Bikini atoll (US$3,000 for two weeks), Jaluit atoll, and Kosrae, so check with him if you have any special requests.

If the thought of combining trekking or rafting in outback Indonesia or Thailand with scuba diving in Belau appeals to you, **In Depth Adventures** (Box 593, Eureka, CA 95501 U.S.A.; tel. 707-443-9842) is worth

checking out. Co-owners Robert Cogen and David Walker—one a trial attorney and the other a licensed private investigator—have 80 years diving experience between them, and they personally lead all trips. There are only a couple of departures a year and at $7,250 (airfare included) it ain't cheap, but you're guaranteed a world-class experience.

Aqua-Trek (110 Sutter St., Ste. 811, San Francisco, CA 94104 U.S.A.; tel 415-398-8990) is another scuba tour operator to try.

See & Sea Travel Service (50 Francisco St., Suite 205, San Francisco, CA 94133 U.S.A.; tel. 415-434-3400) is *the* specialist for live-aboard diving. Their prices are slightly higher than the regular tours mentioned above, but you're offered three or more dives a day plus the selected cream of diving facilities, and all meals are included! For example, nine days of unlimited diving at Belau aboard the *Sun Tamarin* is US$2,200. This boat is popular, so book well in advance. See & Sea's president is the noted underwater photographer and author, Carl Roessler.

See & Sea (and most of the other companies above) will book passage on the two live-aboard dive boats based at Chuuk year-round. The Canadian-owned SS *Thorfinn*, a 50-meter onetime Norwegian whaling ship, is the world's largest live-aboard dive boat. The boat's outdoor hot tub, fireplace in the lounge, and shipboard photo lab add a touch of luxury. Divers are accommodated in 13 double cabins with five- and seven-day Chuuk lagoon cruises with 18 crew members serving the 26 guests! In June 1990 the newer, 10-stateroom *Truk Aggressor* (Drawer K, Morgan City, LA 70381 U.S.A.; tel. 504-385-2416) became the second live-aboard permanently based at Chuuk. A week on either of these boats with meals, accommodations, and unlimited diving included will run US$1,895. Though more expensive than the land-based scuba packages, these boats anchor right at the dive sights and tour prices include unlimited diving and meals.

Ocean Voyages Inc. (1709 Bridgeway, Sausalito, CA 94965-1994 U.S.A.; tel. 415-332-4681) arranges "shareboat" yacht tours throughout Micronesia and scuba diving is

A visitor from Arizona makes new friends on Pingelap, Federated States of Micronesia.

DAVID STANLEY

often possible. This is worth checking out if you enjoy sailing as much as diving and want to get away from the usual scuba sites. Also try the yacht charter brokerage **Cruising Connection** (Box 31496, San Francisco, CA 94131 U.S.A.; tel. 415-337-8330).

Tours For Naturalists

Ecotourism has been slow to come to Micronesia and as yet the only company offering trips which could fall into that category is **Oceanic Society Expeditions** (Fort Mason Center, Bldg. E, San Francisco, CA 94123 U.S.A.; tel. 415-441-1106), a 40,000-member, nonprofit environmental organization founded in 1972. Their two-week hiking and snorkeling tour to Pohnpei, Yap, and Belau is offered only twice a year, between March and July. Groups are limited to 15 participants accompanied by a naturalist/tour escort and the US$3,490 price includes airfare from Los Angeles, boat excursions, accommodations, and some meals. These well-planned trips are ideal for individuals wishing to get close to nature, quickly and briefly, without sacrificing any creature comforts. Participants sleep in standard tourist hotels.

Tours For Veterans

Valor Tours, Ltd. (Box 1617, Sausalito, CA 94966 U.S.A.; tel. 415-332-7850) is one of the only American companies conducting es-

corted package tours to Tarawa (via Majuro). Their annual six-night trip to Tarawa (always in mid-Nov.) is designed for U.S. veterans who want to be present on Betio for the anniversary of the American landings there on 20 Nov. 1943. This trip is always fully booked: when they run out of hotel beds on Tarawa participants are billeted in Marine Corps tents! Valor's president Robert Reynolds has also designed unique tours for veterans to the Solomon Islands and extensions from Tarawa are possible. As the 50th anniversaries of the main WW II battles roll around and new war memorials are dedicated, Valor should have some really interesting trips to offer!

Other Tours

Newmans Tours Ltd., with offices in Los Angeles (tel. 310-277-6401), New York (tel. 212-972-1358), Toronto (tel. 416-923-6444), Sydney (tel. 02-231-6511), and Auckland (tel. 09-31-149), offers seven different packaged vacations to Micronesia. Meals are extra, as is airfare, which must be booked through Newmans. If you want a single room *or* scuba diving included it doubles the price; both these *and* superior accommodation triples it. Airport transfers are covered. This is fine if you only want your hotel rooms arranged, but scuba divers will get a better deal from one of the specialists listed above.

Swingaway Holidays (22 York St., Sydney, NSW 2000, Australia; tel. 02-237-0300) has beach holiday packages to Guam, Saipan, Pohnpei, Chuuk, Belau, and Yap from Australia. They use the best hotels available and prices include airfare but not meals. Participants travel individually on any flight departing Sydney/Brisbane for Guam. This is much cheaper than buying a regular ticket and paying for your accommodation directly. The **Pacific Island Travel Center**, 20 Loftus St., Sydney (tel. 27- 4525), also offers these trips.

In Canada check with **Adventure Treks Ltd.**, in Calgary, Edmonton, Toronto, and Vancouver, for packages and plane tickets to Micronesia. Their Canada-wide toll-free number is (800) 661-7265.

GETTING AROUND

By Air
Local **commuter airlines** such as Air Marshall Islands, Air Mike Express, Air Tungaru, Caroline Pacific Air, Freedom Air, Pacific Missionary Aviation, and Palau Paradise Air operate domestic services within the individual island groups. These flights are described in the respective chapters.

By Ship
The best way to really get the feel of Micronesia is to take a field trip by ship. These depart fairly frequently from Majuro, Pohnpei, Chuuk, Yap, and Tarawa; you should be able to get on if you're flexible. You'll also need a sense of humor because no one seems to know anything until just a few days prior to departure. It's useless to write ahead requesting reservations. If you happen to be there as the ship's about to leave, you're in luck.

The purpose of the field trips is to transport local passengers, freight, and USDA free food, and to pick up copra, the only export. Field trips are for the adventurous: there are few comforts. Deck space is about four cents a km. The cabins are usually reserved by government officials, but if you manage to net one it's six cents a km, plus another US$10 a day for meals. The cheapest way to go is to stretch your own mat and sleeping bag out on deck and eat your own food. When buying your ticket, don't ask for a complete roundtrip as they'll compute it by adding up all the interisland fares. Pick one of the farthest islands and buy a ticket there. Buy another OW ticket at the turn-around point, or just fly back. The ships visit many islands twice, on the outward and inward journeys, so you could stop off, and pick it up on the return.

DAVID STANLEY

two-wheeled transport on Mokil Atoll, Federated States of Micronesia

A ship might stop at each island for anywhere from a few hours to four days. You can sleep on board or go ashore and camp (ask the island mayor or chief for permission—usually no problem). As sailing time approaches, keep a close eye on the ship. Rely only on the captain or Field Trip Officer (FTO) for departure information. Even so, cases have been reported where a ship got an emergency call from another island, gave one blast of its horn, took up the tender, and sailed away. Travelers off walking at the far end of the island have been left to catch a flight back. The ships are usually full at the beginning and end of their journeys, but comparatively empty at the turnaround point.

The islanders and crew on board may give you food, so have something to give back. If you give the cook rice, he may be kind enough to cook it for you. A jar of instant coffee will come in handy as there's always plenty of hot water. The hot water is also good to heat up bags of Japanese ramen or oatmeal, but you'll need a bowl. Open a can of mackerel and you've got a favorite island meal. Take some peanut butter and bread for the first few days. You'll often be invited to feast ashore.

By Canoe
Never attempt to take a dugout canoe through even light surf: you'll be swamped. Don't try to pull or lift a canoe by its outrigger: it will break. Drag the canoe by holding the solid main body. A bailer is essential equipment. If you get off the beaten track, it's more than likely that a local friend will offer to take you out in his canoe. Interisland travel by sailing canoe is sometimes possible in Kiribati.

By Ocean Kayak
Ocean kayaking is experiencing a boom in Hawaii, but Micronesia is still virgin territory. Virtually every island has a sheltered lagoon ready-made for the excitement of kayak touring, but this effortless new transportation mode hasn't yet arrived. So you can be a real independent 20th century explorer! Continental Air Micronesia accepts folding kayaks as checked baggage at no charge.

Companies like **Long Beach Water Sports** (730 E. 4th St., Long Beach, CA 90802 U.S.A.; tel. 310-432-0187) sell inflatable one- or two-person sea kayaks for around US$1,800, fully equipped. If you're new to the game, LBWS runs four-hour sea kayaking classes (US$55) every Sat. morning and all-day advanced classes (US$80) every couple of months—a must for L.A. residents. They also rent kayaks by the day or week. Write for a free copy of their newsletter, *Paddle Strokes.*

Since 1977 **Baidarka Boats** (Box 6001, Sitka, AK 99835 U.S.A.; tel. 907-747-8996) has been a leading supplier of mail-order folding kayaks by Klepper and Nautiraid. **Aire** (Box 3412, Boise, ID 83703 U.S.A.; tel. 208-344-7506) makes the Sea Tiger self-bailing touring kayak which weighs only 16 kilograms. Write these companies for their free catalogs.

For a better introduction to ocean kayaking than is possible here, check at your local public library for *Sea Kayaking, A Manual for Long-Distance Touring* by John Dowd (Seattle: University of Washington Press, 1981) or *Derek C. Hutchinson's Guide to Sea Kayaking* (Seattle: Basic Search Press, 1985).

By Road
Car rentals are available at all the airports served by Continental Air Micronesia. At Guam and Saipan airports several well-known rent-a-car companies compete for your trade, while operators on some of the other islands are of the "rent-a-wreck" variety. Generally, only the agencies on Guam and Saipan accept reservations and sell insurance. The price is usually calculated on a 24-hour basis (around US$35), so you get to use the car the next morning. Mileage is usually included in the price. Avoid any company which charges extra for miles/km.

Shared taxis prowl the roads of Majuro, Ebeye, and Chuuk, offering lifts along their routes at low rates. You don't really need to rent a car on those islands. Taxi vans and minibuses on Pohnpei also charge per head, but elsewhere taxis are expensive. Yap, Guam, Saipan, and Tarawa have public bus services of varying quality which are described in those chapters. See the individual airport and hotel listings for information on airport transfers. Hitchhiking is fairly easy throughout Micronesia, except on hard-nosed Guam. On Guam it's suspicious even to walk!

By Bicycle

Cycling in Micronesia? Sure, why not? You'll be able to go where and when you please, stop easily and often to meet people and take photos, save money on taxi fares—really *see* the islands. It's great fun, but it's best to have bicycle touring experience beforehand. Most roads are flat along the coast but be careful on coral roads, especially inclines: if you slip and fall you could hurt yourself badly. Rainy islands like Pohnpei can start to seem inhospitable.

A sturdy, single-speed mountain bike with wide wheels, safety chain, and good brakes might be best. Thick tires and a plastic liner between tube and tire will reduce punctures. Know how to fix your own bike. Take along a good repair kit (pump, puncture kit, freewheel tool, spare spokes, chain links, etc.) and a repair manual; bicycle shops are few to nonexistent in the islands. Don't try riding with a backpack: sturdy, waterproof panniers (bike bags) are required. You'll also want a good lock and refuse to lend your bike to *anyone*.

Continental Air Micronesia will carry a bicycle free as one of your two pieces of checked luggage within Micronesia. On domestic U.S. flights such as Los Angeles to Hawaii, however, Continental charges US$30. Get around this by checking your bike straight through to your first stop in Micronesia, in which case it's free. Take off the pedals and panniers, turn the handlebars sideways, and clean off the dirt before checking in (or use a special bike-carrying bag). Interisland commuter airlines usually won't accept bikes on their small planes. Boats sometimes charge a token amount to carry a bike; other times it's free.

A reader, Kik Velt, sent the following report:

Majuro and Kwajalein have excellent paved roads, but on Kosrae they're bad and especially slippery after rains. Avoid Pohnpei unless you have extra tires; outside Kolonia, not only are the roads steep, but they're so full of stones it's like riding on a riverbed. On Weno and Yap only the airport roads are paved—the rest are full of mud, stones, and holes. The steep Yapese roads follow the hilltops, with feeders down to coastal villages connected by pedestrians-only footpaths. In Belau it's easy to cycle from Koror to Airai, but forget all the other roads on Babeldaop. On Guam and Saipan almost all roads are paved and excellent to bike. The hills of Guam are long, though not too steep. Take care when descending from the top to Umatac. The coastal road around Nauru is great, as is the South Tarawa road, but beware of trenches cut across it. On the outer islands of Kiribati the hard coral roads are a joy to cycle and many people have bicycles. Traffic is on the left!

Since Kik was there the roads of western Kosrae and northern Pohnpei have been paved and a major new highway has been built on Yap.

GORDY OHLIGER

REPUBLIC OF THE MARSHALL ISLANDS

INTRODUCTION

This scattered group of low coral islands and atolls floating on the wide Pacific became famous during a well-publicized series of nuclear tests just after WW II. Its strategic position as the first island group west of Hawaii led to bitter battles in 1944, and the military muscle-flexing continues today. The indigenous inhabitants—converted, colonized, and irradiated—have now been assigned the role of dependent consumers, and local leaders with an eye for easy money even want to turn the country into a dump site for municipal garbage shipped from the U.S. west coast!

Majuro, the capital and commercial center, will not please those seeking the unspoiled South Seas. The ugly, overcrowded slums and heaps of debris are a fascinating case study in direct American impact on a central Pacific environment. The striking juxtaposi-

tion of wretched refuse against the backdrop of a still-beautiful atoll—such as the fiery tropical sun plunging into the Majuro lagoon behind piles of trash—is nearly surreal.

Take the time to get away from Majuro to the other atolls, however, and you'll soon discover a typical Pacific paradise with beautiful beaches, breadfruit, palms, and pandanus, but no hotels, taxis, or tourists—just a happy, friendly people living simple, natural lives. A guidebook is unnecessary on the outer islands; you'll soon know all you need to know.

The Land
The 1,225 Marshall Islands are grouped together in 29 atolls, five low islands (Jabat, Jemo, Kili, Lib, and Mejit), and 870 reefs. The atolls are narrow coral rings with white sandy beaches enclosing turquoise lagoons. The

southern atolls' vegetation is thicker due to heavier rainfall. Although the land area comes to only 181 square km, the Marshall Islands are scattered over two million square km of the Central Pacific Ocean. They lie between 4° and 19° North latitude, 160° and 175° East longitude.

The largest atolls in the world are found in this group, arrayed in two chains 240 km apart and 1,300 km long. The Northeastern or Ratak ("Sunrise") Chain includes the large atolls of Mili, Majuro, Maloelap, Wotje, and Likiep; the Southwestern or Ralik ("Sunset") Chain includes Jaluit, Ailinglaplap, Kwajalein, Rongelap, Bikini, Enewetak, and others. The Marshall Islands' government also claims the U.S.-held island of Wake (Enenkio) to the north.

Climate
The climate is tropical oceanic, cooled year-round by the northeast trades. The only seasonal variation in rainfall or temperature is from Jan. to March: the climate is slightly

THE MARSHALLS AT A GLANCE

	pop. (1988)	land area (sq km)	lagoon area (sq km)
RATAK CHAIN			
Tsongi	0	3.2	78.0
Bikar	0	0.5	37.4
Utirik	409	2.4	57.3
Taka	0	0.6	93.1
Mejit	445	1.9	none
Ailuk	488	5.4	177.3
Jemo	0	0.2	none
Likiep	482	10.3	424.0
Wotje	646	8.2	624.3
Erikub	0	1.5	230.3
Maloelap	796	9.8	972.7
Aur	438	5.6	239.8
Majuro	19,664	9.2	295.1
Arno	1,656	13.0	338.7
Mili/Knox	854	15.9	763.3
RALIK CHAIN			
Enewetak	715	5.9	1,004.9
Ujelang	0	1.7	66.0
Bikini	10	6.0	594.2
Rongerik	0	1.7	143.4
Rongelap	0	8.0	1,004.3
Ailinginae	0	2.8	106.0
Wotho	90	4.3	94.9
Ujae	448	1.9	185.9
Lae	319	1.5	17.7
Kwajalein	9,311	16.4	2,173.8
Lib	115	0.9	none
Namu	801	6.3	397.6
Jabat	112	0.6	none
Ailinglaplap	1,715	14.7	750.3
Jaluit	1,709	11.3	689.7
Kili	602	0.9	none
Namorik	814	2.8	8.4
Ebon	741	5.7	103.8
MARSHALL ISLANDS	43,380	181.1	11,672.2

MAJURO'S CLIMATE

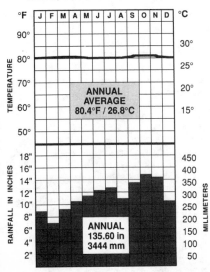

ANNUAL AVERAGE 80.4°F / 26.8°C

ANNUAL 135.60 in 3444 mm

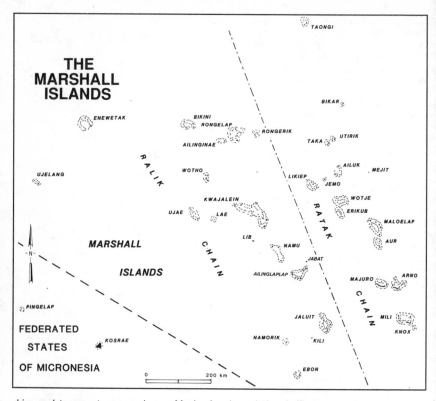

THE MARSHALL ISLANDS

TAONGI

ENEWETAK

BIKINI
RONGELAP
RONGERIK
AILINGINAE

BIKAR

TAKA UTIRIK

RALIK

UJELANG

WOTHO

AILUK MEJIT

LIKIEP

JEMO

KWAJALEIN

UJAE LAE

WOTJE
ERIKUB

MALOELAP

LIB

NAMU

MARSHALL

CHAIN

RATAK

AUR

-N-

ISLANDS

JABAT

AILINGLAPLAP

MAJURO ARNO

PINGELAP

JALUIT

MILI

KNOX

CHAIN

FEDERATED

KOSRAE

NAMORIK KILI

STATES

OF MICRONESIA

0   200 km

EBON

drier and temperatures are lower. Much of the rain falls by day. The northern islands of the Marshalls are cooler than the southern atolls, and receive far less rainfall. Typhoons are rare, although March, April, Oct., and Nov. can be stormy.

HISTORY AND GOVERNMENT

Origin Of The Marshalls

Long ago, the first humans, Uelip and his wife, lived on the island of Ep. One day a tree began to grow on Uelip's head and split his skull. Through the crack were born two sons, Etau and Djemelut. Etau quarreled with his father and decided to build a home of his own. He took a basket of soil and flew off through the air. Through a hole in the basket, soil drained slowly out into the sea, forming the Marshall Islands.

Discovery And Settlement

Humans arrived in the Marshalls about 4,000 years ago. Like most other Micronesians, they created a society ruled by powerful chiefs. Skilled navigators, the Marshallese used stick charts showing wave patterns to sail their large outrigger canoes between atolls indicated by cowrie shells. No single chief ever controlled the entire group, although the Ralik Chain was occasionally united. The most important possession of a Marshallese has always been land, and tribute in the form of the produce of the land had to be rendered to the chiefs.

The White Man Comes

First European on the scene was the Spaniard Alvaro de Saavedra, in 1528. Spain made a vague claim to the Marshalls in 1686, but never attempted to colonize the region. The islands were named for British Capt. John Marshall of the HMS *Scarborough,* who charted the group in 1788. The Russian explorer, Otto von Kotzebue, made two trips to the Marshalls (in 1817 and 1825); his careful observations provided the first clear picture of the Marshallese and their atolls. The ensuing whalers were repelled by the islanders.

The first German trader established himself on Ebon in 1861; in 1878 Chief Kabua of Rongelap signed a treaty with the Germans giving them exclusive use of Jaluit and protection for their traders. The German government declared a protectorate over the Marshalls in 1885, and two years later arrived to set up their headquarters on Jaluit. The Germans ruled indirectly through the Marshallese chiefs. The small European staff was primarily concerned with copra production.

In 1888 the traders merged into the Jaluit Gesellschaft, which agreed to cover the costs of administration in exchange for a monopoly. By 1899 the Jaluit company had 10 stations in the Marshalls and ships which purchased copra throughout the Carolines. But in 1905 a devastating hurricane swept across the Marshalls, destroying buildings and plantations. Unable to recover, the company returned control of the area to the German government in 1906, which joined it to other Micronesian islands purchased from Spain in 1899.

West Meets East

The Japanese, who had been interested in the area since 1890, took the islands from the Germans in 1914 and set up a naval administration. In 1920 Japan received a mandate from the League of Nations to administer Micronesia, and the copra trade was turned over to a company called Nanyo Boeki Kaisha. The number of Japanese officials present increased steadily as direct Japanese rule replaced the authority of the traditional chiefs. In 1938 Japan annexed Micronesia outright.

The Japanese began building military bases on some of the atolls in 1935. The Marshalls were a staging area for the Japanese invasion of Kiribati in 1941. The U.S. captured Kwajalein and Enewetak in Feb. 1944, after bloody battles; the 36,000 shells fired at Kwajalein amounted to the heaviest

M.G.L. DOMENY DE RIENZI

a Marshallese village visited by the Russian explorer Kotzebue in 1817

artillery barrage of the war. Japanese bases on Jaluit, Maloelap, Mili, and Wotje were neutralized by aerial bombardment, and the survivors left to sit out the war on these isolated atolls. From Kwajalein and Majuro the U.S. Navy struck west into the Japanese-held Carolines and Marianas.

In 1947 the Marshall Islands became part of the Trust Territory of the Pacific Islands, administered by the U.S. Although under U.N. auspices, the Trust Territory was a "strategic" trust, and the U.S. was allowed to create military bases. From 1946 to 1958 the U.S. carried out a massive atmospheric nuclear-testing program on the northern atolls of Bikini and Enewetak. The continuing effects of radioactive contamination on both land and people are still very much an issue in the Marshalls. In 1961, Kwajalein became the army's Pacific Missile Range, a target for ICBMs test fired from California.

Recent History

In a plebiscite on 12 July 1978, Marshallese voters chose to separate from the other districts of the Trust Territory of the Pacific Islands. They approved a constitution of their own the following year, and on 1 May 1979 a Marshall Islands government was formed. Economically, the country has always been dependent on direct U.S. aid and payments from the U.S. military for the use of Kwajalein. In fact, Marshallese unwillingness to share the payments, tax revenues, and jobs at Kwajalein with other Micronesians compelled them to split with the Caroline islanders in 1978.

In a Sept. 1983 vote 58% of the Marshallese electorate supported a Compact of Free Association, which will bring in $1 billion in U.S. economic aid over 15 years (including rent on the Kwajalein Testing Range for 30 years). Opponents consisted of the Kwajalein landowners and the victims of nuclear testing, who feared that their claims for financial compensation by the U.S. would be compromised. Indeed, the U.S. government was eager to conclude the compact as a way of terminating further claims from the Bikini refugees, who will receive $90 million for the

rehabilitation and resettlement of their islands. Other Marshallese who suffered radiation poisoning during the testing got a total of $150 million compensation (no further claims against the U.S. will be possible due to an espousal clause in the compact). The Nuclear Claims Tribunal set up to distribute the money has been subject to constant political interference from local politicians.

Most importantly, the compact grants Kwajalein to the U.S. on fixed terms for the next 30 years, with the central government exercising eminent domain, something the Pentagon considers vital if its development of new high-tech weapons is to proceed smoothly. Another plus is the removal of Kwajalein from U.N. scrutiny, and the establishment of a local government unable to challenge U.S. interests. In July 1986 the U.S. Congress passed legislation which allowed President Reagan to declare the compact implemented on 21 October that year. The relationship of free association between Marshall Islands and the U.S. will continue indefinitely, although economic aid must be renegotiated in the year 2001. In Dec. 1990 the United Nations Security Council formally terminated the trusteeship arrangement in these islands, and the following Sept. Marshall Islands was accepted as a U.N. member.

Government

The legislature is modeled on the British parliamentary system with the strong, clan-dominated traditional hierarchy grafted onto an American-style republican democracy. The constitution provides for a 33-senator Nitijela (Parliament), elected every four years. Majuro has five seats, Kwajalein three, Ailinglaplap, Arno, and Jaluit two each, and 19 other districts one each. The voting age is 18.

The Nitijela elects the president from its ranks; the president chooses his cabinet from elected members of the Nitijela. The president must dissolve the Nitijela and call new elections if the house passes two votes of nonconfidence in the cabinet by a simple majority. All legislative powers are centralized in the Nitijela (there are no states or provinces).

The two political groupings are the ruling RMI party, and the Ralik-Ratak Democratic Party opposition. Just prior to the Nov. 1991 election the cabinet placed severe restrictions on opposition use of the single AM radio station, the most important source of news and information in the country. Many of the elected members of the Nitijela are also customary chiefs *(iroij)*. The traditional high chief Amata Kabua, first president of the Marshall Islands, has exercised firm personal leadership since self-government began in 1979. Numerous members of his family hold key positions in the administration.

The Council of Iroij (consisting of 12 hereditary traditional leaders) deliberates on matters relating to land, custom, and tradition. A Traditional Lands Court rules on title and land rights.

The capital of the Marshall Islands is D-U-D (Darrit-Uliga-Delap) on Majuro; Ebeye (Kwajalein), Jaluit, and Wotje are administrative subcenters. Each of the 24 inhabited islands and atolls has a mayor and Island Council organized according to municipal constitutions, which govern the consumption of alcoholic beverages, among other things.

ECONOMY

The Marshall Islands is almost totally dependent on financial aid from the United States, which accounts for two-thirds of the government's budget. Heavy debts for an airline, a British-built 12-megawatt black oil-burning power plant, a fuel-storage tank farm, and a new dock on Majuro have kept Marshallese politicians in line. Construction of the power plant was dogged by revelations of kickbacks, "finder's fees," and a lack of competitive bidding. Much government-financed economic development is wasteful and inefficient; for example, the bankrupt powdered milk factory on Majuro, which cost millions, and Air Marshall Islands's money-losing DC-8 service to Honolulu.

Most of the $70 million received annually as grants, funding, and aid is spent on Majuro itself. In 1986 Ebeye started getting a fairer piece of the pie when it was realized that the former "slum of the Pacific" was giving the U.S. Government a bad name. But even today not much American largess filters down to the outer islands, and only about one percent of the money in the Marshall Islands General Fund goes to the outer island local governments.

The local bureaucracy itself represents over half the economic activity of the country: government workers outnumber those in the private sector three to one. A majority of the population, however, is engaged in subsistence agriculture (coconuts, breadfruit, pandanus, bananas, taro, sweet potatoes, yams, pigs, chickens, reef fish). Unemployment stands at 22% among males, 27% among females.

The Marshall Islands imports 11 times what it exports. During the Japanese colonial period the Marshallese developed their present taste for imported tea, rice, and soya sauce. Consumer items such as tinned food, tobacco, and beer account for about 60% of imports, which totaled $29.2 million in 1985.

Copra and coconut oil are the only significant agricultural exports (about $2 million a year), yet the outer-island copra producers themselves earn only about $68 per capita a year from it. Low prices for copra have discouraged efforts to replant the old German and Japanese coconut plantations. Almost all trade is with the U.S. and Japan, and the country buys $32 million more than it sells.

The Kwajalein Missile Range brings in over $22 million a year in salaries paid to Marshallese workers at the base, $9 million annual "rent" paid by the military, and taxes on the salaries of American expatriates.

Two hundred Japanese fishing boats pay close to $1 million a year to pull $150 million worth of tuna out of Marshallese waters. Some of the canned catch is sold back to the islanders, who now prefer it to fresh fish. Majuro has recently developed into a transshipment point for chilled skipjack tuna sent to Japan by air via Hawaii. Projects underway on Arno, Mili, and Likiep farm giant clams (Tridacna) and Japanese-funded black pearl farms have been initiated on Arno and Namorik. Live tropical fish are exported from Mili to aquarium stores in the U.S. With the world market for copra in a depressed state, these worthy projects provide new income for many outer islanders.

Marshall Islands offers a ship registry service, similar to those of Liberia and Panama, to large shipping companies wishing to avoid taxation, labor controls, government regulation, etc. Some four million tons of shipping are registered under the Marshallese flag in exchange for annual fees.

Marshallese citizens have unrestricted entry to the U.S., and to raise cash the Marshall Islands government sells passports for US$250,000 each. The catch is that U.S. Immigration stipulates that naturalized citizens must have resided in the Marshalls for five years. Only 4,895 people visited the Marshalls in 1990, though this was a 50% increase over 1989.

In recent years Marshall Islands has been targeted as a potential waste dump by persons attracted to the big profits to be made disposing American nuclear and municipal wastes. A proposal to store high-level American and Japanese nuclear reactor wastes on highly contaminated Bikini Atoll seems to have been shelved after it was accepted that, with the expected rise in sea levels over the next century due to the greenhouse effect, these wastes might eventually be washed directly into the sea.

In 1988 the *Marshall Islands Journal* revealed that an American company, Admiralty Pacific Inc., was proposing to use the lagoon of uninhabited Taongi (Bokaak) Atoll as a dump site for millions of tons of solid household waste barged from the U.S. west coast where the garbage dumps are filling and new landfills are restricted due to environmental protection regulations. Additional garbage was to be used to create causeways at Ebeye and reclaim lagoon area at Majuro. The promoters of the scheme offered millions of dollars in fees to the Marshallese, plus additional dry land area for future use. Opponents pointed out that such urban wastes are laced with hazardous materials such as paints, solvents, motor oil, pesticides, lead, and cleaning fluids, and as these substances leach out

the dump sites become permanently contaminated. The controversial proposal fell apart when a secret company plan to export nuclear wastes to the Marshalls was uncovered, and in 1990 another "waste management" company, Micronesian Marine Development Inc., began competing with Admiralty for the business. At last report powerful political leaders, who stood to profit personally from the deal, wanted the garbage to begin arriving in the Marshalls as soon as possible.

A future source of wealth may be undersea deposits of cobalt, manganese, nickel, and platinum in 800-2,400 meters of water within the Marshalls' 200-nautical-mile exclusive economic zone (EEZ). It's estimated that a million tons of exploitable ocean crust or nodules await further advances in mining technology.

THE PEOPLE

Of the 34 atolls and islands, 24 are inhabited. Almost half the population of the Marshalls lives on Majuro and another quarter is on Ebeye, placing them among the most densely populated islands in the Pacific. Large groups also live on Arno, Ailinglaplap, and Jaluit. The birth rate is a high 4.24% and over half the population is under age 15, the highest such ratio in the Pacific islands.

Westernization, the breakdown of the traditional family structure on the outer islands, and the experience of colonialism have led to alcoholism, hypertension, and high rates of suicide among young males and pregnancy out of wedlock among young females. The consumption of imported refined foods and sugar has led to widespread obesity, diabetes, dental problems, and infant malnutrition.

A growing imbalance exists between the affluence of the Americanized group on Majuro and the more traditional outer islanders. Growing numbers of outer islanders are migrating to Majuro and Ebeye. To many Marshallese, *jaba* (hanging out) is more than a way of life, it's a philosophy. They're prone to all the temptations, excitements, and vices of an island people.

Although most Marshallese are Protestant, missionaries of every shape, color, and creed are active on Majuro. Many social activities focus on the church. Education is compulsory up to the eighth grade or age 14. High schools teach in English. For postsecondary education, students go on to the College of the Marshall Islands, a teacher-training facility on Majuro which in 1991 became affiliated with the University of the South Pacific in Fiji. Under this new arrangement selected students will go on to study at the USP and university extension services will be created at Majuro. The School of Nursing for the whole of Micronesia is also on Majuro.

Marshallese society is matrilineal: chiefly titles descend through the mother. Each Marshallese belongs to the *bwij* (clan) of his/her mother and has the right to use the land and other property of the *bwij*. Alongside this is "blood" lineage *(bodokodok)* which is inherited from the father. The *dri jerbal* till the land. The head of the *bwij* is the *alab,* a spokesman between commoners *(kajur)* and the chiefly families *(iroij).* The paramount chiefs *(iroijlaplap)* are the Marshallese equivalent of royalty. As the money culture expands, Marshallese women are losing effective control of the land as family property is sold off to local men. Only Marshallese can own land in the Marshall Islands, although outsiders may lease it.

Language
Marshallese, the official language, belongs to the Austronesian family of languages (formerly known as Malayo-Polynesian) and is closely related to Gilbertese and the languages of the Carolines. People of the Ratak and Ralik chains speak mutually comprehensible dialects. *Yokwe* (pronounced YAG-way) is the Marshallese greeting; "thank you" is *kommol.* Kids often shout *"belle"* or *"dribelle"* (foreign people) at visitors; answer them with *"yokwe."*

Arts And Crafts
The Marshalls are a good place to pick up traditional handicrafts. Plentiful supplies of pandanus and coconut fiber, plus the relaxed pace of atoll life, have led to a variety of handicrafts. The best baskets in Micronesia are made in the Marshalls, especially those made by the Bikini refugees on Kili. Also available are woven coasters, wall hangings, pandanus hats, grass skirts, belts, purses, headbands, necklaces, fans, and mats—all made by the Marshallese women.

The men do carvings of sharks, eels, and canoes. Marshallese stick charts *(wapeepe),* which record the way ocean swells reflect and bend as they near land, make unique souvenirs. The charts, once used to train navigators, include shells to represent specific islands, and thin strips of wood for wave patterns.

Holidays And Events
Public holidays include New Year's Day (1 Jan.), Memorial Day and Nuclear Victim's Remembrance Day (1 March), Good Friday, Constitution Day (1 May), Fisherman's Day (first Friday in July), Labor Day (first Monday

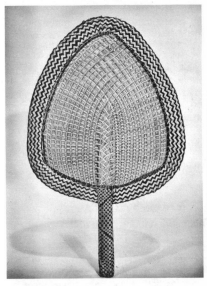

a Jaluit fan made of coconut, pandanus, and hibiscus fibers

INSTITUT ROYAL DU PATRIMOINE ARTISTIQUE, BRUSSELS

Marshallese stick chart: *To travel to islands over the horizon, the people of the Marshalls learned to read the wave patterns of the sea. When uniform ocean currents and wind drifts are interrupted and reflected by numerous atolls and reefs, they form certain kinds of swells which show the direction of land, This phenomenon can be clearly seen today on aerial photographs and pictures taken from weather satellites. The patterns could be felt by an experienced navigator as waves slapped against the side of the canoe, and it's said that even a blind man could navigate by means of a Marshallese stick chart. These charts were used to train young people in the art, and there were several types of these navigational aids.*

in Sept.), Manit Day (last Friday in Sept.), Independence Day (21 Oct.), President's Day (17 Nov.), Thanksgiving (last Thurs. in Nov.), and Christmas Day (25 December).

Constitution Day, commemorating the Marshallese constitution which took effect 1 May 1979, is a good time to see Marshallese singing and dancing, canoe races, etc. Aging Week (last week in May) features exhibitions of handicrafts, traditional Marshallese medicines, and cooking. Fisherman's Day marks the beginning of a famous fishing tournament organized by the Marshalls Billfish Club. Alele Week (last week in Aug.) also hosts dancing, singing, handicrafts, and other cultural activities. At Christmas singing and dancing unfolds in the churches all day.

PRACTICALITIES

Accommodations And Food

The only regular hotels and restaurants are on Majuro and Ebeye, and occasionally all 121 rooms on Majuro and 29 rooms on Ebeye are full. Add three percent government room tax and $2 daily local government tax to all the accommodations rates listed in this chapter. Outside D-U-D camping is generally acceptable, provided you first obtain permission of the landowner (usually no problem).

Accommodations for visitors are available on Mili and a few other atolls, but reliable information can be hard to obtain. One way to arrange a stay on an outer island is to go to the Nitijela and ask for the senator from the atoll of your choice. He/she will be able to outline the accommodations situation and perhaps suggest local contacts. Although you can simply show up on the outer islands, to be assured of a good reception it's much better to make prior arrangements with the Island Council. The Ministry of Interior and Outer Islands Affairs (Box 18, Majuro, MH 96960; tel. 3225) has a radio link with most of the atolls and is experienced in arranging stays. Give them as much lead time as possible to contact the island's mayor and make the arrangements.

If you'll be staying with someone as a guest, ask whoever made the arrangements what they think you should take along as gifts (a large jar of instant coffee, T-shirts, music cassettes, or flashlight and batteries, for example—but not alcohol). Although Marshallese hospitality is genuine, adequate payment (monetary or otherwise) is customary. Airline baggage limits permitting, take your own food and bottled water with you to the outer islands, as local cooperative stores carry only basics like sugar and flour.

Visas

U.S. citizens do not require a passport to enter the Marshalls, although proper identification must be shown. Everyone else must have a passport. No visa is required for a stay of up to 30 days. Anyone intending to stay over 30 days should obtain a Marshalls entry permit in advance through their local sponsor. Visa extensions beyond the initial 30 days are hard to come by, although they might grant you one if you have a valid reason (such as being on a field trip). Everyone other than U.S. and Canadian citizens must already have a U.S. visa if they're going on to Hawaii. All visitors must have an onward or return air ticket and are forbidden from engaging in political activity.

After clearing Customs at Majuro, visiting yachts must obtain a permit from the Ministry of Interior and Outer Islands Affairs to cruise to the other atolls.

Money And Measurements

American currency is used. Food and essentials can cost almost twice as much on the outer islands as they do in Majuro, if they can be found at all. Bargaining is not customary in the Marshalls and tipping is done only in tourist-oriented establishments.

To phone direct from the U.S. to a telephone on Majuro dial 011-692-9, then the local four-digit telephone number. The Marshall Islands issues its own colorful postage stamps, but U.S. domestic postal rates apply. Due to a growing marijuana industry most packages mailed to the U.S. from the Marshalls are opened for postal inspection. The electric voltage is 110 volts/60 cycles and American appliance plugs are used.

The Marshall Islands is the first country west of the International Date Line, so you lose a day if you're coming from Hawaii. The American military base on Kwajalein, however, follows the U.S. day, a 24-hour difference with neighboring Ebeye. Whatever the day, you'll be on "Marshallese time," which means "slow down!" Government offices are most reliably open weekday mornings.

Health

A vaccination certificate against cholera or yellow fever is required if arriving from an infected area. Typhoid and polio shots are not required, but recommended. There's a large new hospital on Majuro and a field hospital at Ebeye. Only dispensaries are available on the outer islands.

Be aware: the sexually transmitted disease and tuberculosis rates on Majuro and Ebeye are high! Marshall Islands also has an incidence of ciguatera (seafood poisoning) three times as high as in any other part of Micronesia.

If you've got a weak stomach, don't drink the tap water in D-U-D or on the outer islands. At best the water is brackish, and it's usually contaminated, so buy bottled water if you can. On Ebeye the distilled tap water is excellent. From Jan. through April water is rationed on Majuro.

Information

Upon request, the Tourism Office, Ministry of Resources and Development, Box 1727, Majuro, MH 96960, will send you their brochures. Their Hawaii office is at 1441 Kapiolani Blvd., Suite 1910, near the Ala Moana Shopping Center, Honolulu.

The Alele Museum (Box 629, Majuro, MH 96960; tel. 3226) sells hard-to-find books such as *Collision Course at Kwajalein* (1984, $8), by Giff Johnson, and *Man This Reef* (1982, $11), by Gerald Knight. They also have the 100-page *Marshall Islands Guidebook* ($7) which includes a Marshallese dictionary, maps of all the atolls, and much background information on the country. These books can be shipped by airmail— write for a complete list.

The weekly, privately owned *Marshall Islands Journal* (Box 14, Majuro, MH 96960) comes out on Fridays (50 cents) in English

the supply ship
Micro Pilot *at Majuro*

and Marshallese. Annual subscription rates to the *Journal* are $77 to the U.S., $205 elsewhere (airmail). The *Journal* includes a wealth of interesting local news from an independent perspective, so be sure to pick up a copy first chance you get.

The *Marshall Islands Government Gazette* is an official publication issued monthly by the Ministry of Interior and Outer Islands Affairs (Box 18, Majuro, MH 96960).

The Guam-based *Pacific Daily News* is usually available in D-U-D. One AM (WSZO) and two FM radio stations broadcast in English and Marshallese. A private cable TV station runs video tapes of commercial Hawaiian programming. The Armed Forces Radio Television Service (AFRTS) beams out from Kwajalein 24 hours a day.

The many Peace Corps volunteers in the Marshalls are an excellent information source on the outer islands.

What To Take

You're allowed to bring in one bottle of liquor and two cartons of cigarettes—a good idea if you need them, as they're heavily taxed. Cosmetics are also expensive locally. Color print film can be purchased in D-U-D, but color film must be sent back to the States for processing, so bring mailers. Female visitors should be aware that the only local women wearing shorts above the knee are prostitutes, so conservative dress is in order.

GETTING THERE

Continental Air Micronesia (tel. 3209) has flights to Majuro four times a week from Honolulu and Guam, thrice weekly via Kosrae. Since it costs about the same to fly Honolulu-Majuro ($565 OW) as Honolulu-Guam with stops in Majuro, Kwajalein, Kosrae, Pohnpei, and Chuuk ($630 OW), buy a through ticket. The local Air Mike office has finally computerized, so you can now get instant confirmations on flight bookings out of Majuro. Reconfirm your onward flight well in advance at the Air Mike office below the RRE Hotel in Uliga or at the airport on arrival.

There's a weekly **Air Marshall Islands** flight from Majuro to Tarawa (US$170 OW), Funafuti (US$409 OW), and Fiji (US$510 OW), which allows a sidetrip to the Republic of Kiribati or a connection to the South Pacific. A 23-day roundtrip excursion fare between Majuro and Fiji is US$709. This airline also flies between Honolulu and Majuro/Kwajalein (US$555 OW) four times a week. Special roundtrip fares from Honolulu are available. For toll-free information on Air Marshall Islands in the U.S. call (800) 543-3898.

Air Nauru (tel. 3259) has an office at the Eastern Gateway Hotel in Delap, but only charter flights from Nauru to Majuro. It's possible to link up with their services at Tarawa and their fares are much lower than those of Air Marshall Islands (see the main "Introduction").

GETTING AROUND

By Air

Government-owned **Air Marshall Islands** (Box 1319, Majuro, MH 96960; tel. 3733) uses safe, reliable German-made Dornier propeller aircraft to provide punctual service to all 26 airstrips in the Marshalls weekly or twice a month. AMI flies from Majuro weekly to Airok ($72) and Jeh ($59) on Ailinglaplap, also weekly to Likiep ($98), twice weekly to Jaluit ($65), Kili ($76), Maloelap ($54), and Wotje ($76), three times a week to Ine ($22) and Tinak ($19) on Arno, and six times a week to Kwajalein ($114). The one-way fares are given above. Their current schedule appears in the *Marshall Islands Journal* each week. Checked baggage limits are 30 pounds on domestic flights, 44 pounds international. Often the flights are full.

Special services sometimes make possible weekend trips to Arno and Jaluit. Occasionally AMI has Sunday day-trips to outer islands like Maloelap or Mili for about $75 including a lunch of local foods—a great opportunity if your travel plans are lucky enough to coincide. A flight arrival on an outer island is the main social event of the week. Some outer islands (such as Maloelap) charge $1 pp departure tax.

By Boat

The most leisurely way to experience the Marshall Islands is on a field trip aboard the *Micro Pilot, Micro Chief,* or *Micro Palm.* These 600-ton ships make five different field trips from Majuro: west (2,430 km), north (1,120 km), south (1,095 km), central (850 km), and east (280 km). Theoretically the ships visit all the atolls every month or two. Fares run 16 cents a km cabin, 10 cents a km deck. The cabins are usually full. Meals are $10 a day extra, but the food served is poor and overpriced so it's best to take along your own.

To find out what's available, inquire at the **Government Transportation Office** (tel. 3469), beside the old dock, as soon as you arrive on Majuro. If something's leaving that same day, don't hesitate—get right on. You might have to wait a couple of weeks otherwise. Another possibility is to fly out to an island that the field trip ship will be visiting shortly and ride back to Majuro. In fact, this is a much surer way to go. Note that alcoholic beverages are prohibited on many outer islands.

Airport

Majuro airport (MAJ) is 13 km west of town—no bank or tourist information and the restaurant is usually closed. Handicrafts are sold at two shops which open at international flight times. A shared taxi to D-U-D costs $2 pp, although most of the hotels offer free shuttles. The runway aprons serve as Majuro's water catchment. The airport tax is $10 on international flights.

MAJURO AND THE RATAK CHAIN

Majuro, 3,658 km southwest of Honolulu, is a long finger of islands joined together by causeways which enclose the whole south side of the Majuro lagoon. Originally 64 islands surrounded the oval lagoon but causeways now enable you to drive the 56 km from Rita to Laura, at opposite ends of the atoll. The WW II code names for Darrit and Majuro islands, Rita and Laura respectively, have stuck (another version claims they're named for Hollywood stars Rita Hayworth and Lauren Bacall). Before the war Majuro was just another outer atoll, but on 1 Feb. 1944 the Americans landed unopposed on Majuro and built a fighter strip near where Gibson's Shopping Center is now, while naval units anchored in the lagoon. The striking shapes of the clouds over Majuro make up for the lack of mountains.

The present capital of the Marshall Islands bears the imaginative title D-U-D Municipality. Actually, the initials stand for Darrit-Uliga-Delap, three islands now joined by roads. D-U-D is five km long and only 200 meters wide. It's a conglomeration of administrative buildings, businesses ranging from department stores/supermarkets to small grocery/beer outlets, and densely packed houses of plywood and corrugated iron with tin roofs. Coconuts have been largely replaced by colas, cans, and cars, and the litter overflows. Twenty thousand Marshallese from every atoll in the country and a couple of hundred Americans live here.

SIGHTS

Majuro

The **Alele Museum** (open weekdays 1000-1200/1500-1700, donation) at Uliga has a collection of artifacts and some fascinating turn-of-the-century photos on permanent display. A few books on the Marshalls, first-day postal covers, and T-shirts depicting local legends are sold in the museum and adjoining **library**, which has a good reference section on Micronesia and recent American newsmagazines.

The largest remaining relic of the Japanese period in D-U-D is a long concrete **bunker**, a relic of a wartime Japanese seaplane base half hidden among the houses in the middle of Rita village between Marshall Is-

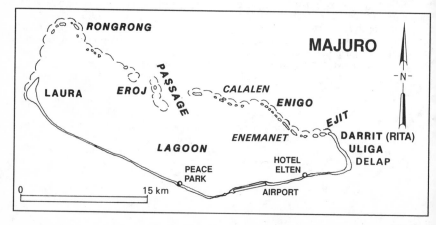

the Japanese typhoon monument in Laura village near the west end of Majuro Atoll

Take a taxi to the new container dock, where the Marshallese navy is moored next to rusted hulks such as the *Mieco Queen.* The **Majuro Long Line Fish Base Operation** here is a joint venture with MMG of Hawaii. Oriental (mostly Taiwanese) fishing boats deliver fresh fish to the cold storage facility for immediate export to Japan (the fish are chilled, not frozen). The large icemaking plant also supplies ice to the boats; in fact, it's the largest such plant in the Pacific, producing 200 tons of ice every 24 hours. Also overlooking the dock is the government-subsidized **Tobolar Copra Processing Plant**, where copra is processed into coconut oil and copra cake. Wander through the plant at will and observe the process.

Just west of the copra plant is the **Majuro Bridge,** built with Japanese aid money in 1983—the highest point on the atoll. The channel was cut through the lee side to allow better access to the sea for small boats, avoiding the long detour around Calalen Island. Dangerous currents in the channel have caused accidents leading to several drownings; a serious erosion problem has also developed.

To Laura

Continue along the excellent 56-km road from Rita to Laura. The **Japanese Peace Park,** created a couple of km west of the airport in 1984, would be a nice picnic spot if it weren't so filthy. **Laura,** a quiet little settlement with a Taiwanese experimental farm, contained a majority of the population of Majuro before WW II. Beyond the end of the paved road at Laura is the three-meter-high Japanese **typhoon monument,** which memorializes Emperor Hirohito's assistance to Majuro after a typhoon in 1918.

Farther along, at the end of the island, is a beautiful beach and **snorkeling** locale. You could camp here, although many locals arrive for picnics on weekends. Ask for Atlan Tobey, a local teacher who lives just beyond the typhoon monument; he will help you find a place to camp. There are several stores in Laura, but the village retains its outer-island flavor despite its accessibility to raucous D-U-D.

lands High School and Rita Elementary School. Take the first road to the right just north of the high school compound and ask. It's easy to climb the **water tower** at the high school for the view.

South Of Town

Opposite Gibson's Shopping Center in Delap is the new $9 million **capitol complex,** construction of which was halted in 1991, when the concrete foundations cracked. The president owns the land on which the complex was built, so his family will be collecting rent on the property for the next couple of thousand years.

Mieco Beach, between Gibson's and the Nitijela, is strewn with beer cans and refuse, but it's the best D-U-D has to offer. As you might have gathered, garbage collection is erratic in D-U-D. The **Nitijela** (parliament) meets at the Cabinet Building farther west. (Persons wearing shorts or shirts without collars are not allowed on the Nitijela grounds!)

Beyond The Road

It's possible to walk west along the reef from the end of the road at Rita to the next few islands. Start two or three hours before low tide—tide tables are published in the *Marshall Islands Journal*. If you're lucky enough to coincide with a very low tide, you'll be able to walk on the dry sand on the ocean side; otherwise you may have to wade up to your waist. Many small islands dot the reef, and you can cross as many as 12 before it comes time to turn back. Take care not to become stranded, and beware of killer currents!

About 200 of the Bikini refugees from Kili live on **Ejit**, the second island; **Enemanet**, much farther along, has the best beach. Private speedboats run back and forth from the beach at Rita to Ejit (offer to contribute for gas). Bring food and water, and camp. Alternatively, bring snorkeling gear and swim your way west. You'll soon find everything you'd hoped to find in the Marshalls—the bustle of D-U-D quickly fades. A cold beer awaits you at the Yacht Club (closed Sunday) upon your return.

PRACTICALITIES

Accommodations

The **Majuro Hotel** (Box 185, Majuro, MH 96960; tel. 3324), above the Majuro Hut Restaurant in the center of Uliga, charges $40 s, $45 d for its 15 a/c rooms. The four rooms with only fan and shared bath (some without windows) are about $27 twin, but they can be unbelievably hot.

The **Ajidrik Hotel** (Box E, Majuro, MH 96960; tel. 3171), behind the Downtown Restaurant right next to the Majuro, has 14 a/c rooms ($40 s, $45 d). It's $5 extra pp for more than two persons. All rooms have private bath and fridge and a few also have TV. Apartments at the Ajidrik are $750 s, $820 d a month. If things are slow they might give you a discount. Both of the above hotels are basic, but okay for those on a budget.

A hit with businesspeople, the **RRE Hotel** (Box 1, Majuro, MH 96960; tel. 3250), also known as the Robert Reimers Enterprises Hotel, is atop Ace Hardware in Uliga. They offer 18 comfortable a/c rooms with private bath and stocked fridge. The six windowless inside rooms are $70 s, $75 d, while the 12 lanai-side rooms with balcony are $85 s, $95 d (credit cards accepted). In addition there are 12 prefabricated beach units that cost the same as the lanai rooms. Play rented video tapes on your own VCR! The hotel has its own generator for use during power failures. Their Tide Table Restaurant, upstairs off the lobby, serves excellent meals with a lagoon view (daily 0700-1400/1700-2200). Try the sashimi here—happy hour is 1700-1800.

The **Seamen's Corner Motel** (Box 382, Majuro, MH 96960; tel. 3491), also known as "Willy's Hotel," doesn't have a sign outside, so look for a two-story wooden building almost opposite the Lanai Club in Delap. The six a/c rooms with shared bath are $35 s or d. It's the cheapest place on the island if the budget rooms at the Majuro are full.

The noisy **Eastern Gateway Hotel** (Box 106, Majuro, MH 96960; tel. 3337) on the lagoon in Delap, a couple of km south of the business center, is overpriced: the 13 a/c rooms in the old motel section are $50 s, $55 d. Coffee-making facilities are provided in the rooms. Construction of the adjacent three-story, ferro-concrete structure, begun way back in 1976 with Nauru money, is now showing serious signs of being completed!

Also a poor value is the 19-room **Capital Terrace Hotel** (Box 107, Majuro, MH 96960; tel. 3527), opposite the Nitijela. Here you pay $47 s, $57 d for an a/c room with private bath and fridge. This two-story hotel is a bit of a dive, with drunks stumbling through the corridors.

Much nicer is the **Royal Garden Hotel** (Box 735, Majuro, MH 96960; tel. 3701), on the ocean a couple of km west of the Majuro Bridge, at $60 s, $75 d for one of the 24 a/c rooms. There's a 10% discount offered to government employees. It's in clean, pleasant surroundings, but you'll need to rent a car to get around. Their seaside restaurant is expensive, so stroll a few hundred meters east to Japanese Flavor Garden Restaurant for lunch or dinner. Credit cards are accepted.

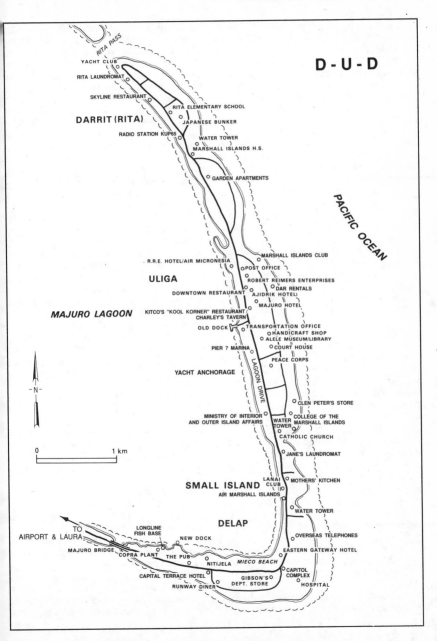

Also on Long Island by the ocean a km west of the U.S. Embassy is **Hotel Elten** (Box 1254, Majuro, MH 96960; tel. 3858) with eight a/c rooms with private bath at $47 s or d. It's a laid-back place in a garden setting—great if you have wheels. There's no restaurant nearby but there is a laundromat next to the Mobil station just east and a small shop on the premises.

The **Airport Motel** (Box 786, Majuro, MH 96960; tel. 3088), farther west near the airport, has been converted into long-term apartments and is not available at the moment.

For a longer stay on Majuro, call Brian and Nancy Vander Velde (Box 1603, Majuro, MH 96960; tel. 3811) well in advance. They rent self-contained units at their **Garden Apartments** in Rita for $600 a month and up.

Camping in D-U-D is not recommended, unless someone's family allows you to pitch your tent near their home. In the past people have camped west of the airport on the road to Laura and beyond the end of the road itself.

Food

Majuro has many inexpensive restaurants of varying quality. One of the best is the **Majuro Hut** below the Majuro Hotel in Uliga and the meals have a Chinese flavor reflected in the decor. **Kitco's "Kool Korner" Restaurant** nearby has been serving dishes like hotcakes and eggs ($2) and fried chicken with chips ($3) for years, but take care, they fry their eggs in the same oil as their fish. Similar is the **Downtown Restaurant** near the Ajidrik Hotel. **The Deli**, between Robert Reimers Enterprises and the post office, offers fast-food-style breakfasts, sandwiches, and pizza at sidewalk picnic tables—nothing special. Also check the **Dar Coffee Corner**, on the back street behind Robert Reimers Enterprises, which is reasonable.

Before ordering at any of the above, be aware that the **Tide Table Restaurant** at the RRE Hotel is only 50% more expensive but 100% better.

Further afield, the **Skyline Restaurant** in Rita offers tasty curries. The chopped tuna or tuna steak ($3.50) at **Mother's Kitchen,** next to Momotaro's store in Delap, is good. This is about the only place where vegetarians have a choice on entrees. The **EGH Restaurant,** next to the Eastern Gateway Hotel in Delap, has pseudo-American fare similar to that offered at Kitco's.

A much better place than the EGH is **Quik Stop Coffee Shop** (daily 0700-2100), nearby at Gibson's. Lunch specials ($5) are posted outside the kitchen. The sandwiches, steaks, and salads are fine, and breakfast is also good here. It's a/c and most of the tables have a lagoon view. The local American expat community seems to hang out here—a good recommendation.

The **Runway Diner** behind the shiny five-story Majuro Central Building opposite the Nitijela features fast service, reasonable prices, and local dishes such as reef fish. Their menu is surprisingly extensive but much is unavailable. Their coffee is good and it's one of the better budget places.

Japanese Flavor Garden Restaurant (open 1100-2200), near the Royal Garden Hotel one km west of the Majuro Bridge, serves reasonable take-out meals which you carry back into the lagoonside garden and eat at the covered picnic tables. You can sample coconut crabs here. It's a good place to stop if you're driving.

Blue Lagoon Take-Out, near the airport, has local take-away foods ready-made for picnics.

Tipping is expected at the American-style restaurants, such as the ones at the RRE and Royal Garden hotels and Quik Stop Coffee Shop, but not in the Marshallese restaurants.

Entertainment

Most bars on Majuro have a happy hour, with reduced prices on drinks weekdays from 1700 to 1830. On weekend nights, the streets are active and the discos start hopping around 2300. Sundays all of the places mentioned below are closed.

Upper-echelon locals and expatriates drink at **Charley's Tavern,** next to Kitco's Restaurant in Uliga, while local government workers usually buy beer and play cards behind **Clen Peter's store,** oceanside near the College of the Marshall Islands.

A true Majuro institution is the **Marshall Islands Club** (tel. 3756; open Mon.-Sat. from noon to midnight), behind Robert Reimers Enterprises in Uliga. You can see across to Arno from their breezy back porch overlooking the sea, and there's a pool table and long bar. Happy hour runs 1700-1800 with free pu-puu's (snacks). Order a pizza or try their $2 snacks anytime: sashimi, fried fish pieces, chicken wings, nachos (chips with a cheese dip), and giant-clam meat. A live band plays after 2200 on certain nights ($3 cover), as advertised on signs at the door.

Also excellent is the **Yacht Club** (tel. 3117: open Mon. to Sat. 1400 to midnight), at the north tip of Rita which serves beer and other drinks in a pleasant outdoor ambience; the perfect place to catch a sunset. Ask for a Majuro Mule (rum or vodka mixed with the milk in a green coconut). After 1600 they bake the best pizza on Majuro. You can play Ping-Pong and pool here.

The **Lanai Club,** on Delap's Small Island, and **The Pub,** near the new dock in Delap, are other favorite drinking and dancing establishments. The live music comes with a cover charge. The Pub is open Wed.-Sat. 2000-0300; Thursday is Ladies Night with free admission for women. Persons wearing shorts are not admitted to The Pub. On Wednesday and Thursday T-shirts are okay, but on Friday and Saturday you must wear a shirt with a collar.

Sports And Recreation

Matt Holly (Box 319, Majuro, MH 96960; tel. 3669) runs an unreliable scuba operation out of an abandoned power plant at Pier 7 Marina, not far from the Alele Museum. Since Matt's boat sank he takes people beach diving from his pickup truck, which often involves wading into the ocean over the reef (dangerous). If you know what you're doing, it's better just to rent tanks and gear from Matt and head off on your own in a rental car. That's assuming, of course, that Matt's air compressor is working—check the equipment carefully before leaving.

Otherwise ask at the fisheries office near the new dock in Delap. Several people working there have boats for rent, and the tourism office (tel. 3262) in the same building can provide further leads. The drift diving is good in the pass off Calalen I., with some shark action; there are a few wrecks in the lagoon, including the freighter *Kabilok* just off D-U-D. Laura is a good place for shore diving. The underwater attractions of Majuro beat the above-water sights fins down. Take special care with ocean currents if you do any snorkeling or diving on the ocean side of the atoll!

Charter boats for deep-sea fishing can be arranged through the RRE Hotel ($150 half day, $300 full day) or the fisheries office mentioned above. Majuro is becoming known for its sportfishing, and game fish such as blue marlin, mahimahi, sailfish, tuna, and wahoo are said to abound off the east tip of Arno. Line fishing in the lagoon and night fishing for flying fish are also possible.

Shopping

The largest department stores and supermarkets are **Robert Reimers Enterprises** in Uliga and **Gibson's Department Store** in Delap. A three-percent government sales tax is added to all sticker prices at the cash register.

For traditional handicrafts there's the **Marshalls Handicraft Shop** (open weekdays; Box 44, Majuro, MH 96960; tel. 3566), just behind the Alele Museum. They have a good selection of baskets, fans, coasters, mats, Kili bags, wall hangings, stick charts, and model canoes at reasonable prices. Their outlet at the airport opens for Continental Air Micronesia flights.

Some crafts are also sold at the **Busy Hands Club** (theoretically open Wed. and Fri. 1000-1200; Mon., Tues., Thurs., Sat. 1500-1700), behind the Catholic church. This is a good place to purchase baskets, fans, and old Japanese bottles.

Services

The Bank of Guam (tel. 3322) and the Bank of Marshall Islands (tel. 3636) have branches opposite one another near Robert Reimers

Enterprises in Uliga. The Bank of Hawaii (tel. 3741), at the Gibson's complex in Delap, is the only place you can get a cash advance with a credit card. The banks are open weekdays 1000-1500, Fri. till 1700.

The downtown post office next to the RRE complex in Uliga has Marshallese stamps and first-day covers (open weekdays 0800-1200/1300-1600, Sat. 0800-1000). There's a branch post office at Gibson's in Delap.

Collectors abroad can order Marshall Islands stamps from the Stamp and Philatelic Center of the Republic of the Marshall Islands, One Unicorn Center, Cheyenne, WY 82008-0009 U.S.A. (tel. 800-443-4225).

Long-distance telephone calls can be made at the white concrete building marked "Overseas Telephone," beside the Satellite Communications Station in Delap. Weekends you may have to wake up the operator (not an easy task). Calls to the U.S. are $2.50 a minute, station to station, to Guam $3 a minute, to Europe $5 a minute. There's a three-minute minimum to Europe but no minimum to the U.S. You can also make overseas calls from the RRE Hotel for an additional $2 service charge. Sometimes both the satellite and high-frequency radio links can be "down" for extended periods of time.

To place radiotelephone calls to the outer islands, go to radio station KUP65 near Marshall Islands High School in Rita. They're open 24 hours a day and the charge is 50 cents a minute.

The Consulate of Israel is on the ocean side behind Robert Reimers Enterprises, the U.S. Embassy (tel. 4011) is on Long Island between the airport and D-U-D, and the Chinese Embassy (tel. 3275) is near the airport.

There are several laundromats (50 cents) around D-U-D, one of the best of which is Jane's Laundromat in Delap. It's a/c, they have more machines than the others, and soft drinks are sold. Others are opposite the Bahai Center near the tip of Rita, next to The Pub out toward the new dock, and near Hotel Elton on Long Island. There's a small coin laundry directly between the Majuro and Ajidrik hotels. Take along some reading material, as the lines can be long. You often see local women occupying four or five machines at a time, doing the wash for entire villages! The laundromats are less crowded in the morning.

Health

The Majuro Hospital (tel. 3399) in Delap provides X-ray, laboratory, emergency, outpatient, and inpatient services. The staff includes American Health Service Corps, Filipino, and Marshallese doctors. Outpatients are treated 1300-2100. There's also a pharmacy at the hospital.

D-U-D tap water is unsafe to drink unless boiled for 20 minutes; buy bottled water at a supermarket.

Information

You can pick up brochures at the tourism office (tel. 3206) in the fisheries building near the new dock at Delap.

The Alele Public Library (Box 629, Majuro, MH 96960; tel. 3226) is open Mon.-Thurs. 1000-1730, Fri. 1000-1700, Sat. 0900-1300. It has a good selection of current magazines from around the Pacific and many interesting books on the region, so it's well worth a few hours.

TV station METV, beside the Marshalls Handicraft Shop behind the library, rents videocassettes of Marshallese dancing and singing at $2 a day. They'll also copy the same tapes for $30 apiece.

Radio station WSZO-AM Majuro broadcasts over 1098 kHz.

Local Transport

Swarms of shared taxis prowl up and down Lagoon Drive in D-U-D, 30 cents pp a ride anywhere between the new dock at Delap and the end of the road at Rita. Flag one down anywhere, though the taxis are often full. Cruising buses charge 25 cents a ride within D-U-D. A taxi to Laura is $10 pp each way.

Theoretically, blue-and-white minibuses run four times a day between D-U-D and Laura ($1.50 pp one way), but no service on Sunday. Look for them in the parking lot in front of the RRE Hotel in Uliga; the stop is marked with a sign reading "Bus Parking Only."

Small Japanese cars rent for $40 daily including insurance at **DAR Sales and Service** (Box 153, Majuro, MH 96960; tel. 3174), also known as Domnick Auto Rental, behind Robert Reimers Enterprises and at the airport. It's convenient because you can drop the car off at the airport.

The **RRE Hotel** in Uliga rents cars at $36 daily, plus $7.50 for insurance. **Deluxe Rent-a-Car** (tel. 3665), opposite The Pub in Delap, is more expensive at $52.50 including insurance, but they're a lot more likely to have cars. There's a $5 extra charge for additional drivers at Deluxe.

Foreign driver's licenses are accepted for one month and at most agencies you must be at least 25 years old to rent a car. The excellent taxi service and limited roads make renting a car optional. In fact, Majuro (along with Chuuk) has the best public transportation in Micronesia.

THE RATAK CHAIN

Arno

You can see Arno, one of the five most populous atolls in the Marshalls, as a thin line along the horizon 56 km east of D-U-D; small outboard motorboats often journey between the old dock on Majuro and Arno ($5). Both Ine and Tinak islands have airstrips, with flights from nearby Majuro three times a week—the easiest way to escape city life. These frequent flights make a brief stay on the atoll quite easy, but surprisingly there's no guesthouse on Arno, so you have to camp or stay with friends.

Over a hundred islets sit on Arno's peculiarly shaped barrier reef, which twists around three lagoons! The beautiful beaches and quiet communities make a visit worthwhile. Arno lobsters are famous. The oyster and clam farm on Enerik I. may be visited with persistence. Black pearls are harvested here. A Japanese government-financed fishing project functions on Arno, with local fishermen using small boats to supply a cold-storage facility.

The locals on Arno, still back in the macho era, have a school at Longar village to teach young Marshallese women how to be good wives. One technique involves a girl lying in the bottom of a canoe to feel the motion of the sea—useful in lovemaking. Naturally, the graduates are in high demand.

Mili

After Kwajalein, Mili Atoll, 150 km south of Majuro, is the largest atoll in land area in the Marshalls. A wartime anti-Japanese revolt on Mili was brutally suppressed. Mili still has a lot of old Japanese war relics, including submerged wrecks for diving enthusiasts, cannons, bunkers, and intact Zero aircraft. Mosquitos breed in wartime bomb craters on Mili, so bring coils or repellent. A giant-clam hatchery is on Wau Island. The Knox Islands, just southeast of Mili, are uninhabited.

Five fan-cooled rooms are for rent at $25 s, $40 d above a store on the lagoon beach, very near the airstrip. It's the only two-story building on the island and is locally known as the "Whitehouse." There's an electricity generator and cooking facilities, also a twin-engine boat available for diving, fishing, or picnics. The place has the same owner as the Capital Terrace Hotel on Majuro, so you could make inquiries there.

Ben Chutaro at Gushi Brothers Warehouse (Box 11, Majuro, MH 96960; tel. 3688), next to Charley's Tavern, can also arrange accommodations on Mili.

AMI flights from Majuro ($44 one way) are twice a week and there's a speedboat once every two weeks ($40). The island mayor charges visitors a $5 pp entry fee. Camping is no problem. Food supplies on Mili are very limited so it's best to bring your own. Take care with the drinking water here.

Maloelap

Maloelap Atoll, 170 km north of Majuro, has the largest lagoon in the Ratak Chain, with 71 islands on the reef. AMI flies from Majuro to Taroa ($54 one way) twice a week, to Kaven every other week. To charter a speedboat for the ride across the lagoon between the two islands costs about $40 (four hours).

The village on Taroa I. is only a few minutes' walk from the airstrip. The mayor has a simple thatched guesthouse in the center of the village, where one can stay for about $5 pp a night. Toilet and washing facilities are outside. Advance arrangements must be made through the Ministry of Interior and Outer Islands Affairs on Majuro, which has radio contact with Taroa. In the past visitors have also slept in the empty classroom at the school in summer.

In 1941 Maloelap became the easternmost Japanese bastion in the Pacific, but on 29 Jan. 1944 a U.S. air strike from the carrier *Enterprise* against the X-shaped runways on Taroa terminated Maloelap's role as a fortified fighter/bomber base. The U.S. never bothered to land on neutralized Maloelap; the 3,116 Japanese stranded there were used for bombing and strafing practice by U.S. pilots until August 1945. Only 1,070 survived: 566 were killed in the air raids, 76 died of wounds, 1,251 of starvation, and 153 from disease.

Today numerous Japanese guns, bunkers, bombs, aircraft, and large concrete buildings are hidden in the thick undergrowth of Taroa. Two Zero aircraft lie beside the airstrip and a large concrete Japanese power plant, its rusted generators still inside, is between airstrip and village. Right in the middle of the village is a reinforced three-story Japanese radio station, presently used as a church and living quarters by the locals. In the bush not far from the village is an aircraft graveyard, with over a dozen wrecked Japanese fighters and bombers. Along the ocean side at the far end of the airstrip are a string of coastal defense bunkers and at least six large 150 mm guns, three on each side of the airstrip. Many more Japanese ruins are half swallowed in the bush; a full week would be required to explore all the wreckage.

It's also fun to snorkel around the twin masts of a Japanese freighter, the *Toroshima Maru*, which poke out of the lagoon just off the beach, only about 100 meters from the large Japanese wharf in the middle of the village on Taroa.

Wotje

Wotje is a large atoll between Maloelap and Likiep, 240 km east of Kwajalein. During WW II Wotje was a Japanese military base, and it's said soil was brought in from Japan in an effort to make the atoll self-supporting. Wotje is still known as the garden island of the Marshalls. Numerous war relics remain in the lagoon and on some of the 72 islands of Wotje. The Wotje people often travel to uninhabited Erikub Atoll by speedboat to fish and make copra. Plan on camping or staying with the locals if you visit.

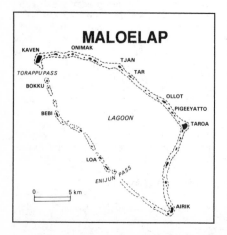

MALOELAP

KAVEN ONIMAK
TJAN
TORAPPU PASS
BOKKU
TAR
OLLOT
PIGEEYATTO
BEBI
LAGOON
TAROA
LOA
ENIJUN PASS
0   5 km
AIRIK

Likiep

Likiep is another sizable atoll, with 65 islands ranged around its shallow lagoon. About a century ago a German named Adolph Capelle and a Portuguese named Anton deBrum bought Likiep from the chief; their descendants still jointly own the atoll. The deBrum mansion, former headquarters of Likiep's coconut plantation, has been restored with support from the Endowment for Historic Preservation of the Micronesia Institute, Washington, D.C. Thousands of glass-plate photos taken by Joachim deBrum are kept at the Alele Museum on Majuro.

After WW II Likiep had a Catholic intermediate school with 700 students, but it closed in 1962. Now there's a project to teach traditional Marshallese canoe building and a giant-clam hatchery has opened. With the mayor's permission you can stay in the Island Council guesthouse. Otherwise, camping and being someone's guest are the only accommodation options on this atoll.

THE RALIK CHAIN

Jaluit

The Germans set up a trading post on Jaluit in 1878, and when the Marshalls became a colony in 1885 the Germans headquartered here. In 1914 Jaluit became the Japanese administrative center; later they built an airstrip on nearby Emidj Island. The Japanese shipped tons of soil from Kosrae and Pohnpei to create vegetable gardens on the island. By 1941 the population of Jabwor village was 3,000. The U.S. bombed and bypassed the Japanese base on Jaluit during WW II and some war wreckage remains.

Today bananas and breadfruit are grown; copra, seashells, and handicrafts are exported. There's a new high school in Jabwor, at the north end of Jaluit, one of 91 reef islands comprising the atoll. Swept channels

lead from three passes to lagoon anchorages off Emidj and Jaluit islands. The new dock and petroleum storage facility at Jaluit sports a big Mobil Pegasus sign. Jaluit is accessible twice weekly by air from Majuro ($65 OW), 90 km northeast.

In January 1992 a small scuba diving resort opened at Jabwor on Jaluit. The reefs, marinelife, and WW II wrecks here are said to be unsurpassed. For information ask at the RRE Hotel on Majuro.

Ailinglaplap

Ailinglaplap, 240 km west of Majuro, is a large, highly populated, copra-growing atoll. Several passages provide entry into the lagoon. Phosphate deposits have been located on some of the 56 islands. Traditionally the high chiefs of the Ralik Chain resided on Ailinglaplap, which is located halfway between Majuro and Kwajalein.

Airstrips are at Airok on the south side and at Jeh on the east side of the atoll. Weekly flights between Kwajalein and Majuro call at both airstrips, making Ailinglaplap a possible stopover en route. Majuro-Jeh-Kwajalein would cost $111 OW, stopover included; Majuro-Airok-Kwajalein would be $124 OW. No organized accommodations are available, so you'd have to camp or stay with the locals.

KWAJALEIN

Kwajalein, 441 km northwest of Majuro, is the largest atoll in the world: its 283-km-long coral reef encloses a boomerang-shaped lagoon of 2,173.8 square km. On 4 Feb. 1944 the atoll was seized from the Japanese and converted into a U.S. military installation. Until 1958 the U.S. Navy used Kwajalein as the main support facility for its nuclear-testing program. When the 1963 Limited Test Ban Treaty drove the testing underground, the accuracy of the delivery system became

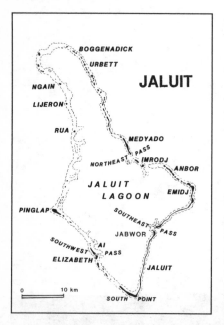

JALUIT

BOGGENADICK
URBETT
NGAIN
LIJERON
RUA
MEDYADO
NORTHEAST PASS
IMRODJ
ANBOR
JALUIT
LAGOON
EMIDJ
PINGLAP
SOUTHEAST PASS
JABWOR
SOUTHWEST PASS
AI
ELIZABETH
JALUIT
SOUTH POINT
0   10 km

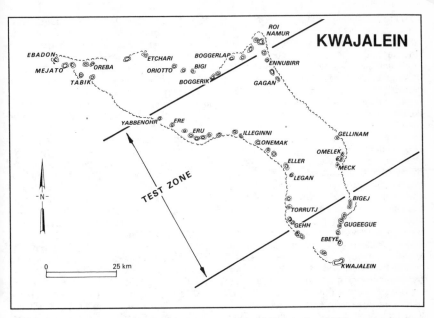

KWAJALEIN

more important than the blast of the war-head. By the late 1980s the U.S. had gained a huge advantage over the U.S.S.R. in missile accuracy, largely thanks to Kwajalein.

In 1964 control of the atoll passed from the Navy to the U.S. Army, which set up the multibillion-dollar Kwajalein Missile Range (Box 26, APO San Francisco, CA 96555-2526 U.S.A.), now officially called USAKA (U.S. Army Kwajalein Atoll). The central two-thirds of this shark-infested lagoon is used as a target for intercontinental ballistic missiles test-fired from Vandenberg Air Force Base in Santa Barbara County, California, 6,900 km distant. Each year about a dozen ICBMs are selected at random from actual U.S. firing sites, the warheads replaced with dummies, then fired at Kwajalein. Streaks of light illuminate the sky as the "reentry vehicles" crash into the lagoon. Previously the missiles were fired into the South Atlantic from Cape Canaveral, Florida. Submarine-launched missiles are also shot at Kwajalein.

Missiles aimed at Kwajalein are often themselves used as targets for new kinds of anti-ballistic-missile (ABM) weapons, thus testing both offensive and defensive systems. On 10 June 1984 a missile fired from Kwajalein's Meck Island destroyed a California-launched Minuteman 160 km out in space, the first time in history that a non-nuclear ABM had been successfully tested.

Kwajalein continues to play a key role in the development of the Pentagon's Maginot Line in the sky, the notorious Star Wars system. In mid-1991 it was revealed that the U.S. Army was preparing to fire an additional four missiles a year at Kwajalein from the Hawaiian island of Kauai over the next 10 years. These rockets pierce the earth's ozone layer twice, and the boosters carry highly toxic payloads which land within 25 km of inhabited areas.

Kwajalein is also an essential element in the Pacific Barrier radar system, which detects and tracks orbiting satellites to be destroyed in anti-satellite (ASAT) warfare. Top-secret Altair radar installed on Roi-Namur, an islet at the north tip of the atoll, can track a five-meter-square object at an altitude of

~0,000 km. The information is relayed by microwave to Kwajalein Island, largest of the atoll's 90 islands, then by satellite to North American Defense Command (NORAD) headquarters in Colorado. Pacific Barrier can pick up satellites on their first orbit after launch.

Only about 50 military personnel are stationed on Kwajalein; the other 3,000 are Americans who work for private American corporations conducting research for the U.S. Defense Department. They lead a charmed existence, with a golf course, swimming pools, a bowling alley, a high school for their children, a library, a supermarket, a department store, free movies, use of boats from the marina, plus full sports and laundry facilities. In 1986 the high school was finally desegregated with the admission of five Marshallese students. No private cars are allowed on Kwajalein and everyone gets around by bicycle or on a shuttle. The number of Americans on Kwajalein continues to grow as President Bush continues to pour billions into Reagan's Strategic Defense Initiative, despite the collapse of the Cold War.

Information
Radio stations CPN-AM (1224 kHz) and CPN-FM (100 MHz) broadcast 24 hours a day from Kwajalein.

Getting There
All **Continental Air Micronesia** flights between Majuro and Kosrae/Pohnpei touch down on Kwajalein. The base itself is closed

> *"Every gun that is made, every warship launched, every rocket fired signifies, in the final sense, a theft from those who hunger and are not fed, from those that are not clothed."*
> —*Dwight D. Eisenhower*

to everyone other than invited guests, but you get a good view from the aircraft window—it's just a sterile expatriate camp. People with a permit to visit Ebeye are also allowed to disembark here.

On arrival at Kwajalein all luggage is lined up and sniffed by drug-detecting dogs. A military policeperson then gives a brief speech explaining the rules and regulations of the base, and those proceeding to Ebeye are referred to Marshall Islands Immigration. After clearance they're bused to a lagoonside wharf and sent on by free ferry to Ebeye.

Kwajalein serves as the northwestern hub of the Marshalls, with weekly **Air Marshall Islands** flights to Airok and Jeh on Ailinglaplap ($52), and six a week to Majuro ($114). There are also flights twice a month to Enewetok ($140), Mejit ($96), Ujae ($57), Wotho ($60), and others (all fares are OW). Passengers in transit from Ebeye may patronize the snack bar on Kwajalein, but not the **Yokwe Yok Club** or **Pacific Dining Room**.

When planning itineraries keep in mind that although Kwajalein is west of the International Date Line, it follows the U.S. day to avoid bungling by the missilemen. Thus it's one day behind all the other Marshall Islands, neighboring Ebeye included. No departure tax is collected on flights from Kwajalein.

Ebeye
Only five km from the country-club affluence of the American settlement on Kwajalein is Ebeye (pronounced EE-bye), the Marshallese reservation. In 1951 construction of the Naval station on Kwajalein Island required the evacuation of the 450 Marshallese inhabitants to Ebeye, a coral islet 13 times smaller. Another 400 Marshallese were brought to Ebeye from other islands of the atoll for security reasons in 1964 and given $25 a month for their trouble. When they complained, the amount was increased to $40. By 1967, 4,500 people were jammed onto Ebeye's 33 hectares amid appalling sanitary conditions. Almost 9,000 live there today. A smaller Marshallese ghetto like Ebeye is located on Sando Island at the north tip of the atoll for laborers employed at Roi-Namur.

Nearly a quarter of the population of the Marshall Islands lives in the cramped plywood and sheet-metal houses on Ebeye. After a storm blew away many of the shanties in 1988, cinderblock housing was put up in their place. Every day 950 Ebeye workers commute to the base by boat. Due to the lack of other sources of employment in the Marshalls, the population of Ebeye has grown rapidly as Marshallese from other atolls arrive looking for jobs on the base or handouts from "wealthy" relatives already established here.

The amount of their compensation has always been a bone of contention between the Marshallese and Americans. A 1969 "sail-in" reoccupation of the test zone by 200 islanders won enhanced recognition of their rights. During a second sail-in in 1979 landowners occupied missile range facilities on Kwajalein and Roi-Namur until lease payments were dramatically increased. Operation Homecoming in 1982 saw 1,000 Marshallese protesters reoccupy 11 islands inside the security zone where they camped for four months.

After a 1986 "camp-in" during which 150 protesters were forcibly removed from Kwajalein and a state of emergency declared, the U.S. levied a $1 million fine against the landowners' association, the Kwajalein Atoll Corporation (to be deducted from land-use payments). The Marshall Islands Government in Majuro (labeled U.S. "puppets" by the landowners) then broke the association, rechanneling land payments through about 80 senior landowners (the KAC had previously distributed the money on a per capita basis). Under the 1986 Compact of Free Association, $9 million a year "rent" is to be paid for the military use of Kwajalein Atoll for 30 years. The senior landowners are expected to share the $6 million a year they receive with their relatives, though there is no legal obligation for them to do so. The U.S. Government refuses to deal directly with the 5,000 Kwajalein landowners any further, insisting that all negotiations be conducted through the national government on Majuro.

To provide stability for the base and improve the U.S. image, a $3-million-a-year

redevelopment plan is being implemented on eyesore Ebeye by the Kwajalein Atoll Development Corporation (KADA) with a new power and desalination plant, container pier, housing, schools, community centers, sporting facilities, and sanitation improvements. The population density may be eased if the planned 10-km reef causeway from Ebeye to Gugeegue, the sixth islet to the north, ever gets built. After Typhoon Roy left 3,000 people homeless in 1988, $2 million in federal disaster relief assistance was spent building nice new homes for 300 of them on Gugeegue. Once proper services and communications are in place at Gugeegue this extension may make Ebeye even more of a magnet for Marshallese outer islanders and the cycle of overcrowding may begin all over again.

Dr. William J. Alexander described a Christmas play he saw at an Ebeye church in 1975. The theme was "God destroys all evil." As the choir sang, a dummy bomb descended from the church ceiling; when it hit the floor, wads of dollar bills inside spewed forth to demonstrate God's power.

Getting There

To visit Ebeye one must obtain an "Entry into Ebeye" permit from the Immigration office in the Nitijela building in Delap on Majuro. The permit is issued automatically if you have hotel reservations or some other place to stay on Ebeye. It's also possible to request the permit by writing Ministry of Foreign Affairs, Division of Immigration, Ebeye, Kwajalein, MH 96970 (tel. 3010). The exact dates of entry and return must be specified on the permit.

Since these formalities are more easily handled in person on Majuro, a visit to Ebeye is really practical only if you're traveling westbound and have Kwajalein included as a free stop on your Continental Air Micronesia Island Hopper ticket. Hotel reservations at Ebeye can be made by either calling the hotel directly or visiting the Kwajalein Atoll Local Government office upstairs at Gibson's.

The northern field-trip ships call at Ebeye; by air you transit Kwajalein. The U.S. shuttle boat between Kwajalein and Ebeye (free and

᾽ only to employees or air ticket ᾽) takes 25 minutes, making a round-trip every three hours or so.

It takes less than an hour to walk right around Ebeye. Yet on an island 1½ km long and 200 meters wide you'll find, believe it or not—taxis! For 25 cents a ride you can "jaba" around Ebeye in a vehicle crammed with as many as it can hold!

Practicalities

Advance hotel reservations are recommended. The **Anrohasa Hotel** (Box 5039, Ebeye, Kwajalein, MH 96970; tel. 3161), formerly known as the Fountain Hotel, opened in mid-1988 by the lagoon near the ferry landing and quickly became the hotel of choice on Ebeye. They offer eight a/c rooms with TV, fridge, and private bath at $40 s, $50 d. There's a restaurant/bar and laundromat on the premises.

North of here is the **A & D Hotel** (Box 159, Ebeye, Kwajalein, MH 96970; tel. 3199), also known as the "Midtown Hotel." The 10 a/c rooms go for $40 s, $45 d, and there's a restaurant/bar. At the south end of Ebeye is the **DSC Hotel** (Box 5097, Ebeye, Kwajalein, MH 96970; tel. 3194). The eight a/c rooms with private facilities are $40 s or d. There's a grocery store downstairs.

The **Ebeye Restaurant** near the dock is the best of Ebeye's several small restaurants. The **Formosa Restaurant** offers Chinese food. **Mon La-Mike's** is a quiet place to drink and, on an island with few trees, this bar has plants and bushes inside! Take care with aggressive drunks on Ebeye.

BIKINI

When the bikini was invented in 1946, it took the name of this denuded island, an apt choice considering the garment's explosive effect on men. From 1946-1958, 23 nuclear blasts in the atmosphere shook Bikini atoll, at a cost of $91 billion in today's dollars; they're feared to have left behind a legacy of contamination, cancer, leukemia, thyroid problems, miscarriages, "jellyfish" babies, and ir-

reversible genetic damage, though the full effects are unknown due to the absence of independent studies by researchers not affiliated with the U.S. government or its pro-nuclear agencies.

For the initial series a captured Japanese war fleet was positioned in the Bikini lagoon to test the use of atomic weapons against naval forces. On 1 July 1948 "Able" was dropped on 90 ships by a B-29 from Kwajalein; on 25 July an underwater explosion code-named "Baker" permanently contaminated the atoll. "Charlie," the third test, was canceled when it became apparent that the radiation endangered U.S. personnel.

In Feb. 1946 American officials informed the inhabitants of Bikini and Enewetak that their islands were needed—temporarily—"for the good of mankind and to end all world wars." The 166 Bikinians were taken to uninhabited Rongerik atoll, but in just two years it became apparent that Rongerik lacked the resources to support them, and they had to be evacuated again.

After a few months on Kwajalein, the Bikinians were resettled on Kili Island, an isolated dot in the ocean just southwest of Jaluit. There 602 of them remain to this day, even though Kili is quite a step down for the Bikinians. Bikini's 36 islands are six times larger than Kili in land area; rat-infested Kili doesn't even have a protective lagoon, and fishing is often impossible due to weather conditions. Other Bikinians live on Ejit Island at Majuro.

In the 1960s repeated requests from the Bikinians and considerable controversy induced the U.S. Government to clean up Bikini so the people could return home. It's now clear that the cleanup was done in a haphazard manner, and that the Atomic Energy Commission failed to take sufficient tests before they declared, in 1969, that Bikini was once again safe for habitation.

Nuclear Nomads

In 1972, the Bikinians began to move back to their home island; by 1978, out of a total population of 600 Bikinians, 139 were living there again. At this point it was discovered that these 139 had ingested the largest dose of plutonium ever monitored in any population, and the "nuclear nomads" were once again re-evacuated to the "prison island," Kili, where they subsist today. Experts estimate that it will be at least a century (if ever) before the radioactive content on Bikini naturally diminishes to the point where it will be fit to consider for human habitation once more.

After lawsuits and pleas to American benevolence, a $6 million trust fund was set up by Washington in 1978, and a further $20.6 million placed in a resettlement fund. In 1984 the U.S. promised to spend $42 million on another cleanup, and in 1988, $90 million was allocated by Congress for a final cleanup. Decontamination alternatives include flushing sea water through the soil to leach out the contaminants, scraping off the top half meter and replacing it with uncontaminated soil, and applying potassium-rich fertilizer to block the uptake of cesium-137 by plants. The Bikinians favor the drastic method of topsoil removal, fearing the other two would make them guinea pigs in continuing experiments.

In April 1992, the scuba wholesaler Tom Jacobus of Innerspace Adventures (13393 Sorrento Dr., Largo, FL 34644 U.S.A.) scored a first by leading a group to Bikini to dive on the Japanese battleship *Nagato,* the U.S. aircraft carrier *Saratoga,* the destroyer *Anderson,* and the submarine *Apogon*. These groups also get to stay on Ebeye and dive on Japanese wrecks in the Kwajalein lagoon—not your everyday scuba tour!

ENEWETAK

Enewetak (Eniwetok) is an almost perfectly circular atoll 32 km in diameter. In Dec. 1947, officials in Washington announced that it was to be used for nuclear tests and the 145 inhabitants were to be moved immediately. They were taken to Ujelang Atoll, an island with a quarter the land area and a fifteenth the lagoon area of Enewetak. There they lived in exile for over 30 years. Due to the limited resources, they soon faced starvation and became dependent on USDA food handouts.

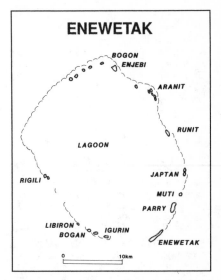

From 1948-1958, 43 nuclear tests rocked Enewetak, which the U.S. began using after Bikini became too highly contaminated for their purposes. On 1 Nov. 1952 the world's first hydrogen bomb was tested here, unleashing more explosive force than all the wars of history combined, and completely vaporizing one of the islands of Enewetak; in 1958 another H-bomb destroyed a second.

In 1976, the U.S. Congress appropriated funds for a $110 million cleanup operation on Enewetak by the Defense Nuclear Agency. The contaminated waste was scraped off the surface of the atoll and buried in a bomb crater on Runit Island under a gigantic cement dome 45 cm thick. The most dangerous waste there is radioactive plutonium, a cancer-causing agent active 24,000 years—the period Runit will be out-of-bounds to human beings. The dome is already reported to be cracking, with material leaking through the base of the crater.

The Department of Energy reports that the southern islands of the atoll are now safe for habitation, but the northern islands will be unsafe for the next 300 years. In 1980, 542 people returned from Ujelang to Japtan Island on Enewetak, and some have gone to live on the northern islands where they are today. Like the people of Bikini, the Enewetakese remain a sociologically disrupted community whose future is clouded by uncertainty. Added to the sociocultural disruptions is the volatile new ingredient of compensation money and how it should be divided.

RONGELAP

On 1 March 1954, 15-megaton "Bravo," largest and dirtiest of the hydrogen bombs, was tested on Bikini. This was the most colossal manmade explosion in history, with an explosive force equal to 1,200 Hiroshima-type bombs, more than twice what its designers expected. The blast sent up a 35-km-high cloud which dropped 3.8 cm of fine white dust on Rongelap atoll four to six hours later, turning the water yellow, contaminating the food, and burning the unprepared people standing in the open. Children played in the radioactive material as if it were snow. The U.S. Navy destroyer *Gypsy,* which had been stationed a mere 30 km from Rongelap lagoon on the day of the test, quickly sailed off.

After 48 hours of exposure to fallout, the population of Rongelap was evacuated to Kwajalein by Americans wearing protective suits; the people of Utirik atoll were exposed an additional 24 hours. The evacuees experienced all the symptoms of radiation exposure. One victim, Etry Enos, told anthropolo-

gist Glenn H. Alcalay: "When we arrived, we were starting to get burns all over our bodies. After two days, my fingernails came off and my fingers bled. We all had burns on our ears, shoulders, necks and feet, and our eyes were very sore."

At the time U.S. officials blamed the contamination on an unexpected wind shift, but 27 years later four retired U.S. airmen who had operated the weather station on nearby Rongerik shed new light on the matter. They reported that the test was allowed with full knowledge that for weeks previous the prevailing wind had been blowing directly at these islands. Said Gene O. Curbow, senior weather technician on Rongerik at the time and now stricken with leukemia: "The wind had been blowing straight at us for days before the test. It was blowing straight at us during the test, and straight at us after it. The wind never shifted." (See *The New York Times,* 20 Sept. 1982, page B15.)

Whether this was done deliberately to "offer a most valuable source of data on human beings who have sustained injury from all possible modes of exposure" (wording from a Brookhaven, N.Y. National Laboratory report) may never be known for sure, although Marshallese Senator Ataji Balos charged U.S. officials with "knowingly and consciously allowing the people of Rongelap and Utirik to be exposed so that the United States could use them as guinea pigs in the development of its medical capabilities to treat its citizens who might be exposed to radiation in the event of war with an enemy country." An article by Alcalay in the 1987 issue of *Third World Affairs* comes to the same conclusion.

Paradise Contaminated
The Utirik people were moved back to their "lightly contaminated" atoll shortly after the "Bravo" test. In Jan. 1957 U.S. officials decided to allow the Rongelapese to return to Rongelap, although no cleanup had been carried out and the island was still heavily contaminated.

In 1978 the Dept. of Energy placed a quarantine on the northern half of Rongelap,

DAVID ROBIE

THE *RAINBOW WARRIOR*

The *Rainbow Warrior,* onetime flagship of the Greenpeace fleet. Beginning in 1978 the ship confronted whalers, sealers, and nuclear-waste dumpers in the North Atlantic. In 1980 the *Rainbow Warrior* was seized in international waters by the Spanish Navy while interfering with the Spanish whale kill. After five months under arrest in Spain the ship made a dramatic escape. In 1981-82 *Rainbow Warrior* led the struggle against the Canadian harp seal slaughter, bringing about a European Economic Community ban on the import of all seal products. The next year the ship battled Soviet whalers in Siberia, finally escaping to Alaska with naval units in hot pursuit. In 1985, fresh from being fitted with sails in Florida, the *Rainbow Warrior* reentered the Pacific to rescue nuclear victims from Rongelap in the Marshalls (see photo). In July, 1985, as the ship lay at anchor in Auckland Harbor, New Zealand, externally attached terrorist bombs tore through the hull in the dead of night, to prevent a voyage to Moruroa to protest French nuclear testing in the Pacific.

which was discovered to have even higher radiation levels than Bikini, but claimed the southern islands were safe. The people were told to stop eating fish and coconuts, and surplus food was shipped in from the U.S. to keep them alive. Often the supply ship arrived months late. In 1983 the Nitijela voted unanimously in favor of relocation after persons not present during Bravo began developing thyroid tumors.

Despite an upswing in radiation-related medical problems, repeated pleas for re-evacuation were denied by U.S. officials. In desperation, Rongelap Senator Jeton Anjain (whose nephew Lekoj died of leukemia in 1972) turned to Greenpeace for help. Said Anjain: "Our land is our most sacred possession, but our children are more important to us than the land itself." In May 1985 the legendary *Rainbow Warrior* (later sunk in New Zealand by French terrorists) was sent to evacuate over 300 "guinea-pig" islanders to Mejato Island near Ebadon at the west tip of Kwajalein atoll.

Medical Studies

Money appropriated by the U.S. Congress for health care of the Marshallese was turned over to the Brookhaven and Livermore laboratories, which have examined only a small portion of the Marshallese population affected by the fallout—and even these victims were *studied* rather than treated. The U.S. Government doctors continue to refuse to look for second- or third-generation effects, or to release personal medical histories. Many experts believe that the long-term effects of the radiation damage, including cancer and genetic damage, will peak in the 1990s and early 21st century.

Despite widespread medical problems ranging from cataracts to numerous miscarriages, the scientists have restricted their studies to thyroid problems. Nineteen out of 21 children on Rongelap at the time of the blast have had thyroid tumors removed; all face premature death from cancer.

In 1971 the U.S. Government terminated a study of the Marshalls begun by a Gensuikin

medical team from Japan, and despite numerous requests from the Marshallese no independent health survey has ever been carried out. Instead, information from official U.S. studies has been concealed. Distrustful of Dept. of Energy scientists, the Rongelapese say they want an independent radiological assessment of the atoll before they will agree to return. German scientists are to carry out the task. If required, a cleanup of Rongelap could cost $93 million.

In 1978 the Dept. of Energy admitted that a total of 14 atolls in the Marshalls had been contaminated during the U.S. testing, yet only the people of Rongelap and Utirik have ever been checked for radiation-related sickness by U.S. doctors. Thousands of other Marshallese were also exposed to the fallout and many islanders still live in a radioactive environment today. Many critics of U.S. policy allege that the extreme pressure to endorse the 1983 compact—with its termination of pending lawsuits of up to $6 billion against the U.S.—was a maneuver by the U.S. to prevent further revelations about the full extent of its nuclear-test program. The 42,000 U.S. servicemen present at the Operation Crossroads testing on Bikini were also exposed to significant radiation, yet this situation has never been recognized by the government, nor any compensation paid.

The well-publicized events at Rongelap shocked the world, leading to the formation of the Campaign for Nuclear Disarmament in England, the Pugwash movement in Nova Scotia, the National Committee for a Sane Nuclear Policy in the United States, and International Physicians for the Prevention of Nuclear War (which won the Nobel Peace Prize in 1985). Public protests forced the U.S. to halt its tests in 1958 and sign the Limited Test Ban Treaty with Britain and the U.S.S.R. in 1963. The anniversary of "Bravo," March 1, is commemorated throughout the region as Nuclear Free and Independent Pacific Day. The member churches of the Pacific Conference of Churches all around the Pacific hold special services on the Sunday closest to 1 March.

GORDY OHLIGER

FEDERATED STATES OF MICRONESIA

INTRODUCTION

The Federated States of Micronesia (henceforth referred to as FSM) is the largest and most populous political entity to emerge from the Trust Territory of the Pacific Islands. It includes all of the Caroline Islands except Belau. Although they share a common history, each of the four state centers of the Federated States has a character and geography of its own. Pohnpei (formerly Ponape) is a lush, volcanic island with much to entice the hiker and historian, while Kosrae has better beaches and a friendly, easygoing people. Chuuk (formerly Truk) is best known for its underwater war wreckage, although its real attraction is a rare chance to get off the beaten tourist track. Yap is a stronghold of traditional Micronesian culture.

The towns where the planes drop you offer most conveniences of modern American life. The adventurer willing to forgo these comforts, however, should explore the outer islands—the remote, unspoiled Pacific, which is still the essence of Micronesia: men in loincloths, bare-breasted women, palm-thatched huts, outrigger canoes, coconut trees, coral reefs, and sparkling, azure lagoons—a South Sea stereotype for the few fortunate travelers willing to look for it, able to find it, and ready to enjoy it.

Life is idyllic on the outer islands, with no hotels, cars, electricity, drugs, crime, rich or poor; lots of food for everyone; and an almost money-free existence based on fishing and gardening. Where else would you be "lent" an uninhabited island with dazzling white-powder sand for as long as you wish to stay? Micronesia is much less developed touristically than the main South Pacific islands because few Americans ever get beyond Hawaii, and few Japanese ever get past Saipan

THE FSM AT A GLANCE

	population (1989)	land area (sq. km)
STATE OF KOSRAE	7,177	109.6
STATE OF POHNPEI	32,884	345.4
Ant	nil	1.9
Kapingamarangi	577	1.3
Mokil	305	1.2
Ngatik	644	1.7
Nukuoro	450	1.7
Oroluk	nil	0.5
Pakin	nil	1.1
Pingelap	840	1.8
Pohnpei	30,068	334.2
STATE OF CHUUK	47,871	127.4
Chuuk Lagoon	38,341	99.9
East Fayu	nil	0.4
Ettal	420	1.9
Houk	346	2.8
Kuop	nil	0.5
Losap	795	1.0
Lukunor	1,279	2.8
Murilo	694	1.3
Nama	897	0.7
Namolik	310	0.8
Namonuito	944	4.4
Nomwin	624	1.9
Pulap	541	1.0
Pulawat	477	3.4
Satawan	2,203	4.6
STATE OF YAP	10,139	118.4
Eauripik	99	0.2
Elato	70	0.5
Fais	253	2.8
Faraulep	182	0.4
Gaferut	nil	0.1
Ifalik	475	1.0
Lamotrek	278	1.0
Ngulu	26	0.4
Olimarao	nil	0.2
Pikelot	nil	0.1
Satawai	465	1.3
Sorol	nil	0.9
Ulithi	847	4.7
West Fayu	nil	0.1
Woleai	794	4.5
Yap	6,650	100.2
TOTAL FSM	**98,071**	**700.8**

and Guam. Everywhere in the Federated States you'll encounter a natural, relaxed affability. The best schedule is no schedule—the Micronesian way.

The Land
The Eastern Caroline Islands include Kosrae, Pohnpei, and Chuuk states, while Yap and Belau form the Western Caroline Islands. It's over 2,500 km from Kosrae to Yap, yet the FSM totals only 700 square km land area, with Pohnpei alone accounting for almost half of it.

This huge insular group, named for King Charles II of Spain, includes almost every type of oceanic topography: high volcanic islands such as Pohnpei and Kosrae; Yap, a large island of sedimentary rock; Fais, an elevated atoll; and Chuuk—an atoll-to-be, with remnants of its volcanic core still poking out of the lagoon. Nearly a thousand smaller coral islands and reefs complete the scene.

The vegetation is also varied. Coconut palms, pandanus, casuarina, and breadfruit flourish on the low islands. On the high islands mangrove swamps along the coasts feature salt-resistant plants, while inland are coconut groves on the flats, rainforest up the slopes, and ferns or grasslands on the summits. Other than fruit bats, most of the terrestrial fauna was introduced by man. Numerous shore- and seabirds make up for the lack of land birds. The marine life is abundant. Elderly Yapese believe fireflies to be spirits of the dead.

Climate
Heavy rainfall drenches the Carolines, although the quantity decreases as you move west from Pohnpei to Yap. Pohnpei gets measurable rainfall 300 days a year, with a wetter period from March through December. At Chuuk the rain falls mostly at night, hardest just before sunrise. The rain often comes in short, heavy downpours, presenting only a temporary inconvenience to travelers, while providing the inhabitants with water for washing and cooking, as well as assuring the food supply.

January-March are the drier months, although the humidity is high year-round. The

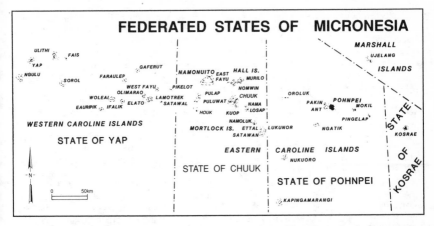

FEDERATED STATES OF MICRONESIA

ULITHI · FAIS

YAP

NGULU · SOROL

FARAULEP

GAFERUT

WEST FAYU

OLIMARAO · PIKELOT

WOLEAI · ELATO · LAMOTREK

EAURIPIK · IFALIK · SATAWAL

NAMONUITO EAST · HALL IS.
FAYU · MURILO

NOMWIN

PULAP · CHUUK

PULUWAT · NAMA

HOUK · KUOP · LOSAP

NAMOLUK

MORTLOCK IS. · ETTAL · LUKUNOR

SATAWAN

OROLUK

PAKIN · POHNPEI
ANT · MOKIL

PINGELAP

NGATIK

MARSHALL

UJELANG

ISLANDS

WESTERN CAROLINE ISLANDS

STATE OF YAP

EASTERN · CAROLINE · ISLANDS

NUKUORO

STATE OF CHUUK

STATE OF POHNPEI

KAPINGAMARANGI

STATE OF KOSRAE

KOSRAE

-N-

0   50km

Northeast Trades blow across the Eastern Carolines Dec.-April; July-Sept. southeast winds prevail. Yap gets northeast winds Nov.-May, changing to southwest July-Oct. (the rainier season).

The Western Caroline Islands spawn more tropical typhoons than any other area on earth, an average of 19 a year! September-Nov. is peak typhoon season, and most of the storms move northwest toward Asia. Typhoons rarely occur in the Eastern Caroline Islands, although Typhoon Nina raged across Chuuk on 21 Nov. 1987. On Pohnpei, the sun rises just after 0600 and sets just after 1800 every day of the year.

Toward Self-government

Until 1978 the FSM, along with most of Micronesia, was administered as part of the Trust Territory of the Pacific Islands. Thus the history of the region up to that point must be treated as a whole (see the main introduction to this book). In July 1978 a draft FSM constitution was approved by voters in Kosrae, Pohnpei, Chuuk, and Yap. The constitution was defeated in votes in Belau and the Marshalls, which then became separate political entities.

On 1 Oct. 1982, American and FSM negotiators at Honolulu signed the Compact of Free Association. This 15-year treaty nets the FSM $60 million annually for the first five years, $51 million annually the second five years, and $40 million the third five, all adjusted seven percent for inflation. In the year 2001 the economic aid provisions must be renegotiated. In exchange the compact gives the U.S. military access to the FSM while denying such access to other powers.

In a June 1983 plebiscite on the compact, 79% of the total FSM electorate voted in favor. Pohnpeians, however, who judged that the intent of the compact was to keep Micronesia under American control, voted against. A second section of the same ballot asked the electorate what status they would prefer should the compact not be approved. Fifty-four percent picked independence, while only seven percent wanted commonwealth status, and another seven percent asked to be annexed by the U.S.

The compact was passed by the U.S. Congress in 1985 and implemented by President Reagan on 3 Nov. 1986; in 1991 the FSM was admitted to the United Nations.

Government

The FSM constitution came into effect on 10 May 1979 (now celebrated as Constitution Day). Under it, each of the four states has a locally elected governor and legislature, while the central government meets at Palikir on Pohnpei. The 14-member National Congress of the FSM includes one member at large elected from each state for a four-year term. The president and vice-president are chosen by the congress from among these senior members, thus president and vice-president cannot be from the same state. The other 10 members serve two-year terms, apportioned according to population: Chuuk five members, Pohnpei three, Kosrae one, and Yap one. There are no political parties. The national government has primacy over state governments. In Chuuk, Pohnpei, and Yap states the role of the traditional chiefs is recognized in the state constitutions; Kosrae has no traditional chiefs. The chiefs often play an important role in municipal government.

Economy

The FSM will receive more than $1.3 billion from the U.S. during the 15-year Compact of Free Association. Initially much of the money is to be spent on construction projects, already the largest element in the private sector of the economy. About the only other private businesses are retail outlets, selling imported food and consumer goods, and a few service industries. Under the compact, textiles manufactured in the FSM may be imported into the U.S. free of quotas, and one Taiwanese company set up a factory on Yap in 1989 to take advantage of this. The company's entire workforce has been imported from mainland China and Sri Lanka.

The government is by far the largest employer, with two-thirds of the workforce. About $100 million of the annual budget comes from U.S. federal grants and around $10 million a year is collected locally. Any reduction of the U.S. subsidy has an immediate impact. In 1983, 83.9% of the gross domestic product went into private consumption, with food and beverages accounting for 73.5% of it. Savings are minimal. In the towns there's a widening gap between rich and poor as businessmen and local officials cash in on American aid intended to benefit the majority of Micronesians, who are still without electricity, running water, proper housing, or jobs. The minimum wage on Pohnpei is $1.35 an hour in the private sector, $1.50 in government.

Food and almost all the elements of modern life are imported. Outside the towns reef fishing and subsistence agriculture continue to be the main occupations. Tourism is being encouraged—wisely, slowly. There's no rush to jump on the Waikiki/Saipan bandwagon. Instead smaller, locally controlled developments are going ahead. Land can only be leased (not purchased) by outsiders, and new businesses must have 51% local ownership. In 1990 Pohnpei got 9,534 visitors, Chuuk 7,654, and Yap 3,984, nearly half of them from the U.S. and another quarter from Japan.

In 1988 the main exports were fish ($1,524,000) and copra ($743,000); imports that year totaled $67.7 million. More revenue comes in through fishing licenses. In 1989 a couple of hundred foreign fishing boats paid $10 million in fees to take $200 million in tuna from the FSM's 200-nautical-mile Exclusive Economic Zone. Another $1.2 million was collected in penalty fines from boats caught fishing illegally. In 1990 the government-owned National Fisheries Corp. ordered a fleet of longline fishing vessels and combined with a Franco-Australian company to form the Caroline Fishing Corp., with three purse seiners. The Compact of Free Association allows the entry of duty-free FSM canned fish to the U.S. market, up to 10% of U.S. consumption. To take advantage of this, canneries are planned for some islands, a fish processing plant was erected near Pohnpei Airport, and an aquiculture center opened on Kosrae. In 1991 the Australian government presented the patrol boat FSS *Palikir* to the FSM to police its rich fishing grounds.

The People

All of the 98,071 people (1989) are Micronesians, except for over a thousand Polynesians on two outlying atolls in Pohnpei State and in Kolonia. Less than a third of the population lives in urban or semi-urban areas. Eight different languages are spoken in the FSM: Chuukese, Kosraean, Kapingamarangi, Nukuoran, Pohnpeian, Ulithian, Woleaian, and Yapese. English has become the common language. Traditionally the societies have been matrilineal, although the influence of missionaries has created a patrilineal system on Kosrae. The Polynesian islands of Kapingamarangi and Nukuoro have always been patrilineal.

The Yapese are Catholic, the Kosraeans Protestant. Pohnpei and Chuuk are split between Catholics and Protestants, with Chuuk leaning toward Catholicism. Nearly half the population is under 15, three-quarters under 25, and the total population is growing at the rate of 3.5% annually. The life expectancy is 58-59 for men, 62-64 for women. The suicide rate among young Micronesian males ages 15-24 is high. In 1985 it was reported there were 1,000 leprosy cases in the FSM. FSM citizens have unrestricted entry to the U.S. and its territories (U.S. citizens don't have such rights in the FSM).

Holidays And Events

The list of national public holidays changes from year to year according to the whim of the legislature, but days to watch out for include New Year's Day (1 Jan.), President's Day (third Monday in Feb.), Traditional Culture Day (31 March), FSM Constitution Day (10 May), Micronesian Day (12 July), United Nations Day (24 Oct.), FSM Independence Day (first Friday in Nov.), and Christmas Day (25 Dec.).

There are also state holidays such as Kosrae Constitution Day (11 Jan.), Sokehs Rebellion Day (24 Feb.), Yap Day (1 March), Kolonia Independence Day (17 May), Kosrae Liberation Day (8 Sept.), Pohnpei Liberation Day (11 Sept.), Chuuk Charter Day (26 Sept.), Kosrae Self-Government Day (3 Nov.), Pohnpei Constitution Day (8 Nov.), and Yap Constitution Day (24 Dec.). Try to be in Colonia on 1 March or Kolonia on 11 Sept. to see canoe races, customary dancing, and other traditional events. There are the various municipal Constitution Days on Pohnpei. On Kapingamarangi, Taro Patch Day is celebrated on 15 March.

PRACTICALITIES

Conduct

Micronesians expect Western women to dress modestly; you're asking for trouble if you don't. Male visitors calling on government offices should avoid dressing too casually. Observe how the officials are dressed. Micronesians are friendly, so a big smile and a hello are never out of place.

Accommodations And Food

The only regular hotels are in the state capitals, although beach resorts are now springing up in the outlying areas of Kosrae, Pohnpei, and Chuuk. Inexpensive restaurants are found in all the towns. In rural areas you'll have a choice of camping or staying with local families; both require permission from the local landowner, householder, chief, or government representative. Try to find some way to repay any kindnesses received. Nonmonetary gifts are always very welcome.

Visas

Since the FSM is not part of the U.S., its entry requirements are not the same as those of Guam and Hawaii. Tourists don't need a visa for a stay of up to 30 days, although the officials will want to see your passport and onward ticket. If you don't have an onward ticket they may insist that you purchase one on the spot (this applies to everyone, Americans included).

U.S. citizens don't need a passport, only proof of citizenship such as a birth certificate or naturalization papers (driver's license and social security card are not sufficient). For Americans too, a passport eases the formalities and saves time. All nationalities other than Americans and Canadians going on to Hawaii must already have a valid U.S. visa in their passport.

Each state has its own immigration controls, so you get a new entry permit every time you cross a state boundary. This works to your advantage, as you'll start on another 30 days without actually having to leave the Federated States. Visa extensions are a nuisance, so always ask for 30 days (the maximum) when you arrive. Yap Immigration is reluctant to grant you the full 30 days, however, and may wish to grant only the exact time until your onward air reservation. You can get up to three 30-day extensions at a cost of $10 per extension.

Anyone considering arriving by cruising yacht should apply for an FSM vessel permit in advance from: Chief Immigration Officer, FSM National Government, Palikir, Pohnpei, FM 96941 U.S.A. (tel 691-320-5844; fax 691-320-2234). Ports of entry are Lelu and Okat on Kosrae, Kolonia on Pohnpei, Weno on Chuuk, Ulithi, and Colonia on Yap. Upon sailing from one state to another, yachts must clear customs again.

Money And Measurements

U.S. currency is used. Credit cards are not widely accepted anywhere in the FSM, not even at banks. Everything must usually be paid for with U.S. cash or dollar traveler's checks.

Standard American 110-volt, 60-cycle appliances are used. The FSM issues its own postage stamps, but U.S. domestic postal rates apply. To call direct from the U.S. to a telephone number in the FSM dial 011-691 and the regular seven-digit number. To call from one FSM state to another put a one before the seven-digit number. Calls within the FSM are fairly cheap at $1 a minute (50 cents a minute from 1800 to 0600). There's a time difference of one hour between Kosrae, Pohnpei, and Chuuk/Yap.

Most public telephones in the FSM accept FSMTC telephone cards, not coins. The same card can be used in Kosrae, Pohnpei, Chuuk, and Yap, so consider investing in a $10 card (good for 40 local calls) if you'll be using the phone much.

Getting There

Almost all visitors arrive on **Continental Air Micronesia's** Island Hopper service between Hawaii and Guam. The flights operate four times a week in each direction Honolulu-Majuro-Kwajalein-Pohnpei-Chuuk-Guam. The same flight calls at Kosrae three times a week. Three additional weekly services run Pohnpei-Chuuk-Guam. Yap is on the Guam-Koror route and a change of planes at Guam is necessary. Coming from the U.S. Mainland one must change planes at Honolulu. For more information on these flights see the main introduction to this book.

In July 1991 **Air Nauru** inaugurated a weekly service Nauru-Kosrae-Pohnpei-Chuuk-Yap-Guam and return with stopovers allowed at all intermediate points. This is of interest mostly to those arriving from or traveling to Australia, New Zealand, and all South Pacific points via Nauru, though the Nauru flights are the only direct connection between the FSM and Kiribati. For more information see the main introduction to this book.

Continental offers half-price, point-to-point fares for their Chuuk and Pohnpei services on Friday nights and Sundays, Yap on Thursdays. As through tickets are required by Immigration, it's hard for visitors to take advantage of this situation. It might be of use for a RT from Guam to Yap or Chuuk, however. The through ticket with free stopovers is just as good a deal. Always reconfirm your onward ticket upon arrival at an island.

STATE OF KOSRAE

Formerly Kusaie, Kosrae (pronounced kor-SHY) is a single 109-square-km island-state, 559 km southeast of Pohnpei. Kosrae is the easternmost of the Carolines and second-largest island in the FSM (after Pohnpei). It's one of the most beautiful islands in Micronesia, with a lush green interior and plenty of white coral beaches around the rim. The rugged interior, inaccessible except with a guide, is crowned by Mt. Finkol (629 meters). A broad valley between Finkol and Mt. Mutunte divides the island in two, with a deep harbor at each end. Legend tells how Kosrae was shaped by the gods from the transformed figure of a sleeping woman. Check out the skyline from Lelu to see her head and breasts in silhouette.

Orientation

Five villages are found along the coast: a road around the east side of Kosrae links Utwe (Utwa) to Tafunsak; Walung is accessible by boat. A U.S. Army Civic Action Team (CAT) is sealing the coastal road on Kosrae, and pavement already extends from the airport to Tofol.

The largest village is on Lelu (also spelled Lela, Lele, Leluh), a small island connected to the main one by a 730-meter-long causeway. The view from Lelu of jungle-covered volcanic peaks in profile on the western horizon rivals Pohnpei's soaring Sokehs Rock in majestic beauty.

Most government offices, the hospital, tourist office, post office, Communications Center, police station, banks, Continental Air Micronesia office, and high school are centered at Tofol, Kosrae's hodgepodge administrative center, about four km from Lelu by road. The seat of government was moved from Lelu to Tofol in 1980.

History

Hundreds of years ago Kosrae was ruled by a feudal aristocracy who lived on Lelu. They built for themselves a great stone city called Insaru, the ruins and canals of which are still seen. In the 17th century the legendary Isokelekel sailed with his 333 warriors from Kosrae to Pohnpei and conquered Nan Madol.

During the 19th century Kosrae became a well-known whaling port. The present-day

Prismatic basalt "logs" stacked atop giant volcanic blocks demonstrate the architectural evolution of Kosrae's Lela ruins. This impressive wall of Kinyeir Fulat appears on our map of the site.

DAVID STANLEY

Kosraean term for foreigner, *ahset,* stems from an expression commonly used by early whalers: "ah, shit." In a final episode of the American Civil War, the Confederate cruiser *Shenandoah* captured four Yankee whalers at Lelu on 1 April 1865, only one week before the surrender of the Army of North Virginia.

The whalers brought diseases which reduced the numbers of Kosraeans from about 5,000 to 300 in just a few decades. They were followed in 1852 by Protestant missionaries from Hawaii who came to convert the survivors and finish obliterating their culture. Unscrupulous traders came too, including the notorious blackbirder Bully Hayes, whose ship Leonora sank at Utwe Harbor in 1874. Hayes is thought to have buried his treasure in the vicinity, but nothing has ever been found.

Thousands of Japanese immigrants developed Kosrae in the prewar period, forcing the Micronesians to abandon their villages and move to the interior. The U.S. military forces bypassed strategically isolated Kosrae and all Japanese guns were removed from the island after WW II. Until Jan. 1977 Kosrae formed part of Pohnpei District, but the island demanded separation and the squeaky wheel got the grease. The U.S. government recently financed an $18 million airport and commercial harbor at Okat, built by a Korean contractor. Since 1984 jet aircraft and container ships have been able to call at Kosrae, and in 1986 Air Mike added the island to its Island Hopper service.

The People

Kosrae (pop. 7,177) is by far the most religious part of Micronesia—95% Congregational. In the 1850s missionaries and whalers from far-off Boston competed for influence. The New England hymns one hears today in the churches tell which side won. Churches are packed to overflowing on Sunday and choir practice is a big social event. Shops and offices are closed that day.

Handicrafts made by the locals include woven bags, hats, fans, headbands, trays, food utensils, taro pounders, purses, model canoes, carved sharks, coconut- or pandanus-fiber briefcases, and decorative wall hangings.

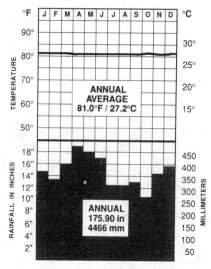

KOSRAE'S CLIMATE

ANNUAL AVERAGE
81.0°F / 27.2°C

ANNUAL
175.90 in
4466 mm

SIGHTS OF KOSRAE

Lelu

Lelu town is a ramshackle collection of corrugated shacks and Wild West storefronts, almost unreal when seen at night from the back of a cruising pickup. The tall concrete building on the main street near Thurston's Enterprise dates from 1915; it was the storehouse of an American trader who dumped stones from the nearby ruins into Lelu Harbor to extend his dock. This historic building is now the **Kosrae Museum** (weekdays 0900-1500, donation). Guided tours of the prehistoric ruins nearby can be arranged here.

Lelu Ruins

One of the most impressive yet least-known archaeological sites in the Pacific, similar to Pohnpei's Nan Madol yet much more accessible, sits right in the center of Lelu. The heart

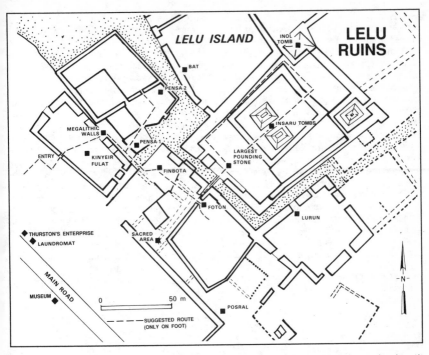

LELU ISLAND

LELU RUINS

INOL TOMB

BAT

PENSA-2

MEGALITHIC WALLS

INSARU TOMBS

ENTRY

KINYEIR FULAT

PENSA-1

LARGEST POUNDING STONE

FINBOTA

FOTON

LURUN

THURSTON'S ENTERPRISE

LAUNDROMAT

SACRED AREA

MAIN ROAD

MUSEUM

0   50 m

–N–

POSRAL

– – – SUGGESTED ROUTE (ONLY ON FOOT)

of the site is just a few minutes' walk down a footpath which begins beside Thurston's Enterprise on the main street. The access path runs along the security fence on the side farthest away from the museum.

Lelu flourished as the feudal capital of Kosrae from 1400 to 1800; the king and high chiefs had their residences here. The city once covered the entire flat portion of Lelu Island and included 100 large walled compounds. Its power was such that warriors from Lelu were able to invade Pohnpei, overthrow the tyrannical Saudeleurs, and conquer Nan Madol.

The present ruins, made up of crisscrossed hexagonal basalt logs, permit a striking glimpse of the medieval city. Coral walkways have been laid out through the site. Wear sturdy shoes as the rocks can be slippery. The prismatic, stacked basalt architecture often rests on walls of massive basalt boulders. These walls reach as high as six meters, megalithic monuments as imposing as those of Peru. The network of canals which brought canoe traffic through the city can still be seen.

Note especially the flat grooved *sakau*-pounding stones at Pensa-1 and at the entrance to Insaru. **Insaru** holds the truncated pyramid tombs of the kings, whose bodies were placed in crypts there. When the corpse had completely decayed, the bones were taken to a reef off Lelu and dropped into a deep hole.

If these ruins were in Hawaii they'd be world famous, but because they're on Kosrae nobody has heard of them! This irony makes them all the more fascinating. If you appreciate archaeology, the Lelu ruins alone make a stop on Kosrae worthwhile.

Lelu Hill

A trail behind a small cemetery not far from the old wharf leads to the summit of Lelu Hill (108 meters), which the Japanese fortified during WW II. You pass a couple of their air raid shelters near the trailhead, then proceed straight ahead on the main trail until reaching a switchback as you approach the summit. A short distance along this trail, a **tunnel** hewn from solid rock winds 30 meters back into the hill. Continue along the same overgrown track toward the south side, where another tunnel, a little more difficult to find, cuts right through the hill. Japanese trenches, fox-holes, and caves still girdle Lelu Hill in rings, but all wartime guns have been removed from Kosrae. Be prepared to do some bush-whacking if you want to explore Lelu Hill, and take a flashlight.

Along The Coast

Swarms of swiftlets inhabit a **cave** at the back of the quarry near Tafunsak. Nearby, not far from the Horizon Hotel, is **Yekula Falls**, not very impressive since much of the flow has been diverted to a water supply. It's still worth seeing after rains, however, and it's possible to bathe in the pool at the foot of the falls.

Several small Japanese tanks are bogged down on the beach at **Sansrik** on the south side of Lelu Harbor. Behind a house at Sansrik is a long concrete stairway up the hillside to what was once a Japanese weather station. Several large reinforced buildings erected by the Japanese military sit cracked and crumbling on the beach at **Malem**.

Utwe is a pleasant Kosraean village at the mouth of the Finkol, Kosrae's largest river. It

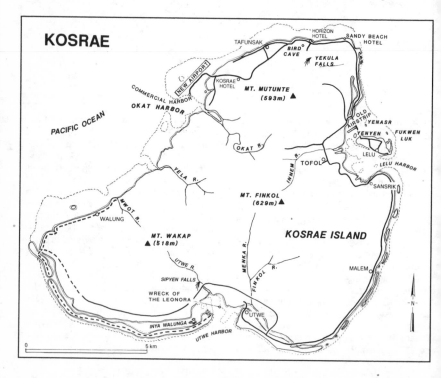

KOSRAE

*early 19th century
houses at Kosrae*

makes a perfect base for exploring the south side of the island, but there's no hotel at Utwe so plan on camping. The tourism office in Tofol can arrange canoe rentals, a guide for Mt. Finkol, camping, and even paid accommodations with a local Utwe family.

Walung

The best trip to be made on Kosrae is the backwater canoe journey on the Inya Walunga (Walung Channel) from Utwe to Walung. You begin by traversing a wide lagoon with a magnificent view of the jungle-clad mountains, then enter a shallow channel through a mangrove swamp of fantastically twisted roots. If the tide is low you'll have to travel along the coast outside the lagoon (much less interesting).

Walung, with its long, palm-fringed beach, is a paradise unknown to tourists: no roads, stores, or electricity. Ask your canoe operator to take you as far as abandoned Mwot Mission, which affords a view back toward the new airport.

When negotiating a price for a motorized canoe at Utwe (about $30), remember that three or four gallons of gas are needed for the roundtrip. It's a good idea to arrange your canoe for the Walung trip in advance through the tourist office in Tofol.

You can also walk from Utwe to Walung in about five hours, along the reef islands bordering the lagoon. Someone will have to ferry you from Utwe to the first island, but you can wade, in knee-deep water at low tide, to the second island and from the second to Walung itself. Speedboats from Okat Harbor also come this way. Alternatively one can drive to the end of the road, 10 km beyond Utwe, and walk to Walung along the main trail in a couple of hours.

Mountaineering

It's possible to scale **Mt. Finkol** (629 meters), highest peak on Kosrae, and return to Utwe in a day. You'll need a guide: Tomic Anshin Tilfas of Utwe takes people up at $50 per group. You wade up the Finkol River quite a distance, then scramble through the slippery rainforest to the top. Wear rubber booties or some old tennis shoes. The sweeping view of the entire island from the grassy summit compensates for the exhausting climb.

For a much easier glimpse of the interior, take a stroll up the road which leaves the main Tofol-Lelu highway just beyond a small bridge near the Mobil service station, not far from Tofol. The way leads up past lush tropical gardens onto the plateau between Mt. Finkol and Mt. Mutunte. This road may even-

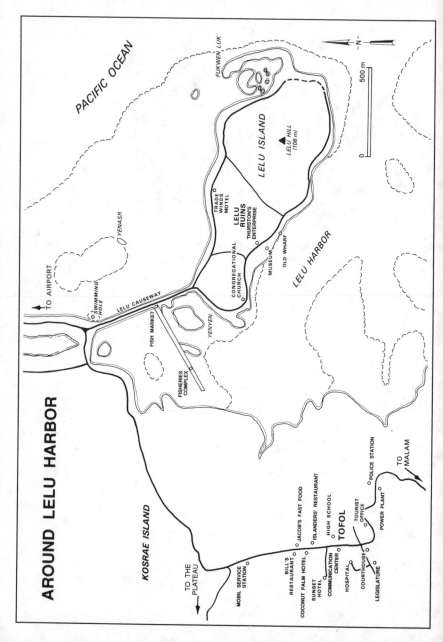

tually be extended across to Okat Harbor and the airport; meanwhile it's idyllic.

PRACTICALITIES

Accommodations

The closest hotel to the airport is the nine-room **Kosrae Hotel** (Edison Nena, Box 231, Kosrae, FM 96944; tel. 370-2145), between the airport and Tafunsak. The owner, Edison Nena, is a Customs officer who often receives flights at the airport. The four upstairs rooms with private bath are $30 s, $46 d, while the five downstairs rooms with shared facilities are $25 s, $30 d. The upstairs rooms are quite large and comfortable. Hot water is supplied free for making coffee or ramen. Though the hotel is far from town, Edison will give you a ride in the morning and hitching is fairly easy. The verdant, jungly location far from the squalor of Tofol, and friendly, helpful staff give a pleasant atmosphere to the place.

The next place you reach as you ride in from the airport is the **Horizon Hotel** (Eugene Palsis, Box 71, Kosrae, FM 96944; tel. 370-3456), right on the beach at Tafunsak. The eight rooms with private bath in this two-story concrete structure cost $28 s, $38 d for a mountainview room, $33 s, $48 d for an oceanview room. All rooms have a/c and private bath, and there's a restaurant right on the premises.

A kilometer east of the Horizon Hotel, facing the same beach, is the **Sandy Beach Hotel** (Donald Jonah, Box 6, Kosrae, FM 96944; tel. 370-3239)—about halfway between the airport and Tofol. The nine thatched cottages with private bath are all $30 s, $45 d—beware the price the two units with no a/c, which cost the same price. This was one of the first hotels on the island and the cottages are beginning to show the signs of age, but it's a favorite with scuba divers.

Those interested in closely observing village life or the Lelu ruins can consider the **Trade Winds Motel** (Thurston K. Siba, Box TE, Kosrae, FM 96944; tel. 370-3054), on the seaward side of Lelu Island. The four units with private bath are $30 s, $50 d, $80 t, or

$60 s, $80 d, $100 t for a room and rental car package. Make sure the a/c works. Some of the bungalows have small kitchens, which is handy as the nearest restaurants are in Tofol. The adjacent shore is thick with mangroves. This motel is managed by Island Office Supply in Tofol; if you show up unexpectedly it's unlikely you'll find anyone around who knows anything.

If you're here on business, stay at the two-story, 11-room **Coconut Palm Hotel** (William Tosie, Box 87, Kosrae, FM 96944; tel. 370-3181) beside Bill's Restaurant in Tofol for $37 s, $47 d. Double occupancy of a single room is $42. If there doesn't seem to be anyone around, ask at Bill's Restaurant, as it's under the same ownership. Advance room reservations are sometimes not honored here.

Your last choice is the two-story, concrete **Sunset Hotel** (Lucian Robert, Box 62, Kosrae, FM 96944; tel. 370-3076), also known as the SS Hotel, above their restaurant at Tofol. They have only two rooms with shared bath at $36 s or d—more than this dreary place is worth.

There's an acute accommodations shortage on Kosrae, and the hotels in Lelu and Tofol are often booked well in advance by business travelers, while the Sandy Beach fills up with scuba divers. Getting a room at the Kosrae or Horizon hotels is usually easier. The hotels get expensive if you stay longer than a few days, so ask at the tourist office about private accommodations.

Food

None of the places to eat on Kosrae is outstanding, and the service is usually incredibly slow. The four restaurants in Tofol tend to the needs of wage-earning bureaucrats and visiting businesspeople; there are no restaurants at all in Lelu.

The preferred place to eat is **Bill's Restaurant** (tel. 370-3181), opposite the Coconut Palm Hotel in Tofol. It's not that much more expensive than the other Tofol eateries, and the hamburgers, chicken and fish are okay, but the coffee is awful. After the bright, pleasant decor inside, the wretched toilets attached to this establishment are a surprise.

a river on Kosrae as seen by French visitors in 1824

Jacob's Fast Food (JFF) Citizen's Restaurant (open daily), across the street from Bill's, is basic but okay. It's the cheapest of the lot.

Islanders' Restaurant (also known as the Pacific Awane) just up the street from the Coconut Palm is similar to Bill's but no cheaper, and they're closed weekends. The restaurant at the **Sunset Hotel** nearby is about the same price but far less appealing; they're also closed weekends.

The most expensive place on Kosrae is the restaurant at the **Horizon Hotel**, which even has crab and lobster on the dinner menu! It's the only place serving beer (no takeout beer), but they only open at meal times.

If you have access to cooking facilities or are staying with a local family, buy fish, crabs, and lobster at the **Fishing Coop** on the Lelu causeway near the old airstrip. The adjacent **farmers' market** (open irregularly) sells oranges, tangerines, limes, lime juice, watermelons, Chinese cabbage, and cucumbers. Kosrae is known for its citrus fruit; these are often sold at the airport. If you can, try *fafa*, Kosraean poi.

Entertainment
Religious fervor has thus far prevented the opening of a public bar on Kosrae. As usual, this misguided puritanism has led to public drunkenness and littering as plenty of take-away beer is available at supermarkets such as Thurston's in Lelu and Webster's at Tafunsak. Most hotels sell cold bottles of beer to guests.

Sports And Recreation
Dive Caroline (Box DC, Kosrae, FM 96944; tel. 370-3239; fax 370-2109) is a full-service dive shop based at the Sandy Beach Hotel. Two-tank boat dives are $65 (minimum three persons) while night dives are $45 (minimum two persons). They also fill tanks and rent equipment.

Scuba diving can also be arranged with Roger Emerson or Jack Sigrah at the Division of Marine Resources (tel. 370-3031), behind the fish market on the Lelu causeway. Several American planes and Japanese ships are submerged in Lelu harbor. During the December mating season large numbers of sea turtles congregate at Kosrae.

One of the best beaches near Lelu/Tofol is at the northwest end of the Lelu causeway, where there's also a platform for diving and a natural hole in which to swim. Good beaches extend all the way from this causeway to Tafunsak, and are also at Malem and Walung.

In summer the reef near the Sandy Beach Hotel is good for snorkeling. In winter Utwe is preferable. The best reef surfing is at Malem, at high tide from Aug. to September.

Shopping

The **JAL Gift Shop** (closed Sun.) next to the Trade Winds Hotel in Lelu has some very nice things: fans, baskets, wall hangings, woodcarvings, coconut products, women's clothing, T-shirts, model canoes, etc.

Services

A Bank of Hawaii branch (tel. 370-3230) is next to the Islanders' Restaurant at Tofol. They give a very poor rate for foreign currency. Below the nearby Coconut Palm Hotel are the Bank of the FSM (tel. 370-3225), the post office, Air Nauru (tel. 370-3013), and Continental Air Micronesia (tel. 370-3024).

Overseas calls can be placed at the Communications Center (open 24 hours) below the hospital in Tofol.

There's a coin laundry at Thurston's Enterprise in Lelu.

Kosrae state government employees are on a four-day work week, so don't count on getting much business done on Friday (national government offices are open Friday).

Information

You can pick up brochures on Kosrae at the tourist office (tel. 370-2228), in a traditional-style thatched building at Tofol. They also sell the book *Kosrae, The Sleeping Lady Awakens* by Harvey Gordon Segal ($8), and William H. Stewart's *Tourist Map of Kosrae* ($2.50). You're more likely to find someone there early in the morning Monday through Thursday. Madison Nena and Justus Alokoa in this office are good sources of information and can help with practical arrangements.

Radio station V6AJ-AM broadcasts from Kosrae over 1500 kHz.

Getting There

Continental Air Micronesia calls at Kosrae six times a week, three times weekly in each direction between Honolulu and Guam. Reconfirm your onward flight at their Tofol office (tel. 370-3024), below the Coconut Palm Hotel.

In July 1991 **Air Nauru** began direct weekly service from Nauru (A$176) and Pohnpei (US$92), the best connection between Kosrae and Kiribati or anywhere in the South Pacific.

The **Kosrae Terminal and Stevedoring Company** (tel. 370-3085), at Okat Harbor near the airport, runs a monthly cargo/passenger ship, the *Mutunlik,* to Pingelap ($9.36), Mokil ($13.50), Pohnpei ($18.30), Ebeye ($20.70), Majuro ($30), and Nauru ($25.20). The quoted fares are deck class, and meals are $10 a day extra for all three (optional). No cabins are available. For information on departures call the office above or the Public Works Dept. (tel 370-3011) in Tofol.

For some reason yachties are not extended the usual Kosrae welcome by local officialdom, but Ted Sigrah, who lives across the street from Thurston's Enterprise in Lelu, does his best to make up for this and keeps a register of all visiting yachts. Private yachts can dock at either Lelu or Okat harbors.

lily (Crinum moorei)

Getting Around

There's no bus service, but hitching is fairly easy. If you're sure you want a rental car, ask your hotel to book one for you when you're reserving your room. The only time you'll really need one is to go to Utwe. There's not much traffic at all beyond Malem.

Cars can be rented at **Island Office Supply** (tel. 370-3226), across the street from the Coconut Palm Hotel in Tofol, at $40 a day (no insurance), but they're often all taken.

A better bet is **Webster's Enterprise** (tel. 370-3116) at Tafunsak, which rents cars at $33 daily. Look for their counter at the airport upon arrival.

Airport

All flights land at the new airport (KSA) at Okat, eight km west of Lelu/Tofol. Visitors with hotel reservations are usually picked up at the airport; those without reservations will have no trouble hitching a lift. A few over-priced handicrafts and a good snack bar with coffee, ramen, popcorn, and cold drinks grace the terminal. There's a $5 departure tax.

STATE OF POHNPEI

INTRODUCTION

The big island of Pohnpei (spelled Ponape until 1984) along with eight outlying atolls and Minto Reef make up the State of Pohnpei, about halfway between Honolulu and Manila. Of the state's 345 square km, Pohnpei Island accounts for 334. This 19-by-23-km island is the second largest of the Carolines, just slightly smaller than Babeldaop (Belau). Local author Gene Ashby calls it "the outer edge of Paradise."

The rugged, rainforested slopes of the interior rise to 772 meters at Nahnalaud (Big Mountain) and Ngihneni (Giant's Tooth), shrouded in lush tropical vegetation nurtured by endless precipitation. Pohnpei's peaks generate the island's high precipitation by catching passing clouds and wringing the moisture from them. The torrential rains swell the 42 streams and rivers, which thunder down from the uplands in high cascades. Pools at the feet of the falls, and the rivers themselves, present excellent opportunities for freshwater swimming.

Don't look for beaches on Pohnpei proper, although there are a few on nearby reef islets. Much of the land is skirted by mangrove swamps. At Kitti, the mangrove swamps are over a kilometer wide and canoes must wind through twisting channels to reach the lagoon. Pohnpei is surrounded by a barrier reef and over 25 islets, many of them volcanic.

Aside from the main town, Kolonia, the most heavily populated areas on Pohnpei are Sokehs Island and Madolenihmw (pronounced mad-o-LEN-ee-um). Under both the Spanish and the Germans, Pohnpei was the capital of Micronesia (the Japanese had their headquarters at Koror, the Americans had theirs at Guam and then Saipan).

For the history buff, Pohnpei is one of the only islands in the Pacific with monumental ruins from every period of its history: Micronesian, Spanish, German, Japanese, and American. The present inhabitants go about their languid lives slightly amused at visitors parading out to see these castoff relics, half covered by the luxuriant vegetation of this rich volcanic island. *Kaselehlia,* like *aloha,* translates into hello or goodbye, but to visitors it means "Welcome to Pohnpei!"

Climate

Even though Pohnpei is one of the wettest and greenest places on earth, water is rationed due to massive leakage from the mains. Kolonia gets 4,917 mm of annual rainfall, but twice that amount falls on the mountains of the interior. January and Feb. are the driest months; April and May the wettest. Most days are cloudy with alternating sunny spells and showers. The temperature is al-

POHNPEI'S CLIMATE

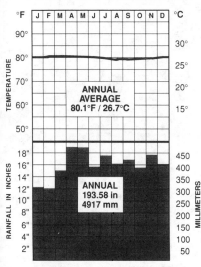

ANNUAL AVERAGE 80.1°F / 26.7°C

ANNUAL 193.58 in 4917 mm

most steady at 26.7° C year-round. The northeast trades die down July-Nov., and the humidity goes up. Much, though by no means all, of the rain falls at night.

The Foundation Of Pohnpei

Long, long ago a group of people sailed from a far island in search of new land. On their way they met an octopus who told them of a shallow place in the sea stretching from north to south. They reached the place, but found only a tiny coral islet which fit between canoe and outrigger. So they used magic to call coral and rocks to help build up the island, but the waves broke the stones. So they planted mangroves to protect their work, and put a reef around the island to keep the sea away. As more soil was brought, the island grew. An altar was built and rock piled on top of it. Thus Pohnpei got its name from *pohn* (on) *pei* (the altar).

Most of the people then went back to their home island, but one couple remained and had many children. A second group arrived and helped enlarge Pohnpei, but all still lived in caves. Finally, a third group landed on the island bringing vegetables, and they taught the others how to build houses of grass and small trees. Later other groups came, each contributing to the Pohnpei of today.

History

Pohnpei was divided into three kingdoms by a line of native kings, the Saudeleurs, who ruled jointly from Nan Madol beginning in the 13th century. The Saudeleur dynasty was overthrown by the legendary warrior Isokelekel, who arrived from Kosrae with 333 comrades. Isokelekel established the first line of Nahnmwarkis, who are the current traditional chiefs.

MICRONESIA REGIONAL TOURISM COUNCIL

Pohnpei's Kepirohi waterfalls are a great place to swim.

a Japanese anti-aircraft gun in a bamboo thicket on Sokehs Mountain (Pohndolap)

Pohnpei was sighted by Alvaro de Saavedra in 1529. Quiros, leader of a Spanish expedition, passed Pohnpei on 23 Dec. 1595 but didn't land. The islanders were left in peace until the second quarter of the 19th century, when whalers arrived and exacted a price: in 1854 a smallpox epidemic brought to Pohnpei by the American whaler *Delta* wiped out half the population and led the Pohnpeians to abandon Nan Madol. A few years later the American ship *Pearl* brought measles, which killed many more. Whaling declined after 1865 when the Confederate raider *Shenandoah* sank 40 Yankee whaling ships in the North Pacific, four of them at Pohnpei.

One chance arrival, James F. O'Connell, shipwrecked here off the *John Bull* in 1827, entered the local lore as the "Tattooed Irishman." O'Connell danced an Irish jig to ingratiate himself with the local chiefs. His book, *A Residence of Eleven Years in New Holland and the Caroline Islands*, is a colorful mix of sailor's tales and interesting facts about old Pohnpei. In 1828 Capt. Fedor Lütke of the Russian ship *Senyavin* named Pohnpei and its adjacent atolls the "Senyavin Islands."

The Spanish had laid vague claim to these islands in the 16th century but only arrived to occupy Pohnpei after the Germans claimed the Carolines in 1885. The Spanish built a town wall and fort at Kolonia, the remains of which are still evident. The Germans bought the islands from Spain in 1899, took over the outpost at Kolonia, and developed the copra trade.

German rule was often harsh. In 1910 four German officials were killed by members of the Kawath clan of Sokehs in a dispute over forced road-building, among other things. The Germans brought in Melanesian soldiers from New Guinea to capture those responsible. Seventeen Pohnpeians were executed and 426 exiled to Angaur Island, Belau, to work in the phosphate mines. Land owned by the rebel clan at Sokehs and Palikir was confiscated and given to outer islanders.

The next period, which began with a bloodless Japanese occupation in 1914, saw completion of a road fit for vehicles a quarter of the way around the island. Thousands of Japanese colonists arrived and by 1941 they outnumbered the Pohnpeians three to one. Pohnpei was not a strategic base during WW II, and the U.S. chose to bypass it after bombing the airfields. During much of the Trust Territory period Pohnpei was a quiet backwater; after so many years of neglect, it's now the capital of the FSM.

Economy

Government plays a dominant role in the local economy, but education is also important. The Community College of Micronesia on Pohnpei offers the only two-year post-secondary program in the FSM, and the Pohnpei Agricultural and Trade School (PATS) is the only one of its kind in the region. Over the next few years the Community College is to be moved from Kolonia to a brand new complex out at Palikir. The Pacific Basin Medical Officer Training Program is based across the road from Kolonia's hospital.

With all the U.S. grant money flowing in things are humming on Pohnpei, with textile factories, a brewery, and many other small industries envisioned for a new industrial park at Palikir. In 1990, however, a Taiwanese company canceled plans to build a major garment factory at Palikir after the Pohnpei and FSM governments announced they would restrict the importation of foreign labor, thus making the project unworkable. Though there's only 30% employment on Pohnpei at the moment, most Pohnpeians are unwilling to put in long hours of exacting work for minimum pay. Japanese interests are threatening to build a paper mill between Sokehs and Palikir to convert the island's excellent hardwoods into cheap pulp, wreaking the

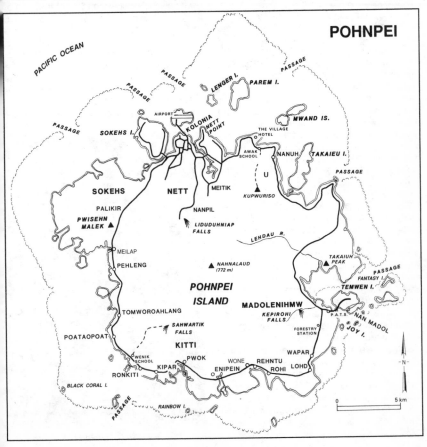

usual ecological havoc in the process. The new Pohnpei Fisheries Complex, built by the Economic Development Authority near the airport, includes a large fish-processing plant supplied with tuna by Oriental fishermen.

In the past agriculture has fared badly. A scheme to develop cacao as an export crop failed due to falling world prices, disease, and U.S. withdrawal of the subsidy program. The desired increase in pepper production never materialized due to a failure of the Trust Territory administration to budget funds for its development. Instead, hundreds of unproductive jobs were created in offices and public works, courtesy of Uncle Sam. Now things seem to be picking up, with two new private pepper processing plants on Pohnpei.

Pohnpei is famous for its yams *(kehp)*, which grow up to three meters long—a cluster can weigh nearly 500 kilos. Other traditional crops are taro, breadfruit, cassava, and sweet potatoes.

A few local processing industries around Kolonia are of particular interest to visitors. Pohnpei black pepper is bagged and exported by Island Traders (Box 704, Pohnpei, FM 96941), beside the Public Market in Kolonia. A branch of Island Traders behind the Chinese Embassy nearby makes buttons from trochus shells and mother-of-pearl. You're welcome to wander in and inspect both these small factories set up by Bob and Patti Arthur, owners of the Village Hotel.

Kaselel shampoo and Oil of Pohnpei soap are made from coconut oil by Pohnpei Coconut Products Inc. (Box 1120, Pohnpei, FM 96941), near PATS in Madolenihmw. This company also produces Marekeiso oil for use on body and hair and Oil of Pohnpei suntan oil (with a protection factor of 3). All these excellent products are sold at handicraft outlets around Kolonia. (According to Gene Ashby, bars of Pohnpei soap "give more suds than anything this side of Budweiser.")

Genuine Pohnpei pepper can be ordered through the mail from Albert Roosevelt, Pohnpei Agricultural Development, Inc., Box 1479, Pohnpei, FM 96941. Both white and black pepper, ground or unground, is available at $2 a bag.

The People

Of the 32,884 (1989) inhabitants of the State of Pohnpei, over 10,000 live in Kolonia. Pohnpeians outside Kolonia don't live in villages, but in groups of individual houses with land around them. The people are languid and friendly—they always return a smile. Bare-breasted women are still seen along country roads (no photography without permission).

Influential lines of chiefs and nobility control five of the six municipalities on Pohnpei: Sokehs, Nett, U, Madolenihmw, and Kitti. No chiefs or nobles operate in Kolonia. Each of these five has a Nahnmwarki, or High Chief, and a Nahnken, or Talking Chief. Below this hereditary nobility are other social classes of landowners and commoners, a complex social hierarchy. Descent is matrilineal, with the children being accepted as members of the mother's clan and inheriting their prestige and property from it. It's hard to discern differences in caste from appearances; when-

unloading oil drums at Mokil

VICINITY OF KOLONIA

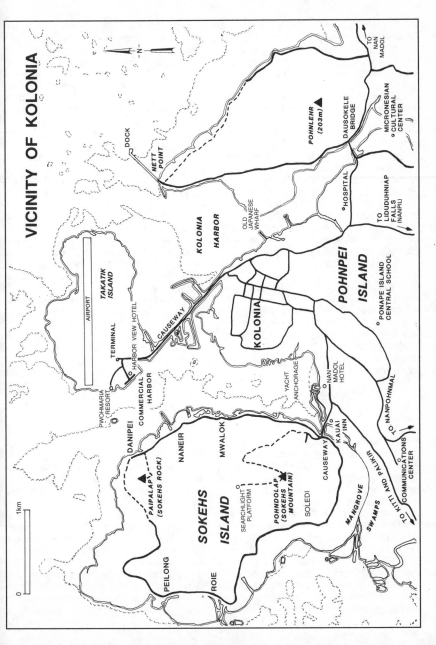

ever in doubt, visitors should address or greet the older people first. Pigs are a form of wealth, so you see them everywhere on Pohnpei; in fact, there are more pigs than people, which doesn't contribute to the fragrance of the island.

Groups of immigrants from outer islands such as Pingelap, Mokil, and the Mortlocks comprise about a quarter of the population of Pohnpei Island. Some have formed separate communities, each with its own language, on Sokehs Island, where they were resettled in 1912 on lands seized by the Germans during the 1910 rebellion. At Porakiet, on the west side of downtown Kolonia, some 900 Polynesians from Kapingamarangi atoll now live. Another 1,027 Polynesians live on the home islands of Kapingamarangi and Nukuoro. Leprosy is endemic in the Polynesian outer islands.

Crafts

Pohnpei is noted for its unique coconut-grating stools and elaborate, carefully scaled model canoes. If you want to go to the trouble of trying to ship them home, full-length outrigger canoes are also available. Other local crafts include carved fish, wall hangings, trays, handbags, baskets, necklaces, fans, and mats.

POHNPEI SIGHTS

Kolonia

Before WW II Kolonia had a population of 10,000 Japanese nationals (in all there were 13,000 Japanese on Pohnpei and only 5,900 Micronesians). Today booming little Kolonia is again approaching that size in population, and it's mostly Micronesians this time.

In the park on the north side of Kolonia is the **old Spanish wall,** mentioned earlier. Built in 1887, it marked the western boundary of Fort Alfonso XIII, which extended north and east to the lagoon. Just across the park is the **Catholic mission**. Only the apse and belfry remain from the original church erected in 1909 by the Capuchin fathers; during WW II material from the structure was used by the Japanese to build defense works.

Due west of this, in a clearing directly behind a new Protestant church, is the **old German cemetery,** with the graves of sailors off the cruiser *Emden* who died putting down the Sokehs revolt of 1910. The mass grave site of 17 Pohnpeians, executed by a German firing squad in 1911, is marked by a simple enclosure on the left near the end of a dirt road at the north end of Kolonia.

Catch a good view of Sokehs Island from the terrace behind the **South Park Hotel**, then take a stroll through the Polynesian village of Kapingamarangans at **Porakiet** on your way back to town. Ninety Polynesians settled here in 1918 after a severe drought on their native island, Kapingamarangi, 586 km southwest of Pohnpei. It's fairly easy to distinguish the big, frizzy-haired Polynesians from the smaller, straight-haired Pohnpeians. The open thatched houses sit on stone platforms and the residents have an outdoor life-style. The **craft shop** here is worth a visit.

A massive **Japanese meteorological building** stands abandoned on the grounds of the Agriculture Station in Kolonia.

Just a little up and across the road from Ace Commercial Center are three small **Japanese tanks** right beside the road. Eight more small tanks are lined up in a pit in the bush directly behind these three. The driveway opposite Ace leads on to a large military dump. The Japanese naval headquarters was in this area.

Pohndolap

The best hike near Kolonia for scenery, war relics, and birdwatching is to the top of **Sokehs Mountain** (250 meters), locally known as Pohndolap. Just after the causeway, take the road straight ahead which winds up the hill to the right. When the paved road turns left, go straight ahead on the overgrown Japanese military road. Follow this for about 25 minutes until it switchbacks steeply up to the mountaintop.

You'll know you're getting there when you start seeing good views of Kolonia. Take care to note which way you came so you can find your way back down! On top are two large double-barreled Japanese AA guns to the right and a six-inch naval gun in a concrete bunker at the back of the hill to the left. The Japanese defense works which ringed the summit is still clearly visible.

At the north end of the mountain, some distance beyond the AA guns, is a metal Japanese searchlight platform which offers stunning views of Sokehs Rock and Kolonia.

Paipalap
The climb to the top of **Sokehs Rock** (200 meters), or Paipalap (Peipapap), is easier than one would imagine from the look of its sheer basalt sides when seen from Kolonia, though you should be in good physical shape. The signposted trail begins a house just before Danipei church, near the end of the peninsula. The rock itself belongs to Pohnpei State but the access trail crosses private land and a $1 pp toll is collected at the trailhead.

Go across the right side of a taro/banana plantation, past and around two large caves, then up to a big tree, the roots of which provide handholds for scaling the cliff. By this time you'll have encountered a black power cable. Follow this up the back of the Rock to the top. The view from the summit is the best on the island—even Pakin atoll is visible on the horizon to the northwest. Go slowly, as the rock can be slippery.

If it's not too late when you get back down to the road, you might continue walking around Sokehs Island. The walk (pedestrians only) along a stone trail through the mangroves from Danipei to Peilong is a nice one. The west side of Sokehs Island is far less heavily populated than the east and the two hours spent hiking right around the island are well spent.

To do both climbs described above and the hike around the island in a single day would be strenuous. If you're not that experienced at finding your own way along overgrown jungle trails, you might consider hiring a young boy to guide you on these climbs for a couple of dollars.

Southeast Of Kolonia
On a hot day hike six km south from Kolonia past the rock crusher along the dirt road to **Liduduhniap Falls** at Nanpil (admission charged). The dirt road follows the Kahmar River (good swimming) then climbs, affording a good view of the island's lush interior. The best swimming is in the pool just above the highest falls. The area around the falls has been cleared; the road runs right up to it. After rains, the way can be muddy and cars can bog down. You pass a hydroelectric project on the way to the falls.

Two more Japanese naval guns are atop **Kupwuriso** (630 meters), a tough four-hour

Massive volcanic plugs poke skywards just below the summit of Sokehs Rock (Paipalap).

DAVID STANLEY

RT climb through the jungle opposite Awak School at U. Ask around for someone to guide you (offer $10).

Around The Island

The potholed roads of southern Pohnpei are among the worst in Micronesia. The 80-km, 80-bridge road around the island, begun by the Spaniards in the 1890s and continued by the Japanese in the 1930s, was finally completed by the Americans in 1985. Eastbound the pavement ends at Awak School; the paved road west reaches as far as Meilap. If you plan to drive yourself around Pohnpei rent a pickup truck instead of a car, as the road is steep and slippery on the southeast side of the island.

An impressive new nine-building **FSM capitol complex** opened at Palikir in 1989, thanks to $13 million in U.S. funding. Imitation Pohnpeian basalt stones support the buildings, which house the national government offices, the Congress of the FSM, and the FSM Supreme Court.

Two km beyond Palikir, a volcanic plug known as **Pwisehn Malek** ("Chickenshit Mountain") towers above the road. It's easy to climb for a sweeping view. The prismatic basalt formations are striking when seen from above and indicate the availability of materials to build Nan Madol. When a lava flow is very deep, the material cools slowly into these columnar basalt crystals. Pwisehn Malek got its name from a legendary rooster who relieved himself here (and thereby created the mountain) while racing around the island on an errand from the gods.

Two uncommercialized waterfalls flow off the southwest side of Pohnpei, an hour's hike up a muddy track from Wenik School. Water which feeds the first falls, **Sahwarlap,** passes under the first suspension bridge you encounter. Trouble is, you're above the falls so it's hard to get a clear view. Just beyond the bridge work your way over to the edge of the cliff for a view of **Sahwartik,** higher of the two. There's a very tricky path to the bottom of the falls where you'll find a spectacular, deep swimming pool, but a guide is necessary. Possibilities for swimming on top exist, but aren't outstanding. This hike gives you a glimpse of the interior few tourists ever see. Go even farther up the trail if you have time.

Every Saturday there's a day tour from Kolonia to **Enipein Marine Park** (tel. 320-2693) on the south side of the island ($40 pp including lunch and transportation). Participants tour the mangroves in a small boat, snorkel on a nearby reef, and get to try *sakau*. Advance reservations must be made through the Tourist Commission in Kolonia or your hotel. Also at Enipein, a couple of km east of the Marine Park headquarters, is a large river, with a good swimming hole just above the highway bridge.

Madolenihmw

The **Pohnpei Agricultural and Trade School** (PATS) at Madolenihmw is an 88-hectare Jesuit boys' secondary school, offering 160 Micronesians four-year courses in construction, mechanics, horticulture, and animal husbandry. Tours of PATS are offered 1300-1600. A small **coconut-products plant** near the Temwen Causeway produces excellent coconut-oil soap, shampoo, and skin cream. Sold in tiny pandanus baskets, they make excellent souvenirs.

Four huge **Japanese naval guns** intended to protect the entrance to Madolenihmw Harbor rest swallowed in jungle around the top of Temwen Island. After crossing the causeway, go straight about four km and ask for Bernard Perez, who owns the land where the guns are. Bernard is a kind man and will probably offer to show you around.

Kepirohi Falls (admission $3), just before the turnoff to PATS, pours over basalt cliffs into an idyllic swimming pool. Take the path near the bridge where the boathouses are. Pyramid-like **Takaiuh Peak** rises across Madolenihmw Harbor. The secure yacht anchorage just west of the point of land opposite Temwen's north end makes this a good port of call for yachties.

Joy Island

About the best place to relax in the FSM is Joy Island, a charming resort set on a sandy reef islet near Nan Madol on the southeast side of·Pohnpei. The swimming is great—bring snorkeling gear. Accommodations at Joy are only $5 pp in one of 12 unfurnished thatched cottages. The new cabins are $7 pp. There's ample fresh water for washing, and an electric generator is used at night. Bedding (if required) is $2 pp extra. Just don't expect any luxuries at those prices!

There's no restaurant or snack bar on Joy Island. Unless you're part of a group which has made prior arrangements, you must bring all your own food from Kolonia (the stores at Madolenihmw are poor and unreliable). Hot water to make tea and ramen soup is available on Joy, and cooking over a campfire is possible.

Reservation tickets *must* be purchased in advance at Joy Hotel (Box 484, Pohnpei, FM 96941; tel. 320-2447) in Kolonia. Their brochure states: "No one will be allowed on the Joy Boat or Joy Island without these tickets." Japanese tour groups sometimes stay on the island; you can avoid them by inquiring well

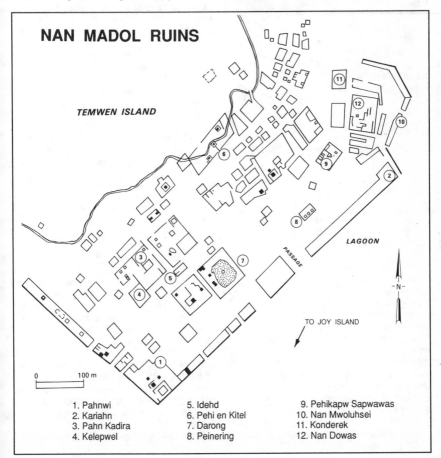

NAN MADOL RUINS

TEMWEN ISLAND

LAGOON

PASSAGE

–N–

TO JOY ISLAND

0   100 m

1. Pahnwi
2. Kariahn
3. Pahn Kadira
4. Kelepwel
5. Idehd
6. Pehi en Kitel
7. Darong
8. Peinering
9. Pehikapw Sapwawas
10. Nan Mwoluhsei
11. Konderek
12. Nan Dowas

000707

NANMDOL VISITORS PERMIT

Ilten Selten
23rd Isopahu of Madolenihmw
since the fall of the Saudeleur Dynasty

$3.00

Ilten Selten

ahead. Also avoid weekends when the locals come out (radios on at dawn). Two nights are probably enough.

Get there by taking a minibus ($2) to PATS, where you connect with a prearranged speedboat ($5 pp RT) to Joy Island. Transport from Kolonia to PATS is most easily found weekday mornings. There have been cases of visitors missing the boat, so the Joy Hotel receptionist may suggest you rent a car to get to PATS (Joy doesn't provide road transportation). If you're unwilling to do this and want to travel by public minibus, they'll ask that you call them once you reach PATS, to say that you've arrived. Then they'll radio for the boat to come over to pick you up on the PATS dock at the foot of Dakota Street. The road from Kolonia to PATS is bad—you

should allow at least one hour by rental car, two hours by minibus.

The Joy Island staff offers a tour of Nan Madol in their launch when the tide is high at $8 pp (Nan Madol fee included). If you visit Nan Madol on your way over to Joy Island or on the way back to PATS, the charge is only $5 pp (Nan Madol fee included). At low tide you could even wade or snorkel across to Nan Madol! Beware of sunburn.

Other Resort Islands
Kehpara or **Black Coral Island,** off the southwest side of Pohnpei, is similar to Joy Island and also popular locally as a weekend getaway. It's also $5 pp to stay on the island, but at $35 RT the boat over is more expensive if there's only one or two of you. For information call 320-2440 or ask at the tourist commission in Kolonia. Also ask if **Fantasy Island** (facing the passage at Madolenihmw) is open.

At Enipein ask for Joseph Paulus, who sometimes provides basic accommodations in thatched huts on Laiap or **Rainbow Island**—he'll take you across in his boat. For advance information about staying on Rainbow Island ask at the Cliff Rainbow Hotel (tel. 320-2415) in Kolonia.

NAN MADOL

The most celebrated ruin in Micronesia is Nan Madol, a group of impressive stone compounds and varied basalt buildings on the east side of Pohnpei, in the lagoon just off Temwen Island. Legend tells how Nan Madol was founded by the magicians Olsihpa and Olsohpa who caused the stones to fly into place by themselves.

A mighty sea wall flanks the site on three sides, with open channels between the 80 artificial islands. Nan Madol is even more amazing considering that all of the huge basalt logs that went into the project had to be brought in on bamboo rafts! Carbon dating at the earliest levels indicates that they were built between 1285 and 1485—surprising evidence of an advanced civilization centuries old. By the time the first Europeans arrived, Nan Madol had already been abandoned.

The main islets to visit are Pahnwi (with a seawall of monoliths), Kariahn (the burial place of priests), Pahn Kadira (the administrative center), Kelepwel (housing servants for Pahn Kadira), Idehd (the religious center), Pehi en Kitel (the burial place of chiefs), Darong (center for ceremonial clamming), Peinering (coconut oil-producing center), Pehikapw Sapwawas (the communication or drumming center), Nan Mwoluhsei (a huge boulder from which warriors jumped to prove their bravery), Konderek (place of funeral rites), and the greatest ruin of all, Nan Dowas (the war temple or fortress). Four or five hours are needed for a thorough visit.

Getting There
Take a boat at high tide, or wade at low tide. Most of the hotels in Kolonia offer tours to Nan Madol for about $50 pp, but they're rather disappointing. First they take you snorkeling in the lagoon, then you spend two hours at Kepirohi waterfall. You finish up with a short stop on Nan Dowas, featuring a five-minute speech by the guide and about 20 minutes to walk around before you return to the hotel.

If that sounds unappealing, consider visiting the site from Joy Island near PATS at Madolenihmw. You can wade or snorkel to the ruins from Joy Island or visit on the island boat. Joy Hotel in Kolonia arranges visits to Nan Madol from PATS for $13 pp (Nan Madol fee and a stop at Joy Island included). A visit if you're staying on Joy Island is $8 pp, or $5 pp if you visit on the way to/from the island. Advance reservations are required.

Alternatively, you could try to charter a motorized canoe from Madolenihmw. Canoes may be found at the bridge near Kepirohi Falls, or ask at the municipal office near the Temwen causeway. Be ready to go well before high tide and agree on the price before you set out. Bargain hard if they ask too much.

If you wade from Joy the first point you reach is Pahnwi, then you proceed along the sea wall to the passage into the site, stop for a look at Peinering, and continue exploring at

will. Great stone walls loom above you out of the mangroves. Beware of becoming stranded by rising waters! As you ride or wade from Joy Island to Nan Madol you'll see a few magnificent manta rays and perhaps an inoffensive reef shark or two.

The High Chief of Madolenihmw, Ilten Selten, 23rd Nahnmwarki since the fall of the Saudeleur dynasty, lives on Temwen and charges a $3 pp fee to visit the ruins (collected at Joy Hotel in Kolonia). A numbered admission ticket is issued.

PRACTICALITIES

Accommodations
The low-budget traveler's Mecca is the **Hifumi Inn** (Elterihna "Likolo" Seiola, Box 811, Pohnpei, FM 96941; tel. 320-2382) in the lower part of Kolonia, with nine fan-cooled rooms at $14 s, $17 d. There's a common shared bath for men and women (no rooms with private bath). It's in a delightful old neighborhood rich in the sounds of pigs, chickens, dogs, and babies. Everyone's very friendly, but fussy visitors should look elsewhere. On weekends there may not be anyone around to give you a room.

Businesspeople like the well-managed **Palm Terrace Hotel** (Box 310, Pohnpei, FM 96941; tel. 320-2392), which offers 11 clean a/c rooms with color TV, fridge, and private bath ($45 s, $52 d) above their retail store in Kolonia. The Palm Terrace has a rather rustic appearance on the outside, but inside the rooms are modern and comfortable. Right on the premises is a full-service restaurant (good breakfast, good prices, large portions), and there's a permanent happy hour in the hotel bar with about the lowest beer prices in town.

Long a favorite with travelers is the **Hotel Pohnpei** (Mercedes Santos, Box 430, Pohnpei, FM 96941; tel. 320-2330), near the Polynesian village of Kapingamarangans, an easy walk from town. Here you're housed in one of 18 modern thatched cottages with garden baths at $30 s, $40 d, $45 t. Not all the rooms are as nice, however, so ask to see the room before checking in. Some of the

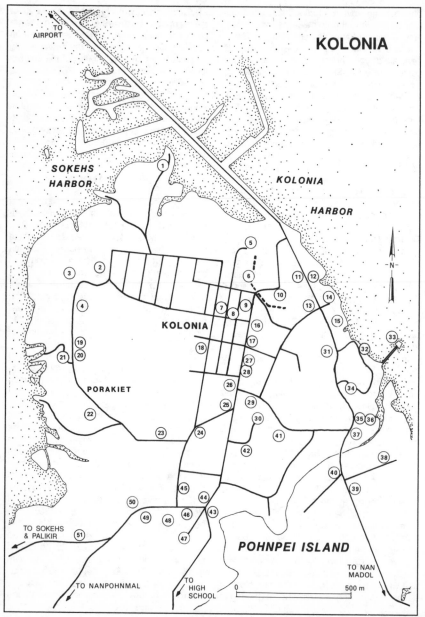

rooms have fridges (suspend food from the ceiling to protect it from pests), and breakfast is available in the dining room from 0700 to 1000. The hotel is beautifully set on a hillside facing Sokehs Mountain. Borrow one of the hotel's outrigger canoes and paddle around the lagoon.

Not far away, the **Cliff Rainbow Hotel** (Box 96, Pohnpei, FM 96941; tel. 320-2415) is $40 s, $48 d in the old building or $60 s or d in the new wing of the main three-story building. It's popular among Japanese tourists and their restaurant specializes in steaks. Unfortunately the 45 rooms don't have the views of those at the nearby Pohnpei or South Park hotels, but at least there may be one available for you when the other places are full.

The **South Park Hotel** (Box 829, Kolonia, Pohnpei, FM 96941; tel. 320-2255) has six rooms in the old wing at $35 s, $42 d; 12 rooms in the new wing at $65 s, $75 d. All rooms are a/c, but the new rooms have better beds, cable TV, and refrigerators. The South Park is undergoing extensive development and will be much bigger by the time you get there. The views of Sokehs from here are unsurpassed.

The efficiently run **Joy Hotel** (Box 484, Pohnpei, FM 96941; tel. 320-2447), a modern, three-story building near the Spanish wall in Kolonia, is the best hotel in town. The 10 a/c rooms with fridge and TV are $53 s, $62 d. Meals are served in the dining room and more independently minded Japanese visitors often stay here.

If your flight is delayed, Continental Air Micronesia might put you up in the three-story **Harbor View Hotel** (Box 1328, Kolonia, Pohnpei, FM 96941; tel. 320-5244). This clean, new hotel has 40 a/c rooms with fridge

KOLONIA

1. Sokehs Rebellion Mass Grave
2. Old German Cemetery
3. South Park Hotel
4. Cliff Rainbow Hotel
5. German bell tower
6. Spanish wall
7. Joy Restaurant
8. Joy Hotel
9. SeAir Shipping
10. state government offices
11. Australian Embassy
12. Chinese Embassy
13. former Japanese department store
14. Public Market/pepper factory
15. Kolonia Coop (KCCA)
16. Ponape House/Tomisiano Martin's Restaurant
17. Telecommunications Corp.
18. Phoenix Marine Sports Club
19. laundromat
20. Happy Landing Sakau Bar
21. Hotel Pohnpei
22. Kapingamarangi Gift Shop
23. Little Micronesia Saloon
24. Nan Uht Sakau Bar
25. Namiki Restaurant
26. Philippine Embassy
27. post office
28. Pohnpei Tourist Commission
29. banks and travel agencies
30. state legislature
31. Protestant Church
32. King's Sakau Bar
33. old Japanese wharf
34. Hifumi Inn
35. Hervis Rent a Car
36. Penny Rent a Car
37. Island Buffet
38. military dump
39. Japanese tanks
40. Ace Commercial Center
41. Community College of Micronesia
42. Island Affairs Office
43. U.S. Embassy
44. Kolonia Dental Clinic
45. laundromat/Micro Car Rental
46. public library
47. Agriculture Station
48. Palm Terrace
49. China Restaurant
50. PCR Restaurant/Car Rental
51. Ocean View Bar

and TV at $47 s, $66 d; a suite is $90. There's a coin laundry on the premises. It's right next to the commercial harbor, just minutes on foot from the airport terminal, so consider strolling over for lunch or a look at their souvenir shop if you check in early for your flight. As at the Palm Terrace, business travelers are well catered to here.

Japanese groups often stay at the more expensive **Pwohmaria Resorts Club** (Box 1416, Kolonia, Pohnpei, FM 96941; tel. 320-2779), on an artificial white sandy beach overlooking Sokehs Rock and just a five-minute walk from the airport terminal. The 12 wooden duplex units (24 rooms) on stilts seem a world away from the busy commercial port right next door.

The bottom end on Pohnpei is the ramshackle, two-story **Kauai Inn** (Carl C. Kohler, Box 745, Pohnpei, FM 96941; tel. 320-5750), at the Kolonia end of the Sokehs Causeway far from town. There are 10 rooms at $15 pp. It's hidden behind Sokehs Island Auto Clinic, hardly an appealing location—except for mechanics. Boat rentals can be arranged ($50). This place is only suitable for someone planning a long stay on a very low budget.

Pohnpei-style thatched bungalows with bamboo walls, oversized waterbeds, ceiling fan, and private bath run $70-90 s, $75-95 d, $80-100 t (depending on the view from the room) at exclusive, American-operated **The Village Hotel** (Box 339, Pohnpei, FM 96941; tel. 320-2797), in undisturbed surroundings at U, 10 km east of Kolonia. Air conditioning is unnecessary here as the trade winds blow through big screens all around the rooms. The Village's **Tattooed Irishman Restaurant** overlooking the lagoon has an elegant island ambience. You'll have to rent a car if you want to stay here, as taxi fares are expensive. Since its opening in 1976 The Village has earned its reputation as an ultimate island hideaway and some people rave about this place.

Add six percent room tax to all prices above. These hotels sometimes offer a free transfer service from the airport, so ask. There's no suitable place to camp in Kolonia itself—you have to go a bit outside. Whenever camping on Pohnpei, get permission from the landowner, especially if houses are near your campsite. Be aware that occasionally every hotel room on Pohnpei is full.

Food

The cheapest place in town is **Tomisiano Martin's Restaurant** (no sign), beside Ponape House on the main street. It's open for breakfast and lunch only (weekdays 0700-1400) and you receive filling local dishes like fried bananas and taro through a hole in the wall.

Island Buffet, on the southeast side of Kolonia a block from Ace Commercial Center, dishes out a good self-service Hawaiian-style lunch weekdays 1000-1500. It's also cheap.

The fan-cooled **Namiki Restaurant**, near the Philippines Embassy, used to be the best budget choice, but they've moved upmarket and are now too expensive for the locals but not good enough for tourists. The food is nothing special and unless you order the lunch special everyone else is having, the service is excruciatingly slow. Color photos of local politicos hang on one wall; a color TV

DAVID STANLEY

President Baily Olter (left) and local author Gene Ashby at the Palm Terrace, Kolonia

pumping out U.S. television tapes hangs from another. They're open for breakfast and lunch 0700-1500 daily. On weekends they also open for dinner from 1700 to 2100.

Bernard's Restaurant, also known as the "Pami Restaurant," on the top floor of the three-story building across the street from the Australian Embassy, is only reliably open for lunch weekdays (call 320-2443 to check if they're serving other meals). They offer Filipino food on a nice terrace with tables overlooking the bay.

The **China Restaurant** (closed Sunday), near the Palm Terrace Hotel, is good for seafood and standard northern Chinese cuisine. They also have special group menus for parties of four and over. Phone ahead (tel. 320-2210) for reservations.

The **PCR Restaurant** (closed Saturday), just down the road from the China, features Japanese food. The steaks and seafood are expensive, but the pizza, spaghetti, chicken, and pork dishes are affordable. Try the seafood pizza. You'll pay more than you would for the more familiar American-style fare (pizza, tacos, salad bar, etc.) at the nearby **Palm Terrace**, but it's nice for a change.

The food and atmosphere at Japanese-operated **Joy Restaurant** (lunch only) are excellent, so be sure to have at least one meal there. They're open daily except Sat. 1100-1500, Sundays also 1730-2100. If they're closed, the restaurant in **Joy Hotel** around the corner is another good place to sample Japanese food.

Finally, if you're only in Kolonia a day or two and can't sample all the restaurants, it's best to have breakfast at the Palm Terrace, lunch at Joy Restaurant, and dinner at the Palm Terrace, China, or PCR. Most eateries other than those at the hotels close on Sundays.

Entertainment

The **Palm Terrace Bar** is the best local watering hole. Weekday afternoons a delightful mix of island characters saunters in after work (ask for Gene Ashby). By 1700 it'll be full of American expats but around 1900 the color of the clientele begins to change, and by 2100 there won't be a white face in sight,

their places having been taken by Micronesians. This is the place to be if you want to meet people.

The **Little Micronesia Saloon**, two blocks north, is another favorite bar. After 2200 *the* place to be is the bar at the **Harbor View Hotel** where *karaoke* is featured.

The places in Kolonia close by law at midnight, but the **Ocean View Bar** (tel. 320-2131), outside city limits on the way to Sokehs, is open until 0230. It attracts a lively young local crowd whenever there's live music, but be aware—it can be rough. Three bars along the 10-km road to The Village Hotel are similar. The minimum drinking age on Pohnpei is 21 years.

The **Micronesian Cultural Center** at Nett offers programs for visitors including local dancing, *sakau* pounding, and craft demonstrations for $12.50 pp (five person minimum). These usually take place Fri. at 1500, but arrangements should be made at least 24 hours in advance through the tourist commission, a hotel, or a travel agency. Another similar cultural center is found in U.

Sakau

Listen for the rhythmic pounding leading to a *sakau* house. *Sakau*, made from a pepper shrub root, is pounded on a flat stone and squeezed through hibiscus fibers to produce a mildly narcotic drink similar to Fijian *kava*, only stronger. The *sakau* is served in a half coconut shell—lots of it. The smooth, woody taste is interesting and getting *puputa* (high) on *sakau* is a strange experience: your head stays completely coherent, but when you try to get up, your knees have disappeared.

Try it out in the villages on Pohnpei, or at a *sakau* house in Kolonia (25 cents a cup). A *nahs* is an assembly house for drinking *sakau*. For genuine hand-pounded *sakau*, visit the **Nan Uht Sakau Bar** a few blocks up the street running directly north from the Palm Terrace: their slogan is "we pound it on the rock." Others are the **Happy Landing** opposite the Hotel Pohnpei, the **JW Bar** down the hill from the Community College, and **King's Sakau Bar** just down the street from the Hifumi Inn. Most nights some form of live music materializes at Happy Landing. The spitting by patrons can be a little unpleasant, however. *Sakau* bars are continually changing locations, so ask around if these places seem closed. Arrive early because the houses often run out of *sakau* by 2030. In Micronesia, *sakau* is found only on Pohnpei.

Sports And Recreation

The biggest dive shop on Pohnpei is the efficient, Japanese-operated **Phoenix Marine Sport Club** (Box 387, Pohnpei, FM 96941; tel. 320-5678) on a back street just down from the tourist commission in Kolonia. Diving on the dropoffs just outside the reef passes costs $95 for two tanks including lunch and drinks (four-person minimum). This includes tanks but all other equipment is an additional charge. Diving at Ant and Pakin atolls is $105 for two tanks. A full day of picnicking and snorkeling, usually at Black Coral Island or Ant, is $55 pp, lunch $5 extra (five person minimum). PMSC also offers deep-sea trolling at $500 half day, $700 full day (lunch and drinks included) for up to seven persons. Pickups are made at all hotels upon request.

Scuba diving can be arranged through **Joy Ocean Service** (Box 484, Pohnpei, FM 96941; tel. 320-2336), based at Joy Hotel.

They charge $85 pp (minimum three persons) for a two-tank dive.

If you want to learn scuba diving, ask for Kenny Omura, a qualified PADI instructor who works out of the Palm Terrace Hotel. Scuba diving from The Village Hotel is $70 pp for three persons, $75 pp for two persons, or $100 for one person.

Divers should bring their own regulator, buoyancy compensator, and gauges with them. A certification card is required for all equipment rentals and scuba trips. Too much sediment from heavy rainfall runoff precludes beach diving off the main island but the channels through the barrier reef offer excellent possibilities to see caves and sharks in good weather. From Dec. through Feb., the waters can be rough.

Shopping

Handicrafts such as baskets, grass skirts, wall hangings, trays, model canoes, and woodcarvings are sold at shops in the **Public Market** on the lower east side of town. Behind this is **Pohnpei Products Mart,** selling local fruits and vegetables plus a few handicrafts and local coconut-oil shampoo and soap. Right next to this store is the pepper-processing factory where Pohnpei pepper is graded, sorted, and bagged. It's okay to go inside and look around. Several general

Boathouses and kitchens line the lagoon side at Mokil; the people sleep in houses on the breezier ocean side.

DAVID STANLEY

stores are also found in this area. Stock up on supplies and color print film at the **Kolonia Coop**, a Wild West general store.

Ponape House (Box 371, Pohnpei, FM 96941) on Main St. has books about Pohnpei and a good selection of handicrafts including baskets, wall hangings, fans, shell necklaces, woodcarvings, headbands, and grass skirts. Pohnpeian black pepper is among the best in the world, and this is a good place to buy a three-oz. souvenir bag of it ($3.50).

Excellent Polynesian handicrafts such as woodcarvings of dolphins and sharks, shellwork, woven wall hangings, coconut graters, model outrigger canoes, canoe bailers, mobiles, food and oil bowls, tackle boxes, and fish or eel traps are available at the **gift shop** at Porakiet. You may see some carvers at work near here. Joy Restaurant also sells crafts.

The **Pohnpei Public Library** (Box 284, Pohnpei, FM 96941) near the Palm Terrace sells calendars, postcards, and posters of Micronesian birds and fish. **Phoenix Marine Sports Club** has colorful T-shirts.

Services

The Bank of Hawaii (tel. 320-2543) and Bank of Guam (tel. 320-2550), both open Mon.-Thurs. 0930-1430, Fri. 0930-1600, have adjacent branches in the commercial block just below the Pohnpei Legislature. A couple of good travel agencies are in offices above them. The Bank of the FSM (tel. 320-2724) is in the lower town.

To make long-distance telephone calls go to the Telecommunications Corporation on the main street near the post office (weekdays 0800-1700). The cost is $7.50 to the U.S. or Guam for three minutes. On Sundays it's only $6 for three minutes, but you must go out to the Communications Center at Nanpohnmal (open 24 hours).

The FSM Immigration office (tel. 320-2606), across from the baseball field and next to the old Spanish wall, will give visa extensions 30 days at a time, up to 90 days maximum.

Several countries have diplomatic missions in Kolonia. The Chinese Embassy (tel. 320-5575) near the Public Market is hard to miss, and above the Bank of the FSM across the street is the Australian Embassy (Box S, Pohnpei, FM 96941; tel. 320-5448). The Philippine Embassy (tel. 320-5474) is on the main street near Namiki Restaurant. The U.S. Embassy (Box 1286, Pohnpei, FM 96941; tel. 320-2187) is near the old Japanese meteorological station on the south side of town.

Phoenix of Micronesia beside PMSC develops all kinds of film on the premises and sells film. There's also a coin laundry here. Another laundromat is behind the Mobil service station next to Ace Commercial Center. Check to make sure there's water before you throw in your clothes and soap.

Information

The Pohnpei Tourist Commission (Box 66, Pohnpei, FM 96941; open weekdays, tel. 320-2421), beside the small Japanese tank on the main street, can provide current information on local resorts on reef islands and cultural events. They also sell William H. Stewart's excellent *Map of Pohnpei and the Ancient Ruins of Nan Madol* ($2.50).

Check out the a/c library at the Community College of Micronesia (Box 159, Pohnpei, FM 96941; tel. 320-2479)—ask to see the Pacific Collection upstairs. The Pohnpei Public Library is near the Palm Terrace Hotel.

Micronesia Office Supply beside the Public Market sells tide tables and used paperbacks at low prices.

By far, the best book on the island is *Pohnpei, An Island Argosy* by Gene Ashby (Rainy Day Press, Box 574, Pohnpei, FM 96941). Gene explores every aspect of Pohnpei, and copies are usually available at souvenir shops and restaurants in Kolonia. Other good local books are *Micronesian Customs and Beliefs* and *Never and Always,* which include fascinating tales told by students at the Community College of Micronesia.

Surprisingly, there's no local newspaper. Guam newspapers, however, are sold at the

Radio station WSZD-AM's big 10-kilowatt transmitter broadcasts from Pohnpei over 1449 kHz.

TRANSPORT

Airport
Pohnpei Airport (PNI) is on Takatik Island, three km northwest of Kolonia. Most of the hotels meet the flights; it's also very easy to hitch a ride across the causeway into town. Two car rental booths, Ellen's Snack Bar, and local handicraft counters open for arrivals and departures. Until construction of the runway here in 1970, all air traffic into Pohnpei was by four-engine "Granny Goose" amphibian utilizing the wartime Japanese seaplane ramp on Lenger Island in the lagoon. Airport departure tax is $5.

Getting There
Continental Air Micronesia touches down four times a week in each direction on its Island Hopper flights between Honolulu and Guam. A total of seven flights a week each way connect Pohnpei to Chuuk and Guam. Three times a week the Air Mike flight calls at Kosrae between Majuro and Pohnpei. Ask about the half-price off-peak midnight flight from Pohnpei to Chuuk and Guam on Fri. nights and Sundays. Reconfirm your onward reservations at the Air Mike office (tel. 320-2424) at the airport upon arrival.

Air Nauru's weekly service to Pohnpei from Nauru (A$238), Kosrae (US$92), Chuuk (US$115), Yap (US$213), and Guam (US$222) is the best connection between Kiribati and anywhere in the South Pacific.

Pacific Missionary Aviation (Box 517, Pohnpei, FM 96941; tel. 320-2796) has an office in their hangar behind the main airport terminal. Their shuttle between Pohnpei and Pingelap ($60 OW) and Mokil ($50 OW) operates on Monday and Friday. The flight between Mokil and Pingelap is $25 OW. You're allowed 22½ kilograms free baggage. Book ahead if possible, as the flights are often full. This company has done commendable work in Micronesia, providing air-sea rescue, medical evacuations, flying health clinics, etc.

An imposing tino *figure from the Polynesian island of Nukuoro, 400 km southwest of Pohnpei. Abstract female images of this kind were draped with flowers and mats during island ceremonies.*

Palm Terrace Hotel. Joan King (Box 1238, Pohnpei, FM 96941) puts out the informative monthly *JK Report on Micronesia,* an independent view of government and business trends in the FSM (annual subscription $70).

The National Union (Box 34, Palikir Station, Pohnpei, FM 96941) is a government newsletter issued twice a month by the Office of the President of the FSM (annual subscription $8).

In late 1991 a new Pohnpei-based carrier appeared. **Caroline Pacific Air** (c/o Village Travel, Box 339, Pohnpei, FM 96941) uses a nine-passenger Beechcraft E-18 to fly twice a week from Pohnpei to Ta Island of Satawan Atoll, Weno in the Chuuk Lagoon, Onoun Island on Namonuito, and back again to Pohnpei the same day.

Field Trips

The **Island Affairs Office** (tel. 320-2710), near the Governor's office behind the Pohnpei legislature, offers two distinct monthly field trips on the MV *Micro Glory*. The four-day eastern trip visits Mokil and Pingelap ($31 cabin RT), while the nine-day southern trip calls at Ngatik, Nukuoro, and Kapinga-marangi ($89 cabin RT). Cabin passengers must also pay $2 pp daily extra for berthing. The ship has seven double cabins, usually booked well in advance; deck fares are about one-third these amounts.

Check with **SeAir Transportation Agency** (tel. 320-2866) downtown for boat tickets to Mokil ($6.24), Pingelap ($9.78), and Kosrae ($18.30). All fares are deck class (no cabins available) and meals are extra.

Boats to the outer islands routinely leave anywhere from 48 hours to a week late. If you're not prepared for this, *take a plane*. Any unpleasantness to the clerks at the shipping agency, the captain, or ship's crew will only spoil things for other travelers who follow.

By Road

Taxis and minibuses around Kolonia or out to the airport charge a flat fare of $1 pp. To Palikir the taxi fare is $2 pp, but to the Village Hotel it's $5 pp even though the distance is about the same. To PATS it's a whopping $30 pp! Just flag down any taxi you see cruising the streets around Kolonia.

Minibuses to Madolenihmw and Kitti are usually found in the lower town around the market or near Ace Commercial Center. On their regular runs these charge about $2 pp to anywhere on the island, and the easiest time to catch them is early morning or late afternoon weekdays. They only leave every couple of hours, so be prepared to wait. The

minibuses don't run all the way around Pohnpei: eastbound they run as far as PATS, westbound as far as Enipein. Other mini-buses run to Sokehs for 50 cents pp.

Hitching on the roads to/from Kolonia isn't too difficult; there's not much traffic, but drivers will take you if they have room. Assume, however, that any pickup truck which stops to give you a ride outside Kolonia will expect you to pay.

Pohnpei Bicycle Rental (tel. 320-2875), on the main street next to Ponape House, rents bicycles for $10 a day.

Car Rentals

About a dozen agencies, large and small, rent cars for $35 and up a day with unlimited mileage. Check the rental time and fuel level marked on your contract before you drive off—and make sure there's a spare tire. Insurance is only sometimes available, so hope that nothing goes wrong! Pickup trucks are better than cars for trips around the island.

Penny Rent a Car (tel. 320-2940), with offices at the airport and near Hifumi Inn, has cars without insurance at $35-45 a day. **Hervis Rent-A-Car** (tel. 320-2784) is also near Hifumi Inn.

Jerry's Car Rental (tel. 330-2769), below the Chinese Embassy near the market, has cars from $40, pickups from $45. **H & E Car Rental** (tel. 330-2413) behind the Australian Embassy nearby is a better bet with cars from $37.50, pickups from $40, tax included (no insurance available).

The **Palm Terrace Hotel** also rents cars at $35, pickups at $40, and they do offer optional collision insurance at $8.50 extra. If they don't have anything, **Micro Car Rental** (tel. 320-2122) nearby has cars for $35, pickups for $45, plus $5-10 for insurance. Also in this area is **PCR Rental** (tel. 320-5252) behind PCR Restaurant with sedans from $40, pickups from $45, $200 deductible collision insurance included.

Speedboats

Speedboats for the islands east of Kolonia (Lenger, Parem, Mwand) leave from the dock near the market. The **Pohnpei Island Transportation Co.**, or PITC (Box 750, Pohnpei, FM 96941; tel. 320-2409) by the Public Market rents a speedboat at $150 per day (gas included) for up to three people (additional persons extra). Take this boat right around Pohnpei, visiting the old Japanese seaplane ramp at Lenger Island, Nan Madol, and Rainbow Island on the way.

If the PITC boat is unavailable, try **Joe Henry** (Box 788, Pohnpei, FM 96941; tel. 320-2339), who lives near the Hifumi Inn. Joe charges about $50 pp (lunch included) for the Nan Madol trip (half an hour at Nan Dowas and a boat ride around the rest).

Mountaineering
A local nonprofit organization, **Micronesia Bound, Inc.** (Aramas Kapw Program, Box 326, Pohnpei, FM 96941; tel. 320-2365), can provide guides for a mountain trek across the center of the island. Prices begin at $100 (two days) and $150 (three days) for two

persons. They also have five- and 14-day expeditions which may include jungle survival training, wilderness treks, "ocean expeditions" (canoe trips—paddling—around the island), camping, community service, etc. A less demanding one-day tour around the island by car including stops at two villages, Sokehs Rock, a waterfall, and a mangrove swamp costs $25 for two people. Their office is next to the Immigration office, not far from the old Spanish wall. This appropriate-technology group deserves your support.

THE OUTER ISLANDS

Fine beaches and excellent scuba diving can be experienced on Pakin and Ant, small atolls just off the west coast of Pohnpei. Numerous seabirds nest on **Ant,** and the diving in the S-shaped pass is superb during slack water (beware strong currents at high and low tides). The 10-unit tourist resort on Nikalap

Sunday school at Pingelap

DAVID STANLEY

Pacific Missionary
Aviation's
nine-passenger
Britten-Norman Islander
STOL (Short Take Off
and Landing) aircraft at
Mokil Atoll

HARVEY A. PACE

Aru, the largest of the 13 islets of Ant, was destroyed by a typhoon but there are plans to rebuild. Ask about trips to Ant at one of the dive shops mentioned above. Yachties must obtain permission from the Nanpei family in Kolonia before visiting.

Ngatik (Sapwuahfik), southwest of Pohnpei, was resettled by Pohnpeians after all the male inhabitants of Ngatik were massacred by the crew of a British whaler in 1837. Only a few people share **Oroluk** atoll with hawksbill and Pacific green sea turtles.

Mokil (Mwoakilloa)

This clean, jewel-like atoll 156 km east of Pohnpei consists of three islands: Coconut, Taro, and Home (where the 305 people live). Lined with coral stones, Main St. runs right down the middle of Home, from the elementary school to the airstrip at the far end. Canoe houses and kitchens line the lagoon side of the road, sleeping houses the ocean side. There's only one store in the village, the MICA—often completely sold out. No dogs are allowed on this island.

The eastern field-trip ship from Pohnpei often calls at Mokil twice, on both the outward and inbound journeys, allowing a stop in between of a couple of days. Camp at the airstrip or ask about accommodations at the Municipal Building. Mokil is mostly for avid snorkelers, as the above-water attractions

are soon exhausted; there's more than enough life in the lagoon to satisfy anyone. Red coral is found washed up on the ocean beaches.

Pingelap

Pingelap, between Pohnpei and Kosrae, is a heavily populated three-island atoll (pop. 840), with a big sunken taro patch *(inipwel)* behind the village. The snorkeling is good off the east end of the airstrip. The wide main island would take several hours to walk around at low tide. At night Jan.-April islanders with hand-held nets catch flying fish attracted by burning torches.

The chief magistrate can arrange accommodations at the Municipal Building, or ask for storekeeper Larry Lundstrum, who sometimes takes in guests. There are several small stores on Pingelap.

Polynesian Islands

The people of Nukuoro and Kapingamarangi atolls are Polynesians. There are 42 tiny islands on the **Nukuoro** reef but most of the 450 people live on the largest, a third of which is planted with taro.

Although 33 islets comprise **Kapingamarangi** atoll, 586 km southwest of Pohnpei, the population lives on the adjacent islets of Touhou and Ueru, which are linked by a concrete bridge. Tiny Touhou, which you can walk right around in 10 minutes, houses the majority. The homes are arranged in clusters, each of which belongs to a different family. Yachts require a pilot to enter the lagoon, where an American plane and a Japanese ship lie sub-merged. The overwater toilets are a quaint part of Kapinga. Recently Kapingamarangi has been hit by a leprosy epidemic, which may eventually reach in some form 40% of the island's 577 inhabitants.

STATE OF CHUUK

INTRODUCTION

One thousand km southeast of Guam, the 127-square-km State of Chuuk (known as Truk until 1990) consists of 11 high, man-grove-fringed volcanic islands in the sap-phire-blue Chuuk lagoon, and a series of 14 outlying atolls and low islands. The Chuuk lagoon covers 2,129 square km and is 64 km across at its widest point. Circled by one of the largest and longest (225 km) barrier reefs in the world, this lagoon holds a captive fleet of half-submerged mountain peaks, as well as over 70 brooding purple sunken hulks, remnants of WW II.

CHUUK'S CLIMATE

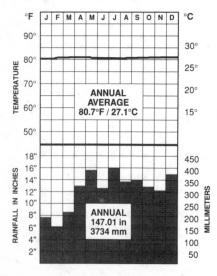

While reef-locked islands in the lagoon compete with Pohnpei's lush peaks, the state's outer-island groups (the Halls, West-erns, and Upper and Lower Mortlocks) close-ly resemble the palm-and-sand atolls of the Marshalls. Thus there are three aspects of Chuuk for the visitor to experience: Weno (formerly Moen), the state administrative center; the islands in the Chuuk lagoon; and the outlying atolls—in all, some 290 islands to choose from.

Chuuk is one of the least explored corners of Micronesia. Almost all tourists to Chuuk come only to scuba dive. They're taken straight from the airport to the Continental Hotel or onto dive boats, and unless you're one of them you won't see all those white faces again until you're checking in for your next flight.

Thus Chuuk, more than any other FSM state, is a land of adventure. There are many opportunities to escape to the outliers. Speedboats and *yamma* boats leave con-stantly for islands around the lagoon and there are several departures a week to more remote outer islands. For budget travelers willing to rough it this is definitely the way to go, as the standard tourist accommodations on Weno are expensive.

Wartime Chuuk
Before WW II Chuuk was the main Japa-nese naval base in the Central Pacific. Al-though in 1942 the emphasis shifted to Ra-baul, 1,500 km due south, Chuuk remained the "Gibraltar of the Pacific," protected by the encircling reef and giant guns in caves and tunnels guarding the passes. Most of the entrenched firepower was taken off ob-solete cruisers and battleships and posi-

tioned on the hillsides. The Japanese had four airstrips at Chuuk: two on Weno and one each on Etten and Parem.

On 17 Feb. 1944, the U.S. unleashed Operation Hailstone, one of the most incisive aerial attacks in history. For two days and a night, aircraft from nine carriers hammered the islands in 30 waves. Submarines posted outside the passes caught fleeing vessels. Japan lost 250 planes, nearly 60 vessels, and thousands of men, compared to a U.S. loss of only 26 aircraft. The 180,000 tons of shipping sunk set a two-day WW II record.

This defeat would have been even more devastating, except for an American reconnaissance flight over the lagoon on 4 Feb. which tipped the Japanese off to the impending attack. On 10 Feb. all the Japanese war-

ships present (including a battleship, two aircraft carriers, five heavy and four light cruisers, and 20 destroyers) were withdrawn to Belau. Most of the wrecks in the lagoon are merchant ships converted to war use.

The 45,000 Japanese survivors on Chuuk were bypassed as the U.S. forces moved on to capture Saipan, and both Japanese and Chuukese suffered famine due to an American blockade. In 1946 the U.S. Navy established a base on Weno, which has been the administrative center ever since.

Economy

Aside from government jobs, it's nearly impossible to find work in Chuuk. In 1991 the state government was $6 million in debt and massive doses of U.S. aid money seemed to

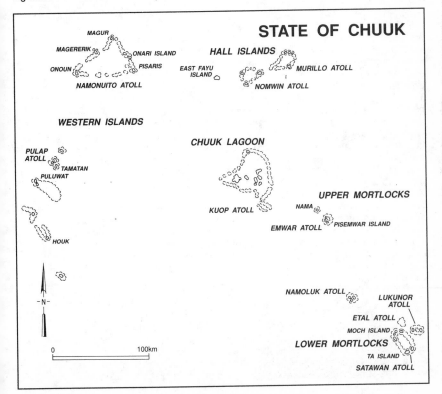

evaporate upon arrival as educational, health, and other public services languished. Power outages are frequent. Nepotism reigns in Chuuk and there's a local saying *ke pach, ke tento* which translates roughly "it's not what you know but who you know." Many local officials have done very well out of self-government, but Chuuk remains as dependent as ever. There are few Filipino laborers here.

The People
Of the 98,071 inhabitants of the FSM, some 47,871 live in the State of Chuuk. Weno, the administrative and commercial center, accounts for 15,253 of these; another 23,088 live on other islands in the Chuuk lagoon. The Hall and Morgan islands to the north and south of Chuuk proper are closely related in language and customs. The Western Islands, however, have always been remote.

On the outer islands most people live in compact villages with the rest of the land used for coconut plantations or taro patches. Breadfruit is the subsistence crop in Chuuk. The most unusual local food is *oppot,* ripe breadfruit buried up to a year in a banana leaf-lined pit *(nas)* before being removed, kneaded, cooked, and served. *Oppot* was kept for the months when fresh breadfruit was not available or to eat on long canoe journeys. The pungent taste is catching and memorable.

The Chuukese love potion or magic perfume *(omung)* is difficult to obtain, but highly effective. The strongest *omung* comes from outer islands such as Satawan in the Lower Mortlocks. Care must be taken as improper use can lead to madness and hysteria. Chuukese magic can also be used as a curse, a form of protection, or a way of exorcising evil spirits.

Chuuk is well known among sociologists for its high suicide rate, the subject of many noted studies by a local priest, Rev. Francis X. Hezel, S.J. Most of the victims are males aged 15 to 24 who seemed to have felt shamed in the eyes of their families. Father Hezel has shown how rapid social change combined with alcohol has magnified an "anger" too often expressed in this way.

Anthropological studies of Micronesia often portray the Chuukese as cantankerous or aggressive in comparison with other Micronesians. From the visitors' point of view this is rather unfair; you'll probably find the Chuukese as helpful as any Micronesians, so don't believe everything you read! Be aware, however, that many hikes around Chuuk involve crossing private property. This isn't usually a problem as visitors interested in hiking are rare. Just ask directions of any adults you meet, then ask if it's okay to continue. There are a couple of places on Weno where you're required to pay a fee to visit a place and these are noted below (please let us know if you encounter others). The Chuukese tend to be a little slow, so be patient.

The Chuukese are very friendly, so smile and say hello to everyone you meet. *Ran annim* is Chuukese for "good day."

Crafts
The people on the outer islands make fine handicrafts, such as the *tapwanu* masks of the Mortlocks, the only masks made in Micronesia. Representing a benevolent spirit, these masks were worn at dances to ward off typhoons, or used to ornament the gable of the men's house. Originally carved from the wood of the breadfruit tree, they're now made from lighter hibiscus wood and have been rechristened "devil masks."

Also unique are the Chuuk love sticks and war clubs. At one time every Chuukese male had an individually designed love stick. Love sticks were up to four meters long, so the young man could thrust the object through the wall of a hut and reach the girl of his affections, who might be sleeping on the other side of the room. He would then entangle her hair in the long stick and tug to wake her. She would know by the feel of the stick whose it was; if she pulled it inside the hut he could enter; if she shook it she was coming outside; and if she pushed it out, he was rejected. Since few houses on Chuuk are constructed of pandanus anymore, love sticks are no longer used.

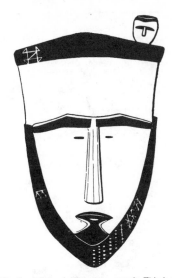

Mortlock Islands' Tapwanu mask: This is the only type of mask known in Micronesia, and may once have ornamented the gable of a men's house. Carved from the wood of the breadfruit tree, it was thought to protect the fruit of that tree during storms.

The frightening wooden war bludgeons and shark tooth-studded knuckle-dusters of Chuuk were designed for less romantic encounters. Handbags, baskets, trays, stools, wall hangings, *lava lava,* and grass skirts complete the crafts scene. Note that many nontraditional objects, such as carved faces and storyboards, are sold. Try to stick to the traditional items.

Health
The lack of proper toilets and a safe, dependable water supply led to a serious cholera outbreak in 1982-83. The danger seems to be over, but still take a little extra care in Chuuk. Don't drink tap water without boiling or chemically purifying it. Keep clean. The quaint overwater outhouses *(benjos)* introduced by the Japanese are still a feature of Chuuk.

SIGHTS OF WENO

Weno is one of the dirtiest islands in Micronesia, with lots of trash scattered along the roads and the heavy smell of urine or human excrement occasionally in the air. The commercial center stretches along the west shore of Weno to beyond the port; Nantaku, the administrative center of Chuuk State, is on the saddle road headed east. Dense forests and grasslands fill the interior of this, the second-largest island in the lagoon. The view from Weno across the lagoon with the sun setting behind the Tol Group can be outstandingly beautiful.

Begin with the **Chuuk Ethnographic Exhibition Center**, accessible from the Chuuk Visitors Bureau, upstairs in the building next to the Japanese war memorial near the center of town (open weekdays 0800-1700, admission $1.50). Here you'll see *tapwanu* "devil masks" of hibiscus wood, *fenai* love sticks of mangrove wood, *tor lava lava* skirts of hibiscus fiber, model canoes, war clubs, fish traps, war relics, and other crafts. The exhibits are nicely labeled.

Western Weno
A big **Japanese gun** is in a tunnel dubbed "Nefo Cave" just a short walk up from the Governor's residence at Nantaku. Follow the road due south from the courthouse as far as a large, green water tank. The tunnel is 50 meters to the right. There's an excellent view of Weno center and the lagoon from here.

The Japanese had an airstrip at **South Field,** the level area just east of the Truk Continental Hotel. A **coconut-processing plant** now graces the vast concrete platform that sloped into the lagoon to permit seaplane traffic. Inside you can see how soap, body oil, and even shampoo are made from copra. Also drop into the Continental Hotel to enjoy the superb lagoon view.

Roads run along the north and west sides of Weno. It's a leisurely three-hour walk on a level footpath along the southeast coast between the ends of these roads. East-

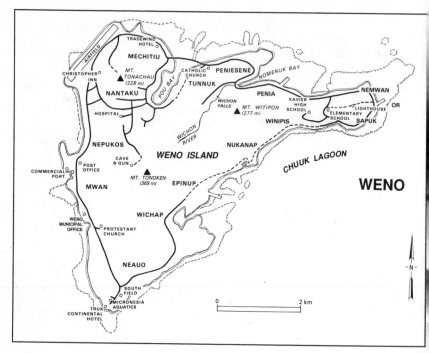

bound you get a good view of grassy Mt. Witipon. There's a beach at **Nukanap**: stop for a swim.

Northern Weno

To climb to the grassy summit of **Mt. Tonachau** (228 meters), take the road beside the rock crusher near the airport up as far as the U.S. Air Force Civic Action Team (C.A.T.) headquarters. The overgrown trail follows the power lines that run up the ridge just before the "Cat House." It's a stiff climb which can be slippery near the top and high sharp grass on the slopes forces you to stay on the trail. Bring your camera. One story explains that Tonachau is a great octopus whose arms once stretched across the lagoon; another claims the hero Soukatau brought the great basalt knob atop Tonachau with him from Kosrae. Soukatau's son, Souwoniras, built his *wuut* (meetinghouse) on the mountain.

The ranking Catholic bishop assigned to the Caroline and Marshall islands resides at **Tunnuk**. The library of the Micronesian Seminar next to Tunnuk Catholic Church is open to the public. At **Fairo** village on the lagoon near Tunnuk is a traditional *wuut* built by Puluwat islanders in 1990 as a community center, with support from the Micronesian Institute. A canoe house stands alongside.

To reach the small yet attractive **Wichon Falls** and swimming hole on the northeast side of Weno, walk about 600 meters up a dirt road from Peniesene and ask directions—it's unmarked. You'll see a cross-section of village life along the way.

Eastern Weno

Near the east end of Weno is **Xavier High School,** once a fortified Japanese radio communications center, as the thickness of the cement walls and the steel hatches on the

a bombed-out Japanese freighter off Weno

windows attest. After the war the Jesuits purchased the building for $1,000 and made it into the best four-year high school in Micronesia, with students from throughout the region. The view of the lagoon from the roof is excellent.

An abandoned **Japanese lighthouse** *(totai)* in reasonably good condition stands on the highest point of the Sapuk Peninsula. Get there by following a footpath from the elementary school near Xavier High School, or from Or village to the east. Someone claiming to be the lighthouse owner may ask $1-2 pp at Or, which is fair enough, but pay only after you're shown the way up to the lighthouse. Ownership of the lighthouse is in dispute and you may be asked for money more than once. The fine view from the lighthouse makes it worth the nuisance.

Just below, at the bottom of the slope to the northeast, are several huge **200 mm naval guns** off an Italian armored cruiser (purchased by Argentina and sold to Japan) in big metal housings. One bears the imprint "Stabilimento Armstrong Pozzuoli 1902." These guns point straight out toward Northeast Pass. Looking at these fearsome weapons you'll appreciate what a wise decision it was to bomb by plane, then bypass Chuuk in 1944.

The Sunken Japanese Fleet

Without doubt, Chuuk has the greatest assortment of Japanese war wreckage of any Pacific island. Giant naval guns poke out from hoary caverns on almost every lagoon island, while a ghost fleet of 180,000 tons of Japanese ships and 270 planes litter the shallow lagoon bed. Little was salvaged from the wartime air strikes; almost all the wrecks lie as they sank, most of them around Tonoas and Fefan. Now shrouded in murky waters and huge soft corals, they form the largest manmade reef in the world.

Sixty ships went down during the 1944 air strike; 40 more from other attacks also lie here. Among the most important wrecks are the *Shinkoku Maru,* a 153-meter oil tanker standing eerily upright just 12 meters down, covered with heavy marine growth; night dives are possible here. The *Yamagiri Maru* is a 134-meter munitions ship loaded with 18-inch shells, now in 15 to 34 meters of water. The holds of the *San Francisco Maru,* in 50 meters of water, are packed with mines and trucks, while three light tanks rest on deck.

The *Dai Na Hino Maru,* between Fefan and Uman islands, is accessible to snorkelers. The 150-meter *Aikoku Maru* was blown in half by an American dive-bomber, itself destroyed in the explosion. The largest wreck in the lagoon, the *Heian Maru,* a 160-meter submarine tender, lies 15 meters down. The stern mast of the *Fujikawa Maru,* a 133-meter aircraft ferry still containing Zero planes, sticks right out of the water just south of Etten—a great dive.

A 113-meter munition ship, the *Sankisan Maru,* full of 50 mm ammunition, is covered with soft coral formations 15 meters down. Submarine I-169 *Shinohara* was lost because someone forgot to close the storm ventilation valve in the bridge when the 100-meter sub dove to avoid a U.S. air raid in April 1944. A number of submerged Japanese planes off Etten can also be visited.

June to Sept. are the calmest months in the lagoon, with all wrecks accessible, al-

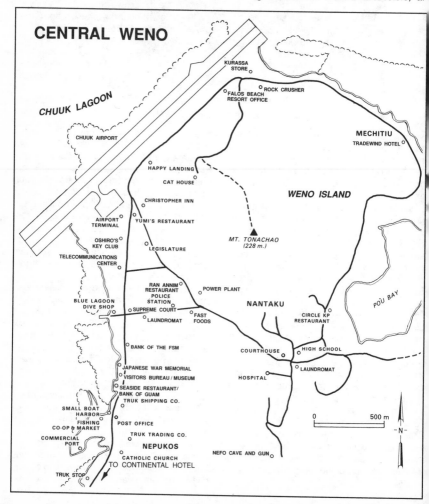

CENTRAL WENO

KURASSA STORE

ROCK CRUSHER

FALOS BEACH RESORT OFFICE

CHUUK LAGOON

CHUUK AIRPORT

MECHITIU
TRADEWIND HOTEL

HAPPY LANDING

CAT HOUSE

WENO ISLAND

CHRISTOPHER INN

AIRPORT TERMINAL

YUMI'S RESTAURANT

OSHIRO'S KEY CLUB

LEGISLATURE

MT. TONACHAO (228 m.)

TELECOMMUNICATIONS CENTER

RAN ANNIM RESTAURANT
POLICE STATION

POWER PLANT

BLUE LAGOON DIVE SHOP

SUPREME COURT

NANTAKU

POÜ BAY

LAUNDROMAT
FAST FOODS

CIRCLE KP RESTAURANT

BANK OF THE FSM

COURTHOUSE

HIGH SCHOOL

JAPANESE WAR MEMORIAL
VISITORS BUREAU / MUSEUM

LAUNDROMAT

SEASIDE RESTAURANT/ BANK OF GUAM

HOSPITAL

TRUK SHIPPING CO.

SMALL BOAT HARBOR

FISHING CO-OP & MARKET

POST OFFICE

COMMERCIAL PORT

TRUK TRADING CO.

0   500 m

NEPUKOS

NEFO CAVE AND GUN

CATHOLIC CHURCH
TO CONTINENTAL HOTEL

TRUK STOP

—N—

though visibility is better the rest of the year. (Micronesia Aquatics recommends Sept., Oct., Feb., and March as the best months for diving here.) To discourage souvenir hunters, all wrecks have been declared parts of an Underwater Historical Monument.

PRACTICALITIES

Accommodations

Hotel accommodations on Weno are expensive and sometimes full. Many lodgings fill up with people on government contracts who stay a long time—this also boosts prices. There are no hotels or guesthouses in Chuuk State beyond Weno, and arranging an overnight stay on an outer island involves either trying to make a contact through someone on the main island or just going blindly in the hope that something will materialize once you get there. On the outer islands local mayors can arrange stays.

The commercial **Christopher Inn** (Box 37, Chuuk, FM 96942; tel. 330-2652), a three-story concrete building near the airport, charges $47 s, $52 d, $61 t for an a/c room with fridge and private bath. As you come out of the air terminal look left across the street to the three-story building marked Stop 'n Shop. The atmosphere is a lot better here than at the tourist-oriented Continental Hotel described below but beware of rooms without windows—ask for a room on the back side of the building. There's a central common lounge where you can sit and watch videos while sipping coffee or soft drinks.

Truk Travel Unlimited (Box 546, Chuuk, FM 96942; tel. 330-2701 or 330-4232) offers four comfortable apartments with TV, fridge, and cooking facilities above their office on the south side of town at $55 s, $61 d, $72 t. They also have a package deal for a room and rental car together for $85 ($75 daily if you stay over five nights). The office is only open weekdays during regular office hours. If you arrive at another time ask if there's anyone from the motel at the airport. This place is locally known as the **"Truk Stop"**.

Several other small places around Weno rent rooms with cooking facilities above retail stores, but their charges are about the same as those of Christopher Inn and they're far less convenient. Rooms are usually unavailable anyway. At $50 s or d they're all grossly overpriced. In this category are the **Tradewind Hotel** (Box 329, Chuuk, FM 96942; tel. 330-2277), above K.S. Pisipis Restaurant on the north coast road two km east of the airport, and the six apartments above **Kurassa Store** (Box 64, Chuuk, FM 96942; tel. 330-4355).

Seaside Restaurant (Box 100, Chuuk, FM 96942; tel. 330-2445) opposite the Bank of Guam has a couple of rooms with shared bath at $25 pp, but they aren't very interested in having you.

Ask around the small boat harbor opposite the post office for rooms to rent by the month. Add 10% room tax to all of the above rates.

Resort Hotels

The pretentious, unfriendly **Truk Continental Hotel** (Box 340, Chuuk, FM 96942; tel. 330-2727), owned and operated by Continental Airlines, charges $98 s, $107 d, $154 t. All 56 rooms in this rambling, two-story, Hawaiian-style luxury resort (opened 1970) have individual balconies. It's rather rundown, often without hot water, but beautifully set in a coconut grove on the beach at the southwest corner of Weno. The hotel staff is rather dull and you may have to repeat yourself several times in order to communicate. The Continental charges $7 pp each way for airport transfers or just walk out onto the road beside the terminal and flag down any southbound taxi, which will take you directly to the hotel for $1 pp. Most packaged tourists are taken straight from the airport to the Continental and only leave the hotel grounds to go out on dive boats around the lagoon. You seldom see them in town and never on the outer islands. Due to the lack of alternatives the Continental is often full, so book ahead if you're sure you want to stay there.

Falos Beach Resort (Kachutosy O. Paulus, Box 494, Chuuk, FM 96942; tel. 330-2606), on a lagoon island surrounded by a white-sand beach, is about 25 minutes from Weno by boat ($10 RT). The 10 tin-roofed cottages cost $39 s, $50 d, $61 t. Couples can take a single room with one bed for the single rate. Barbecue facilities and picnic huts dot the grounds, plus a kitchen with running water, sink, kerosene stove, and cooking utensils. A store at the resort sells cup noodles, tinned food, beer, and handicrafts; still it's best to bring food and bottled water with you. A snack bar serves fast food and alcoholic drinks, but only when groups are present. To get to the island contact Vincent and Brothers Enterprises next to Island Mart by the airstrip, very near the rock crusher. Even if you don't stay, Falos makes a great outing: a day tour costs $45 for two people, lunch not included. Admission to the island is $2.50 pp. Several readers have written in recommending this place.

Food
Unlike accommodations, food is readily available and inexpensive on Weno. The **Roof Garden Restaurant** on the third floor at Christopher Inn is not unreasonable; the **Rainbow Coffee Shop** downstairs has a lunch special ($4) but isn't quite as good. **Yumi's Restaurant** opposite the airport has Filipino dishes.

About the cheapest and friendliest place on Weno is the **Ran Annim Restaurant**—the place beside the bakery between Christopher Inn and the police station. There's no sign, so ask. Don't be put off by the ramshackle appearance—this place serves some of the best food in Micronesia. It's very popular among local hamburgermunching Peace Corps volunteers. It closes around 1900.

Fast Foods across the street from the police station is actually a self-service cafeteria with very reasonable prices. It's good for breakfast.

The **Seaside Restaurant** opposite Susumu's Store is a nice place to stop for coffee. If you eat here stick to the sashimi or Spanish omelettes and avoid the meat dishes. Check the menu carefully before ordering, as the pricing is illogical.

The expensive **Takarajima Japanese Restaurant** is on the road to the Continental Hotel.

Entertainment
Prohibition of a sort has existed on Weno since 1977. The island women got tired of their men spending all their money drinking then coming home and beating them up, so the governor's wife led a campaign for a referendum to vote liquor out. The loophole however, was that as some outer islands were still "wet," and since all imported beverages had to be off-loaded at Weno, it was no coincidence that a lot of beer and liquor was available locally at bootleg prices. Large quantities were consumed on "government picnics" to uninhabited lagoon islands.

Things have opened up a lot since those heady days and you now have the usual choice of licensed speakeasies on Weno (but not on the outer islands). Beer is still harder to find in supermarkets than elsewhere in Micronesia and prices are high. Public drinking is actively discouraged by the police, though you'll often see small groups crowded around a pickup helping themselves from a case or two, tossing the empty cans into the bush one after another.

Official drinkers are required to hold permits ($6), which are sold at the police station, but tourists staying under two weeks are exempt. Bars on Weno operate as private clubs to which only members are admitted, although tourists are quickly ushered in as special guests. They're all closed Sundays.

Oshiro's Bar (tel. 330-4239), right next to the big satellite dish near the airport, is one of the safest places for a cold one, as the owner watches out for his customers. Other local bars include **Naporu** directly behind the post office, **Black Magic** beside ASA Wholesalers just south of the commercial harbor, the **Key Club**, and **Happy Landing** near the airport.

Sports and Recreation
Chuuk offers some of the best WW II shipwreck diving in the Pacific. It's great, but compared to reef diving there's limited visibil-

ity and a lack of natural beauty. To see lots of fish (and small sharks), ask to be taken out to one of the reef passages for a dive, as well as to the wrecks. All scuba divers (but not snorkelers) must pay $3 for the mandatory Chuuk State Diving Permit.

Micronesia Aquatics (Clark Graham, Box 57, Chuuk, FM 96942; tel. 330-2204) has been offering reliable scuba services since 1974. Diving is $45 pp (one tank) or $65 pp (two tanks), snorkeling from the boat $30 pp. Divers should bring their own buoyancy compensator, regulator, and tank pressure gauge, plus other standard equipment. A certification card is required. This company also offers water skiing ($45 an hour pp) and windsurfing lessons ($25). Rental of windsurfing equipment is $10 an hour. If you're staying at the Continental ask Clark to find you a guide for a hike up Mt. Witipon, where many Japanese guns and fortifications remain from WW II. His office is just inside the gate of Continental Hotel—recommended.

If you're staying at Christopher Inn **The Blue Lagoon Dive Shop** (Gradvin K. Aisek, Box 429, Chuuk, FM 96942; tel. 330-2796) is more convenient and prices are similar. Gradvin's father, Kimiuo Aisek, an Operation Hailstone eyewitness who located many of the lagoon wrecks, founded this company in 1973.

If you only want to snorkel, go to the small boat harbor and bargain for someone to take you to one of the many wrecks off Tonoas. Make sure they know of a wreck in shallow water; this way four people can go for about $30.

Two live-aboard dive boats, the SS *Thorfinn* and the *Truk Aggressor,* also service visiting scuba divers. At $275 a day (accommodation, meals, and diving included) it's more expensive than staying at a hotel and diving with the two companies mentioned above, but you get almost unlimited diving and much time is saved by not having to shuttle back and forth from the dive sites. Passage on these boats must be booked ahead, either through one of the scuba wholesalers listed in the introduction to this book or by contacting **Seaward Holidays Micronesia Inc.** (Box DX, Weno, Chuuk, FM 96942; tel. 691-330-4302) or **Aggressor Fleet** (Drawer K, Morgan City, LA 70381-000K U.S.A.; tel. 504-385-2416).

Shopping
Sundance Tours beside the Truk Stop sells baskets, fans, wall hangings, coasters, shell necklaces, T-shirts, love sticks, and woodcarvings. Beware of the black coral and turtle shell products sold here, which are prohibited entry to Guam. Handicrafts can also be purchased at Yumi's Restaurant opposite the airport and the **Small Industries Center** near the Truk Trading Company.

Attractive FSM first-day covers are sold at the post office. Both Blue Lagoon Dive Shop and Micronesia Aquatics sell Chuuk T-shirts. Camera film with a recent date is usually available at the Continental Hotel (but it's expensive).

The **Chuuk Coconut Authority** (Box JQ, Chuuk, FM 96942; fax 330-2777) on Weno produces Misimisi body oil, Tirow suntan oil, Saram shampoo, and Afata bath soap from local copra. These quality products are exported worldwide and the factory adjacent to the Truk Continental Hotel can be visited.

Three percent sales tax is added to all sticker prices in Chuuk.

Services
The Bank of Guam (tel. 330-2331; open Mon.-Thurs. 1000-1500, Fri. 1000-1600) and the Bank of the FSM (tel. 330-2353; open Mon.-Thurs. 0830-1430, Fri. 0830-1600) both have branches on Weno. You'll encounter much shorter lines at the Bank of the FSM and they'll cash U.S. dollar traveler's checks, but only the Bank of Guam will change foreign currencies.

Place long-distance phone calls at the Telecommunications Center (open 24 hours) near the airport. It's $2.50 a minute (three-minute minimum) to call the U.S. or Guam (slightly cheaper on Sunday).

The Chuuk hospital is a place you go to die.

Information

The Chuuk Visitors Bureau (Box FQ, Chuuk, FM 96942; tel. 330-4133; open weekdays 0800-1700), upstairs beside the Chuuk Ethnographic Exhibition Center, has a few maps and leaflets and is a good place to ask questions. They also sell William H. Stewart's *Dive Map of the Ghost Fleet of the Truk Lagoon* ($3.50). The staff here can arrange for you to stay as a paying guest with families on outer islands.

There's an excellent library at the Micronesian Seminar in the Catholic Mission (Box 250, Chuuk, FM 96942; tel. 330-2313). Guam newspapers are sold around town.

There's a sizable Peace Corps contingent in Chuuk and they're knowledgeable about almost everything, should you get a chance to talk.

Radio station WSZC-AM broadcasts from Chuuk over 1593 kHz.

TRANSPORT

Airport

Chuuk International Airport (TKK) is less than two km north of the business center on Weno. A small counter serves cold drinks and coffee at flight times. The only phone at the airport is a card phone (no coins). To get a taxi from the airport turn left as you leave the terminal and walk out into the main street where they pass frequently during daylight hours. The high security fence around the airport terminal is locked at night, so forget trying to crash here if you arrive late from some outer island. Reconfirm your onward flight at the Air Mike office (tel. 330-2424) at the airport (open daily 0800-1700). There's a $10 departure tax.

Getting There

Continental Air Micronesia's Island Hopper calls at Chuuk four times a week on its way between Honolulu and Guam. There are three additional weekly flights to Pohnpei and Guam only. All through passengers must change planes in Honolulu or Guam. Air Mike offers cheaper off-peak fares on certain flights, for example from Chuuk to Pohnpei on Wed. Fri. and Sun. nights. This flight is often late but fares are nearly half the regular price.

In July 1991 **Air Nauru** began a weekly service to Chuuk from Nauru (US$245), Kosrae (US$184), Pohnpei (US$115), Yap (US$130), and Guam (US$153). In Guam there are onward Air Nauru flights to Manila and in Nauru one can connect for Kiribati and all points in the South Pacific.

Since late 1991 **Caroline Pacific Air** has flights twice a week from Chuuk to Onoun, Ta Island of Satawan, and Pohnpei. **Pacific Missionary Aviation** occasionally flies to Onoun from Yap. These services are still in a state of flux, so inquire locally.

Field Trips

The field-trip ships *Micro Trader* and *Micro Dawn* depart Weno approximately every two weeks on a week-long journey along one of four different routes: Upper Mortlocks, Lower Mortlocks, Hall Islands, or Western Islands. The trip to the Westerns is the best, but it only goes once a month at most. There are basically three types of trips: medical evacuations, trips to pick up or drop off high-school students, and regular field trips. On the latter the boat becomes a sailing supermarket selling supplies to the inhabitants of all the islands it visits.

Schedules don't matter much on these trips as the ship can be diverted at any time for emergency evacuations, etc. The ships usually leave in late afternoon but they're often delayed until the next day at the last minute, even after the ship is fully loaded and all the passengers are aboard. In this case everyone has to get off and find somewhere else to spend the night. As a general rule the ship will leave a day or two late and get back a couple of days later than expected.

Passage costs 5 cents a km deck, 16 cents a km cabin (plus $2 a night for berthing). The *Micro Trader* has eight two-berth cabins but government officials have priority on these subsidized trips. Even though you may have been promised a cabin you can't really be sure you actually have one until just before the ship leaves, as they're not assigned earlier. Even once you're underway you may be asked to give up your cabin in case of medical need. You can always travel deck.

Meals are provided at $13 a day for all three. Passengers take meals with the ship's officers, and although the food is overpriced by local restaurant standards you get to meet the crew and pick up morsels of useful information along with what you get on your plate. There's no obligation to take every meal (you only pay for those you consume). Take along a good supply of food of your own and bottled water, and get a cabin if at all possible as the local color of deck passage will wear off completely after a couple of nights. The Chuukese have no environmental consciousness at all—all aluminum or plastic trash is immediately thrown over the side.

The ship usually stops at each island on its route for a couple of hours and you're free to go in on the ship's boat for a look around. In rough weather it can be dicey landing on some islands through the crashing surf. Take along a couple of packs of cigarettes to give to people who show you around their islands.

For field trip information check with the **Transportation Office** (tel. 330-2592) in the warehouse beside the commercial port, as only they can give definite information on cabin availability. The **Truk Shipping Company** (Box 669, Chuuk, FM 96942; tel. 330-2455), upstairs in the back of the two-story building opposite the gasoline station beside the small-boat harbor, sells deck-class tickets and is a good place to make initial inquiries about departures. The field trips are a great experience, not to be missed if you have the opportunity and time.

Other Boats
Smaller municipal boats make more frequent trips from Weno to the outer islands, for example the *Ik No. 3* to Kuttu in the Lower Mortlocks, the *Ik No. 1* to Puluwat, the *Toku* to Tamatam, and the *Fuun Matau* to Pulap. The large motor vessel *Miss Nama* sails to Nama twice a week, leaving Weno Tues. and Fri. afternoons (four hours, $5 OW), and there are similar services to Losap and Pis. There are many others.

Some of the above are actually fishing boats owned by the outer islands themselves and these offer no comforts or safety standards at all. That shouldn't discourage real adventurers, though.

Inside The Chuuk Lagoon
Small boats to the lagoon islands can be found at the small boat harbor opposite the post office, or at the landing across from the Truk Trading Company. Serving commuters who work, shop, or sell their produce on Weno, they leave the lagoon islands in the early morning and depart for the return trip in the afternoon. All of the wooden *yamma* boats which are based in remote villages operate this way—backwards if you're planning a day-trip from Weno.

Finding a village *yamma* boat ($2 OW) to Fefan, Uman, Parem, Udot, or Tol is usually no problem, but you must spend at least one night on each island. Tol is the farthest away, so boats going there leave earlier. Different boats serve the east and west sides of Fefan, and there are several routes to Tol: be sure to clarify exactly where they're going. A few larger boats do make day-trips from Weno, however, departing around 0600, so ask around.

Also ask about barges and cruisers to Tonoas (there are no *yammas*). Tonoas is so close to Weno that most people come over in private outboards in the morning and return about 1500 in the afternoon. For a ride to Tonoas, inquire at the landings mentioned above and offer to share the gas (maybe $2 pp). Since Tonoas has no hotels, some boat owners may hesitate to take you if they think you'll expect them to provide free accommodations on the island. You could get around this by explaining that you'll be camping, or ask if they know of anyone willing to accommodate a paying guest. About $10 pp a night would be fair.

Unfortunately the number of *yamma* boats is declining due to the increasing number of private fiberglass speedboats with four-horsepower Yamaha outboard motors bought with FSM government "fisheries" loans. Weekdays you can see long lines of them tied up in the small-boat harbor or beside the Seaside Restaurant. From a plane you can see large numbers of them plowing across the lagoon. Hitching a ride on one of those should be no problem.

By Road

Weno has one of the best public transportation systems in the Pacific. By day, pickups with taxi signs in the front windows continually cruise the roads, so getting around is cheap and easy. These shared taxis charge 50 cents pp within the town area, $1 pp to Sapuk or the Continental. At night everything stops running, but hitching is easy then.

Rental cars from **VJ Car Rental** (tel. 330-2652) at Christopher Inn are $30 a day plus 13% tax (no mileage charge). **Truk Travel Unlimited** (tel. 330-2701 or 330-4232) has older cars at $35 a day, newer cars at $40-45 a day, plus 13% tax. **Jerry Car Rental** (tel.

330-2487) at the Truk Trading Company has new cars for rent at $35 a day. Considering the excellent taxi service it's not really necessary to rent a car on Weno.

The Continental Hotel will rent mopeds to guests.

ISLANDS IN THE CHUUK LAGOON

Tonoas

From the look of it today, it's hard to believe that Tonoas, the Japanese Natsu Shima or Summer Island, once housed the largest Japanese naval installation outside the home islands. As you walk around the island, however, plenty of evidence surfaces: wrecked buildings, melted oil tanks, an abandoned Japanese hospital, piers, and torn-up railway tracks.

In 1814 a Spaniard, Manuel Dublon, arrived to collect bêche-de-mer and from that

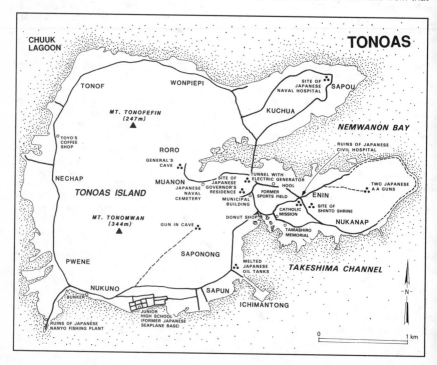

time until the official change back to the original Tonoas in 1990 the island was called Dublon (a name still in common use).

In 1899 the Germans made Tonoas the base for the copra trade. Here too the Japanese built their Chuukese capital, Tokyo, centering on the area between the present Municipal Building and Catholic Mission. Until late 1946 thousands of Japanese prisoners were held on Tonoas awaiting repatriation to Japan. The overcrowding forced the U.S. Navy to build their base on Weno, which has been the administration center ever since.

Most of the worthwhile sights on Tonoas are marked on this book's map. Don't miss the old **Japanese seaplane base** (now the junior high school), with its vast fields of concrete sloping into the lagoon, bomb shelters, and view of the old airstrip on **Etten.** You could even snorkel across to Etten, which is shaped like an aircraft carrier.

A new, $2.2 million American wharf called **Ichimantong** juts out into the lagoon on the south side of Tonoas, within sight of the crumbling remains of a Japanese dock built 40 years earlier. The U.S. wharf is intended to support a freezer and fisheries complex built by the Japanese government.

Two **Japanese antiaircraft guns** are at the top of the peninsula beyond the hospital ruins, but you'll need a guide to find them. Some try to charge $2 pp to visit the hospital itself, which is a bit of a joke!

The most unusual sight on Tonoas is a little out of the way and generally overlooked. It's the **General's Cave**—actually a network of tunnels beginning right beside the road at Roro. Still used as a typhoon shelter, the cave can easily accommodate the entire population of Tonoas. Bring a flashlight and go right under the hill, out the other side, then climb up on top and find your way down to the nearby Protestant Church.

Across the road from the church are two meeting halls. The one nearest the water is the **Hall of the Magic Chickens.** Once upon a time an ancient sorcerer called all the chickens of Tonoas together and had them level the top of the hill behind the church in a single night. Even today it's said that anyone who eats chicken in this hall will assume fowl characteristics, plus other terrifying consequences. Also because of this legend, most people on Tonoas would rather starve than eat a local chicken (imported chickens are okay).

Fefan

Fefan, with a profile like that of a floating woman, is a center for market gardening and handicrafts. Most of the boats from Weno stop at Mesa on the east side. From Sako Store at Fason, just south of Mesa wharf, hike up to the center of the island along an old Japanese road which leads to Unufouchy, where five large **Japanese naval guns** congregate and afford fine views.

After visiting the guns continue down the other side of Fefan to Saporanong on the west coast. Many other Japanese guns still sit in caves on the sides of Fefan's mountains, such as those above Inaka. You can see these if you're very keen. Easier to get to are the three small **field guns** near the road just north of Mesa wharf.

As elsewhere in Chuuk, the guns are a good excuse to go hiking and a way of meeting people as you ask directions, as well as being an end in themselves. Some Chuukese, however, are puzzled at their visitors' interest in a period they would rather forget.

You can walk right around the island on the coastal road in about five hours; to do so is to experience a delightful series of smiles and greetings. On your rounds ask at local stores for *supanchuk,* the homegrown Fefan tobacco. Pickup-truck taxis circle the island occasionally, charging $2 for the complete 1½-hour trip.

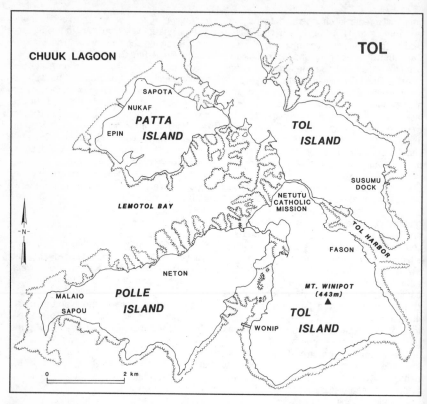

Tol

Tol (34.2 square km, pop. 8,346), largest island in the Chuuk lagoon, is actually three islands (Tol—21.76 square km, Polle—9.07 square km, and Patta—3.37 square km), partly isolated from one another by narrow channels and mangrove swamps. The Japanese forced the Chuukese to dig canals between the islands to allow their patrol boats free circulation. The highest peak in the state (443 meters) is on Tol. The Chuuk greater white-eye, one of the rarest birds of Micronesia, is found in the jungles of Tol.

Known collectively as the Faichuk Islands, a few years ago the inhabitants attempted to secede from Chuuk State and form a state of their own within the FSM. With a third of the population of Chuuk, the Tolese felt they weren't getting their fair share of the state budget. Although the move actually passed the FSM Congress, it was finally stopped by a presidential veto.

The administrative center is at Fason on Tol; the Susumu boat drops you there. More adventurous would be to take a boat over to Polle, leaving Weno almost daily at 1330. The best beaches on Tol are at Sapou and Malaio villages, at the west end of Polle; the local assistant magistrate will give you permission to camp. Giant **Japanese cannons** meant to defend Piaanu Pass still lie in huge caverns chiseled from solid rock, two above Sapou, two more above Malaio. All four can be seen in a morning.

(top) cement-encased Japanese fuel storage, Maloelap, Marshall Is. (Ria de Vos)
(bottom) house on Abemama, Rep. of Kiribati (Rod Buchko)

(clockwise from top) Rock Islands, Rep. of Belau (Gerald A. Heslinga); tropical blossom (Belau Tourist Commission photo by Neil Montanus); taro and papaya (D. Stanley); plantain (D. Stanley); coral reef at Johnston Atoll (U.S. Fish and Wildlife Service photo by Eugene Kridler)

The undulate triggerfish (Balistapus undulatus) *gets its name from a triggerlike mechanism controlling the dorsal fin, which the fish uses to wedge itself into coral crevices when threatened.*

The boat from Malaio to Weno stops at Epin on Patta on the way. If you decide to stop, visit a cave dug by the legendary turtles, Nukaf and Sapota, a short walk from Epin.

A relatively easy three-hour walk along an old Japanese road from Malaio brings you to Netutu Catholic Mission, set on both sides of one of the canals. Netutu is less than an hour's walk from Fason. Hiking north toward Patta is much more difficult.

Only 29 km southwest of Weno, Tol is the outback of the lagoon, with numerous villages and few visitors. A throng of curious children will surround you as you disembark and follow wherever you go. Be prepared to experience a little culture shock if you visit Tol. No matter what happens, don't get angry or show any irritation. Those who have been to remote areas of Indonesia will understand the situation. Female travelers should not visit Tol on their own.

Other Islands In The Chuuk Lagoon
Chuuk Island forms the largest island group in the Carolines. Ninety-eight islands and islets are in the group, 41 of them on the mighty barrier reef which encircles the lagoon, with five major passes that allow shipping to enter. All the other large volcanic islands within the lagoon offer a simpler, more traditional lifestyle than Weno; all are beautiful in themselves and for the views they yield. Although mangrove swamps predominate along the shores, there are also a few beaches.

During Japanese times the lagoon islands were divided into two groups: the Shiki Islands (including Weno, Tonoas, Etten, Fefan, Parem, and Uman) and the Shichiyo Islands (Udot, Fanapanges, Tol, and others). The present administration divides these islands into Northern Namoneas (Weno and Fono), Southern Namoneas (Fefan, Parem, Tonoas, Totiw, Tsis, and Uman), and Faichuk (Eot, Fanapanges, Romanum, Tol, and Udot).

The Japanese reshaped **Etten** Island into an unsinkable aircraft carrier with 200 planes. Some 2,895 people live on **Uman**, the most densely populated lagoon island. The Uman people own Kuop Atoll to the south. **Udot** has three peaks. Many Japanese guns remain on little **Parem** where the Japanese had an airstrip. Planes destroyed during Operation Hailstorm still litter the lagoon beach. You may camp on any of these islands with a local mayor's permission.

OUTSIDE THE CHUUK LAGOON

The Outer Islands
Sizable populations inhabit the 11 atolls and three single islands of the Mortlocks, Halls, and Westerns. No cars clog these very traditional islands, so no highways are needed! The people are extremely hospitable and

CHUUK LAGOON

PIS
NORTH PASS
FALOS
FONO
NORTHEAST PASS
WENO
ROMANUM
EOT
PATTA UDOT
TONOAS
PIAANU PASS
PAREM
ETTEN
POLLE
TOTIW
FEFAN
TOL
TSIS
UMAN
FANAPANGES
SOUTH PASS
SALAT PASS
OTTA PASS
KUOP ATOLL

-N-

0   20km

you'll be invited to stay with embarrassing frequency. Keep in mind, however, that some islands have a limited food supply and are unable to accommodate visitors.

To stay on an outer island it's best to make advance arrangements by radioing ahead to an island mayor. If it's known you're coming there'll be time to spread the burden among several households. The diplomatic way to go about it would be to work through the Chuuk Visitors Bureau on Weno. In past a few problems have occurred with freeloaders taking advantage of the islanders' unreserved hospitality, or sincere visitors who've had difficulty adjusting to island life. The example you set could well determine if others are to be allowed to have the same experience.

Each outer island has both an elected mayor and a hereditary chief. Either can give permission for visitors to stay on the island. If you arrive unannounced on an island it may be better to ask to see the chief, but if arrangements are made prior to your arrival you'll probably work through the mayor, who will be in much closer contact with Chuuk.

The mayor will often speak better English than the chief. If in doubt ask someone from the island who they think you should talk to, but do pay a courtesy call on the other if you're planning to stay. Mostly they only want to know who you are, why you've come, and how long you'll be staying.

The Mortlocks
The Mortlock or Nomoi Islands (pop. 5,904), southeast of the Chuuk Lagoon, include the Upper Mortlocks (Nama and Losap), the Mid-Mortlocks (Namoluk, Etal, and the northernmost islands of Satawan atoll), and the Lower Mortlocks (Lukunor and southeastern Satawan). **Nama** (pop. 897) is a single island without a lagoon.

Satawan atoll's land area totals only 4.6 square km but its lagoon measures 382 square km, second largest in Chuuk State. The old Japanese airstrip was on Satawan Island (pop. 885) but it's now completely planted with coconut and breadfruit trees and the new airstrip is on Ta (pop. 291). You can walk on the Satawan reef from Ta Island to Satawan Island in two hours. **Japanese guns** still lurk beneath Satawan's lush vegetation. You can continue northwest on the barrier reef along the east side of the atoll from Satawan to Moch (pop. 604) in five hours at low tide, eight hours at high tide, passing many small islands along the way. Satawan is one of the only atolls of Chuuk where this is possible. The Mortlocks junior high school is on Satawan.

The Japanese government has built a modern freezer plant on Oneop Island (pop. 534) of Lukunor atoll.

The Hall Islands
A hundred km north of the Chuuk Lagoon, the Hall Islands (Pafeng) consist of twin atolls, Murilo (pop. 694) and Nomwin (pop. 624), and the uninhabited single island East Fayu. The Hall Islanders are closely related to the people of the Chuuk Lagoon, speaking the same dialect. All the houses in the group have tin or concrete roofs and all the boats are of fiberglass with outboard motors.

THE WESTERN ISLANDS

Some of the last vestiges of the old Pacific culture persist on the Western Chuuk and Eastern Yap islands. The inhabitants of the central Carolines have much more in common with each other than they do with the high islanders on Yap proper or inside the Chuuk Lagoon. Here amid the sapphire blue waters and smell of frangipani trees, nearly every house is built of native materials (few tin roofs), most of the men wear loincloths, and the older women are bare breasted.

Many canoes are still outriggers carved from breadfruit logs, though fiberglass boats with outboard motors are increasing. Large thatched canoe houses serve as a combination men's social club, workshop, and school. You'll still find the old navigators here, men who can travel hundreds of km to islands they've never seen, without compass or charts, just from watching the sun, stars, wind, waves, birds, fish, etc. They can predict a typhoon when all seems calm and travel in their sailing canoes between the states of Chuuk and Yap. Yet growing outside influence is reflected in the "video haircuts" of the young men—both sides of the head are shaved clean!

The Westerns include Namonuito, Pulap, and Puluwat atolls, plus Houk (Pulusuk) Island. Chuuk's most skilled navigators reside on Tamatam, Houk, and Puluwat.

Puluwat

Puluwat atoll (pop. 477) is a cluster of five islands, the largest of which are Puluwat and Alet. The one passage into Puluwat's small lagoon leads to an excellent protected anchorage between these two where cruising yachts sometimes drop anchor.

The inhabitants all live on Puluwat Island. The Puluwat islanders were once feared warriors, but missionaries changed that. These days the large thatched canoe houses lining the lagoon are more likely to shelter one of the island's dozen fiberglass outboards than traditional canoes. The atoll's vegetation is dense and there's an ample supply of fish and vegetables.

A tall concrete **Japanese lighthouse,** pocked with bullet holes from wartime strafing, still stands at the west tip of uninhabited Alet, just above the beach. You can climb the spiral stairway almost to the top, but the upper platform is now closed as the lighthouse has recently been returned to service. It's a 1½-hour walk along the reef from the village to the lighthouse; many harmless little blacktip reef sharks patrol the shore on the ocean side. A new junior high school has been built beside the lighthouse.

An overgrown Japanese airstrip is also on Alet and plans exist to clear and reopen it, though it may be many years before this happens due to the compensation sought by

THE CHUUK LAGOON AT A GLANCE

	pop. (1989)	area (hectares)	elevation (meters)
Weno	15,253	1,890	376
Fono	369	33	61
Tonoas/Etten	3,870	931	356
Fefan	3,902	1,322	313
Uman	2,895	470	289
Tsis	438	61	76
Parem/Totiw	350	196	72
Eot	279	48	61
Udot	1,513	493	243
Romanum	679	75	51
Fanapanges	447	157	119
Patta	1,299	337	197
Tol/Wonei	5,720	2,176	452
Polle	1,327	907	207
other lagoon islands	nil	81	4
reef islands	nil	411	4
CHUUK LAGOON	38,341	9,588	452

PULUWAT ATOLL

landowners and the lack of any economic justification for the facility.

In 1990 an outrigger canoe race took place from Puluwat to Chuuk (269 km), with participants navigating by traditional means and often tacking into the wind. The field-trip ship *Island Trader* followed along behind to make sure nobody strayed too far off course. Unfortunately this event was never repeated.

To arrange a stay on Puluwat write Simeon Choffat (Box 372, Weno, Chuuk, FM 96942), a local teacher with family on both Weno and Puluwat.

Houk

Houk (Pulusuk) is a relatively large, heavily vegetated single island with only a fringing reef (no lagoon). Ships sailing between Chuuk and Houk usually call at Pulap or Puluwat first, as the direct route from Weno to Houk is obstructed by dangerous reefs.

Houk is one of the most traditional and isolated islands of Micronesia, though this could soon change when a projected airstrip is built. Meanwhile magnificent outrigger canoes are kept in large thatched boathouses along the beach. The breadfruit trees of Houk are incredibly tall and the food supply is adequate. A brackish lake on Houk is used for bathing and washing clothes. Small fish are found in the lake.

Pulap Atoll

Pulap (pop. 315) and Tamatam (pop. 226) are small islands on the Pulap reef, each with a single village. They lie on opposite sides of the atoll, with about eight km of lagoon between them. Both are so small you can look right through them. When typhoons strip the coconuts and breadfruit from the trees and the residents are forced to depend on taro, they can suffer serious famines.

Tamatam is a very traditional island, clean and breezy with houses along the ocean side and a friendly, welcoming people. The two verdant ends of Tamatam are separated by a narrow sandy strip. The island's many huge outrigger canoes can carry as many as 10 men or more to the outer islands of Yap to hunt turtles. Pulap Island is a less traditional, less happy place.

Namonuito Atoll

Namonuito's huge triangular 1,875-square-km lagoon is the largest in the Caroline Islands. The atoll's five inhabited islands are Onoun (Ulul), Magur, Ono, Onari, and Pisaris. Namonuito is somewhat less traditional than the other Western Islands to the south.

Onoun Island (pop. 513) is a long, broad coral strip at the west end of the lagoon. Coconut-covered Onoun is the largest of the Namonuito islands and the best able to receive visitors. Taro is planted in swampy pits in the center of the island and the food supply is adequate. It's a "developed" island with roads (no cars), stores (closed), an airstrip (no scheduled service), and a large, modern junior high school (many students). The 1,000-meter cement-surfaced airstrip, a 15-minute walk north of the main village, was completed by a U.S. Air Force Civic Action Team in 1991. There's good snorkeling on the lagoon side, cool breezes and fiery sunsets on the ocean side.

The other four Namonuito islands have limited food supplies. Magur (pop. 121) is the northernmost island of Chuuk State. The name means "head," symbolizing a legendary diamond-shaped *pupp* fish formed by all the islands stretching as far west as Fais in

Yap State. Landing on Ono (pop. 91) is dangerous during rough weather. At tiny Pisaris (pop. 139), in the southeast corner of the Namonuito lagoon, visiting ships must anchor far from the island due to treacherous coral shoals in this corner of the lagoon. The shallow waters on the lagoon side do protect Pisaris from heavy seas, so landing itself is easy at high tide. Magur and Onari (pop. 80) are also reasonably approachable.

STATE OF YAP

INTRODUCTION

The 118-square-km State of Yap is comprised of the four large adjoining islands of Yap, Gagil-Tomil, Maap, and Rumung, plus 15 outer islands. Together the outer islands stretch 1,000 km east but total only 18.2 square km. All the outer islands are atolls except Fais (a raised atoll). The influence of the northeast tradewinds makes sandy beaches more common on the west and southern shores, but none are to be found near Colonia, the main town.

Yap Proper is 870 km southwest of Guam. Three of the four big islands are linked by bridges, while Rumung, the fourth, is accessible only by boat. A barrier reef surrounds the cluster and snorkeling possibilities from the main island are limited. Yap, alone among the other large islands of the Carolines, is not volcanic, but of sedimentary structure. The middle and northern portions are hillier. The landscape varies from coastal villages flanked by the most majestic palm trees in the Pacific to the open pandanus and scrub meadows of the upland interior and sheltered thickets of areca palms and bamboo. Other than a few sandy beaches, much of the coast is fringed with the familiar mangrove swamps. Ancient stone paths between taro patches link the villages.

Yap is the most traditional corner of Micronesia and things operate at a much slower pace than on Koror or Guam. The state constitution gives the island chiefs veto power over state legislation relating to culture or matters of tradition. Yapese tourism officials say they want "controlled tourism." Rather than turn their state into another Guam or Saipan, the Yapese are determined to protect their traditions. If this is inconvenient at times remember that it's *they* who are in charge, not tourists. A public outcry recently stopped a major Japanese resort development. Outside Colonia, if you think everything isn't arranged just to please you, you're right.

History

The Yapese were, and the outer islanders still are, the greatest voyagers of the Western Pacific, traveling incredible distances in outrigger sailing canoes, using only the stars and waves as their guides. All of these is-

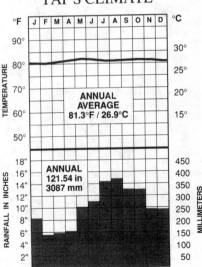

YAP'S CLIMATE

ANNUAL AVERAGE
81.3°F / 26.9°C

ANNUAL
121.54 in
3087 mm

lands were well known to the Micronesians and populated long before the first white men arrived.

The Yapese name for Yap Proper is Wa'ab, while the outer islands are Remetau. The name Yap comes from the Yapese word for "paddle." The story goes that an early European visitor pointed to the island and asked its name. His local informant thought he was pointing at a canoe paddle, hence the error.

Traditionally, all of the outer islands which now belong to Yap State, plus the Westerns and Halls in Chuuk State, and the Marianas, were under the rule of the high chief of Yap. The outer islanders were kept in line by the high chief's magic, which could cause sickness, famine, and hurricanes if tribute was not sent.

In 1869 the Germans set up a trading post. Their claims to the island prompted Spanish

DAVID STANLEY

Stone money and betel palms flank the traditional meetinghouse at Qokaaw on the path across Yap.

from the Philippines to occupy Colonia in 1885, which they ended up selling back to the Germans 14 years later. The Japanese occupied Yap in 1914. WW II was a difficult time for the Yapese as the Japanese forced them to work on defense installations, breaking their stone money if they didn't cooperate. The U.S. bombed Yap Proper, but never bothered to take it.

His Majesty O'Keefe

One of the most unusual characters of the European period was Capt. David O'Keefe, an Irish-American who was shipwrecked on Yap in 1871. Nursed back to health by a Yapese medicine man, he caught a steamer to Hong Kong when he was able. He returned a year later with a Chinese junk, which he used to launch a successful 30-year trading career.

The highly developed Yapese culture of the time had an elaborate scale of values based on stone money. The type of stone used for this money didn't exist on Yap; the stones had to be brought 400 km from Babeldaop by canoe, a perilous undertaking which, of course, gave the stone money its value. O'Keefe used his ship to bring the stone from Belau and traded it for copra and sea slugs, becoming very influential in the process. Taraang, the little island you see in the middle of Tomil Harbor, was once the residence of "His Majesty," built a century ago with bricks imported from Hong Kong. Many years later Burt Lancaster played O'Keefe in a movie about the adventurer.

Government

By agreement, if the elected governor of Yap State is from Yap Proper, then the elected lieutenant governor will be from the outer islands, and vice versa. The Office of Outer Islands Affairs assists the governor in coordinating outer island development.

There are two councils of chiefs: the Council of Pilung from Yap Proper and the Council of Tamol from the outer islands. The chiefs still carry considerable weight and can decisively influence how people vote in free elections. The councils have veto power over legislation affecting traditional customs.

DAVID STANLEY

*Chief John Tamag
takes a betel nut break
while rebuilding the
Bechiyal meeting house
at Maap.*

There are 10 municipalities on Yap Proper: two are separate islands (Rumung and Maap), Tomil and Gagil share an island, and Yap Island has six municipalities.

Economy

The biggest industry on Yap is a Taiwanese-owned textile factory called King Tex (FSM) Inc., which opened in 1989 near Yap Airport. King Tex uses mostly Sri Lankan or mainland Chinese labor to sew "Made in Yap" clothing for export to U.S. department stores under a quota-free, tax-free status granted in the compact of free association. They're not allowed to sell goods on Yap—the clothing is made to order and sold under U.S. brand names. The several hundred workers live in dormitories directly behind the factory and seldom visit Colonia. The Yap government got a new source of tax revenue out of the deal, though the plant does strain the local infrastructure.

The People

Of the 10,139 inhabitants of the state, about a third live on the outer islands, the rest on Yap. The population is 95% Catholic. European- and Japanese-imported diseases caused the number of Yapese to drop from 10,000 in 1869 to 4,717 in 1950. Since then the population has rebounded to its pre-contact levels, although the traditional social structure is breaking down under the onslaught of Americanism.

American education seems fine, but the number of jobs available to graduates is limited. The best students go abroad for schooling and often fail to return, a negative decision that makes the people back home lose confidence in their traditional way of life. For the outer islanders especially, finding a way forward without economic dependence, alcohol, or the need to emigrate is not easy. The feeling out on the atolls is that too much of the state's income is consumed on Yap Proper.

A rigid nine-level caste system governed Yap in the old days. The village accounted for the Yapese caste; those living in strong, powerful villages were of the highest caste. The people take their surnames from their land parcels rather than their parents, which explains why land is so sacred to them. Each village has a chief; the highest chiefs come from the highest caste villages. Traditionally, the women farmed while the men fished.

Although all the Yapese *pebai* (meetinghouses) were destroyed during the war, *faluw* can be seen in many villages. The *faluw* are usually built beside the seashore on large stone platforms with high thatched roofs; traditionally they serve as a school, meeting place, dormitory for young men, and storage area. Prior to WW I, each *faluw* had a *mispil* (resident female) who tended to the sexual needs of members. Women's houses *(dapal)* are found only on the outer islands. Always ask permission before approaching a *faluw.*

Note too the *wunbey* (stone platforms) and *malal* (dancing grounds). Yapese dances include the bamboo, marching, sitting, and standing dances. The dancing could mark the inauguration of a new building, a high school graduation, or the commemoration of the death of an important person *(tayor).* Today few women on Yap Proper still wear grass skirts, but young boys are often seen in the *thu* (loincloth).

Betel nut chewing is universal, even among the children. A green nut is split open, sprinkled with dry lime made from coral, and wrapped in part of a pepper leaf. The bundle is inserted into the mouth and chewed whole. A mild high lasting about 10 minutes is produced. Saliva and teeth are colored bright red by betel nut. The red/black teeth are said to be cavity proof! Top-quality betel nuts are grown on the island and are a big export item, as you'll notice when you check in for your flight to Belau or Guam.

Sap drawn from coconut buds is allowed to ferment into an alcoholic drink called *tuba.* Occasionally you still see people transporting baskets of vegetables along the coast on bamboo rafts. The oranges of Yap are delicious.

Three languages are spoken in Yap State: Yapese, Ulithian, and Woleaian. In Yapese *mogethin* means "hello," *kefel* "goodbye," *sirow* "excuse me," and *kammagar* is "thank you."

Stone Money

Stone money *(rai)* was as much a pillar of Yapese society as gold is of ours. Although cash is starting to get the upper hand, the big circular stone "coins" are still of considerable value to the Yapese. A Japanese count in 1929 revealed 13,281 pieces of stone money; about half that number survive today, and the money may be seen in every village. The money resembles a flat gristmill with a hole in the middle, so two men could carry it on a pole. The largest piece (on Rumung) is four meters across and takes a dozen men to move.

Although important, size is not the only factor in determining the value of a coin; a smaller piece may be worth more due to its age and history. The stones are seldom moved, since who owns what is common knowledge. Stone money was used for traditional purposes, such as to pay workers for building a men's house. Sitting or standing on stone money is forbidden. Stone money cannot be taken out of Yap without the permission of the paramount chief and the state governor.

Crafts

Outer island *lava lava* are woven from hibiscus and banana fibers or cloth in a lined pattern, and along with the Yapese grass skirts are excellent souvenirs. Woven baskets for betel nuts and babies are also good. Distinctive men's combs have long teeth made of bamboo. The *yar* is a large, polished mother-of-pearl shell tied with a handle woven of coconut fiber, also a form of traditional currency.

Other craft items include hair ornaments, carved spoons, shell belts, colorful hibiscus-fiber necklaces *(lap)* and fans, model canoes, and woodcarvings.

Events

A *mitmit* is a traditional festival where one village hosts another in an exchange of gifts and obligations. The completion of a major village project and high school graduations can also occasion traditional singing, dancing, and feasting. Yap Day (March 1) is a celebration with sporting events, traditional dancing, contests, and feasts.

Conduct

Since all land and beaches on Yap are privately owned, ask permission before using a beach, approaching a *faluw,* collecting shells, camping, or walking around a village. The government owns only Colonia and only the main road is public. The Yapese are permission-crazy. You'll be told you need permission to do any number of things, but specifically who can give the needed permission is often hard to determine. Go along with this as best you can, but if you start getting the runaround or no one is there to give permission, use your own judgment to decide what to do. Off the main roads, if you smile and greet everyone you meet, you'll rarely be refused permission to proceed and may make a few friends in the process.

Don't infringe on fishing grounds or disturb the fish traps. Many older people object to having their pictures taken. Don't point at people or pat children on the head. It's considered ill manners to step over another person's outstretched leg or betel basket or to walk in front of someone who is speaking. A group walks single file rather than abreast. Yapese walking through a strange village will tell people they meet the purpose of their visit. They sometimes carry a piece of green vegetation in one hand, to show peaceful intentions, as they pass through a village; carrying a small basket called a *way* (pronounced Y) serves a similar purpose. Traditionally a Yapese not carrying the basket would be considered rebellious. It's a local custom that women do not expose their legs above the knees, so when in Yap. . . .

SIGHTS OF YAP

Colonia And Environs
The Yapese name for Colonia is Donguch, meaning "Small Islands." The point where the government offices and legislature sit, once a tiny island, is now connected to the rest of Colonia by reclaimed land. The offices were built on the foundations of a **Spanish fort;** the state legislature nearby occupies the site of the Japanese **Shinto shrine.**

For a superb view of all of Yap, follow the jeep track from the Catholic mission above Colonia up Medeqdeq Hill to the **Coast Guard Lighthouse** (147 meters). Beyond the lighthouse this track dead-ends at a power line in the valley.

Directly south of Colonia is the outer islanders' colony of Madrich. A Spanish trading post was once here and the place is named after Madrid. A kilometer farther along, **stone money** lines each side of the road in front of the Ruul Municipal Office at Balabat. A few hundred meters beyond, a side road to the left leads in to the **stone money bank** and a *faluw* by the seashore (occasional $2 admission charge).

Continue to the south end of the road where a **dancing ground** *(malal)* rests between two stone platforms *(wunbey)*. A stone path leads off to the right. All this can be seen on foot from Colonia in a couple of hours.

South Of Colonia
The remains of an old **German cable station** still stand beside the Seabee camp beyond the high school between Colonia and the airport. The Germans had an advanced undersea cable system which linked Yap to Guam, Sulawesi, and Shanghai right up to WW I. The first message telegraphed around the world passed through this station. A British gunboat shot down the 61-meter-high steel radio mast in 1914, but you can still see the three huge concrete pylons which supported the tower.

The disused **old airstrip** was built by the Japanese. Over a dozen Japanese planes are in fragments near it, most of them destroyed on the ground by U.S. aircraft. Two planes rest beside the communications center, another three behind the weather station, one on the far side of the pond, and a half-dozen or so are hidden in the bush on the far southeast side of the runway. At last report several of these planes had been removed from Yap by the Japanese. Notice the gun half-hidden in the vegetation between the weather station and the old airport terminal.

Beside the highway, just a hundred meters south of the crossroads and to the west of the road, is a wrecked **Japanese bomber** with German engines. Notice the small insect-eating plants in this area. After exploring the old airport, cool off in the deep freshwater swimming hole at the rock quarry just southwest of the end of the new airstrip. There's a good view from the adjoining hill.

North Of Colonia
The most impressive **meetinghouse** on Yap is at Qokaaw, northwest of Colonia. To get

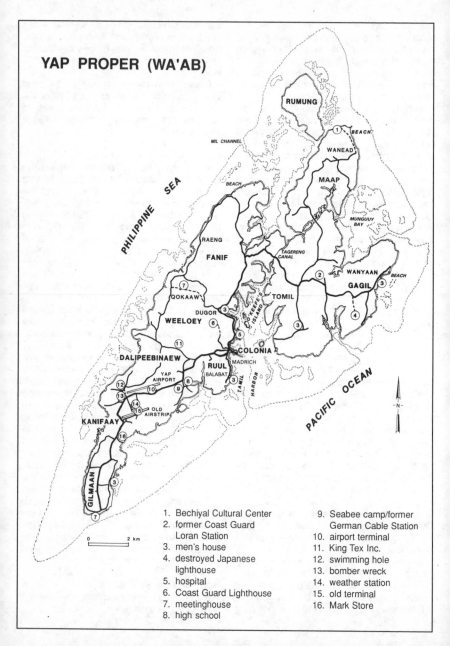

YAP PROPER (WA'AB)

1. Bechiyal Cultural Center
2. former Coast Guard Loran Station
3. men's house
4. destroyed Japanese lighthouse
5. hospital
6. Coast Guard Lighthouse
7. meetinghouse
8. high school
9. Seabee camp/former German Cable Station
10. airport terminal
11. King Tex Inc.
12. swimming hole
13. bomber wreck
14. weather station
15. old terminal
16. Mark Store

there hitch, take a taxi, or drive a rental car around to the west coast and walk in on the short stone path. It's unmarked, but the path begins near a house on the right just before a small bridge after the coastal mangroves join the road. The towering *pebai* (meetinghouse) is surrounded by stone money and platforms in the midst of the luxuriant vegetation.

From here it's possible to continue on the stone footpath right across the island. You follow a stream through a bamboo forest punctuated with immense banyan trees and taro patches up to a new road which will take you down to Dugor on the east coast. This whole trip can be done in about four or five hours on foot from the west coast road.

Gagil-Tomil

The **Tagereng Canal,** dividing Yap Island from Gagil-Tomil, was excavated at the turn of the century by Germans using Japanese labor. There's a strong tidal flow through the channel. The U.S. Coast Guard once had a **loran station** on Gagil-Tomil, and in January 1990 the Micronesian Maritime and Fisheries

a stone money coin on Yap

Academy operated by Pacific Missionary Aviation opened in the converted building.

At **Wanyaan** on the east side of Gagil-Tomil is St. Joseph's Church, one of the prettiest on the island. Just north across a small bridge is an old *faluw* and north again are two huge pieces of stone money right beside the road. At the north end of the road is one of the best beaches on the island ($2 admission), site of a proposed hotel complex.

Maap

At **Bechiyal** near the north tip of Maap (pronounced mop) are three large traditional buildings including a men's house, set on a good beach. The larger building is a reconstructed *pebai* (meetinghouse), and in front of it a *tabinaw* or residence. The *pebai* contains exhibits from the defunct Yap Museum in Colonia, including various kinds of shell money. All construction work here was supervised by Chief John Tamag, a master builder who lives on the site and travels to other villages around Yap to advise on the renovation of traditional buildings. Support for this project was received from the Endowment for Historic Preservation of the Micronesia Institute in Washington, D.C.

The white sandy beach at Bechiyal slopes far out into the lagoon, which makes it very safe for children but snorkelers have to swim quite a distance to reach the reef. A four-passenger speedboat is available for rent for reef snorkeling. Collecting live seashells is not allowed. There are several good short hikes in the vicinity, including walks along the beach to fish traps or mangrove swamps.

The Bechiyal complex is run by the Bechiyal Cultural Center (Box 37, Colonia, Yap, FM 96943), part of a low-impact tourism plan. A $2.50 pp sightseeing fee is charged to enter and those with video or movie cameras pay $25 extra, plus $20 for each local person involved in the filming. A signboard at the entrance lists all fees and the money is used for maintenance and village improvements— an excellent way for the local people to earn a little income while preserving their way of life. Authentic handicrafts are sold here.

To stay in the men's house or the guest cottage at Bechiyal, talk to Alphonse Ganang at the Tourism Office in Colonia or Joe Tamag at the Rai View Hotel. The charge is $10 pp in the men's house, $15 pp in the guesthouse, or $3 pp to camp on the green grass amid the whispering palms. The **guesthouse** is an unfurnished thatched cottage able to accommodate up to 10 persons on floor mats. Groups of three persons or more get a reduced rate of $10 pp in the guesthouse; in the men's house groups of six or more pay only $5 pp. Children are half price. Washing is done in a clean, enclosed bathhouse. Chief Tamag's kind family serves local meals of fried breadfruit chips, bananas, taro, and fish for $3-4; coconuts are 25 cents. Bring insect repellent.

You can easily reach Bechiyal weekdays on the public bus (30 cents) which leaves the Waab Mak'uuf Market at 1700. Otherwise a taxi from Colonia will be about $9 for the car (not pp). It's a 20-minute walk along a beautiful stone path from the end of the road to the village. It's even possible to use Bechiyal as a base from which to visit Colonia (instead of the other way around) as the bus runs into town early on weekday mornings and returns in the afternoon. Bechiyal is about the best place in Yap for friendly people, traditional architecture, and the fine beach—highly recommended.

Bechiyal faces the forbidden island of **Rumung** (accessible only by boat), whose people have decided they're not ready for tourism yet so you'll need an invitation to go there.

PRACTICALITIES

Accommodations

Yap Island has the only hotels in the state, all in Colonia and all with public restaurants. The tap water (called "government water" by the locals) is not suitable for drinking on Yap, and during the dry season there may not be water in the hotel showers all the time. Add 10% room tax to the hotel rates.

The friendly **Rai View Hotel** (Joe Tamag, Box 130, Colonia, Yap, FM 96943; tel. 350-2279), an older two-story wooden building on a hill just above town, has 10 a/c rooms. The two rooms with shared bath are $22 s, $30 d; the eight with private bath cost $28 s, $33 d, $39 t. The rooms look rather basic at first glance but they serve the purpose and it's the cheapest hotel in town. Just don't check in here if you're at all fussy. Four-hour bus tours are $20 pp, boat tours $25 pp (minimum participation two persons on either). The hotel can arrange traditional Yapese dancing for groups at $125. The restaurant downstairs has a colorful island atmosphere, serves big

The Bechiyal men's house at Maap overlooks a sandy beach.

DAVID STANLEY

bowls of ramen and reasonable sandwiches, and beer is available.

The **ESA Hotel** (Elena and Silbester Alfonso, Box 141, Colonia, Yap, FM 96943; tel. 350-2139), a two-story concrete building on the south side of the Chamorro Lagoon, has 16 small a/c rooms with private bath, TV, and fridge at $40 s or d, $45 t. The ESA is dry—no alcohol is served in the restaurant nor is any allowed in the rooms. The restaurant does have a nice lagoon view, though. A tour of southern Yap by private car is $50 for one, $25 pp for two, $20 pp for three. Car rentals are $38.50 a day, airport transfers $3 pp. It's often full.

Perhaps the best place to stay in Colonia is at **The Pathways** (Box 718, Colonia, Yap, FM 96943; tel. 350-2253, fax 350-2223), between the Evangelical Mission and Blue Lagoon Store. The 14 attractive thatched cottages go for $60 s, $65 d, $70 t, plus $10 extra if you use the a/c. Each individual screened unit has a private balcony overlooking the bay, a private bath, ceiling fans, and a king-size bed. They're separated by lush vegetation and connected by picturesque wooden walkways, all set into the hillside. No smoking is allowed in the units. A restaurant and bar are attached. The Pathways is owned by an American doctor, Don Evans, and his Yapese partners, Stan and Flora Fillmed.

Beside the harbor in the center of town is the **Manta Ray Bay Hotel** (Box 177, Yap, FM 96943: tel. 350-2300), a modern three-story building opened in 1990. The 15 a/c rooms cost $95 s or d lagoonside or $85 s or d roadside. Airport transfers are $10 pp RT. Though there's no beach or swimming pool, the Manta Ray Bay serves the needs of scuba divers admirably, as the dive shop is right next to the hotel and their boats leave from a dock behind the hotel reception area. The whole complex is a little claustrophobic, however, a result of the limited space available.

Almost opposite the Manta Ray Bay is the nondescript **Ocean View Hotel** (Box 130, Colonia, Yap, FM 96943), a two-story business hotel with 17 a/c rooms at $50 s or d with private bath, $75 for a suite.

For a longer stay ask at **Blue Lagoon Store** (tel. 350-2136, fax 350-4120) which has seven two-bedroom apartments with cooking facilities at $45 daily, $500 monthly, but they're often full.

In addition to the places listed above, the **Tourism Office** (Box 36, Colonia, Yap, FM 96943; tel. 350-2298) can arrange stays in Yapese homes, costing about $20 pp a day including meals in villages near Colonia, or $10 pp a day and up in more remote villages. Among the local people receiving guests are Martin Datmagurun, Falownug Kenmed, Martin Dugchur (at Toruw village in Maap), and Robert A. Wuyoch (at Ma village in Tomil). This is a good way to meet the people while finding a place to stay provided you don't mind sacrificing some of your privacy and roughing it a little.

In a pinch the best place near Colonia to look for a freelance campsite would be up behind the water tank on the road to the Coast Guard lighthouse. **Campers** will do much better at the Bechiyal Cultural Center described above, the only place on Yap where tenters (and others) are catered to ($3 pp).

Food And Entertainment

Most restaurants in Colonia offer cold coconuts for less than the price of a can of soda. For locally grown vegetables and color check out the **Waab Mak'uuf Market**.

The **Yap Marina** (tel. 350-2211), just beyond the Continental Air Micronesia office, has a breezy terrace overlooking the bay where sandwiches and regular meals are served, plus alcoholic drinks after 1300. Cold coconuts are 75 cents, ice cream $1.25. The cheeseburgers are good but don't order the overpriced French fries. Monday and Wednesday 1700-1900 beer prices are lower, and this is also a good time to try the sashimi (raw fish).

Vicky's Kool Korner, upstairs in the new YCA Complex, is a popular place for lunch, though the surroundings and food are nothing special.

The hotels also have restaurants. The one at the **Rai View** is cheaper and serves drinks, while the one at the **ESA Hotel** has a/c but no booze. Check out the **Yap Evangelical Church Snack Bar** beside the ESA. The pleasant restaurant-bar on the roof of the **Manta Ray Bay Hotel** offers "stone money pizza" (with a hole in the middle) and a bottomless glass of ice tea or cup of coffee.

Drinkers staying on Yap over 30 days must obtain a drinking permit ($5) at the police station. Aside from the places mentioned above, there haven't been any regular bars since O'Keefe's Oasis closed down years ago, so plan on an early night.

Sports And Recreation
Yap Divers (Bill Acker, Box 177, Colonia, Yap, FM 96943; tel. 350-2321), beside the Manta Ray Bay Hotel in Colonia, offers scuba trips. The charge for a two-tank dive including a sandwich and beverages is $85 (minimum of two persons), night diving $45. Certification cards are carefully scrutinized. Snorkelers may go along with the divers for $35 pp.

Yap is one of Micronesia's most popular new scuba destinations and depending on the time of year, diving takes place at sites all around the island. One of the favorites is Gilmaan Wall off the southwest tip of the lagoon. From a depth of 10-12 meters a vertical wall plunges 200 meters. Large fish abound, including barracuda, tuna, and jacks, plus eagle rays, turtles, moray eels, and sharks (harmless). The waters off southern Yap are clearest because of prevailing ocean currents from the south. Yap's most famous dive sites are Mil Channel and nearby Manta Ridge, off the northwest side of the island, home to some 40 manta rays. The mantas are filter feeders that hover here, catching the nutrient-rich waters of the outgoing tide as small wrasses remove parasites from their bodies.

Shopping
The **YCA** (Yap Cooperative Assn.) store in the center of town sells Yap T-shirts. A very enjoyable afternoon can be spent sitting on the bench in front of the YCA, talking to shoppers and passersby.

Family Chain Store offers a wide selection of goods and keeps the longest hours in Colonia (0730-2000 daily). The hardware department around the side in back sells masks and snorkels.

The **Women's Association Handicraft Shop** in the unmarked yellow building beside the Manta Ray Bay Hotel is a good place to buy crafts such as grass skirts, pandanus baskets and hats, necklaces, model canoes, miniature stone money, fish traps, and woodcarvings.

You can buy an "Island of Stone Money" Yap State license plate at the police station for $5. Philatelic stamps and first-day covers are available at the post office.

Services
The Bank of Hawaii (tel. 350-2129) has a branch in Colonia ($6 commission to change foreign currency into U.S. cash). The Bank of the FSM (tel. 350-2329) is in the new YCA Complex.

Place long-distance telephone calls at the Telecommunications Corporation (open 24 hours) up the road toward the Rai View Hotel. It's $3 for three minutes within the FSM, $7.50 for three minutes to Guam and the U.S., $9 for three minutes to Belau and the Philippines. Rates are cheaper 1800-0600 and on Sunday. The area code, when phoning Yap from abroad, is 691.

The FSM Immigration office (tel. 350-2126) is upstairs near Vicky's Kool Korner in the new YCA Complex.

Free public toilets and showers are found in the Marina Center beside the Continental Air Micronesia office.

There's a laundromat (open weekdays 0800-1630, Sundays 1200-1630) in an unmarked building between the Yap Divers office and the Health Corner.

Information
Alphonse Ganang in the tourism office (tel. 350-2298) opposite the Mak'uuf Market has information leaflets on Yap, can answer questions, and will even arrange paying-guest accommodations in local homes.

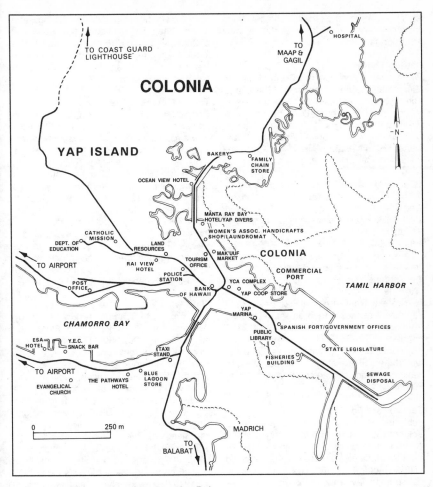

The Land Resources office near the Rai View Hotel sells large printed topographical maps of Yap and Micronesia for $4 each.

The Yap State Public Library (Box 550, Colonia, Yap, FM 96943; tel. 350-2793) near the old Spanish fort is open Mon., Wed., and Fri. 1330-1630.

Radio station WSZA-AM's powerful 10-kilowatt transmitter broadcasts from Yap over 1494 kHz.

TRANSPORT

Airport
Yap Airport (YAP) is six km southwest of town. All hotel keepers meet the flights at the airport and provide transfers at about $3 pp each way, or you can easily hitch a ride into town. Immigration officials on Yap are stricter than those in the other FSM states and usu-

ally only give you the length of time till your onward reservation. At last report there was no airport tax.

Getting There

Three times a week Yap is a **Continental Air Micronesia** stopover between Guam and Koror, so the cheapest way to get there is to include Yap in a through ticket between Honolulu and Koror. From Southeast Asia, a Continental ticket Manila-Koror-Yap-Koror-Manila will run $628.

Certain Continental flights to/from Yap feature reduced off-peak fares: on Fri. it's $120 from Yap to Guam (compared with $213); on Sun. it's cheaper Guam to Yap; on Wed. it's $80 from Yap to Koror (compared to $141); on Sun. it's cheaper Koror to Yap. A regular roundtrip ticket from Guam to Yap will cost $426.

Reconfirm your onward flight at the Continental Air Micronesia office (tel. 350-2127) in the Marina Center.

In late 1991 Air Nauru included Yap in their weekly Nauru-Kosrae-Pohnpei-Chuuk-Yap-Guam service with fares set at US$130 from Yap to Chuuk or Guam, US$213 Pohnpei-Yap, A$443 Nauru-Yap. This, the first nonstop air link between Yap and the rest of the FSM, is of most interest to those planning a Micronesian trip from the South Pacific via Nauru.

Getting Around

Public buses connect the outlying villages to Colonia (30 cents) weekdays only, leaving the villages at the crack of dawn and departing the Mak'uuf Market, Colonia, around 1700. Hitching is fairly easy. The local pickup taxis have reasonable rates, but ask before getting in. A taxi to Maap is $9, to the airport $3.

Pacific Bus Company (Box 366, Colonia, Yap, FM 96943; tel. 350-2266) in the hardware department behind Family Chain Store rents cars and pickups at $40 a day, tax and mileage included (no insurance). The hotels in Colonia also rent cars.

In 1991 a Korean construction company built an excellent paved highway northeast

from the airport to Colonia, Tomil, Gagil, and Maap. When driving observe the speed limit of 20 mph on roads, 15 mph in villages. The local chiefs often set "sand traps" (holes in the road filled with sand) in their villages to catch speeding cars.

To The Outer Islands By Air

Pacific Missionary Aviation (Box 460, Colonia, Yap, FM 96943; tel. 350-2360) at the new airport flies their twin-engine, nine-passenger planes twice a week from Yap to Ulithi ($50, one hour), weekly to Fais ($75, 1¼ hours) and Woleai ($150, three hours). Free baggage is limited to nine kilograms and no alcoholic beverages may be carried. Tickets are not refundable.

PMA is mainly intended to support medical missionaries, but their flights are available to visitors. This praiseworthy company carries out emergency medical evacuations and transports referral patients, bodies of deceased, and medical supplies at no charge.

Field Trips

The **Yap State Transportation Field Trip Service** (Box 576, Colonia, Yap, FM 96943; tel. 350-2240; fax 350-4113) in the radio room of the government offices in Colonia runs the field-trip ship MV *Micro Spirit* from Yap to Ulithi, Fais, Faraulep, Woleai, Ifalik, Eauripik, Sorol, and Ngulu about every five weeks. Actually there are two field trips: a short one from Yap to Ulithi and perhaps one other island, and a long one to all the inhabited islands of Eastern Yap.

Try to be there a week before departure to arrange any required permits, extension of stay, trip bookings, shopping, and acclimatization to Yapese life-style. On an outer island the radio operator will know the estimated time of arrival of the ship.

Seven simple double cabins are available on the first deck, but 95% of the passengers travel deck. Fares are 3 cents a mile deck or 15 cents a mile cabin. Bookings have to be made a few days in advance, otherwise an additional fee may be charged. Meals in the officers' mess are $3 for breakfast, $4 for lunch, and $4.50 for dinner.

Take plenty of food with you from Yap (soups, coffee, tea, tinned food) and be self-sufficient. The locals always have rice, taro, breadfruit, dried or smoked fish, and bunches of fresh coconuts, and they're always inviting you to meals. In return offer them canned food or meat, which they can't get without spending their very limited money.

Drinking water is not abundant, so take a few 10-liter plastic containers along and fill them with rainwater at the villages, when possible. Smokers should bring enough cigarettes, as the number of people asking is infinite. The captain has a small shop where cigarettes, biscuits, and cold drinks are sold at fair prices. Toward the end of the trip it will run out of stock, so plan ahead.

On deck a straw mat and a thin sleeping bag will do for a bed and should be rolled out early upon boarding. The washing facilities are poor and only a half-hour of water daily is supplied from the military-type shower (usually 1830-1900). There's always a line, so be quick and don't arrive last, or you could end up with a soapy body and no water.

The Field Trip Officer (FTO) is the one responsible for the itinerary, payments, and cargo. He also has a cupboard with medications, and a doctor is usually aboard to check the island people at short stops. A field trip can seem very long if you're not making friends on deck and taking the supply boat ashore at stops. Always make sure to catch the last trip back to the ship, as they could easily leave without you! Keep in mind that the field trips are meant to serve the outer islanders, not tourists. If you'd like to charter the ship it can be arranged for $2,000 a day.

THE OUTER ISLANDS

The Outer Islanders
The Western Caroline Islands east of Yap are among the most traditional in the Pacific. The men still pierce their ears and noses and often practice tattooing. They can still sing the chants of their forefathers and are able to travel long distances by sailing canoe.

Instead of the grass skirts of Yap, the women wear knee-length *lava lava* held in place by a string of shells or a girdle belt. The men wear a *thu* (loincloth) consisting of a long piece of cloth wrapped around the waist and between the legs. Neither men nor women wear any upper garment. Every outer island has a men's house or two. During menstruation the women resort to the *pal* (women's house). Most of the people are Catholic.

Permissions
If you'd like to take the plane to Ulithi, Fais, or Woleai and stay a couple of days, you must first get clearance in Colonia from the Office of the Governor. The same procedure is required to spend time on an outer island between visits of the field-trip ship. The Outer Islands Affairs Officer at the governor's office will contact the chief of the outer island you wish to visit to obtain his permission and announce your arrival.

You're supposed to apply one month prior to your arrival at the outer island. If you're really serious about going call ahead at (691) 350-2108, or write two months in advance to the Office of the Governor, State of Yap, Colonia, Yap, FM 96943, stating precisely which atoll you'd like to visit and when. Upon arrival in Yap check with the Outer Islands Affairs office at the governor's office.

They'll usually grant the permission if they believe you're a legitimate visitor intending only a brief stay. You'll be expected to take enough food for your duration of stay, pay a courtesy call on the island chief upon arrival, and respect local customs. An "entry fee" of $20 pp must be paid to the chief upon arrival at each island.

Advance permission is not required to visit the outer islands on a field-trip ship as a through passenger, provided you only get off at the islands for a couple of hours to look around while the ship's there. Tourists are not allowed to disembark on an outer island for an indefinite stay without prior consent of the governor.

People on the outer islands are not used to tourists and will therefore think, What do these people want here? So far nearly every

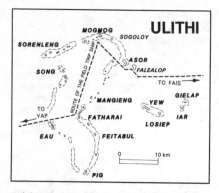

arriving foreigner has been a missionary, Peace Corps volunteer, anthropologist, fisheries researcher, etc. Nobody is interested in tourism yet, so you'll be their guest.

Ulithi

Ulithi (pop. 847), 171 km northeast of Yap, has 49 small islets on its reef, which encloses a 473-square-km lagoon. In 1731, a 13-member Jesuit missionary party under Father Juan Antonio Cantova landed on Ulithi. When the Spanish returned the next year, they found the islanders had wiped the Jesuits out.

The Japanese built an airstrip on Ulithi, but evacuated to Yap Proper when an American landing became imminent. On 20 Sept. 1944, the U.S. Navy occupied Ulithi unopposed. A thousand U.S. warships assembled in the Ulithi lagoon ("Flattop Row") just prior to the landings on Iwo Jima and Okinawa in early 1945.

The presently inhabited islands of Ulithi are Asor, Falealop, Fatharai, and Mogmog. The airstrip, radio transmitter, administrative offices, post office, and Outer Islands High School are all on Falealop Island. The high school buildings were once part of a U.S. loran station, now closed. Students from all the outer islands of Yap come here to further their education.

PMA flies in from Yap three times a week and an outboard from Mogmog usually runs to Falealop to meet the plane. The field-trip ship calls at Ulithi on both the outward and inward journeys. It delivers supplies to all the villages on the way out, but may stop only at Falealop on the way back.

Mogmog is the chiefly island, where men once went to have their bodies covered in tattoos. The chief of Mogmog rules the atoll, except Falealop where the government representative is in charge. A certain rivalry continues between the two areas. At low tide you can wade from Mogmog to neighboring, uninhabited Sogoloy.

Western clothing and alcohol are prohibited on Mogmog; on Falealop the women are covering up. As hurricanes destroy the old thatched houses, dwellings of tin and concrete appear. Much of the work is still done communally. The men catch fish and the women cook vegetables from their gardens. If any fishing boats haven't returned by 1800, a rescue mission is launched.

If you visit Ulithi, ask permission of the chief to stay in one of the two *fal* (men's houses). The stock in the couple of small stores often runs out, so bring food if you're coming by boat. Cigarettes, coffee, and betel nuts make welcome gifts.

Fais

Fais (pop. 253) was once mined by the Japanese for its phosphate: the ruins of machinery and railroad can still be seen. Today the inhabitants live from fishing, vegetable gardening, and copra production. USDA food supplements the diet. This raised atoll has no lagoon—hardly a place for foreign visitors. Access is fairly easy with weekly PMA flights from Yap ($75) and Ulithi ($25).

Eauripik

Large ships cannot enter Eauripik's long, fish-filled lagoon. The hundred inhabitants crowded into the tiny islet at the east end of the atoll don't make copra because they need the coconuts to eat. Instead they smoke fish to exchange at Woleai, which they visit by sailing canoe. A passing freighter which lost a few big tropical logs recently was much appreciated by the skilled Eauripik canoe builders. They also make beautiful wood carvings and other handicrafts of turtle and

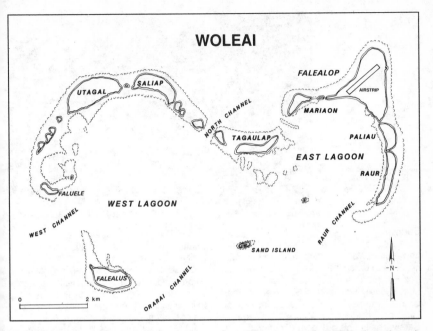

WOLEAI

FALEALOP

AIRSTRIP

UTAGAL SALIAP

MARIAON

NORTH CHANNEL

TAGAULAP

PALIAU

EAST LAGOON

RAUR

FALUELE

WEST LAGOON

WEST CHANNEL

RAUR CHANNEL

SAND ISLAND

FALEALUS

ORARAI CHANNEL

0   2 km

-N-

seashell. Their houses are built on massive stone platforms to resist hurricanes, which flush waves over the islands.

Woleai

Woleai (pop. 794) is roughly in the center of the eastern outer islands. Five of the 22 islands around Woleai's two connected lagoons are inhabited. The others are used for copra and taro production. Woleai has the most breadfruit and the largest reef islands of any of the Yap atolls.

A junior high school and old Japanese airstrip are found on Falealop where the high chief resides. Thousands of bypassed Japanese soldiers starved on Woleai in 1945. Wrecked planes, cannon, bunkers, and dumped heavy equipment are still found in the bush. Former railway tracks are used as curbs along the roads or as supports for cooking pots on Falealop.

In Sept. 1991 Pacific Missionary Aviation began flying into Woleai's wartime airstrip

from Yap once a week ($75, three hours). The FSM government hopes eventually to have internal flights from Chuuk to Yap without passing through Guam, and Woleai would make an ideal stop. Many islanders fear the changes this would bring.

The Japanese government recently donated a modern iceplant to Woleai, but it's seldom in use due to maintenance problems and enormous fuel consumption. Aside from American education, the school on Woleai teaches youngsters more appropriate skills like weaving, rope- and canoe-making, fishtrap manufacturing, dancing, etc. The graduation ceremony is the biggest event on Woleai with dance practice beginning weeks before, beside palm-leaf fires.

Falealus with its cool lagoon breeze has beautiful houses and the largest canoe. There are Japanese guns on Utagal and four oceangoing canoes. More Japanese guns are on uninhabited Mariaon, which can be reached from Falealop on foot at low tide.

a downed Japanese Zero near the old airfield on Yap

DAVID STANLEY

Satawal

Satawal (pop. 465), the easternmost inhabited atoll of Yap, is overpopulated so many Satawal islanders have emigrated to work on Yap Proper. Some of the old Pacific navigators still live on Satawal, still setting their course by the ocean swells and relative positions of the stars. In 1988 Lino Olopai of Satawal sailed his outrigger canoe to Saipan in this way. A new consulting industry has developed supporting inquisitive museums, writers, and filmmakers eager to learn the ways of Satawal. Mau Piailug, navigator of the famous Polynesian sailing canoe *Hokule'a,* is from Satawal.

Others

Sorol atoll has only two or three resident families, among the most isolated families on earth. The rusty tin houses give Sorol an unattractive appearance, even though the atoll is quite beautiful.

Outboard motors are banned on highly traditional **Ifalik** atoll (pop. 475). Fish are mostly caught on an outer reef about 15 km north of Ifalik, always by outrigger canoes. The Phallus of Maur stood in the meeting house (Tan Nap) on Ifalik until Catholic missionaries managed to engineer its removal.

Elato (pop. 70) and **Lamotrek** (pop. 278) are two of the most beautiful atolls of Yap with an unspoiled traditional way of life and sailing canoes. Lamotrek is well known for the traditional magic still practiced there. Together with Satawal these islands have been hard hit by typhoons in recent years and there still could be a serious shortage of food and water, so check before heading that way.

REPUBLIC OF BELAU

INTRODUCTION

With only 15,122 (1990) inhabitants, the Republic of Belau is the smallest of the four political units to emerge from the Trust Territory of the Pacific Islands. Belau is the indigenous name of the group. The Spanish called it Los Palaos, which the Germans shortened to Palau, a form still often used.

The Belau cluster consists of 343 islands strewn along a line which begins with Kayangel in the northeast and ends with Angaur, 200 km southwest. This spectacular group, at the southwest corner of the Western Caroline Islands, offers great diversity, from tiny dots to 396-square-km Babeldaop, second-largest island in Micronesia (Guam is bigger). In addition there are the far-flung Southwest Islands, home to less than 100 people.

Together, the Republic of Belau totals 488 square km of land area. Only nine islands are inhabited. Two-thirds of the population resides in the present capital, Koror. This pic-turesque town 1,300 km southwest of Guam is only 1,200 km north of Biak (Indonesia) and 880 km east of Mindanao (Philippines).

Belau's strategic position explains the bitter battles fought over it during WW II and continuing U.S. military interest today. Though the struggle between traditional and imported values has led to tense political divisions in recent years and alcohol and marijuana remain problems, Belau is still the "Charm of Micronesia."

The Land
The 105-km-long barrier reef down the west side of Belau from Kossol to Peleliu shelters a wide lagoon, the east side of which is riddled near the middle with hundreds of tiny umbrella-shaped islands—the Rock Islands. These rounded, undercut mounds of limestone float like emerald mushrooms on a turquoise-fringed sapphire lagoon. Formed from the weathering of ancient uplifted reefs,

they're spectacular for their secluded beaches, tranquil channels, gin-clear water, and unbelievable coral formations.

Today this uninhabited 200-island complex south of Koror is thickly jungled, with dark greenhouse vegetation engulfing its arches and caves and hiding the interior marine lakes. The coral and marinelife in the lagoon are rich, as Belau's big two-meter tides keep the water clean. Although Chalbacheb (the Belauan name for the Rock Islands) is a scenic highlight of the Pacific, alone worth a visit to Belau, aluminum and plastic pollution left behind by visitors is a growing problem. Speed- and fishing boats, spear guns, hunters, and anglers are beginning to take their toll.

In contrast, the 213-meter-high volcanic interior of 43-by-13 km Babeldaop consists of impenetrable jungle fringed by crocodile-infested mangrove swamps. Add Babeldaop's freshwater Ngardok Lake (900 meters long) to Belau's perfect coral atoll (Kayangel) and two elevated limestone islands (Angaur and Peleliu), and you have one of the most compact and varied physical environments to be found in any ocean. In addition, the Palau Visitors Authority promises, "At night the bright Southern Cross in clear sky will not fail to bring you a romantic mood."

Climate

Belau has only two types of weather, alternately sunny and rainy. Due to the southerly location, temperatures here tend to be slightly higher than elsewhere in Micronesia. Daily and seasonal variations in temperature are small. February through April are the driest months; the northeast trades blow from Nov. through April, varying to easterlies in May and June. From July through Oct. the westerlies prevail: this southwest monsoon season is the wettest period. The heaviest rains occur early in the morning, with a second peak just after sunset. The rain cools off temperatures but the humidity remains a relatively high 82%.

Fauna

Belau's flora and fauna are the richest in Micronesia. The variety of habitats and proximity to the Indo-Malay faunal region explain the tremendous diversity of marinelife in the Belau Lagoon. Scientists have found that as distance from Southeast Asia increases, the number of species both above and below water decreases. Hawaii, for example, has only one-half to one-third as many varieties of fish and coral as Belau. Three nutrient-carrying ocean currents merge here. In all, some 1,500 species of tropical fish and 700 different types of coral and anemones may be seen at Belau. (Collecting corals and seashells is prohibited.)

In addition there are giant clams weighing up to 450 kilos, sea snakes, sharks, dugongs, monitor lizards, fruit bats, a hundred different kinds of birds, and huge sea turtles which land on the Rock Islands to lay their eggs. The birds and turtles are suffering from a lack of government protection.

Belau's seagoing crocodiles, which inhabit the rivers and mangrove swamps of Babeldaop, probably arrived here from New Guinea. They grow up to five meters long—big

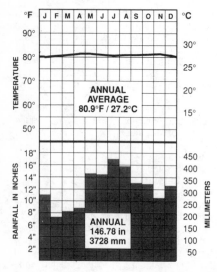

KOROR'S CLIMATE

ANNUAL AVERAGE
80.9°F / 27.2°C

ANNUAL
146.78 in
3728 mm

enough to swallow a man. Like all wild animals, they're shy and will flee from people if they can. Not a single crocodile incident has been reported since 1965, although men attack crocodiles constantly.

HISTORY

Creation Myth
Once upon a time on the isle of Angaur there lived a child named Uab, who had a voracious appetite. An average meal consisted of 50 large baskets of food, plus dozens of basins of spring water and coconut juice. Reaching manhood, Uab grew so fat that he could no longer feed himself, and men had to climb ladders to force food into his mouth. His size increased to the point where only his head would fit into the large house built just for him; his body stretched out along the beach.

The people of Angaur became frightened and decided to kill him. One night while he slept, they tied him up and set fire to his house. Uab roared and kicked, and Angaur shook. The struggle was so fierce that his body broke into many pieces which were scattered to the north, forming the islands of Belau.

One leg became Peleliu, another formed Aimeliik. Babeldaop was his body. Today Ngiwal State is attributed to Uab's stomach, which explains why the inhabitants there eat seven times a day. Ngarchelong was his head, so those people are the smartest and most talkative in the republic. The location of Uab's pubic area explains why Aimeliik gets more rain than any other part of Belau.

Prehistory
The first humans may have arrived from Indonesia as early as 2500 B.C. Carbon dating of abandoned village sites on the Rock Islands proves human habitation in Belau by 1000 B.C. The terrace culture on Babeldaop climaxed about A.D. 1000; by 1600, the terraces had been abandoned. The function of these great earthworks and the reason for their abandonment are still being studied.

At the time of European contact, the Belauans resided in inland villages associated in regional alliances. The social system was complex and highly organized. A Council of Chiefs from the 10 clans was headed by two chiefs: High Chief Reklai of Babeldaop (Upper Ocean) and High Chief Ibedul of Youldaop (Lower Ocean), seated at Melekeok and Koror respectively. Traditionally it was the elder women who decided who the chief would be.

Belau was self-sufficient: the women tended the taro swamps while the men hunted, fished, and harvested breadfruit and betel nuts. Foreign affairs centered around the export of stone money to Yap. Coral bead money (udoud) was a symbol of wealth. The legends, which explained the universe to these people, appeared on men's meeting houses (bai) and were painted in limestone caves.

European Impact
Although Spanish and Portuguese navigators had visited as early as 1543, it was Capt. Henry Wilson of the East India Company's ship Antelope, wrecked in the Rock Islands in 1783, who first publicized Belau (Pelew) in Europe. Abba Thulle, one of the chiefs of Belau, befriended Wilson and helped him build a schooner in which he was able to return to Macau. Abba Thulle's son, Prince Lee Boo, sailed to London with Wilson, and the published account of the events made Belau briefly as famous in contemporary Europe as Captain Cook's Tahiti. Sadly, Lee Boo died of smallpox after five months in England.

British traders introduced guns to the islands. During the century from 1783 to 1882, the population declined from 40,000 to only 4,000, due to influenza and dysentery epidemics. Early Spanish colonialists were mostly concerned with spreading Catholicism, while the Germans, who succeeded them in 1899, concentrated on taking phosphates from Angaur and producing copra.

The Japanese Period
The Japanese, who seized Micronesia from the Germans in 1914, pursued economic de-

an inlaid wooden food bowl collected at Belau in 1914

velopment, largely for the benefit of masses of Japanese immigrants and the motherland—they paid their Belauan laborers seven yen a month. Phosphate and bauxite mines, rice paddies, and pineapple plantations flourished. The Belauans were taught to speak Japanese, their lands alienated, and the traditional chiefs replaced by Japanese bureaucrats.

Under the Japanese, Koror became the capital of all Micronesia, and had a mostly Japanese population four times as large as at present. Before the war, a streetcar line ran through the city. In the late 1930s military bases were erected and after 1938 the area was closed to outsiders (a status which continued under the Americans until 1962).

In Sept. 1944, a brutal battle exploded over Peleliu, as the Americans sought a base from which to launch their attack on the Philippines. Rather than meet the landings on the beaches, the Japanese entrenched themselves in caves on a tangled limestone ridge. In two and a half months of heavy fighting some 11,000 Japanese were killed. Nearly 2,000 Americans also died, and 8,000 more were wounded.

The U.S. bombed and neutralized Koror and Babeldaop, but never tried to take them and the 25,000 Japanese troops there were left to sit it out. Prior to the Peleliu landings the Japanese concentrated the Belauan population in central Babeldaop, where 526 of them (almost 10% of the indigenous popula-

tion of the time) perished. Memories of this period are still vivid in Belau, and the islanders don't want to get caught between two crocodiles again.

RECENT HISTORY

A Nuclear-free Belau

Belauans have been struggling against American military domination since 1972, when the Pentagon first announced its interest in bases in Belau. In July 1978 Belau voted to separate from the rest of Micronesia, and in Jan. 1979 the first Belau Constitutional Convention convened to write a constitution for a self-governing republic.

To the dismay of American officials, the delegates incorporated provisions banning nuclear materials from Belau, preventing the government from using eminent-domain powers for the benefit of a "foreign entity," and declaring a 200-nautical-mile territorial sea zone around the entire archipelago. A 75% referendum vote would be required to override or alter the antinuclear provisions of the constitution, the high level reflecting the Belauan tradition of consensus.

Although 35 of 38 delegates signed the draft, the U.S. had the Belau Legislature repeal the legislation providing for the Constitutional Convention. Despite this, the planned referendum went ahead on schedule, and on 9 July 1979, 92% of voters approved the world's first nuclear-free constitution.

After the referendum, the Chief Justice of the Trust Territory High Court ruled that the legislature had the right to repeal the convention, and declared the result of the referendum void. The legislature then prepared a "revised" constitution without the antinuclear provisions, but on 23 Oct. 1979 this document was rejected by 70% of those who voted in a second referendum.

On 14 July 1980 a third referendum was held, and 78% of voters once again approved the original nuclear-free constitution. A few

THE BELAU REFERENDA

Date	Turnout	Yes	No	Description
9 July 1979		92%	8%	Approval of nuclear-free Constitution (not accepted by U.S.)
23 Oct. 1979		30%	70%	Replacement of first Constitution with another the U.S. found more acceptable (not nuclear-free)
14 July 1980	68%	78%	22%	Re-affirmation of first nuclear-free Constitution
10 Feb. 1983	88%	62%	38%	First Compact vote—75% required to pass
4 Sept. 1984	71%	67%	33%	Second Compact vote—75% required
21 Feb. 1986	71%	72%	28%	Third Compact vote—75% required. A court case was needed to uphold defeat of the Compact.
2 Dec. 1986	82%	66%	34%	Vote on Feb. 1986 Compact—75% required
30 June 1987	78%	67%	33%	Vote on Feb. 1986 Compact—75% required
4 Aug. 1987	70%	73%	27%	Vote to amend nuclear-free Constitution. Courts rule election unconstitutional.
20 Aug. 1987	75%	73%	27%	Vote on Feb. 1986 Compact—75% required
6 Feb. 1990	69%	61%	39%	Vote on 1986 Compact with a subsidiary agreement—75% required

days later, U.S. Ambassador Rosenblatt rejected the vote and declared the constitution "incompatible with the concept of free association." Yet on 1 Jan. 1981 self-government was achieved under the nuclear-free constitution, which remains in effect today, 11 referenda later, with a 75% popular vote still needed to change the nuclear prohibition.

The Compact

The strong Belauan opposition to the military stems from their WW II experience, when Belau was a battleground for the Japanese and Americans, and from the experience of the Marshall Islanders. The controversy revolves very much around land. The influential traditional chiefs oppose the withdrawal of lands for U.S. military use. The U.S. government has insisted that Belau revise its constitution and accept a compact of free association, which would allow the transit of its nuclear-powered or armed military forces and give the U.S. eminent-domain rights for the establishment of military installations.

In Aug. 1982 the compact was signed and on 10 Feb. 1983 a referendum held. The 15,000 Belauans were offered about $428 million in U.S. aid over 15 years (nearly $30,000 per head) in exchange for tax-free military use of a third of the national territory for 50 years, plus the *permanent* strategic denial of Belau to the navies of other countries without U.S. consent (the Monroe Doctrine extended clear across the Central Pacific). Only 62% voted in favor, less than the 75% required to override the constitution. The strongest opposition was in Koror and southern Babeldaop.

Another referendum on a revised compact was hastily held on 4 Sept. 1984 but only 67% voted yes despite hundreds of thousands of U.S. dollars spent on "political education" campaigns, millions in subsidies offered, and even promises of free entry to the U.S. for all Belauans.

At this point the compact negotiators changed tack and offered Belauans an "improved" compact which they claimed was consistent with the constitution in that it banned the "use, storage, testing, and disposal" of nuclear weapons, although American nuclear forces were to be allowed to "operate" in Belau. On 21 Feb. 1986 this version received a 72.2% favorable vote, in part due to shock in the aftermath of the assassination of President Haruo I. Remeliik (see below).

Chief Ibedul Yutaka M. Gibbons and others filed suit against the compact and in July 1986 the Belau Supreme Court ruled it unconstitutional as 75% in favor had not been obtained. Another referendum on this same compact took place on 2 Dec. 1986, obtaining only 66% approval. The U.S. government responded to these affronts by reducing its subsidy to Belau as expenditures mushroomed, leading to a crisis in which the government payrolls could not be met.

Hard Tack

In early 1987 President Lazarus E. Salii increased pressure for the compact by ordering nightly electricity blackouts, reduced hospital service, and wage reductions for government employees. When the compact was defeated for the fifth time on 30 June 1987 Salii laid off about 900 of the 1,300 government employees, throwing Belau into chaos. It's now believed that Salii's intention was to declare a state of emergency and dispense with the constitution. By remaining calm in the face of unprecedented provocations the antinuclear side forestalled these plans.

The furloughed government workers camped outside the legislative building and sent death threats to defenders of the constitution. The home of Bena Sakuma, Press Information Officer of the Belau House of Delegates, was firebombed after he made a radio broadcast stating the pro-constitution position. Shots were fired into the home of the Speaker of the House of Delegates, Santos Olikong, by a former Special Assistant to President Salii (later convicted and sentenced to 15 years for the act). On 8 July 1987, when Belau police failed to curb the excesses, High Chief Yutaka Gibbons asked the United Nations to deploy a peacekeeping mission. The U.N. failed to act and the situation deteriorated.

On 16 July an intimidated House of Delegates began the process of amending the constitution, lowering the approval level for nuclear materials from 75% to 50%. This amendment got 73% of the vote in a snap referendum on 4 Aug. and the compact itself was declared approved after another hurried referendum on 20 August. High Chief Gibbons promptly challenged these acts in court but increasing mob violence forced him to withdraw his suit. A group of outraged Belauan women quickly reinstated the suit.

In September 1987 the government-sponsored reign of terror moved into high gear with new firebombings of the homes of opponents of the compact. On the evening of 8 Sept. 1987 Bedor Bins, aged 71, father of constitutionalist lawyer Roman Bedor and educator/activist Bernie Kelderman, was murdered by a pro-compact death squad outside the Belau Pacific Center in Koror. No one has ever been charged with this crime, although Roman claims that the red sedan driven by the gunmen in the Olikong case was the same car used by his father's killers. The same evening the home of Gabriela Ngirmang, leader of the women's group challenging the compact in the courts, was firebombed. The Belauan women tearfully withdrew their suit the next day.

Desperation And Deliverance

Seen in retrospect, the events of mid-1987 were acts of real desperation by the pro-compact elements. Shocked by the violence, the U.S. House Interior Committee delayed ratification of the compact and in March 1988 the women reinstated their suit. On 23 April 1988 Judge Robert A. Hefner ruled the 4 Aug. 1987 vote void and the nuclear-free constitution still in place. Without Belau's gun control laws (15-year mandatory jail sentence for possession) the disorders would have been far worse.

The IPSECO Scandal

From 1945 to 1982 three U.S. military diesel generators provided Belau with its electricity. Then the U.S. suddenly announced it was taking its generators back. In May 1983, with

State Department encouragement, Belau made a deal with the British firm International Power Systems Co. Ltd. (IPSECO) to build a 16-megawatt black-oil-burning electric generating plant and six-million-gallon oil storage facilities in Aimeliik state.

No competitive bids were taken for the project and IPSECO charged Belau $32 million, double what it should have cost to build the plant. The generating capacity was way above the four megawatts Belau actually needs, and the government has had to ration power due to a lack of funds to purchase fuel for the plant. The British operator had promised the plant would pay for itself through energy sales. Only a U.S. military base could consume that much power—the purpose, of course, for which the plant was intended.

By April 1985 Belau had defaulted on the power-plant debt, which had been financed by a British banking consortium. In Dec. 1985 five banks sued the Belau government for their money and on 5 Aug. 1988 a District Court in New York City ruled that Belau would have to pay $45 million (interest included)—about $3,000 each for every man, woman, and child—for the uneconomic plant, on which the Belau Government lost $2.4 million in fiscal 1987-88. In Feb. 1991, however, a New York court of appeals ruled that the $60-million case required a jury trial, which Belau stood a good chance of winning. British banker Richard Halerow declared, "We're absolutely flabbergasted."

After IPSECO declared bankruptcy in Britain in March 1986 the San Jose *Mercury News* uncovered illegal payments of more than $1 million by the contractor to officials in Belau and the Marshall Islands. A $250,000 kickback went to Carlos Salii, brother of the president. (As Speaker of the Belau House of Delegates from 1981 to 1984, Carlos Salii had chaperoned the power plant deal.) A $100,000 payment went to President Salii himself. In Dec. 1987 the U.S. House Subcommittee on Asian and Pacific Affairs asked Salii if such payments were normal in Belau. His now-famous reply: "In my experience, yes it is."

The Remeliik Assassination

The 1980 presidential elections were won by former Trust Territory District Administrator Haruo I. Remeliik over Airai State Governor Roman Tmetuchl and chief compact negotiator Lazarus Salii. Remeliik, a moderate, had helped frame the nuclear-free constitution, but later supported the compact as a means of gaining an income for Belau. In 1984 Remeliik was reelected when the anti-nuclear vote was split between Roman Tmetuchl and High Chief Yutaka Gibbons.

Just after midnight on 30 June 1985 Remeliik was shot four times outside his Koror home, the first Pacific head of state ever to be assassinated. Four persons were charged, including Roman Tmetuchl's son Melwert, his nephew, and two Tmetuchl associates. The suspects were convicted even though the main prosecution witness failed FBI lie-detector tests. The American Civil Liberties Union called the trial a "miscarriage of justice" and a "frame-up" and sent a New York lawyer to Belau. In July 1987 Tmetuchl's relatives were acquitted, as the appellate court found no credible evidence against them. (Melwert Tmetuchl later pleaded guilty to drug trafficking after a July 1989 raid by Guam narcotics agents.)

In the fall of 1985 chief compact negotiator Lazarus E. Salii, a faithful servant of Washington, was elected to replace Remeliik. Until his suicide on 20 Aug. 1988, Salii (nicknamed "mini-Marcos") ruled Belau amid increasing accusations of mismanagement and corruption. At the time of his death nearly a dozen lawsuits were pending against Salii, alleging misuse of government funds and illegal construction contracts.

It's now believed that Remeliik was murdered as he was about to make public charges of corruption against Salii associates. Remeliik was scheduled to appear on TV the next day to expose the IPSECO kickbacks. With one blow Remeliik was removed from the scene and Tmetuchl disgraced, leaving the way clear for Lazarus Salii's rise to power. Remeliik's killers have gone free.

American Designs On Belau

Belau straddles the north-south lines of communication between America's most important allies in the western Pacific: Australia and Japan. When the strategic value of Belau was recognized in 1944, the U.S. took Peleliu and Angaur from the Japanese at terrible cost. Even today the military "fallback arc" stretches from Saipan to Guam to Belau.

The Pentagon originally wanted Angaur for the Air Force, Koror for the Navy, and Babeldaop for the Army and Marines. The end of the Cold War has made major new bases on these islands unlikely, but Belau would still provide a useful springboard for U.S. military adventures in the Indian Ocean, Persian Gulf, and Asia, and rapid deployment forces may yet be installed here if the compact is approved. Airai Airport could become a base for Japanese antisubmarine aircraft, operating in coordination with U.S. forces.

Rumors (denied by the U.S.) persist that a top-secret forward Trident submarine base is desired for Koror's Malakal Harbor. The 8,000-meter-deep Belau Trench just east of the group would allow submarine movements invisible to satellite observation. Plans to dredge the harbor are waiting to be put into operation.

The U.S. continues to demand free entry for its ships, planes, and personnel, storage of nuclear weapons, renunciation of the archipelagic concept, and a "denial clause" designed to keep rival powers out of the area forever. Free passage through the archipelago for U.S. nuclear ships is considered essential, as American nuclear weapons are being increasingly redeployed aboard ships and submarines, a fact the U.S. will "neither confirm nor deny."

Japanese Designs On Belau

During the mid-'70s there was an attempt by corporations such as Nissho-Iwai and the Industrial Bank of Japan, backed by U.S. and Iranian interests, to create a $325 million central terminal station for oil storage on Belau's Kossol Reef. "Superport" was to have been used for transferring and storing oil from jumbo tankers between the Middle East and Japan.

Although the U.S. military supported the plan as very compatible with its own, local protests and the Environmental Protection Act managed to halt the project. The Japanese may yet revive this controversial project, despite the havoc Superport would wreak on the seas around Belau.

Recent Events

In the November 1988 presidential election, the pro-compact candidate, businessman Ngiratkel Etpison, won by only 31 votes in a seven-candidate race. The antinuclear vote was split between Airai governor Roman Tmetuchl, High Chief Ibedul Yutaka Gibbons, and Speaker Santos Olikong. Anti-compact candidates won the vice-presidency and a majority in both houses of the legislature.

In May 1989 Belauan and U.S. negotiators added a subsidiary agreement to the compact designed to protect Belauan lands, and the U.S. offered extra millions to investigate corruption in Belau and pay off the IPSECO debt. This was approved by the U.S. Congress in June 1989, but in a seventh compact referendum in Feb. 1990 the compact garnered only 60% in favor and was deemed defeated.

The 1990 vote convinced most observers that ratification of the present compact of free association had become impossible. Alternatives were independence, annexation as a U.S. commonwealth, or a nonnuclear compact of free association—something the U.S. has never been willing to grant. The U.S. continues to insist that provision for the transit and storage of nuclear weapons must be included and refuses to renegotiate. And now, with the Cold War over and military bases no longer so important, the U.S. is even suggesting that independence is an option for Belau, after all!

After testifying before the U.N. Trusteeship Council in early 1990, antinuclear activist Charles Scheiner wrote:

> Throughout the meeting, the U.S. repeated its big lie—that Belau has not approved the compact because the Constitution requires 75% voter approval. In fact, as I told the Council, it is only the entry of weapons of mass destruction into Belau that requires 75%. A peaceful compact, absent section 324, would need only 50% and would have been approved years ago as part of a normal decolonization process.

nuclear-free zone advocate Roman Bedor

DAVID STANLEY

In Aug. 1989 the U.S. General Accounting Office (GAO) confirmed reports of financial mismanagement in Belau, causing the U.S. Department of the Interior to announce that it would play a more active role in the internal affairs of Belau. In mid-1990 officials in Washington assumed veto power over Belauan laws and the budget, evoking loud protests against this renewed colonialism from Belauan officials. Meanwhile the U.S. government has succeeded in having the trust territory terminated in the Marshall Islands, the Federated States of Micronesia, and the Northern Marianas, leaving Belau as the last remaining U.N. Trust Territory. Heavy pressure is being applied to Belau to finally find its place in the world.

GOVERNMENT

The three branches of government are executive, legislative, and judicial. The president and vice president are elected by the people for four years; the president chooses his cabinet. The Olbiil Era Kelulau is a bicameral legislature consisting of an elected house of delegates (one delegate from each of the 16 states) and a senate (14 senators elected from districts based on population). A presidential veto can be overridden by a two-thirds majority in both houses. There are two political parties, the pro-compact Ta Belau (One Belau) Party, and the opposition Coalition for Open, Honest, and Just Government. The Chief Justice of the Supreme Court is appointed by the president and confirmed by the senate.

For its population Belau is one of the most overgoverned places on earth. Aside from the national government and chiefs, each of the 16 states has a governor, chosen according to its state constitution, and a legislature. Some state governors are elected directly by the people, while others may be the highest-ranking traditional leaders of the states. One governor is picked from among members of the state legislature. In addition there's a traditional Council of Chiefs, with one chief from each state; the authority of the chiefs is increasing under self-government.

ECONOMY

A net exporter in the 1930s and 1940s, Belau now depends almost exclusively on the money it receives for operations from the U.S. Dept. of the Interior as a Trust Territory. This accounts for 95% of its budget and between 1981 and 1991 the U.S. government subsidized Belau to the tune of US$227 million. At $2,384 per capita (1987) Belauans received three times as much money as citizens of the Marshalls or FSM but slightly less than people in the Northern Marianas. Yet since constitutional government came into effect on 1 Jan. 1981, Belau has continually faced bankruptcy, the result of shrinking U.S. subsidies to a burgeoning bureaucracy. The compact of free association would greatly increase funding for 15 years.

Upon self-government in 1981 Belau had 34 farmers and 1,227 public servants, and today nearly half of employed Belauans work for the government. Agricultural development was never encouraged by the Americans, and dependence on imported food and drink is growing. Consumer-oriented sales outlets are flourishing as U.S. money goes into imported goods. Merchandising is dominated by the locally owned Western Caroline Trading Company (WCTC). Filipinos do much of the petty work as maids and manual laborers.

Belau receives a half million dollars a year in license payments from some 290 Asian fishing boats. Thirty tons of fresh tuna for sashimi is flown directly from Koror to Japan every week by Palau International Traders Inc. Their cold-storage base is at the commercial port on Malakal and you may see their DC-8 cargo plane at the airport. Despite U.S. eagerness to "defend" Belau from a hypothetical foreign invasion, the U.S. has failed to provide adequate surveillance of Belau's valuable 200-nautical-mile fisheries zone.

Japan continues to have a keen interest in its former colony, and Japanese businesses are mushrooming. Tourism is being developed by Japanese interests in the same capital-intensive, exploitive manner as on Guam and Saipan. In 1990, 30,317 tourists and business travelers visited Belau, 20% of them from Japan and 35% from the U.S. The number of European and Australian visitors is increasing rapidly. The $40-million Palau Pacific Resort complex, completed in 1984 by the Japanese Tokyu group, caters mostly to expense-account Americans and packaged Japanese. Plans have been laid to build a new $100-million airport in central Babeldaop to open the country to jumbo jets and 160,000 tourists a year within two decades. A Japanese corporation offered to build the airport and access roads at no cost to Belau if they were given control of tourism for 30 years.

In recent years Belau became a transshipment point for counterfeit $100 bills produced in the Philippines, along with Southeast Asian heroin, being smuggled into the U.S. Top Belauan officials have been involved in the heroin trade. Out of a population of 15,000, there are 400 heroin addicts in Belau. Marijuana *(udel)* grown illegally on Peleliu and Angaur remains the country's only cash crop. Customs inspectors on Guam know all about Belau's drug problems, and thorough spot checks are carried out.

A plan to sell Belauan passports to Hong Kong and Taiwan residents at $250,000 each flopped when spoilsport American officials insisted on five years' residency in Belau as a condition for free entry into the U.S. Another wild scheme would have floated a $398 million bond issue with a New York firm to provide borrowed money for a whole range of nonproductive prestige projects. The deal fell through when the broker was indicted in the U.S. for fraud. Dirtier yet, in 1990 a company called Underwater Systems Australia Limited proposed to build an incinerator in western Babeldaop to burn garbage from Australia and Southeast Asia. Carpetbaggers and opportunists with sordid get-rich-quick schemes are turning up in Belau by the dozen.

PEOPLE

Belauans *appear* to be the most Americanized of Micronesians, but beneath the sur-face they're extremely tradition-oriented. In the face of conflicting outside influences, their identity as Belauans has grown in importance. Like other Micronesians they've learned the subtle art of seeming to comply while outlasting those who would control them.

Don't expect to see any Belauans in native dress—they all wear American-style clothes. They're short and stocky with broad heads and almost no necks. A little lump of betel nut is often stuck in one cheek. They're very friendly people but they'll usually check you out by waiting for you to smile or say hello first.

In 1990 Belau had 15,122 inhabitants. In addition some 1,562 Filipino and 315 Asian workers are present and much of the $6 million a year they earn is sent out of the country. Foreigners may lease Belauan land but not purchase it (in a 1990 decision the Belau Supreme Court ruled that 99-year leases by foreigners were the equivalent of ownership and therefore illegal). A fifth of all Belauans live abroad, many on Guam. Two distinct languages are spoken, Belauan and Sonsorolese-Tobian. Both Belauan and English are official languages. The Micronesian Occupational College (Box 9, Koror, PW 96940), founded in Koror in 1969, provides two years of vocational training for students from all across Micronesia.

Belau is a matriarchy in which the women choose which males will be the clan chiefs. Women own and divide land traditionally. Chiefly titles are inherited through the mother, and some of today's queens are extremely powerful.

One of the only indigenous religious movements remaining in Micronesia is found in Belau. The United Sect or Ngara Modekngei was founded by Temedad on Babeldaop in 1915. Traditional Belauan beliefs are mixed with ancestor worship and faith in protective spirits. Almost a third of the population is said to adhere to the religion. The Modekngei High School at Ibobang village in Ngatpang State, Babeldaop, was founded in 1974 with funding from the School of the Pacific Islands, Thousand Oaks, California. The emphasis is on teaching self-sufficiency and preserving Belauan culture, history, and language. For more information call Mr. Otoichi Besebes at 488-2741.

Arts And Crafts

The storyboard, among the most striking of Pacific art forms, originated in the early 1930s. The Japanese folklorist, Hisakatsu Hijikata, taught the men of Belau to take their histories and legends, incised and painted on rafters and gables of the ancient council houses *(bai)*, and reproduce them on portable planks. The emphasis has since evolved from bright colors to deeply carved relief, and the genre is flourishing as never before. Following tradition, the scenes can be blatantly erotic. In addition, these scenes are carved on branches, stumps, roots, tables, doors, etc., or can be shaped like fish, turtles or animals. Mahogany, ironwood (rare), and mangrove (lighter color) wood are used.

Replicas of traditional Belauan money *(udoud)* are made from pink and black coral and used as necklaces. The real money, still used in customary exchanges, was made from bits of glass or ceramic of unknown origin. Today some island women wear a string of *udoud* as a necklace.

Also unique are the Tobi Island monkey men, representing small guardian spirits that originally accompanied the deceased on their journey by canoe from this world. Among the other creations are the small model *bai* and canoes, wooden money jars, shell and coral jewelry, and woven pandanus bags and purses. Beware of turtle-shell jewelry, which is prohibited entry into the United States.

Holidays And Events

Public holidays include New Year's Day (1 Jan.), Youth Day (15 March), Senior Citizens' Day (5 May), President's Day (1 June), Nuclear-free Constitution Day (9 July), Labor Day (first Mon. or Tues. in Sept.), United Nations Day (24 Oct.), Thanksgiving (fourth Thurs. in Nov.), and Christmas (25 December).

Youth Day features open air concerts and sporting events, while on Senior Citizens' Day there are dancing contests, handicraft exhibitions, and a parade with floats. Senior citizens are remembered on the fifth day of the fifth month because in Belau one attains official senior citizenship at age 55! The Belau Arts Festival on Nuclear-free Constitution Day is also great for its traditional dancing, popular music performances, an arts and crafts show, and a culinary competition featuring local produce and cuisine.

During the *ngloik* dance, lines of Belauan women, their bodies glistening with coconut oil, chant legends to rhythmic movements. The Belauan men dance the *ruk* to celebrate a victory or inaugurate a new *bai*.

PRACTICALITIES

Accommodations

All of the regular hotels are in or near Koror. No obvious campsites present themselves in central Koror, but you could try the village behind the Palau Nikko Hotel at Ngermid, down by the water. There's no problem camping on Peleliu, Angaur, and Kayangel, and the likelihood of being able to stay with a family is good. On Babeldaop get permission before pitching your tent, or camp in the bush out of sight. Drunks are occasionally a problem on Babeldaop. Many of the states have offices in Koror which may be able to advise on village accommodations in their areas.

Peleliu and Angaur offer small village guesthouses, but Paradise Air in Koror can be rather evasive about the price and availability of accommodations at them, and the guesthouse operators sometimes charge as much for food as they feel their guests will pay. Clarify prices in advance. You may be permitted to cook at the guesthouses, otherwise you can eat straight from the tin if you have a can opener. Buy ship biscuits for hiking or camping. Some guesthouse keepers base their prices on what the restaurants and hotels in Koror charge, even though the quality isn't comparable. The local Paradise Air agents on Angaur and Peleliu will try to find a bed for you at one of the guesthouses upon arrival.

(clockwise from top) barbecued chicken, Majuro, Marshall Is. (Ria de Vos); children near Kolonia, Pohnpei, FSM (M. Dennis Gee); a fisherman at Gilmaan, YAP FSM (Karl Partridge); dancers at the Micronesian Cultural Center, Pohnpei, FSM (Eugene Kridler); an old man sharpening his fishing spear at Maap, Yap, FSM (Karl Partridge)

(clockwise from top) red-footed boobies on Hikina Island, Johnston Atoll (Gerald M. Ludwig); fairy terns, Midway Atoll (R.J. Shallenberger); red-footed booby, brown phase, Wake Atoll (R.J. Shallenberger); Layson albatrosses, Midway Atoll (R.J. Shallenberger); male frigatebird (Eugene Kridler); all photos this page courtesy U.S. Fish and Wildlife Service)

All hotel accommodations are subject to a 10% room tax which is added to the bill. Some hotels also have a five-percent service charge.

Visas

No visa is required for a stay of 30 days or less, although an onward ticket must be shown. Visa extensions cost $50 each, so ask for the full 30 days upon arrival. Extensions are not automatic and will only be done twice, so three months is the very longest you'll be able to stay. A U.S. visa may be required if you'll be transiting Guam, but not if you're making a roundtrip from Manila.

Money And Measurements

U.S. currency is used. Restaurant tipping is optional but appreciated. Most government offices are closed for lunch 1130-1230. When arriving in Belau from Manila, Guam, or Yap remember the one-hour time difference.

Although U.S. domestic postage rates apply, Belau has its own colorful postage stamps bearing the name "Palau." Collectors can order sets from the Palau Philatelic Bureau, G.P.O. Box 7775, New York, NY 10116 U.S.A. They don't provide standing-order accounts: issues must be ordered individually.

Information

For a brochure and list of hotels write the Palau Visitors Authority, Box 256, Koror, PW 96940 (tel. 488-2793). The *Pacific Daily News* is flown in from Guam. The *Belau Tribune* is published every Thursday on Saipan, and copies can be purchased in Koror at the souvenir counter in Ben Franklin Department Store in Koror. There's a government-run radio station (WSZB) and a cable TV network which shows San Francisco programming and commercials on 12 channels operating around-the-clock.

The 167 pages of *A Guide to the Palau Islands* (available to U.S. addresses *only* for $20 postpaid from NECO Tours, Box 129, Koror, PW 96940) by Mandy Thyssen, are jammed full of fantastic color photos, line drawings, and useful information. Mandy works as a diving instructor at the Palau

Pacific Resort, so all the main scuba locales are described along with excellent coverage of the flora and fauna. Nancy Babour's *Palau* (Full Court Press, 511 Mississippi, San Francisco, CA 94107 U.S.A.) is similar.

Try to see one of these devastating documentaries: *Belau, the Price of Independence* by Franco-Australian filmmaker Michel Bongiovani, *Strategic Trust: The Making of a Nuclear Free Belau* by James Heddle, or *Trouble in Paradise* by Sylvia Collier.

Charlie Scheiner (Box 1182, White Plains, NY 10602 U.S.A.) issues a *Belau Update* with news of political developments in the country, and he'll put you on the mailing list for a donation of $20.

Getting There

Continental Air Micronesia has daily flights to Koror from Guam and three a week from Manila. Connections can be made easily from the major cities of Asia, Japan, Europe, and the U.S. by way of Guam and Manila. Three times a week Yap is included as a stopover on the Guam-Koror flight. Continental flies Koror-Saipan nonstop once a week, but not Saipan-Koror.

Koror is the last stop on Continental's Micronesian island hop. A through ticket Honolulu-Majuro-Kosrae-Pohnpei-Chuuk-Guam-Yap-Koror costs about $795 OW; from California the same ticket is $1,026 OW. All passengers must change planes on Guam and often spend the night there at their own expense.

Some off-peak evening Air Mike flights to Koror from Yap and Guam are considerably cheaper than the regular fare, so ask plenty of questions if you don't already have your ticket. From Koror the half-price flight to Guam departs on Mon., Thurs., and Sun. evenings ($166 OW).

Getting Around

Palau Paradise Air (Box 488, Koror, PW 96940; tel. 488-2348) offers commuter service to Peleliu and Angaur. The flight between Peleliu and Angaur allows you to combine both islands in a single visit. The Koror-Peleliu-Angaur service operates twice a day (on Sat. only the morning flight operates), making even day-trips from Koror possible. The Wed. services are reserved for charters.

Fares run $20 Koror-Peleliu, $15 Peleliu-Angaur, and $26 Angaur-Koror. The plane passes directly over the Rock Islands—spectacular from the air. You can also charter the six-seater Palau Paradise Air plane at $295 an hour for some spectacular aerial sightseeing. Credit cards are not accepted.

Paradise Air reservations must be reconfirmed on the islands, otherwise the local agent could give your seat to someone else. You're allowed 20 pounds of luggage free; $2 for each additional pound. Transfers be-tween Airai Airport and Palau Paradise's Koror office are free.

Airport

Airai Airport (ROR) is on Babeldaop, 12 km east of Koror by road. The taxi into town is $13. Some hotels charge $10 RT for airport transfers; others are free. Car rental agencies are also located at the airport. The Visitors Authority operates a desk at the airport, which opens for all arrivals, and they'll give you a complete hotel list with current rates. There's a pay telephone (25 cents) against the wall beside the exit from the customs area. The departure tax is $10 on international flights.

an early 19th century view of Belau

KOROR

Despite lacking a beach, Koror is by far the most scenic town in Micronesia. From several points you get excellent views of the fabulous Rock Islands stretching out to the south. A paved road leads to Koror, political and economic center of Belau, from Airai Airport on southern Babeldaop. About two-thirds of the country's population now live in Koror (pop. 10,501). The bustling prewar Japanese city was leveled by American bombing, although isolated relics remain. Today Koror throbs again with a steady stream of traffic along the main road through town. Bridges and causeways linking Koror Island to Babeldaop, Arakabesan, Malakal, and other islands make it a perfect base and an interesting place to explore.

SIGHTS

Begin by visiting the **Belau National Museum** (tel. 488-2265; open weekdays 0800-1100/1300-1600, Sat. 1000-1400; admission $2). Founded in 1955, this is the oldest museum in Micronesia. The exhibits of local artifacts, crafts, painted storyboards, frag-

ments of old *bais,* traditional money, and models of *bai* and dugout canoes occupy a two-story concrete building which was once a Japanese weather station. Notice especially the original paintings by Rechucher Charlie Gibbons (1894-1988), Belau's most famous artist. A varied botanical collection and a statue of the late President Haruo I. Remeliik (1933-85) spruce up the museum grounds. The traditional *bai* near the museum was erected in 1991 to replace an earlier one built in 1969 that burned down in 1979.

North of the museum near the center of town is the Olbiil Era Kelulau or Belau **legislature,** a former Japanese power plant built in the 1930s. Both the senate and house of delegates meet here.

Malakal
Malakal Island, Koror's industrial suburb and commercial port, has a cold-storage plant for tuna exported to Japan. The nearby **Fisheries Co-op** sells fresh fish daily. The Belau Boat Yard is nearby.

At the end of the road on Malakal is the **Micronesian Mariculture Demonstration Center** (MMDC), locally known as the "ice

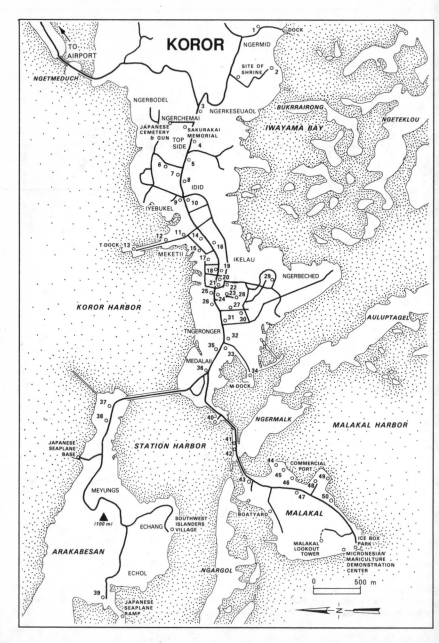

box" for a long-gone Japanese ice-making plant. The concrete steps down to the water from the park by the MMDC would make this a good place to snorkel if it weren't for the nearby sewage-treatment plant. It's a perfect picnic spot.

The MMDC, a major mariculture research center established in 1974, is the world's largest commercial giant-clam farm. Through hatching and rearing the MMDC hopes to save from extinction the giant Tridacna clam, a species ravaged by Taiwanese poachers who take only the abductor muscle (an aphrodisiac) and leave the rest to rot. Millions of seed clams have been distributed throughout Belau and to 17 foreign countries to support low-cost, low-technology projects raising giant clams for profit. Aside from four major

clam species, hawksbill sea turtles are reared in tanks here for release, and other marinelife such as commercial trochus and reef fish may be seen in outdoor tanks—visitors welcome weekdays 0800-1100/1300-1600, $2 donation requested.

(For information on the MMDC's visiting scientist program, which provides laboratory space, boat rentals, and accommodations for marine researchers, write: Box 359, Koror, PW 96940. A $100 Scientific Research Permit must be obtained, but the other rates are reasonable.)

Climb to the top of Malakal for a stunning **view** of the Rock Islands crowding Koror. Take the dirt road uphill from the sewage plant to the water tank, then bushwhack through the forest to the high metal tower at the sum-

VICINITY OF KOROR

1. Mother & Child Stone
2. Nikko Palau Hotel
3. U.S. Liaison Office
4. T & O Motel
5. Lee Bros. Motel
6. Protestant Mission
7. West Motel II/West Laundromat
8. Palau Paradise Air
9. Island Mart
10. Catholic Mission
11. Sure-Save Mart
12. West Motel I
13. T-Dock Guesthouse
14. Koror State Government
15. Yokohama Inn
16. New Koror Hotel
17. Lebuu Gift Shop
18. WCTC Shopping Center/ Ben Franklin Dept. Store
19. Palau Hotel
20. West Motel Plaza
21. post office
22. Continental Air Micronesia/ VIP Guest House
23. police station/jail
24. Belau Legislature
25. Bank of Guam/Arirang Restaurant
26. Micronesian Occupational College (MOC)/Bookstore
27. ball park
28. Civic Center
29. Belau National Museum
30. old hospital
31. Bank of Hawaii/ Furusato Restaurant
32. public library
33. Judicial Building
34. Fish 'n Fins/Marina Hotel
35. D.W. Motel/Senior Citizens Center
36. Palau Visitors Authority
37. Overseas Communications/ new hospital
38. Office of the President
39. Palau Pacific Resort
40. Peleliu Club
41. Cave Inn
42. Blue Line
43. King's Car Rental/Studios
44. NECO Marine
45. Carp Sea Food Restaurant/ Palau Diving Center
46. Fisheries Coop/Royal Belau Yacht Club
47. Longshoremen Restaurant
48. freezer plant
49. Belau Transfer
50. Malakal Central Hotel

mit (124 meters), once used by the Japanese as a lighthouse. On one side you can see right across Babeldaop; on the other you look down on the great green arms enfolding the harbor. Very few places in the Pacific give you as much of an eyeful as this tower.

Arakabesan

The Japanese evicted all the Belauans from Arakabesan Island and turned it into a military base. Great concrete football fields sloping down into the water remain from the **seaplane bases**, one beyond a school at Meyungs village not far from the causeway from Koror, two more on the west side of the island by the Tokyu Corporation-owned, $40-million **Palau Pacific Resort.**

On the south side of Arakabesan is a Southwest Islander's village accessible via a dirt road. Notice the outrigger canoes.

East Of Town

On each side of the Koror State Government office are stone platforms and backrests, once used for chiefly meetings. Walk east along the highway to Top Side. Just beyond a couple of Japanese stone lanterns, go down a dirt track on the left beside the house marked "QTR. NO. 03" to the evocative **Sakurakai Memorial**. The old Japanese cemetery and a cannon are just below.

Continue along the main highway (keep right) toward the **Palau Nikko Hotel**. Near the hotel turnoff, past more stone lanterns, is a stone stairway leading to the recently restored Japanese **Shinto shrine.** When opened in 1940 this was the largest of its kind outside Japan. Continue to the hotel, which offers excellent views of Rock Islands-studded Iwayama Bay and a few old guns at the top of the hill.

Ngermid village, beyond the hotel turnoff, is attractive and well worth strolling through. Halfway down to the dock at Ngermid are some old stone platforms and pathways and beyond the houses, in a field to the left, the stone figure of a woman and child frozen on this spot when caught snooping on a gathering of men in a *bai*. Visible on the hillside is a Japanese cave containing a double-barreled

AA gun. Several other Japanese guns are in the bush beyond the canoe dock at Ngermid.

The best natural **beach** near Koror accessible by road is directly under the north end of the K-B Bridge. An old dredge lies beached here and there's also a bar.

PRACTICALITIES

Accommodations

The cheapest place to stay is the **T-Dock Guest House** (Box 1728, Koror, PW 96940; tel. 488-2369), beside Oh's Fish Market at T-Dock. A very simple room with fan and shared bath is $15 s or d, plus a one-time $5 charge for linens. Monthly rates are $175 d. Communal cooking facilities are available. This place is very basic compared to the other hotels around Koror, but it may appeal to rock-bottom, low-budget travelers.

The locally owned **D.W. Motel** (Box 738, Koror, PW 96940; tel. 488-2641), a clean three-story building nicely set back from the busy highway to Malakal, is a big step up in quality. The 17 clean, a/c rooms with private bath and hot shower go for $25 s, $30 d, $35 t. Those staying over 15 days may get a 10% discount. The beds are firm and comfortable and each room has a fridge. The hot water available in the common lounge is great for instant cereals and soups; free tea and coffee are also available here. A coin laundry adjoins the motel. Airport transfers are free—recommended.

Right above the Continental Air Micronesia office in central Koror is the **V.I.P. Guest Hotel** (Box 18, Koror, PW 96940; tel 488-1502). The 10 a/c, balconied rooms in this pink three-story building are $65 s or d. At this price it's worth trying only if everything else is full.

The **West Motel** (Box 280, Koror, PW 96940), a subsidiary of the Western Caroline Trading Company, has three branches. Motel I (tel. 488-1780), a three-story building at T-Dock, offers nine a/c rooms, $50 with kitchenette, $45 without. Motel II (tel. 488-2529) at Top Side (Ngerchemal) has 11 a/c rooms with cooking facilities at $45, plus two

two-bedroom apartments for $50. **West Motel Plaza** (tel. 488-1671) in downtown Koror charges $55 and up. At the airport information is available from the Toyota Rent-a-Car agency.

The **Palau Hotel** (Box 64, Koror, PW 96940; tel. 488-1703) in central Koror is a four-story building built by Taiwanese interests. The 38 a/c rooms with TV and fridge go for $35 s, $40 d, $45 t. The Omball Restaurant on the premises is probably the worst in Koror. This hotel caters to Asian businesspeople.

The bottom-end **New Koror Hotel** (Box 339, Koror, PW 96940; tel. 488-2231), also in the heart of Koror town, offers 26 a/c rooms with private bath at $27.50 s, $33 d. Car and boat rentals can be arranged; airport transfers are $4. The hotel owner, Fumio Rengiil, is a former senator and chief of police—he's an interesting person to talk to.

Also try the **T & O Motel** (Box 1383, Koror, PW 96940; tel. 488-2883), above T & O Enterprise at Top Side near the place where Japanese stone lanterns are set on each side of the road. The five a/c rooms are $35 s or d, $45 t.

King's Studio Apartments (Box 424, Koror, PW 96940; tel. 488-2964) on Malakal has 10 a/c rooms with TV and private bath at $35 s, $45 d. Its location is a little too far to walk to from town and not an especially attractive area.

Visiting scientists and students involved in marine science research programs should apply in advance to stay in the a/c dormitory rooms at the **Micronesian Mariculture Demonstration Center** (Box 359, Koror, PW 96940; tel. 488-2266) on Malakal Island for $20 s, $30 d. Bed linen is provided but bring your own towel. A refrigerator and cooking facilities are available. Without advance reservations you won't get in, as the MMDC doesn't cater to vacationers. If you tell Customs you intend to stay at the MMDC they'll ask to see your research permit ($100).

For a longer stay inquire at the mayor's office in the Koror State Government building (Box 116, Koror, PW 96940; tel. 488-2853 or 488-2576; ask for Scott Yano) about apartments for rent by the month ($150-600 a month).

Expensive Hotels
The Japanese-owned, Hawaiian-style **Palau Pacific Resort** (Box 308, Koror, PW 96940; tel. 488-1603) on Arakabesan Island is popular among civil servants and executives on expense accounts and packaged tourists from Japan and the States. This $40 million complex operated by the Pan Pacific hotel chain has 100 a/c rooms from $160 s or d, or $450 for a suite, plus two restaurants, tennis courts, a swimming pool, and an artificial beach. The resort's Meduu Ribtal Restaurant offers lobster and mangrove crab at $18.50 a pound, sashimi platter $18, bouillabaisse $16, and fresh fish $12, plus a different buffet every night—very good, but expensive. "Commercial rate" discounts are said to be available on room prices. All the scuba boats pick up divers off the hotel's long concrete pier.

The four-story **Malakal Central Hotel** (Box 6016, Koror, PW 96940; tel. 488-1117) adjoins the commercial port, and for $140 s or d you can do better than this. The clientele is almost exclusively Japanese.

The three-story **Marina Hotel** (Box 142, Koror, PW 96940; tel. 488-1786), also known as the Hotel Sunroute, at M-Dock is mainly of interest if you've booked scuba diving with Fish 'n Fins. The 28 a/c rooms begin around $80 s or d. The Southern Cross Restaurant at this hotel is known for its poor service and high prices. The location is convenient for sightseers, though the walk into town from the hotel passes a smelly public dump.

Until the Palau Pacific Resort went up in 1984, Belau's top hotel was the atmospheric **Hotel Nikko Palau** (Box 310, Koror, PW 96940; tel. 488-2486), the former TraveLodge built by Continental Airlines in 1971. Now owned by Japan Air Lines, the Hotel Nikko is spectacularly set on a hillside just east of Koror, with a breathtaking view of the Rock Islands. The 51 small, mildewed rooms with private bath cost $95 s, $105 d, or $75 d if you ask for the commercial or government rate. The hotel restaurant/bars are pricey and the meals aren't up to scratch, though the Sunday dinner buffet (1800-2100) draws local expatriates (reservations suggested).

The hotel swimming pool is small and there's no beach, but dive boats can pick up/drop off passengers just below the hotel (the hotel tour desk is very expensive). It's mostly Japanese groups who stay here.

Food

Koror boasts quite a few restaurants, with new ones appearing all the time. Locally caught fish, fresh produce, and inexpensive plate lunches are often available. Buy local foods such as cold coconuts, hot tapioca, fried fish, and fresh fruit at **Yano's** beside WCTC Shopping Center. Fresh fish is sold daily at the fish market on the Fisheries Coop dock at Malakal.

The coffee bar inside **Sure-Save Mart** on the road to T-Dock is great for coffee and donuts or inexpensive chicken and rice. They're open daily and there's a cozy little corner where you can sit and watch CNN Headline News as you sip your bottomless cup of coffee.

The locally oriented **Yokohama Inn** on Lebuu St. serves inexpensive lunches, including fried fish and Japanese dishes from around $5. **China Snack Bar** opposite West Motel Plaza in the center of town has cheap lunch specials.

The **Arirang Restaurant** above the Bank of Palau serves excellent Japanese and Korean dishes but at $8-10 a plate it's rather expensive.

A good medium-priced choice is the **Furusato Restaurant** (tel. 488-2689) beside the Bank of Hawaii, a Koror favorite with an extensive menu, good Japanese and American food, and reasonable prices. The local fat cats congregate here for leisurely business breakfasts.

Ben Yore Snack Bar beside Family Mart, just below the old hospital, is good for breakfast (0730-1000 daily) and offers reasonable Chinese and American food other times.

One of the cheapest places for lunch is the **Longshoremen Restaurant** on Malakal, which has a cold buffet with some Belauan dishes, and you only pay for what you eat. Everything's gone by 1230.

The **Carp Sea Food Restaurant** (tel. 488-2978), near the Fisheries Co-op on Malakal, serves authentic Japanese dishes like tofu stew, sukiyaki, and tempura. Included is a plate of fruit for dessert. The portions are large and prices very reasonable, with most things around $5. This rustic island restaurant, full of colorful Gauguin-style art by painter/diver/chef Johnny Kishigawa, is a real little hideaway; in fact you'll never find it at night unless you know the way in. They're only open for lunch (1100-1400) and dinner (1800-2100). Recommended.

Also full of local favor is the nearby **Royal Belau Yacht Club** overlooking the Fisheries Co-op dock. You can get a good breakfast here from 0600 to 1000, and the lunch or dinner specials begin around $6.50. It's a great place for a drink, especially at happy hour (1700-2000), and there's a nice open terrace from which to observe the action on "Pirate's Cove." Otherwise enjoy the a/c inside. Their specialty is pizza (pepperoni $9, $12 for the special), and they'll even deliver.

Entertainment

The day action around Koror consists of cruising up and down the one main street and touring huge, customerless department stores. Koror's nightlife kicks in after 2100 by the Malakal causeway. The **Peleliu Club** and **Kosiil Landing** (open 1730 to midnight) nightclubs are adjacent on an island off the causeway, but it's a local scene and can get rough (expats hang out at the **Royal Belau Yacht Club** mentioned above). Learn how to dance the local cha-cha. Women should wear jeans and high heels to look "native."

Everything closes down when midnight curfew rolls around, but you're given another hour to get home after the bars close. Many restaurants in Koror offer Japanese *karaoke*-style entertainment in the evening.

The Belau National Museum (Box 666, Koror, PW 96940; tel. 488-2265) can arrange **traditional dance programs** for visiting groups with two weeks' notice and payment of a $100 fee. Slide shows for groups are available, and the museum can provide a tutor to those wishing to learn Belauan. The Ngara Bngungau Dance Troupe also performs traditional dances for visiting groups for a flat fee of $100.

There's an occasional "island night" at the **Palau Pacific Resort** at 1800 with a buffet of local food and traditional dancing ($24 plus 10% tax). Call 488-1603 for information and reservations.

Sports And Recreation

Belau is one of the most sought-after scuba locales in the Pacific. The diving season is year-round with 60-meter visibility. A dozen blue holes are found along the southwest barrier reef, along with 60 identified dropoffs; Ngemelis Dropoff on Barnun Bay is considered the world's best. One minute you're standing knee-deep on the reef, the next you're plunging into 250 meters of warm tropical ocean! This nearly vertical wall is almost covered with crimson/yellow sea fans, sponges, and soft corals. At Denges Dropoff is a plateau with giant tabletop corals.

Want to see fan coral, giant clams, or sharks? Just ask—the local divemasters know over 50 good diving spots including blue holes and at least a dozen channel dives (drift dives). Special trips can be arranged to the underwater cave system off Koror or the saltwater Rock Island lakes connected to the lagoon by tunnels. At Jellyfish Lake on Eil Malk you can swim among the non-stinging creatures. Also ask about submerged Japanese ships and aircraft, including the well-preserved Zero sitting on a reef at Koror Road. The hospital has a recompression chamber if you need it.

Fish 'n Fins Ltd. (Box 142, Koror, PW 96940; tel. 488-2637) beside the Palau Marina Hotel at M-Dock is a very experienced scuba operator with daily trips and safe boats. Francis Toribiong at Fish 'n Fins offers the best price on a snorkeling trip to the Rock Islands—$45 pp, lunch included. Scuba diving is $50 with one tank, $85 with two tanks. Night dives are $45 and NAUI scuba diving certification courses are available at $450. They'll pick up at the Palau Pacific Hotel, but nowhere else.

The **NECO Marine** (Shallum and Mandy Etpison, Box 129, Koror, PW 96940; tel. 488-2206) on Malakal Island is Koror's largest and most expensive dive shop: one tank $60, two tanks $90, night dives $60. Transfers from the hotels are free. Full-day boat rentals to the Rock Islands are $230 for up to three persons, $264 for four persons. NECO also offers PADI certification courses with three to seven days of theory and two dives for $450 all-inclusive. Their branch office at the Palau Pacific Resort caters mostly to Japanese divers.

Sam's Tour Service (Sam Scott, Box 428, Koror, PW 96940; tel. 488-1720; fax 488-1471) isn't as big as the other scuba operators, so you'll receive more personalized service (one tank $50, two tanks $80, night dive $50, all-day snorkeling $50). Trips to northern Babeldaop are a specialty. Sam operates out of his own home, so give him a call and he'll pick you up at your hotel the next morning. Ask if lunch is included.

For *serious* divers, **Micronesian Yachts Co. Ltd.** (Box 1216, Koror, PW 96940; tel. 488-1363) operates a dive and sail charter operation at Koror with their 20-meter sloop, the *Sun Tamarin*. Its three double staterooms are outfitted for six scuba divers. The price is $1,895 pp all-inclusive for the seven-day tours, but four or five dives a day are common. One diver managed to pack 67 dives into 10 days! Dives among the currents and dropoffs at the south end of Peleliu are featured. Reservations must be made several months in advance through Sea and See Travel, 50 Francisco St., Ste. 205, San Francisco, CA 94133 (tel. 415-434-3400). Capt. Michael D. Meares and his Aussie/Kiwi crew are based next to NECO Marine at Malakal.

Island Base Camps

To avoid the long commute by speedboat from Koror to the dive sites, many divers choose to stay at one of the island base camps closer to the action. The **Carp Island Resort** (Box 5, Koror, PW 96940; tel. 488-2978), on Ngercheu Island near the fabulous Ngemelis Dropoff, offers three duplex cottages with private bath, $55 s, $65 d, $75 t.

Bunkbed accommodations are available in a large "divehouse" of 10 four-bed dorms with shared bath ($22 pp). The island restaurant serves breakfast ($7.50), lunch ($7.50), and dinner ($20), but seafood specials ($25 pp) must be requested the day before. If owner Johnny Kishigawa is there to do the cooking you're in for a real treat; bring food if you want to cook for yourself. Scuba diving at Carp Island is $65 for one tank, $90 for two tanks, and $65 for night diving. Boat transfers from Koror $30 pp (free for scuba divers). Information is available from the **Palau Diving Center** at Carp Restaurant on Malakal.

A less expensive choice would be the **Ngerchong Island Boat-tel** (Box 94, Koror, PW 96940; tel. 488-2691) which also caters mostly to groups. They have one large building, or *abai*, with cooking facilities at $50 a night for up to 10 persons, $100 for up to 20 persons. A separate four-person unit is $35. Bathroom facilities are shared. Rafting, plus line and spearfishing, are among the activities offered. A charter boat to Ngerchong might cost $80 RT, or you can try to get the Peleliu boat to drop you.

You can also camp free on one of the Rock Islands, where shelters have been erected by the Koror government. Fish 'n Fins will drop you off at the end of a snorkeling tour with a promise to take you back to Koror a day or two later at no additional charge. Be sure to take enough water and pack out your garbage. An ocean kayak would be just the thing here, as most of the Rock Islands are inaccessible due to their limestone structure. The few Rock Islands with sandy beach areas are crowded with divers and picnickers most of the day. Don't expect an "uninhabited" island all to yourself!

Shopping
The **Belau National Museum** in Koror sells quality storyboards, Tobi Island monkey men, other handicrafts, and books on Belau. First-day covers, postcards, and prints designed by noted local artists Simeon and Samuel Adelbai are available. By making purchases here you support this worthy institution.

The talented prisoners held in the **Correction and Rehabilitation Division Jail** (open 0800-1600 daily) behind the police station downtown carve outstanding storyboards. Since the guards get a 10% cut, purchases can be made on the spot; work is also done to order. (Prisoners on lesser charges may keep pets and are allowed to go home on weekends or attend courses. Most willingly return to the ramshackle structure.) Medium-sized storyboards cost $100-225 and up.

The **Senior Citizens Center,** beside D.W. Motel, and **Lebuu Gift Shop** also sell storyboards and other crafts. **George Market** beside Belau Medical Clinic has Belauan traditional money as well as storyboards. **Shell Museum Souvenirs** near the Bank of Hawaii has storyboards, Tobi monkey men, and other carvings. The gift shop at the **Hotel Nikko** is more expensive but the quality is good. **Duty-Free Shoppers** at the Palau Pacific Resort sells storyboards, first-day covers, T-shirts, Belau videos ($30), etc.

The post office sells Belau postage stamps and first-day covers at face value, and what's available is displayed. They're only allowed to sell items less than one year old, however, and after a year they must destroy leftover covers. Most souvenir shops on Koror sell older stamps and covers.

The **Ben Franklin Department Store** upstairs in WCTC Shopping Center has a wide assortment of clothes, consumer goods, and cheap snorkeling gear, plus souvenirs such as storyboards, first-day covers, etc. There's a large supermarket downstairs at WCTC but **Sure-Save Mart** has a better selection of groceries. It's best to bring your own camera film with you to Koror.

Services
The Bank of Hawaii (tel. 488-2602), Bank of Palau (tel. 488-2638), and Bank of Guam (tel. 488-2697) have branches in Koror. All are open Mon.-Thurs. 0930-1430, Fri. 0930-1700. To cash traveler's checks expressed in currencies other than U.S. dollars costs US$8 commission (U.S. dollar checks cashed free). There's seldom a line at the

Bank of Palau where U.S. traveler's checks are cashed but there's no foreign exchange.

The post office in central Koror is open weekdays 0800-1600. If you're considering mailing a storyboard, be aware that it can't be over 108 inches total length and breadth. To the U.S. the maximum weight is 70 pounds ($75.35 by airmail), to Great Britain the maximum is 66 pounds ($97.25 for the first 22 pounds, then $3 for each additional pound, by air).

Phone long-distance from the PNCC Overseas Communications office just above the new hospital on Arakabesan (open 24 hours). Charges are $9 for three minutes to all Micronesia, $12 for three minutes to the Philippines and U.S., and $15 for three minutes to Europe.

The Immigration Office (tel. 488-2498) is upstairs in the Judicial Building (entry from the back side).

Dr. Victor Yano's Belau Medical Clinic (Box 822, Koror, PW 96940; tel. 488-2688) just up from WCTC Shopping Center charges $13 for consultations, but appointments are required. Prices are lower but you get less attention at the new hospital out on Arakabesan.

Palau in Prints (tel. 488-1488) on the street leading inland from Furusato Restaurant develops color and black-and-white film on the premises.

Tngeronger Laundromat is beside the National Development Bank of Palau on Lebuu St. below WCTC Shopping Center. There's also a small laundromat behind the reception area at D.W. Motel.

Information

The Palau Visitors Authority (Box 256, Koror, PW 96940; tel. 488-2793) is at the junction of the Malakal and Arakabesan roads. Watch for William H. Stewart's *Tourist Map of Palau* and *Battlefield Map of Peleliu* at souvenir outlets.

The Kltal-Reng or Belau Pacific Center (Box 58, Koror, PW 96940; tel. 488-2745), a grass-roots citizens' group, was established to spread awareness of nuclear and independence issues, while reintroducing young Belauans to fishing and gardening. Get in touch by asking for attorney Roman Bedor at Meyungs village on Arakabesan. The Otil A Beluad (Box 273, Koror, PW 96940; tel. 488-2831), led by Gabriela Ngirmang and Cita Morei, is a women's organization formed to defend Belau's nuclear-free constitution.

There's an a/c public library (Box 189, Koror, PW 96940; open weekdays 0730-1130/1230-1630, Mon.-Thurs. also 1900-2100, weekends 0900-1100) opposite the high school. Before the war the Japanese administration building stood on the site of the present library.

Blue Line (tel. 488-2679) opposite the Mobil station on Malakal has topographical maps of Babeldaop and Koror for $10 a sheet, also a few nautical charts.

The MOC Book Store at the Micronesian Occupational College sells cheap novels and better books on Micronesia, this book included.

Radio station WSZB-AM broadcasts from Koror over 1584 kHz.

GETTING AROUND

Field Trip

Belau Transfer (Box 318, Koror, PW 96940; tel. 488-2432) at the commercial port may have information on the quarterly field trip to the Southwest Islands (Sonsorol, Pulo Anna, Merir, Helen Reef, and Tobi). A Belauan fishing patrol boat also travels there occasionally.

Local Boats

Boats to Peleliu and Angaur leave from the dock by the **Fisheries Co-op** on Malakal.

The state boat to Peleliu leaves Tues. and Fri. ($3, two hours); it also sometimes makes special trips. Due to varying tide conditions, it's best to check the precise departure times with the boat captain, either the night before or early on the morning of the day you wish to leave. Occasional fishing boats also head out from Fisheries to Ollei and Melekeok on Babeldaop.

Fisheries is also the place to hitch rides to the Rock Islands, when speedboats come in for gas. Boats between Peleliu and Angaur are rare, although you might arrange for an Angaur boat to drop you off on Peleliu on its way back to Koror. Private boats to Peleliu leave from the anchorage beside the Peleliu Club.

Boats for Babeldaop and Kayangel leave from **T-Dock.** Although a few of the state boats to the north have regular schedules, the only sure way to get on is just to be there, ready to leave when they do. Friday afternoon and early Sat. morning are good times to look for speedboats to northern Babeldaop (up to $5 OW). Even if they tell you they're full, persist.

Surprisingly, Monday is a good day to head north, as the crowds are smaller and some boats which brought commuters may be returning empty. There's a concrete waiting pavilion by the dock. Quickly accept a ride to any place in Ngaraard or Ngarchelong states, or to Kayangel if you're lucky.

Every other week a boat makes the four-hour trip to Kayangel ($6 pp). It usually leaves Koror on Sat. morning, returning Thurs. afternoon a week and a half later. On its way back, the boat calls at Ollei, the northernmost village on Babeldaop, and sometimes another village halfway down—a good connection for those wanting to get off. Rides are scarce on the off weeks, but sometimes available from speedboats and fishing boats.

By Road

There's no bus service, but nearly everyone travels by car so hitching is easy. Taxis are not unreasonable. Standard fares from the center of Koror are $2 to Ice Box Park, $3 to the Nikko Hotel, $4 to the Palau Pacific Resort, and $13 to the airport. Most taxis carry a printed rate card which lists all fares. Be sure to ask the price in advance, and ask to see the card if it seems too high. Taxis are individual, not shared, and the price is for the whole car, not pp. To call a radio-dispatched taxi, dial 488-1519, 488-2510, or 488-2691.

Several companies rent cars at around $20 a day with unlimited mileage. **D.W. Rent A Car** (tel. 488-2641) at the D.W. Motel charges $20 a day for their one and only compact sedan without a/c, $37.50 a day for a medium sedan with a/c.

Toyota Rent-a-car (Box 280, Koror, PW 96940; tel. 488-1551), beside WCTC at T-Dock, has cars for $35-50 a day, plus $8-10 daily for insurance. They're represented in the U.S. by National Car Rental. **King's Car Rental** (Box 424, Koror, PW 96940; tel. 488-2964) has new cars from $35-41 daily, plus $6 optional collision insurance.

Most rental agencies want their cars driven only along the paved roads on Koror and as far as the airport. You're not supposed to drive on the unpaved roads on Babeldaop so if you do, drive very slowly and stop to clean off the mud before returning the car. Take care with uneven driveways, which can scrape car bottoms. Speed limits in Koror are 20-25 km per hour. Some rental cars carry no liability insurance, so ask.

OTHER ISLANDS

BABELDAOP

Southern Babeldaop

Since 1979 Koror has been connected to Babeldaop Island by the 235-meter-long cantilever **K-B Bridge,** one of the longest of its kind in the world. Ten states are on the coastal plains of Babeldaop. A network of roads covers the bottom half adjacent to Koror, as far as Ngatpang and Melekeok; beyond that, access is by boat only.

The **Palau Crocodile Farm** at the south end of the K-B Bridge has 41 Belau crocodiles kept for their skins (admission $3 adults, $2 children, $5 camera, $10 video camera). It's only 50 cents to see the four live crocodiles held in some concrete pens behind **Crocodile Lounge**, between the bridge and Airai Airport (entry through the adjacent laundromat). The attendant may throw the crocs some fish or water to wake them up for you.

The paved highway passes the airport and extends almost as far as the concrete shell of the huge **Japanese Communications Center** at **Airai** (Irrai) village, split by American bombs in 1944. A Japanese tank and several AA guns lie dumped beside the structure. A kilometer beyond this is an authentic old *bai,* built in 1890, with painted facades, thatched roof, and finely carved beams. One is sometimes, though not always, asked to pay $5 to walk around it, $10 to take photos inside. This is the only original building of its kind left in Belau.

Near the *bai,* at the junction of four stone pathways leading in from the cardinal points, is the compass platform. The south path leads to the modern concrete **Bai ra Mlengl** (1983), painted with traditional scenes (notice the quarrying of Yapese stone money). Below this new *bai* is a dock from which you'll get a good view.

Middle Babeldaop

A dirt road leads north from near the K-B Bridge to Aimeliik, Ngatpang, and Ngchesar states. Ten km north of the bridge the road divides, with Aimeliik to the left and Ngchesar to the right. If you keep left toward Aimeliik, after one km you'll reach a turnoff to the left to Ngerkeai village. Three km beyond this turnoff is the Chinese Agricultural Mission at **Nekkeng**, with the Oisca agricultural training school one km to the right.

North from Nekkeng another road climbs to a lookout above central Babeldaop with a view of a large bay which at first appears to be a lake. Visible on the east side of the bay is the Belau Modekngei High School at Ibobang and south of it the solitary white triangle of a large Japanese war memorial. Six km north of Nekkeng on this road is the **Ngatpang** State Office and a km beyond it, over a hill to the right, a fisheries dock constructed with Japanese aid money in 1990.

The road to the left from Nekkeng runs five km to **Ngchemiangel** village and terminates at the scandal-ridden **IPSECO power plant** on the coast, about 25 km from Koror by road. You get a good view of the ancient Aimeliik terraces from here. A short feeder road to the north runs to **Medorm** village, where old *bai* platforms may be seen: one on the ridge just before the village, another accessible from the dock. There's a store at Ngchemiangel where you can buy cold drinks and food.

If back at the turnoff to Ngchesar you had turned right, after four km you would have reached a group of collapsed metal towers dating from Japanese times. Here the road divides again with **Ibobang** and the **Japanese war memorial** to the left and Ngchesar to the right.

At last report the roads beyond the collapsed towers were in bad shape and four-wheel-drive was required. In dry weather,

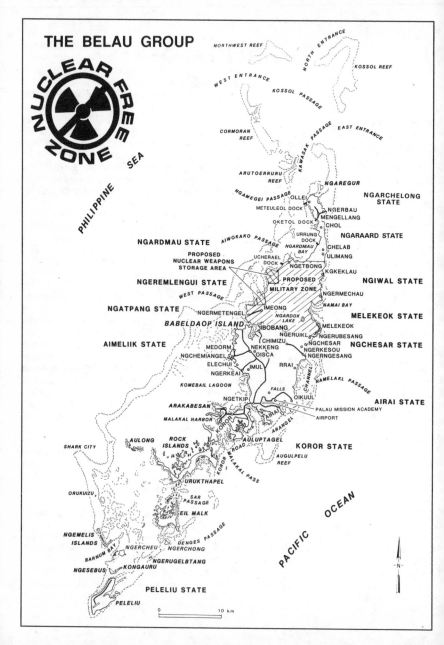

however, one may be able to drive through Ngchesar as far as Melekeok and road-building is proceeding slowly north. Be aware that all the dirt roads on volcanic Babeldaop can get very muddy and even become impassable after heavy rains.

Northern Babeldaop
During the Japanese period, northern Babeldaop was connected to Koror by roads, but these have long been overgrown and the locals now commute by speedboat. You can sometimes walk along jungle trails from one coastal enclave to the next, but it's not easy and you'll probably need a guide. The east coast offers the most possibilities for hikers, but there's an incomplete causeway north of Melekeok, plus rivers and crocodile-infested mangrove swamps to contend with. A project is now underway to rebuild these old roads and causeways, so get recent information upon arrival. From Melekeok one can rent a boat to Ngiwal State for around $20.

Melekeok was once the seat of the high chief of Babeldaop; ruins of an old village and stone *bai* platforms can be seen. Also see a circle of huge stones in the vicinity, one carved into a great face. There are grandiose plans to build a new capitol complex and international airport at Melekeok.

South of Melekeok is **Ngchesar** village, which boasts a traditional war canoe and inland, crocodile-inhabited **Ngardok Lake,** a two-hour walk from Ngchesar. A trail once ran from the lake to Ngardmau State, on the northwest side of the island.

Ngardmau is noted for the highest point in Belau (213 meters), the tallest waterfalls, and remains (including locomotives) from the prewar Japanese bauxite mine. At Taki Falls the Ngardmau River tumbles 25 meters into a lush jungle pool. The trail to the falls follows the three-km route of an old Japanese mining railway through the rainforest.

The highlight of Babeldaop is the northern tip; excellent **beaches** extend down the east coast from Ngaraard to Melekeok, while most of the rest of the island is fringed by mangrove swamp. A road crosses the narrow neck of Ngaraard State from Urrung dock to

Chelab and Ulimang villages. Walking north from Ulimang to Ngarchelong State is easy and there are many stone paths to explore.

Visit the awesome five-ton Easter Island-like basalt **stones of Badrulchau,** on a hilltop between Mengellang and Ollei, the northernmost villages. The story goes that spirits were working in the night to build a great *bai* at this spot. Then the sun came up, roosters crowed, and the spirits scattered, so the building was never finished. Today all that remains are 37 monolithic blocks arranged in two rows, which may once have supported an immense *bai.* Carved faces are seen on six of the stones and pot sherds are found here.

An old **Japanese lighthouse** stands on a hill at Ollei. Boats for Koror leave Ngarchelong and Ngaraard states fairly often.

Accommodations
The only official place to stay on Babeldaop is the **Ngaraard Traditional Resort** (Box 773, Koror, PW 96940; tel. 488-1788 evenings), run by Hanson Shiro on the beach at Ulimang village, Ngaraard State. They offer three thatched cottages, each with two bedrooms, sitting room, and kitchen (bring food). The toilets and washing facilities are outside and there's no electricity. The price is $25 s, $45 d, $60 t, plus tax. For four people it's $70 and groups of five or more pay $15 pp. Local meals are $19 pp extra for all three. Getting there from Koror by boat costs $100 RT per group and boat tours ($25-30 pp) of northern Babeldaop can be arranged. This locally owned resort has all the attributes of a genuine island hideaway, and it's reasonable if you can get a small group together.

KAYANGEL

The same geological movement which uplifted Angaur and Peleliu was probably part of the tilt which submerged Kayangel and the northern reefs. Kayangel, an idyllic atoll 25 km north of Babeldaop, has only one village (137 people) and no electricity, plumbing, or cars—just peace and quiet, and beauty. Alas,

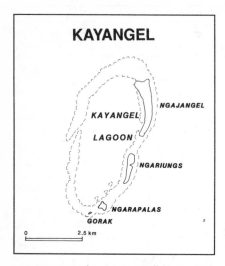

KAYANGEL

NGAJANGEL

KAYANGEL

LAGOON

NGARIUNGS

NGARAPALAS
GORAK

0   2.5 km

motor scooters have appeared! Untouched beaches surround the four islands of the atoll, and you can walk from island to island on the reef at low tide. Snorkeling in the lagoon is exquisite. Unfortunately the island's traditional *bai* was destroyed by Typhoon Mike in Nov. 1990 and replaced by a concrete *bai*.

Upon arrival, ask one of the two chiefs to help find a family willing to accommodate you; they would welcome the money. Although the island has two tiny stores, bring plenty of canned food, ramen, and insect repellent. Bread and coffee are appreciated but no beer is allowed on Kayangel. High-quality pandanus handbags are woven here.

PELELIU

The little island of Peleliu (pop. 601), 50 km southwest of Koror at the south end of the Belau Lagoon, was a scene of intense combat from Sept. through Nov. 1944. Mercifully, the Japanese evacuated the Micronesian inhabitants to Babeldaop before the battle began. The defense of Peleliu marked a change in Japanese military tactics, as the 10,000 defenders holed up in entrenched positions in the island's tangled rocky interior, instead of facing the Americans on the beaches. This strategy led to a drawn-out 2½-month struggle, with far heavier casualties on the U.S. side than had been previously experienced. After this battle the U.S. made no attempt to capture Koror and Babeldaop, which remained in Japanese hands until peace came. Military historians now agree that the whole campaign was ill-advised and that the capture of Peleliu contributed nothing to the eventual defeat of Japan.

Today you can visit the invasion site at Bloody Beach, and the interior limestone caves and tunnels where the Japanese held out till the fatal end. A wartime airstrip and a good system of crushed-coral roads are found on the island. These roads are ideal for walking—two full days are necessary to cover the island on foot.

All the inhabitants live in three adjacent flower-filled villages at the north end of the island. Before the wartime evacuation people also lived in the south. Some Peleliu islanders are rather reserved and suspicious of outsiders, but as a whole the people are as friendly as ever. Apart from visiting the battle sites, swim at white-sand beaches and an inland cave with a saltwater swimming hole. Remember, a maximum $15,000 fine and one year imprisonment applies to anyone caught removing war relics from the island.

Sights

Some interconnecting **Japanese caves** are right by the road near Elochel Dock at the north end of the island. The massive two-story reinforced concrete structure of the former **Japanese communications center** looms among the houses at Klouklubed village, just south of the school. The large blue and white **grave** of Haruo I. Remeliik, a native of Peleliu, is on the corner opposite the baseball field in Klouklubed.

A miniature Shinto shrine stands before the limestone cliffs of **Bloody Nose Ridge,** where the fiercest fighting took place. The Americans poured aviation fuel into caves sheltering diehard Japanese who refused to surrender and blew them away. Three large

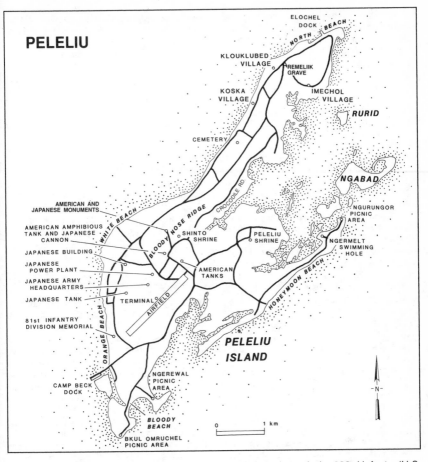

PELELIU

ELOCHEL DOCK
NORTH BEACH
KLOUKLUBED VILLAGE
REMELIIK GRAVE
KOSKA VILLAGE
IMECHOL VILLAGE
RURID
CEMETERY
NGABAD
AMERICAN AND JAPANESE MONUMENTS
CROCODILE RD
NGURUNGOR PICNIC AREA
AMERICAN AMPHIBIOUS TANK AND JAPANESE CANNON
WHITE BEACH
BLOODY NOSE RIDGE
SHINTO SHRINE
PELELIU SHRINE
NGERMELT SWIMMING HOLE
JAPANESE BUILDING
JAPANESE POWER PLANT
JAPANESE ARMY HEADQUARTERS
AMERICAN TANKS
JAPANESE TANK
TERMINAL
AIRFIELD
HONEYMOON BEACH
81st INFANTRY DIVISION MEMORIAL
ORANGE BEACH
PELELIU ISLAND
CAMP BECK DOCK
NGEREWAL PICNIC AREA
-N-
BLOODY BEACH
0   1 km
BKUL OMRUCHEL PICNIC AREA

war memorials have been erected on Bloody Nose Ridge. On the lowest terrace is the U.S. Marine Corps monument. From there a road winds up to the Japanese monument on a high terrace almost surrounded by jagged limestone peaks. This monument was erected in Feb. 1989 on the site of the Japanese last stand where Colonel Nakagawa of the elite 2nd Infantry Regiment of the Imperial Japanese Army committed *seppuku* after burning the regimental colors on 24 Nov. 1944. At the very top of the ridge, acces-

sible by a stairway, is the 323rd Infantry (U.S. Army) memorial and a flagpole on the uppermost peak. There's a superb view of the entire island from up there.

Several huge **Japanese buildings** stand half swallowed in the jungle northwest of the airfield. **Orange Beach** is where the American landings took place on 15 Sept. 1944. At **Camp Beck Dock** are an assortment of abandoned U.S. ships and vehicles, plus wrecked planes bulldozed into mangled heaps of bent aluminum sculpture.

Near Honeymoon Beach is the **Ngermelt Swimming Hole**, a natural limestone sinkhole full of water which rises and falls with the tides—dive into the clear salt water and enjoy a refreshing swim.

Practicalities

Peleliu has no hotels or restaurants, but several of the inhabitants rent rooms with shared bath (occasional running water) to visitors. A brief stay with any of them is the ideal way to observe contemporary outer-island Micronesian life. Charges average $15 pp, plus another $18 for all meals, but ask first. There are five small stores in the villages, some open on Sundays. Electricity operates 1800-0600.

The best choice is **Keibo's Place** near the beach at Koska village. Mayumi and Keibo Rideb rent rooms beside their store and offer minibus tours. Keibo's place is good if you want a little privacy, as they have a separate four-room building just for guests. Don't believe the airport minibus driver if he tells you Keibo's place is full or more expensive—check for yourself. Nearby is **Wenty's Inn,** run by Wenty Tongmy. Back near the school in Klouklubed ask for Reiko Kubarii, the Palau Paradise Air agent, or Hiroichi Ucherremasch.

Camping is possible on any of the excellent beaches away from the villages. Orange and Honeymoon beaches are the closest to the airport, if you arrive by air. Honeymoon is more centrally located for sightseeing; it also gets more of a breeze. There's good snorkeling on this side of the island when the wind is right, but beware of strong currents at the southern tip of Peleliu. The Ngrerewal Picnic Area is also an idyllic campsite. Your main problems at these beaches are finding drinking water and avoiding mosquitos and sand flies.

Omsangel Nightclub between Elochel Dock and Klouklubed is open nightly.

Transport

The minibus to the airstrip, eight km southwest of Klouklubed village, is $2. The plane parks near the water-treatment area beside Peleliu's gigantic wartime runway. **Palau Paradise Air** has flights from Koror and Angaur daily except Wednesday.

The passenger boat *Nippon Maru* from the Fisheries Co-op in Koror lands at Elochel Dock at the north end of Peleliu. It leaves Koror Mon., Thurs., and Fri. mornings, and departs Peleliu Wed., Thurs., and Sun., $3 OW (two hours). Sometimes extra trips are made, so ask. It's a good plan to fly one way and take the boat the other.

The guesthouse owners can arrange pickup-truck rentals for about $30. There are only 25 motor vehicles on the island but everyone has a motor scooter. Ask around for someone willing to rent you one (about $10). Tangie Hesus offers minibus tours of Peleliu at $40 for the vehicle (not pp). He works with Keibo Kubarii (the Paradise Air agent) and often meets the flights.

ANGAUR

Angaur (pop. 206) is a quiet coral island, with no tourists or traffic to distract you. This was also a major WW II battlefield, so you'll find the same sort of relics and caves as on the larger and more populated island of Peleliu, 11 km northeast. The 18 Sept. 1944 American landings on Red Beach on the northeast side of Angaur were unopposed. The Japanese garrison had withdrawn to caves in the mined-out area, which they held for over a month. The Americans built the huge airstrip, which runs right across Angaur, in just 30 days, and B-24 Liberators became the main occupants.

Today the island is noted for the casual life in the one village, the attractive coastal scenery and beaches, and Micronesia's only crab-eating macaque monkeys (which bred from two escaped German pets), found mainly in the northern half of the island. Large monitor lizards are also seen. Belauans consider the monkeys pests so it's illegal to take them to other islands. Like Peleliu, Angaur is a prime marijuana-growing area and the producers tend to be rather suspicious of strangers, so don't take it personally.

Sights

Several half-submerged **American tanks** reinforce the breakwater of Angaur's harbor. The Japanese government recently spent $2.2 million on the harbor's new pier, but this reduced the available space, making it difficult for large fishing boats to maneuver, and the entrance is still treacherous. **Phosphate mining**, begun by the Germans in 1909 and continued through the Japanese period, finally ended under the Americans in 1954. The ruins of the bulk-loading pier are just north of the harbor. Follow the remains of the fallen conveyor belt back through the bush to the skeleton of the phosphate-crushing plant.

A ruined **Japanese lighthouse** rises high above the harbor, but it's not visible from the road, so it can be hard to find. Get there by taking the coastal road north from the phosphate plant less than a kilometer, to a point where the route cuts between cliffs and begins to drop. Retrace your steps a little till you find your way into a small coconut grove on the southwest side of the road. Go in and look for a stone stairway leading past a square concrete water tank to the highest point. Your effort is rewarded with a good view of the island from the second-story roof. This place is perfect at sunset, and chances are you'll have a grandstand view of the antics of the local monkeys.

Northern Angaur

A pleasantly shaded coral road runs right around Angaur, which you can easily cover on foot in a day (take something to drink). The most attractive stretch skirts the stark limestone cliffs at the northwest corner of the

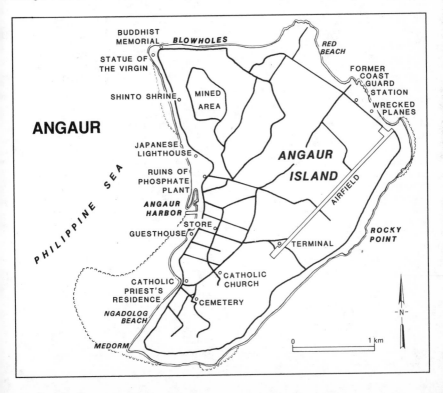

island. This is where the Japanese army made its last stand during the American invasion; Shinto and Buddhist memorials mark the event. The miniature **Shinto shrine** is especially striking, with a good beach opposite. The snorkeling is good here when the weather's very calm, but beware of high surf and undertow when it's not. Today this area is inhabited by large bands of monkeys, which dwell in the many huge banyan trees.

The ocean crashes relentlessly into the northwest cape of Angaur. A statue of the **Virgin Mary** was erected at this point in 1954 to protect the islanders from rough seas. Several spectacular **blowholes** blow on the north coast, and the beat of the waves against the uplifted coral terraces is almost hypnotic.

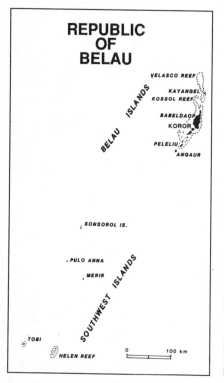

Between the abandoned buildings of the **former Coast Guard station** and the northeast end of the airstrip, a number of **broken aircraft** are found between the road and the coast. Included in this WW II aviation dump are fragments of a Corsair fighter and the wings of B-24 Liberators, half swallowed among the pandanus and ironwood trees.

Southern Angaur

Angaur is outside the protective Belau Reef. The meaning of this can be appreciated at **Rocky Point** on the east side of the island: a blowhole and smashing surf. The south end of the island is calmer with sandy beaches.

By the road at the north end of **Ngadolog Beach** is the former hospital, now the residence of the Catholic priest, just behind which are two large concrete platforms. Beyond the platforms look for a long depression in the ground near some large trees. The souls of all Belauans come to this pit after death to ascend to heaven up the trees or descend into hell through the ground. The place is haunted and screams are heard in the night; a ghost is often seen in the priest's residence.

Practicalities

The two guesthouses in the village are both within easy walking distance from the airstrip. **Julio's Guest House** (Box 261, Koror, PW 96940), the house beside the store closest to the airfield, has a few rooms at $15 pp. Meals are $5 (breakfast), $8 (lunch), and $12-15 (dinner), or buy groceries at one of the two stores on Angaur. You share all facilities with the locals.

Masao's Guest House, a pleasant beach bungalow with a large verandah, has two rooms at $15 pp and floor space for groups. All meals are $18 extra or you can cook your own food. The water supply is variable. Masao's is right on the east coast at the end of the road across the island from the airstrip. Here you're more or less on your own. At $15 pp accommodations on Angaur are reasonable if you're alone, a little high for two. Bargaining is not possible—it's take it or leave it.

Camping is okay almost anywhere on the island. The pine-covered southwest tip of Angaur beside Ngadolog Beach, the island's best, makes a perfect campsite. It's easy walking distance from town, yet far enough away from local houses. The beach is protected by a wide reef, so enjoy the swimming and snorkeling. Don't go off and leave valuables lying around, though.

Both camping and snorkeling depend on the direction of the wind: if it's out of the east Ngadolog Beach will be calmer, but when it's out of the west Rocky Point or the promontory between Red Beach and the former Coast Guard Station will be preferable. Much of the year Ngadolog Beach will be best, except during the Southwest Monsoon from July through Oct., when this side of the island gets the most rain and wind.

The two small stores on Angaur are closed on Sundays.

Transport

The plane stops at the southwest end of Angaur's gigantic wartime airfield on the east side of town, a few minutes' walk from everything, or catch a ride with the Palau Paradise Air agent for $2. **Palau Paradise Air** offers convenient flights to Peleliu ($15) and Koror ($26).

The channel between Angaur and Peleliu can be rough. The *Yamato Maru,* a modern Japanese-made motor vessel given to Angaur as war reparations, sails to Angaur from the Fisheries Dock, Koror, Mon. and Fri. afternoons, returning from Angaur to Koror on Thurs. and Sun., $5 OW. It doesn't stop at Peleliu on the way.

THE SOUTHWEST ISLANDS

These five tiny islands between Koror and Indonesia are among the most remote in the Pacific. **Tobi Island** (Hatohobei), 599 km southwest of Koror, is just 250 km from the Indonesian island of Morotai. In 1990 Sonsorol State, which includes Tobi (60 hectares) and Sonsorol (1.9 square km) islands, had 61 inhabitants. About a dozen people may be on **Pulo Anna** (80 hectares) at any one time, while Merir (90 hectares) and Helen (2 square km) are usually uninhabited. The main source of income is the sale of copra. **Sonsorol** consists of two islands, Fana and Sonsorol, about a kilometer apart.

The people of the Southwest Islands speak the language of Woleai atoll, Yap State; Belauans cannot understand them. These islanders retain more of the traditional Pacific culture (leaf houses, canoe making, handicrafts, etc.) than any other group in Belau.

On remote **Helen Reef**, a sand spit east of Tobi, thousands of seabirds and turtles live in undisturbed bliss. Helen Reef has a 101.2-square-km lagoon, but the other Southwest Islands are all low islands with only fringing reefs. Papua New Guinea also claims Helen Reef.

TERRITORY OF GUAM

INTRODUCTION

If you've been island-hopping west across the Micronesian islands, Guam comes as a bit of a shock. You suddenly find yourself back in the hard commercial world of high-rise hotels, traffic jams, shopping centers, convenience stores, subdivisions, television, hostess bars, Coca-colonialism, hamburger imperialism, and money. You notice immediately how people just ignore you instead of saying hello. You've suddenly come upon a little chunk of California or Hawaii marooned in the mid-Pacific—the U.S. without the tension between blacks and whites, the poor social conditions, and the homeless.

The Agana-Tamuning corridor has all the flavor of suburban Los Angeles. Agana's main street, Marine Drive, is bumper-to-bumper with rush-hour cars and buses packed with Japanese groups. The middle part of the island is Suburbia, U.S.A. Along Tumon Bay north of the airport is a large Japanese tourist ghetto. Most of the rest of northern Guam, the best beach on the island included, is a military base inaccessible to civilians.

It's the southern portion of Guam, still the sleepy South Sea island, which is more attractive to the traveler. Unfrequented hiking trails south of Agat lead along the coast and into the interior; offshore, kaleidoscope reefs brim with marinelife. If you're fresh from Tokyo or Hong Kong, Guam may even appear laid-back. As America's westernmost possession in the Pacific, it's been a crossroads and impact point of diverse cultures for almost a century. Guam is the western gateway to Micronesia—its business, educational, and travel hub.

THE LAND

The Pacific ends at Guam; on its western shores begins the Philippine Sea. The Marianas Trench separates Guam from the Carolines, 400 km south. This 541-square-km, 14-by-48-km island at 13 degrees north latitude is the largest in Micronesia, the southernmost link in the 685-km-long Marianas Chain. Guam's position on the circum-Pacific Ring of Fire makes it prone to earthquakes, 16 of which have shaken the island since the 1800s. The island's name comes from the Chamorro word *guahan* (we have).

Shaped like a footprint, Guam was formed by the union of two volcanoes: the older northern one was already capped with limestone when the southern volcano joined it. It's less than seven km across its narrow instep, from the University of Guam to Agana, the commercial center. Legend holds that a great fish had been eating away at the middle of the island until the Virgin Mary restrained it with a hair from her head, saving Guam from destruction.

The flat northern two-thirds of Guam is a high limestone plateau with no permanent rivers or streams, and steep 175-meter cliffs at the coastline. The southern one-third consists of mountainous, volcanic terrain with a ridge of red clay hills reaching 406 meters at Mt. Lamlam. When you visit Guam, you get two different islands for the price of one.

In the south are crashing waterfalls, seldom-visited jungles, and languorous villages along the coast (Umatac, Merizo, and Inarajan are the most picturesque). The beaches on the west side of the island are calm and safe, while those on the east experience the high waves that draw surfers. The best **surfing spots** on Guam are reputed to be Rick's Reef at Tamuning, the Agana Boat Basin, the entrance to Merizo harbor, and Talofofo Beach Park. Optimum surfing conditions exist from Dec. through June.

Climate

Guam is a land of endless summer, generally warm and humid with little seasonal temper-

GUAM'S CLIMATE

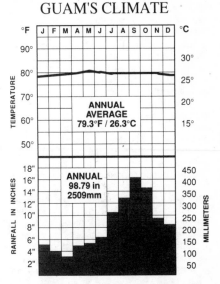

ature variation. January through April, the dry season, are the best months to come, with lower humidity and temperatures as the northeast and east tradewinds blow. Two-thirds of the rainfall occurs during the southwest monsoon from July to mid-Nov., with measurable rain on 20-25 days of each of these months. Hottest months are May and June.

Guam is located within the breeding grounds of the western Pacific typhoons (June to November). Between 1948 and 1977 approximately 80 tropical storms and typhoons passed within 300 km of Guam. Over one billion dollars of damage has been caused by these storms, attracting millions in federal disaster relief. The world's lowest air pressure (870 millibars) was recorded 482 km from Guam on 12 Oct. 1979.

FLORA AND FAUNA

Salt-tolerant vegetation grows along the coastal strands, with swamps and marshes on some southern coasts and rivers. In the southern ravines are ferns and palms, then swordgrass-sided valleys which give way to high savanna. Dense forests once covered the northern limestone plateau.

The territorial tree is ironwood or *ifil,* a slow-growing, termite-resistant evergreen. Its timber turns black with age. In 1947 *tangan tangan* brush *(Leucaena)* was seeded from aircraft to protect the defoliated island from erosion. *Tangan tangan* now grows in impenetrable thickets over much of the north end of the island, although it's seldom found on the volcanic southern slopes of Guam.

The only indigenous mammals on Guam are two species of bats. Other unique creatures are nonpoisonous centipedes and scorpions (though their bites are painful), stinging ants, 1.8-meter-long iguanas, and a variety of crabs. The giant African snail *(Achatina),* imported by the Japanese during WW II for food, is now an occasional pest, destructive to plants and crops.

Two endangered species of sea turtles, the green and the hawksbill, may be found in

M.G.L. DOMENY DE RIENZI

Guam waters. Guam's reefs harbor one of the most diverse fish populations in the world, with 110 families, and 800 species of inshore fish identified so far. (The Philippines has over 2,000 species, Hawaii 450.) Guam sharks rarely attack humans. Over 300 species of coral are present. The gathering of live coral is prohibited by law.

Guam may be one of the first places on earth to lose *all* its endemic birds, a disaster which could have serious ramifications on the pollination of native plants, dispersal of seeds, insect populations, etc. In 1979 the governor of Guam asked the U.S. Fish and Wildlife Service to list several of the island's birds on the Endangered Species List, which would have brought federal support for their protection. Five years later, the paperwork was completed and the birds listed. Meanwhile Guam's bridled white-eye, 2,000 of which remained in 1981, and the Guam broadbill had disappeared forever. The flightless Guam rail or *koko* has since become extinct; only a few hundred Guam fruit bats, locally known as the *fanihi,* survive.

Introduced diseases, pesticides, hunting, and habitat loss have all been factors in the dramatic decline in birdlife over the past two decades. But in 1983 biologist Julie Savidge identified the main culprit as the brown tree-climbing snake *(Boiga irregularis),* introduced from the Solomon Islands in the hold of a navy ship toward the end of WW II. The nocturnal snakes were first identified in the harbor area in the 1950s and only began multiplying in 1960s. Now some forested areas of the island may have up to 12,000 snakes per square mile. The snakes can grow up to two meters long but are no danger to adults as their fangs are far back in their jaws. They feed mainly on eggs, chicks, chickens, ducks, quail, kittens, puppies, caged birds, and young fruit bats. Until the brown tree snake arrived, Guam's only serpent had been a blind, earthworm-like snake. Guam's native forest birds were helpless in the face of bird-eating *B. irregularis,* which also climbs telephone poles and often shorts out electric lines, causing millions of dollars in damage. A few Guam birds may be seen in

U.S. zoos, but the forests of Guam are silent. Several hitchhiking snakes have been found at Hawaii airports and it's feared the snake has also spread to Saipan.

HISTORY

Early History

It's possible that the indigenous inhabitants arrived in the Mariana Islands from the Malay Peninsula around 3000 B.C. The people lived in small villages. The basic social unit was the extended, matrilineal family. After marriage the man moved to the woman's house; land was inherited from the mother's brother. There were three social classes: nobles, commoners, and outcasts. Spirits of the ancestors were venerated.

The most intriguing remains left by the *taotaomona* ("spirits of the before-time people") are latte stones, megalithic monuments up to six meters high which once supported residences of the *matua* (upper class). The latte occur in double rows of six to 14 stones, each composed of a *haligi* (pedestal) and a *tasa* (cap). The *tasa* are natural coral heads placed atop the *haligi* with the spherical side down; they look like giant mushrooms with the tops inverted. Burials and artifacts are found in the vicinity of latte, with local variations in the stonecarving. Latte stones are found throughout the Marianas, the biggest on Tinian.

A Spanish Colony

Guam's written history dates from 1521 when Ferdinand Magellan discovered the island on the first circumnavigation in history. Magellan landed 3½ months after rounding the tip of South America; his scurvy-ridden crew had been reduced to a pitiful diet of rats and leather after crossing the Pacific without sighting land. Magellan named Guam the Isle of Thieves when his skiff was stolen at Umatac. He recovered the boat after personally leading a raid ashore, during which seven or eight islanders were killed and their village burned. The meddlesome explorer was himself killed at Mactan in the central Philippines

a little less than two months later when he intervened in a local war.

Miguel Lopez de Legaspi, colonizer of the Philippines, claimed Guam for Spain in 1565, but it was not until 1668 that Jesuit missionaries arrived to implant their faith. When persuasion failed, the Spanish resorted to force. From 1680 to 1695, troops under Captain Jose de Quiroga waged a war of extermination against the native Micronesians and, with the help of introduced diseases like smallpox and syphilis, reduced their numbers from 80,000 in 1668 to below 5,000 by 1741.

Today, a church-inspired monument to the pro-Spanish collaborator Quipuha graces Agana's Marine Drive, while resistance leader Chief Matapang is not commemorated. Father Diego Luis de San Vitores, who used Spanish soldiers to carry out forced baptisms of Chamorros and was finally speared by them in 1672, is now in the process of canonization!

The survivors, mostly women and children, were relocated in controlled settlements where they intermarried with the Spanish and Filipino troops and adopted much of their cultures, becoming the Chamorros of today. Clan-held lands were divided among individuals. In 1769 a power struggle between the king of Spain and the Jesuits led to the expulsion of the order from Guam and all other Spanish colonies. The decline of the Chamorros continued and by 1783 their population was down to 1,500.

Changing Hands

For 200 years, Guam was a source of food and water for Spanish galleons plying between Mexico and the Philippines. It took three months to sail from Acapulco to Manila, and six months to return. Gems and spices of the Orient were traded for the silver of America. The annual journeys ended in 1815 when Mexico became independent from Spain. After 1822 Yankee whalers became regular visitors.

Guam, Puerto Rico, and the Philippines became American possessions as a result of the Spanish-American War. On 20 June 1898 the USS *Charleston* entered Apra Harbor, firing as she came. The Spanish governor sent word to the American commander that he was sorry but he could not return his polite salute as he was out of gunpowder. Informed that their countries were at war, the Spaniard promptly surrendered.

Military Rule

From 1898 to 1941 Guam was run as a U.S. naval station under a captain. General proclamations and numbered orders were the law, U.S. Marines the constabulary. Trial by jury was denied. To avoid provoking Japan, no attempt was made to fortify the island. Just prior to WW II Guam's defenses consisted of a few machine guns and several hundred rifles.

The Americans surrendered to a Japanese invasion force on 10 Dec. 1941, just three days after Pearl Harbor. The Japanese immediately forced the 2,000 Chamorro inhabitants of Sumay village on the Orote Peninsula to evacuate their homes. They still live elsewhere on Guam; the area is a U.S. naval base today. The Japanese renamed Guam "Omiyajima" (Great Shrine Island), part of an empire which was supposed to last a thousand years.

In March 1944 the Japanese deployed 18,500 troops to Guam to meet an expected American invasion. Guamanians were conscripted to work alongside Korean labor battalions. On July 12th the Japanese beheaded 30-year-old Father Jesus Baza Duenas and three others accused of aiding a fugitive U.S.

Navy radioman. A few days later all 21,000 local residents were herded into concentration camps such as the one at Manengon near Yona, a fortunate move which separated the Chamorros from the crossfire.

Some 55,000 army and navy personnel were involved in the American landings at Agat and Asan on 21 July 1944. Organized resistance by the outnumbered and outgunned Japanese ended on 10 Aug., although some remained in the interior for years—one diehard Japanese straggler, Sergeant Shoichi Yokoi, held out in the jungle near Talofofo until 24 Jan. 1972, unaware that the war had ended! The final cost to the U.S. came to 2,124 dead and 5,250 wounded, most of them marines. Only 1,250 Japanese were captured; the other 17,000 perished.

The U.S. then turned Guam into an armed camp; by mid-1945 there were 200,000 U.S. servicemen present. Large tracts of land appropriated at that time remain in the hands of the military today, and the private owners have never been fairly paid. While the U.S. spends millions to lease bases elsewhere, it gets those on Guam for free. In the late '70s former landowners or their heirs launched a $300 million lawsuit against the U.S. demanding compensation. The final $39.5 million out-of-court settlement paid in 1986 has not been accepted by everyone.

From 1945 to 1949, 144 defendants were tried by the U.S. Navy in a Quonset hut on Nimitz Hill, Guam. Two Japanese lieutenant

The governor's palace at Agana, erected in 1885 on the site of the 1736 palace, was destroyed in 1944.

FLORES MEMORIAL LIBRARY, AGANA

*marines taking cover
during the landings on
Guam, 21 July 1944*

generals, two rear admirals, five vice admirals, and the commanding officers in the Marshalls, the Marianas, Tungaru, Bonin, Belau, and Wake were among the 136 convicted of war crimes; fifteen of the 111 convicted murderers were executed on Guam. The rest served various sentences at Sugamo Prison, Tokyo.

In 1946 the U.S. granted independence to the Philippines but decided to hang onto Guam. Control was transferred from the navy to the Dept. of the Interior in 1950, at which time the inhabitants became U.S. citizens and started paying income tax. But right up until 1962 a military security clearance was required to enter the territory.

Military Use

Guam's incredibly strategic position is readily appreciated when you consider that three major powers, Russia, Japan, and China, have common borders just north of this U.S. island. Though the posture is gradually changing, Guam today is still one of the most heavily militarized islands on earth: the U.S. Defense Dept. spends $800 million a year here, with 23,600 military personnel and dependents present.

In 1954 Guam became the main Strategic Air Command (SAC) base in the Pacific with Andersen Air Force Base, headquarters of the Eighth Air Force, the only B-52 base

outside the continental U.S. The 16 B-52G Stratofortress bombers of the 43rd Strategic Wing were fitted with nuclear-tipped cruise and short-range attack missiles directed against airfields in the Soviet Far East. Then in 1989 the aging bombers were stripped of their nuclear capacity and Andersen's command was downgraded from the SAC in Colorado to the Pacific Air Force in Hawaii. In 1990 the Defense Department announced it planned to scale back this presence even more and the U.S. Congress voted to withdraw the planes entirely. In 1991 the headquarters of the 13th Air Force was moved to Andersen from Clark Air Force Base in the Philippines.

Meanwhile the navy still controls a 2,400-meter runway at the Agana Naval Air Station beside the international airport, with two squadrons of Fleet Air Reconnaissance EP-3 Orion aircraft, and one squadron of P-3C ASW aircraft, all fitted with nuclear depth charges. The Government of Guam has asked the Pentagon to transfer these units to Andersen to make room for airport expansion, a request strongly opposed by the navy.

Guam is the Communications Area Master Station for all U.S. naval forces in the Western Pacific. In 1964 Polaris nuclear submarines carrying missiles with a range of 2,000 km were deployed to Guam. Although these obsolete subs have now been scrapped,

Naval Base Marianas at Apra Harbor is still the largest U.S. naval homeport outside the 50 states. It's also the westernmost naval ship repair facility on U.S. territory. The naval magazine at Lake Fena, largest lake in Micronesia, includes 250 earth-covered bunkers storing conventional and nuclear weapons, the most important nuclear weapons storage area in the western Pacific. An array of underwater antisubmarine SOSUS hydrophones are positioned just off the island.

With the collapse of the Cold War, the closing of U.S. bases in the Philippines, and a reduced U.S. presence in South Korea, the military situation in the western Pacific is changing. What this will mean to Guam in the long run is still undecided, but the emphasis is shifting away from American military use toward Asian business.

Government

Guam is a permanent, unincorporated territory of the United States. It's called "unincorporated" because not all provisions of the U.S. Constitution apply to Guam. Continuing efforts are underway to strengthen self-government by replacing the outdated Organic Act of 1950 with a deal similar to that granted the Commonwealth of the Northern Marianas in 1976. With all of its neighbors (except Belau) now enjoying the benefits of stable legal relationships with the U.S., Guam remains a virtual U.S. colony. Guam's present local government is by the grace of the U.S. Congress and can be revoked at any time.

In a 1979 referendum 81.7% of the voters rejected a draft constitution because they felt it did not adequately protect Chamorro rights. In a 1982 plebiscite another substantial majority rejected statehood in favor of commonwealth status. In 1987 voters approved a draft Guam Commonwealth Act which has been before the U.S. Congress since March 1988 where it's bogged down by a provision granting Chamorros the exclusive right of self-determination. The proposed Commonwealth Act also gives Guam control over immigration, veto power over federal laws, and a say in defense policy relating to the island.

At present Guam has only one level of government: a 21-senator unicameral legislature elected every two years. The people of Guam elected their own governor for the first time in 1970; both governor and an elected lieutenant governor serve four-year terms. Since 1972 an elected, *nonvoting* congressman has represented Guam in Washington. Guamanians cannot vote in U.S. presidential elections, yet any U.S. citizen can vote in a Guam election as soon as he/she gets off the plane.

The Government of Guam controls certain territorial departments and autonomous agencies such as the Commercial Port of Guam, Guam Airport Authority, Guam Power Authority, Guam Telephone Authority, University of Guam, etc., but has no say in the running of federal agencies such as the departments of the Interior, Defense, Justice, Labor, and Health and Human Services, and the General Services Administration.

Political infighting on Guam, usually centered around personalities rather than policies, is brutal. Candidates are divided between the Democratic and Republican parties. The big bureaucracy is very much in evidence on Guam and in past corruption has been the order of the day. Japanese developers get their projects speedily approved by putting the right money in the right pockets. The legislature has a tendency of granting big pay raises to government employees just prior to elections to buy votes. Meanwhile the infrastructure languishes. Just under half the people work for the government, while many others are involved in service industries related to government.

ECONOMY

Guam is hamstrung by federal regulations, often totally inappropriate and arbitrarily applied. Regulations such as the Jones Act, which requires that all goods shipped between the West Coast and Guam be carried on U.S. ships, result in sky-high shipping charges. Guam's clothing and watchmaking industries were squelched when federal bureaucrats changed the customs definitions under which Guam's products could be shipped to the U.S. Mainland. Development of a fishing industry (freezer plants and canneries) is stymied by a regulation which prohibits foreign tuna boats from off-loading in U.S. ports; nearly all fish consumed on the island is processed abroad and imported. However, much chilled tuna is unloaded from U.S. boats at Guam and air-freighted to Japan for the sashimi market. Control of the marine resources and undersea minerals within the 200-nautical-mile Exclusive Economic Zone (EEZ) around Guam remains in Washington.

Almost none of Guam's food is locally grown. Just after WW II the U.S. government took over the best agricultural lands for military bases, leaving the inhabitants dependent on federal handouts. The large military reservations account for 30% of the surface area of the island; over half of this area is held for "contingency purposes" and not even used. The Guam government holds another 25% of the land and the remaining 45% is privately owned.

There's strong local opposition to plans for expanding the bases or moving military operations from the Philippines here. Expansion might conflict with the islands' booming tourist trade and the importation of large numbers of support workers (mostly Filipinos) would upset the local ethnic balance. The military bases contribute less to the local economy than might at first appear since they're tax-free, and most personnel shop at base/navy exchanges (PX) at subsidized prices. Off-base housing by military dependents has already pushed local rents through the ceiling.

Tourism is the biggest private business on the island, bringing in $700 million a year and directly or indirectly responsible for 31% of jobs. Not many people realize that Guam gets more tourists than any other Pacific territory except Hawaii. Eighty-five percent of the 780,404 tourists in 1990 were Japanese, often honeymooners, who arrived on Japanese planes, stayed at Japanese-owned ho-

tels, and ate Japanese food; 75% of these stayed three days or less. In 1990 alone the Japanese invested $1.1 billion on Guam, 75% of it in resort properties, and the present 4,000-plus hotel rooms are expected to increase to 10,000 over the next few years. Guam's high-impact tourism is similar to that of Saipan, yet Guam is much bigger than Saipan and not as overwhelmed by Japanese tourism. Prices on Guam have increased substantially in recent years and even the free-spending Japanese have now begun searching for cheaper destinations farther afield.

Guam is a free port and does not form part of the U.S. Customs area. Import duties are charged only on tobacco, liquor, and liquid fuel. Local car dealers make millions transshipping Japanese automobiles to the U.S. to evade voluntary import quotas (cars shipped via Guam don't count). Industry is concentrated at Cabras Island, Tamuning, and Harmon. Oil refining accounts for about 90% of manufacturing receipts, producing jet fuels for the military and gasoline. Guam is totally dependent on petroleum as a source of energy and the private automobile as the primary means of transport. There's been talk of developing alternative energy sources, but as yet next to nothing has been done.

Manufactured goods with at least 30% value added by assembling or processing on Guam can be exported duty-free to the U.S. Combined with the ability to import components duty-free this should have stimulated huge finishing industries, but variable U.S. Customs regulations have stymied such development. Only commonwealth status would provide the required long-term stability. The local government also hopes to make Guam a financial center from which American corporations could direct their Asian operations.

Guam's economy is booming and the severe labor shortage means any American can easily find a job. Thousands of jobs in the construction and service industries are going begging and large numbers of workers have had to be imported from the Philippines, Korea, etc. However, for most people other than professionals salaries begin at $3.75 an hour, and housing is expensive and in very short supply. Anyone interested in working on Guam should send a resume of his/her background and experience to the Director of Labor, Government of Guam, Agana, GU 96910. Employment agencies on Guam include Accessible Services (tel. 649-1859), Andrus Associates (tel. 646-5379), and Executive Typing (tel. 646-3541). Guam residents pay normal U.S. income tax but are not eligible for federal social security benefits.

THE PEOPLE

The pre-European people of the Marianas were racially and culturally the same as other Micronesians. The Chamorros of today are a mixed race with Micronesian, Filipino, and Spanish blood. Ninety-eight percent are Roman Catholic. They continue their traditional custom of living in flower-filled villages, but commute to work in Agana and elsewhere by car. About 90% of the civilian inhabitants live within 26 km of Agana.

In March 1990 the Guam legislature passed, and Governor Ada signed, the strictest antiabortion law in the U.S. after the island's Catholic archbishop threatened to excommunicate any legislator who voted against the bill. Simply to advise a woman to have an abortion became a crime. There was an immediate backlash in the U.S. Congress as key members questioned Guam's quest for commonwealth status in light of this assault on freedom of speech, due process, equal treatment, and women's right to privacy. In Aug. a federal judge declared the law unconstitutional despite an argument from Ada that the separation of church and state had no place on Guam since Roman Catholicism is a "custom!"

Under a succession of colonial rulers the focus of Chamorro life shifted from the traditional men's clubhouse to the village church, the school, and finally the shopping mall. As wholesale Americanization proceeds, the Chamorros are undergoing an assimilation crisis. By age 60, 30% of the population have

hypertension. The Community Mental Health Center estimates there are 650-800 heroin addicts on Guam. Traffic accidents are the third-highest cause of death on Guam (after heart disease and cancer).

Of the total population of 133,152 (1990), almost 20% are U.S. military personnel and dependents. In 1962, the security clearance requirement was withdrawn to allow the importation of cheap Filipino labor to build up the military facilities and infrastructure. The population grew rapidly, with a 50% increase from 1960 to 1975, largely due to military spending during the Vietnam War. By the end of the century the population will double again to 200,000.

Aside from Chamorros a mixture of other nationalities, including statesiders (15%), Chinese, Filipinos, Japanese, Koreans, and Micronesians, also live on Guam. The number of immigrants from the Federated States of Micronesia is increasing fast. Filipinos comprise almost a quarter of the population, most of them legal nonimmigrant aliens working in construction, agriculture, and tourism, while the Chamorros hold government jobs. Koreans and Taiwanese control the retail trade while most other business is run by U.S. statesiders or Japanese. The Chamorros share a very real fear that the growing influx of immigrants from east and west will make them a small minority on their own island. In 1940 they comprised 90% of the total population; today they're only 45%.

Language

Chamorro is a rhythmic, melodic tongue with many repeated syllables and just enough guttural sounds to make it interesting to listen to. Numerous Spanish, Tagalog, and English terms have entered the language, and although much of it *looks* like Spanish, a Spanish speaker is soon lost. There are two systems of spelling: the church way and the school way. Chamorros are always surprised and pleased by a visitor who attempts a few words of their language.

Start by saying *hafa adai,* which sounds like "half a day" but means something like "hello, how are you?" If you'd like to ask how someone is, try *hafa* or *fa,* but smile as you say it or it could be interpreted as a threat. To ask the time say *Que hora?* Other easy phrases include *si yuus maasi* (thank you), *buenos dias* (good morning), and *adios* (goodbye). *Bai falak y . . .* (pronounced "bay fa lak' ee") means "I'm going to . . ." Add the name of the place *(banko* is bank, *checho* is work, *tenda* is store) and you're speaking Chamorro! To stress something, simply repeat the last syllable or two. Hence *dikiki* is little, and *dikikikiki* is very little.

Although everyone on Guam can speak English as well as you or I, there's a third language called Eyebrow. A greeting can be sent or received merely by lifting the eyebrows and smiling. Raising both eyebrows can also indicate surprise, or ask a question. Raising and lowering the eyebrows quickly several times can mean "want to?" The same technique in response means "Sure!" Furrowing the eyebrows means "no" or "don't." If an islander squints at you as you're talking, either he's got the sun in his eyes or he doesn't believe a word you're saying.

Holidays And Events

Banks and government agencies remain closed on the following public holidays: New Year's Day (1 Jan.), Martin Luther King's Birthday (third Mon. in Jan.), President's Day (third Mon. in Feb.), Guam Discovery Day (first Mon. in March), Good Friday (March/April), Memorial Day (last Mon. in May), Independence Day (4 July), Guam Liberation Day (21 July), Labor Day (first Mon. in Sept.), Columbus Day (second Mon. in Oct.), Veteran's Day (11 Nov.), Thanksgiving Day (fourth Thurs. in Nov.), Feast of the Immaculate Conception (8 Dec.), and Christmas Day (25 December).

Around March 6 a fiesta at Umatac village commemorates Magellan's landing. Many events take place in July to celebrate Guam's liberation in 1944, culminating in a large parade and fireworks on 21 July. Merizo's Water Festival is held in August. Feasts are commonly held to celebrate anniversaries, marriages, and births. The biggest procession of the year occurs on 8 Dec. in Agana, to honor

Our Lady of the Immaculate Conception, patron of the island. Fireworks at the Hilton mark New Year's Eve.

All 19 Chamorro villages on Guam celebrate their patron saint's day; since some villages have more than one saint there are 32 recognized fiestas a year. The best-known fiestas are those of the Santo Nino Perdido, Asan (Jan.); Nuestra Senora de la Paz y Buen Viaje, Chalan Pago (Jan.); Our Lady of Lourdes, Yigo (Feb.); St. Joseph, Inarajan (May); Assumption of Our Lady, Piti (Aug.); San Roque, Barrigada (Aug.); Santa Rosa, Agat (Aug.); Dulce Nombre de Maria, Agana (Sept.); San Miguel, Talofofo (Sept.); St. Teresita, Mangilao (Oct.); St. Jude, Sinajana (Oct.); Our Lady of the Blessed Sacrament, Agana Heights (Nov.); and Santa Barbara, Dededo (December). A complete list of village fiestas with exact dates is provided on the last page of the Guam telephone directory.

Most of these feature a religious procession through the streets, followed by a mammoth feast. The people are very hospitable on these occasions and you stand a good chance of being invited if you're in the right place at the right time. "Come and eat" is the usual greeting. For a full description of a typical Chamorro fiesta, see the "Northern Marianas" chapter. A complete three-month *Calendar of Events* is available from the Guam Visitors Bureau on request.

ACCOMMODATIONS

The 4,000-plus hotel rooms on Guam generally cost about the same single or double, but don't count on finding much under $50. A 13% government room tax is added and some places collect another 10% service charge to bring prices up to Tokyo/Osaka levels. Tips are extra. Since the second edition of this book in 1989 hotel prices on Guam have almost doubled. Some large hotels and car rental agencies will give you a "corporate rate" discount of around 20% if you say you're there on business (a business card helps).

Most rooms have a/c, private bath, color TV, phone, etc. Most of the high-rise tourist hotels serving packaged Japanese are along Pale San Vitores Road, a five-lane boulevard running up Tumon Bay. If you're on your own you'll do better at one of the smaller commercial hotels in Tamuning or Agana. The ITC (International Trade Center) Building on Marine Drive, Tamuning, is a landmark. Be sure to call ahead to check for vacancies. Bookings can be tight in Feb./March (Japanese winter), August (peak holiday time), Oct./Nov. (Japanese honeymoon time), and at Christmas/New Year's. Most of the listings below specify the total number of rooms to help you evaluate your chances, and the full address so you can write for reservations.

For a long stay check the yellow pages of the telephone directory under the heading "Apartments" and start calling. One agency with many such apartments is Six D Enterprises Inc. (tel. 646-5606; fax 646-5929).

Inexpensive Hotels In Tamuning

If price is your main concern, a few nondescript places along busy Route 1 in Tamuning are worth a call upon arrival to check availability. There are plenty of pay phones in the airport terminal. As on Saipan, many of the cheaper hotels are run by Koreans or Chinese whose English may not be that hot, so speak slowly and try to understand. Some places are "love hotels" which advertise hourly rates, but these often have separate sections for normal travelers.

The 20-room **Hafa Dai Hotel** (Box 4293, Agana, GU 96910; tel. 646-6542) is good value at $40 s or d. It's the two-story white building just south of and on the opposite side of the highway from the large McDonald's at Tamuning, just two km from the airport. Only two people are allowed in one room.

Another good choice is the 36-room, Korean-operated **Midtown Hotel** (Box 1263, Agana, GU 96910; tel. 649-9882) behind Ben Franklin Department Store in Tamuning ($40 s or d). Get a room on the third floor as the downstairs rooms are used by "short-timers."

The **Gold Motel** (Box 10328, Tamuning, GU 96911; tel. 649-5662), on Hospital Rd. two blocks west of Gibson's Department Store, has 18 rooms at $45 s or d. The VIP room features a round double bed and a Jacuzzi bath.

The two-story, 41-room **Pagoda Inn** (Box 4285, Agana, GU 96910; tel. 646-1882) charges $50 s or d for a room with a double bed, $55 s or d for twin beds. It's a little out of the way, just off Marine Dr. in Upper Tumon, so you'll need to rent a car.

Inexpensive Hotels Near Agana

The three-story **International Marina Hotel**, (470 West Soledad Ave., Agana, GU 96910; tel. 477-7836), is conveniently located at 470

Built in the late 1960s, the 475-room Hilton International Guam is one of the largest hotels on the island.

(clockwise from top left) disembarking from the *Micro Spirit* at Mogmog, Ulithi Atoll, Yap, FSM (Paul Bohler); setting sail, Woleai Atoll, Yap, FSM (Paul Bohler); unloading drums of fuel from the landing craft *Monaraoi*, Rep. of Kiribati (Rod Buchko)

(clockwise from top left) the largest *maneaba* in the Gilberts, Nonouti Atoll, Rep. of Kiribati (Rod Buchko); small shop at Betio, Tarawa, Rep. of Kiribati (Rod Buchko); houses on Eauripik Atoll, Yap, FSM (Paul Bohler); outriggers at Tarawa, Rep. of Kiribati (Rod Buchko); private residence, Nauru (Rod Buchko)

West Soledad Ave. off Marine Dr. overlooking the lagoon in central Agana. The 53 rooms with fridge begin at $52 s or d. The hotel has its own car rentals.

The **Island Hotel & Motel** (Box 3956, Agana, GU 96910; tel. 477-7380), a neat two-story building on West O'Brien Dr. just west of central Agana, has 40 rooms at $45 s or d with double bed, $55 s or d with twin beds.

Motel Orange (Box 4411, Agana, GU 96910; tel. 477-4677), a two-story orange and white building in East Agana, has 10 rooms at $35 s or d with a double bed or $45 d with two single beds. It's within sight of the junction of Marine Dr. and Route 8.

A little further up Route 8 and also within walking distance from central Agana is the **Plumeria Garden Hotel** (Box 7220, Tamuning, GU 96911; tel. 472-8831), a pleasant, motel-style establishment with lots of parking. They have 78 rooms for $51 s, $57 d. A laundromat is on the premises. This is a decent place.

The **Maite Garden Hotel** (Box 2925, Agana, GU 96910; tel. 477-0861) on Route 8, Maite, behind the Maite Shopping Town Plaza just east of the Micronesia Hotel, has 47 units beginning at $51 s, $63 d. A two-bedroom apartment with cooking facilities (double bed in each room) is $102.

If saving money is your only concern, consider the rather run-down **Micronesia Hotel** (Box 3177, Agana, GU 96910; tel. 477- 8225; fax 477-5662) on Route 8, Maite, two km east of Agana. The Micronesia was built by the military in 1944 and later became headquarters of the U.S. Trust Territory administration. The daily rates for the 60 rooms begin around $36 d (a/c and private bath), studio apartments $45 d, 30% discount if you stay a week, monthly rates even lower. An $8 all-male dormitory is sometimes available. A huge sign warns "No Refunds"; beware of cockroaches and leaky roofs. As the name suggests, it's patronized mostly by students from Micronesia and there have been several bad fires caused by cooking in the rooms. A laundromat and grocery stores are nearby.

Farther along the same way, the **Kina Court Hotel-Motel** (Box 804, Agana, GU 96910; tel. 477-1261) in Barrigada is a lot more pleasant. This three-story hotel, owned by a local family, is at 1241 Toto-Canada Road. The 31 spacious rooms with full cooking facilities begin at $62 s or d. Coin-operated washing machines, unlimited free local telephone calls, and free airport transfers are features. This hotel is often used by military personnel.

Upmarket again is the **Cliff Hotel** (178 Francisco Javier Dr., Agana Heights, GU 96910; tel. 477-7675), near Government House above central Agana. For $77 s, $83 d you'll get one of the 41 rooms, each complete with work desk and an individual balcony with a view of Agana. The Cliff is an excellent choice for businesspeople.

Bed And Breakfast

An excellent alternative to the hotels is the **Guam Garden Villa** (Box 10167, Sinajana, GU 96926; tel. 477-8166) at 193 Ramirez Dr., Ordot, off Route 4 southeast of Agana. This local homestay is run by Mrs. Herta K. Laguana, a German expat married to Romy, a local Chamorro. The charge for bed and breakfast is $35 s, $45 d with shared bath. Book well in advance—there are only three rooms and they're usually taken. Airport transfers are available at $10 each way, but you're better off renting a car upon arrival as the house, on spacious, flower-filled grounds, is isolated. It's also hard to find, so call Herta for detailed directions.

Also call Ann Concepcion, who rents rooms adjacent to her shop, the Treasure Chest (tel. 472-8380) in Piti. Ann and her husband are extremely helpful hosts.

Moderate Hotels In Tamuning

The only hotel near the airport is the **Hotel Mai'ana** (Box 8957, Tamuning, GU 96931; tel. 646-6961), good if you only need a place for one night. The U-shaped, three-story building (78 rooms) encloses a pleasant courtyard with pool. Studios with cooking facilities are $83 s or d, while spacious two-bedroom apartments go for $114 s or d, $133 t. They'll pick you up free at the air terminal, but it's often full with military personnel.

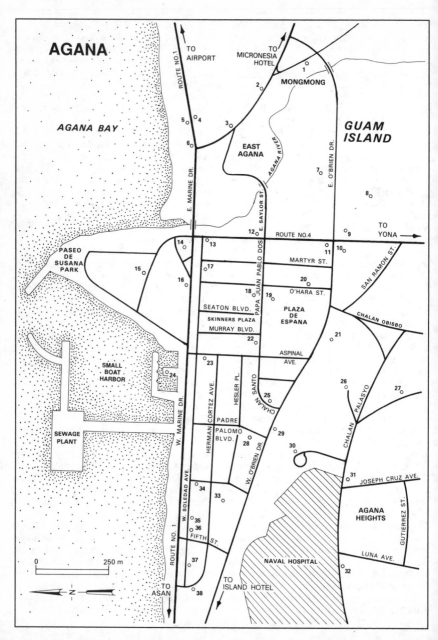

AGANA

1. Nining's Tavern
2. Plumeria Garden Hotel
3. Orange Motel
4. Hafa Books
5. Naval Cemetery
6. Padre Palomo Park
7. public swimming pool
8. Agana Shopping Center
9. Sizzler Steak House
10. Superior Court of Guam
11. public library
12. Bank of Guam
13. Papalagi Divers
14. Chief Quipuha Statue
15. Paseo Baseball Stadium
16. public market
17. Bank of Hawaii
18. Guam Legislature
19. Catholic Cathedral
20. Pacific Daily News Bldg.
21. Latte Stone Park
22. post office
23. San Antonio Bridge
24. Agana Boat Basin
25. Mini Cafe
26. Government House
27. Cliff Hotel
28. Lujan House
29. Japanese caves
30. Fort Santa Agueda
31. Simply Food
32. Dept. of Parks and Recreation
33. Julale Shopping Center
34. Mongolian Hut Restaurant
35. Korean Consulate
36. Agana Cinema
37. International Marina Hotel
38. Kentucky Fried Chicken

The **Polynesian Hotel** (Box 9014, Tamuning, GU 96931; tel. 646-7104), on Ypao Rd. between the airport and Tumon Bay, has 13 rooms above a convenience store at $74 s or d.

The 40 rooms at the **Tamuning Plaza Hotel** (Box 2925, Agana, GU 96910; tel, 649-8646) are $74 s or d. It's a new three-story hotel set back off Marine Dr. near Ben Franklin Department Store.

Moderate Hotels Near The Beach
If you're lucky you might get a hotel near Tumon Beach for only slightly more than the places listed above. If you're driving watch for the **Grand Hotel** (1024 San Vitores Rd., Tumon, GU 96911; tel. 649-1161), a four-story building on the inland side of Route 14. The 98 comfortable rooms here are $100 s, $115 d.

Better value (if you can get a room) is the **Terraza Tumon Villa Hotel** (Box 8588, Tamuning, GU 96911; tel. 646-6904), just up the road leading to the beach from near the Grand. The 12 rooms are $80 s or d, $91 t. The rates of the eight suites with cooking facilities are negotiable. Reservations recommended.

Across the street from the Terraza Tumon and right on the beach is the **Fujita Tumon Beach Hotel** (153 Fujita Rd., San Vitores, Tumon, GU 96911; tel. 646-1811) with 283 rooms at $110 s, $115 d, $135 t. They may offer commercial rates. Consider reserving.

Guam's largest hotel, the 520-room **Guam Plaza Hotel** (Box 7755, Tamuning, GU 96911; tel. 646-7803), is further north along the Tumon Bay strip. At $101 s, $113 d, $130 t, it's considerably cheaper than the luxury hotels listed below, and noisy Japanese groups on low-price package tours crowd in. This Waikiki-style hotel is on the inland side of the road away from the beach.

Expensive Hotels Near The Beach
Most of Guam's big tourist resorts face Tumon Bay. The first luxury hotel on Guam was the **Hilton International Guam** (Box 11199, Tamuning, GM 96911; tel. 646-1835), a seven-story, 486-room, mock-Hispanic complex which snakes along Ipao Beach between the hotel strip and the Tamuning business district. Planned after air service from Japan commenced in 1968, this former Guam Continental Hotel opened in 1970. Rooms without a view begin at $175 s, $210 d, $240 t, and prices go up from there. The Polynesian song and dance show by Jimmy Dee and the Chamorritas is on Wednesdays ($32). Free shuttle buses connect the Hilton to the airport.

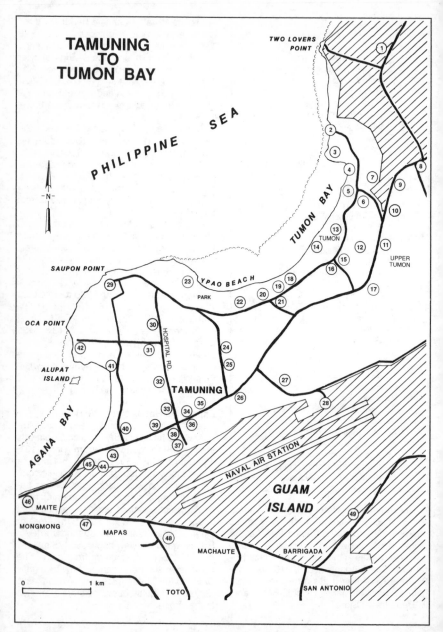

The 498-room **Pacific Islands Club** (Box 9370, Tamuning, GU 96931; tel. 646-9171) on Ipao Beach is supposedly styled after France's Club Med, though the mock Spanish church, concrete latte stones, and artificial waterfall facing the pools make it more like Disneyland. If staying in a 32-story hotel tower appeals to you, it's $246 s or d, $369 t, some recreational activities included. Meals are extra. Almost all the guests are Japanese.

Next door to the PIC is the stylish **Pacific Star Hotel** (Box 6097, Tamuning, GU 96911; tel. 649-7827), a 19-story pyramid owned by the Republic of Nauru. The $55-million complex opened in 1987 with 436 deluxe rooms and suites beginning at $175 s, $200 d. Special features of the hotel are six restaurants and a 24-hour coffee shop on the fourth floor, three bars, a 600-seat ballroom, a computerized business center, and a complete health club on the premises. A dinner show unfolds nightly except Sun. at 1800 in the Galaxy Theater on the first floor ($48 pp); after 2100 the locale becomes a disco. Free airport transfers are provided for guests. It's an excellent choice for those on expense accounts. A new 291-room **Holiday Inn Hotel** was being built across the street from the Pacific Star in 1992.

All the other hotels farther northeast on Tumon Bay are intended for Japanese tourists: for example, the **Dai-Ichi Hotel** (Box 3310, Agana, GU 96910; tel. 646-5881) with 333 rooms from $135 s, $146 d, and the adjacent **Sotetsu Tropicana Hotel** (Box 8139, Tamuning, GU 96911; tel. 646-5851) sporting 198 rooms at $150 s or d (no airport transfers available).

Hotel Joinus (Box 8139, Tamuning, GU 96911; tel. 646-6801), under the same man-

TAMUNING TO TUMON BAY

1. Youth With A Mission
2. Rick's Reef/Gun Beach
3. Hotel Nikko Guam
4. Okura Hotel
5. Reef Hotel
6. Plaza Hotel
7. Sunroute Hotel
8. Micronesia Mall
9. Guam Visitors Bureau
10. Horizon Hotel
11. Chuck's Steak House
12. Pia Resort Hotel
13. Hyatt Regency Hotel
14. Fujita Beach Hotel/Terraza Tumon
15. Joinus Hotel/Tumon Sands Plaza
16. Grand Hotel
17. Pagoda Inn
18. Royal Palm Resort
19. Dai-Ichi Hotel/Sotetsu Tropicana
20. Pacific Star Hotel
21. Holiday Inn Hotel
22. Pacific Islands Club
23. Hilton Hotel
24. Seventh-day Adventist Clinic
25. Polynesian Hotel
26. Hafa Dai Hotel
27. Mai'ana Hotel
28. airport terminal
29. Guam Memorial Hospital
30. Guam Greyhound Park
31. CSS Thrift Shop
32. Golden Motel
33. Gibson's Guam Shopping Center
34. Toyota Rent a Car
35. Denny's Restaurant
36. Hafa Dai Exchange
37. Tamuning Post Office/Coral Reef Marine Center
38. ITC Building
39. Shakey's Pizza Parlor
40. Memories Vietnamese Restaurant
41. Onward Agana Beach Hotel
42. Palace Hotel
43. Ben Franklin Dept. Store/Mark's Sporting Goods
44. Tamuning Plaza Hotel
45. IT&E Overseas Inc.
46. Citibank
47. Micronesia Hotel
48. Kina Court Hotel
49. Guam Main Facility (GMF) Post Office

agement as the Sotetsu Tropicana, charges $125 s, $140 d, $160 t, for one of the 36 mountain-view rooms with fridge. It's hidden on the third floor of the Tumon Sands Shopping Arcade—take the elevator. The luxurious shopping center downstairs is worth a look.

In 1992 the 448-room **Hyatt Regency Guam** (Box 12998, Tamuning, GU 96911) was still under construction on an ancient Chamorro burial site by the beach in central Tumon. Despite the American name this $150-million Hyatt belongs to EIE International of Japan and it's destined to become one of Guam's leading hotels.

The **Pia Resort Hotel** (Box 8874, Tamuning, GU 96931; tel. 649-5530), a huge 12-story building on the hillside above Tumon Bay, has 54 rooms occupied by Japanese tourists ($150 s, $160 d) and another 61 condominiums with permanent residents. The road in to the hotel is poorly marked.

Overlooking Tumon Beach is the 18-story **Guam Reef Hotel** (Box 8258, Tamuning, GU 96911; tel. 646-6881), owned by Japan Air Lines. You get excellent views from the balconies of the 458 rooms at the Reef, $170 s, $190 d. The Polynesian dinner show is $44.

The **Guam Hotel Okura** (Box 7118, Tamuning, GU 96911; tel. 646- 6811) is a five-story, V-shaped building belonging to the Okura Hotel Chain. It's quite elegant with a large crystal chandelier hanging in the lobby and a convention/banquet facility seating 450 guests. The 350 rooms at the Okura go for $160 s, $175 d, $200 t.

In late 1991 the $81-million **Hotel Nikko Guam** (Box 12819, Tamuning, GU 96931; tel. 649-8815) opened just beyond the Okura. The 500 rooms in this Japan Air Lines-owned hotel begin at $180 s, $190 d.

The **Hotel Sunroute Guam** (Box 10839, Tumon, GU 96911; tel. 649-9670) has 69 spacious rooms in their hillside building at $180 s or d.

All of the above are on Tumon Bay. The **Palace Hotel** (Box 12879, Tamuning, GU 96931; tel. 646-2222) is on Oka Point overlooking Agana Bay, accessible via Farenholt Ave., Tamuning. The 403 rooms ($195 s, $215 d) of this 10-layer, $64-million hotel

open onto an inner atrium complete with artificial waterfall. The guests are almost exclusively Japanese.

Hotels In Southern Guam

As yet there are only three hotels in southern Guam. The **Inn on the Bay** (Box 7387, Agat, GU 96928; tel. 565-8521), a new apartment hotel on the coast at Agat, caters mostly to people with business at the nearby Naval Base Marianas. The 70 rooms go for $117 s, $141 d, and there's a Denny's Restaurant on the premises. Commercial, military, and local discounts are available.

Cocos Island Resort Hotel (Box 7174, Tamuning, GU 96911; tel. 828-8691), on a small island off the south tip of Guam, was devastated by Typhoon Ross in 1990 and still closed in 1992 but may have reopened by the time you get there. The hourly boat which connects Merizo to Cocos is $20 (locals $5). You'll have to patronize the two restaurants or assorted snack and beach bars on the island as no outside food or drinks are allowed. Cocos's main draw is the best beach on Guam; water sports (including scuba diving) are available.

The **Inarajan Garden House** (Box 23548 GMF, Barrigada, GU 96921; tel. 828-2608), a three-story hotel complex on the beach three km south of the Saluglula Pool, Inarajan, is used mostly to house guests of the parent company in Japan and isn't usually open to the public. This could change.

Camping

Camping is allowed in all public parks administered by the **Department of Parks and Recreation** (tel. 477-9620 or 477-7825). Visit their office (open weekdays 0800-1700) at 490 Chalan Payaso Rd., Agana Heights, GU 96919, to pick up a $2-a-night camping permit. Facilities are extremely basic—only Ypao Beach Park has a public shower.

The accessible parks include Tanguisson Beach Park (near Two Lovers Point), Ypao Beach Park (Tumon Bay), Afflege Park (Agat), Nimitz Beach Park (Agat), Fort Soledad (Umatac), Saluglula Pool (Inarajan), Talofofo Beach Park, Ipan Beach Park (Talofofo), Tagachang Beach Park (Yona), and Francisco F. "Gonga" Perez Park (Pago Bay). At Fort Soledad pitch your tent inside the walls of the old Spanish fort. You may also camp anywhere in Guam Territorial Seashore Park (administered by Parks and Recreation), which includes much of the coast between Merizo and Nimitz Beach.

Camping is also possible in Danos Park at the west end of Cocos Island. Get there on the hourly Cocos Island Resort ferry ($20 RT, locals $5) or look for the regular shuttle boat to Danos from Merizo pier ($10 pp RT). Take food and drink.

Remember, however, it's unwise to leave your tent unattended. Be prepared to be blasted by high-volume music from cars parked nearby late at night. Camping is rather new to Guam, so set a good example by not leaving behind a mess.

Other options are to sleep in a rental car or on a bench at the airport. There's also a special $15 lounge at the airport (see "Airport," below). If you're car camping, coin laundromats are good places to sit around in the evening and chat with the local people or read. Most stay open late.

FOOD AND ENTERTAINMENT

As everywhere, the restaurant scene changes fast, so check *TV Guam* magazine's comprehensive weekly "Taste of Guam" restaurant listings if you're big on eating out. Tipping is expected in full-service restaurants (unless a service charge is added to the bill).

The **Public Market** (closed Sun.) on Marine Dr. is worth a visit to meet some local people, peruse the local produce, or eat a takeaway Chinese, Filipino, or Chamorro lunch at one of the picnic tables provided. Good vibes. **Shirley's Coffee Shop** (closes at 1500) next to the International Marina Hotel is good for breakfast.

For something different try the bar-B-Q [sic] buffet at the **Mongolian Hut Restaurant** (tel. 472-8056; closed Sun.) on Marine Dr., Agana. You pay according to the weight of food you select (about $6).

Despite the unpretentious appearance, the **Mini Cafe** downtown (see map) is very popular for its weekday Cantonese lunch combination specials (closed Sun.).

Sizzler Steak House (tel. 477-7112) at the Agana Shopping Center has a good all-you-can-eat salad bar for $7. Sizzler's steaks begin around $9.

Guam's only vegetarian restaurant is **Simply Food**, beside the Seventh-Day Adventist Church in Agana Heights. They're open for lunch weekdays 1100-1400. No smoking.

Tamuning/Upper Tumon

The **Furusato Restaurant** (tel. 646-5969; closed Sun.) on Marine Dr. right in front of Ben Franklin Department Store is one of the least expensive places to sample Japanese food, and **Tony Roma's** (tel. 646-9034) across the street is *the* place for ribs. Both these are mildly splurgy, but not unreasonably so. Nearby on Camp Watkins Rd. is **Memories Vietnamese Restaurant** (tel. 649-2864) with an all-you-can-eat lunch buffet weekdays 1100-1400 ($7).

Shakey's Pizza Parlor opposite the ITC Building offers all the pizza, chicken, soup, salad, spaghetti, nachos, and more you care to eat for $6, 1100-1700, or $7, 1700-2100. If you don't wish to stuff yourself it's better to order pizza or chicken from the posted menu, as the buffet tends to be cold while individual orders are specially prepared and served hot. Big 48-oz pitchers of beer are available. Shakey's is full of locals and has a lively atmosphere. Also try **Marty's Mexican Merienda** (tel. 646-5533) in the adjacent bowling alley. Happy hour there is from 1600 to 1900.

Another American institution is **Denny's Restaurant** farther up Marine Dr., with fast, cheerful service, big portions, and a bottomless cup of coffee. Have breakfast here when you're starved and want to experience a thick slice of stateside life. A special reduced menu is available for senior citizens (age 55 and over). They're open 24 hours a day!

King's Restaurant (also open 24 hours) in Gibson's Guam Shopping Center is similar to Denny's but slightly cheaper, and they offer breakfast specials weekdays. The portions are huge, so order conservatively. It's very popular with the locals.

Chuck's Steak House (tel. 646-1001) off Marine Dr. in Upper Tumon serves a good, filling lunch 1130-1400 weekdays and thick, juicy steaks in the evening. Their bar is worth a visit anytime (happy hour 1400-1800 weekdays).

The **Dragon Restaurant** (tel. 646-8959), in a plaza on Route 16 just east of the Micronesia Mall, has a self-service lunch special Monday through Saturday for around $4.

Out On The Island

The **USO**, in Piti near Cabras Island, has a cheap public snack bar. The **International United Seaman's Service Club** (tel. 472-4247), beyond the power plant on Cabras Island, has a good inexpensive dining room open till 2100 daily and a bar open till 2300. Turn off the main coastal highway at USO.

One of the only places to get lunch (chicken and steaks) on the way around the island is **Jeff's Pirates Cove** (tel. 789-1582; closed Mon.), just north of Ipan Beach Park. All the Japanese bus tours stop there so it's not cheap, but the cold beer at the bar is not overpriced.

Entertainment

Karaoke or "video sing-along" is all the rage at many bars and restaurants on Guam and Saipan. Customers are offered a microphone and the chance to sing rock songs, following the text displayed on a video screen. It's great fun and hostesses are often available to do the singing for tips. "Polynesian" dance shows ($45 including dinner) are staged at the big hotels for Japanese tourists. Be aware that these artificial productions have nothing to do with Micronesian culture. Guam's many "sleaze and disease" striptease clubs and massage parlors are best avoided.

Tumon's most exclusive dinner theater and discotheque is the **Sand Castle** (tel. 649-7469), next to the Hyatt Regency Hotel in Tumon. This $30 million entertainment center, which opened in 1990, features a Las Vegas-style musical review dinner show at 1900 nightly except Wednesday. It's $100 pp if you arrive at 1730 for dinner, $50 pp for the show alone. At 2000 daily Sand Castle's three-level, 750-person capacity, New York-style **Onyx Disco** cranks up with two huge video screens and black light beneath a six-story ceiling ($12 pp admission). Dress sharp or you'll be out of place here. Call ahead for information about reservations and the shuttle-bus pickup.

A good local bar complete with shuffleboard and pool table is **Mom's Place** (tel. 477-7585) on Route 8, Maite. **Ninings Tavern** (no sign), on a side street down from Mom's, has lots of local atmosphere and very cheap beer.

Among the more offbeat events is **dog racing** every Tues., Wed., Fri., and Sun. at 2000 at Guam Greyhound Park, Tamuning (admission for overseas tourists $5, local customers $2.50, minimum bet $3, tel. 646-9700). About 13 races are held per night.

A number of shooting galleries exist around Tumon where Japanese tourists have the fun of firing handguns, shotguns, and even machine guns for around $65 for 42 rounds. You can easily get the attendants to knock $25 off the posted price when there aren't any Japanese present.

Sports And Recreation

Guam is one of the best places for scuba diving in Micronesia, thanks to the excellent facilities available. There are no less than five five-star PADI dive centers on the island! Prices at the dive shops are competitive and it's even cheaper just to rent tanks and beach dive from a rental car. Tanks can be rented for $15 at the **Coral Reef Marine Center** opposite USO in Piti (tel. 477-6335) or behind the ITC Building in Tamuning (tel. 646-4895), and diving equipment is sold locally at duty-free prices. An estimated 400 local scuba freaks head for the reefs on any given weekend, so you'll have no trouble getting in on the action. For a description of a few dive sites see "Scuba Locales" at the end of this chapter.

Papalagi Divers (Box 11226, Tamuning, GU 96911; tel. 472-3232), 110 West Soledad

Ave. in downtown Agana, offers two-tank dives daily for $90 including equipment and lunch. Also excellent is **Guam Divers** (Box 3361, Agana, GU 96910; tel. 477-7621), whose dive shop is on Marine Dr. opposite Ace Hardware on the south side of Agana. Their two-tank boat dives are $85 (lunch included), beach dives $65 (two tanks) or $55 (one tank). One-tank night dives are $65.

One of the biggest scuba operators on Guam is the **Micronesian Divers Association** (Box 24991, GMF, GU 96921), founded in 1975 by Pete Peterson. Full-day scuba trips (two tanks) are $85 pp, transportation and lunch included, provided you book directly with them upon arrival on Guam. They frequent Blue Reef, Haps Reef, Crevice, and the twin shipwreck in Apra Harbor. MDA has three dive shops on Guam: the main one at Agat (tel. 565-2656) near Gaan Point and others in Tumon (tel. 649-9870) and Yigo (tel. 653-1665). MDA rates as a "PADI Five-Star Instructor Development Center," the highest qualification possible.

Diving may work out cheaper on a charter boat, such as the motorized trimaran *Pura Vida* based at the Aqua World Marina on Apra Harbor. Their two-tank dives at 0900 daily are only $45, but you must supply your own tanks. Wednesdays at 1800 there are night dives ($20). Call the *Pura Vida* at 472-3852 for information.

The 46-passenger *Atlantis* submarine takes visitors on 45-minute reef rides for $89 pp. The sub departs the Aqua World Marina, Piti, 10 times a day and information is available at their office (tel. 477-4166) opposite the Sotetsu Tropicana Hotel on Tumon. Hotel transfers are included.

Jet Skis are for rent at Merizo pier ($20 for 25 minutes). Admission to the **public swimming pool** (closed Mon.) opposite the Agana Shopping Center is 50 cents.

The **Marianas Yacht Club** (Box 2297, Agana, GU 96910; tel. 472-1739), behind Dry Dock Point at Apra Harbor, provides two-week guest privileges for visiting yachts and temporary membership at $100 a month. Facilities include washing machines and showers, and the Friday night barbecues here are

fun and open to everyone. An annual race and regatta calendar is available from the club. The Continental Cup from Japan to Guam occurs around Christmas, with the Guam-Japan Goodwill Regatta in Feb. or early March.

Golf

The Japanese are crazy about golf and Guam has three public courses to serve them. The most "local" of the three is the **Country Club of the Pacific** (tel. 789-1362), an established 18-hole golf course which opened in 1971. It's in pleasant rolling countryside just north of Ipan Beach on Route 4 south of Yona. Greens fees for 18 holes are $30 for locals and $55 for tourists weekdays, $40 for locals and $85 for tourists weekends. If you want to do only nine holes it's cheaper. Rental clubs are $20, shoes $7, and a cart is $15 pp (two-person minimum). The clubhouse is impressive.

The 18-hole **Takayama** or **"Windward Hills" Golf Club** (tel. 789-2474), west of Talofofo in the center of the island, is similar though somewhat less appealing as far as facilities and scenery go. Packaged Japanese are its main clientele.

Another slick modern course custom-made for Japanese tourists is the 27-hole **Hatsuho International Country Club** (tel. 632-1111) on Route 9 in northern Guam. A round of golf here will cost $50 for greens fees, $30 cart fee, $20 club rental fee, and $7 shoe rental. On weekends and holidays the greens fee is $84. There's also a flat "local price" of $59 ($62 weekends) which includes greens fee, the cart fee, and maintenance—ask for it if you're from the States.

At all three courses call ahead to check whether reservations are necessary. A dozen golf tournaments a year are held on Guam.

OTHER PRACTICALITIES

Shopping

Since a wide range of American-made products are available on Guam, it's a good place to restock and refit. Make up a shopping list before you arrive. There's still no sales tax on Guam so the marked prices are what you really pay! Watches, photography and stereo equipment, perfumes, jewelry, liquor, and chinaware are found everywhere. As on Saipan, most of the handicrafts you see here are made in the Philippines.

The Agana Shopping Center will warm the hearts of stateside suburbanites, but the Ben Franklin Department Store in Tamuning has a better selection of merchandise. Gibson's Shopping Center in Tamuning has degenerated into a souvenir mart for Japanese tourists and is of little interest to anyone else. Micronesia Mall, at the intersection of Routes 1 and 16 in Upper Tumon, is Guam's biggest shopping center. A shuttle bus connects the Tumon Bay tourist hotels to Micronesia Mall every 30 minutes—ask the hotel doorman.

Slide or black-and-white film is hard to find and expensive on Guam. Only color print film is usually available. Kimura Camera (tel. 646-4631) in the ITC Building is a competitive place to buy a camera.

CSS Thrift Shop on Farenholt Ave. (weekdays 0900-1200/1300-1600) sells second-hand clothes. There's a flea market at the USO (tel. 333-2021) in Piti the first and third Sundays of each month beginning at 0700 (by 0830 the best things are gone). The USO snack bar serves a $1 breakfast special on flea market days.

Returning U.S. residents are allowed a duty-free exemption of $800 (instead of $400) on consumer items acquired in Guam. Four liters of alcoholic beverages may also be taken back (instead of one liter). An invoice or bill of sale may be necessary to prove where you purchased the articles. The company **Duty-Free Shoppers**, with 10 stores on Guam, has a government-sanctioned monopoly over the duty-free business on the island.

Visas

Entry requirements are similar to those of the rest of the U.S.: almost everyone other than Americans requires a passport and visa. The loophole is that as of Oct. 1988 tourists from Australia, Brunei, Burma, Hong Kong, Indonesia, Malaysia, Nauru, New Zealand, Papua New Guinea, Singapore, Solomon Islands, Vanuatu, and Western Samoa may now enter Guam visa-free for stays of up to 15 days provided they have passports and onward tickets. In Oct. 1990 South Koreans also became eligible for visa-free entry, and tourism officials are lobbying to extend the same facility to Filipinos and Taiwanese. Citizens of Germany, Italy, Japan, Sweden, Switzerland, and the United Kingdom can stay up to 90 days without a visa.

American citizens are required to show proper identification such as a certified birth certificate or voter's registration card unless they're arriving directly from the U.S. (driver's license or social security card may not be enough). Americans will require a passport should they wish to continue to any Asian country. Canadians need the passport but not a visa. All passengers flying from Guam to Hawaii must pass U.S. Immigration controls at Honolulu. As always, the more affluent you look the better. No vaccinations are required.

Money, Measurements, And Services

Nineteen different banks have branches on Guam which open from 1000 to 1500 Mon. through Thurs., 1000-1800 Fri., 0900-1300 Saturday. Major credit cards are accepted. The American Express representative on Guam is Travel Pacificana, 207 Martyr St., Agana, GU 96910 (tel. 472-8884). You can receive mail c/o this office provided you have American Express traveler's checks or their credit card, but registered letters and parcels are not accepted.

U.S. domestic postal rates apply, which makes this a cheap, dependable place to mail things. To North America the price difference between air and sea mail is minimal, but parcels take two to four months to travel by boat. General delivery mail is held at the inconveniently located Guam Main Facility (GMF) post office on Route 16 in Barrigada. The new Tamuning post office behind the ITC Building is open weekdays 0800-1600, Sat. 0900-1200. For postal information call 734-2921.

Long-distance phone calls can be made at IT&E Overseas Inc., on Marine Dr. between Agana and Tamuning. A direct-dial call to Hawaii or the U.S. Mainland from a booth at their office will cost only $1.75 for the first minute, plus about $1 per additional minute—cheap. Prices are a few cents lower evenings and weekends. To call direct from the U.S. to a telephone number on Guam, dial 011-671 and the regular seven-digit number. Remember, Guam's a day ahead of the rest of the U.S., so if it's noon Monday in Merizo it's 6 p.m. Sunday in Seattle.

The consulates general of Japan (tel. 646-1290) and the Philippines (tel. 646-4620) are in the ITC Building at Tamuning. If you have a personal problem and need help, call the Crisis Hot Line (tel. 477-8833), which is answered 24 hours. The electric current is 110-120 volts AC, 60 cycles.

The travel consultants at Gem Travel (tel. 477-9022), below the International Marina Hotel, 470 West Soledad Ave., Agana, can reserve rooms at Hawaiian hotels belonging to the Outrigger chain for about $60 d plus tax, rental car included. This is much less than the usual "rack rate" you'd be charged if you just showed up in Hawaii without reservations, but you must have a valid credit card.

Information

The Guam Visitors Bureau (tel. 646-5278), 1270 North Marine Dr., Suite 201, Boons Building, Harmon, an orange and green two-story building near Micronesia Mall, can supply glossy brochures. Their accommodations list only includes their members, however—not the cheapest places. Ask for their excellent *A Guide to the War in the Pacific Sites,* the *Island of Guam Highway Map,* and William H. Stewart's *Pacific Explorer's Map of Guam,* all available free of charge. You can obtain the same material through the mail by writing the Guam Visitors Bureau, Box 3520, Agana, GU 96910.

For an informative brochure on Guam's WW II history write:, War in the Pacific National Historic Park, Box FA, Agana, GU 96910.

Weather information is available by dialing 117.

If you need to see a doctor your best bet is the Seventh-Day Adventist Clinic (tel. 646-5301) on Ypao Rd., Tamuning.

The N.M. Flores Memorial Library (tel. 472-6417), 254 Martyr St., Agana, GU 96910, is open Mon., Wed., and Fri. 0930-1800, Tues. and Thurs. 0930-2000, Sat. 1000-1600, and Sun. 1200-1600.

Faith Book Store (tel. 472-1265) in the Agana Shopping Center sells topographical maps of Guam and books on Micronesia. Hafa Books (tel. 472-8034), 222 East Marine Dr., sells secondhand books at half price; they also exchange books. The Coral Reef Marine Center (tel. 646-4895), below the ridge behind the ITC Building, sells nautical charts ($20 each). For a price list of academic publications on the whole region write: Micronesian Area Research Center, University of Guam, UOG Station, Mangilao, GU 96923.

Guam is lucky to have two good newspapers, the *Pacific Daily News* (Box DN, Agana, GU 96910), owned by the conservative Gannett chain, and the twice-weekly *Guam Tribune* (Box EG, Agana, GU 96910). The *Pacific Daily News* circulates throughout Micronesia; read Joe Murphy's provocative column, "Pipe Dreams," in this paper. The monthly *Guam Now!* tourist magazine (free) includes extensive restaurant listings.

Three quality magazines are published on Guam: *Guam & Micronesia Glimpses, Hafa,* and *Guam Business News* (see the "Booklist" at the end of this book).

There are seven radio stations on Guam: KGUM-AM (567 kHz), KUAM-AM (612 kHz), KTWG-AM (801 kHz), KUAM-FM (93.9 MHz), KSTO-FM (95.5 MHz), KZGZ-FM (97.5 MHz), and KOKU-FM (100.3 MHz). All but KTWG-AM broadcast 24 hours a day.

Volunteers

Youth With A Mission (Box 1245, Agana, GU 96910; tel. 646-7180), an international, interdenominational Christian missionary organization with close ties to the U.S. Christian

Right, has been operating on Guam since 1977. YWAM welcomes young volunteers interested in performing a three-month "summer of service" as Christian missionaries. Their "mobile teams" travel constantly throughout Micronesia and this would be an excellent way to see the area and meet the people, provided you're a sincere believer. Volunteers who take the two-week orientation course at Youth With A Mission's Guam headquarters, beside the Belauan meetinghouse and baseball field at Harmon, just beyond the Two Lovers Point turnoff, pay $5 a day for room and board. Accommodations are limited, so it's important to write in advance to let them know you'll be arriving. (This listing is provided for information purposes only and does not imply an endorsement.)

GETTING THERE

The transportation hub of the Central Pacific, Guam's Tamuning airport receives most flights through Micronesia. Air Nauru (tel. 649-7107), All Nippon Airways (tel. 646-9069), Continental Air Micronesia (tel. 646-0220), Japan Air Lines (tel. 646-9195), Korean Airlines (fax 649-9683), Northwest Orient (tel. 649-8384), and Philippine Airlines all provide service. Guam's big-four carriers are Air Micronesia (66% of passenger departures), Japan Air Lines (16%), Northwest (10%), and All Nippon (7%). None of the others account for more than one percent of departing passengers.

All **Continental Air Micronesia** flights terminate on Guam. San Francisco and Los Angeles passengers must change planes in Honolulu. If an overnight stay at any of these points is required between connecting flights it will be at your own expense. Continental flights stop at Majuro, Kwajalein, Kosrae, Pohnpei, and Chuuk between Honolulu and Guam. Continental also serves Yap and Koror and flies three times a week to Brisbane and Sydney in Australia. Points in Asia served by Continental directly from Guam include Denpasar (Bali), Hong Kong, Manila, Port Moresby, Seoul, Taipei, and many Japanese cities.

Regular OW Continental fares from Guam are $708 to Los Angeles or San Francisco, $320 to Koror, $331 to Japan. Certain off-peak flights from Guam offer reduced OW fares; for example, $120 to Chuuk instead of $242, $177 to Pohnpei instead of $367. See the main Introduction to this book for more tips.

Continental also offers reduced VRIP Micro$aver roundtrip fares from Guam ($64 to Rota, $73 to Saipan, $229 to Yap, $352 to Koror, $266 to Chuuk). The restrictions on these rock-bottom fares are that you must book and pay on the same day; the dates are fixed and cannot be changed; you must spend at least one Saturday at your destination; and the tickets are nonrefundable. These tickets are valid one year.

Many airlines fly between Japan and Guam/Saipan (compare prices). All Nippon Airways, Continental, Japan Air Lines, and Northwest Airlines fly from Tokyo: Continental also serves Fukuoka, Nagoya, Okinawa, Sapporo, and Sendai, and Japan Air Lines has nonstop flights from Nagoya and Osaka. Northwest arrives from Fukuoka and Nagoya. All these airlines would like to greatly increase the frequency of their services between Japan and Guam but are hampered by inadequate airport facilities in Japan. Interestingly, JAL and Northwest offer direct connections to Guam from many North American cities via Tokyo (Narita), instead of the usual Los Angeles/Honolulu routing.

Air Nauru at the Pacific Star Hotel has a weekly flight Nauru-Guam-Manila and return. The OW point-to-point fare out of Guam is $168 to Nauru. From Nauru, Air Nauru has onward flights to Australia, New Zealand, and Fiji. Continental charges $286 Guam-Manila while Air Nauru asks only $248 for the same flight; with stops on Yap and Koror it's $416 on Continental.

In July 1991 Air Nauru began a new weekly service from Nauru to Guam via Kosrae, Pohnpei, Chuuk, and Yap. Stopovers are allowed but all the interisland fares are added up (see the main Introduction to this book for details).

An Air Micronesia subsidiary, **Air Mike Express**, flies several times a day between Guam and Rota ($58), Tinian, and Saipan ($66). Lower off-peak fares exist here too, so ask.

You can charter a four-seater Apache plane from Guam direct to Pagan in the Northern Marianas from **Freedom Air** (Box 1578, Agana, GU 96910; tel. 646-8009) for $1,600 RT plus $30 an hour waiting time on the island.

GETTING AROUND

A **public transit service** operates along nine routes, with important transfer stations at Micronesia Mall, Guam Shopping Center (Gibson's), and the Agana Shopping Center. One of the most useful routes for visitors is the hourly Express Line from Micronesia Mall to the Tumon Bay tourist strip, then up to Gibson's, Tamuning, and down Marine Dr. to the Agana Shopping Center. This service will stop anywhere along its route, so just flag down a bus and try getting a schedule from a driver.

Route PT-3 from Micronesia Mall to Gibson's via Marine Dr. runs only six times a day. Routes PT-4 and PT-5 from the Agana Shopping Center to the University of Guam run once an hour. Routes PT-6 and PT-7 from the Agana Shopping Center do a circular loop right around southern Guam seven times a day in opposite directions. This two-hour ride is Guam's best bargain island tour and you can easily stop off at points along the way after confirming onward bus times with the driver.

Fares on all routes are 75 cents, plus 25 cents per transfer, exact change required. Service ends around 1900 and there are no buses on Sun. and holidays. For information call 472-2173 from 0530 to 2030 Mon.-Saturday.

Other than this, you've got a choice of hitching, taking taxis, or renting a car. Guamanians are rather mean about giving rides, however, and taxi fares in sprawling Agana/Tamuning become a major expense. All taxis have meters and charge $1.80 flag fare, plus 60 cents every half mile, plus $1 a piece for luggage. Sample fares from the airport are $7 to the Pacific Star Hotel, $15 to Micronesia Hotel (same fare day and night). Insist that the meter be used.

The **USO** (or United Service Organizations—a military social club) has an organized "boonie stomp" hike every Sat. at 1145 from their center at Piti near the Cabras Island causeway. Civilians are welcome upon payment of a $1 transportation fee (phone 333-2021 for details).

Nobody walks anywhere on Guam if they can help it; pedestrians are considered un-American subversives and most roads don't even have sidewalks!

Car Rentals

Several car rental companies such as Avis (tel. 646-1801), Budget (tel. 646-5494), Dollar (tel. 646-7000), Gordon's (tel. 565- 5827), Hertz (tel. 646-5875), Islander (tel. 646-8156), National (tel. 649-0110), Nippon (tel. 646-1243), and Toyota (tel. 646- 1876) have offices on Guam. Their rates are fairly standard: $40 a day with unlimited mileage, plus five percent tax, plus $8-15 for $500-deductible collision insurance (optional). If you take a car for a week, the seventh night is sometimes free. Always ask if they have any special discounted or business rates, or lower rates for older non-a/c cars. Avoid any agency which tacks a mileage charge onto the daily rate.

The car rental agencies at the airport (Avis, Hertz, Islander, Toyota) are supposed to be competitive, but in practice they're all about the same (though Toyota may be cheaper). The companies with offices along the Tumon strip are Avis, Budget, National, and Nippon. Cars are in short supply on Guam so try to reserve a few days ahead, especially if you want one of the cheaper models. Tourist magazines like *Guam Now!* advertise special deals on car rentals.

Toyota Rent-a-car (tel. 646-1876), 443 South Marine Dr. not far from the ITC Building, has cars beginning at $28 a day, plus $8 CDW and five percent tax.

Gordon's Rent a Car (tel. 565-5827) in Agat doesn't have a regular office and their cars are often all taken, but they do offer the cheapest rates on Guam: $16 a day plus $3 daily for CDW. Call them up to arrange a delivery to your hotel.

Your home driver's license (U.S. or foreign) is valid on Guam for 30 days. The speed limit on Guam is 40 mph (65 kph); if nothing is posted then 35 mph (57 kph) is the limit.

The Gorgo Shooting Gallery (tel. 646-8729) near the Fujita Beach Hotel rents **bicycles** at $15 a day, **mopeds** at $30 a day (gas included). This is for a 1000-1900 day only.

Airport

Won Pat International Airport (GUM) at Tamuning is six km northeast of downtown Agana. There's no bus service but a taxi should be under $10 to most hotels. If you only have a backpack it's quite feasible to walk down to the Tamuning or Tumon Bay hotels (two or three km). Notice the latte motif in the airport architecture.

Strangely, there's no tourist information at the airport, nor any foreign currency exchange office for arriving passengers. The airport "bank" is in the departure lounge on the second floor, past the security clearance, but its only purpose is to change excess U.S. dollars back into foreign currency for those departing ($1 minimum commission). They won't cash U.S. dollar traveler's checks. Have some quarters ready for the airport pay phones and watch for the dollar bill changing machine. No coin lockers are available at the airport.

Reconfirm or change your onward Continental Air Micronesia reservations at the helpful Service Center (tel. 646-9101) opposite the check-in counters.

All travelers transiting Guam between Hawaii or the FSM and Yap, Koror, or Saipan will have to change planes here and this often requires an overnight stay. If you aren't interested in leaving the airport, check your luggage straight through to your final destination and spend the night in the transit lounge amid clouds of cigarette smoke. In the case of westbound passengers from the FSM to Yap or Koror, this could entail a wait of 12 hours or more, so check the schedules carefully.

The terminal is open 24 hours a day, so you can spend the night on one of the yellow plastic benches if you're leaving in the very early morning, provided you can bear the relentless Muzak. A better bet is the a/c **Hafa Adai Lounge** on the third floor at the airport (take the elevator). Here you can stretch out on a nice, soft sofa, though the airport loudspeakers still broadcast jarring flight announcements directly into the lounge in Chamorro and Japanese! It's $5 pp for two hours or less with free coffee and nonalcoholic drinks, $15 pp for eight hours including four alcoholic drinks.

The single duty-free shop in the departure lounge is stocked with insipid luxury items. There's no departure tax.

SIGHTS OF GUAM

· AGANA

Founded in 1668, Agana (pronounced agan-ya) is the oldest European city in the Pacific. Although leveled during the 1944 American invasion and rebuilt on a different plan, a few reminders of the Spanish era remain. First sightseeing stop is **Plaza de Espana,** the heart of downtown Agana and center of spiritual and temporal power during Spanish colonial times. Of the Casa de Gobierno (Governor's Palace), built in 1736 and enlarged in 1885, little survived the war. However, one can still see the *azotea* (terrace), the arches of the arsenal (1736), and the "Chocolate House," a summerhouse where Spanish ladies once gathered for late-afternoon *meriendas* (teas). The former Spanish garden house, also in the Plaza, is now the **Guam Museum** (open Mon. to Sat. 0900-1200/1300-1600, $1 admission). Here you'll read the amazing story of Corporal Shoichi Yokoi who hid in an underground hideout in a bamboo grove near Talofofo until discovered by two Guamanians on 24 Jan. 1972.

To one side is the **Cathedral,** first erected here in 1669 and rebuilt in 1955. The image above the main altar is Santa Marian Camalin. Legend says that this statue miraculously floated ashore on the beach at Merizo over 200 years ago, guarded by two golden crabs bearing lighted candles in their claws. A revolving statue of Pope John Paul II (who said Mass here in 1981) watches over Plaza de Espana.

Nearby, at the foot of Kasamata Hill, is **Latte Stone Park,** where eight ancient latte pillars, originally from the vicinity of Lake Fena in south central Guam, were reerected in 1955. These timeworn monoliths could once have been the foundation stones of prehistoric buildings, though their precise history is obscure. Along the cliffs behind the park are **caves** where the Japanese ensconced themselves.

Back near Marine Drive, northwest of the Plaza de Espana, is the **San Antonio Bridge** (1800). In 1676 the Presidio Agana, a small settlement surrounded by a stockade, was located between this bridge and the waterfront. The river itself was filled in after WW II.

a view of Umatac in the early 19th century

M.G.L. DOMENY DE RIENZI

Paseo de Susana Park, on land reclaimed with bulldozed WW II rubble, is worth a stroll. Japanese tourists have their pictures taken in front of the **miniature Statue of Liberty** in the park. If the surf is up, walk out to the end of the breakwater and feel the waters roar around you as **surfers** defy waves at the mouth of Agana Boat Basin.

On the corner of Marine Drive and Route 4 near the park is the **Chief Quipuha Statue,** where on 31 Jan. 1990 two-term Governor Richard J. Bordallo wrapped himself in the Guamanian flag and shot himself through the head just three hours before he was due to board a plane to the U.S. to begin serving a four-year prison term for corruption. In the **U.S. Naval Cemetery,** just east on Marine Dr., are the graves of a number of German sailors off the SMS *Cormoran,* scuttled in Apra Harbor on 7 April 1917.

Above Latte Stone Park at Agana Heights is **Government House** (1952), residence of the governor. Inside you may visit the Governor's Museum, with its interesting displays on Guamanian history, and enjoy the view from the terrace. Just beyond this is the site of **Fort Santa Agueda** (1800). Although very little is left of the fort, you do get a splendid view of Agana from this hill.

AROUND THE ISLAND

The West

Heavy fighting took place near Agana in July 1944. The main landings were at Asan and Agat; the Japanese commander directed the defense from the Fonte Plateau above Asan. **War in the Pacific National Historical Park Visitor Center** at Asan, 2½ km west of Agana, offers a photo display and a 15-minute slide show on the war (tel. 477-9362; open weekdays 0730-1530, weekends 0830-1400, free).

Three large 14-cm **Japanese guns** are perched in a row up a concrete stairway and along a short trail behind the community hall on the north side of Piti Catholic Church. The mahogany trees near the guns were planted in the 1920s and 1930s.

From Nimitz Hill high above Piti, an excellent hike follows a jeep track south from Mt. Chachao to the summit of **Mt. Tenjo** (313 meters), with panoramic views along the way. (As you drive up to Nimitz Hill from Piti turn right onto Larson Rd., the next street after Trans World Radio, and right again on Turner Road. Keep straight as far as Mt. Chachao where the road swings left to the relay station atop Mt. Alulom. The rough jeep track to Mt. Tenjo, impossible for a car, is straight ahead, a 1½-hour hike roundtrip.)

Apra Harbor, between Asan and Agat, is one of the largest protected harbors in the world. Guam's commercial port is here, though most of the south side of the harbor is taken up by a giant U.S. naval base. At **Gaan Point,** Agat, a couple of guns and tunnels recall the WW II fighting. Just beyond Nimitz Beach Park is **Taleyfac Bridge** (1785), part of the old Spanish road from Agana to Umatac.

The South

By far the best hike on Guam is along the coast from near Nimitz Beach Park to Umatac. Although the coconut plantations at the heads of bays are private property, much of this area is within **Guam Territorial Seashore Park.** You'll have to wade on the reef around the points and ford knee-deep streams emptying into the bays, but you can make it through to Umatac in a day. Wear shorts and rubber booties or old tennis shoes you don't mind getting wet. It's also quite feasible to hike down to the coast from the **Sella Bay lookout,** which avoids a lot of houses but can be very slippery after rain.

A drive around the south end of the island is an essential part of any visit to Guam. The main road turns inland from beyond Nimitz and climbs along the slopes of **Mt. Lamlam** (406 meters), Guam's highest peak. A viewpoint above Sella Bay looks down on grassy red ridges trailing into the sea. A trail departing from the **Cetti Bay Overlook** leads up to the large cross atop Mt. Lamlam, (45 minutes OW), with a sweeping view of the entire island. On Good Friday a religious procession parades to this cross. It's possible to hike south along the ridge to Merizo or Inarajan.

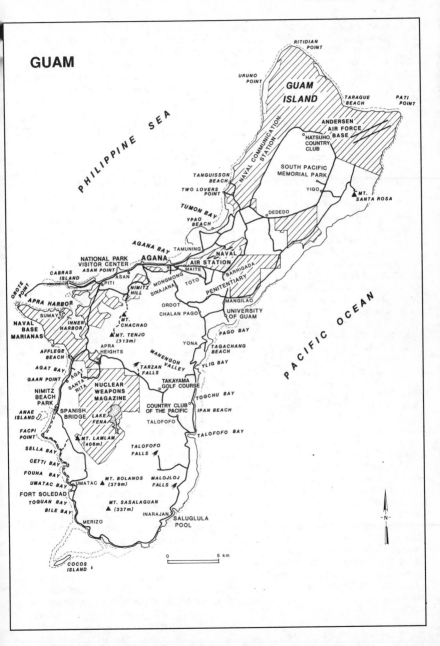

Umatac, the first unspoiled Chamorro village you encounter on your way around the island, was the docking site used by the Spanish galleons; several forts built there in the early 19th century protected the area from English pirates. **Fort San Jose** was on the north side of the bay, **Fort Soledad** on the south; not much is left of either, but the view from Fort Soledad is great. Magellan landed at Umatac on 6 March 1521; there's a monument to record the event.

Merizo is the halfway point around the island—about 35 km from Agana either way. Busloads of Japanese tourists are sent over from Merizo to Cocos Island Resort in an hourly shuttle boat—join them if you wish, but have your $20 RT boat fare ready (locals $5). The west end of Cocos is a public park, but you'll need to hire a boat ($10 pp) to get there.

The **rectory** (El Convento) in front of the Merizo village church was occupied by the parish priest beginning in 1856; across the road is a **bell tower** built in 1910. The **Massacre Monument** in front of the church memorializes 46 Chamorros murdered by Japanese troops near here as the American invasion became imminent.

Saluglula Pool, a popular saltwater swimming hole, is right beside the road at **Inarajan.** Founded by Governor Quiroga in 1680, this is the best-preserved village on Guam, so take time to stroll around. Father Jesus Baza Duenas, the Chamorro priest beheaded by the Japanese in 1944, is buried beneath the altar in the parish church.

Four km north of Inarajan is the turnoff for **Talofofo Falls Park** (admission $4), another four km down the NASA road. The impressive falls tumble 10 meters over a black cliff set in the emerald-green vegetation of central Guam. The swimming and picnicking are good.

Tarzan Falls is near the center of the island. It takes 20 minutes to hike down a muddy track to the crest of the falls, then there's a slippery climb down the side through long, sharp sword grass to a pool. The bottom of Tarzan Falls is idyllic (admission free).

The North

Get a good view of the cliffs of Guam's windy east coast from **Tagachang Beach Park** just below Yona. At Mangilao beyond Pago Bay is a large educational complex. The **University of Guam** (founded in 1952 as a teachers' college) has a Micronesian Area Research Center (MARC), a marine research laboratory, and a university library with a small collection of local artifacts. Guam Community College is nearby.

Much of the north and west of Guam is occupied by the U.S. Air Force and Navy. From **Andersen Air Force Base** B-52s targeted Vietnam. (After 1975 Guam continued to reap the whirlwind as tens of thousands of Vietnamese refugees passed through on their way to the U.S.)

Toward the end of the battle for Guam in 1944, the Japanese withdrew northward. They made their last stand near Yigo; **South Pacific Memorial Park** marks the spot. Lt. General Hideyoshi Obata, commanding general of the Japanese 31st Army, had his headquarters in a network of tunnels below the park. On 11 Aug. 1944 American soldiers tossed white phosphorous hand grenades into the tunnels and sealed the openings with blocks of explosives. When the tunnels were reopened four days later, 60 Japanese bodies were found inside, though Obata was never identified. Several of the tunnels can still be seen at the bottom of the hill behind the monument.

Beyond the north end of Tumon Bay is **Two Lovers Point,** a 100-meter basalt cliff where two young Chamorro lovers are reported to have tied their hair together and jumped to their deaths to avoid separation. A deep cave drops to the sea. **Gun Beach,** beyond the Hotel Nikko on Tumon Bay, directly below the cliffs, is a favorite for swimming, snorkeling, scuba diving, and surfing. Tumon Bay curves around between Two Lovers Point and the Hilton.

Scuba Locales

Guam's greatest attraction is its surrounding sea—a virtual paradise for snorkelers, scuba divers, and surfers, or just plain swimmers and beach loafers. For accessibility, cost, and ease of diving, Guam is outstanding. Proximity to the Marianas Trench means the offshore waters are constantly flushed, resulting in 60-meter-plus visibility in the dry season, 30-meter-plus in the wet. There are 15 to 20 good walk-in locations.

For beginners, **Bile Bay** provides a gradual slope out, and some cave diving. Farther north a Japanese **Zero aircraft** rests in 18 meters of water off Umatac Point.

Blue Hole just off the south side of the Orote Peninsula, right under the cliffs, is also only 18 meters down. You pass through the 5- by 10-meter entrance and drop 40 meters, then make a 90-degree turn straight ahead out an immense opening onto a sheer dropoff—excellent visibility and plenty of shark action. Near Blue Hole is the crevice, also an exciting experience.

A navigational buoy in **Apra Harbor** marks two wrecks right next to one another at about 30 meters: the WW I German auxiliary cruiser SMS *Cormoran*, and the WW II Japanese freighter *Tokai Maru*. This is the only place in the world where two enemy vessels from two different wars can be seen on a single dive! Visibility, however, is much better at the wreck of a sunken U.S. tanker 1½ km farther out.

Guam's most colorful scuba spot is **Double Reef** off Uruno Point near the northwest end of the island. The 120-meter cliffs along the shore and the military base create a restricted access; you have to come in by boat. Two parallel reefs about 300 meters apart have a channel 12-18 meters deep between them, with excellent visibility of the fine coral beneath. The most exciting dive of all is into 30-meter-square **Shark Grotto,** about three km south of Double Reef. Sharks are best seen at night (they usually don't bite).

COMMONWEALTH OF THE NORTHERN MARIANAS

INTRODUCTION

The Commonwealth of the Northern Mariana Islands (CNMI) stretches north from Guam in a 685-km-long chain. The 14 islands are weathered tips of a massive mountain range rising over 10 km from the depths of the Marianas Trench. The southern islands are limestone with level terraces and fringing coral reefs; the northern islands are volcanic. Saipan reaches an altitude of 471 meters, while a peak on Agrihan soars to 965 meters, highest in Micronesia.

The Marianas are the Pacific island group closest to Japan. Saipan is 2,600 km due east of Manila, 2,424 km south-southeast of Tokyo, and only 206 km northeast of Guam. This location made it a battleground during WW II. The planes which nuked Hiroshima and Nagasaki took off from North Field on Tinian. Today Japanese tourists fill the high-

rise hotels along Saipan's west coast. They come to enjoy the beaches and coral-crammed lagoon, but also to make the pilgrimage to Suicide Cliff.

Saipan is the business, government, and tourism center of the Northern Marianas, while Tinian and Rota are still relatively quiet and unspoiled. The 20th century hovers like a helicopter slowly descending on Saipan, where most of the homes have cable TV. But while thoroughly Americanized, the Northern Marianas islands are friendlier and more inviting than Guam.

The Land

The three largest islands of the 478-square-km Commonwealth are Rota (85 square km), Tinian (102 square km), and Saipan (123 square km). These islands (along with northern Guam) are actually raised coral reefs. Once volcanoes, they sank below the sea and became capped by limestone. As they were lifted back out of the water, flat tops and steep cliffs appeared. Later, lava broke through Saipan's coral cap once more to create a rolling landscape.

Saipan, second largest of the Mariana Islands, is a 23- by 8-km block of towering shell-pocked cliffs on the north, east, and south, gently sloping to white sandy beaches on the west. A barrier reef protects the wide western lagoon, making this side of the island the favorite of swimmers, snorkelers, and windsurfers. Sunsets seen from these beaches are spectacular.

Except for a short stretch at Laulau, no reefs are off the east coast, and huge breakers fanned by the Northeast Trades crash into this shoreline during Saipan's winter (Nov.-April), cutting deep scars. Small bays, tidal pools, blowholes, and craters dot the

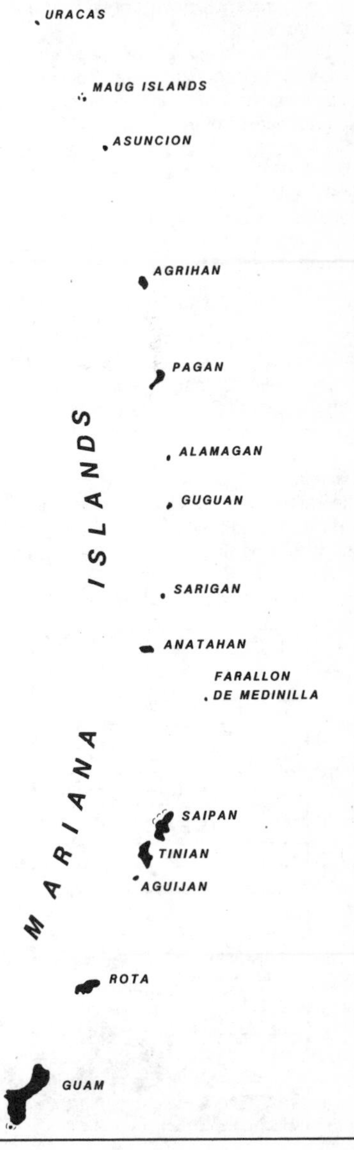

THE MARIANAS AT A GLANCE

	land area (sq km)	highest point (meters)
NORTHERN MARIANAS	477.9	965
Uracas	2.0	319
Maug Is.	2.1	228
Asuncion	7.3	891
Agrihan	47.4	965
Pagan	48.3	572
Alamagan	11.3	744
Guguan	4.2	301
Sarigan	5.0	549
Anatahan	32.3	788
Farallon de Medinilla	0.9	81
Saipan	122.9	471
Tinian	101.8	186
Aguijan	7.2	168
Rota	85.2	491
GUAM	541.0	406

THE MARIANAS

URACAS

MAUG ISLANDS

ASUNCION

AGRIHAN

PAGAN

ALAMAGAN

GUGUAN

SARIGAN

ANATAHAN

FARALLON DE MEDINILLA

SAIPAN

TINIAN

AGUIJAN

ROTA

GUAM

ISLANDS

MARIANA

rocky, broken east coast. The highest cliffs are in the Marpi area of northeast Saipan, now intimately entwined with the tragic events of 1944.

The other big islands of the Marianas are similar to Saipan, with Rota especially noted for its beautiful, crashing coastline and upland plateaus, and Tinian outstanding for its fertile soil. The towering northern islands, some still actively volcanic, are mostly uninhabited. There have been eruptions on Uracas, Asuncion, Pagan, and Guguan this century.

The Marianas Trench just east of the chain is the deepest of the world's trenches, a circular arc extending 3,000 km from Japan to Ulithi atoll. The 75-km-wide trench was discovered in 1899 when the Nero Deep was sounded at 9,636 meters. It's eight times longer, six times deeper, and 2½ times wider than the Grand Canyon, and as deep as Mt. Everest is high.

Climate

The rainiest months are July through Oct.; June is the hottest. The best months for a visit would be Jan.-March, when conditions are best for swimmers and sailboarders. This is also the period when most tourists arrive to escape the Japanese winters. The Northeast Trades blow across the Marianas from Nov. through March; easterly winds predominate from May through October. The Marianas get an average of one typhoon a year, usually between July and January. Saipan has the world's most equitable annual temperatures (lowest monthly variations), but the humidity is high.

Flora And Fauna

Saipan isn't a lush tropical island like those farther south. To prevent erosion the Americans sowed *tangan tangan* brush over the defoliated landscape from aircraft soon after the war. Saipan's soil was saved, although it's now difficult to see it, so voraciously has the *tangan tangan* rooted itself. The flame or poinciana trees along Saipan's Beach Drive bloom red and orange from May through August.

There have been sightings on Saipan of the brown tree snake which has ravaged Guam's birdlife. If you come across a snake anywhere in the Northern Marianas (not on Guam), try to kill or capture it, and report the incident to police. The flightless Guam rail, which the snake wiped out on Guam, has been introduced to Rota from U.S. zoos in an attempt to save the bird from extinction.

HISTORY

Early History

The earliest known archaeological remains date from about 2000 B.C. The people of Guam and the Northern Marianas were one race. They lived in small beach villages organized into matrilineal clans. Children belonged to the clan of the mother, and inheritance was through the female line. (Colonialism later altered this organization, and the present Chamorros are patrilineal.)

In 1668 Charles II of Spain dispatched Jesuit missionaries to Guam and named the group for his mother, Queen Maria Ana of Austria. After unsuccessfully resisting Span-

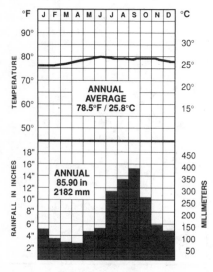

SAIPAN'S CLIMATE

ANNUAL AVERAGE 78.5°F / 25.8°C

ANNUAL 85.90 in 2182 mm

Various war relics have been set up near the Last Japanese Command Post at the foot of Saipan's Suicide Cliff.

ish soldiers, the inhabitants of the Northern Marianas were relocated to Guam in 1698. There they intermarried with the Spanish and adopted much of their culture.

In 1816, the Chamorros began returning to the Northern Marianas, where they found communities of Carolinians from Lamotrek and Woleai which had established themselves in their absence. These people lived peacefully together—the Chamorros farming, the Carolinians fishing.

Germany purchased the Northern Marianas from Spain in 1899. Governor Fritz had roads built and required every family to plant a quarter-hectare of their land with food crops. Guamanians were offered free land on Saipan for homesteading. Germany's main interest in the area was copra production.

Japan seized the islands from Germany in 1914. An influx of Japanese, Okinawans, and Koreans led to the development of sugarcane and pineapple cultivation. The Nanyo Kohatsu Kaisha (South Seas Development Co., Ltd.) built sugar mills fed by extensive rail networks on Saipan, Tinian, and Rota.

By 1935 as many Asians were present as Micronesians; by the outbreak of war Japanese nationals outnumbered Chamorros two to one. Garapan, on Saipan, was both the German and Japanese capital of the Marianas. Just before WW II the town had a

Japanese population of 15,000. After WW II all were repatriated.

The War

In June and July 1944 the U.S. took the Marianas from the Japanese. The landings at Chalan Kanoa on the southwest side of Saipan on 15 June led to a brutal three-week struggle for the island. After securing the south, the GIs began fighting their way up both sides of the island, hoping to meet on the Marpi plain below Suicide Cliff.

On 19 June the Japanese Navy sent three Zero-laden aircraft carriers to rescue their forces. The U.S. had no less than 16 carriers waiting west of the Marianas. During the Battle of the Philippine Sea (the "Great Marianas Turkey Shoot") 402 Japanese planes and all three carriers were destroyed in a single day, against a loss of only 17 U.S. aircraft.

On 6 July the remaining Japanese troops launched a fanatical banzai charge across the Tanapag plains, which continued until all 5,000 Japanese attackers had been killed. Of the 30,000-strong Japanese garrison on Saipan, only about 600 survived to be repatriated in 1945. Over 3,000 Americans were killed and another 11,000 wounded during the campaign. Some 419 Saipanese also died. Saipan suffered the worst devastation of any Pacific island. The sugar industry had been destroyed for good.

With Saipan in their hands, the U.S. landed on Guam on 21 July and Tinian on 24 July. Rota was bombed but not considered worth invading, so it remained in Japanese hands until the end of the war.

The islands then became airbases from which American B-29s leveled the cities of Japan. At the height of the bombing campaign, North Field on Tinian was the busiest airfield in the world, with two B-29s taking off abreast every 45 seconds for the seven-hour ride to Japan. The nuclear age began here when the *Enola Gay* left Tinian for Hiroshima.

The Americanization Of The Marianas

With the rest of Japanese-held Micronesia, these islands became part of the Trust Territory of the Pacific Islands in 1947. Until 1962 the Northern Marianas were under U.S. naval administration and used as a training facility by the CIA. That year the TTPI headquarters was relocated to Capitol Hill, Saipan, from Guam. Partly because of this, the Northern Marianas, which accounted for only about 12% of the total TTPI population, received 32% of the territorial income. Much of this was passed on to the inhabitants in the form of welfare-state benefits such as free food, subsidized housing, and government jobs.

Political-status negotiations began in 1969; in Feb. 1975 the Marianas Covenant was signed, slicing the Northern Marianas from the Trust Territory to become a U.S. Commonwealth somewhat like Puerto Rico. In a hurried plebiscite in June of that year, 79% of the approximately 5,000 voters approved the covenant and annexation.

A factor in the favorable vote was a desire to become eligible for a federal food-stamp program, which feeds a third of the population. There's also Medicaid, school lunches, education, and old-age assistance. Federally subsidized housing starts at $8 a month. No other area under U.S. sovereignty gets services like these!

On 24 March 1976 President Ford signed the Marianas Covenant, making the Northern Marianas the first territory acquired by the U.S. since the purchase of the Virgin Islands

from Denmark in 1917. A governor and legislature were elected in Dec. 1977, and on 9 Jan. 1978 the Commonwealth constitution came into effect.

The covenant creates a political union between the U.S. and the Northern Marianas. The U.S. has full control of defense and foreign affairs, while the Commonwealth is internally self-governing. The agreement can only be terminated by mutual consent. On 3 Nov. 1986 the U.S. implemented the covenant and the inhabitants were declared American citizens and given U.S. passports. In May 1988 a CNMI Supreme Court was established.

Military Use

Why all the interest in such a remote island group? After the end of the Vietnam War, the Pentagon started planning a fallback arc of island-based military installations around the perimeter of Asia. The giant U.S. bases in the Philippines, South Korea, and Japan were politically sensitive and nearby Guam was already overloaded with weaponry. An island like Tinian with its strategic position and low population seemed ready-made for a base with wartime airfields and roads just waiting to be recycled!

Under the Commonwealth Covenant, the U.S. Department of Defense obtained leases on the northern two-thirds of Tinian, all of the tiny island of Farallon de Medinilla (used by Guam-based aircraft for target practice), and a tract at Saipan harbor. The U.S. was granted the 50-year Tinian lease (renewable for a second 50 years) for a one-time payment of $33 million.

The 7,203 hectares on Tinian were to have become a vast airbase and supply center where nuclear weapons would be kept to reequip U.S. forces in Asia. The end of the Cold War seems to have put these plans on hold, though Tinian is still being used as a marine amphibious training area.

Waste Dumping

In 1979 the Japanese government announced plans to dump 10,000 cement-solidified 200-liter metal drums of "low-level" nuclear wastes into the Marianas Trench halfway between Tokyo and the Northern Marianas. This was to be an "experimental" dump, followed by larger and continuous dumping in the future. With 36 nuclear reactors operating, and 21 more under construction or in the planning stages, Japan has a serious nuclear-waste storage problem. By the year 2000 some three million drums of wastes will have accumulated, so the pressure is building.

The drums contain cobalt-60, strontium-90, and cesium-137, which present a major threat to the food chain in the northwest Pacific. Ocean currents from the dump site flow directly to Saipan, and leakages could eventually cause thousands of human cancer deaths a year. For the wastes to lose even half their radioactive potency, over 1,500 years must pass. No assurance can be forthcoming from the Japanese that the containers will resist the corrosive action of the sea anywhere near that long. Once deposited, the barrels themselves are unrecoverable, but escaping radiation would soon reach humankind. The ecological consequences are irreversible. The dumping places all future generations in grave peril.

Widespread opposition to the Japanese plan erupted throughout the Pacific. The governor of the Northern Marianas commented, "We reap no benefits from nuclear energy but are being forced to share its hazards." A 1983 law created a 200-nautical-mile no-dumping zone around the Northern Marianas. Those convicted of disposing of nuclear or chemical wastes in Marianas waters are now liable to a maximum fine of $1 million and up to 10 years imprisonment. The Japanese dump site is outside this area, however.

An open-ended moratorium on nuclear-waste dumping at sea, adopted by the London Dumping Convention in 1983, has delayed the program, but the Japanese have declared they will go ahead with their plans "at an appropriate time in the future." The U.S. government has repeatedly denied any obligation on its part to honor the LDC moratorium, raising the suspicion that the U.S.

might also try to use the same dump site should the Japanese succeed. One U.S. official even remarked that the location might be a suitable spot to dump all the nuclear wastes of the entire world!

Government

The autonomous Commonwealth of the Northern Marianas has a governor and lieutenant governor elected every four years. The bicameral legislature is made up of nine senators, three elected at large from each of the main islands every four years, and 15 representatives elected every two years, two each from six districts on Saipan and one each from Rota, Tinian, and the northern islands. A two-thirds vote in both houses is required to impeach a governor. Each of the four municipal jurisdictions is headed by a mayor. Commonwealth residents aren't represented in the United States Congress and can't vote in presidential elections. Both the Democratic and Republican political parties are active. Corruption among officialdom is rampant.

ECONOMY

The Commonwealth of the Northern Marianas' greatest resource is its position between Japan, Guam, and the Philippines. The beaches, relaxed entry requirements, and easy access bring in 435,454 (1990) tourists a year, 75% of them from Japan. About 37% of the Commonwealth's income comes from tourism.

Japanese tourism is largely prepaid in Japan and the $120 million spent by Japanese tourists each year doesn't bring the benefits the numbers might suggest. Package-tour food coupons discourage most Japanese tourists from patronizing local restaurants. Most of the major hotels, tour companies, and restaurants on Saipan are owned by Japanese businessmen. Japanese investments in the Northern Marianas are worth billions. In past locals have been given few opportunities to assume managerial positions or even work in these businesses, although the Commonwealth government is fighting to correct this.

Between 1986 and 1992 the Northern Marianas received $228 million in federal grants and assistance, and other forms of aid arrive indirectly. At $2,958 per capita (1987) the CNMI received more U.S. aid than any other part of Micronesia. The $7 million annual U.S. subsidy to the Economic Development Loan Fund is used mostly to develop retail outlets selling imported goods. Federal tax laws don't apply in the CNMI and local residents pay only two to nine percent income tax! (Income generated in the U.S. itself *is* subject to federal tax, however.)

In contrast to the privileged position of officials, the educational system is overwhelmed by the population explosion and a lack of qualified local teachers. The hiring of American teachers, common practice in past, is now discouraged. Today only 243 hectares of land are farmed, as compared to 16,000 hectares under the Japanese. A provision in the Commonwealth Covenant prohibits the sale of land to persons of non-Marianas descent during the first 25 years (until 2011), although aliens may lease land for up to 55 years. The 25-year prohibition was meant to protect the locals from Americans; instead the Japanese have come in and leased all the most valuable property.

While wages on Guam are similar to those on the U.S. mainland, Northern Marianas wages are only about half the U.S. minimum rate. Despite widespread underemployment, foreigners (mostly Filipinos, Chinese, and Koreans) comprise 82% of the work force in the private sector. The sort of jobs they hold are exempted from the $2.15 minimum wage (maids, construction workers, fishermen, and

The Nauru Building at Susupe is Saipan's largest office block.

nese. The local government earns $2 million a year in tax money without having to worry which way the workers will vote. The employers make nice profits by paying their employees Asian wages and shipping the products to Sears, Macy's, and Bloomingdale's. Feeling the strain on the water, sewage, power, and social-service infrastructures, the Commonwealth government halted construction of new industry in 1987 and required the existing firms to train and employ more local staff. By 1990 the overburdened public utilities commission was allowing millions of gallons of raw sewage a day to be discharged into the Saipan lagoon.

Many of the factories are sweatshops where minimum-wage and labor laws are often violated. Garment workers are often paid using a quota or piecework system without overtime, and after deductions are made for housing and food there isn't a lot leftover. The workers are confined to barracks during nonworking hours and sent home if they protest the many violations of their human rights.

Although graceful in the air, the white-tailed tropicbird (Phaethon lepturus) *must crawl on its belly to move about on land. During courtship male and female glide and circle one another high in the air, the upper bird sometimes touching the back of the lower with its two long, streaming tail feathers. Tropicbirds often spend months at sea when not nesting, ranging hundreds of kilometers in search of food. Their bills have teethlike notches to help them hold their catch.*

farmers get about $150 a month). Filipinas are often brought in under false circumstances, then they don't have money to leave and are forced into prostitution.

Anxious to expand the private sector, in 1984 the Northern Marianas offered tax incentives to Hong Kong and Korean textile manufacturers in search of quota-free and duty-free access to the U.S. market through an insular possession. Business-license applications were given immediate approval and the companies allowed to bring in their own personnel. Knit shirts, sweaters, dresses, jeans, sports outfits—you name it, it's "Made in the Northern Mariana Islands." In 1989 garments worth $153.9 million were exported to the Mainland U.S. (in return the Commonwealth imported goods of equivalent value from the U.S.).

Today the 26 garment factories on Saipan employ thousands of non-resident aliens (mostly Filipinos and Thais), but few Saipa-

THE PEOPLE

The inhabitants of the Mariana Islands, the present-day Chamorros, differ considerably from their ancestors, whose skeletal remains indicate a tall, large-boned people. Modern Chamorros are actually the descendants of those original Micronesians who intermarried with Spanish, Filipino, Chinese, German, Japanese, and American peoples over the past three centuries, producing the present Chamorro physical type. Spanish influence was particularly strong, and to this day family names, social customs, and personal appearance reveal a deep Hispanic legacy.

A fourth of the indigenous population of the Northern Marianas is descended from Carolinians who arrived over a century ago by canoes. You can sometimes spot the Carolinians by the flower lei *(mwarmwar)* they wear in their hair. Since citizens of the FSM gained free entry to the U.S. and its territories in 1986 there's been a second wave of Carolinian immigration to Saipan.

Some 43,345 people live in the Commonwealth, mostly on Saipan (38,896), Rota (2,295), and Tinian (2,118). Only 31 people live on the islands north of Saipan. Included in the total are some 18,766 registered alien residents. During the 1970s the population of Saipan doubled, and it jumped from 16,780 in 1980 to 43,345 in 1990, an increase of 158%! Nonresident alien workers are not allowed to stay in the Marianas over four years.

The Chamorros of today have their minds very much on the present. They want the money *now*. Government jobs are given out as political favors, and it's much more important who you know than what you know. It's said the local greeting *hafa dai* is really how long a government employee works. The Marianas government is very good at asking for federal handouts but the money often disappears into private pockets. To qualify for extra disaster relief benefits, people have gone to the extreme of bulldozing their own homes after typhoons. The Japanese are buying back the island they lost during the war, piece by piece. They've gained control of large areas through Chamorro fronts who buy up land for them. Many locals appear naive and greedy, unwilling to learn the lesson of the Hawaiians.

Crafts

Grotesque lacquered and mounted turtles and coconut crabs are sold, as well as jewelry, dolls, wall hangings, and carved coconut masks. Most of these souvenirs are imported from the Philippines.

Fiestas

Village fiestas take place in Guam and the Northern Marianas every month of the year, except during Lent. These offer an excellent opportunity to try typical Chamorro food and get to know the people in an informal atmosphere. Since most of the population is Catholic, each fiesta begins with a procession and Mass on the Sat. closest to the day of the village's patron saint, followed by feasting into the night. Sunday is the village open house when the people open their homes to one and all. Precise dates of fiestas can be obtained from the Marianas Visitors Bureau, or just watch for a large group of cars parked beside a rural road.

St. Joseph's Day (early May) is celebrated with great fervor at San Jose villages on both Saipan and Tinian. Other important fiestas include those dedicated to Our Lady of Lourdes (early Feb.), San Vicente (early April), San Isidro (at Chalan Kanoa in mid-May), San Antonio (June), Our Lady of Mt.

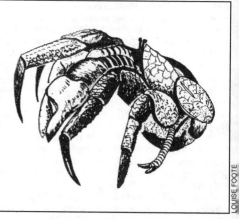

The coconut crab (Birgus latro) *is a nocturnal creature which lives under logs, in holes, or at the base of pandanus or coconut trees. The females lay their eggs in the sea and the tiny crabs float around a few months, then crawl into a seashell and climb up the beach. When a crab is big enough, it abandons the shell and relies on its own hard shell for protection. Its food is ripe pandanus or coconut. The crab will appear dark blue if it's a coconut eater, rich orange if it feeds on pandanus. First it will husk a coconut using its two front claws, then break the nut open on a rock. It might take a crab two nights to get at the meat. Coconut crabs, which can grow up to a meter across, make good eating.*

LOUISE FOOTE

Carmel (at Chalan Kanoa in mid-July), San Roque (late Aug.), San Francisco de Borja (on Rota in Oct.), and Christ the King (at Garapan in mid-November). Other similar gatherings might commemorate a marriage, birth, or funeral—you're never sure what. If you get invited to one, you'll long remember the hospitality of the local people.

Holidays

Public holidays include New Year's Day (1 Jan.), Commonwealth Day (9 Jan.), President's Day (third Mon. in Feb.), Covenant Day (24 March), Good Friday (March/April), Memorial Day (last Mon. in May), Liberation Day (4 July), Labor Day (first Mon. in Sept.), Columbus Day (second Mon. in Oct.), Citizenship Day (4 Nov.), Veteran's Day (11 Nov.), Thanksgiving Day (fourth Thurs. in Nov.), Constitution Day (8 Dec.), and Christmas Day (25 December).

Commonwealth Day (9 Jan.) gives occasion to arts and crafts displays, entertainment, and feasts. Liberation Day (4 July) commemorates the day in 1946 when the indigenous inhabitants were released from Camp Susupe at Chalan Kanoa, the U.S. internment camp, *not* the American military liberation. The Flame Tree Festival occurs during the week leading up to 4 July, with sporting events, handicraft shows, an agricultural exhibition, traditional food, and arts performances. On Liberation Day itself expect a parade, firecrackers, carnival events, and feasting on Saipan. On All Souls' Day (1 Nov.), cemeteries are visited and the graves are cleaned and adorned with candles and flowers.

Sporting Events

Hobie sailors and sailboarders should write the Northern Marianas Amateur Sports Association (Bill Sakovich, Box 2476, Saipan, MP 96950; tel. 234-1001; fax 234-1101) for information on sailboat and sailboarding races off Saipan. Locally you can contact Bill in the large gymnasium beside the baseball field in Susupe. There are regular basketball (Jan.-May), baseball (Feb.-June), soccer (April and May), and volleyball (June-Nov.) league games.

Annual events include the Saipan Sails Hobie Cat Regatta (Jan.) and the Hobie Cat Laguna Regatta (mid-Feb.). The Tagaman Triathlon in May includes a 1½-km swim, a 60-km bicycle race, and a 15-km footrace, all without any rest between. Bill can also advise on the Saipan Ocean Swim (half mile to a mile and a half) on the Saturday before Easter (March/April). Participants for these events come from Guam, Japan, and sometimes the States, and you'd be welcome.

PRACTICALITIES

Chamorro Food

A typical Chamorro feast consists of roast suckling pig cooked on a spit, red rice (white rice colored with achote seeds), a selection of fish, taro, coconut crabs, pastries, and *tuba*—a coconut wine fermented from sap drawn from a palm sprout. Another favorite is chicken *kelaguen* (minced and prepared with lemon, onions, shredded coconut meat, and a touch of that super-hot *finadene* sauce that goes well on everything).

Also try *escabeche* (fried fish with cooked vegetables and soya sauce), *cadon guihan* (fish cooked in its own juices with coconut milk), *lumpia* (pork, shrimp, and vegetables in a pastry wrapping), *pancit* (fried noodles), *poto* (ricecake), *bonelos aga* (fried bananas), and *bonelos dago* (deep-fried grated yam served with syrup). For dessert it's *kalamai* (sweet coconut milk pudding) or *ahn* (grated coconut boiled in sugary water).

Visas

Everyone entering the Commonwealth must have a passport, except U.S. nationals, who still must carry proof of citizenship such as a birth certificate or naturalization papers. Passports must be valid 60 days beyond the date of entry. Foreign tourists do not require visas for stays of up to 30 days provided they hold onward or return tickets and sufficient funds. If required, you must already have a visa for your next destination after the Northern Marianas. Since this is American territory,

U.S. citizens are allowed to live and work in the Northern Marianas without restrictions.

Money And Measurements

U.S. currency, credit cards, and U.S. postage stamps are used (there are no local stamps). The electricity is 110 volts, 60 cycles. To telephone direct from the U.S. to a number in the Northern Marianas dial 011-670 plus the regular seven-digit number. There's no sales tax in the Northern Marianas.

Information

Before arrival you can obtain a packet of colorful brochures and a "Travel Information Sheet" listing hotel prices by writing the Marianas Visitors Bureau, Box 861, Saipan, MP 96950 (tel. 234-8325). Ask for a free copy of their *Historic and Geographic Map of Saipan,* by William H. Stewart, which contains much information on the island's war record. Mr. Stewart has also produced a *Geographic Atlas and Historical Calendar of the Northern Marianas,* which can be obtained from the Office of the Governor, Commonwealth of the Northern Marianas, Saipan, MP 96950.

Getting There

Saipan is linked to Tokyo by Continental Air Micronesia, Japan Air Lines, and Northwest Airlines. Continental also arrives nonstop from Fukuoka, Guam, Koror, Manila, Nagoya, Sapporo, and Sendai, and Japan Air Lines from Nagoya and Osaka. Japan Air Lines and Northwest Airlines have direct connections in Tokyo to/from Atlanta, Cincinnati, Los Angeles, New York, Seattle, and other North American cities.

Continental passengers connect in Guam with flights to/from Honolulu. To fly Continental between Saipan and San Francisco or Los Angeles involves changing planes in both Honolulu and Guam. Those continuing on Continental to the Federated States of Micronesia or Koror may have to overnight on Guam at their own expense (catch one of the Guam flights leaving Saipan just after midnight and sleep in the transit lounge at Guam airport).

Local Flights

Commuter airline service between Guam and the Northern Marianas has had a tumultuous history with at least 16 local carriers operating flights to Saipan for a few years before declaring bankruptcy. These include Guam Airlines (1960-1962), Inter-Island Air Service (1963-1965), Micronesian Airlines (1964-1965), Guam Airways (1968), Island Air (1972-1982), Tinian Air Service (1973), Air Pacific (1973-1976), Fox Air (1977-1980), Trans Micronesian Airways (1981), South Pacific Island Airways (1982-1987), Air Marianas (1983), Air Guam (1984), Royal Hawaiian Air Service (1984-1985), Maui Airlines (1985-1988), Blue Pacific Air (1987-1988), and Guam Marianas Air (1988-1990). Most failed because they were undercapitalized or suffered air crashes. In 1989 Air Mike Express, a subsidiary of Continental Air Micronesia, began providing the Northern Marianas with reliable air service for the first time in years. In 1992 yet another commuter airline, Alliance Air, is scheduled to give these routes a try. Freedom Air has provided service to the Northern Marianas since 1974.

The **Air Mike Express** (Box 138, Saipan, MP 96950; tel. 234-3272) has direct Guam-Saipan flights several times a day, and daily via Rota. On the regular OW fare between Guam and Saipan ($66) you can get free stops on Rota and Tinian. Some off-peak nonstop OW flights Saipan-Guam are $35 OW (departing Saipan at 1500 and midnight). Special 21-day roundtrip excursion fares between Guam and Saipan are also usually available ($101). Check carefully for special deals.

Freedom Air (Box 239 CK, Saipan, MP 96950; tel. 234-8328) flies Saipan-Tinian ($25 OW) seven times a day. This commuter airline doesn't require reservations; just be at their office 45 minutes before flight time. You can charter one of their four-seater Apache planes to the Japanese fighter strip on Pagan for $1,400 RT, plus $30 per hour waiting time on the island. Ask if any charters to Pagan are coming up—there may be a spare seat.

Airport

Saipan International Airport (SPN) is 13 km south of Garapan. Some hotels offer free transfers, others charge up to $12 OW, so ask. A taxi to Garapan would be about $13. Numerous car rental companies have offices in a kiosk in front of the airport terminal. Freedom Air and Air Mike Express flights leave from the commuter terminal next to the main terminal.

This is the former Aslito Airfield of WW II vintage, and over a dozen Japanese bunkers are scattered around the airport area. One of them is now occupied by the Marianas Visitors Bureau, on the left side of the road leading from the airport. The money-exchange counter is in the departure lounge and only intended for foreign tourists wishing to get rid of leftover dollars. There's no bank available to arriving passengers, nor are there any coin lockers. There is one duty-free shop in the departure lounge. The terminal building is open 24 hours a day. There's no departure tax.

SAIPAN

With its paved roads, big hotels, and white-sand beaches, Saipan is Guam without the military bases. The fast track to paradise runs right up the island's protected west coast to Banzai Cliff, where Japanese dreams of conquest crashed headlong into the sea. Chalan Kanoa/Susupe, with banks, post office, law courts, and large stores, is the commercial center of Saipan.

Most of the hotels are along Beach Rd. with Garapan the main tourist center. Saipan's main commercial port is farther north at Charlie Dock. The Marpi area in northern Saipan is a tourists' mecca. Rugged, isolated beaches are found along the east, while the airport is in the south. Some 20,000 Saipanese live on the island along with tens of thousands of alien workers. Today Saipan is a war shrine and honeymoon resort for the Japanese, Tokyo's Miami Beach. Yet despite Japanese tourism Saipan seems more relaxed than Hawaii or Guam.

SIGHTS

Garapan

Garapan, Japanese capital of the Marianas, was almost totally destroyed in WW II, and only recently has it again surpassed Chalan Kanoa in population. A couple of wartime tanks and guns stand outside the former Saipan Museum (closed), beside the Hyatt Regency Hotel in Garapan. Nearby **Micro Beach** with its gentle lagoon and resort hotels is a great place to catch the sunset or have a swim.

Just south of the main tourist center you'll find **Sugar King Park,** complete with a 1934 statue of Haruji Matsue, head of the South Seas Development Company, which developed the sugar industry in the Marianas prior to the war. In the same park is a red-painted **Japanese locomotive** used to haul cane to the large sugar mill at Chalan Kanoa before WW II. This park is now a botanical garden with a reconstructed Japanese shrine and examples of various tropical trees (open 0800-1600 daily, free). Don't confuse this botanical garden with another one on the east side of the island which charges a rip-off $10 admission!

Across the road are the imposing ruins of the **old Japanese hospital,** and nearby on a back street to the south the **old Japanese jail**. In a 1966 book, author Fred Goerner claimed aviatrix Amelia Earhart was held here after being captured on a spy mission in the Marshall Islands in 1937. Several decades later Goerner has thrown out the spy theory, but he's still seeking evidence to place Earhart on Saipan.

Northern Saipan

The north end of Saipan was the scene of the last desperate Japanese resistance in mid-

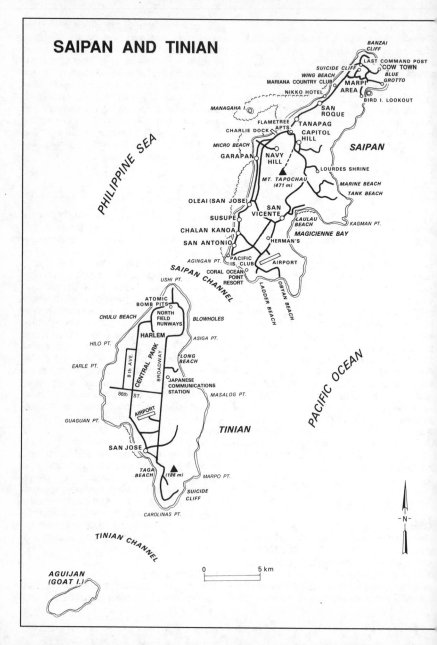

SAIPAN AND TINIAN

PHILIPPINE SEA

BANZAI CLIFF
LAST COMMAND POST
SUICIDE CLIFF
COW TOWN
WING BEACH
BLUE GROTTO
MARIANA COUNTRY CLUB
MARPI AREA
NIKKO HOTEL
BIRD I. LOOKOUT
MANAGAHA I.
SAN ROQUE
FLAMETREE APTS.
TANAPAG
CHARLIE DOCK
CAPITOL HILL
MICRO BEACH
SAIPAN
GARAPAN
NAVY HILL
LOURDES SHRINE
MT. TAPOCHAU (471 m)
MARINE BEACH
TANK BEACH
OLEAI (SAN JOSE)
SAN VICENTE
SUSUPE
LAULAU BEACH
KAGMAN PT.
CHALAN KANOA
MAGICIENNE BAY
SAN ANTONIO
HERMAN'S
AGINGAN PT.
PACIFIC IS. CLUB
AIRPORT
CORAL OCEAN POINT RESORT
LADDER BEACH
OBYAN BEACH

SAIPAN CHANNEL

USHI PT.
ATOMIC BOMB PITS
CHULU BEACH
NORTH FIELD RUNWAYS
BLOWHOLES
HARLEM
HILO PT.
ASIGA PT.
8th AVE.
CENTRAL PARK
LONG BEACH
EARLE PT.
BROADWAY
JAPANESE COMMUNICATIONS STATION
86th ST.
MASALOG PT.
GUAGUAN PT.
AIRPORT
TINIAN
SAN JOSE
TAGA BEACH
(186 m)
MARPO PT.
SUICIDE CLIFF
CAROLINAS PT.

PACIFIC OCEAN

TINIAN CHANNEL

–N–

0   5 km

AGUIJAN (GOAT I.)

(top) Japanese tankette, Tarawa, Rep. of Kiribati (Richard Eastwood);
(bottom) Zero aircraft, Pisaris, Chuuk, FSM (Ria de Vos)

(clockwise from top left) Gayan, a chief of Maap, Yap, FSM (Karl Partridge); girl at the Yap Day celebrations, Yap, FSM (Paul Bohler); Rooiti and Tikoa gathering firewood at Nonouti Atoll, Rep. of Kiribati (Rod Buchko); Katween, a girl from Falealop, Woleai Atoll, Yap, FSM (Paul Bohler)

Many Japanese families committed suicide by jumping from Saipan's Banzai Cliff rather than surrender.

1944 and mass suicides by Japanese soldiers and civilians to avoid capture. Later this area became an ammunition stockpile zone which was only cleared and reopened to the public in 1968. No stores are north of San Roque, so come prepared.

The **Last Japanese Command Post** is in a cave just below high cliffs next to the **Okinawa Peace Memorial**. Here Gen. Yoshitsugo Saito ordered his men to take seven lives for the emperor, then committed harakiri. From this post follow the Banadero Trail for an hour up to the top of **Suicide Cliff** where, high above the post, hundreds of Japanese soldiers jumped 250 meters to their deaths rather than surrender. (You can also drive to the top of Suicide Cliff, so one person could go around with the car—five km.)

At **Banzai Cliff,** near the north end of the island, large numbers of Japanese civilians did the same. Entire families lined up, the elder pushing the younger. The Saipanese claim the white terns which ride the winds over these cliffs didn't exist before the war, that they bear the souls of the dead. Today tourist helicopters also hover above. After the war the U.S. military pushed tanks, trucks, and other surplus war materiel off Banzai Cliff rather than ship it home. Scuba divers call the place Million Dollar Hole.

Many war memorials have been erected at these and other places around the island,

and every day busload after busload of Japanese tourists arrive to have their pictures taken in front of them. Also included on the bus tours is the **Bird Island lookout** from which you get a good view of the small cliff-girdled island the Japanese more poetically called Moon Viewing Island.

The 4½-km road from the Last Command Post to Bird Island lookout passes the turnoff to the **Blue Grotto,** a sunken pool connected to the ocean by twin underground passages. Steep concrete stairs lead down to this cobalt blue pool and a variety of fish reside here—a favorite of scuba divers.

Also in this area is **Cow Town**, a Wild West theme park for Japanese. There's horseback riding ($35 an hour), a driving range ($3 a basket), a rodeo (Sat. and Sun. at 1400), and movies (at an open air cinema nightly at 2000—$5).

Central And Southern Saipan

From 1951 to 1962 the CIA had a $28 million base on **Capitol Hill** where Nationalist Chinese guerrillas were trained. The trainees arrived blindfolded so they wouldn't know where they were. Later Capitol Hill became the headquarters of the High Commissioner of the U.N. Trust Territory, and a ghetto for American expatriates. Today most Commonwealth government offices are found here.

From behind the Civil Defense Energy/ MPLC office (the former Congress of Micronesia building) at Capitol Hill, follow a rough road three km up to the top of **Mt. Tapochau** (471 meters) for a good 360-degree view. A small statue of Christ was erected on the summit at Easter 1987, and the Saipanese carry several wooden crosses up here every Easter. The road up is possible for a sturdy car, or park and walk when it gets too difficult.

Southeast of Capitol Hill is **Our Lady of Lourdes Shrine,** marking an area where the Saipanese took refuge during the American invasion. It's a kilometer off the main highway. A number of remote beaches on the east coast are accessible from the Cross Island Road. **Laulau Beach** near San Vicente has good coral and tends to be calm.

The best conditions for walk-off scuba diving and snorkeling are found at the southern beaches of Saipan: Ladder and Obyan (don't leave valuables unattended on the beach). **Obyan Beach** features garden eels (no danger). An ancient Micronesian settlement at Obyan has been carbon-dated at 1527 B.C. and the remnants of taga (latte) stones can still be seen, as well as a concrete Japanese pillbox.

Managaha Island

Managaha Island, in the Tanapag Lagoon due north of Micro Beach, is the most popular snorkeling site on Saipan. A white sandy beach runs right around Managaha, which was captured from the Japanese only after the main island had fallen. Three Japanese artillery pieces are still there, and a great array of sunken barges, landing craft, ships, planes, and guns can be seen among the coral heads near the island, on a sandy bottom in only six to 12 meters of water. Look in particular for the Japanese Zero, the sub chaser, and the four-engine bomber.

Numerous local tour operators run glass-bottom boat trips over to Managaha Island, $43 pp with barbecue lunch.

ACCOMMODATIONS

Almost all of the hotels are along the west coast sunbelt. They're listed here in geographical sequence from the airport. The highrise luxury hotels invariably cater to Japanese tour groups, and individuals will do better at one of the smaller, less expensive selections below. Many of the least expensive are under Korean or Chinese management. New hotels are popping up on Saipan all the time, and prices at the existing hotels also keep popping up. Hotel rates in the Northern Marianas and on Guam are much higher than elsewhere in Micronesia. Saipan has a much better selection of reasonably priced beach hotels than Guam, however.

Many luxury hotels and car rental agencies on Saipan will give you a discount if you ask for the "local rate" (tell them you live on Guam). This only works for Americans and Micronesians—not Japanese. You must ask for the "local rate" in person. Telephone callers are usually quoted the higher tourist rate.

Prices are for the room only with no meals, but many units have refrigerators. Most of the rooms have air-conditioning and private bath. Rooms in the highrise hotels usually have balconies with ocean views. The price difference between a single and a double is small, so try to link up with other travelers. Add 10% hotel tax to all of the hotel rates listed in this chapter. Some hotels quote rates including tax, others without tax, so ask.

Inexpensive Hotels

One of the cheapest places to stay on Saipan for many years has been the **Sun Inn Motel** (Box 920, Saipan, MP 96950; tel. 234-6639), behind the ballpark beside Susupe's Marianas High School. The 18 a/c rooms here are $44 s, $50 d, $52 t.

The **New Seoul Motel** (Box 1694, Saipan, MP 96950; tel. 234-5551), a new three-story hotel beside Korea Town Restaurant in San Jose, is competitive at $44 s, $55 d, $77 t with a/c, private bath and fridge. When things

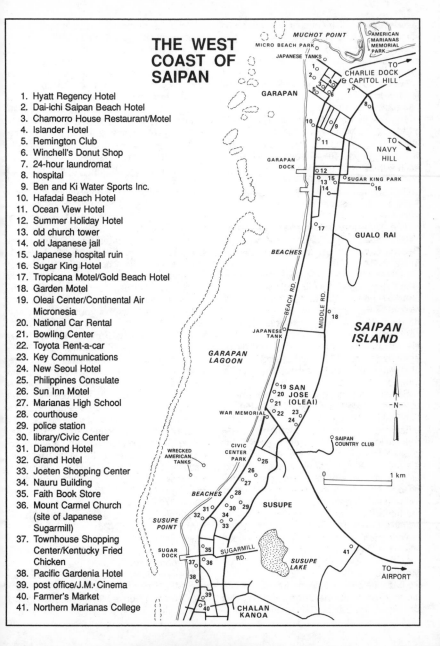

THE WEST COAST OF SAIPAN

1. Hyatt Regency Hotel
2. Dai-ichi Saipan Beach Hotel
3. Chamorro House Restaurant/Motel
4. Islander Hotel
5. Remington Club
6. Winchell's Donut Shop
7. 24-hour laundromat
8. hospital
9. Ben and Ki Water Sports Inc.
10. Hafadai Beach Hotel
11. Ocean View Hotel
12. Summer Holiday Hotel
13. old church tower
14. old Japanese jail
15. Japanese hospital ruin
16. Sugar King Hotel
17. Tropicana Motel/Gold Beach Hotel
18. Garden Motel
19. Oleai Center/Continental Air Micronesia
20. National Car Rental
21. Bowling Center
22. Toyota Rent-a-car
23. Key Communications
24. New Seoul Hotel
25. Philippines Consulate
26. Sun Inn Motel
27. Marianas High School
28. courthouse
29. police station
30. library/Civic Center
31. Diamond Hotel
32. Grand Hotel
33. Joeten Shopping Center
34. Nauru Building
35. Faith Book Store
36. Mount Carmel Church (site of Japanese Sugarmill)
37. Townhouse Shopping Center/Kentucky Fried Chicken
38. Pacific Gardenia Hotel
39. post office/J.M. Cinema
40. Farmer's Market
41. Northern Marianas College

are slow they'll give couples a single at the single rate. The lighting in the rooms isn't that bright but there are often vacancies, and airport transfers are free. It's just up Middle Rd. off the airport highway.

Further up Middle Rd. is the **Garden Motel** (Caller Box PPP 134, Saipan, MP 96950; tel. 234-0320) with 17 rooms at $54 s, $58 d.

The **Sugar King Apartment Hotel** (Box 1939, Saipan, MP 96950; tel. 234-6164) near Garapan is set back a few blocks behind Sugar King Park. The 27 cottage-style units, each with its own verandah, fridge, and double bed, are $48 s or d. There's a swimming pool. Long-term rates of $288 weekly and $450 monthly are sometimes available. It's rather basic.

The two-story **Tropicana Motel** (Box 1489, Saipan, MP 96950; tel. 234-5550) on Beach Rd. has 20 rooms with twin beds and fridge at $54 s, $60 d.

Business travelers often pick the **Islander Hotel** (Box 1249, Saipan, MP 96950; tel. 234-6071) on Beach Rd., Garapan, with 32 rooms on the second floor of a commercial building. A single room with fridge but no cooking facilities costs $50 s, $60 d. A double with kitchen facilities, living and dining areas is $72 d, $77 t. A two-bedroom suite, also with kitchen and all facilities, is $105 for four persons.

Saipan's best budget find is the **Remington Club** (Box 1719, Saipan, MP 96950; tel. 234-5449), opposite the Dai-ichi Hotel in the entertainment district of Garapan. The 14 regular rooms are $39 s or d; rooms with cooking facilities are $55 s or d. The rooms are on the second floor above their bar and, aside from being the cheapest, it's near the beach and right in the heart of the action. There can be communication problems with the front desk over minor matters, however. Martin's Ocean Bar and Grill nearby offers the opportunity to escape the Japanese tourists in this area.

Moderate Hotels

Perhaps the best of Saipan's beach hotels is the three-story **Marine Sports Hotel** (Caller Box PPP 158, Saipan, MP. 96950; tel. 234-

1462) adjacent to the Chalan Kanoa Beach Club right on the beach south of Chalan Kanoa. Their 14 rooms with cooking facilities are $88 d and a "local price" is often available. If the hotel's front door seems locked, go around the side. There's a pleasant beach bar.

The **Pacific Gardenia Hotel** (Box 144, Saipan, MP 96950; tel. 234-3455) at Chalan Kanoa calls itself "Saipan's Biggest Little Hotel." The 14 spacious rooms with cooking facilities and TV are $100 s or d. There's a coin laundry here. Transfers to the nearby airport are free. During "Beach Fun" on Mon., Wed., and Fri. evenings a local band plays on the sandy beach behind the hotel as guests wine, dine, and dance. Happy hour at the beach bar is 1630-1830 Monday through Saturday.

The Korean-operated **Gold Beach Hotel** (Box 2232, Saipan, MP 96950; tel. 235-5501), next to the Tropicana Hotel south of Garapan, has 46 rooms at $88 d. It's only good value if you get the 15% "local rate" discount. The rooms have cooking facilities, but you have to supply your own pots and pans!

The locally owned **Summer Holiday Hotel** (Box 908, Saipan, MP 96950; tel. 234-3182) is behind Club Imperial on Beach Rd., Garapan. The 19 rooms with fridge and cooking facilities in the attractive three-story building are $76 s, $86 d, $96 t. A coin-operated laundromat is on the premises and Martha's Store next to the hotel is open 24 hours. They mostly cater to American business travelers.

The Chinese-owned **Saipan Ocean View Hotel** (Box 799, Saipan, MP 96950; tel. 234-8900) is a new three-story hotel on Beach Rd. above the East Ocean Chinese Restaurant, Garapan. The 20 rooms with fridge are $60 s, $72 d.

Another locally owned place is the **Chamorro House Motel** (Box 975, Saipan, MP 96950; tel. 234-7361) in central Garapan with 14 spacious rooms at $66-72, or $165 for a three-room suite.

The **Joy Motel** (Caller Box PPP-155, Saipan, MP 96950: tel. 234-8710), right beside the Chamorro House Motel, has 20 rooms at $50 s, $88 d.

Japanese-owned **Hotel Blueberry Saipan** (Box AAA 205, Saipan, MP 96950: tel. 234-7437), on a back street in Garapan, has 27 rooms at $72 s, $93 d, $110 t. Larger "deluxe" rooms are about $20 more. It's overpriced.

Expensive Hotels

The stuffy, pretentious **Pacific Islands Club Saipan** (Box 2370, Saipan, MP 96950; tel. 234-7976) in San Antonio has 220 standard rooms at $370 d. All meals, airport transfers, and a wide range of recreational activities are included in this price. It's mostly packaged Japanese tourists you see here, though many "local rate" Americans do stay for $130 d without meals and activities.

Saipan's smallest luxury hotel is the **Chalan Kanoa Beach Club** (Box 356, Saipan, MP 96950; tel. 234-7829) at the south end of Chalan Kanoa. The 28 deluxe units arranged in two-story buildings around the pool are $155 d, $180 t. There's a swimming pool, cocktail lounge, and restaurant on the premises.

The **Saipan Grand Hotel** (Box 369, Saipan, MP 96950; tel. 234-6601) on Susupe Beach has 152 rooms from $130 s or d, $160 t.

Also dedicated to Japanese tourism is the adjacent **Saipan Diamond Hotel** (Box 66, Saipan, MP 96950; tel. 234-5900) opposite Joeten Shopping Center, Susupe. It occupies the site of the old 60-room Royal Taga Hotel, the first luxury hotel to appear on Saipan (in 1967). All 265 rooms in this 10-story structure face the sea and cost $175 s or d, although the suites are $350. Three freshwater swimming pools face the beach.

The highrise **Hafadai Beach Hotel** (Box 338, Saipan, MP 96950; tel. 234-6495), on the beach just south of Garapan, is another of the packaged Japanese variety. The 162 rooms in the main building are $160 s or d, while the 118 rooms in the tower run an additional $45.

The 180 rooms at the **Dai-ichi Saipan Beach Hotel** (Box 1029, Saipan, MP 96950; tel. 234-6412) in Garapan are $175 s or d, $200 t. This yellow three-story building was built for Japanese groups.

The **Hyatt Regency Saipan** (Box 87 CHRB, Saipan, MP 96950; tel. 234-1234), formerly owned by Continental Airlines (opened 1974), serves a more international clientele. The 255 rooms with balcony and fridge in this plush seven-story hotel begin at $200 s or d, $240 t. It's nicely set on landscaped gardens facing Garapan's Micro Beach. Three wings of the hotel face a lush tropical garden with screeching parrots in cages and colorful fish in the ponds. During happy hour from 1800 to 1900 drinks in the lobby lounge are half price. There's a Tahitian show in the Hyatt's Gilligan's Disco at 1830 daily except Wed. and Sunday. Admission is $30 for locals, $40 for tourists. It's also possible to see the show from the bar but there's a $15 cover charge. Airport transfers are free.

The **Aqua Resort Club** (Box 9, Achugao, Saipan, MP 96950; tel. 322-1234), a low-rise complex right on the beach between Tanapag and San Roque in northern Saipan, opened in 1989. The 91 rooms begin at $175 d and airport transfers are $12 RT. The Aqua resort does have class and it's patronized almost exclusively by Japanese. The highrise **Plumeria Resort** is right next door.

The largest and most isolated of Saipan's hotels is the **Hotel Nikko Saipan** (Box 152 CHRB, Saipan, MP 96950; tel. 322-3311) on the northwest coast near San Roque. Rates for the 313 rooms are from $200 s or d, $230 t. This 13-story, Japan Air Lines-owned resort is patronized almost exclusively by JAL tour groups.

Long Stays

Flame Tree Terrace Apartments (Box 86 CHRB, Saipan, MP 96950; tel. 322-3366; fax 322-3886) in Lower Capitol Hill rents its nicely furnished condominiums on a monthly basis only. There are 35 apartments available: $750 for a one bedroom, $1,050 for a two-bedroom, and $2,000 for a four bedroom. There's a swimming pool. This is just what you need if you're moving to Saipan but everything tends to be fully booked, so write or call as far in advance as possible to get on the waiting list. Another condo development is going up a little farther along the same road toward Capitol Hill.

As-Teo Mini Mart (Box 302, Saipan, MP 96950; tel 322-9871), beside Our Lady of Lourdes Shrine, has one room behind the store which rents at $110 a month.

Camping

The parks along the west side of Saipan are for day use only so if you want to pitch a tent consider the remoter east coast beaches, such as Laulau. On the south coast Ladder Beach, just 2½ km from the air terminal, has caves with picnic tables you could sleep upon, otherwise camp by the Bomb Wing Memorial nearby. Obyan Beach would be a better campsite, but it's another three km farther along.

No permit is required at these beaches and none has any facilities. Try to keep out of sight of motorists and don't go off and leave your gear unattended.

OTHER PRACTICALITIES

Food

A number of restaurants advertise $4 lunch specials weekdays. Tips are extra but at least restaurant meals aren't taxed. For locally grown fruit and vegetables it's the **Farmers' Market** opposite the post office in Chalan Kanoa. **Kentucky Fried Chicken** is in the Townhouse Shopping Center on the main drag in Chalan Kanoa.

Herman's Modern Bakery on the airport road serves breakfast and lunch specials (open 0600-1500 Monday through Saturday). It's popular among the locals.

The large **supermarket** at Joeten Shopping Center is open until 1900 Sundays, 2100 other days. **Aiko's Coffee Shop**, in the corner between this supermarket and Ace Hardware, serves a good breakfast or ramen soup and sandwiches anytime. They're open till 1930 daily except Sundays, when they close at 1400. This is your best bet if you only want a snack.

J's Restaurant, at the Bowling Center in San Jose, is open 24 hours a day. It's good

for breakfast and has cheap lunch specials 1100-1230, though the service tends to be dull. Many locals eat here.

The **Marianas Trench Restaurant** (Box 1074, Saipan, MP 96950; tel. 234-3146), above the *Marianas Review* office on Beach Rd. just south of Garapan, has a $4.50 lunch special weekdays 1100-1300. The international special is $4.50 (lunch) and a local Chamorro plate is offered for $3. A different plate is offered every day but there's no choice. The attractive dining room overlooks the lagoon—recommended. The five hotel rooms adjoining the restaurant are $72 d.

Another excellent choice is the **Canton Restaurant** (tel. 234-7236) opposite the Mobil Station on Beach Road near central Garapan. Their $4 lunch special weekdays includes a choice of six different dishes. This large dining room features efficient service and good food—their lunch special is the best deal on the island.

Poon's Restaurant, on Middle Rd. just north of Sugar King Park, serves Indonesian dishes (small servings). Avoid the Chinese selections on their menu.

For local Chamorro food try the lunch special ($7) at the **Chamorro House** near the Saipan Beach Hotel. The higher price may be worth it.

Entertainment

The Carolinian residents of Saipan transmit their oral traditions through dance songs; one group, the **Aghurubw Society Dancers**, performs stick war dances *(dokia)* and marching dances *(maas)*. Try asking at the Marianas Visitors Bureau, though you probably don't stand much chance of seeing them as the big hotels only stage the "more dramatic" Polynesian dance shows tourists expect. If you'd like to be culturally carried across the Pacific to Tahiti catch the dinner show around 1800 ($40 pp) at the **Saipan Diamond Hotel** (Wed., Fri., and Sun.) or the Hyatt's **Gilligan's Disco** (daily except Wed. and Sun.).

Many of the large tourist hotels have happy hours at their bars with reduced drink prices, usually around 1730. Many tourist discos have admission charges of $25 and up. There are also plenty of *karaoke* clubs with hostesses, such as the raunchy **Starlite Disco Club** near the Chamorro House Restaurant in Garapan.

JM Cinema (tel. 234-6950) beside the post office in Chalan Kanoa opens at 1930 daily ($6 pp).

Sports And Recreation
Saipan's only locally owned dive shop is **Ben and Ki Water Sports Inc.** (Box 31 CHRB, Saipan, MP 96950; tel. 234-6664; fax 235-5068). They charge $70 for beach diving (two tanks) or $80 for boat diving (two tanks). Snorkelers can join the divers for $25 pp, lunch and gear included. This is the way to visit the waters around Managaha Island—better than glass-bottom boats and cheaper. A seven-hour scuba expedition to Tinian and Goat islands is $100; a four-day scuba certification course runs $350. Water-skiing is $30 for 20 minutes and trolling $350 for four hours (up to six persons). The manager, Ben Concepcion, and his son Lawrence are very helpful. Visit their store behind the Blueberry Hotel in Garapan (see the map). They also have a kiosk facing the beach beside the public toilets between the Dai-ichi and Hyatt hotels. They pick up at hotels anywhere on Saipan—recommended.

Many of the 25 other scuba outfits on Saipan are geared mainly to Japanese tourists: they're highly regimented and expensive. You can buy your own mask and snorkel at Joeten Shopping Center for less than you'd pay to rent a set.

Between dynamite and bleach fishermen, sedimentation from eroded soil, dumped waste pollution, and a crown-of-thorns starfish epidemic, the diving at Saipan is not as great as you might think. On the other hand, Anatahan, Sarigan, and Pagan are wonderful and untouched.

The surfing is poor on Saipan, but the sailboarding's good in the wide western lagoon. Lessons and equipment are available. For example, **Marianas Aqua Sports** (Bill Sakovich, Box 100 CHRB, Saipan, MP 96950; tel. 234-9308) offers **sailboarding** ($15 an hour), Hobie Cat sailing ($20 an hour), Managaha transfers ($25 RT), etc. They're in the same beach kiosk as Ben and Ki Water Sports Inc. (see above).

For something different, board the 46-passenger *Mariea-I,* the first commercial **submarine** in the Pacific. A 45-minute, $77 dive into the Saipan lagoon brings you face-to-face with war relics, coral, and maybe even "killer sharks" (if they're cooperating). The **Dosa Sub-Sea** (Box 2183, Saipan, MP 96950; tel. 234-9600) shuttle boat leaves from Lower Base near the power plant in San Jose.

Golf
Of Saipan's three public golf courses, the nine-hole **Saipan Country Club** (Caller Box PPP 130, Saipan, MP 96950; tel. 234-7300) is the most "local." They have varying greens fees for varying clients: $10 for Chamorro locals, $20 for white locals, $30 for white tourists, $40 for Japanese tourists. You can rent a full set of clubs for $15 and a pull cart for $7. On fairway no. 4 a ball passing to the left of a coconut tree is considered out of bounds, irrespective of where it comes to rest!

Saipan's top-end golf course is the **Coral Ocean Point Resort Club** (Box 1160, Saipan, MP 96950; tel. 234-7000) on the south coast at Koblerville. This golfers' paradise has 72 rooms at $165 d. The resort's fantastic 18-hole golf course right on the coast is $70 a round if you're staying at the hotel, $120 a round otherwise.

The **Mariana Country Club and Resort Hotel** (tel. 322-3054) at Marpi has another 18-hole golf course overlooking the sea.

Services
The Bank of Hawaii (tel. 234-6102; open weekdays 1000-1500, Friday 1000-1800) in the Nauru Building is in Chalan Kanoa. There are also branches of the Bank of Guam (tel. 234-6467), Bank of Saipan (tel. 234-7694), Marine Merchant Bank (tel. 234-7773), and the Union Bank (tel. 234-6559) on Saipan.

Many private companies on Saipan offer facilities for making overseas telephone calls. Always ask about lower direct-dial rates, 25 cents a minute to Tinian, $2.25 a minute to the U.S. Mainland. Rates may be lower from Friday 1800 through Sunday. For example, try Key Communications just up Middle Rd. from the New Seoul Motel (open daily 0800-midnight), MTC Micronesian Tel behind Xerox just beyond Key Communications (only open during business hours), and Marianas Communication Services opposite the New Seoul Hotel.

The main post office is opposite the market in Chalan Kanoa and there's another, less crowded post office beside the CNMI Convention Center on Capitol Hill.

The Immigration and Naturalization Office (tel. 234-6178) is on the fourth floor at the Nauru Building in Chalan Kanoa.

The Japanese Consulate is on the fifth floor, Yarikuchi Building, opposite Garapan dock (open weekdays 0900-1700). The Philippines Consulate (tel. 234-1848) is in the CTC Building in Susupe (Mon. to Thurs. 0800-1200/1400-1630). You'll need a Philippines visa only if you want to stay longer than 21 days.

The main Continental Air Micronesia reservations office (tel. 234-6491) is in the back of the Oleai Center in San Jose. They also have an office at the airport.

Information

The helpful Marianas Visitors Bureau (Box 861, Saipan, MP 96950; tel. 234-8325; open 0800-1700 Mon. to Sat.) is found in a former Japanese communications bunker at the airport. Ask for a free copy of William H. Stewart's *Tourist Map of Saipan.* Their *Saipan Battlefield Map—1944* ($3.50) is also excellent. Unfortunately the Visitors Bureau's brochures only list their members (not the cheaper places) and the quoted room rates are unreliable.

For information about social or political matters, talk to Frank S. Rosario in the Public Information/Protocol office (Box 216 CHRB, Saipan, MP 96950; tel. 322-5094), just inside the Administration Building on Capitol Hill.

Faith Book Store opposite the Saipan Community Church on Beach Rd. has a large selection of books on Micronesia.

There are two twice-weekly newspapers, the *Marianas Variety* (Box 231, Saipan, MP 96950) and the *Marianas Review* (Box 1074, Saipan, MP 96950), both published on Tues. and Friday. The *Saipan Tribune* (Caller Box AAA-34, Saipan, MP 96950) is published every Thursday. The Guam-based *Pacific Daily News* puts out a special Saipan edition on Fridays.

The two Saipan AM radio stations are commercial KCNM-AM (1035 kHz) and nonprofit KSAI-AM (936 kHz); commercial KZMI-FM (93.9 MHz) dominates the FM bands. The local cable TV plays commercial Los Angeles tapes.

Volunteers

The **Summer of Service Program** (Youth With A Mission, Box 230 CHRB, Saipan, MP 96950; tel. 322-9891) accepts volunteer workers for one- to three-month periods. The group has a youth-oriented collective poultry farm at Capitol Hill, Saipan, where interns do manual labor alongside local students from 0600 to 1630 Tues. through Saturday. Participants must pay their own way to Saipan, plus a $150 monthly fee which covers food, accommodations, and local transportation.

If you're a born-again Christian, this could be the way to break a long Pacific trip, or a good reason to visit Saipan. You can arrive any time of year, but you're supposed to apply by mail a couple of months ahead. Otherwise, just take potluck that they'll accept you when you happen to arrive on Saipan. (This listing is provided for information purposes only and does not imply an endorsement.)

GETTING AROUND

By Boat

The **Commonwealth Marine Leisure Corporation** (CMLC, Box 369, Saipan, MP 96950; tel. 234-9157) at the Saipan Grand Hotel runs the ferry Emerald from Sugar Dock in Chalan Kanoa to San Jose village on Tinian daily except Tuesday at 0815 ($14 OW for locals, $65 RT for tourists). The tourist price includes a pickup at any Saipan hotel and free drinks on the boat. This red-and white-striped motor cruiser caters mostly to Japanese tourists on day-trips to Tinian, but it's a good alternative to the plane for everyone.

By Road

Theoretically a **Saipan Rapid Transit** (SRT) bus runs along Beach Rd. from the Hafadai Hotel, Garapan, to San Antonio every 30 minutes from 0600 to 2200. In practice the service is irregular. Bus stops are marked but drivers will stop almost anywhere along their route if you wave. Buses will also pick up or drop passengers in San Roque, Capitol Hill, and San Vicente upon request, but you must call their office at 234-2788 or 234-2789 to request this service. The SRT bus will also pick you up at the airport, but you must call for a bus to be dispatched and it's $4 pp (unless you're alone it's just as cheap to take a taxi). The buses won't go to the Marpi area. Tickets cost $2 if you pay cash on the bus, or you can buy $1.25 coupons at their main office at Ko-Star Travel below Arirang Restaurant on Beach Rd. not far from Garapan Dock (Caller Box PP-237, Saipan, MP 96950). Dollar Up Mart opposite the Townhouse Shopping Center in Chalan Kanoa also sells bus coupons.

Taxi fares begin at $3 and go up to $42, depending on distance. Ask to see the official rate chart every taxi must carry. From the airport it's $11 to Joeten Shopping Center, $13 to Garapan. Hitching is much easier on Saipan than on Guam.

Tasi Tours (Box 1023, Saipan, MP 96950; tel. 234-7148) in the Oleai Center above Continental Air Micronesia offers a three-hour Gray Line island sightseeing tour three times a week ($30), the only one in English.

Car Rentals

Unless you're really ready to rough it, you'll have to rent a car upon arrival at Saipan. All the main sights of the island can be seen in one day by rental car, and the car rental companies at the airport are competitive. Standard non-a/c subcompacts begin at $20 a day with unlimited mileage and increase to $40 daily, plus $6-10 collision insurance. When calling around ask about additional service charges, collision insurance (usually optional), mileage charges (seldom levied), and weekly and monthly rates. There's no tax on car rentals in the Northern Marianas. Most agencies will want to sell you PAI (personal accident insurance) with the car—a feature you can easily pass up. If you're under 21 they won't rent to you at all. The speed limit on Saipan is 35 mph (57 kph) unless otherwise posted. Your home driver's license is valid for 30 days after arrival.

Of the more than 10 car rental companies on Saipan, ESPN Rent-A-Car, Hertz, Islander, and Thrifty have offices at the airport. As usual, **Hertz** (tel. 234-8336) is the most expensive, but **Islander** (tel. 234-8233) also charges $40 a day, plus five percent insurance. **Thrifty Car Rental** (Box 487, Saipan, MP 96950; tel. 234-8356) is also expensive at $34 a day plus $9 for insurance.

ESPN Rent-A-Car (Box 569, Saipan, MP 96950; tel. 234-8232) at Saipan Airport offers the lowest rates, provided you're lucky enough to get one of their $20 subcompacts. Additional charges are $6 for collision insurance and a onetime $5 service charge.

Forget renting mopeds, which cost more than cars and are unreliable. At $15 daily bicycles are also a rip-off, but Japanese tourists pay whatever is asked.

OTHER ISLANDS

The Northern Islands

Pagan, 324 km north of Saipan, has a formidable volcano, hot springs, and winding beaches of glistening black sand. Bandeera village is on Apaan Bay, backed by the narrow isthmus that separates explosive Mt. Pagan (570 meters) in the north from the two dormant volcanoes in the south. When the mountain exploded in May 1981, blowing a section off the summit, the 54 Chamorro inhabitants of Pagan escaped the flow of molten lava by huddling together in bat-infested caves until they were rescued by a Japanese freighter. A wrecked Japanese bomber and AA gun remain beside Pagan's airstrip.

The 36 people on **Agrihan** and **Alamagan** are mostly dependent on USDA food (pork, rice, flour, shortening, corn, milk, orange juice, peanut butter). The group on Agrihan are Carolinians, while Chamorros reside on Alamagan. The Chamorros made a last stand against the Spanish *conquistadores* on Agrihan in the 17th century. A hot spring is at the north end of Alamagan's west coast.

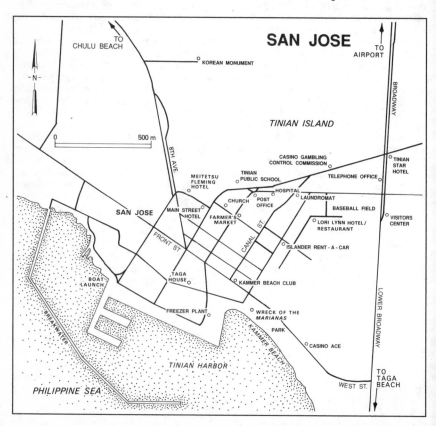

A wide caldera was created at the center of **Anatahan** when its volcano blew up. On the crater wall are two peaks, 714 and 788 meters high, on its northeast and west sides, respectively. In 1990 the island's 22 inhabitants had to be evacuated due to continuing volcanic activity.

Asuncion's active volcanic cone rises to 891 meters. **Maug** is comprised of three steep islands, which were left when its volcano exploded and the sea flooded the caldera. The Japanese once used the submerged caldera as an anchorage and had a weather station here, but Maug is now abandoned. The Tropic of Cancer slices right through Maug. **Uracas** (Farallon de Pajaros), northernmost of the Marianas, is a cinder-covered active volcano.

TINIAN

Only five km south of Saipan, Tinian consists of a series of layered limestone plateaus covered by *tangan tangan*. Tinian was once the world's greatest producer of cane sugar, but only scattered clumps of it grow wild today. The Bar K Ranch, built by Ken Jones on leased land, runs 4,500 beef cattle across a third of the island. Butterflies and dragonflies abound on Tinian.

U.S. and Asian fishing boats use Tinian's spacious harbor to transfer tuna caught in FSM and PNG waters to refrigerated freighters bound for U.S. canneries. This presence, together with explosive-laden vessels of the U.S. Military Sealift Command which often visit, explains the number of bars with Filipina hostesses in San Jose. Many Filipino laborers are employed in construction on Tinian.

Before WW II Tinian had a population of 15,000 Japanese and Korean civilians. All were repatriated, and in 1948 the inhabitants of the present Chamorro village, San Jose, were resettled here from Yap. The U.S. military pulled out of Tinian just after the war but for a while it looked like they might be making a comeback after the U.S. paid $33 million for a 50-year lease on everything north of the present airport (7,203 hectares) in 1983.

Though the end of the Cold War has made the projected airbase unnecessary, the island is still used occasionally for amphibious exercises by Okinawa-based Marines and areas are closed at these times.

In Nov. 1989 an 86% majority on Tinian voted in favor of gambling casinos on the island, causing land prices to soar and several dozen families sold out for around a million dollars each. Though gambling has yet to be approved by the Commonwealth government, the administrative offices of the Tinian Gaming Control Commission (Box 143, San Jose, Tinian, MP 96952; tel. 433-9288) are already prominent at the entrance to town and "security services" offices and an Alcoholic Beverage Control Board headquarters are seen. Casino Ace, which opened with five-card-draw poker machines in 1990, was Tinian's first mini-casino and five much larger casinos are planned for the hillside just east of San Jose, the Tinian Hills Casino Hotel among them. If this development ever gets fully underway, Tinian's present quiet character will be gone forever.

Sights

San Jose village has the air of a sleepy Spanish-American town complete with Mexican-looking church, flower gardens around the homes, and Spanish arcades on the larger buildings. The town's main sight is the **Taga House,** in a taga stone park not far from the harbor. These stones, thought to have been supports for an ancient building, are much larger than the latte stones of Guam. Who carved the 12 mammoth taga stones and then managed to erect them is a mystery of the Pacific. Next to the Taga House is a small Japanese war memorial.

Nearby lies the wreck of the freighter *Marianas,* thrown up onto the beach by a typhoon in the late 1960s. From here you can look across to uninhabited Aguijan (Goat Island), eight km southwest. Another much larger shipwreck marks the entrance to the harbor. Several large purse seiners may be tied up in San Jose's wartime harbor, the metal and concrete structure of which is continuously eroded by typhoons.

The **Korean Monument** off 8th Ave. just outside San Jose bears an evocative inscription on the back dedicated to the 5,000 Koreans who "suffered by chains of reckless imperial Japanese army, by whom they were deprived of their rights, and were taken to the islands here and there like innocent sheep, and then were fallen to this ground leaving behind them an eternal grudge."

Taga Beach at the foot of Broadway offers good views from the limestone bluff and is a good place to sit and watch the sunset. You can swim at **Tachogna Beach** nearby. At **Suicide Cliff** on the southeast side of the island die-hard Japanese troops in caves held out for three months after the rest of Tinian had fallen. Now there are Japanese and Okinawan peace memorials here.

Northern Tinian

On the east side of Broadway, halfway between San Jose and North Field, is the massive concrete structure of the former **Japanese Communications Station,** now the slaughterhouse of Bar K Ranch.

In 1944, even before the island had been secured, American Seabees began rebuilding a captured Japanese airstrip at the north end of the island in one of the largest engineering projects of WW II. Less than one year later **North Field** was the largest airfield in the world, with four vast 2,600-meter runways and a total of 19,000 combat missions launched against Japan. To carry the huge quantities of bombs up from the port at San Jose, two divided highways were built across Tinian. As the island was shaped something like Manhattan, the GIs gave the roads names like Broadway, 8th Ave., and 86th Street.

On the north side of the runways a large concrete platform is flanked by two Japanese air raid shelters on the west side, another concrete Japanese building on the east side, and three white American war memorials. In the bush behind the middle memorial is the Japanese **air operations command post**, a massive, two-story reinforced concrete building complete with a Japanese bathtub. Beyond it a road to the right (east) leads to the poorly marked **atomic bomb loading pits**. At No. 1 Bomb Loading Pit the atomic bomb was loaded aboard an American B-29 dubbed *Enola Gay* on the afternoon of 5 August 1945, to be dropped on Hiroshima the next day. At nearby No. 2 Bomb Loading Pit a second atomic bomb was loaded on 9 Aug. 1945 and dropped on Nagasaki. On 10 Aug. 1945 Emperor Hirohito decided to end the Pacific war without his cabinet's consent.

West again is Chulu or **Invasion Beach** where 15,000 U.S. soldiers landed on 24 July 1944. A concrete Japanese bunker stands watch.

Accommodations And Food

The various restaurants and snack bars of Tinian are expensive. The best deal for accommodations is probably **Lori Lynn's Hotel** (Box 50, Tinian, MP 96952; tel. 433-3256), a little east of the center, where a comfortable, large a/c room with TV and fridge will be $30 s, $45 d downstairs, $50 d upstairs. Reduced weekly and monthly rates are available. Lori Lynn's has more local atmosphere than the other hotels and its coffee shop (reasonable Japanese food) is the only eatery on the island worth seeking out.

The five-room **Main Street Hotel** (Box 92, Tinian, MP 96952; tel. 433-9212) near the Fleming Hotel is $41 s or d.

The Japanese-oriented **Meitetsu Fleming Hotel** (Box 68, Tinian, MP 96952; tel. 433-3232) in central San Jose has 13 overpriced rooms at $60 s, $70 d, $80 t. Try for one of the slightly cheaper non-a/c rooms downstairs. The Fleming complex also sports a restaurant, a grocery store, a laundromat, and a bank.

At last report the motel-style **Tinian Star Hotel** (Box 57, Tinian, MP 96952; tel. 433-3229), on Broadway at the entrance to San Jose from the airport, was closed.

No permit is required to **camp** on Kammer Beach near the Taga House in San Jose, which has a shower, toilet, and running water. The beach is good, and a few picnic tables down by the wrecked ship even have electric lighting, though many locals hang out here until late at night.

Camping is also possible at Taga and Tachungnya beaches. For something more secluded try Chulu Beach at the north end of 8th Ave., or Long Beach halfway up the east coast. Bring water to these.

Kammer Beach Club (tel. 433-0475) in San Jose has happy hour from 1600 to 1800 daily except Sunday. Their terrace is just the place to sit and watch the sun go down. Upstairs is an expensive restaurant.

Sports And Recreation

Suzuki Diving (Box 100, Tinian, MP 96952; tel. 433-3274), across the street from the Fleming Hotel, takes scuba divers out in their cabin cruiser, the *Haromi*. They know over 18 superb dive sites off the west coast of Tinian, including war relics, coral grottoes, and drop-offs. It's $80 for a one-tank dive, $100 for a two-tank dive, and $60 for snorkeling.

At high tide Long Beach is probably the best place for freelance snorkeling.

Services

The Bank of Guam (tel. 433-3258) is beside the Meitetsu Fleming Hotel. Overseas telephone calls can be made at the Tinian Center on Lower Broadway.

Transport

West Field Airport (TIQ) is four km north of San Jose village, but it's not hard to hitch into town. There's a pay phone in the terminal you can use to call your hotel to ask about airport pickups. The toilets at the airport are free and they're unlocked early. A couple of old Japanese guns stand outside the terminal.

Freedom Air's (tel. 433-3288) five-passenger Cessnas fly from Saipan to Tinian seven times a day. This commuter carrier runs extra flights whenever the traffic demands. The **Air Mike Express** (tel. 433-9400) calls at Tinian on its way from Saipan to Rota and Guam twice a week.

The CMLC cruiser *Emerald* departs San Jose for Sugar Dock, Saipan, at 1500 daily except Tuesday, $14 OW for "locals" (for more information see "Transport," in the Saipan section above). Due to the action of the Northeast Trades the channel between the islands can get rough!

Tinian Rental Service or **Jim & Cris Co. Ltd.** (tel. 433-3207) at the airport rent cars at $40-50 a day, plus $7.50 collision insurance. **Islander Rent a Car** (tel. 433-3025) in San Jose charges about $40 a day plus $9.95 for optional insurance. **Hans Rent a Car** (tel. 433-9412) across the street from the Main Street Hotel rents cars at $46 daily.

Hitching north of the airport or south of San Jose is dicey.

ROTA

Halfway between Tinian and Guam, Rota is an attractive, friendly island. Shaped like a hand with a finger pointing at Guam, the flat mountain atop the finger is known as Wedding Cake because that's what it looks like. The U.S. felt no need to recapture Rota during WW II, so the Japanese garrison was bombed and left to sit it out. Today Japanese tour groups hit the island on short excursions from Saipan and Guam.

The locals call their island Luta and its flower-filled main Chamorro village, Songsong, offers a better glimpse of Chamorro life than the villages on Saipan. A second village is being constructed at Sinapalo near the airport by homesteaders. The best time for a visit is the Sunday before Columbus Day (in Oct.), Rota's fiesta in honor of patron saint San Francisco de Borja. The sea around Rota is very clear and the sunsets superb.

Rota doesn't have a good harbor and this limits development, though mass tourism is now threatening to flood the island. A 54-hole golf and country club is on the drawing boards and there's even talk of gambling casinos—come soon.

Songsong

Songsong is spread along a narrow neck of land between two harbors. The brick shell of an **old Japanese sugar mill** still stands beside Songsong's West Harbor, an old steam locomotive from the operation parked along-

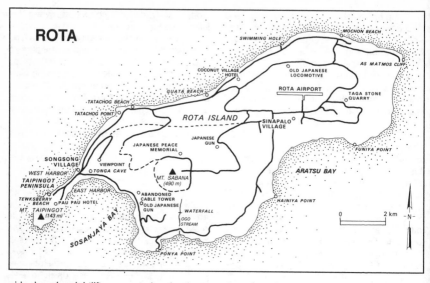

side. Local weightlifters use train wheels as barbells.

At the end of the road west of Songsong is **Tweksberry Beach Park** below Mt. Taipingot (Wedding Cake). Tweksberry is very attractive and a good place to snorkel at high tide; at low tide you can wade along the shore quite a distance.

Just above Songsong is **Tonga Cave,** with stalactites and stalagmites. The Japanese used it as a hospital during the war, and the locals still take shelter here during typhoons. There's a perfect short hike up the jeep track to the white cross directly above Tonga Cave. You'll get a great view of Songsong and Wedding Cake Mountain from this viewpoint but it's too steep to drive a car up there.

Other Sights

A huge **Japanese cannon** in a bunker beside the road five km east of Songsong overlooks Sosanjaya Bay. The abandoned **cable car towers** nearby once brought ore down from the phosphate mines in the interior.

The road along the south coast from Ponya Point to Hainiya Point is very rough but can be negotiated in any car if you go

slow. It's also a panoramic half-day hike; you'll easily be able to hitch a ride back to Songsong from Sinapalo.

From Sinapalo a good dirt road climbs to the **Japanese Peace Memorial** on the Sabana Plateau near the highest point on Rota (491 meters), passing a Japanese cannon on the way. From the memorial the same deteriorating track continues northwest and eventually comes out on the coastal highway near Tatachog Beach. Rugged hikers could walk all the way from Sinapalo to Tatachog in about five hours and see a good cross section of Rota's vegetation, though scenic views from the plateau are few. Now a proposed golf course threatens the wild beauty of the Sabana.

At the **Taga Stone Quarry** east of the airport are the massive shapes of nine megalithic taga or latte stone pillars, and seven capstones still lying unfinished in their trenches.

If you have a car, the stalactite-covered cliffs and blowholes (best at low tide) of **As Matmos Cliff** at Rota's northeast point are worth the drive. The **swimming hole** west of here and three km off the main airport highway is a large, natural swimming hole in the reef and a perfect campsite.

Accommodations

Accommodations on Rota are limited and expensive. **Penny's Meitetsu Hotel** (Box 539, Rota, MP 96951; tel. 532-0468), formerly the Blue Peninsula Inn or "B.P. Hotel," in the middle of Songsong village, charges $55 s, $61 d for one of the 21 rooms with a/c and private bath. They levy a $10 key deposit, then keep the "deposit" to pay for your airport transfer. Penny's has just remodeled but it's still pretty basic, with leaky roofs and sometimes no hot water. Just below the hotel is a bank and a supermarket.

The two-story **Rota Pau-Pau Hotel** (Box 503, Rota, MP 96951; tel. 532-3561) stands on a terrace below Mt. Taipingot at the south end of town looking like a rundown Travelodge. All 50 rooms have a fridge and bathtub and Japa-

nese tourists generally stay here, which explains the prices: $139 s, $161 d, $190 t. They provide free airport transfers for guests, their poolside bar is reasonable, and the setting below the cliffs of Taipingot evocative.

Rota's nicest hotel without doubt is the well-managed **Rota Coconut Village** (Box 855, Rota, MP 96951; tel. 532-3448) on the coast west of the airport. An individual Japanese hot tub *(ofuro)* comes with each of the 18 bungalow-style rooms, $77 s, $88 d, $104 t—probably the best value on the island. There's a pleasant swimming pool on a terrace overlooking the sea, but no beach, just a rocky shore graced by a shipwreck. Dive Rota bases its dive packages at the village, so scuba nuts will be well attended here. It is a little out of the way, so rent a car at airport upon arrival. Airport transfers are $5 OW. Another Japanese golf course is to be built nearby, but for now it's idyllic.

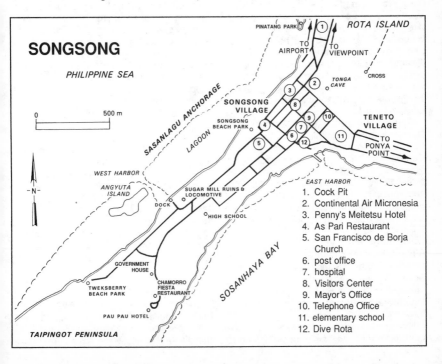

1. Cock Pit
2. Continental Air Micronesia
3. Penny's Meitetsu Hotel
4. As Pari Restaurant
5. San Francisco de Borja Church
6. post office
7. hospital
8. Visitors Center
9. Mayor's Office
10. Telephone Office
11. elementary school
12. Dive Rota

The only other official place to stay on Rota is the five dumpy, bare rooms at Calvo's Insurance Agency/Hita Travel (Box 875, Rota, MP 96951; tel. 532-3429), overlooking Songsong's East Harbor. At $65 d they're way overpriced.

Camping possibilities include the park in front of Tonga Cave, Tweksberry Beach Park, Guata Beach Park, Tatachog Beach, and the Swimming Hole. A lot of traffic passes Guata and Tatachog, and Tonga Cave is probably better than Tweksberry as there are no picnic tables to attract late-night visitors with loud radios. No permit is required to camp on Rota, though you could check in at the Parks & Recreation Division (tel. 532-4001), behind the police station on the hill in Songsong.

Food And Entertainment

Unlike on Tinian, there are several good restaurants in Songsong. The **Chamorro Fiesta Restaurant** beside the Pau-Pau Hotel serves a good bowl of ramen soup, and it's also good at breakfast as they have a bottomless cup of coffee. You can have steak for dinner for $10 but reservations are required. This place is being remodeled and slowly going upmarket but it's still a good place to eat, it's open afternoons, and in the evening the Filipina hostesses will teach you to sing *karaoke*.

Leng's Restaurant (tel. 532-0717) near Penny's Meitetsu Hotel is a lot nicer inside than the exterior implies. It's a little expensive but they serve a very good breakfast (open daily 0600-1400/1800-0200).

Just a few meters away is the **AS Pari Restaurant** (tel. 532-3356), with Rota's most extensive menu including everything from pizza to Mexican food, though their specialties are steaks, lobster, seafood, and Filipino dishes. They close afternoons from 1300 to 1800.

Also in Songsong, the **South China Restaurant** prepares tasty meals but the portions are small. The Pau-Pau Hotel and Coconut Village have restaurants if you've got a big yen for Japanese food.

The Mobil station at the entrance to Songsong from the airport sells groceries and is open till 2200 daily. There are several grocery stores and even a coin laundry in Sinapalo village near the airport. The water on Rota is drinkable.

The **Rota Cock Pit**, across the street from Pinatang Park at the north entrance to Songsong, functions on Fri. and Sat., entry $2 regular, $5 derby.

The **North Wind Restaurant & Bar** (tel. 532-0402) in Sinapalo isn't cheap but it's a good place to stop for drinks and there's *karaoke*.

Sports And Recreation

Dive Rota (Box 941, Rota, MP 96951; tel. 532-3377) at East Harbor, Songsong, charges $50 for a one-tank morning or afternoon dive ($70 for two dives the same day). Americans Mark and Lynne Michael also offer night dives ($60), water-skiing, and trolling. They'll happily take snorkelers out in their boat for $20 pp, plus $5 for mask, snorkel, and fins (if required). Dive Rota has a dive package including RT airfare from Guam, two nights' accommodations at the Rota Coconut Village, three boat dives, and two picnic lunches at $261 s, $418 d. Even if you aren't a diver it's worth visiting their dive shop in Songsong for the wide selection of island T-shirts.

Most of the dive sites are near Songsong. The wreck of the WW II Japanese freighter *Shoun Maru* stands upright in about 30 meters of crystal-clear water in East Harbor. The wreck has been blown open to reveal trucks, bicycles, a deck crane, a bathtub, and two steam engines. Divers also inspect the underwater debris near the phosphate-loading cableway on the same bay and, of course, the usual marinelife on the reefs. It's possible to surface inside Senhanom Cave, among the moray eels, squirrelfish, and bronze sweepers. Wall diving is done at Harnom Point.

Services

The Bank of Guam (tel. 532-0340) is below Penny's Meitetsu Hotel. International phone calls are more cheaply and easily placed on Saipan than on Rota and Tinian. There are several coin-operated laundromats in Songsong.

Information

The Rota office of the Marianas Visitors Bureau (tel. 532-0327) is up on the hill across the street from the police station in Songsong. The *Luta Pa'go* (Box 555, Rota, MP 96951) is published weekly on Rota.

Transport

Rota International Airport (ROP) is 13 km northeast of Songsong. The excellent highway along the north coast from the airport to Songsong was built with federal dollars. Hitching to the airport is easy, but little traffic runs along the other roads. Car campers should note that the toilets at the airport are open long hours. The Mayflower Restaurant upstairs in the terminal is nice for a cup of coffee.

Air Mike Express flies an F-27 turboprop to Rota from Guam three times a day, from Saipan twice a day, and from Tinian twice a week. Ask about special deals on airfares. Reconfirm your flight at the Air Mike Express office (tel. 532-0397) at the airport.

All the hotels offer guided island tours by minibus, though you're better off renting a car and finding your own way around. Most of the car rental companies have counters at the airport, including **Budget** (tel. 532-3535), **Islander** (tel. 532-0901), **ESPN** (tel. 532-0343), and **Paseo Drive Car Rental** (Box 555, Rota, MP 96951; tel. 532-0406). Expect to pay around $40 with unlimited mileage plus $8 for optional collision insurance. ESPN has subcompacts without a/c at $20 a day, plus a onetime $5 service charge, plus five percent tax, plus $6 for optional insurance.

REPUBLIC OF NAURU

INTRODUCTION

Tiny, 21-square-km Nauru (Naoero) is the richest island in the Pacific, its A$20,000 per capita annual income among the highest in the world. This is thanks to large deposits of easily accessible, high-grade phosphates. For millions of years billions of birds nested on Nauru, and the excrement or guano (phosphoric acid and nitrogen) they left behind reacted through leaching with the coral (lime) of the upraised atoll to form a hard, odorless, colorless rock, averaging 85-88% pure phosphate of lime. This material is an outstanding fertilizer, helping to keep the fields of New Zealand green and the farms of Australia productive. Ironically, the phosphate has never had any impact on the fertility of Nauru itself, as it must be treated with sulfuric acid before it's of any use as a fertilizer.

The Land

Oyster-shaped Nauru is one of the three great phosphate-rock islands of the Pacific (the others are Banaba in Kiribati and Makatea in the Tuamotus). A fringing reef, bare at low tide, borders a glistening white-sand beach. The island's 100- to 300-meter-wide coastal belt bears its only cultivable soil, although a short distance inland are gardens around the small Buada Lagoon. Coral cliffs encircle an elevated interior plateau which reaches 65 meters in altitude. Punctuated by white coral pinnacles of worked-out phosphate fields, the barren, moonscaped interior is now a scene of utter desolation, in striking contrast to the lush, tropical coastline.

Climate

Only 53 km south of the equator, there's no seasonal variation in Nauru's temperature. November through Feb. (the westerly monsoon) are the wettest months; drier northeasterly trade winds blow the rest of the year. Rainfall varies greatly from year to year with occasional prolonged droughts.

History

The first European ship to happen upon Nauru was the British whaler *Hunter,* which arrived in 1798. Capt. John Fearn named it Pleasant Island for the friendly welcome he received. During the 1830s whalers began calling more often and a number of crew members deserted to become beachcombers. These men allied themselves with rival chiefs and after 1878 there was continual fighting among the 12 tribes.

Germans from New Guinea landed in 1888 and suppressed the savage tribal warfare which had decimated the population over the preceding 10 years. Arms and ammunition were confiscated; liquor was banned. The Germans set about running their new colony as part of the Marshall Islands Protectorate, unaware of the wealth beneath their feet. The first missionaries showed up around 1899.

Then a strange chain of events began which was to change the island forever. While visiting Nauru in 1896 trader Henry E. Denson picked up a nicely stratified rock which he assumed was from a petrified tree. He took the rock back to Australia thinking perhaps it could be made into children's marbles. It kicked around the office of Denson's Pacific Islands Company a couple of years and was being used as a doorstop when Albert Ellis, a young company employee in Sydney, noticed the strange-looking rock. In Jan. 1899 Ellis decided to have it analyzed and discovered to Denson's amazement that it contained 80% pure phosphate of lime. (The original rock may now be seen in Auckland Museum.)

Unfortunately the Germans had already claimed the island and set up a tiny trading post and coconut plantation. As mineral-rights negotiations proceeded on Nauru, an employee of the Sydney trading company was dispatched to Banaba, 306 km east, where he found additional vast quantities of the same material, so Britain annexed Banaba on 28 Sept. 1901. (The subsequent history of Banaba is given in the Kiribati chapter.)

It was finally agreed that the phosphates of Nauru would be exploited under joint British-German auspices, and the Pacific Phosphate Company came into being in 1902. Profits were to be shared with the German firm Jaluit Gesellshaft with no provision for direct bene-

fits for the Nauruans. Mining began in 1907. The Germans lost their share when the Australians took Nauru without a fight on 9 Sept. 1914, at the beginning of WW I. A Japanese warship arrived soon after with the same intent, but turned back when it found the Australians in control.

After the war, the League of Nations granted Australia the right to administer Nauru on behalf of Britain and New Zealand. In 1920 the British Phosphate Commissioners (BPC), controlled by these three governments, bought out all rights to the deposits for 3.5 million pounds and carried on with the mining operations. Far from benefiting the Nauruans, the early days of phosphate mining witnessed a series of epidemics introduced by the foreign labor force: dysentery (1907), polio (1910), influenza (1919), pneumonia (1920). Some 400 Nauruans died from these diseases, lowering the population by 25% to only 1,210 in 1920. In 1927 agreement was reached between the company and the island chiefs that a royalty of 7½ pence per ton would be paid. Mining land

NAURU'S CLIMATE

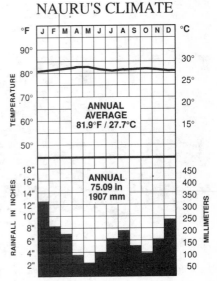

land was to be leased at 40 pounds an acre and 25 shillings paid for any food-producing tree cut down.

WW II came to the island on 6 Dec. 1940, when the German raider *Orion* captured and sank the BPC vessel *Triona*, bound for Nauru. The next day the *Orion* and its companion, the *Komet,* arrived at Nauru and sank four more phosphate freighters drifting offshore. On 27 Dec. 1940 the *Komet* returned to Nauru and shelled the cantilever loader, putting it out of commission until 1948. On 9 Dec. 1941 a Japanese plane bombed the radio station on Nauru, and with the war situation deteriorating the British Phosphate Commissioners had personnel and their families evacuated to Australia by a French destroyer on 23 Feb. 1942. The ship also took off 391 Chinese laborers but some 194 Chinese and 149 I-Kiribati had to be left behind.

On 26 Aug. 1942 a Japanese invasion force landed on Nauru and began building the present airport, which was operational by Jan. 1943. After an American air raid on 25 March the Japanese executed five Europeans who had been captured on the island. Of the 1,850 Nauruans present when the Japanese arrived some 1,200 were eventually deported to Chuuk to serve as forced labor. On 31 Jan. 1946 some 737 survivors returned to their island. The Japanese solved Nauru's leprosy problem by loading the 49 lepers into a boat, then taking it out and sinking it. The Allies bypassed Nauru; some 500 Japanese Marines held it until the end of the war.

Recent History

In 1947 Nauru became a United Nations trust territory administered by Australia. Phosphate shipments recommenced in July 1947 and payments to the Nauruans were increased. Yet right up to 1965 only a 2½% royalty was paid to the Nauruans for the devastation of their island.

The first elected Local Government Council was formed in 1951, at which time the Nauruans began to press Australia more strongly for a greater share of the profits from phosphate mining. Expenditures by the BPC administration for health, housing, and education increased nearly fivefold between 1951 and 1955. In 1953 public service employees launched a four-month strike led by Hammer DeRoburt, who was elected Head Chief in 1956.

In 1963 DeRoburt turned down an offer of Australian citizenship for his people and resettlement somewhere on Australian territory, such as Fraser or Curtis islands off the coast of Queensland. In Jan. 1966, with the

These New Guinea soldiers made up the German garrison on Nauru at the outbreak of WW I.

AUCKLAND INSTITUTE AND MUSEUM

establishment of legislative and executive councils, Nauruans became almost totally self-governing. The next year, it was agreed that the Nauruans could buy themselves back from the British Phosphate Commissioners for A$21 million, payable over three years. On 31 Jan. 1968, the 22nd anniversary of the return from Chuuk, Nauru became the world's smallest independent republic. DeRoburt was elected president in May 1968 and on 30 June 1970 the mines were formally transferred to the Nauru Phosphate Corporation at a ceremony in Melbourne.

Government

Two levels of government coexist here. The Nauru Government, run by the elected president and his ministers, owns the Nauru Phosphate Corporation and Air Nauru, while the Nauru Local Government Council (NLGC), under an elected head chief and his councillors, controls trade, including the Nauru Insurance Corporation, the Civic Center complex, the Menen Hotel, and the Lands Committee. Nauru has an 18-member Parliament which elects the president from its ranks. The five cabinet ministers are chosen by the president. Elections are held every three years. The Nauru Party, founded in 1975, was reformed as the Democratic Party in 1987. The Nauru Local Government Council consists of nine elected members under a Head Chief. There are 14 districts (indicated on the map), each headed by a councillor (formerly the chief of the clan).

Mismanagement and waste are a way of life on Nauru, a situation usually blamed on ex-president Hammer DeRoburt, who ran Nauru with an iron fist for all but two of the years between 1968 and 1989 and who is said to have spent much of his time at his penthouse in Melbourne or in a suite at London's Savoy Hotel. In Oct. 1991 Parliament debated abolishing the NLGC after it was revealed that it had run up a debt of A$300 million.

Economy

Until recently Nauru exported two million tons of phosphate a year to Australia, New Zealand, Korea, and the Philippines each year,

bringing in A$100 million. In 1990 shipments declined sharply, partly due to economic recession and alternative agricultural techniques, but more because the phosphate reserves are quickly being exhausted. It's now thought that by 1995 this gold carriage will have turned back into a pumpkin, and with all Nauru's phosphate played out the island could become a deserted hulk, 80% of its area completely devastated.

The Nauru Government takes half the revenue from phosphate sales; the rest is split between the Local Government Council, the Nauru Phosphate Royalties Trust, and landowners. The trust fund is now worth over A$1 billion, designed to provide the inhabitants with a future income. Investments include flashy office buildings in Melbourne ("Birdshit Tower"), Honolulu, Manila, and Saipan, two Sheraton hotels in New Zealand, Fiji's Grand Pacific Hotel, the highly successful Pacific Star Hotel on Guam, the disastrous Eastern Gateway Hotel on Majuro, housing developments in Oregon and Texas, and a seven-story "Pacific House" in Washington, D.C.

Though financial reports are never published, Nauru is believed to have lost A$70 million on a fertilizer plant in the Philippines and millions more on a similar plant in India. Much money is also spent on prestige items such as Air Nauru's fleet of Boeing 737s, which loses thousands of dollars per Nauruan annually but is convenient for jet-set officials. Nauruans also play the Australian and Japanese stock markets. In 1991 Nauru filed a formal complaint with the Japanese Government when the Japanese stock market crashed and they lost 40% of their investment!

Belatedly Nauru has tried to get the governments of Australia, Britain, and New Zealand to accept responsibility for rehabilitating the island and in 1989 filed suit against Australia before the International Court of Justice in The Hague for A$72 million in damages. Australia rejected the court's jurisdiction and said Nauru had already been adequately compensated. The cost of replacing the island's topsoil is estimated at A$216 million and as yet the Nauru Government has declined to spend any of its own money on it.

IKIMAGO

7c

REPUBLIC OF
NAURU

The People

Of the 8,902 (1988) people living on Nauru, 58% are indigenous Nauruans. The rest are a mix of Australians, New Zealanders, Chinese, Filipinos, and other Pacific islanders doing the dirty work connected with phosphate mining. The lower-caste contract workers are housed in long, squalid blocks of Soweto-style tenements at Location, just north of the company's noisy Bottom Side phosphate-crushing plant. They find this lifestyle appealing: guaranteed income, no quarrels over land ownership, and availability of Western food and consumer goods compel the laborers and their families to stay. Perhaps they're better off, and so are their extended families back home, to whom they remit part of their income. Because of this, Kiribati and Tuvalu will feel the inevitable crunch when the phosphate runs out, far more than Nauru.

The Nauruans reside in single-story tin-roofed family dwellings strung all along the coastline and around the Buada Lagoon. It's fairly easy to distinguish the heavyset Nauruans, with their flattop Land Rovers and overpowered speedboats, from the guest workers, who ride big articulated trailer buses and fish for tuna just offshore in dugout canoes. For now, the Nauruans' education, hospitalization, electricity, and housing are provided free by the government, and there's no income tax, sales tax, or customs duties.

Only the I-Kiribati, Tuvaluans, Indians, and Chinese are permitted to keep their wives and children with them on Nauru; others such as the Filipinos must stick it out alone. And it's

mandatory that foreign workers must marry any live-in companion. Even so, marriage to a Nauruan woman is no passport for a foreign male to remain on the island without a job. Such relationships, in fact, are officially discouraged, and special dispensation is required for the ceremony to be performed on Nauru itself.

The Nauru Phosphate Corporation still runs a tight little colonial system with no interfering unions, and employees are paid according to ethnic origin. The Pacific island and Chinese laborers are at the bottom of the scale, the Filipino tradesmen next up, and the European management and technicians near the top. Everybody beefs about the lousy deal they're getting, but no one seems in a hurry to leave. Indians willing to work for lower wages are quickly replacing expatriate Europeans at the management level, and there are more Solomon islanders employed as laborers (and fewer I-Kiribati) due to complaints about working conditions and pay.

The Nauruans

The native Nauruans are, like Tongans, physically huge. They're a mixed Polynesian/Melanesian/Micronesian/European bunch—5,000 people who found themselves sitting on the richest bed of bird do in the world. The affluence, decadence, and accompanying wastage is astounding. Four-wheel-drive Land Rovers and fancy Australian cars dominate the roads; blaring stereo and video systems dominate the airwaves. Not all families are rich, however. Those who come from smaller, more heavily populated districts where the phosphate was mined first receive less in royalties than people who possess large tracts of land with phosphate reserves.

Nauruans have the world's highest incidence of diabetes—a shocking 30.3%. Medical journals cite Nauru's epidemic as a classic case of junk-food-induced, as opposed to hereditary, diabetes. The special diabetic section in the supermarket says it all. High blood pressure, heart disease, alcoholism, and obesity are rampant. The heaps of jetti-

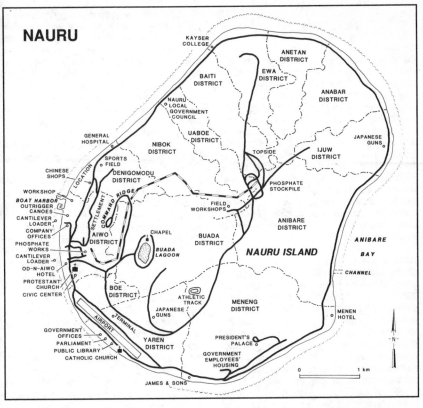

NAURU

KAYSER COLLEGE

ANETAN DISTRICT

EWA DISTRICT

BAITI DISTRICT

ANABAR DISTRICT

NAURU LOCAL GOVERNMENT COUNCIL

UABOE DISTRICT

JAPANESE GUNS

GENERAL HOSPITAL

NIBOK DISTRICT

TOPSIDE

IJUW DISTRICT

SPORTS FIELD

CHINESE SHOPS

DENIGOMODU DISTRICT

PHOSPHATE STOCKPILE

WORKSHOP

BOAT HARBOR OUTRIGGER CANOES

FIELD WORKSHOPS

CANTILEVER LOADER

COMPANY OFFICES

CHAPEL

AIWO DISTRICT

BUADA DISTRICT

ANIBARE DISTRICT

PHOSPHATE WORKS

CANTILEVER LOADER

BUADA LAGOON

NAURU ISLAND

ANIBARE BAY

OD-N-AIWO HOTEL

CHANNEL

PROTESTANT CHURCH

CIVIC CENTER

BOE DISTRICT

ATHLETIC TRACK

MENENG DISTRICT

JAPANESE GUNS

MENEN HOTEL

TERMINAL

AIRPORT

GOVERNMENT OFFICES

PARLIAMENT

PUBLIC LIBRARY

CATHOLIC CHURCH

YAREN DISTRICT

PRESIDENT'S PALACE

GOVERNMENT EMPLOYEES' HOUSING

0   1 km

-N-

JAMES & SONS

LOCATION

SETTLEMENT

COMMAND RIDGE

---

soned Foster's beer cans have led to suggestions that Nauru be renamed "Blue Can Island" or "Foster's Island." Traffic accidents on the one road (!) and the high mortality rate make a 50th birthday a big event for Nauruans. Few males live much beyond this age and only 1.2% of the population is over 65—the lowest such ratio in the Pacific islands. Visit a cemetery and note the ages on the tombstones.

Holidays And Events

Public holidays include New Year's (1 Jan.), Independence Day (31 Jan.), Easter, Constitution Day (17 May), Angam Day (26 Oct.), and Christmas (25 December). The Independence Day celebrations last three days, beginning 31 Jan., and include fishing competitions, sports events, a parade by students, and a speech from the president. Angam Day commemorates the times (in 1932 and 1949) when the local population regenerated back up to the 1,500 level, the minimum necessary for the maintenance of a collective identity, according to the Nauruans. Other major events include the Australian Rules Football Grand Final Day in Sept. and the Melbourne Cup horse race the first Tues. in November. Large amounts of money change hands between gamblers on these days as most Nauruans sit glued to their radios or TV sets.

PRACTICALITIES

Conduct

Be aware that the Nauruans do not take kindly to pushy, argumentative people. No matter how bad things seem, a friendly, low-key approach is the most likely to be crowned with success. Topless sunbathing and skimpy dress are frowned upon. As in Kiribati, don't openly admire a possession of a Nauruan or he/she may feel obligated to give it to you, an old custom known as *bubuti*. Except at the Menen Hotel, theft is no problem on Nauru. Western males seen driving around late at night with Nauruan women receive special attention from the police. Be careful walking down the street after dark, as the Nauruans train their dogs to attack passersby.

Accommodations

Of the two hotels on Nauru the family-operated **Od-N-Aiwo** (Tim John Enterprises, Box 299, Nauru; tel. 3555 or 3591), near the Civic Center and phosphate works downtown, is best if you're into sightseeing and observing local life. The 20 a/c rooms go for $40 s, $46 d, $64 t. The meals served in the restaurant downstairs vary in quality and a small, well-stocked supermarket is on the premises but no alcoholic beverages are sold at either. Check the expiry date before purchasing film here. The free Od-N-Aiwo airport bus meets all flights. If you're alone, look for someone on your flight to share a room with you.

The 65-room, government-owned **Menen Hotel** (Sandip Mukhejee, Box 298, Nauru; tel. 3210 or 3595), at the south end of Anibare Bay four km east of the airport terminal, is preferable for those who are only waiting for an onward flight. If it looks like there's nobody on duty at the reception desk, look behind the counter; the clerk may be asleep on the floor. Rooms go for A$30 s, A$40 d with ceiling fan, or A$45 s, A$55 d with a/c. Unfortunately the Menen has fallen on hard times, the rooms are deteriorating from corrosion and lack of maintenance, and you may have to change rooms twice before you're

given one with everything in working order. If you want to be able to make your own tea and coffee ask for a "jug." Beware of noisy neighbors as the partitions separating the rooms are very thin. Put a chair in front of your door to prevent the maids from coming in unannounced and lock your valuables up in your luggage or carry them with you when you go out. If you get a room at ground level make sure your sliding balcony door is securely locked.

The restaurants and bars attached to the Menen operate on a capricious timetable. Although the food is sometimes good, the portions are small and the service abysmal. Avoid ham steak—canned ham sliced and fried. Sometimes the Menen actually runs out of food and the head cook has to replenish his supplies from the empty shelves at the Civic Center supermarket, and catering for Air Nauru gets first priority. If there's no one on duty in the dining room when you arrive, have a look outside or stick your head in the kitchen or bar—the staff may be on gossip/smoke break.

Some of the Nauruans at the Menen are aloof and arrogant—an exception on this island. Avoid the Reef Bar when it's full of drunken Nauruans; other times barman Frank Limen is a fertile source of information on the island. If you're interested in fishing, just ask Frank. Nothing pleases him more than an exotic addition to his collection of foreign bank notes displayed behind the bar. The Menen does have a comfortable lobby should you happen to arrive on Nauru in the middle of the night. Take the free bus there and hang loose. If your flight out is at an odd hour don't rely on the hotel staff for a wake-up call as they often just forget.

As this book goes to press the Menen is undergoing a complete renovation in preparation for the 1993 South Pacific Forum on Nauru, so expect the facilities to have improved and prices to have gone up.

At the back of a parking lot just north of the Menen, across the road from the channel on nearby Anibare Bay, is a trail up into the interior. If you're staying at the Menen this is an excellent shortcut to the phosphate workings. If desperate, you could find somewhere to pitch a tent in there, but avoid hassles by keeping it well out of sight and off the trails. Beware of packs of stray dogs which have been known to attack people on their own at night. Mosquitos are abundant.

Food

Several inexpensive Chinese restaurants are found among the Chinese shops near the workers' housing area at Location. A good lunch of beef and rice goes for around $2. The **Triton Restaurant** near the Od-N-Aiwo is good, and if you wish to spend a little more the **Star Twinkles Restaurant** at Nibok is worth a try. The **Frangipani Cafe** at Boe is very reasonable. A series of small Chinese cafes is dotted around the island, but no Nauruan cafes. Nearly all food is imported from Australia, and even water is shipped in. You can drink all the coconut milk you want if you care to take the trouble of climbing for the nuts yourself; the locals just leave them where they are, although the I-Kiribati sometimes make toddy from the trees.

Entertainment

Nauru is not organized for tourists, so you'll have to entertain yourself. Actually, a little imagination reveals plenty to do. The best bar is the **NPC Staff Club,** just beside the larger cantilever at Aiwo. One of the "tropo" Aussies will probably offer to sign you in (it's a private club) if you look respectable enough. The beer is cheap and there's an excellent snack bar here.

The wildest places on Nauru are the **Bula Bar** behind the Civic Center, the **Ace of Diamonds Club** near the Menen Hotel, and the **Sailing Club** at Anabar. Beware of aggressive drunks at all three. The friendly **East End Club** almost opposite Kayser Church at Baiti has two good snooker tables. The beautiful new theater in the **Civic Center** shows only kung fu and Rambo-style movies. Many people stay up all night watching rented videos in their homes.

Nauru is the only country in the world where the national sport is Australian Rules football. Games at the sports field by the road

just north of the Chinese shops are played all day Saturday and some evenings. Admission is free. If you enjoy tennis or volleyball, go to the courts at Location any evening and ask the locals if you may join in a game. A nine-hole golf course mingles among the phosphate buildings at Aiwo. A reader, John Connell, writes: "Setting off at 0600 one morning I ran around the island without too much interference from dogs. I now claim to be one of the few people to have run around a country (even a republic) before breakfast!"

Other activities in Nauru include betting on Australian horse races that are broadcast live over the radio. You can place bets at any one of around five illegal bookie joints. Many of the bookies provide patrons with a complimentary meal. Bingo games are ubiquitous on Fri. and Sat. nights.

If you have Nauruan friends, ask about joining a Black Noddy hunt. The birds are attracted to prerecorded Black Noddy calls on a cassette tape and as they pass, two Nauruans standing on raised platforms catch them in nets attached to long poles. The hunt takes place in the interior at night and complete silence must be maintained if the birds are to come. The captured birds are then plucked and roasted and are quite a treat if you haven't tried them before. To avoid wiping out the species the Nauru Government limits the hunt to only a few weeks a year and severe penalties are applied to anyone caught violating this.

Shopping

Nauru has three kinds of shops. Those operated by the Local Government Council (such as the ones in the Civic Center) resemble Eastern European stores for their shoddy goods, irregular hours, and poor selection. The better-stocked Chinese shops will be familiar to anyone who has been to Southeast Asia (trinkets, loads of clothes and material, etc.). In recent years a few Nauruan general stores have been set up, one of the best of which is Capelle and Partners at Ewa with frozen foods, ice cream, liquor, fruit juices, camera film, etc. A similar two-story store is at the Menen end of the airport runway. Fresh fruit and vegetables can sometimes be found at James and Sons Store between the airport and the Menen Hotel.

Most of your business needs can be tended to in the dilapidated **Civic Center** at Aiwo, which includes the Air Nauru office, the bank, the post office and Philatelic Bureau, a cinema ($1), and a barren but cheap supermarket, which features out-of-date canned goods and weevil-infested flour. Note the rat and cockroach droppings around the shelves! The lack of local taxes means a lot of things—for example, cassettes ($3-4), cigarettes ($5-6 a carton), and alcohol are cheaper here than in their countries of origin.

The Central Pacific Bookshop near the Od-N-Aiwo sells magazines and some good postcards of Nauru. The post office may also have postcards. Color print film is available at a small store opposite the Civic Center, with 24-hour processing available, but their slide and black-and-white film is usually expired.

Visas

All visitors must have a passport. A visa is not required if you'll be continuing to a third country on the first connecting flight and hold a confirmed seat reservation. Since all flights begin or end in Nauru, a little planning will allow you a visa-free two- or three-day stopover—quite sufficient. Even if your connection is immediate, immigration will sometimes allow you to stay until the next flight a few days later without a visa, although in 1991 such requests were being denied due to problems with overstayers. Showing money to prove you're able to support yourself may help, and mentioning the name of a Nauruan friend works even better. Applying for a tourist visa in advance is hopeless and a waste of time. If you know a Nauruan family willing to sponsor you, a one-month visa may be possible, but application must be made at a Nauruan diplomatic office well before your planned arrival.

Visiting yachts must tie up to a ship's buoy and someone must stay on the boat at all times. It's much too deep to anchor. Spending the night moored here is not allowed, however, and yachts must stand offshore overnight if they wish to stay a second day. Dinghies can land in the shallow small boat harbor, though it does experience quite a surge. Diesel fuel is usually available, but little water.

Services

Australian currency is used on Nauru. The hotels change traveler's checks at a noticeably poorer rate than the Bank of Nauru. Credit cards are not accepted. Place overseas telephone calls from the Telecom Nauru offices beside the satellite dish next to the government buildings opposite the airport. The post office provides public telex services. Postage is inexpensive. The electric voltage is 240 volts, 50 cycles AC, and the Australian three-pin plug is used.

Free consultations are available weekdays at the general hospital at Denig just up the road from the NPC staff hospital. A haircut at Backside Barber No. 3 near the Chinese shops at Location is $2. Nauru doesn't have a tourist information office. The Australian High Commission (tel. 5230) in the Civic Center has a decent library where you can relax in comfort and learn about the wonders of Oz.

Information

The *Central Star News* (Box 429, Nauru), Nauru's only newspaper, is published every two weeks. There are no tourist brochures of any kind available on the country.

Radio station C2AM-AM broadcasts from Nauru over 1323 kHz.

Getting There

Air Nauru, the only airline to land on the island, has flights to Auckland ($444), Chuuk (A$330), Fiji ($198), Guam ($227), Honiara ($140), Kosrae ($176), Manila ($340), Melbourne ($389), Noumea ($211), Pohnpei (A$238), Sydney ($335), and Tarawa ($103). All fares are in Australian dollars, one-way economy from Nauru. To calculate the cost of transiting the Pacific via Nauru, add together any two of the fares listed above. A more detailed examination of the routes is provided in the book's main Introduction.

Air Nauru has been restructured after a near-two-year grounding resulting from a pilot's strike in May 1988. Services have been revamped and over 90% of all flights now run on schedule—a far cry from the old days of routine cancellations and passenger-bumping.

Be sure to reconfirm your onward flight soon after you arrive, even though your transit time may be less than 24 hours, as flights departing Nauru are sometimes overbooked. Arrive at the airport early, as the check-in counter closes 30 minutes before departure time and anyone arriving later is refused passage. If any sudden changes occur and you happen to be staying at the Menen, try asking one of the New Zealand flight engineers lodged there for information. If your Air Nauru flight is delayed or canceled, politely ask the employee at the airport to give you a voucher for a paid room at the Menen Hotel with meals.

Getting Around

Without your own transport, touring Nauru can be difficult, unless you like walking. The taxis on Nauru are not overly expensive, once you've found them. The Od-N-Aiwo Hotel serves as the taxi stand of sorts. If plane connections allow only a couple of hours on Nauru, hire a taxi up into the interior.

Car rental is difficult as resident expatriates usually have all the vehicles out on lease, but try Mr. B. Waqa at PPH (tel. 3472), or Mr. Clodumar (tel. 3411). They charge around $35 a day with unlimited kilometers. The manager of the Menen Hotel rents out the hotel bus for island tours at a reasonable rate.

Airport

Nauru International Airport (INU) is one km southeast of the Civic Center at Aiwo. Both hotels provide free transfers. Facilities at the airport are poor, with a limited snack bar (often closed) and filthy, unlit public toilets (the ones in the departure lounge are the best). There's a basic grocery store in the building next to the terminal. Unless a flight is scheduled, the terminal is locked. Another Nauru peculiarity: traffic lights are set up to stop cars on the circumferential road when aircraft are on the runway.

The Nauruans have finally realized that the bird shit's really running out, so everyone transiting Nauru (including those continuing on the same aircraft and only on the ground one hour) must disembark, have their passport stamped, and pay the A$10 airport departure tax—unless, of course, you're a Nauruan, and pay nothing.

SIGHTS OF NAURU

Bottom Side

The phosphate mined on the hot, dusty interior plateau (Top Side) is brought down by train to the works near the **cantilever loaders** (Bottom Side). Here the material is crushed, screened, roasted, and stored. A new **calcination plant** removes all carbon and most cadmium (a pollutant) from the phosphate.

The **buoys** off Aiwo are connected to the deepest deep-water moorings in the world (518 meters). Two ships can be loaded from the cantilevers at a time. The **small boat harbor** nearby remains from the pre-1927 days when ships were loaded by lighter.

Location, the workers' housing area, is just north of the boat harbor, while management housing sits on the hilltop above at Settlement.

Top Side

A look at the mined-out **coral pinnacles** of the interior is an essential part of any tour of the island. You may also visit the **phosphate fields** on foot. There are no restrictions on entry. Head inland from the Od-N-Aiwo Hotel and turn right on the dirt road at the top of the hill. You may be lucky and get a lift for most of the way to the phosphate-mining area, where great cranes load giant trucks at quite a slow pace due to the small size of the grab buckets on the crane. You'll often see lengths of steel cable protruding from the coral pinnacles with a grab bucket cut loose below. It's easier simply to abandon jammed buckets than to spend time trying to retrieve them. One of the few **railways** in the Central Pacific operates here. The long phosphate trains traverse the narrow-gauge tracks from the interior loader at Stockpile to Bottom Side below.

The interior of Nauru is ecological chaos. Photographers will be especially intrigued but there's no water on Top Side, so take something to drink. If you aren't into hitchhiking or walking long distances along a hot, dusty road, ask at your hotel about a taxi tour or car rentals. Cross-country hiking off the road through the pinnacles is challenging, but very dangerous. If you fall into a pit you might never be found, so don't go alone. Unaccompanied women should pay attention while wandering about the mining area, especially on weekends.

War Relics

Just beyond the garbage dump, about a km along the dirt road to the phosphate fields, are a couple of big **Japanese antiaircraft guns** to the left of the main roadway, clearly visible at the top of a hill. There's also an excellent view from there, and a stone fort is hidden in the undergrowth just behind. Backtrack to the paved road and continue down to the **Buada Lagoon,** where banana and coconut trees border the brackish water. Many Nauruans live in houses around the lagoon; fishing rights are divided according to family. There's a small store and mini-supermarket where you could buy a cold drink.

Between the lagoon and the west coast is **Command Ridge,** accessible via a dirt track to the right just before the road to the phosphate fields. If you miss it, follow the railway line which crosses the track about 20 minutes inland. A short distance inland to the left of the track is a huge **machinery dump** hidden in the undergrowth. Thousands of dollars worth of machinery is discarded here, cheap-

Nauru phosphates are loaded onto ships for Australia and New Zealand from these giant cantilever loaders at Aiwo.

er to replace than to repair! Carry a stick, as wild dogs frequent this area. Among the pinnacles behind the equipment dump are the remains of a U.S. Flying Fortress aircraft shot down during WW II. If you decide to look for it, take care as you risk getting lost or falling in a pit.

The dirt track then takes you across the railway line where you start to climb Command Ridge. The Japanese had their headquarters up here during the war, and the ridge is still riddled with trenches, bunkers, and intact naval guns, although much is hidden among the thick growth. The extremely deep **pits** between the adjacent coral pinnacles were dug out with pick and shovel by Chinese coolies during the early days of phosphate mining. Take a shortcut down to **Settlement,** along the pipeline which feeds three large water tanks at the end of the access road. Some intact concrete pillboxes can be recognized around these tanks near the radio transmitter shack. The management housing you'll pass contrasts strikingly with the crowded workers' tenements on the coastal plain directly below. Carry a big stick for the dogs.

Around The Island

The better part of a day can be spent walking around the island (19 km). A cement sidewalk borders the road much of the way, and small stores and restaurants are well distributed so you're never far from a cold drink or snack. Although reserved, the Nauruans are basically friendly and will return a smile, wave, and word of greeting when you catch their eyes.

Frigate birds (some tame enough to eat fish from your hand) are often seen soaring above the shoreline. Until recently each district had its own **Frigate bird roost,** huge elevated platforms on wooden legs where the birds would perch. Some are still to be seen, sadly falling apart as interest is diverted elsewhere. One fine example remains at Anabar, to the right of the road near the beach, and you're welcome to feed or photograph the 100 birds—preferably in the early morning or an hour before sunset. The perch

is privately owned so do ask permission of anyone there.

Many wartime **Japanese pillboxes** dot the coastal fringe and more are slightly inland. Just a little north of Anibare Bay, on the inland side of the road adjacent to some houses on the crest of a hill, are two large coastal defense guns. One is hard to find as a large workshop has been erected right next to it, but the other is in the open. The barrels were "spiked" by the Australian Army after the Japanese surrender in 1945.

Many Japanese bunkers are to be found around the Menen Hotel, including a well-hidden pillbox just off the steps to the tennis courts and a larger two-story observation post directly below the courts. An underground bunker is behind the volleyball court near the hotel entrance. A number of camouflaged bunkers are on the interior side of the airport runway. During runway extensions in 1990 a number of war relics were dug up, including an intact engine from a Japanese plane, but they were either reburied or pushed into the sea.

The Bureaucracy

If you've got some extra time, visit the government offices opposite the airport terminal. If **Parliament** is in session you may observe from the large public gallery; the meetings in May and June on the budget are the liveliest as backbenchers heckle and mudslinging matches start. The debates are supposed to be in English but some strong Nauruan can be heard when things get hot! Nearby is the **courthouse,** where you're welcome to sit in on a trial. A very poor public library is also here.

Waterfront

The swimming is good in the boat harbor at Aiwo, especially at high tide. **Surfers** should check out Gabab Channel, at the end of the airport runway closest to the Civic Center, and Menen Point near the hotel—rides are short and only possible at high tide. **Reef walking** at low tide along the coast near the Menen Hotel is fascinating. Corals, sea urchins, crabs, and small fish can be seen in abundance at the edge of the intertidal zone where the breakers crash. You might even find some cowrie shells if you're lucky.

The best beach on Nauru borders **Anibare Bay,** but beware of dangerous currents. Be especially wary when swimming in the cut channel (boat ramp) about 500 meters north of the Menen Hotel, as there's often a strong outflow of water from waves which have broken over the reef. Never swim alone here and if you get caught don't try to fight it, but float out and come back in over the reef to the south. Saturdays after 1600 watch for aggressive drunken locals and don't leave personal effects unattended.

LOUISE FOOTE

Since the frigate bird doesn't have the oily waterproofing of other seabirds, it spooks other species into disgorging their catch in mid-air.

REPUBLIC OF KIRIBATI

INTRODUCTION

Legend tells how the god Nareau picked flowers from the ancestral tree and threw them north of Samoa to mark the place where the islands of Tarawa, Beru, and Tabiteuea appeared. Today, these islands and 30 others combine to form the independent Republic of Kiribati. The name, pronounced "kir-EE-bas," is an indigenous corruption of the name "Gilberts." To further confuse you, the Kiribati name of the Gilbert Islands group is Tungaru. Originally the Gilbertese wanted to call their country Tungaru, but the Ellice Islanders had already chosen Tuvalu; Tungaru sounded too similar. In this book we use Tungaru to refer to the group of 16 atolls forming the Gilbert Islands, and apply Kiribati to the country as a whole. The people of Kiribati, the Gilbertese, are known as I-Kiribati, and speak a language also called Kiribati.

A visit to the republic is like stepping back to the Pacific of half a century ago. Here, in this most unspoiled corner of Micronesia, sailing canoes have not yet been replaced by outboards, and tourists are extremely rare. The I-Kiribati are friendly, embarrassingly bold and inquisitive, and terribly hospitable. They're also fun-loving, easygoing, and somewhat languorous. They don't have to spend all day working in order to survive; their requirements are minimal. In Kiribati visitors can participate in the daily activities of the village—mingling with the people; observing their customs, lifestyles, and behavior; and of course learning the language. This is no place for the energetic, hyperactive traveler!

The Land
The 33 low-lying coral islands of Kiribati total only 817 square km land area, but 3,550,000

square km sea area (included within Kiribati's 200-nautical-mile Exclusive Economic Zone or EEZ). No other political unit on earth is made up of such a large sea-to-land ratio. Largest atoll state in the world, it straddles the equator for 3,218 km from Banaba to Christmas Island and crosses the International Date Line. Tarawa, the capital, is 2,800 km north of Fiji.

The islands are arrayed in three great groups: the 16 Gilbert Islands (Tungaru), the eight Phoenix Islands, and the eight Line Islands, with little Banaba alone to the west between Tarawa and Nauru. Tungaru contributes 279 square km and most of the people to the country. The flat, palm-studded Tungaru isles are characterized by a uniform environment of crushed-coral surface, magnificent white beaches, lagoons, and reefs. Most of these atolls are no more than 200-300 meters wide, but may be anywhere from 15 to 100 km long. Due to the action of the

TARAWA'S CLIMATE

prevailing winds, the atolls' northeast coasts are generally higher than the west, but nowhere do they reach more than a few meters above sea level. The west sides are encumbered by shoals and reefs, making it safer for ships to navigate the east coasts. All except Makin, Kuria, Nikunau, Tamana, and Arorae have central lagoons.

Banaba, 440 km west of Tarawa, is a raised limestone island. To the southeast of Tarawa is the uninhabited Phoenix Group, and farther east the Line Islands stretch between Hawaii and Tahiti. Christmas Island, largest atoll in land area in the world, accounts for nearly half the republic's dry land.

A United Nations report on the greenhouse effect (the heating of earth's atmosphere and resultant rise in sea level due to industrial pollution) lists Kiribati as one of the countries that could disappear completely beneath the sea in the 21st century unless drastic action is taken. At the 1989 South Pacific Forum meeting on Tarawa, Australia agreed to fund a series of monitoring stations to be established throughout the Pacific islands in 1990.

Climate

Robert Louis Stevenson wrote that Tungaru enjoys "a superb ocean climate, days of blinding sun and bracing wind, nights of heavenly brightness." The best time to visit is March-Nov. when the southeast trades blow; from Nov. to March the westerlies bring much of the rainfall, in sharp irregular squalls. This is also the typhoon season, though typhoons are extremely rare. Droughts occur in southern and central Tungaru; considerably more rain falls on the northernmost atolls (Butaritari gets 3,114 mm of annual rainfall, compared to only 1,177 mm at Onotoa). The reduced rainfall in the south is caused by the upwelling of cold oceanic water which reduces evaporation from the ocean surface (nutrients also brought to the surface make this a prime fishing area). The climate of Kiribati is hot but not humid; cool sea breezes often moderate the temperature.

HISTORY AND GOVERNMENT

Prehistory

Perhaps 3,000 years ago, the ancestors of the Micronesians arrived in Tungaru from Southeast Asia via the Caroline Islands. Several thousand years later Polynesian navigators came and intermarried with the original inhabitants. Gilbertese legends tell how the spirits left Samoa and journeyed to Tungaru, where they remained a long time before changing into humans.

Continual contact among the atolls by canoe led to a homogeneous culture. The inhabitants were fierce warriors, equipped with shark's teeth daggers and swords, body armor of thickly plaited coconut fiber, and porcupine fish helmets. On the islands north of the equator district chiefs predominated; south of the equator councils of old men *(unimane)* ruled.

European Contact

Some of the islands may have been sighted by Spanish explorers in the 16th century. In 1765 Commodore John Byron of the HMS *Dolphin* chanced upon Nikunau. Tungaru received its European name from Capt. Thomas Gilbert of the British ship *Charlotte,* who passed in 1788. The first detailed observations and charts were made by Capt. Charles Wilkes of the U.S. Exploring Expedition (1840).

By this time whalers were active in the area. Although they had many skirmishes with the islanders, they also traded tobacco and rudimentary manufactured goods for supplies and women's favors, and some deserted to become beachcombers. Resident Europeans maintained continual contact with the outside after 1850, trading bêche-de-mer (edible sea slugs), turtle shells, and coconut oil. Blackbirders recruited I-Kiribati laborers to work European plantations in other parts of the Pacific between 1850 and 1875.

American missionaries from Hawaii arrived in northern Tungaru in 1857; it was not until 1870 that the London Missionary Society sent representatives from Samoa to southern Tungaru. Catholic missionaries

KIRIBATI AT A GLANCE

	pop. (1990)	land area (sq km)
TUNGARU		
(Gilbert Is.)	**67,187**	**279.23**
Abaiang	5,314	17.48
Abemama	3,218	27.37
Aranuka	1,002	11.61
Arorae	1,440	9.48
Beru	2,909	17.65
Butaritari	3,786	13.49
Kuria	985	15.48
Maiana	2,184	16.72
Makin	1,762	7.89
Marakei	2,863	14.13
Nonouti	2,766	19.85
Nikunau	2,048	19.08
Onotoa	2,112	15.62
Tabiteuea (North)	3,275	25.78
Tabiteuea (South)	1,325	11.85
Tamana	1,396	4.73
North Tarawa	3,648	15.26
South Tarawa	25,154	15.76
BANABA (Ocean I.)	**284**	**6.29**
PHOENIX IS.	**45**	**28.64**
Birnie	0	1.21
Kanton (Abariringa)	45	9.15
Enderbury	0	4.53
Gardner (Nikumaroro)	0	4.14
Hull (Orana)	0	3.91
McKean	0	1.21
Phoenix (Rawaki)	0	1.21
Sydney (Manra)	0	3.28
LINE IS.	**4,782**	**496.52**
Caroline	0	2.27
Christmas (Kiritimati)	2,537	388.39
Fanning (Teraina)	1,309	33.73
Flint	0	2.43
Malden	0	43.30
Starbuck	0	16.19
Vostock	0	0.66
Washington (Tabuaeran)	936	9.55
REP. OF KIRIBATI	**72,298**	**810.68**

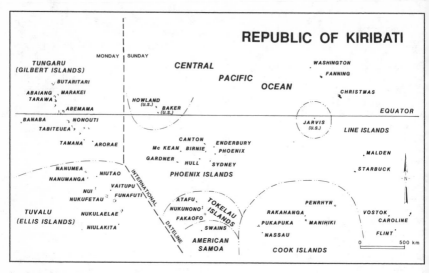

landed at Nonouti in 1888. When the Americans withdrew in 1917, the Catholics extended their influence in the north.

Colonialism

Britain established a protectorate over the Gilbert and Ellice islands in 1892, to halt encroachment by American traders. When phosphates were discovered on Banaba (Ocean Island) in 1900, the British quickly annexed the island. From 1908 to 1941, the British governed the group from Banaba; the administration was not shifted back to Tarawa (where it had been before 1908) until after WW II. The protectorate became a colony in stages between 1915 and 1916. In 1919 Christmas Island was joined to the colony, and in 1937 the Phoenix Islands were added.

In the Guano Act of 1856 the U.S. claimed 14 islands in the Line and Phoenix groups, a subject of amicable dispute with the British until 1939, when they agreed to jointly control Kanton and Enderbury.

The British ended factional and religious warfare in Tungaru, and brought the security of justice evenly applied. The people, who had always lived in scattered family *(kaainga)* settlements, were concentrated in clean, orderly villages connected by roads. Land ownership was registered, and the inhabitants were protected from disruptive outside influences.

The War

Most Europeans and Chinese were evacuated from the area by a French cruiser soon after the outbreak of WW II. The Japanese occupied Tarawa, Butaritari, Abemama, and Banaba on Christmas Day, 1941, but did not fortify the islands or establish large garrisons until after an American raid on Butaritari on 17 Aug. 1942. That day, 221 Marines under Col. Carlson landed from two submarines on the south side of the atoll, in a move to divert Japanese attention from the concurrent invasion of Guadalcanal in the Solomons. The Marines dug in and easily wiped out an attack by the 150 Japanese on the island the next day. The U.S. force then withdrew before the Japanese could retaliate from their strongholds in the Marshalls. Nine unfortunate Marines left behind in a mix-up were captured and beheaded. Even worse, two days after the raid Japanese planes bombed a Gilbertese village in which they thought some Americans were hiding, killing 41 islanders.

As a response to the Carlson raid, Tarawa's Betio islet was heavily fortified by the Japanese, who built an airstrip right down its middle. On 20 Nov. 1943 a strong force of U.S. Marines landed at Betio and cleared the island in a brutal three-day struggle. During this Battle of Tarawa 4,690 Japanese soldiers and Korean laborers were killed (only 17 Japanese and 129 Koreans were captured); the number of U.S. troops killed, wounded, or missing reached 3,314. This was the war's first great amphibious landing against fortified positions and, though costly, provided valuable lessons for later operations. The Americans retook Butaritari at a cost of several hundred lives; the 22 Japanese on Abemama committed hara-kiri to avoid capture. The U.S. didn't consider it worthwhile to land on strongly defended Banaba and Nauru, which they bypassed, although air attacks continued.

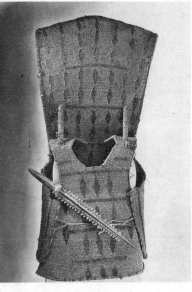

Gilbertese warriors wielding shark-tooth swords once donned heavy armor made from coconut fibers and human hair.

INSTITUT ROYAL DU PATRIMOINE ARTISTIQUE, BRUSSELS

Throughout the war Gilbertese civilians were forced to work for the occupying armies, first Japanese, then American. The great quantities of supplies brought in by the Americans so impressed the Gilbertese that a cargo cult soon materialized and delegations were sent to the U.S. military commanders requesting permanent American rule. This, of course, was denied, and several persistent petitioners were arrested. The British were not amused.

To Independence

The Gilbert and Ellice Islands Colony fell under the British colonial Western Pacific High Commission, until 1953 headquartered in Fiji, then in the Solomon Islands. In 1972 this administrative arrangement ended and the British resident commissioner on Tarawa became a governor responsible directly to London.

The first move toward self-government came in 1963 when the British appointed islanders to executive and advisory councils. In 1967 the Advisory Council was replaced by a House of Representatives with a majority of elected members. In 1971 this was expanded to a Legislative Council with greater powers. The creation of the post of chief minister and a House of Assembly in 1974 was the next significant advance.

That same year the Polynesian Ellice Islanders voted in a plebiscite to be administered separately from the Micronesian Gilbertese, and in 1975 an independent Tuvalu was born. Banaba attempted, unsuccessfully, to secede from the colony about the same time; the dispute still simmers. Even so the British granted full internal self-government to the Gilbert Islands in 1977.

Official independence followed on 12 July 1979. The British had timed this carefully to coincide with the playing out of the phosphate deposits on Banaba (the mine closed in 1980). With no other easy resources to exploit, and a growing, impoverished population, the British were more than happy to get out. Probably no other former British colony got such a lousy deal at independence; even Tuvalu had seceded from the Gilberts.

Dead marines strewn along the beach at Betio, 22 Nov. 1943: some 990 Americans died in the battle of Tarawa.

Also in 1979 the U.S. relinquished to the Republic of Kiribati all claim to the Phoenix and Line islands in a Treaty of Friendship, which specified that none will be used for military purposes by third parties without consultation. Kiribati didn't reach its present extent until 1982 when the country was able to buy Fanning and Washington atolls back from the transnational Burns Philp.

Government

The Republic of Kiribati has a 41-member Maneaba ni Maungatabu (House of Assembly), elected every four years. The speaker is not a member but an outsider chosen by the Maneaba. The Beretitenti (president) is elected by the people from among three or four candidates nominated by the Maneaba from its ranks. The Beretitenti chooses an eight-member cabinet from the Maneaba. Kiribati's first president, Ieremia Tabai, who served from independence in 1979 until his statutory retirement in 1991, worked hard to make his country self-reliant.

The main political parties are partly divided along religious lines, with Protestants in the ruling National Progressive Party and Catholics supporting the opposition Christian Democratic Party. The Liberal Party and the New Movement Party complete the scene. Many voters have vigorously opposed the creation of a defense force. Although government is

centralized at Bairiki on Tarawa, small administrative subcenters are run by district officers on Abemama, Beru, Butaritari, Christmas, and Tabiteuea.

ECONOMY

Cash Economy

Kiribati has a simple agricultural economy based on copra-making on the outer islands. Coconut Products Ltd. (Box 280, Tarawa) uses the copra to make coconut oil soap and cosmetics. In the Line Islands copra production is run by the government, while village cooperatives handle production in Tungaru. The large trading companies left the Gilberts during WW II and never returned.

Until 1980, phosphates from Banaba provided 80% of exports and over half the local tax revenue, plus several hundred jobs. Since the loss of this income, Kiribati has faced financial ruin. A trust fund of phosphate revenues accumulated between 1956 and 1980 is presently worth A$200 million and brings in about A$7 million a year in interest, however.

In 1989 Kiribati exported A$3.1 million worth of copra and A$2.7 million in fish. A record trade deficit of US$24 million was announced in 1990 with food imports alone contributing A$8.59 million to it.

When Queen Elizabeth II visited Kiribati for 24 hours in 1982 the British government paid Kiribati a handsome sum to prepare for the visit by painting all the houses along the road pink, among other absurdities, while cynically continuing to reduce aid grants. Aid from Britain has been replaced by development assistance from Australia (which also supplies most of Kiribati's imports), Japan, New Zealand, South Korea, and the European Community.

In 1989 a small garment factory opened on Betio (Tarawa) with South Korean aid, and a year later British aid was used to establish a small industrial center on Betio producing garments, footwear, and *kamaimai* (coconut molasses). Solar-evaporated salt production on Christmas Island reached 20,000 tons in 1986. The main market for the salt was expected to be fishing vessels using brine refrigeration systems.

In 1984 a trial seaweed farm on South Tarawa was declared successful and expanded to 200 hectares. In 1988, 70 metric tons of seaweed were produced and the project widened to Abaiang and other atolls. Seaweed farming has become more popular because it brings better returns for less work compared to copra, and in 1990 Kiribati exported a half million dollars worth of dried seaweed to Europe and Asia, where it is used in food emulsifiers and pharmaceuticals.

About 1,500 I-Kiribati are still employed in the phosphate operation on Nauru, but those jobs will disappear when Nauru's mines are worked out in about five years time. Remittances from I-Kiribati seamen serving on German ships are an important source of income for outer-island families, and some I-Kiribati are employed on South Korean trawlers licensed to fish within Kiribati's EEZ.

Sales of stamps to collectors by the post office's philatelic bureau (Box 494, Betio, Tarawa) bring in a little revenue. Package tourism is insignificant and unlikely to develop due to unreliable air service, lack of facilities, and competition from more accessible destinations. The only really hopeful sign for the economy is rich manganese nodules in the sea near the Line Islands, which could one day become a major source of income.

Fisheries

Kiribati's greatest resource is its EEZ, encompassing 3,550,000 square km of the richest fishing grounds in the Western Pacific. The A$2 million in annual royalties paid by about 300 South Korean, Taiwanese, Japanese, and American fishing vessels represents about 25% of the country's budget. Collecting fishing-license fees from the tight-fisted Americans has been a frustrating task. In 1987 the U.S. tuna boat MV *Tradition,* caught poaching in Kiribati waters, was ordered forfeit by the Kiribati High Court. The Kiribati government later sold the vessel back to its owners for US$1.5 million.

For many years Kiribati was unable to get a fair deal from California purse seiners working local waters because the U.S. considered tuna "migratory" and not subject to licensing fees. The Americans also refused to recognize the EEZ, although they claimed similar zones around their own shores. In Oct. 1985, to help the U.S. see things in better perspective, Kiribati signed an agreement giving the U.S.S.R. the right to operate 16 fishing boats in its EEZ that year for A$2.4 million. Although the Soviets agreed to stay outside the 12-mile territorial waters of Kiribati and not to land on any island, the mere specter of their presence led to a dramatic increase in U.S. and New Zealand aid to the country. In 1986 the Soviet-Kiribati fishing agreement was not renewed, and in April 1987 the U.S. government finally agreed to recognize the EEZs of 16 Pacific island states and pay regular licensing fees.

To ensure easy access to the EEZ for their 400 fishing boats, Japan provides Kiribati with millions of dollars in aid related to fisheries development. Eight Kiribati pole-and-line tuna-fishing boats based at Betio (Tarawa), belonging to the government-owned Te Mautari Ltd., transfer their frozen catch to a mother ship, which delivers the fish to canneries in American Samoa or Fiji. In 1990, however, this company declared bankruptcy, with a debt of A$7 million built up over three years—a situation blamed on poor management. Fish ponds, such as those near Tarawa Airport, are being developed to supply milkfish for use as bait.

Subsistence

Most I-Kiribati live from subsistence agriculture and fishing, and by collecting seafood from lagoon and reef. Small amounts of copra are made and seaweed is farmed to earn extra cash for essentials such as sugar, flour, cigarettes, kerosene, etc. Farmland is often divided into scattered mini-holdings and this, combined with a shortage of land, overpopulation, and a lack of services and opportunities, has led many to migrate to Tarawa, where the best jobs are concentrated.

Away from the South Tarawa conurbation of Betio-Bikenibeu, however, life moves at a deliberately sedate pace. Activities are directed toward securing the necessities of life (which are few), and no one exerts him/herself unnecessarily. Fishing, cooking, tending the *babai* (taro) pits, and socializing are the main preoccupations. The tranquility is disturbed only by the omnipresent motor scooter and the infrequent Air Tungaru plane. Outside of South Tarawa, only the government compound at Beru and the main settlement on Christmas Island have electricity. Because of the limited soil, the only vegetable which grows is taro, and this must be cultivated in deep organic pits. Coconuts, however, proliferate on all the islands (except some of the Phoenix Group), and the pandanus palm, breadfruit tree, banana, and papaya plants all provide food. Pigs and fowl are common, and fish plentiful, although in 1988-89 it was reported that the use of driftnets by South Korea, Taiwan, and Japan had seriously depleted tuna stocks.

THE PEOPLE

Of the 72,298 inhabitants of Kiribati, about a third live in South Tarawa, with half these on Betio and almost another half on the Bairiki-Bikenibeu strip. The other Tungaru atolls average 1,000-4,000 inhabitants each. The Phoenix and Line groups were never inhabited by Gilbertese; people have only inhabited them since the arrival of Europeans. To relieve the population pressure on South Tarawa the Kiribati government announced in 1989 that nearly 5,000 people would be resettled on outlying atolls, mainly in the Line Islands.

Between 1985 and 1990 the population grew at an annual rate of 2.24%, and 40% of the people are aged 14 or under. The northern atolls of Kiribati are predominantly Catholic, the southern mostly Protestant. The total population is 53% Catholic, 39% Protestant, 2% Seventh-Day Adventist, and 1½% Mormon. Over 2,000 I-Kiribati are on Nauru and overseas, and another 275 work aboard ships. Most of the 155 resident Europeans and 360 Tuvaluans live in South Tarawa.

The ribbonlike I-Kiribati villages stretch out along the lagoon side of the Tungaru atolls. Although thatched roofs still predominate, hot tin roofs are becoming popular because they require little maintenance and can be used as water catchments. The *maneaba,* a community meetinghouse, is the focal point of the village. Its huge, lofty thatched roof rests on low coral pillars with open sides. Place mats *(boti)* line the earthen floor, each belonging to a specified member of a clan or extended family *(ka-ainga)*. Intermarriage within a *ka-ainga* is not allowed, so an individual always has another family to turn to in case of domestic strife. Most I-Kiribati own land, and extreme poverty is normally unknown.

banana tree (Musa cavendishi)

LOUISE FOOTE

The I-Kiribati are excellent seamen and build large, swift, seagoing outriggers with canvas sails. To reverse direction one must lift the mast and sail and swing them around to the other end of the canoe. Pointed windward, the canoes are manned by the lightest men, who constantly shift their bodies to keep the outrigger skimming just above the surface of the water. Racers can exceed 16 knots, able to turn at great speeds. At night, smaller canoes can be seen netting flying fish by the light of dried-coconut-frond torches or kerosene lamps.

Language
English is understood by many on South Tarawa. It's also the official language, but once you leave Tarawa, only government officials and a few men are willing to speak English. Others are reticent, stemming perhaps from the custom of not being boastful or desirous of elevating oneself above others. Egalitarian society: if everyone present does not understand English, it's not used. This custom is pervasive, and it can occasionally be difficult to get I-Kiribati to speak English in group (especially family) situations. But also observing this custom, they do become more communicative in one-to-one situations with you.

English is taught in all schools, from primary through secondary levels, although the children quickly forget what they've been taught, mainly through lack of use. English is generally used in government departments and business, but not at home. Unless a child is being "groomed" for a government or business job later in life, the learning and maintenance of English isn't taken too seriously. However, they don't seem to have much trouble remembering those nasty four-letter words picked up from watching videos!

Kiribati is one of the Malayo-Polynesian group of the Austronesian family of languages, and it resembles many of the Micronesian languages as well as Polynesian. Pronunciation of Kiribati is divided into northern and southern Tungaru dialects. The northern dialect is used on Abemama,

an old photo of an I-Kiribati couple

Aranuka, Kuria, and all the islands northward, while the southern version applies on Nonouti, Beru, and the islands to the south. It's interesting to note that the northern dialect is also used on Mili atoll in the Marshalls and the southern dialect in the Line Islands and Nui in Tuvalu. On South Tarawa both dialects are used.

Both pronunciation and spelling are different. In the north the word for "one" is spelled *touana* while in the south it's *teuana*. "To sit" is *takataka* in the north and *tekateka* in the south. A few common words are entirely different: "satisfied" is *buu* in the north and *ngae* in the south. If you stay on an outer island long you'll soon pick up a few words and there's always someone willing to serve as your teacher. Kiribati has no letters "s" or "c" in their 13-letter alphabet, so "ti" is used for these and pronounced as an "s." Thus the word *otintaai* (sunrise) is pronounced "oh-SIN-tie."

Holidays And Events

The I-Kiribati are renowned dancers with flawless rhythm; the emphasis is on movement of the hands, head, and eyes, rather than the body or feet. A classical Kiribati dance is the *ruoia,* while the more vigorous *batere,* parts of which resemble a Samoan *siva,* was introduced from Tuvalu centuries ago. Children learn the technique early and practice all their lives. The *ruoia* was banned by the missionaries but it has made a comeback in recent years. It's said that *ruoia* composers had special powers and could inflict curses and spells through their songs and chants.

Traditional dancing is performed during Easter or Christmas, during Independence Days, or on special occasions such as when opening a new building, greeting special visitors, etc. Talcum powder may be sprinkled on the backs of the necks of guests and performers at these gatherings, as a gesture of appreciation. To maintain the purity of Kiribati dancing the Cultural Affairs Office has prohibited the performance of Polynesian dances such as the *tamure, hula,* and *siva* before tourists.

The young and middle-aged love to dance *"te tuitit"* (the twist). It's hard to believe that these fundamentally languid people could have such a passion for this energetic dance, yet they go absolutely nuts doing the twist. The four-stringed ukulele is the most common musical instrument. Just before dusk, youths often form a circle and attempt to keep a soccer ball in the air by kicking it with the side of the foot. Just as the ball is about to strike a foot, everyone claps simultaneously.

Independence Day (12 July) features a parade at the Bairiki National Stadium (Tarawa), traditional dancing, and canoe races. Interschool sports and dance contests are held on Youth Day (first Mon. in August). Other public holidays include New Year's Days (1 and 2 Jan.), Good Friday, Easter Monday, Independence Days (12, 13, 14 July), Human Rights Day (10 Dec.), and Christmas Days (25 and 26 December).

PRACTICALITIES

Conduct

Whenever you're outside South Tarawa, always have a supply of black stick tobacco and matchboxes to repay anyone who invites you in for a drink of toddy or a meal. In the morning, in addition to the tobacco and matches, a package of tea leaves and a tin of condensed milk should also be presented to any family you might happen to stay with, as this is a local custom and is happily accepted; in fact, it's the very least you can do to show your appreciation and respect. If you stay more than one night with the same family, check out the village trade store and purchase something more substantial to give them. Those staying over a week somewhere should contribute a large bag of rice. Spend at least what you figure your meals were worth, then a little more. *Te ga'am* (chewing gum) is popular with children and young adults. If you're invited to a meal at a *maneaba,* take a can of corned beef as your contribution.

Don't verbally admire an islander's possession or he/she may feel obligated to give it to you, a custom known as *bubuti.* I-Kiribati are naturally curious people who won't hesitate to ask your age, marital status, occupation, etc. Don't react as if they're invading your privacy, because they only want to know you better in order to feel more comfortable. Enlightening them about your country will be appreciated, and it's always handy to have photos of your family, home, workplace, etc., to show. Take care, however, of your rubber thongs (zories), even in a private home, as "borrowing" another person's pair is not considered a sin at all. Keep all your personal gear locked up in your bag, as sharing is customary among I-Kiribati families and the children may go through your things while you're out. Be careful too with your western time values, as the I-Kiribati are likely to be more relaxed and easygoing than you, something you'll no doubt experience in most Pacific islands.

In The *Maneaba*

When moving about in the *maneaba* it's proper to stoop. Never stand upright, especially in front of seated people. Maintaining a low profile is a sign of respect to the *unamane* (old men) and others present. It's also polite to back out of the *maneaba* when exiting; never turn your back on the occupants. It's considered disrespectful to place your hands on the beams and roof or to point with an outstretched finger or arm (the locals point with their head and a wrinkling of the nose).

While business is being discussed in a *maneaba* everyone sits cross-legged and it's considered disrespectful to sit with legs outstretched pointing toward someone. After the official "business" is over everyone relaxes and stretches out their legs, though it's still rude to step over someone's legs.

If a celebration or special event is in progress at a *maneaba,* you may be placed up front with the guests and dignitaries, even though you have nothing to do with what is occurring. You'll be expected to make a short speech as a formality. Someone will translate. Tell them why you've come and how you're enjoying their island. When driving past a *maneaba* in a car or motor scooter, it's polite to slow down if something's happening inside. Notice how the older men and women dismount from their bicycles when passing an occupied *maneaba.*

Accommodations

The only hotels are on Abemama, Abaiang, Christmas, and Tarawa—they're often fully booked. A five percent hotel tax is added to the bill.

Many of the Tungaru atolls have basic Island Council rest houses constructed from local materials, most charging $5-15 pp. Cooking facilities and mosquito nets are usually provided, and other amenities may consist of a wooden table and bench, outhouse toilet, washbasin, sleeping mat, and perhaps a chair. Toilet paper, towels, plates and cutlery, linen, beds, mattresses, shower, and a kerosene lamp may or *may not* be provided. Don't expect any luxuries whatever: these

facilities are for the convenience of visiting officials, not tourists.

To book a rest house send an urgent telegram to the council clerk of your chosen island, stating your estimated arrival time. Also mention if you require transportation from the airstrip. The Ministry of Home Affairs (Box 75, Bairiki, Tarawa; tel. 21-092) on Tarawa can be of assistance in making these arrangements. An alternative is just to hope the facility is available and make arrangements on arrival, but you could be out of luck. There are no rest houses on South Tarawa or Abemama.

Another possibility is to stay with the locals, but one must keep in mind that this means adapting to their way of doing things, including squatting on the beach to do your "daily business." Toilet paper is unobtainable on the outer islands, and visitors should also bring their own mosquito net and repellent, as these are often not found in local trade stores. Extra pillows and mattresses may also be lacking. Beware of unboiled water!

You could ask permission of a family to sleep in their *boti* (place) in the village *maneaba,* or ask for the church *maneaba.* If you've got a tent, get permission before you pitch it in a coconut grove or on a deserted beach, as all land is owned by someone. It's unlikely you'll be refused; in fact, you'll probably be invited to stay with the family. Village people don't like visitors to camp beside their homes, which confers a loss of face—they'll insist you stay in the house. If you think you'll be in this position, plan to repay their hospitality. Take along a few gift items such as T-shirts, colored cloth, or inexpensive wristwatches.

The first evening you spend in a private home neighbors will come to visit. As a guest you'll eat first, having the choice of the best food. Once you're finished, the men will be served. The women and children are the last to eat, and sometimes not much is left for them. Expect to sacrifice much of your privacy: custom dictates that members of your host family accompany you everywhere you go, and you'll seem rude if you resist. On

Sun. you'll be expected to accompany them to church—the wonderful singing will be your reward. In some churches the men sit separately from the women, and you'll realize why when the singing begins.

Food

Te babai (swamp taro) is cultivated in large pits below the water table; it's eaten either boiled or made into several different puddings. Breadfruit is a staple which is boiled or fried in butter; fried as chips, they make a terrific snack. Boiled pumpkin, papaya, and plantain are used to supplement the diet. The harsh, dry climate of most of the atolls limits the variety of produce. On the southern islands *te roro,* a wafer-like food made from the boiled fruit of the pandanus tree, tastes like dates. It's eaten with coconut cream spread on the surface. Formerly *te roro* was eaten only in the *maneaba.* Ripe pandanus fruit is dark yellow or orange, and sweet like pineapple.

A fantastic variety of fish can be caught in the lagoon or on the reef. You'll usually eat them fresh since there's no refrigeration, but salted or dried fish are also delicious. Crayfish, the tasty coconut crab, eels, and a couple of kinds of shellfish are also eaten. Unfortunately, the women only boil or fry them, which does little to enhance the flavor. Sea turtles are only consumed on special occasions.

As usual, rice is consumed in phenomenal quantities, and when possible, canned corned beef. The latter is substandard—too salty and fatty. The I-Kiribati go to great lengths to please foreigners (I-Matang); for example, the frequent serving of cold, uncooked corned beef from the can! Chickens, eggs *(buni-moa),* and pork are not popular foods. Remember that food and all the basics can be in short supply on the outer islands, due to erratic shipping and incompetence of the cooperatives. Take as much with you as you can.

Toddy

The drink of the islands is *te karewe* (sweet toddy), extracted from the coconut palm early in the morning and evening. The spathe of the tree is bound and cut, then the sap is collected in a coconut shell or bottle. It can be drunk immediately—not sweet, but very refreshing—or used in cooking. It's usually taken after meals and is even used to wean babies.

Te kamaimai, molasses extracted from boiled *karewe,* is great in rice; diluted with water it makes a pleasing drink called *te katete. Te kamaimai* mixed with grated coconut and coconut cream makes a tasty sweet called *kati ni ben. Te karewe* fermented three days becomes *te kaokioki* (sour toddy), a very smooth, potent drink. *Te kaokioki* can be readily obtained on most outer islands, and the color varies from a milky white to light brown.

A local sweet bread is made from *te kaokioki* yeast which is left in the sun to rise and cooked in an earthen oven. *Kabubu* is a mixture of toddy, pandanus, and grated coconut, dried in the sun and pounded, which can be stored for long periods.

Toddy-cutting is a male profession passed from father to son and the cutters are well respected in their village. In the 1990 census 1,638 I-Kiribati men listed their occupation as "tree workers," the high number in any occupational category. As they go about their business high up among the coconut palms they often sing Christian hymns or songs of praise for toddy, wives, girlfriends, lost loves, or even the adventures of the previous night. Said Robert Louis Stevenson, "They sing with a certain lustiness and Bacchic glee."

Visas

All visitors must have a passport and an onward ticket. Visa regulations are simple: nationals of countries which require a visa of I-Kiribati travelers must themselves possess a visa to visit Kiribati. Thus Americans, Australians, Dutch, French, Germans, Japanese, and New Zealanders (among others) must obtain a visa in advance at a British diplomatic mission.

The visa costs anywhere from A\$20 to £60 sterling (two photos required) and may be used anytime within three months of the date of issue. Kiribati has honorary consular offices in Auckland (New Zealand), Honolulu

(Hawaii), Leicester (England), Sydney (Australia), Seoul (South Korea), and Tokyo (Japan).

In Australia apply at any Australian passport office or contact Mr. Bill Franken, Consulate-General of Kiribati, 35 Dover Road, Rose Bay, Sydney, NSW 2029, Australia (tel. 371-7808). At this office visas cost A$20 and only one photo is required. In Hawaii contact Mr. William E. Paupe, Honorary Consul for Kiribati, Suite 503, 850 Richards St., Honolulu, HI 96813 U.S.A. (tel. 808-521-7703). For Californians it's the British Consulate-General, Suite 312, 3701 Wilshire Blvd., Los Angeles, CA 90010 U.S.A. (tel. 213-385-0252). In Japan it's Mr. Tokugoro Kuribayashi, Honorary Consul for Kiribati, Room 684, Marunouchi Building, 2-4-1 Marunouchi, Chiyoda-ku, Tokyo, Japan (tel. 03-201-3487). In Europe it's Mr. Maurice Chandler, Honorary Consul of Kiribati, Rutland House, 8 Brookhouse St., Leicester, LE2 0JB, England. Otherwise contact any British consulate or write: Principal Immigration Officer, Ministry of Foreign Affairs, Box 69, Bairiki, Tarawa. Visas are *sometimes* available upon arrival at the airport ($20).

Most British subjects and nationals of some European countries do not require visas. Among those who *do not* need a visa are nationals of Canada, Denmark, Fiji, Hong Kong, Iceland, India, Korea, Malaysia, Norway, Philippines, Samoa (both American and Western), Singapore, Solomon Islands, Spain, Sweden, Switzerland, Tonga, Tuvalu, and the United Kingdom (except Northern Ireland). Holders of passports issued in Guam and the Micronesian associated states may enter visa-free for 20 days. Those on prepaid package tours *may* be able to obtain their visas from immigration upon arrival. Check this with the tour operator.

Upon arrival you'll usually be granted a stay until the date of your onward flights, although you can ask for one month. Extensions are obtained from the Immigration Office at the Office of the Beretitenti, Bairiki, one month at a time for up to four months in any 12-month period (bring along your onward ticket). If you're on an outer island you must cable your request to this office in advance. Extensions are free. The officials may not be overly pleased with visitors living with the locals and may seek verification that you've been staying at a hotel or rest house.

Ports of entry for cruising yachts are Banaba, Tarawa (Betio), Fanning, and Christmas. At Tarawa yachts can obtain permission to cruise the outer islands of Tungaru but must return to Tarawa again to clear out of the country. Occasionally yachts en route to Majuro are allowed to stop at Butaritari without having to return to Tarawa.

Money And Measurements

Australian paper currency is used, although some Kiribati coins circulate. Beware of the Kiribati $1 coin—exactly the same size as the Australian 50-cent piece. Most prices in this chapter are in Australian dollars. It's usually impossible to change traveler's checks on the outer islands, so take enough cash in small-denomination banknotes. It's nearly impossible to change $50 and $100 bills on the outer islands. Don't expect to be able to use your credit cards in Kiribati, although the Bank of Kiribati accepts MasterCard for cash advances. Tipping is not practiced.

Take stamps to the outer islands if you want to post any mail from there; local post offices can be sold out of all values. Know how much to put on, too, as island postmasters are only familiar with local rates. Never mail anything from Kiribati by surface: it could be months until the next ship leaves! Even airmail takes well over a month to travel from Kiribati to North America.

The electric voltage is 240 volts, 50 cycles, and the Australian three-pin plug is used. On Tarawa both the metric and imperial measurement systems are in use, although distances are usually measured in kilometers.

Health

When walking about, be careful of the sun—coconut palms provide little continuous shade, and the white sand on the lagoon side creates a tremendous glare. Wear a broad-brimmed hat and sunglasses. Shirts with collars and long sleeves may be advisable.

There's no malaria in Kiribati, but outbreaks of dengue fever sometimes occur. After prolonged dry spells there are outbreaks of pinkeye, a form of conjunctivitis, on South Tarawa. This highly contagious eye infection is easily contacted through using the pillow or towel of another person, and during epidemics all medication is soon exhausted. Anyone contemplating staying with the locals should have a mosquito net and a shampoo for head lice.

With very few toilets in Kiribati, unless you're staying at a hotel or can find a government building with a bathroom chances are you'll have to squat on the beach with the locals. Toilet paper is scarce. The Tarawa lagoon looks inviting, but unacclimatized swimmers could get stomachaches. The overcrowding on South Tarawa has led to appalling sanitary conditions. Diarrhea and hepatitis are common, so take care with the water. Carry Lomotil and drink boiled water or coconut juice. Cholera, typhoid fever, tetanus, and immune globulin (for viral hepatitis A) vaccinations are recommended (but not mandatory).

Fish poisoning is also common in Kiribati. Take care with the small red ants common on South Tarawa as they have a nasty sting. Centipedes should also be treated with respect.

Information

Tourist brochures on the country (including whole sections copied from the 1985 edition of this book) are available from the Kiribati Visitors Bureau, Ministry of Natural Resource Development, Box 251, Bikenibeu, Tarawa (tel. 28-287; fax: 686-21-120). For information on Christmas Island, contact the Tourism Office, Ministry of Line and Phoenix Development, Christmas Island, Republic of Kiribati.

Topographical maps of Kiribati can be ordered from the Lands and Surveys Division, Box 7, Bairiki, Tarawa. A good selection of books on the country is available from the National Library, Box 6, Bairiki, Tarawa.

The bilingual newspaper *Te Uekera* (30 cents) is published twice a month by the Broadcasting and Publications Authority (Box 78, Bairiki, Tarawa).

Getting There

The easiest way to get to Kiribati is on **Air Nauru**, which flies Nauru-Tarawa (A$103) weekly. At Nauru there are weekly connections to Kosrae, Pohnpei, and Chuuk in the FSM. **Air Marshall Islands** also has a weekly flight Majuro-Tarawa-Funafuti-Fiji. Fares to Tarawa are US$170 from Majuro, 770 Fiji dollars from Fiji. The flight calls at Funafuti (Tuvalu) but in order to stop you must pay A$340 Tarawa-Funafuti, plus A$340 Funafuti-Fiji. Unless you're dead set on seeing Funafuti it's much cheaper to fly to/from Fiji via Nauru (A$301 total). AMI flights are often fully booked weeks ahead, so confirmed reservations are essential.

In Jan. 1992 **Air Tungaru Corporation** (Box 274, Bikenibeu, Tarawa; tel. 28-088; fax: 686-28-277) and Air Nauru launched a joint Nauru-Tarawa-Christmas-Honolulu weekly flight. Fares were set at US$299 Honolulu-Christmas, US$403 Honolulu-Tarawa. As this service is heavily subsidized by the Kiribati government it's unknown how long it will last, so check carefully before making any plans.

Getting Around By Air

Air Tungaru operates a subsidized domestic air service to all the Tungaru atolls. Each island is allotted a portion of the seats along the route, and every atoll gets at least one flight a week, some several. It's best to book all your flights before you leave Tarawa, although radio communication between the airstrips and Tarawa has improved recently. The Air Tungaru "office" on the outer islands usually operates out of the agent's attaché case when a flight is due in at the airstrip! Reconfirm your onward reservation with the local agent immediately upon arrival at an outer island. If you want to change your reservation, simply go to the airstrip when the next flight is due and ask the agent to radio in your request. At other times the radio shack is closed. You could also try forwarding written requests to Tarawa with the pilot. Plan your itinerary carefully, as it will be hard to make changes. Fares from Tarawa vary between A$28 (Maiana) and A$153 (Arorae), and some outer islands levy a $1 airstrip departure tax. The baggage allowance is 15 kilos. Be prepared for schedule irregularities and canceled flights.

Getting Around By Sea

The **Shipping Corporation of Kiribati** (Box 495, Betio, Tarawa; tel. 26-195) at Betio harbor has five cargo/passenger ships which service the outer islands of Tungaru about every two weeks. Every two or three months trips are made to Kanton and the Line Islands. Fares range from $11 deck to Abaiang up to $123 deck to Christmas Island. Cabins (when available) are double fare, but the meals are better than deck class. Since these ships are always at sea two or three days longer than scheduled, it works out as a good value. Every two months there are sailings to Fiji ($94 deck OW, meals included, eight days). The only way to find out about these services is to personally go to the upstairs office at Betio: don't trust local gossip!

MATS Shipping and Transport (Box 413, Betio; tel. 26-355) in Betio runs their copra boat, the *MATS-1*, to the outer islands every couple of weeks, with occasional voyages to Christmas Island, Fanning, Washington, Fiji, and Majuro. Fares are similar to those charged by the Shipping Corporation. Another possibility is **Waysang Kum Kee** (tel. 21-036) at Bairiki, whose converted fishing boat also plies Tungaru. He charges slightly higher fares but his boat is also faster. **Compass Rose Enterprises** (tel. 26-305) is also worth a try.

Baurua (large twin-sailed catamarans) travel between Tarawa and Abaiang ($6 OW) two or three times a week; visitors can arrange to go along by asking at the harbor at Betio. Also ask about a boat to Abaiang at Borata's Club in Bairiki.

A final possibility is to try traveling as unpaid crew on a cruising yacht. Most private yachts sail north from Fiji and Tuvalu to Tarawa, then continue on to Majuro. From Tarawa to Hawaii is a long haul. As yachts are required to clear customs at Betio on both the inward and outward journeys, you may be lucky enough to be accepted for a cruise around the Tungaru atolls. Be prepared to do your share of the work and contribute a per diem toward costs. Yachts anchor in the lagoon just off Betio and the only way to get on is to convince a captain you're a hand worth having aboard.

Others

On the outer islands, ask the Island Council clerk if he knows of anyone who might be willing to rent you a motorbike (te rebwe-rebwe). If you can borrow a bicycle (te batika), you've got great and leisurely local transportation, and a barrier-free way of meeting people. Otherwise bring your own. George Kum Kee at the Kiribati Hotel on Betio sells bicycles, and he'll probably agree to buy it back from you later. Walking is also good.

Airport

Bonriki Airport (TRW) is five km northeast of Bikenibeu on Tarawa. The airport bus to the Otintaai Hotel costs $2 pp, or wait for a public bus in front of the terminal. When returning to the airport from Betio or Bairiki by public bus, allow at least 1½ hours traveling time. A small snack bar and a souvenir shop open for international flights. The airport tax is $5 on international flights.

TARAWA

Tarawa atoll, just 130 km north of the equator, is the main center of the Tungaru group and capital of Kiribati. Most of the people live along the bottom side of this huge open triangle of long, low islands facing a jade green lagoon. A single passage pierces the barrier reef along Tarawa's west flank, the route for contemporary shipping and a wartime American invasion force.

Continuous ribbon development is apparent all along the 24-km lagoon-side road from Bonriki to Betio. Most of the structures are traditional, save for pockets of European-style buildings in the larger villages and the government complexes at Bikenibeu and Bairiki. The most important government offices are at Bairiki, though the health and education facilities are at Bikenibeu and communications at Betio. The government departments of agriculture and fisheries are on Tanaea Island, just northwest of the airport. Densely populated Betio is the heart of

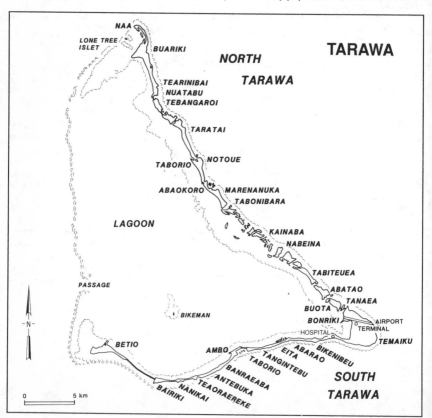

Kiribati. It has stores, bars, war relics, and the port where the fishing and shipping industries are centered: affluence as well as squalor.

Overcrowding is common in South Tarawa, where the population has increased fifteen-fold since the war. South Tarawa residents collect about three-quarters of the total cash income in the country, which explains the continuing influx of outer islanders toward the "bright lights." Along with the population explosion, South Tarawa is experiencing a religious explosion: successive missions, churches, and theological colleges of every sect and denomination are evident along the road from the airport to Betio.

The four-km, A$10-million Nippon Causeway, built with Japanese aid, opened in June 1987 connecting Betio to the rest of South Tarawa. The construction of causeways between the islands of South Tarawa may be convenient for getting around, but a serious pollution problem has developed as wastes accumulate in the murky, cut-off waters of the lagoon. Local fishermen complain that the causeways choke the lagoon and cause formerly clear passages to silt up. The use of large quantities of coral rock and sand to build the causeways also disrupts the ecology of reef and lagoon, and leads to fast erosion. Still, there's nice swimming under the Betio causeway bridge when the tide's coming in. As of 1991 there were still no causeways north of Tanaea, though plans exist to link all the remaining islands once outside funding is obtained. Meanwhile it's still fun to wade to the north tip of Tarawa at low tide. To really see Kiribati life, you have to get out of South Tarawa.

SIGHTS

Betio

In 1943, over 4,000 Japanese soldiers on Betio were sheltered underground in concrete blockhouses with walls 1½ meters thick, reinforced by palm trees and steel rails, roofed by a three-meter blanket of sand and coral. Facing the U.S. Marines, who landed on 20 Nov. 1943, was a solid wall of enemy gunfire coming from inside these pillboxes.

Today you can visit the four eight-inch **Japanese coastal defense guns** at the southeast and southwest ends of Betio. One of the guns has collapsed and is now half-buried in the sand, another was restored in 1989. These guns bear British markings but were sold to Japan in 1904, *not* captured at Singapore as some assert.

A series of bunkers, dugouts, and trenches is found along the ocean side of the island, where the Japanese expected the landings, but the Americans came ashore on the northern and western beaches. About 20 rusting **landing vehicles** (LVT), visible at low tide, still lie stalled on the reef where they got bogged down in 1943 due to a miscalculation of the tides. All that remains of them today is rusting engines and broken tracks. A relatively intact Sherman tank may be visited at low tide on the beach just west of Betio hospital.

The two-story **concrete bunker** of Rear Admiral Keiji Shibasaki was captured only after a fierce struggle. Even a direct hit from an American warship just offshore failed to shatter the bullet-pocked walls. In 1989 it was announced the bunker would be made into a war museum, but as yet nothing has been done. Even without any displays it would be a major point of interest if the locals didn't use it as an outhouse—the stench is almost unbearable. Another large bunker containing the remains of an electric generator is behind the Betio police station between here and the port. Spent cartridges are scattered about.

On the south side of Betio, surrounded by smashed cement bunkers and fallen guns, is the local cemetery, with a simple **memorial** to the 22 British coastwatchers beheaded here by the Japanese. Their epitaph reads, "Standing unarmed to their posts they matched brutality with gallantry, and met death with fortitude." Beware of the drunks sleeping on the graves.

The **Marine Training Center**, also on Betio, is partially financed by German shipping companies, which train young islanders to man their vessels. This excellent program has given hundreds of I-Kiribati an opportu-

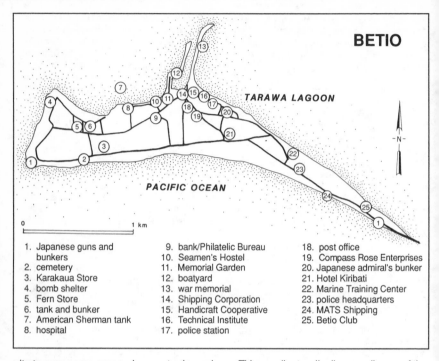

BETIO

TARAWA LAGOON

PACIFIC OCEAN

- N -

0   1 km

1. Japanese guns and
   bunkers
2. cemetery
3. Karakaua Store
4. bomb shelter
5. Fern Store
6. tank and bunker
7. American Sherman tank
8. hospital
9. bank/Philatelic Bureau
10. Seamen's Hostel
11. Memorial Garden
12. boatyard
13. war memorial
14. Shipping Corporation
15. Handicraft Cooperative
16. Technical Institute
17. police station
18. post office
19. Compass Rose Enterprises
20. Japanese admiral's bunker
21. Hotel Kiribati
22. Marine Training Center
23. police headquarters
24. MATS Shipping
25. Betio Club

nity to earn some money, learn a trade, and see a bit of the world. Some of the buildings of the school are vintage WW II American—note the Japanese bunker converted into a squash court.

To North Tarawa

The South Tarawa bus service extends from Betio to Tanaea, just beyond the airport. A bridge links Tanaea to Buota Island (good swimming in the channel), and from Buota it's easy to wade northward at low tide through the knee-deep water, across passages separating the string of reef islands as far as Tabonibara. There, another continuous coral road begins, and you can walk right to Naa at the atoll's northern tip without getting your feet wet again. A few trucks ply irregularly between Abaokoro and Buariki, or charter a minibus for the trip for about $10 a group.

This excellent walk allows a glimpse of the real Kiribati, especially in villages such as Nabeina and Kainaba. There's a Catholic mission at Taborio. Set out from Buota three hours prior to low tide. You could camp on uninhabited islands, stop at the rest house in Abaokoro, or sleep in a village *maneaba*. Be prepared to sing or give a speech for your supper! An unreliable launch runs back to South Tarawa approximately twice a week from Buariki and Tearinibai ($4 pp), or just walk back. This trip is the perfect way to spend a couple of extra days on Tarawa and meet some friendly people in the bargain.

In 1991 the Kiribati government announced plans to build causeways linking South Tarawa to North Tarawa, so traveling conditions could have changed. At last report large trucks could already drive all the way north at low tide. North Tarawa is also to be connected to the electricity grid.

PRACTICALITIES

Accommodations

The **Otintaai Hotel** (Borerei T. Uriam, Box 270, Tarawa; tel. 28-084), on the lagoon at Bikenibeu, was totally renovated in 1989 to accommodate the South Pacific Forum meeting that year, and there are now 40 a/c rooms with fridge and fan at $60 s, $70 d in the refurbished east wing or $70 s, $80 d in the new west wing, continental breakfast included. Airport transfers are $2 pp each way. The Otintaai has a large indoor/outdoor restaurant facing the lagoon. The food tends to be good, though the waiters sometimes mix up their orders at busy times. The Wed. evening barbecue is $9 and sometimes there's traditional dancing (ask).

A new place to stay is the **Tarawa Motel** (Baakoa Ieremia, Box 59, Bairiki, Tarawa; tel. 21-445), near the Stewart Club by the ocean at Ambo. The four rooms with clean, shared bath and cooking facilities go for $35 s or d. Long-term rates are negotiable. Baakoa runs a small store out front.

Mary's Hotel (Mary Teanako, Box 12, Bairiki, Tarawa; tel. 21-164) is a neat, two-story, concrete-block building near the landing at Bairiki. The three a/c rooms with private bath and fridge are $40 s, $48 d, whereas the one room without a/c goes for $32 s, $38 d. Meals in the restaurant downstairs are $5 and up, and airport transfers in the hotel van cost $7 pp. The walls are rather thin, so a lot depends on who your neighbors are.

The **Kiribati Hotel** (George Kum Kee, Box 462, Tarawa; tel. 26-048) on Betio charges a bit less than the Otintaai for its 10 a/c rooms with bath ($50 s, $60 d), but the facilities aren't as good and it can get noisy. You do get to observe the local life-style, however, and it's nearer the sightseeing, stores, nightlife, and ships to the other atolls. Ask George about renting a bicycle, moped, or car. Airport transfers are not provided. An expensive Chinese restaurant, rowdy bar, and beer garden are on the premises. Beware of getting shortchanged at the cash register if you eat here.

"Good-time" girls often frequent the bar and on payday the place is full of drunks. Watch for the large rat that often runs along the windowsill behind the bar!

Jong Kum Kee Brothers, opposite the Co-op in Betio, offers two a/c rooms with private bath adjacent to their restaurant upstairs for $50 s or d. Unfortunately it's right next to the Paradise Club and on weekends the noise is deafening.

The **Seamens Hostel** (Box 478, Betio; tel. 26-133), near the wharf at Betio, has 10 guest rooms with fan at $20 pp. Yachties get a reduced rate of $10 pp, and those who choose to stay on their boat get free showers and use of the facilities. The rooms are in one block with four shared toilets and showers (dirty).

Budget travelers can do no better than the **Tarawa Youth Hostel**, run by Mr. Biteti Tentoa at Antebuka opposite Tarawa Motors, the Toyota agency. The charge is $15 pp with all meals (mostly fish), or $10 pp without meals. The hostel has been under construction for several years and the toilet facilities are primitive, but Biteti (pronounced BEE-tis) is a most attentive host who more than makes up for any material shortcomings. Once the leader of an I-Kiribati dance group, Biteti became a furious Seventh-Day Adventist in May 1987 and gave up dancing. He'll still direct you to other dancers, though. He'll also teach you how to sail the *te wa* (outrigger) and arrange for someone to take you fishing or out into the lagoon collecting shellfish at night. Biteti has relatives on Nonouti and Kuria atolls, and he'll gladly arrange for you to stay with them ($5 pp without meals), if you like. (A reader, Kik Velt, wrote, "Visiting Kuria was one of the most rewarding experiences I have had in the Pacific.")

For a longer stay, contact the housing department at one of the town councils on South Tarawa for houses to rent by the month (about $500 for up to six people). Even if they don't have any available at the moment, someone working in the office may overhear your request and come forward offering private accommodations.

Food

The local expats dine on Chinese and European food at the **Tarawa Restaurant** (tel. 28-018), on the lagoon side at Bikenibeu. The Chinese food at **Susie's Restaurant**, at the end of the causeway in Bairiki, is also good, though there sometimes isn't enough of it on your plate. **Borata's Store**, also at Bairiki, serves plates of cold rice and fish for $1.50, plus tea or Milo for another 30 cents.

The restaurant atop **Jong Kum Kee Brothers** store, opposite the Co-op in downtown Betio, is quite pleasant although the service is often erratic. The Chinese restaurant across the street from the Co-op is also worth a try and the beer here is always cold. The snack bar in the supermarket is cheap and has a jukebox.

For lunch weekdays watch for the women with pushcarts dispensing fish and rice with tea or *kamaimai* ($1.50) opposite the library in Bairiki or around the high court offices in Betio. Throngs of hungry office workers congregate here, and beggar dogs take care of the leftovers. If you have access to cooking facilities, fresh fish can always be purchased at the outdoor market in Betio or from vendors outside the Co-op in Bairiki. In the evening many stores sell fresh donuts for 20 cents—**Karakaua Store** near the cemetery at Betio is said to have the best.

Entertainment

Two groups of traditional dancers practice on Betio, though it takes investigating and luck to get to see them. If someone tells you about "dancing," be sure to clarify if it's traditional I-Kiribati or modern disco dancing—otherwise you could be in for a surprise!

The expat clubs at Betio, Bairiki, and Ambo sometimes have film nights and dances (cover charge). Honorary membership at one of these is about $2 and the beer is inexpensive. The **Betio Club** has tennis courts. The **Bairiki Club** has the best chips in town and complete lunches for $2-4. (If you need someone to sign you in, ask for Peter Jackson.) This is a good place to meet some colorful expats and locals, the beer is cold, and there are darts, snooker, and pool.

The **Ambo Club** is the last bastion of the expat era though standards are fast declining as more jobs are localized. You ought to come respectably dressed. Monday at 1930 there are movies ($2), Fri. at 1830 a barbecue ($5—bring your own meat and eating utensils). Darts, snooker, and table tennis competitions are also on Fri. night. If you visit during the day there'll only be Erote, the I-Kiribati caretaker, present, but he'll fill you in on what's happening. The beach here is good at high tide. The **Stewart Club**, also at Ambo, is predominantly I-Kiribati, and they have dances on Fri. and Sat. nights.

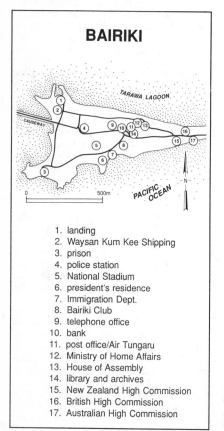

BAIRIKI

1. landing
2. Waysan Kum Kee Shipping
3. prison
4. police station
5. National Stadium
6. president's residence
7. Immigration Dept.
8. Bairiki Club
9. telephone office
10. bank
11. post office/Air Tungaru
12. Ministry of Home Affairs
13. House of Assembly
14. library and archives
15. New Zealand High Commission
16. British High Commission
17. Australian High Commission

The hottest nightlife unfolds in the bars of Betio where the sailors gather. **Club Paradise** next to the Bank of Kiribati is a fight a minute but worth checking out provided you go with locals. During "island nights" on Fri. and Sat. they have live bands and everybody gets drunk and fights. Not recommended for unescorted female visitors! The **Nikon Bonn Club** opposite the roundabout in Betio is okay for a quiet drink during the day but at night it seems to attract drunks who have been thrown out of the other bars. Beware of shortchanging by the bar girls here. The **Seamens Club** has live music on Friday night.

Most *maneaba* show kung fu or Rambo-style movies or videos in the evening ($1.20). Bring your own mat and insect repellent. Each village has a large billboard hanging from a tree adjacent to the road, advertising forthcoming attractions.

Soccer matches take place most evenings at the Betio police headquarters games field or the stadium at Bairiki, and you'll be welcome to join in if you're able. In the villages volleyball matches with "boys" versus "girls" also occur most evenings, and if you hang around watching too long you're certain to be asked to play. They'll be thrilled to have you on the team and it's great fun.

On weekends the young and young at heart race model outrigger canoes with plastic sails down the beaches at high tide. Look for these at Taborio, near the small causeway at Teaoraereke, or at Nanikai. You'll be amazed how fast they go when the breeze is right.

Shopping

Several cooperative stores have limited selections at Bikenibeu and Bairiki; and some better, cheaper ones are at Betio. Prices for the same items vary a lot. The AMS stores at Bairiki and Betio and Fern Store at Betio offer some of the best prices. When buying mosquito coils check to see that they aren't broken, and inspect the packaging of biscuits carefully as they're often infested with weevils. Avoid plastic-wrapped cheese unless it's clearly dated. Every village and housing agglomeration has a small store selling tobacco, matches, kerosene, corned beef, rice, flour, beef drippings, tinned butter, sterile milk, etc. Stock up on *te rauara,* black "twist" tobacco, finely grated and rolled in pandanus leaf (20 cents each).

It's safer to bring all your own film as the supply here is variable and it's often expired. Causeway Traders in Betio and Chinese shops often have color print film. Business hours are 0830-1200/1300-1600 weekdays, though many stores remain open during lunch hour and for reduced hours on weekends. The **Philatelic Bureau** above the bank branch on Betio sells Kiribati postage stamps—excellent gifts or souvenirs.

Several places sell handicrafts at Bikenibeu, including the gift shop at the Otintaai Hotel (inflated prices), the **Cooperative Society** and **Girl Guide** shops across from the police station, and the **Women's Federation** shop, just a few hundred meters farther down the road. The hours are irregular, so just keep trying. Sleeping mats, sun hats, baskets, and fans are good buys. And check these shops regularly as new items are always coming in. Most of Kiribati crafts are related to day-to-day usefulness, such as woven mats and thatch. There's no pottery or woodcarving (except model canoes). On the outer islands, the co-op stores display items made by I-Kiribati families. Artifacts over 30 years old and traditional tools cannot be taken out of the country.

Services

The Bank of Kiribati (a joint venture with Australia's Westpac Banking Corporation) operates branches on Tarawa at Bikenibeu, at Bairiki, and Betio, all open weekdays from 0900 to 1400. They give a poor rate for anything other than Australian or U.S. dollars, but they are the only places to change traveler's checks in Tungaru.

Bikenibeu, Bairiki, and Betio have post offices. When picking up general delivery mail, check under your first initial as well as your surname. Cables, telexes, and long-distance calls can be placed at the Telecommunications Office beside the bank at Bairiki, at the Ministry of Communications next to Betio

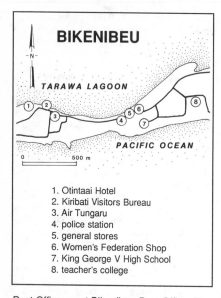

BIKENIBEU

-N-

TARAWA LAGOON

PACIFIC OCEAN

0   500 m

1. Otintaai Hotel
2. Kiribati Visitors Bureau
3. Air Tungaru
4. police station
5. general stores
6. Women's Federation Shop
7. King George V High School
8. teacher's college

Post Office, or at Bikenibeu Post Office. The charge is $18 for three minutes to Europe or the U.S., $9 to Australia, New Zealand, and the Pacific islands.

Immigration is at the Office of the Beretitenti in Bairiki. Australia, China, Korea, New Zealand, and the United Kingdom maintain diplomatic missions on Tarawa.

The new Japanese-funded Tungaru Central Hospital (tel. 28-081), between the airport and Bikenibeu, and the branch hospital at Betio offer free medical service, although medical supplies are limited.

Warning
The South Tarawa strip from Betio to Bikenibeu is experiencing a crime wave of sorts in the form of burglaries by unemployed youths in search of money with which to buy beer. Drunks are becoming an increasing nuisance and domestic violence and vandalism are growing, a sure sign that Western "civilization" is taking hold. Clothes hung out to dry are often stolen from the line. The police are slow to react and not much help in retrieving lost property. Tarawa is still a safe place to visit; just keep an eye on your gear. Village elders and the church blame all this on the impact of videos, which make money seem more important than traditional values. These problems haven't reached the outer islands yet where the family unit is very solid.

Information
The Kiribati Visitors Bureau office (tel. 28-287) is across the road from the Air Tungaru headquarters in Bikenibeu. The receptionists at the Otintaai Hotel are very helpful.

Tourist information is also dispensed at the Ministry of Natural Resources and Development above the post office at Bairiki. The National Library and Archives at Bairiki stocks the latest magazines and newspapers. The library also sells some interesting books on Kiribati. The Lands and Surveys office above the archives has excellent colored maps of most of the islands.

The student bookshop in the forecourt area of the Catholic mission at Teaoraereke has a comprehensive Kiribati dictionary ($3.50). The University of the South Pacific Center is also at Teaoraereke. Visit the bookstore at King George V School, Bikenibeu, for books on the country and Kiribati grammars.

Radio Kiribati's powerful 10 kilowatt transmitter broadcasts from Tarawa seven hours a day over the 846 kHz AM band. These same programs are relayed over 14917 kHz in the Line Islands.

GETTING AROUND

By Road
Bus stops are indicated by black and white stripes painted on coconut trees. You can also flag them down anywhere along the road, provided they're not full. When you want out, just shout *kai*. Although buses are supposed to run between Bonriki and Betio every 15 minutes, you can wait five minutes or more than an hour. Sometimes four or five buses arrive simultaneously, or they might be nicely staggered, or there may be none for excruciatingly long periods of time. At rush hours (0730-0830, 1330-1430, and 1630-

1700) they're often overcrowded with workers and schoolchildren—it's not uncommon to see passengers hanging out of a jam-packed bus. They run daily 0600-2000 and the fare is about $1.20 for the longest trip (Betio-Tanaea). On Betio there's a 30 cents flat fare. You pay the conductor—the person with the money box on his/her lap. Unmetered taxis are also available, though much more expensive than the buses. If you take a taxi for the day, agree on the price beforehand (write it down).

Others
The **Air Tungaru** office (tel. 28-088) in Bairiki handles international bookings; other offices handling domestic flights are at Bikenibeu and Betio.

Tuesday and Sat. catch a launch to North Tarawa ($4). You can also rent a small launch from people at the wharf in Betio for about $5 an hour with driver. Bikeman, a small islet in the lagoon, is a popular destination for picnics.

The Otintaai Hotel rents cars and motorbikes. Several other companies rent cars at about $40 a day with unlimited kilometers, or $25 a day plus 20 cents a kilometer. When available, insurance is about $10 extra. The Visitors Bureau has a list of car rental companies and may offer to call around to help you find a car. A foreign driver's license is valid on Tarawa for two weeks, and driving is on the left. Beware of speed humps.

Scuba divers should bring all their own equipment as there's still no dive shop on Tarawa. Privately owned compressors do exist, and a good place to inquire about both diving and sportfishing is Betio Hardware (tel. 26-130) in Betio.

OTHER ISLANDS OF TUNGARU

Abaiang
Abaiang, 51 km north of South Tarawa, is the most easily accessible outer island, with Air Tungaru flights three times a week ($29). The Island Council truck often meets the flights. A more exciting way to come would be on the Island Council *baurua* (catamaran canoe), which departs Betio on Tarawa two or three times a week, a very pleasant three-hour journey in good weather. Fishing canoes sometimes cross the narrow passage between Buariki on North Tarawa and Tabontebike on Abaiang.

In 1989 the Island Council built four traditional thatched guest bungalows ($30 pp) at Tabontebike village near the southern tip of the atoll. The bungalows are quite comfortable with mosquito nets provided, but toilet and washing facilities are shared. Fishing and snorkeling off an outrigger canoe and trips to uninhabited Teirio island are arranged, and traditional dancing is staged for groups. Local meals are served. For reservations call the Abaiang Island Council clerk from South Tarawa.

An older rest house is at Taburao, a few km north of the airstrip. At Koinawa, farther north, is an old Catholic church with a tower. Ask permission to climb up for the view. Heavily populated, villages are squished together all the way up the thin strip of land along the

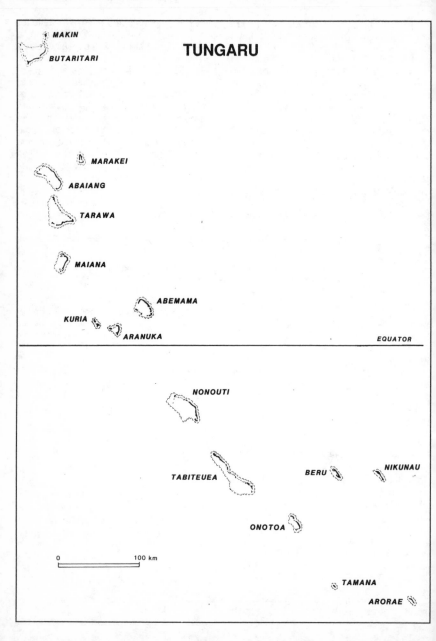

TUNGARU

MAKIN

BUTARITARI

MARAKEI

ABAIANG

TARAWA

MAIANA

ABEMAMA

KURIA

ARANUKA

EQUATOR

NONOUTI

TABITEUEA

BERU

NIKUNAU

ONOTOA

0   100 km

TAMANA

ARORAE

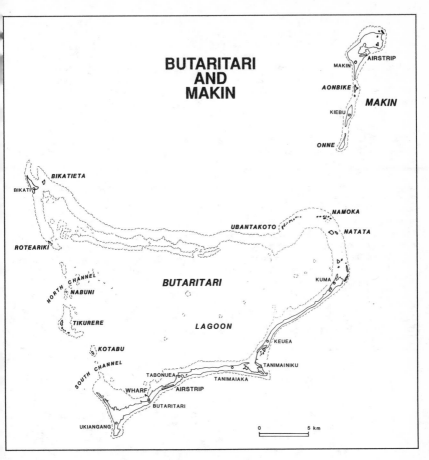

BUTARITARI AND MAKIN

lagoon's east side. Abaiang sour toddy has a distinct flavor. In 1991 Teatao Teannaki from Abaiang was elected president of Kiribati.

Marakei

Marakei has an enclosed interior lagoon; two passages connect it to the sea at high tide, but at low tide it's entirely landlocked. It's customary for visitors to travel counterclockwise around Marakei (27 km) immediately upon arrival. The airstrip is at the north end of the atoll, not far from Rawannawi village, which has the rest house.

Butaritari

Due to the regular rainfall, Butaritari is a very green island. The abundant vegetation and foods are in striking contrast with the dry, parched islands to the south. Butaritari is well known for its flavorful bananas, large quantities of which are shipped to South Tarawa. A causeway joins the two larger portions of the atoll, making it possible to walk the 30 km from Ukiangang to Kuma. At Kuma, near the east end of Butaritari, men call dolphins from the sea.

Butaritari has had long contact with Europeans; the first permanent European trading post in Tungaru was established here in 1846. At one time during the 19th century 20 traders operated on the atoll. Many Western-style buildings remain today, intermingling with Chinese and local architectural styles. Americans and Japanese fought several battles here during WW II, and rusted pillboxes still mar the island. The skeleton of a **Japanese seaplane** (minus wings and tail) lies beside the lagoon, opposite the small hospital in Butaritari village.

There's good anchorage for ships in the lagoon. Father Gratien Bermond, the Catholic priest in Butaritari village, also runs a small two-room **guesthouse** ($15 pp including all meals). There's a co-op and numerous privately owned shops on the island. Take care with the water on Butaritari, and always wear thongs, as the wetter climate encourages parasitic hookworms, etc. Air Tungaru flies to Butaritari three times a week ($61).

Makin

Butaritari's near neighbor, Makin, is the northernmost Tungaru island, 190 km north of Tarawa. (Formerly, Butaritari was known as Makin and the present Makin was "Little Makin.") Tradition holds that the spirits of dead I-Kiribati pass this way on their journey to hell or paradise. Nakaa, the Watcher-at-the-Gate, waits at the northern end of Makin to catch the dead in his net. The rest house is at Makin village, south of the airstrip.

Kuria

Kuria consists of a pair of triangular islands connected by a causeway; the airstrip and rest house (at Buariki) are on the southern one. Kuria has a fringing reef but no central lagoon. Near the north tip of the island are remnants of a former whale station. Air Tungaru flies from Tarawa to Kuria on Mon. and Wed. ($48 OW).

Abemama

Abemama (Island of Moonlight), just north of the equator 152 km southeast of Tarawa, is a crescent-shaped atoll with a lagoon on its west side. No outlying shoals or reefs skirt the island, and two passages give access to an excellent anchorage. There's good snorkeling here, if you don't mind the company of a few black-tipped sharks.

Transportation on Abemama consists of three trucks, one based at Tabaiang near the airstrip, one at Kariatebike, and the last at Manoku. At least one of them meets the plane. They're often hired by groups of people to transport their copra, thus temporarily terminating public service. You may also be able to hitch a ride on the government tractor-trailer or a local motorbike. Kariatebike is the government center with a small hospital, administrative building, police station, and co-op. Causeways have been built linking Kariatebike to the islets south, making it possible to drive all the way to Kabangaki.

Near Tabontebike, north of the Catholic *maneaba,* is the tomb of the tyrant chief Tem Binoka. Robert Louis Stevenson, who lived just north of Kariatebike for several months in 1889, made Tem Binoka famous (read *In The South Seas*). War relics on Abemama include the airstrip at the north end of the atoll and a wrecked Corsair fighter aircraft set up in front of the hotel.

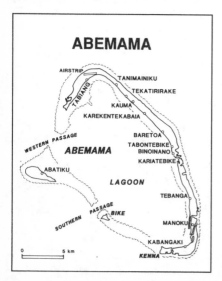

ABEMAMA

AIRSTRIP
TABIANG
TANIMAINIKU
TEKATIRIRAKE
KAUMA
KAREKENTEKABAIA
WESTERN PASSAGE
BARETOA
TABONTEBIKE
ABEMAMA
BINOINANO
KARIATEBIKE
ABATIKU
LAGOON
TEBANGA
PASSAGE
BIKE
SOUTHERN
MANOKU
KABANGAKI
0   5 km
KENNA

The **Robert Louis Stevenson Hotel** at Kariatebike has six thatched bungalows ($30 pp daily for bed and breakfast). A room with shared bath is $25. The three-course dinner at the hotel is $8.50. Irish manager Brian Orme is a colorful island character who came to Kiribati many years ago after a spell on Nauru. He'll keep you entertained with many a yarn about island life and local politics. Airport pickups are $5—radio ahead to announce your arrival. On Tarawa ask at Compass Rose Enterprises on Betio, which is in regular radio contact with Brian. Unfortunately the RLS is slowly falling into disrepair and Brian lacks the capital required to make improvements.

Not far from the RLS, Henry Schutz has five rooms built from local materials beside his store. Henry also owns the Causeway Traders store under the Nikon Boon Club opposite the roundabout on Betio (Tarawa), so that's where to ask.

Traditional dancing is popular and there are groups at most villages. A Chinese shopkeeper has a portable generator with which he runs a projector. He tours the villages, doing the circuit every two weeks or so: 20-50 cents for kung fu and Rambo-style movies. Mosquitos swarm on Abemama at nighttime; hordes of flies arrive by day—both a result of so many *babai* pits. Abemama is also the most productive copra island in Tungaru, although seaweed farming has recently been introduced.

Air Tungaru flies to Abemama three or four times a week ($45), but the flights are often full. After heavy rains the journey from Kariatebike to the airport can be very slow due to potholes and water on the road, so allow extra time when leaving. The island council charges a local airport departure tax of $1.

Nonouti

The Government Rest House at Matang, four km south of the airstrip, faces the ocean and is cooled by the prevailing winds. The manager can provide food, if you need it. Nearby are a post office, a couple of small shops, and a local hospital with a nurse. The cooperative store is located at the government wharf at Aubeangai, just south of Matang. One bus, if running, provides an erratic, unscheduled service the length of the road—two trips each way daily; there's also a government tractor-trailer. Most people travel by motor scooter.

Visit Kiribati's largest *maneaba* at Umantewenei village. The Makauro *maneaba* is the oldest on Nonouti; visitors traditionally spent their first night on the island here, although this practice is no longer universally followed. A monument in the form of a ship at Taboiaki village recalls the arrival of the first Catholic missionaries to Tungaru in 1888. At the northern extremity of the atoll are several small islets, accessible by boat, where large numbers of seabirds nest; inquire at the council offices for a visit. Kiribati's first president, Ieremia Tabai, hails from Temotu village on Nonouti.

Tabiteuea

The name Tabiteuea means "Forbidden to Kings"—a society in which kings are forbidden, a system different to all the other islands. Fences erected around the houses delineated private property. If anyone entered without first seeking the owner's permission (i.e., by calling out), they could be attacked or punished. One can still see vestiges of this in the well-maintained flower gardens surrounding the houses, and in the more evident retention of fences. At one time theft was deemed a more serious crime than murder.

In 1881 the population of Tabiteuea South was almost wiped out by an army from Tabiteuea North, organized by a pair of Protestant Hawaiian missionaries desirous of spreading their faith by force. Most of the inhabitants of the atoll are now Catholic! This 72-km-long island, 294 km southeast of Tarawa, is the longest in Tungaru. Rest houses are at Utiroa, near the airstrip on Tabiteuea North, and at Buariki, near the airstrip on Tabiteuea South. Tabiteuea is known for its dancers.

TABITEUEA

Onotoa

Onotoa is named for six giants who created the island by throwing stones into the sea. Its houses and *maneaba* are still built on coral slabs. A lot of land has been reclaimed from the lagoon by building coral walls around an area, then filling it in with broken shells, coconut husks, etc. There's no causeway to the southernmost islands of the atoll, so you must wade at low tide or borrow a canoe. The postman delivers mail to the southern villages once a week and he might give you a lift. The rest house is at Buraitan, seven km southeast of the airstrip. The mission truck charges 60 cents for the trip to/from the airstrip if it has already been hired, otherwise $5 for locals and $20 for tourists. The stores are poorly stocked. Ask about bingo games at the Catholic mission.

Beru

The bones of Kourabi, a famous 18th-century Beru warrior, hang in a basket in the Buota Maneaba Atianikarawa, with a huge turtle shell suspended above. Once every eight years they are washed in the ocean, and the villagers celebrate a great feast. The London Missionary Society ran its Tungaru mission from this island for many years. Beru is the only place in Tungaru outside South Tarawa that has electricity. The well-furnished rest house is at Tabukiniberu, a few km northwest of the airstrip. Ships cannot enter the lagoon. Every Tues. evening an informal get-together at the *maneaba* in Tabukiniberu gives visitors and residents the chance to meet and perhaps learn something from one another. Ask the council clerk about this. It can be profoundly boring if you don't speak Kiribati, however.

Others

The three small islands at the southeast end of the Tungaru group, Nikunau, Tamana, and Arorae, are all without central lagoons. To stay at the rest house in Rungata village on Nikunau, see the manager of the co-op. The rest house on Tamana, smallest atoll of the Tungaru group, is cooled by the sea breezes. The deep *babai* pits, about a 15-minute walk northeast of the government center, are impressive. Arorae, 620 km from Tarawa, has a basic rest house opposite the co-op at Taribo, three km south of the airstrip. At the northwest tip of Arorae are seen the Atibu ni Borau, large coral "navigation stones." The ruins of an old village and a cemetery are nearby.

BANABA

Banaba (also known as Ocean Island) is a tiny, six-square-km raised atoll which claims the highest point in Kiribati—86 meters. It lies 450 km southwest of Tarawa, closer to Nauru. Like the latter, it was once rich in phosphates, but from 1900-1979 the deposits were exploited by British, Australian, and New Zealand interests in what is perhaps the best example of a corporate/colonial rip-off in the history of the Pacific islands.

After the Sydney-based Pacific Islands Company discovered phosphates on Nauru and Banaba in 1899, a company official, Albert Ellis, was sent to Banaba in May 1900 to obtain control of the resource. In due course "King" Temate and the other chiefs signed an agreement granting Ellis's firm exclusive rights to exploit the phosphate deposits on Banaba for 999 years in exchange for 50 pounds sterling a year. Of course, the guileless Micronesian islanders had no idea what it was all about.

As Ellis rushed to have mining equipment and moorings put in place, a British naval vessel arrived on 28 Sept. 1901 to raise the British flag, joining Banaba to the Gilbert and Ellice Islands Protectorate. The British Government reduced the term of the lease to a more realistic 99 years and the Pacific Phosphate Company was formed in 1902.

Things ran smoothly until 1909, when the islanders refused to lease the company any

additional land after 15% of Banaba had been stripped of both phosphates and food trees. The British government arranged a somewhat better deal in 1913, but in 1916 changed the protectorate to a colony so the Banabans could not withhold their land again. After WW I the company was renamed the British Phosphate Commission (BPC), and in 1928 the resident commissioner, Sir Arthur Grimble, signed an order expropriating the rest of the land against the Banabans' wishes. The islanders continued to receive their tiny royalty right up until WW II.

On 10 Dec. 1941, with a Japanese invasion deemed imminent, the order was given to blow up the mining infrastructure on Banaba, and on 28 Feb. 1942 a French destroyer evacuated company employees from the island. In August some 500 Japanese

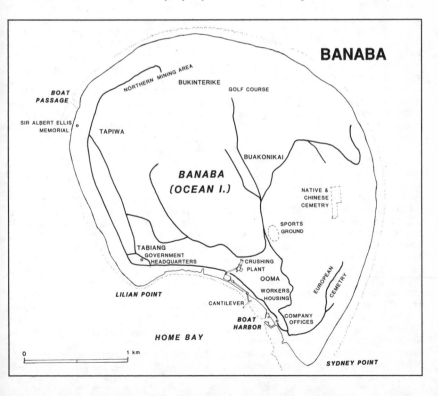

troops and 50 laborers landed on Banaba and began erecting fortifications. The six Europeans they captured eventually perished as a result of their treatment by the Japanese, and all but 150 of the 2,413 local mine laborers and their families present were eventually deported to Tarawa, Nauru, and Kosrae. As a warning the Japanese beheaded three of the locals and used another three to test an electrified anti-invasion fence.

Meanwhile the BPC decided to take advantage of this situation to rid itself of the island's original inhabitants once and for all to avoid any future hindrance to mining operations. In March 1942 the commission purchased Rambi Island off Vanua Levu in Fiji for 25,000 pounds as an alternative homeland for the Banabans. In late Sept. 1945 the British returned to Banaba with Albert Ellis the first to step ashore. Only surrendering Japanese troops were found on Banaba and the local villages had been destroyed.

Two months later an emaciated and wild-eyed Gilbertese man named Kabunare emerged from three months in hiding and told his story to a military court:

We were assembled together and told that the war was over and the Japanese would soon be leaving. Our rifles were taken away. We were put in groups, our names taken, then marched to the edge of the cliffs where our hands were tied and we were blindfolded and told to squat. Then we were shot.

Kabunare either lost his balance or fainted, and fell over the cliff before he was hit. In the sea he came to the surface and kicked his way to some rocks where he severed the string that tied his hands. He crawled into a cave and watched the Japanese pile up the bodies of his companions and toss them into the sea. He stayed in the cave two nights and, after he thought it was safe, made his way inland where he survived on coconuts until he was sure the Japanese had left. Kabunare said he thought the Japanese had executed the others to destroy any evidence of their cruelties and atrocities on Banaba.

As peace returned the British implemented their plan to resettle all 2,000 surviving Banabans on Rambi, which seemed a better place for them than their mined-out homeland. The first group arrived on Rambi on 14 Dec. 1945 and in time they adapted to their mountainous new home and traded much of their original Micronesian culture for that of the Fijians. They and their descendants live there today.

During the 1960s the Banabans saw the much better deal Nauru was getting from the BPC, mainly through the efforts of Hammer DeRoburt and the "Geelong Boys," who were trapped in Australia during the war and thus received an excellent education and understanding of the white man's ways. Thanks to this, the Nauruan leadership was able to hold its own again colonial bullying while the Banabans were simply forgotten on Rambi.

In 1966 Mr. Tebuke Rotan, a Banaban Methodist minister, journeyed to London on behalf of his people to demand reparations from the British for laying waste to their island, a case which would drag on for nearly 20 bitter years. After some 50 visits to the Foreign and Commonwealth offices, he was offered (and rejected) £80,000 sterling compensation. In 1971 the Banabans sued for damages in the British High Court. After a lengthy litigation, the British government in 1977 offered the Banabans an ex gratia payment of A$10 million in exchange for a pledge that there would be no further legal action.

In 1975 the Banabans asked that their island be separated from the rest of Kiribati and joined to Fiji, their present country of citizenship. Kiribati politicians, anxious to protect their fisheries zone and wary of the dismemberment of the country, lobbied against this, and the British rejected the proposal. The free entry of Banabans to Banaba was guaranteed in the Kiribati constitution, however. In 1979 Kiribati obtained independence from Britain and mining on Banaba ended the same year. Finally, in 1981 the Banabans accepted the A$10 million compensation money, plus interest, from the British, though they refused to withdraw their claim to Banaba. The present Kiribati government rejects all further claims from the Banabans, asserting that it's something between them and the British. The British are trying to forget the whole thing.

In 1990 an Australian company studied the viability of restarting phosphate-mining operations on Banaba on a small scale but found the plan unworkable due to the high cost of replacing obsolete equipment and depressed phosphate prices on the world market. It was estimated, however, that there was a potential for profits as high as A$24 million, which would have been shared equally by the company, the Kiribati government, and the Banabans. It's possible this scheme will be revived someday.

A more sinister proposal came from another Australian company, which in 1991 wanted to build an A$12 million treatment plant on Banaba for liquid industrial wastes from Italy. The company said it was willing to pay A$3.5 million a year to dispose of three million tons of the chemicals, the residue from which would be dumped in the island's mined-out interior. The irony that poor, devastated Banaba should have been selected by these unscrupulous opportunists is almost surreal. As yet nothing has been done.

Some 284 people now practice a subsistence life-style on Banaba. There's no airstrip so the only way to get there is on the quarterly supply ship from Tarawa ($25 deck OW). Anyone wishing to spend three months on Banaba must obtain advance permission from the Home Affairs Office in Bairiki (Tarawa), but no permit is required to visit the island for a few hours while the ship is in port.

THE PHOENIX ISLANDS

Archaeological remains indicate that some of the Phoenix and Line islands were once inhabited, probably by Polynesians. By the time the first Europeans arrived, however, these people had died or left. Guano was collected on these islands during the mid-19th century, but the deposits were soon exhausted. Britain annexed the group in 1889, although the U.S. had a vague claim dating from the guano-collecting era.

In 1937 Phoenix was joined to the Gilbert and Ellice Islands colony, and a year later, to reinforce their claim, the British resettled about a thousand people from overcrowded southern Tungaru on Gardner, Hull, and Sydney. Americans visited Kanton and Enderbury in 1938; in 1939, as their value as stopovers on the trans-Pacific aviation route between Fiji and Honolulu became apparent, the two islands were placed under joint British/U.S. administration for 50 years.

By 1952 the strategic value of the islands had declined, and the colonists were undergoing serious difficulties due to saline well water and droughts. They also suffered from isolation and unrealistic expectations. Some returned to Tungaru, but most were taken to the British Solomon Islands Protectorate, where large numbers of them live today. By 1964 all the Phoenix islanders had left.

Kanton
Kanton (Canton) is the largest and most northerly of the Phoenix Group. The 14-km-long lagoon is surrounded by a narrow triangular strip of land, broken only on the west side. Despite strong currents, large ships can enter the lagoon. The island was named for the New Bedford whaling boat *Kanton*, wrecked here in 1854. The 32 survivors sailed from Kanton to Guam in an open boat, a distance of 2,900 nautical miles. (Capt. Bligh's epic, open-boat journey from Tonga to Timor totaled 3,618 nautical miles.)

Pan American Airways used Kanton's lagoon as a stopover for its trans-Pacific seaplanes in the 1930s. In 1938 they built an airstrip on the atoll and cleared the coral heads from a seaplane runway in the lagoon. During WW II the U.S. Air Force built a new airstrip at the island's northwest end. This was maintained as an emergency

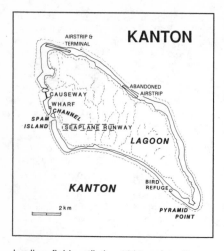

landing field until the 1960s when it was abandoned.

A NASA satellite tracking station established in 1965 closed in 1967, when the island passed to the U.S. Air Force. The unused facilities stand intact on Kanton, taken care of by an I-Kiribati family. An American-built wharf on Kanton is capable of handling large freighters. The U.S. has turned these abandoned facilities over to the Kiribati government, which has fantasies of using them one day for fisheries development.

In 1990 the government installed firefighting equipment and refueling capacity beside Kanton's airstrip to provide emergency landing facilities for flights between Tarawa and Christmas Island. There are no scheduled flights, but Shipping Corporation of Kiribati ships sometimes call on their way to Christmas Island every three months. On the return voyage the ship will bypass Kanton unless there's enough cargo or passengers to be picked up. Ask about this before disembarking or be prepared to pay a substantial "diversion fee" if the ship is forced to return only to evacuate you.

Fauna
Wildlife on Kanton consists mostly of birds, fish, and rats. Large colonies of white fairy terns and red-footed boobies nest on the atoll. Giant hermit crabs are plentiful all over Kanton and, together with the frigate birds, are useful scavengers. Tiny insect-eating lizards dart through the ruins of the U.S. base. A kaleidoscope of tropical fish fills the lagoon: triggerfish, damselfish, pufferfish, parrotfish, sharks, and moray eels.

THE LINE ISLANDS

The five central and southern Line Islands, worked for guano over a century ago, are now uninhabited. None of the five (Malden, Starbuck, Caroline, Vostok, and Flint) has a safe anchorage, although landings have been blasted through the reefs at Starbuck and Flint and an airstrip was built on Malden in 1958 as part of a nuclear-testing program.

Plantation workers live on the three northern Line islands: Fanning, Washington, and Christmas. In 1983 the Kiribati government purchased the coconut plantations on Fanning and Washington from the Australian trading company, Burns Philp, and leased them to the former employees, who produce copra for their cooperative on individual tracts.

The extremely isolated nature of these islands has created serious transportation and administrative problems for the present government, yet a major resettlement program in the Line Islands to relieve the overcrowding on South Tarawa is underway. The deep seabed around the Line Islands contains some of the richest deposits of cobalt, nickel, platinum, and manganese in the world.

Washington

Washington (Tabuaeran) is an oval-shaped island about seven km long with a large freshwater lake surrounded by peat bogs on its eastern side. Washington is the wettest of the Kiribati Line Islands and after heavy rains the lake is drained into the sea through a sluice. Coconut palms cover the island with pandanus in the damper areas. Taro and breadfruit do well on Washington, providing a steady food source. Tangkore and Nanounou villages are at Washington's west end. Landing can be difficult due to strong currents and heavy surf.

Fanning

Fanning (Teraina) is an 18- by 11-km atoll, 285 km northwest of Christmas Island and 140 km southeast of Washington. Three channels lead into the wide lagoon. Discovered by Capt. Edmund Fanning in 1798, the island is 3,000 km east of Tarawa. It was once the mid-ocean station of the undersea cable from Fiji to Vancouver (now closed). Most of the land area is planted with coconuts. The number of seabirds nesting here is limited due to the activities of feral cats. A British six-inch gun was mounted on Fanning during WW II but its present state is unknown. The main village, English Harbor, is on the southwest side of the island.

Visiting yachts are charged $3 a day to anchor at English Harbor in the Fanning lagoon. The Shipping Corporation of Kiribati supply boat visits Fanning three times a year. One-way deck fares are $17 from Christmas, $116 from Tarawa, double fare for a B-class cabin, triple for A class. There's an airstrip on Fanning.

CHRISTMAS ISLAND

This large island—2,100 km southeast of Honolulu, 2,700 km north of Tahiti, and 3,200 km east of Tarawa—accounts for nearly half the

FANNING

NORTH CAPE

FANNING ATOLL

WHALER ANCHORAGE

ENGLISH HARBOR

LAGOON

AIRSTRIP

0   10 km   GREIG POINT

CHRISTMAS ISLAND

land area of Kiribati. Deserted beaches surround the 160-km perimeter, with many small lakes in the interior. The huge tidal lagoon on the island's west side covers 160 square km. Christmas's southeast "panhandle" has no palm trees, only bushes and many seabirds.

Captain Cook discovered the island on Christmas Day 1777; the British annexed it in 1888. (Another Christmas Island, a dependency of Australia, is in the Indian Ocean.) To the locals, it's known as Kiritimati, the Kiribati spelling of Christmas.

During WW II the U.S. built the airport on Christmas to refuel planes flying southwest toward Australia, and from 1956 to 1962 the U.S. and Britain tested nuclear weapons in the atmosphere at Christmas and Malden islands. The British tested their first hydrogen bomb at Malden on 15 May 1957; over the following 15 months they exploded six more, plus two atomic bombs. The British tests blinded millions of seabirds and exposed some 20,000 British servicemen to cancer and other radiation-related diseases; only now, over a quarter of century after the tests ended, many of these men are paying the price of Britain's nuclear arsenal. (For a full examination of the British testing read *Just Testing* by Derek Robinson,

published in 1985 by Collins Harvill, 8 Crafton St., London W1, England.)

In 1962 Britain "loaned" Christmas to the Americans for a crash program of 40 tests, before the Partial Test Ban Treaty with the Soviets came into effect in 1963. One U.S. missile launched from a Polaris submarine off California exploded a half-megaton bomb over the island. Because the bombs went off high in the air over the ocean no measurable radioactivity remains, only a lot of military junk and ruins to explore.

The 1,265 present inhabitants are mostly indentured I-Kiribati laborers employed on the government copra plantation. They live in three villages: London, Banana, and Poland; Paris village has been abandoned. The roads on Christmas date from the testing period, while the airstrip was built during WW II. Ships must anchor off Cook Island; only small punts can enter the lagoon. There's a small wharf at London.

Sights

Large **colonies of seabirds** nest on Cook Island and Motu Tabu; about 18 species of rare migratory birds are found, all very tame. Christmas Island has the world's largest known colony of sooty terns; the eight million birds nest in June and December. Other tame birds nesting on the ground at camera level include noddies, fairy terns, boobies, tropicbirds, frigate birds, wedgetailed shearwaters, and petrels. The seabirds have breeding seasons spread throughout the year, though especially good months to visit are March-July and Oct.-December. It's illegal to hunt them, and possession of birds, nests, eggs, and even feathers is prohibited.

The island swarms with scavenging land crabs and the reefs teem with fish. Christmas Island is famous among sportfishermen/women for the **Pacific bonefish** found on the coral flats of the shallow interior lagoon. The anglers wade out watching for a bonefish, then cast their fly toward it and experience the fight of their lives. Gray sharks are numerous along the drop-off beyond the reef and papio, ulua, waho, marlin, stingrays, and lobster are abundant.

The lee shore between Northwest Point and London is the safest scuba-diving or snorkeling area. It can be dangerous fighting your way through the pounding surf, but the coral "canyons" (surge channels through the reef) teem with fish. Combine a little snorkeling with your visit to the bird sanctuary on Cook Island. The surfing is also good around here (best in January).

At the north end of the island the National Space Development Agency of Japan (NASDA) has a downrange **satellite tracking station,** which controls satellites launched from Tanegashima, Japan, during the early stages of orbit. Thirty Japanese personnel are present. The Japanese government is considering developing a US$8 billion (yes, US$8 *billion)* "nonmilitary" space center on Christmas, complete with a space shuttle, research center, space studies university, hotels, and golf course. A 10-km causeway would lead to a mammoth commercial rocket launcher in the middle of the lagoon. The island's position 190 km north of the equator makes it an ideal satellite launching pad with reduced orbital maneuvering and velocity loss during launches.

Practicalities

Any way you look at it, Christmas Island is expensive. The 36-room **Captain Cook Hotel,** four km northwest of the airstrip, is the only hotel. Formerly a Royal Air Force officers' quarters, its architecture and rates would not be out of place beside a motorway in Britain. All rooms have twin beds and private bath, $80 s or d with a/c, $70 s or d with fan. Fairly expensive American-style food and local fresh fish are served in the dining room. The bar is open every evening, and Mon. night is Island Night with typical food cooked in an *umu* (underground oven). Kiribati dance shows are arranged if a large enough group is present. Airport transfers are $4.20 each way. The Hawaii tour operator lobbied successfully to prohibit camping on the island.

There are plantation stores in all the villages, plus a hospital in London. A large map of the island is available from the Land Development Officer. There are no telephones, local or overseas, nor any telex facilities on Christmas. The hotel will change U.S. cash or traveler's checks, but credit cards are not accepted.

Getting There

Christmas Island has transportation problems. After Air Tungaru suspended its weekly Boeing 727 Tarawa-Christmas-Honolulu service in 1985 due to heavy financial losses, a Honolulu tour operator, CHR Ltd., began offering all-inclusive fishing and birding packages from Hawaii to Christmas using a chartered Aloha Airlines Boeing 737, as part of a joint venture with the Kiribati government. This plane only shuttled back and forth between Hawaii and Christmas and Kiribati citizens wishing to travel from Tarawa to Christmas had to go via Honolulu, where a U.S. visa was required of them.

In 1989 Air Tungaru tried to restart the Tarawa-Christmas-Honolulu service with the same Aloha 737, but the U.S. Federal Aviation Administration (FAA) stipulated that either an alternative airport such as Kanton had to be available for emergencies or a larger aircraft was needed for the four-hour flight from Tarawa to Christmas. The Kiribati government was told that firefighting equipment and refueling capacity had to be installed on Kanton and major improvements carried out at the airports on Christmas and Tarawa. Meanwhile Aloha Airlines discontinued its service to Christmas Island on 27 March 1991.

In May 1991 Air Tungaru attempted to recommence service Honolulu-Christmas-Tarawa (with an extension from Tarawa to Fiji) using a Boeing 737 chartered from Valtec Airlines of Hawaii, but the deal fell through after the first flight when Valtec's owner was arrested in Hawaii for allegedly infringing FAA rules.

Meanwhile the facilities on Kanton were made ready and in Jan. 1992 Air Nauru began a weekly Nauru-Tarawa-Christmas-Honolulu and return service using Air Tungaru's landing rights in Hawaii. Fares are Tarawa-Christmas A$448, Christmas-Honolulu A$404, and Tarawa-Honolulu A$544. This service is heavily subsidized by the Kiribati government, which is hoping air freight will compensate for the lack of passenger traffic, but how long it will last is anyone's guess. Current information should be available from the Honorary Consul of Kiribati in Honolulu, Mr. William E. Paupe (tel. 808-521-7703).

Fishing tours to Christmas Island are offered by **Fish and Game Frontiers** (Box 959, Wexford, PA 15090 U.S.A.; fax 412-935-5388).

The Shipping Corporation of Kiribati has a supply ship from Tarawa to Christmas ($123 deck) every four months to pick up copra. Cabins are double or triple the deck fare. This ship often runs a month late.

Getting Around

To control disturbing the breeding birds, access to some of the seabird areas is restricted. For example, Northwest Point, the area on the ocean side of the road between NASDA and London, is a bird sanctuary and entry is prohibited unless accompanied by a wildlife warden ($200 fine). Escorted boat tours to the accessible reserves, including Cook Island and Motu Tabu, can be arranged at the hotel. Other activities include visiting the milkfish-rearing ponds, fly-fishing for bonefish (permit $35), shelling on the beaches, and attending beach barbecues.

Other breeding areas can be reached by rental Isuzu pickup truck ($75 a day, $450 a week, plus gas), available at the hotel or from **J.M.B. Enterprises** nearby. Collision insurance and unlimited mileage are included in the rates, and your overseas driver's license will be accepted. Motor scooters are also sometimes available. Some of the vehicles are of dubious dependability, and traveling any distance with them is risky. Don't drive a vehicle onto the coral flats, as it will soon sink up to its axles.

CAPSULE KIRIBATI VOCABULARY

mauri—hello
tiabo—goodbye
ko uara?—how are you?
i marurung—I'm fine
kua—tired
taiaoka—please
ko raba—thank you
te raoi—you're welcome
antai aram?—what's your name?
ko nako mai ia?—where do you come from
iraua am ririki?—how old are you?
katokia ikai—stop here
i kani moi—I'm thirsty
i kan amwarake—I'm hungry
e kangkang te amwarake—the meal is delicious
teutana—a little
teutana riki—a little more
e a tau—that's enough
akea riki—no more
akea—none, nothing
eng—yes
tiaki—no

te ika—fish
kikao—octopus
te iriko—meat
te ben—coconut
te moimotu—drinking coconut
te tongo—fermented coconut milk
kabubu—pandanus drink
te babai—swamp taro
katei ni Kiribati—the Gilbertese way
maneaba—meeting place
boti—place in a *maneaba*
uea—chief
unamane—group of elders
ka-ainga—group of extended families
utu—extended family
batua—eldest male in a *ka-ainga*
unaine—old woman
karimoa—the eldest son
I-Matang—Europeans
riri—woman's coconut leaf skirt
tibuta—woman's shirt-sleeved blouse
baangota—spirit-worshipping place

AMERICAN POSSESSIONS

The United States government claims as possessions a number of scattered islands and atolls on Micronesia's northeast fringe; they're included here due to the many historical and geographical links to the rest of the region. Midway Atoll is part of the Hawaiian Chain, although it's not part of the State of Hawaii. Johnston and Wake atolls are stepping-stones to the Marshalls and Guam. Kingman Reef, Palmyra Atoll, and Jarvis Island are part of the Line Islands (the rest of which are included in the Republic of Kiribati). Howland and Baker are just northwest of Kiribati's Phoenix Islands.

Originally uninhabited, many of these islands came under U.S. sovereignty about the same time as Hawaii and Guam (1898). They were not considered important until after 1935 when some began to be used as aviation stopovers or military bases. Today they're administered by a number of different federal agencies with a fascinating variety of uses. None are open to the public, although yachties often call at Palmyra, and Majuro-bound air passengers may get a glimpse of Johnston. Midway, Johnston, and Wake are restricted military bases, while Howland, Baker, and Jarvis as well as Johnston form the **Pacific Islands National Wildlife Refuge** (Box 50167, Honolulu, HI 96850 U.S.A., tel. 808-541-1201). Entry to the refuges is restricted to scientists and educators, who must obtain a permit signed by the Refuge Manager prior to landing.

In 1990 Congresswoman Pat Saiki of Hawaii introduced a bill in the U.S. Congress which would incorporate Baker, Howland, Jarvis, Kingman, Midway, and Palmyra into the State of Hawaii and annex Wake to Guam. Saiki argued that the insular environments would be better protected under regional control than as wards of remote Washington departments, but a desire to control the island's rich 200-nautical-mile Exclusive Economic Zones was the underlying motive. The bill drew strong protests from the Marshall Islands, which claims Wake (Enenkio) as the northernmost of the Ratak Chain.

MIDWAY

Near the northwest end of the Hawaiian Chain, a full 2,350 km from Oahu, Midway measures 5.2 square km. The 24-km-long barrier reef around this circular atoll encloses two small islands, Sand and Eastern. The name refers to the atoll's position midway between California and Japan. Discovered by Capt. N.C. Brooks of the Hawaiian ship *Gambia* in 1859, the atoll was annexed by the U.S. government in 1867. In 1903 Midway became a station on a now-disused submarine cable and Pan Am China Clippers began stopping here to refuel in 1935. Soil was shipped in from Guam, and Norfolk pines were planted, giving Midway a manicured, military look. Pan Am's hotel is still standing, although dilapidated.

In 1941, on the eve of the Pacific War, an important submarine and air base was completed. The Battle of Midway (3-6 June 1942) marked a turning point of World War II. The large military airstrips built then are still a dominant feature of the atoll. At the outbreak of war most of the installations were on Eastern, but these have been completely abandoned and are now off-limits. After 1943 the runways and other facilities were relocated to Sand, the largest island and the only one presently inhabited.

MIDWAY

ISLET

REEF HOTEL

– N –

CENTER LAGOON

SEAWARD ROADS

LANDING

WELLES HARBOR

BROOKS CHANNEL

EASTERN ISLAND

AIRSTRIPS

SAND ISLAND

0   3km

During the Vietnam War, Midway again became an important naval air station with several thousand residents, but after 1978 the population fell sharply. Since 1903 Midway has been controlled by the U.S. Navy, under the command of Barbers Point Naval Air Station, Hawaii 96862-5050 U.S.A. P-3C Orion antisubmarine warfare (ASW) planes are operated from here. In 1988 approximately 45 military and 250 Thai and Sri Lankan contract personnel maintained the runway and facilities on Sand Island.

Hundreds of thousands of gooney birds (Laysan albatrosses) are also on Sand, protected in a national wildlife refuge. As an experiment a few albatrosses were flown blindfolded to Alaska, San Francisco, Los Angeles, Australia, and other points. Upon release they flew back to Midway within 10 days. Naturalists may visit Midway after obtaining naval security clearance (write: Officer in Charge, Naval Air Facility Midway Island, FPO San Francisco, CA 96516-1200).

Radio station KMTH-FM broadcasts from Midway over 94 MHz 24 hours a day.

WAKE

Wake (Enenkio) is located between Guam and Midway, 1,200 km north of Kwajalein. The three islands of this 6½-square-km atoll—Wilkes, Wake, and Peale—enclose a horseshoe-shaped lagoon, sealed on the northwest side by a barrier reef. The channel between Wilkes and Wake islands, now blocked by a solid-fill causeway, once gave entry to the lagoon. A small-boat harbor presently occupies this channel, but ships over 22 meters must moor to buoys offshore.

Marshallese navigators had long visited uninhabited Enenkio to hunt sea turtles and birds, and Marshallese chiefs came to have facial tattoos applied. Though first sighted by the Spaniard Mendana in 1568, Wake is named for the British sea captain William Wake, who arrived in 1796. In 1840 the atoll was charted by Captain Charles Wilkes of the U.S. Exploring Expedition; Peale Island was named for the expedition's naturalist. The Re-

smoke rising from an American installation on Midway, hit by Japanese aircraft in early June 1942

public of the Marshall Islands now claims the atoll, though the U.S. is unlikely to give it up.

The U.S. annexed Wake in 1898 for use as a cable station. A Pan American Airways refueling base and 48-room transit hotel opened on Peale in 1935 and on 26 Nov. that year the first trans-Pacific airmail service in history stopped off at Wake from Midway, carrying 44,346 letters from San Francisco to Manila. On 3 Dec. the great four-engined Martin M-130 flying boat returned from Manila with 74,719 letters for San Francisco. Fred Noonan, navigator on this first flight, later disappeared over the Pacific with Amelia Earhart (see "Howland," below).

At the outbreak of WW II, 1,200 civilian workers were on Wake just completing a major air and submarine base. On 11 Dec. 1941 a Japanese invasion force was repelled. The construction workers and 523 marines put up a valiant defense against air and sea attacks, but on 23 Dec. 1941 Japanese troops from Kwajalein landed in force. They took Wake after 820 of their men were killed, 333 wounded, and 21 planes and four warships lost (the Americans suffered 120 dead, 49 wounded). Some 1,462 captured Americans were sent to POW camps in China and Japan, where 231 died. After an escape attempt the 98 American civilians still prisoners on Wake on 7 Oct. 1943 were beheaded by order of Rear Admiral Sakai-

bara, who was hanged at Guam for the act in 1947 along with Lt. Commander Tachibana and 14 others.

The Japanese held Wake until the end of the war and attempted to use it as a submarine base, though U.S. air raids soon reduced all structures to rubble. The Wake Island rail was hunted to extinction by the 4,500 bypassed and famished Japanese soldiers, who also captured and consumed 54,000 rats (according to meticulous Japanese records) and thousands of seabirds. Every edible morning glory vine was eaten, the reef was stripped of seaweed, and hand grenade

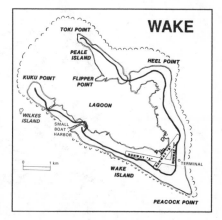

fishermen soon wiped out every fish. Eventually over half the Japanese starved to death and their bodies became fertilizer used in gardens torn apart by bullets from U.S. planes. Eugene Burdick tells the story in "The Puzzle of the Ninety-Eight," in his book *The Blue of Capricorn.*

Today a Japanese midget tank squats outside Air Force Headquarters on Peale, with a couple of rows of Quonsets in back. Other war relics include a Japanese eight-inch gun at Toki Point, a couple of American three-inch guns, numerous machine guns, and bunkers. Four war memorials may be seen on Wake, dedicated to the U.S. Marines, U.S. civilians, the Japanese, and the 98 executed civilian prisoners. One group of ex-POWs occasionally charters a plane to Wake for memorial services (for information write: Chalas Loveland, Survivors of Wake, Guam, and Cavite, Inc., Box 1241, Boise, ID 83701 U.S.A.).

Wake was administered by the U.S. Navy until 1962, when jurisdiction passed to the U.S. Air Force, which controls it today. From 1947 to 1972 the Federal Aviation Administration used Wake as a major refueling stop for trans-Pacific flights but with the development of long-range aircraft Wake became obsolete. In 1975 some 15,000 Vietnamese refugees passed through Wake on their way to the U.S., with some spending up to four months on the atoll. The 3,000-meter runway on Wake is capable of handling the largest aircraft. The facilities are presently maintained by seven Air Force personnel headed by a major, plus 25 American and 152 Thai civilian employees (down from 1,600 during the Vietnam War). Scheduled Military Airlift Command flights from Hickam Air Force Base, Hawaii, call weekly. Wake is more accessible to civilians than Midway and Johnston. Civil aircraft are allowed to land and refuel, but prior permission is required (write Detachment 4, 15th Air Base Wing, APO San Francisco, CA 96501-5000 U.S.A., or contact Hickam Air Force Base).

Radio stations KEAD-AM (1485 kHz) and KEAD-FM (101.2 MHz) broadcast from Wake.

JOHNSTON

Johnston Atoll, 1,324 km southwest of Honolulu, is 19 km around. Its four islets, Johnston, Sand, Akau (North), and Hikina (East), total 2.8 square km and much of the present surface area was created by dredging coral from the lagoon during the early 1960s. Although crew members of the brig *Sally* of Boston first sighted this island in 1796, Capt. Charles James Johnston of HMS *Cornwallis* was the first to land (in 1807). In 1856 John-

A Pan American Airways Martin M-130 at Wake in 1936, the year Pan Am started trans-Pacific passenger service. The first airmail flight from San Francisco to Manila passed through a year earlier.

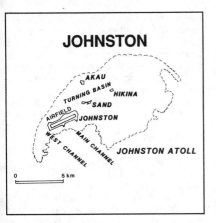

JOHNSTON

AKAU
TURNING BASIN
HIKINA
SAND
AIRFIELD
JOHNSTON
WEST CHANNEL
MAIN CHANNEL
JOHNSTON ATOLL

0   5 km

ston was claimed by both the U.S. and the Kingdom of Hawaii (which called it Kalama Island); that year, an American company began a 50-year extraction of guano. In 1934 the atoll was placed under the U.S. Navy, which transferred it to the Air Force in 1948. Since then the U.S. military has converted this formerly idyllic atoll into one of the most toxic places in the Pacific.

During the late 1950s and early 1960s, high-altitude nuclear testing was carried out at Johnston; in 1958 Air Force planes dropped two H-bombs over the island. Five rockets fired from Johnston in 1962 exploded atomic warheads high above the Pacific. On 9 July of that year the U.S. detonated a nuclear device some 386 km out in space, destroying satellite equipment, disrupting trans-Pacific radio communications for months, and permanently changing earth's Van Allen belts. Atomic Energy Commission Chairman Glenn Seaborg commented at the time: "The results of Starfish (the name of the operation) should have a sobering effect on any who believe that the earth's outer environment could emerge from a full nuclear exchange without severe damage." Already in 1964 the U.S. had nuclear missiles on Johnston capable of shooting down Soviet satellites.

Just in case someone decides to break the 1963 Partial Nuclear Test Ban Treaty with the

U.S.S.R., the U.S. government spends millions of dollars a year maintaining its atmospheric nuclear testing facilities on Johnston on a standby basis.

In 1971 the Army leased an area on Johnston to store thousands of tons of mustard gas, nerve gas, and other chemical warfare weapons left over from the Korean War and held on Okinawa until it reverted to Japanese administration. These were originally to have gone to a military depot in northeastern Oregon but were diverted to Johnston after public protests. In 1977 an incinerator ship burned 17 million liters of the chemical defoliant Agent Orange from Vietnam at Johnston. In 1983 the army began preparations for the incineration of its toxic weapon stockpile held on the island as part of a Johnston Atoll Chemical Agent Disposal System (JACADS). Operations were to have begun on 30 June 1990, with the existing stockpile on Johnston being destroyed initially in a specially built, $260-million incinerator, followed by 435 tons of nerve gas contained in 102,000 artillery shells shipped here in late 1990 from a U.S. base in Germany (together about six percent of the total U.S. stockpile).

Costs have soared and technical difficulties delayed the start-up by over a year, but if JACADS works, similar incinerators may be built at eight sites on the U.S. Mainland as part of a $3.1-billion-dollar scheme to eliminate all obsolete chemical warfare weapons by April 1997. JACADS is linked to an arms control agreement with the former Soviet Union and the technology developed on Johnston will be shared with Russian officials bound to destroy the ex-Soviet chemical warfare arsenal.

These activities drew protests from people around the Pacific who complained that they were once again being exposed to the unpredictable consequences of dangerous military experiments. Fears were raised that the poisons dioxin and furan emitted by the incinerator smokestacks might settle on the ocean surface and enter the food chain and that Johnston could develop into a permanent mid-ocean toxic waste dump for chemical weapons brought from the U.S. mainland (something the U.S. government denies). Critics claim the military hasn't adequately considered the chemical neutralization of these gases and that "quick and dirty" incineration is a mistake. The whole question of weapon destruction on Johnston Atoll has divided advocates of disarmament and environmental protection as never before.

Since 1973 top-secret Johnston has been run for the Defense Nuclear Agency (DNA) by a U.S. Air Force lieutenant colonel, Commander, Johnston Island (address: Johnston Atoll, Field Command, APO San Francisco, CA 96305-5000 U.S.A.). Overall command is exercised from Kirtland Air Force Base in New Mexico (NM 87115-5000 U.S.A.). The population consists of 319 servicemen and 1,010 civilian employees (1990), many of whom work for Raytheon Services Nevada, whose 1991 contract to service the base was worth $17.6 million. All personnel are required to have their gas masks ready. Personnel on "J.I." (as they call it) have been known to go "island happy" and are often sent to Honolulu for "stress seminars." A former commanding officer was shipped out after he ended up in the lagoon attempting to drive off the island in his jeep!

Ironically that portion of the atoll not dedicated to military use is a wildlife refuge under the U.S. Fish and Wildlife Service. President Coolidge designated Johnston a federal bird reserve way back in 1926. Johnston is home to 53 species of birds: wedge-tailed shearwaters, red-footed and brown boobies, red-tailed tropicbirds, sooty terns, brown noddies, and great frigate birds all nest here in abundance. The half-million birds unwittingly foiled a U.S. plot to test biological warfare weapons on Johnston: the migratory fowl might have carried the germs back to the U.S.!

Although some Continental Air Micronesia flights between Honolulu and Majuro touch down on Johnston, nonmilitary passengers are not permitted to disembark. You get to see quite enough of it out the aircraft window—the 1,860-meter runway alone takes up much of the island's surface. Lt. Col. James M. Fowler, Deputy Commander of Johnston Atoll, sent us this: "Due to the active missions on the islands, we will not allow civilian visitors unless they support our operations. As such, we strongly suggest that Johnston not be depicted as a haven for seagoing vessels nor be considered an input to a 'travel guide' since we would deny entry to any such vessel." For more information write: Defense Nuclear Agency, GC 6801 Telegraph, Alexandria, VA 22310-3398 U.S.A.

KINGMAN

Kingman Reef, between Hawaii and Samoa, is a triangular-shaped atoll, the apex of which points northward. On the east side is a barren speck of sand about 40 meters long and only one meter above the high-tide mark. This low

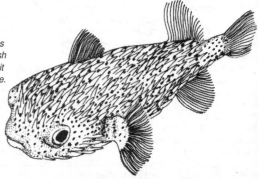

The dozens of sharp spines on the body of the porcupine fish (Diodon holocanthus) make it almost inedible.

profile makes the atoll a navigational hazard. Kingman was discovered by American Capt. Fanning in 1798 but named for Capt. Kingman, who visited in 1853. The U.S. annexed the reef in 1922, and in 1934 turned it over to the Navy, which retains jurisdiction. Pan Am China Clippers bound for New Zealand touched down briefly in the lagoon in 1937-38, but today the Kingman lagoon is abandoned. The only civilian visitors in recent years have been a couple of amateur radio DX-peditions.

Just 250 km northwest of Kingman, within the U.S. Exclusive Economic Zone, is an extinct undersea volcano covered by a two-cm-thick manganese crust containing 2½% cobalt, the richest deposit of its kind ever found. Other rich nickel and platinum deposits lie on the seabed near the Line Islands at depths up to 2,000 meters. As terrestrial de-

posits of these metals are depleted and mining technology develops, this $3 billion worth of metal may become the focus of a major environmental problem. Despite warnings that the millions of tons of released sediment from ocean dredging would devastate marinelife, the Bush administration is pushing ahead with research into ocean-crust strip-mining.

PALMYRA

Palmyra atoll, 53 km southeast of Kingman Reef, is at the north end of the Line Islands, 1,700 km south of Honolulu. The atoll originally consisted of approximately 50 tiny reef islets, which totaled only two square km (now 11.9 square km due to dredging). The barrier reef encloses three distinct lagoons known

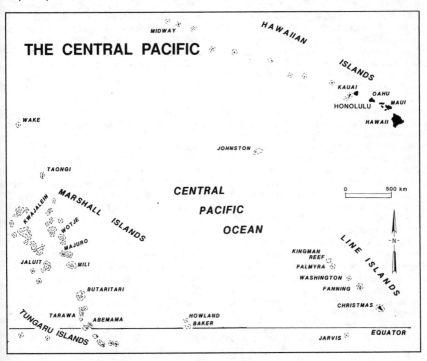

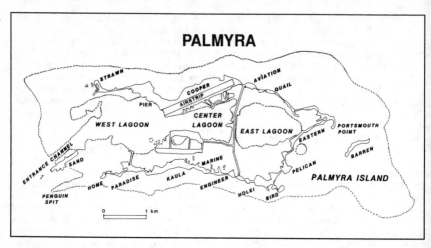

PALMYRA

as West, Center, and East. West Lagoon provides large anchorage areas and can be entered through a narrow dredged channel on the southwest side of the atoll, adjacent to Sand Island. A dredged seaplane landing area connects the West and Center lagoons, while landlocked East Lagoon was cut off by a causeway, now breached.

Fish caught at Palmyra are often poisonous. Several years ago scientists at Tahiti determined that ciguatera (seafood poisoning) was caused by a microalgae called dinoflagellate. Normally these algae are found only in the ocean depths, but when a reef is disturbed, as happened at Palmyra during WW II, they can multiply dramatically in the lagoon and enter the food chain through the fish which feed on them.

A tropical front provoked by the meeting of the northeast and southeast trades brings almost daily rainfall to Palmyra, creating a dense foliage of coconut and balsa-like trees up to 30 meters tall. The humidity is high.

Captain Sawle of the American ship *Palmyra* discovered the atoll in 1802 and it's rumored that Spanish pirates from Peru left buried treasure here in 1816. The Kingdom of Hawaii claimed the atoll in 1862; 36 years later the U.S. annexed it along with the rest

of Hawaii. In 1911 a Judge Cooper of Honolulu acquired title to Palmyra, which he used as a coconut plantation. Before his death in 1929 the judge sold all but tiny Home Island to the Fullard-Leo family of Honolulu. During WW II Palmyra was a 6,000-man naval air station, an important link in the aerial supply route to Canton and Bora Bora in the South Pacific. A 1,800-meter coral airstrip was built on Cooper Island and roads were laid out with causeways connecting most of the islets and islands. A harbor and seaplane landing area were also dredged—transforming the atoll. The sea has now severed the connecting causeways in several places.

Though the U.S. Navy never paid any rent to the Fullard-Leos for the use of Palmyra during the war, in 1947 the U.S. Supreme Court confirmed their private ownership of the atoll. When Hawaii became a state in 1959 Palmyra was specifically excluded and in 1961 President Kennedy placed the uninhabited atoll under the jurisdiction of the U.S. Department of the Interior, where it remains today. In 1979 an American-Japanese scheme to store 30,000 tons of nuclear wastes received considerable publicity but was shelved after strong objections by the Fullard-Leos.

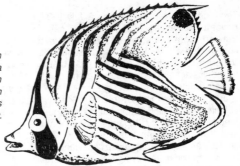

The false eye near the tail of the threadfin butterflyfish (Chaetodon auriga) is a defensive mechanism: a predator's aim might be spoiled if the fish darts off in an unexpected direction. Sharp spines on its back make the butterflyfish hard to swallow.

LOUISE FOOTE

In 1985 a bizarre case unfolded in a San Francisco federal courtroom against one-time yachtie Buck Duane Walker, accused of murdering a wealthy San Diego couple, Muff and Mac Graham, on Palmyra 11 years earlier and stealing their boat, the *Sea Wind*. Oceanographer Norman Sanders, whose craft left Palmyra just prior to the killings, testified that Palmyra "was a place where even the vinyl would rot." Sanders said: "If the 200 inches of rain and rapacious sharks were bad, the culture clash between the hippies and the establishment was worse." Apprehended in Honolulu in late 1974, Walker claimed the victims had been lost during a storm while fishing in their rubber dingy. Then, in 1981, Muff's bones washed ashore in a metal box which was found by a South African yachtsman. Walker, who was already doing time on drug and piracy charges, was convicted and given life imprisonment after a fellow inmate told how he had boasted of making Mac "walk the plank." The full story is in the June 1986 issue of *Pacific Islands Monthly*.

In July 1990 Honolulu realtor Peter Savio (Suite 202, 931 University Ave., Honolulu, HI 96826 U.S.A.; tel. 808-942-7701) leased Palmyra for 75 years from the three Fullard-Leo brothers, with an option to buy the atoll for $36 million. Mr. Savio now has a manager and a team of 16 I-Kiribati laborers housed on Palmyra, and the wartime airstrip has been cleared. Plans call for Palmyra to be developed for "get-away-from-it-all" tourism,

though two-thirds of the atoll will be kept in its natural state. Cruising yachts on their way from Hawaii to the South Pacific have long called here, though Mr. Savio now requires that yachties obtain advance permission from him before doing so. The island's huge wartime rainwater catch-basin is always full.

HOWLAND

Howland Island, 1,150 km east of Tarawa, is only 1.6 square km in area. Pigweed and a few scrawny *kou* trees survive on this dry, flat island 2.4 km long, 890 meters wide, and nowhere over 4.5 meters high. There's no anchorage, but in emergencies small boats can land on the west-side beach. In 1856 the U.S. claimed 48 Pacific islands (15 of them not yet located!) under the Guano Act, including the Northern Cook Islands, Tokelau, part of Tuvalu, and the Phoenix and Line groups. Barren, dry Howland, Baker, and Jarvis were among the islands annexed, and the guano deposits were worked by Americans and British until about 1890. The islands became potentially important as stopovers for trans-Pacific aircraft in the 1930s, and in 1936 American colonists landed on Howland, Baker, and Jarvis to reinforce U.S. claims. Nothing remains on Howland of Itascatown.

In 1937 three dirt airstrips were constructed so that Howland could be used as a refueling stop for Amelia Earhart and Fred Noonan on their around-the-world flight.

They left Lae, New Guinea, on 2 July 1937, never to be seen again. A "lighthouse" called **Earhart Light** in memory of the aviatrix was constructed a year after the loss, some 150 meters inland on the western side of the island. It's actually a day beacon painted with red and white stripes.

Just after Pearl Harbor in Dec. 1941, two colonists were killed during attacks on undefended Howland by Japanese submarines and Kawanishi flying boats from the Marshalls. Although the Japanese didn't land, the remaining colonists were evacuated and the island abandoned for the duration of the war. In 1974 Howland, Baker, and Jarvis were placed under the supervision of U.S. Fish and Wildlife Service; the only inhabitants today are reptiles, crustaceans, green and hawksbill turtles, and about 20 species of seabirds and shorebirds numbering in the millions. Fish and Wildlife makes annual visits to these islands from Hawaii or Samoa, on a Coast Guard ship transiting the area. All three islands have been under the jurisdiction of the U.S. Department of the Interior since 1936.

BAKER

Baker Island, just north of the equator 58 km southeast of Howland, is a flat, oval island of 1.4 square km. Scattered herbs, grass, and low shrubs grace this hot, dry island. A 600-meter-long sandy beach runs along the southwest side, but Baker has no lagoon or anchorage. Feral cats were eradicated on Baker in 1964, and nesting brown noddies are now undisturbed.

In 1839 Capt. Michael Baker of the New Bedford whaler *Gideon Howland* discovered phosphate guano on the island while burying one of his crew and claimed the island for himself and the United States. The American Guano Company later bought his rights and worked the deposits from 1859 to 1878; from 1886 to 1891 a British firm carried the work. In 1935 American colonists landed and founded Meyerton to reassert the U.S. claim, but Japanese air raids following Pearl Harbor prompted their removal in early 1942. The ham radios on both Baker and Howland had been shot up by the Japanese, so the first

Active mostly at night, the fierce-looking leopard moray eel (Lycocontis javanicus) *attacks only when threatened. Since it hides in holes and crevices in rock or coral, this can be done by a diver inadvertently. The flesh of this species is often poisonous to eat.*

rescue-vessel personnel to risk entering the area a few months later were surprised to find any survivors.

On 1 Sept. 1943 Baker was occupied by U.S. forces and an airstrip built using Marston mat (which remains today but is too deteriorated to use). A fighter squadron based on Baker supported bombers flying from Canton and staging through Baker and participated in campaigns in the Gilberts and Marshalls. Howland was used as a target for gunnery practice by Baker-based aircraft; one U.S. airman managed to shoot himself down by flying into bullets ricocheting off the coral surface! A C-47 "Gooney Bird" transport was sent to the rescue. The pilot later returned with a mechanic and spare engine, which they installed to fly the plane back out again (this story supplied by Robert Townsley, Ph.D.). There was also an early loran station on Baker, one of the first facilities to employ this type of electronic navigational aid. After the war the military pulled out.

JARVIS

Jarvis Island is located just below the equator, 400 km southwest of Christmas Island. This saucer-shaped island of coral and sand has an area of only 4.5 square km and no lagoon. The beaches slope steeply to a six-meter-high ridge which entirely surrounds the flat interior. Due to little rainfall, only sparse bunchgrass, prostrate vines, and low shrubs grow. Boat channels cut through the reef on the west and southwest sides of the island lead to landings, but there's no anchorage at Jarvis.

Captain Brown of the English ship *Eliza Francis* discovered Jarvis in 1821. The island has had many names: Brock, Brook, Bunker, Jarvis, and Volunteer. The American Guano Company dug guano from 1858 to 1879. Britain annexed Jarvis in 1889, and leased the island to a London and Melbourne guano company in 1906. Little was extracted and poor-grade deposits remain on the island today. In 1935 the U.S. suddenly landed colonists on Jarvis, who founded Millerville and erected a monument to make a point of the change in ownership. The British didn't respond and the island remains in U.S. hands. A weather station and a radio station were built, but Jarvis was evacuated in 1942 and, except for brief scientific visits, has never been inhabited since.

APPENDIX

INFORMATION AND DIPLOMATIC OFFICES

REGIONAL

Pacific Asia Travel Association, Pacific Division, P.O. Box 645, Kings Cross, NSW 2011, Australia

Pacific Area Travel Association, Micronesia Chapter, 970 South Marine Dr., Ste. 10-PATA, Tamuning, GU 96911 U.S.A.

Office of Territorial and International Affairs, Room 4312, United States Dept. of the Interior, Washington, DC 20240 U.S.A.

Office of Freely Associated States, Dept. of State EAP/FAS, Room 5317, Washington, DC 20520-6310 U.S.A.

MARSHALL ISLANDS

Tourism Office, Box 1727, Majuro, MH 96960 U.S.A.

Embassy of the Marshall Islands, 2433 Massachusetts Ave. NW, Washington, DC 20008 U.S.A.

Permanent Representative of the Marshall Islands to the United Nations, 885 Second Ave., 7th Floor, New York, NY 10017 U.S.A.

Consulate General of the Marshall Islands, 1441 Kapiolani Blvd., Suite 1910, Honolulu, HI 96814 U.S.A.

Embassy of the Marshall Islands, 8th Floor, Ratu Sukuna House, Suva, Fiji Islands

FEDERATED STATES OF MICRONESIA

Dept. of Resources and Development, National Government of the FSM, Capitol Postal Station, Box 12, Palikir, Pohnpei, FM 96941

Dept. of Conservation and Development, Division of Tourism, Kosrae State Government, Box R & D, Kosrae, FM 96944 U.S.A.

Pohnpei Tourist Commission, Box 66, Kolonia, Pohnpei, FM 96941 U.S.A.

Chuuk Visitors Bureau, Box FQ, Weno, Chuuk, FM 96942 U.S.A.

Office of Tourism, Division of Commerce and Industries, Dept. of Resources and Development, Yap State Government, Box 36, Colonia, Yap, FM 96943 U.S.A.

FSM Information Office, Box 490, Kolonia, Pohnpei, FM 96941 U.S.A.

Embassy of the Federated States of Micronesia, 1725 N St. NW, Washington, DC 20036 U.S.A.

Permanent Representative of the FSM to the United Nations, 820 Second Ave., Suite 800-A, New York, NY 10017 U.S.A.

Federated States of Micronesia Consulate, 3049 Ualena St., Suite 408, Honolulu, HI 96819 U.S.A.

Federated States of Micronesia Consulate, Box 10630, Tamuning, GU 96911 U.S.A.
Embassy of the Federated States of Micronesia, 2nd Floor, Reinanzaka Bldg., 14-2

Akasaka, 1-Chome, Minatu-Ku, Tokyo 107, Japan

Embassy of the Federated States of Micronesia, Box 15493, Suva, Fiji Islands

BELAU

Palau Visitors Authority, Box 256, Koror, PW 96940 U.S.A.

Palau/Washington Liaison Officer, Suite 308, Hall of States, 444 North Capitol St., Washington, DC 20001 U.S.A.

Palau Hawaii Office, 1441 Kapiolani Blvd., Suite 1120, Honolulu, HI 96814 U.S.A.

Palau/Guam Liaison Officer, Box 9457, Agana, GU 96911 U.S.A.

GUAM

Guam Visitors Bureau, Box 3520, Agana, Guam 96910 U.S.A.

Guam Visitors Bureau, The Keating Group Inc., 425 Madison Ave., New York, NY 10017 U.S.A.

Guam Visitors Bureau, Kokusai Building, 3-1-1 Marunouchi, Chiyoda-ku, Tokyo 100, Japan

NORTHERN MARIANAS

Marianas Visitors Bureau, Box 861, Saipan, MP 96950 U.S.A.

Resident Representative, Commonwealth of the Northern Mariana Islands, 2121 R St. NW, Washington, DC 20008 U.S.A.

CNMI Liaison Office, 1221 Kapiolani Blvd.; Suite 348, Honolulu, HI 96814 U.S.A.

CNMI Liaison Office, Box 8366, Tamuning, GU 96911 U.S.A.

KIRIBATI

Kiribati Visitors Bureau, Ministry of Natural Resource Development, Box 251, Bikenibeu, Tarawa, Republic of Kiribati

Tourism Office, Ministry of Line and Phoenix Development, Christmas Island, Republic of Kiribati

BOOKLIST

DESCRIPTION AND TRAVEL

Ashby, Gene. *Pohnpei: An Island Argosy.* Rainy Day Press, Box 574, Pohnpei, FM 96941 U.S.A. A comprehensive summary of the history, flora and fauna, culture, and attractions of Pohnpei. The numerous maps, illustrations, and complete subject index make this a very handy book.

Childress, David Hatcher. *Lost Cities of Ancient Lemuria & the Pacific.* Adventures Unlimited Press, Box 22, Stelle, IL 60919 U.S.A. Childress, the Indiana Jones of Pacific archaeology, defies sharks and man-eating groupers as he dives 30 meters below the Pohnpei lagoon to explore the mysterious basalt columns of a sunken city.

Christian, F.W. *The Caroline Islands.* London: Frank Cass & Co., 1967. Christian's detailed account of his journey through Micronesia in 1896, when Spanish colonial rule was still in place.

Daniken, Erich Von. *Pathways to the Gods: The Stones of Kiribati.* New York: Berkley Books, 1982. To the remote atolls of Kiribati, Von Daniken follows the trail of alien beings who may once have colonized the earth.

Fisher, Jon. *Uninhabited Ocean Islands.* Loompanics Unlimited, Box 1197, Port Townsend, WA 98368 U.S.A. This unique book and Fisher's other work, *The Last Frontiers on Earth,* are essential reading for anyone considering relocating in Micronesia.

Grimble, Sir Arthur. *A Pattern of Islands.* London: John Murray, 1952. Grimble served as British resident commissioner in the Gilberts 1926-1932 and left behind this classic narrative of Kiribati life as he observed it during his first six years there (1914-1920). In the U.S. the same book was published as *We Chose the Islands.* A sequel, *Return to the Islands,* dating from his second tour of duty, appeared in 1957.

Hinz, Earl R. *Landfalls of Paradise: The Guide to Pacific Islands.* Western Marine Enterprises, 3611 Motor Ave., Suite 102, Los Angeles, CA 90034-5748 U.S.A. The only genuine cruising guide to all 32 island groups of Oceania.

Kahn, E.J., Jr. *A Reporter in Micronesia.* New York: Norton, 1966. An account of Kahn's travels through the region before the arrival of jet aircraft.

Kluge, P.F. *The Edge of Paradise: America in Micronesia.* New York: Random House, 1991. Kluge's long association with the region began with the Peace Corps and continued as speechwriter for Lazarus Salii, Belau's second president. This sweeping survey, bursting with vignettes of island players and politicians, is a full-length feature portrait of the place.

Lewis, David. *We, the Navigators.* Honolulu: University of Hawaii Press, 1972. A definitive work on the ancient art of landfinding as practiced by Micronesians.

Nakano, Ann. *Broken Canoe: Conversations & Observations in Micronesia.* St. Lucia, Queensland: Queensland University Press, 1984. A traveler's tale of Micronesia as it was a decade ago.

Nude Pacific Travel Guide. Tahanga Research Assn., Box 8714, La Jolla, CA 92038 U.S.A. Though dedicated to "trying to uncover approximately 60 lands," the coverage of Micronesia is scanty.

Price, Willard. *Pacific Adventure.* New York: John Day, 1936. A rare eyewitness account of Micronesia during the Japanese period. An updated abridgement of the same book appeared in 1944 under the title *Japan's Islands of Mystery,* then again in 1966 as *America's Paradise Lost: The Strange Story of the Secret Atolls.*

Rock, Tim. *Diver's Guide to Guam and Micronesia.* Marine Images, Box 24666 GMF, Guam, GU 96921 U.S.A. Describes scuba sites in Chuuk, Yap, Belau, Guam, and the Northern Marianas.

Segal, Harvey Gordon. *Kosrae: The Sleeping Lady Awakens.* Kosrae: Kosrae Tourist Division, 1989. A 382-page compilation of all kinds of hard-to-obtain background information about the island.

Stanley, David. *South Pacific Handbook.* Chico: Moon Publications, 1992. Covers the South Pacific in the same manner as the book you're reading. There's also *Fiji Islands Handbook* and *Tahiti-Polynesia Handbook,* both by the same author.

Stevenson, Robert Louis. *In the South Seas.* New York: Scribner's, 1901. The author's account of his travels through the Marquesas, Tuamotus, and Gilberts by yacht in the years 1888-90. Stevenson's portrayal of life in the Gilberts is especially intriguing, as it was written just prior to the group's annexation by Britain.

Stewart, William H. *Business Reference Guide to the Commonwealth of the Northern Marianas Islands.* James H. Grizzard, Box 330 CHRB, Saipan, MP 96950 U.S.A. An economic atlas which includes 90 maps and 50 charts.

GEOGRAPHY

Coulter, John Wesley. *The Pacific Dependencies of the United States.* New York: MacMillan, 1957. A comprehensive, though dated, geography of Micronesia.

Couper, Alastair, ed. *The Times Atlas of the Oceans.* New York: Van Nostrand Reinhold, 1983. A superb study of the oceans of the world in their contemporary context.

Freeman, Otis W., ed. *Geography of the Pacific.* New York: John Wiley, 1951. Although somewhat dated, this book does provide a wealth of background information on the islands.

Ridgell, Reilly. *Pacific Nations and Territories.* Honolulu: Bess Press, 1988. One of the few high school geography texts to the region. Bess Press (Box 22388, Honolulu, HI 96822 U.S.A.) also publishes Bruce G. Karolle's *Atlas of Micronesia.*

NATURAL SCIENCES

Amesbury, Steven S., and Robert F. Myers. *Guide to the Coastal Resources of Guam: The Fishes.* Guam: University of Guam Press, 1982. A comprehensive, profusely illustrated handbook, useful to both layman and specialist. Unfortunately a matching volume, *The Corals,* is less accessible, as only scientific terminology is used.

DeLuca, Charles J., and Diana MacIntyre DeLuca. *Pacific Marine Life: A Survey of Pacific Ocean Invertebrates.* Rutland, Vt.: Charles E. Tuttle Co., 1976. An informative 82-page pamphlet.

Engbring, John. *Field Guide to the Birds of Palau.* Illustrated by Takesi Suzuki. Koror: Conservation Office, 1988.

Engbring, John, and Peter Pyle. *Checklist of the Birds of Micronesia.* Hawaii Audubon Society, 212 Merchant St., Suite 320, Honolulu, HI 96813-2922 U.S.A; US$2. This excellent six-page publication lists both the scientific and English names of 244 species. A detailed bibliography and precise sighting information are provided. Hawaii Audubon also sells a Checklist of the Birds of the Mariana Islands (also US$2).

Hargreaves, Bob, and Dorothy Hargreaves. *Tropical Blossoms of the Pacific*. Ross-Hargreaves, Box 11897, Lahaina, HI 96761 U.S.A. A handy 64-page booklet with color photos to assist in identification; a matching volume is titled *Tropical Trees of the Pacific*.

Hinton, A.G. *Shells of New Guinea and the Central Indo-Pacific*. Australia: Jacaranda Press, 1972. A photo guide to shell identification.

Martini, Frederic. *Exploring Tropical Isles and Seas*. Englewood Cliffs, N.J.: Prentice-Hall, 1984. A fine introduction to the natural environment of the islands.

Mayr, Ernst. *Birds of the Southwest Pacific*. Rutland, Vt.: Charles E. Tuttle Co., 1978. A reprint of the 1945 edition.

Merrill, Elmer D. *Plant Life of the Pacific World*. Rutland, Vt.: Charles E. Tuttle Co., 1981. First published in 1945, this handy volume is a useful first reference in a field very poorly covered.

Mitchell, Andrew W. *A Fragile Paradise: Man and Nature in the Pacific*. London: Fontana, 1990. Published in the U.S. by the University of Texas Press under the title *The Fragile South Pacific: An Ecological Odyssey*. Andrew Mitchell, an Earthwatch Europe deputy director, utters a heartfelt plea on behalf of all endangered Pacific wildlife in this brilliant book. Micronesia is only briefly touched upon.

Nelson, Bryan. *Seabirds: Their Biology and Ecology*. New York: A & W Publishers, 1979. A fully illustrated manual.

Pratt, Douglas. *A Field Guide to the Birds of Hawaii and the Tropical Pacific*. Princeton, N.J.: Princeton University Press, 1986. The best of its kind—essential reading for birders.

Tinker, Spencer Wilkie. *Fishes of Hawaii: A Handbook of the Marine Fishes of Hawaii and the Central Pacific Ocean*. Hawaiian Service, Inc., Box 2835, Honolulu, HI 96803 U.S.A. A comprehensive, indexed reference work; US$30.

HISTORY

Burdick, Eugene. *The Blue of Capricorn*. Honolulu: Mutual Publishing, 1986. Chapter three, "The Puzzle of the Ninety-eight," describes the fate of 98 Americans imprisoned by the Japanese on Wake Island during WW II.

Hanlon, David. *Upon a Stone Altar*. Honolulu: University of Hawaii Press, 1988. A history of Pohnpei to 1890 by a person who lived seven years on the island.

Hezel, Rev. Francis X. *The First Taint of Civilization*. Honolulu: University of Hawaii Press, 1983. A History of the Caroline and Marshall islands in precolonial days, 1521-1885.

Hezel, Rev. Francis X., and M.L. Berg, eds. *Micronesia: Winds of Change*. Saipan: Omnibus Social Studies Program of the Trust Territory, 1980. A huge book of readings on Micronesian history intended as a textbook for social studies cultural heritage courses.

Kiribati: Aspects of History. Suva, Fiji: Institute of Pacific Studies, 1984. A collection of papers by 25 I-Kiribati writers.

Lessa, William A. *Drake's Island of Thieves: Ethnological Sleuthing*. Honolulu: University of Hawaii Press, 1975. A fascinating examination of Drake's 1579 visit to Micronesia aboard the *Golden Hinde*.

Meller, Norman. *Constitutionalism in Micronesia*. Honolulu: University of Hawaii Press, 1986. An account of the factors which led to the fragmentation of the Trust Territory of the Pacific Islands.

Nevin, David. *The American Touch in Micronesia*. New York: W.W. Norton, 1977. A story of power, money, and the corruption of a Pacific paradise. Nevin provides good documentation on the U.S. educational system in Micronesia.

Nufer, Harold. *Micronesia Under American Rule: An Evaluation of the Strategic Trustee-*

ship (1947-1977). Hicksville, N.Y.: Exposition Press, 1978. Includes interviews with Micronesians about WW II.

Oliver, Douglas L. *The Pacific Islands*. Honolulu: University of Hawaii Press, 1989. A new edition of the classic 1951 study of the history and economies of the entire Pacific area.

Oliver, Douglas L. *Native Cultures of the Pacific Islands*. Honolulu: University of Hawaii Press, 1988. A text for college-level courses on the precontact societies of Oceania.

Parmentier, Richard J. *The Sacred Remains*. Chicago: University of Chicago Press, 1987. Myth, history, and society in Belau.

Peacock, Daniel J. *Lee Boo of Belau*. Honolulu: University of Hawaii Press, 1987. The story of a 20-year-old island prince taken to London by an English sea captain in 1784.

Peattie, Mark R. *Nan'yo*. Honolulu: University of Hawaii Press, 1988. The rise and fall of the Japanese in Micronesia, 1885-1945.

Sanchez, Pedro C. *Guahan: The History of Our Island*. Guam: Sanchez Publishing, 1989. "Doc" Sanchez's *Complete History of Guam,* a primary source for over two decades, has been carefully updated in this well-illustrated new volume.

Stewart, William H. *Ghost Fleet Of the Truk Lagoon*. Contains 60 photos and maps of the Feb. 1944 bombings, plus considerable general information on Chuuk. Other similarly well-illustrated books from Pictorial Histories Publishing Co. (713 South Third West, Missoula, MT 59801 U.S.A.) include *A Glorious Page In Our History,* about the 1942 battle of Midway, and *Amelia Earhart: What Really Happened at Howland.*

Tetens, Capt. Alfred. *Among the Savages of the South Seas: Memoirs of Micronesia, 1862-1868*. Stanford: Stanford University Press, 1958. The account of a German sea captain in Belau and Yap.

White, Geoffry M., and Lamont Lindstrom, eds. *The Pacific Theater: Island Representations of World War II*. Pacific Islands Monograph Series, No. 8. Honolulu: University of Hawaii Press, 1989. An outstanding portrayal of what the war meant to the indigenous peoples of the Pacific.

PACIFIC ISSUES

Dibblin, Jane. *Day of Two Suns: U.S. Nuclear Testing and the Pacific Islanders*. New York: New Amsterdam Books, 1990. Dibblin links human rights and nuclear disarmament in this provocative review of American military activities past and present in the Marshall Islands.

Firth, Stewart. *Nuclear Playground*. Honolulu: University of Hawaii Press, 1987. The story of the nuclear age in the Pacific.

Garrison, Randall, ed. *Readings on Canada and the South Pacific, 1991*. South Pacific Peoples Foundation, 415-620 View St., Victoria, B.C. V8W 1J6, Canada. This 77-page dossier covers a wide range of issues equally relevant to Micronesia and of concern to everyone.

Johnson, Giff. *Collision course at Kwajalein: Marshall Islanders in the Shadow of the Bomb*. Honolulu: Pacific Concerns Resource Center, 1984. Though rather dated, this referenced study continues to provide useful background information on the effects of past U.S. nuclear testing and present Star Wars research in the Marshall Islands.

Jones, Peter D. *From Bikini to Belau: the nuclear colonization of the Pacific*. War Resisters' International, 55 Dawes St., London SE17 1EL, England. This 40-page pamphlet published by the WRI in 1988 touches on many Pacific issues.

Hayes, Peter, Lyuba Zarsky, and Walden Bello. *American Lake: Nuclear Peril in the Pacific*. Australia: Penguin Books, 1986. How the nuclear buildup in the cause of "peace" fuels the threat of war.

Marshall, Mac, and Leslie B. Marshall. *Silent Voices Speak: Women and Prohibition in Truk*. Belmont, Calif.: Wadsworth Publishing Company, 1990. Fascinating reading for anyone interested in the role of women in Micronesian society and the influence grass-roots community groups can exert on the political process.

Robie, David. *Blood on their Banner.* London: Zed Books, 1989. Robie's incisive account of nationalist struggles in the South Pacific also includes a chapter on Belau. In the U.S. it's available from Zed Books, 171 First Ave., Atlantic Heights, NJ 07716; in Britain from Zed Books, 57 Caledonian Rd., London N1 9BU; in Australia from Pluto Press, Box 199, Leichhardt, NSW 2040. Highly recommended.

Robie, David. *Eyes of Fire: The Last Voyage of the Rainbow Warrior.* Philadelphia: New Society Publishers, 1985. Robie was aboard the Greenpeace protest vessel as the Rongelap islanders were evacuated to Kwajalein. His photos and firsthand account tell the inside story.

Roff, Sue Rabbitt. *Overreaching in Paradise: United States Policy in Palau Since 1945.* The Denali Press, Box 021535, Juneau, AK 99802 U.S.A., 1991. An outstanding new history of the political impasse in Belau.

Walker, Ranginui, and William Sutherland, eds. *The Pacific: Peace, Security & the Nuclear Issue.* London and New Jersey: Zed Books Ltd., 1988. Published as part of the "Studies on Peace and Regional Security" program of the United Nations University, Tokyo. Among the 12 fully-referenced papers is "Kiribati: Russophobia and Self Determination" by Uentabo Neemia.

SOCIAL SCIENCE

Alkire, William H. *An Introduction to the Peoples and Cultures of Micronesia.* Menlo Park, Calif.: Cummings Publishing Co., 1977. An anthropological survey.

Colletta, Nat J. *American Schools for the Natives of Ponape.* Honolulu: University of Hawaii Press, 1980. A study of education and culture change in Micronesia.

Howell, William. *The Pacific Islanders.* New York: Scribner's, 1973. An anthropological study of the origins of Pacific peoples.

Kiribati: A Changing Atoll Culture. Fiji: Institute of Pacific Studies, 1984. A team of 14 I-Kiribati writers examines island life in the context of present-day changes.

Kiste, Robert C. *The Bikinians: A Study in Forced Migration.* Menlo Park, Calif.: Cummings Publishing Co., 1974.

Koch, Gerd. *Material Culture of Kiribati.* Fiji: Institute of Pacific Studies, 1987. The English translation of a classic work; dozens of line drawings of everyday objects.

Ward, Martha C. *Nest in the Wind: Adventures in Anthropology on a Tropical Island.* Prospect Hills, Ill.: Waveland Press, 1989. Ward spent several years managing a scientific research project on Pohnpei in the early 1970s and her very personal account of how she adapted to Pohnpeian ways will make fascinating reading for anyone thinking of "going native" in outback Micronesia.

ART AND LITERATURE

Ashby, Gene, ed. *Micronesian Customs and Beliefs.* Rainy Day Press, Box 574, Kolonia, Pohnpei, FM 96941 U.S.A. A treasure trove of Micronesian legends and traditions, as related by the students of the Community College of Micronesia. This and the volume below are among the only cultural writings by Micronesians presently in print!

Ashby, Gene, ed. *Never and Always: Micronesian Legends, Fables and Folklore.* Rainy Day Press, Box 574, Kolonia, Pohnpei, FM 96941 U.S.A. Another 86 traditional stories by CCM students.

Feldman, Jerome. *The Art of Micronesia.* Honolulu: University of Hawaii Art Gallery, 1986. An exhibition catalog.

Knight, Gerald. *Man This Reef.* Majuro: Micronitor Press, 1982. This translated autobiography of a Marshallese storyteller takes more concentration to read than others of its kind because Knight went out of his way to retain the language patterns and structure of the original. This gives the book its depth and indirectly conveys the Marshallese concept of life.

Luelen, Bernart. *The Book of Luelen.* John L. Fischer, Saul H. Riesenberg, and Marjorie G. Whiting, eds.; Honolulu: University of Hawaii Press, 1977. The old traditions of Pohnpei.

Tator, Elizabeth, ed. *Call of the Morning Bird.* Honolulu: Bishop Museum, 1985. This unique cassette bears the chants and songs of Belau, Yap, and Pohnpei collected by Iwakichi Muranushi in 1936. It's a basic document for the study of Micronesian music.

Te Katake. Fiji: Institute of Pacific Studies. Traditional Kiribati songs.

REFERENCE BOOKS

Douglas, Ngaire, and Norman Douglas, eds. *Pacific Islands Yearbook.* Australia: Angus & Robertson Publishers. Despite the name, a new edition of this authoritative sourcebook has come out about every three years since 1932. Copies may be ordered through *Pacific Islands Monthly,* GPO Box 1167, Suva, Fiji Islands.

Far East and Australasia. London: Europa Publications. An annual survey and directory of Asia and the Pacific. Provides abundant and factual political, social, and economic data; an excellent reference source.

Fry, Gerald W., and Rufino Mauricio. *Pacific Basin and Oceania.* Oxford: Clio Press, 1987. A selective, indexed Pacific bibliography which actually describes the contents of the books, instead of merely listing them.

Goetzfridt, Nicholas J., and William L. Wuerch. *Micronesia 1975-1987: A Social Science Bibliography.* Westport, Conn.: Greenwood Press, 1989.

Jackson, Miles M., ed. *Pacific Island Studies: A Survey of the Literature.* Westport, CT:

Greenwood Press, 1986. In addition to comprehensive listings there are extensive essays which put the most important works in perspective.

Marshall, Mac, and James D. Nason. *Micronesia 1944-1974: A Bibliography of Anthropological and Related Source Materials.* New Haven: Hraf Press, 1975.

Oceania: A Regional Study. Washington, D.C.: U.S. Government Printing Office, 1985; extensive bibliography and index. This 572-page volume forms part of the area handbook series sponsored by the U.S. Army and intended to educate American officials. A comprehensive, uncritical source of background information.

The Pacific Business Telephone Directory. Micronesian Publishing Co., Box 23097, Guam Main Facility, GU 96921 U.S.A. Includes businesses and government listings in the FSM, Belau, Guam, and the Northern Marianas in both alphabetical and classified sections. Revised annually.

Uludong, Francisco T. *American Pacific Business Directory.* Pacific Information Bank, Box 1310, Saipan, MP 96950 U.S.A. A telephone-book-style directory, giving the addresses and phone numbers of businesses, government offices, and organizations throughout Micronesia and American Samoa.

BOOKSELLERS AND PUBLISHERS

Many of the titles listed above are out of print and not available in regular bookstores. Major research libraries should have a few; otherwise, write to the specialized antiquarian booksellers or regional publishers listed below for their printed lists of recycled or hard-to-find books on the Pacific. Sources of detailed topographical maps or navigational charts are provided in the following section.

Alele Museum Booklist. Alele Museum, Box 629, Majuro, MH 96960 U.S.A. A complete mail-order list of books on the Marshall Islands.

Australia, the Pacific and South East Asia. Serendipity Books, Box 340, Nedlands, WA 6009, Australia. The largest stocks of antiquarian, secondhand and out-of-print books on the Pacific in Western Australia.

Boating Books. International Marine Publishing Co., Box 220, Camden, ME 04843 U.S.A. All the books you'll ever need to teach yourself how to sail.

Books from the Pacific Islands. Institute of Pacific Studies, University of the South Pacific, Box 1168, Suva, Fiji Islands. A number of books on Kiribati are included in this 12-page catalog. Their specialty is books about the islands written by the Pacific islanders themselves.

Books, Maps & Prints of Pacific Islands. Colin Hinchcliffe, 12 Queens Staith Mews, York, YO1 1HH, England. An excellent source of antiquarian books, maps, and engravings, mostly on the South Pacific.

Books on Africa, Archaeology & Anthropology, Asia, & Oceania. Michael Graves-Johnston, Bookseller, Box 532, London SW9 0DR, England. Though most of the recycled books in Graves-Johnston's catalog are on the South Pacific, he's still worth a try.

Books & Series in Print. Bishop Museum Press, Box 19000-A, Honolulu, HI 96817-0916 U.S.A. An indexed list of publications on the Pacific available from the Bishop Museum.

Catalogue of Pacific Region Books. Pacific Book House, 17 Park Ave., Broadbeach Waters, Gold Coast, QLD 4218, Australia. A Queensland source of out-of-print books on the Pacific, including many on Micronesia.

Hawaii and Pacific Islands. The Book Bin, 2305 NW Monroe St., Corvallis, OR 97330 U.S.A. (tel. 503-752-0045). An indexed mail-order catalog of hundreds of rare books on the Pacific. If there's a particular book about the Pacific you can't find anywhere, this is the place to try.

Hawaii and the Pacific. University of Hawaii Press, 2840 Kolowalu St., Honolulu, HI

96822 U.S.A. Lists many new and current titles on Micronesia.

Pacificana. Messrs Berkelouw, "Bendooley," Hume Highway, Berrima, NSW 2577, Australia (tel. 048-77-1370). A detailed listing of thousands of rare Pacific titles. Payment of an annual subscription of A$25 entitles one to 25 catalogs a year.

Pacificana. Books of Yesteryear, Box 19, Mosman, NSW 2088, Australia. Another good source of old, fine, and rare books on the Pacific.

Publications Price List. Micronesian Area Research Center, University of Guam, UOG Station, Mangilao, Guam 96923 U.S.A. Reprints or translations of old classics, bibliographical references, and specialized studies all figure in MARC's extensive mail-order list.

Polynesian Bookshop Catalogues. Box 68-446, Newton, Auckland 1, New Zealand. Mostly new books on the South Pacific, but a good starting point for New Zealanders.

The "Nesias" & Down Under: Some Recent Books. The Cellar Book Shop, 18090 Wyoming, Detroit, MI 48221, USA. A wide range of new books on the Pacific.

MAP PUBLISHERS

American Pacific Islands Index. U.S. Geological Survey, NCIC, M/S 532, 345 Middlefield Road, Menlo Park, CA 94025 U.S.A. A complete list of recent topographical maps of Micronesia.

Charts and Publications, United States Pacific Coast Including Hawaii, Guam and the Samoa Islands. National Ocean Service, Distribution Branch (N/CG33), Riverdale, MD 20737-1199 U.S.A. Nautical charts put out by the National Oceanic and Atmospheric Administration (NOAA).

Defense Mapping Agency Catalog of Maps, Charts, and Related Products: Part 2—Hydrographic Products, Volume VIII, Oceania. Defense Mapping Agency Combat Support Center, ATTN: DDCP, Washington, D.C.

20315-0010 U.S.A. For a copy of this complete index and order form for nautical charts of Micronesia send US$2.50.

Index to Topographic Maps of Hawaii, American Samoa, and Guam. Distribution Branch, U.S. Geological Survey, Box 25286, Denver Federal Center, Denver, CO 80225 U.S.A.

Pacific Historical Maps. Economic Service Counsel, Inc., Box 201 CHRB, Saipan, MP 96950 U.S.A. These fascinating tourist maps by William H. Stewart are literally packed with information. Copies are available from local tourist offices.

PERIODICALS

Asian-Pacific Issues News. American Friends Service Committee, 2249 East Burnside, Portland, OR 97214 U.S.A (US$12 a year in the U.S., US$15 overseas). An informative monthly newsletter with good coverage of political events in Belau.

Atoll Research Bulletin. Washington, D.C.: Smithsonian Institution. A specialized journal and inexhaustible source of fascinating information (and maps) on the most remote islands of the Pacific. Consult back issues at major libraries.

Bulletin of Concerned Asian Scholars. 3239 9th St., Boulder, CO 80302-2112 U.S.A. The Volume 18, Number Two, 1986, issue is devoted entirely to the antinuclear movement in the Pacific.

Commodores' Bulletin. Seven Seas Cruising Assn., 521 South Andrews Ave., Suite 10, Fort Lauderdale, FL 33301 U.S.A. (US$29 a year worldwide by surface mail). This monthly bulletin is chock-full of useful information for anyone wishing to tour the Pacific by sailing boat. All Pacific yachties and friends should be Seven Seas associate members!

The Contemporary Pacific. University of Hawaii Press, 2840 Kolowalu St., Honolulu, HI 96822 U.S.A. (published twice a year, annual subscription US$25). Publishes a good mix of articles of interest to both scholars and general readers; the country-by-country "Political Review" in each number is a concise summary of events during the preceding year. Those interested in current topics in Pacific Island affairs should check recent volumes for background information. Recommended.

Earth Island Journal. Earth Island Institute, 300 Broadway, Suite 28, San Francisco, CA 94133, U.S.A. Outstanding coverage of environmental problems, including some relating to the Pacific.

German Pacific Society Bulletin. Feichmayrstr. 25, 8000 München 50, Germany. At DM 70 a year Society membership is a good way for German speakers to keep in touch.

Globe Newsletter. The Globetrotters Club, BCM/Roving, London WC1N 3XX, England. This international travel newsletter, published six times a year provides lots of practical information on how to tour the world "on the cheap." Club membership (US$18 plus a US$5 joining fee) includes a subscription to *Globe*, a globetrotter's handbook, a list of other members, etc. This is *the* club for world travelers.

Globetrotter-Magazin. Postfach, 8023 Zürich, Switzerland. If you can read German, you won't find a more informative travel magazine than this and its companions, *Ticket-Info* and *Travel-Info*, all published quarterly. A subscription to all three is included in the Globetrotter Club membership fee (Fr 20 in Switzerland, DM 20 elsewhere).

Guam & Micronesia Glimpses. Box 8066, Tamuning, GU 96931 U.S.A. (annual subscription US$16 to the U.S., US$20 to Canada, US$32 elsewhere). A quality, quarterly photo magazine with a smorgasbord of articles on Western Pacific themes.

Guam Business News. Box 3191, Agana, GU 96910 U.S.A. An informative newsmagazine published monthly on Guam (US$36 a year).

Hafa, The Magazine of Guam. Local, Inc., Suite 211, Ada Commercial & Professional Center, 130 East Marine Dr., Agana, GU

96910 U.S.A. (monthly, $28 a year). Carries a variety of articles on island life.

Isla, A Journal of Micronesian Studies. Isla Editorial Office, Graduate School and Research, UOG Station, Mangilao, GU 96923 U.S.A. (twice a year, $15 annually).

Journal of Pacific History. Division of Pacific and Asian History, RSPacS, Australian National University, GPO Box 4, Canberra, ACT 2601, Australia (annual subscription US$35). Since 1966 this publication has provided reliable scholarly information on the Pacific. The volume XXI 3-4, 1986 issue includes several scholarly articles on recent events in Micronesia. Outstanding.

Micronesian Investment Quarterly. Box 3867, North Potomac, MD 20885 U.S.A. A newsletter for investors interested in setting up joint ventures. Subscriptions are free to anyone involved in business development in the islands.

Micronesica. The Marine Laboratory, University of Guam, UOG Station, Mangilao, GU 96923 U.S.A. (twice a year, $15). A journal devoted to the natural sciences in Micronesia.

NFIP Bulletin. Jan Symington, 52 Salisbury Road, Crookes, Sheffield S10 1WB, England (£10 a year). This bulletin of Women Working for a Nuclear Free and Independent Pacific appears six times a year.

Pacific Affairs. University of British Columbia, Vancouver, B.C. V6T 1W6, Canada (quarterly, $25 a year). The Vol. 64, No. 1 (Spring, 1991) issue of this journal contains a fascinating article by Joseph E. Fallon, "Federal Policy and U.S. Territories: The Political Restructuring of the United States of America," which attempts to demonstrate that the entire structure of U.S. Government ties to Micronesia is unconstitutional.

Pacific Arts Newsletter. Pacific Arts Foundation, Box 19000-A, Honolulu, HI 96817-0916 U.S.A. (monthly, $20 a year).

Pacific Islands Monthly. GPO Box 1167, Suva, Fiji Islands (annual subscription A$30 to Australia, US$45 to North America, and A$63 to Europe). Founded in Sydney by R.W. Robson in 1930, *PIM* is the granddaddy of regional magazines. In June, 1989, the magazine's editorial office moved from Sydney to Suva.

Pacific Magazine. Box 25488, Honolulu, HI 96825 U.S.A. (every other month; US$15 annual subscription). This business-oriented magazine, published in Hawaii since 1976, will keep you up to date on what's happening around the Pacific, and in Micronesia in particular. The January/February 1990 issue carried an excellent series of articles on Ebeye Island of Kwajalein Atoll.

Pacific News Bulletin. Pacific Concerns Resource Center, Box 489, Petersham, NSW 2049, Australia (A$12 a year in Australia, A$25 a year elsewhere). A 16-page monthly newsletter for use worldwide by members of the Nuclear Free and Independent Pacific Movement.

Pacific Report. Box 25, Monaro Cres. P.O., ACT 2603, Australia (A$120 for six months). This fortnightly newsletter edited by Helen Fraser is very good on Kiribati.

Pacific Research. Research School of Pacific Studies, Coombs Building, Australian National University, GPO Box 4, Canberra, ACT 2601, Australia (A$20 a year). A monthly periodical of the Peace Research Center.

Pacific Studies. Box 1979, BYU-HC, Laie, HI 96762-1294 U.S.A. (quarterly, US$30 a year). Funded by the Polynesian Cultural Center and published by Hawaii's Brigham Young University, this scholarly journal often carries articles on Micronesia.

Skin Diver. Petersen Publishing Co., Circulation Division, 8490 Sunset Blvd., Los Angeles, CA 90069 U.S.A. (annual subscription US$22 in the U.S., C$39 in Canada, and US$36 elsewhere). This monthly magazine carries frequent articles on Micronesian dive sites and facilities.

The Surf Report. Box 1028, Dana Point, CA 92629 U.S.A. (US$35 a year). A monthly summary of worldwide surfing conditions with frequent feature articles on the islands.

Third World Resources. 464 19th St., Oakland, CA 94612-9761 U.S.A. (two-year subscription US$35 to the U.S. and Canada, US$50 overseas). A quarterly review of books, articles, and organizations involved with development issues in the Third World.

Tok Blong SPPF. South Pacific Peoples Foundation of Canada, 415-620 View St., Victoria, B.C. V8W 1J6, Canada ($25 a year). This quarterly of news and views focuses on regional environmental, development, human rights, and disarmament issues. Recommended.

Undercurrent. Atcom Publishing, 2315 Broadway, New York, NY 10024-4397 USA (US$58 a year). A monthly consumer-advocate newsletter with valuable tips on scuba diving conditions and facilities around the world.

The Washington Pacific Report. Pacific House, 1615 New Hampshire Ave. N.W., Suite 400, Washington, DC 20009-2520 U.S.A. (published twice a month, $150 a year, $175 outside the U.S.). An insider's newsletter highlighting the insular Pacific.

AN IMPORTANT MESSAGE

Authors, editors, and publishers wishing to see their publications listed here should send review copies to: David Stanley, c/o Moon Publications Inc., 722 Wall St., Chico, CA 95928 U.S.A.

GLOSSARY

AIDS—Acquired Immune Deficiency Syndrome

archipelago—a group of islands

atoll—a low-lying, ring-shaped coral reef enclosing a lagoon

bai—a traditional Belauan men's meetinghouse

bareboat charter—the chartering of a yacht without crew or provisions

barrier reef—a coral reef separated from the adjacent shore by a lagoon

bêche de mer—sea cucumber; trepang; an edible sea slug

benjo—an overwater toilet

betel nut—the fruit of the Areca palm, chewed together with pepper leaves and a little lime

blackbirder—European recruiter of island labor during the 19th century

breadfruit—a large, round fruit with starchy flesh, grown on a breadfruit tree (*Artocarpus altilis*)

cassava—manioc; a starchy edible root from which tapioca is made

CDW—collision damage waiver; a type of insurance which limits one's liability for damage to a rental car

Chamorro—the indigenous inhabitants of the Mariana Islands

ciguatera—a form of fish poisoning caused by microscopic algae

coastwatchers—Australian intelligence agents who operated behind Japanese lines during WW II, spotting approaching planes and ships

coir—coconut husk sennit used to make rope, etc.

confirmation—A confirmed reservation exists when a supplier acknowledges, either orally or in writing, that a booking has been accepted.

copra—dried coconut meat used in the manufacture of coconut oil, cosmetics, soap, and margarine

coral—a hard, calcareous substance of various shapes, comprised of the skeletons of tiny marine animals called polyps

coral bank—a coral formation over 150 meters long

coral head—a coral formation a few meters across

coral patch—a coral formation up to 150 meters long

cyclone—Also known as a hurricane (in the the U.S.) or typhoon (in the Pacific). A tropical storm which rotates around a center of low atmospheric pressure; it becomes a cyclone when its winds reach 64 knots. In the Northern Hemishere cyclones spin counterclockwise, while south of the equator they move clockwise. The winds of cyclonic storms are deflected toward a low-pressure area at the center, although the "eye" of the cyclone may be calm.

dapal—a Yapese women's meetinghouse

direct flight—a through flight with one or more stops but no change of aircraft, as opposed to a nonstop flight

dugong—a large, plant-eating marine mammal; called a manatee in the Caribbean

ecotourism—a form of tourism which emphasizes the natural environment, participation, and limited impact

EEZ—Exclusive Economic Zone; a 200-nautical-mile offshore belt where a state controls mineral exploitation and fishing rights

endemic—something native to a particular area and existing there only

FAD—fish aggregation device

faluw—a Yapese young men's house

FIT—foreign independent travel; a custom-designed, prepaid tour composed of many individualized arrangements

fringing reef—a reef along the shore of an island

guano—manure of sea birds, used as a fertilizer

guyot—a former atoll, the coral of which couldn't keep up with the rise in sea level

karaoke—video sing-along, in which restaurant or bar customers take the mike and sing words shown on the screen to the accompaniment of recorded music

lagoon—an expanse of water bounded by a reef

latte stones—limestone pillars used as building supports by pre-contact Chamorros

lava lava—a wraparound skirt

leeward—downwind; the shore (or side) sheltered from the wind; as opposed to windward

Loran—Long-Range Aids to Navigation

maneaba—a Kiribati community meetinghouse

mangrove—a tropical shrub with branches that send down roots forming dense thickets along tidal shores

manioc—*see* cassava

matrilineal—a system of tracing descent through the mother's familial line

Melanesia—the high island groups of the western Pacific (Fiji, New Caledonia, Vanuatu, Solomon Islands, Papua New Guinea)

NFIP—Nuclear Free and Independent Pacific

omung—Trukese love potion

OTEC—ocean thermal energy conversion

overbooking—the practice of confirming more seats, cabins, or rooms than are actually available to ensure against no-shows

Pacific rim—the continental land masses and large countries around the fringe of the Pacific

PADI—Professional Association of Dive Instructors

pandanus—screw pine with slender stem and prop roots. Fiber from the sword-shaped leaves is used for weaving.

parasailing—being carried aloft by a parachute pulled behind a speedboat

pass—a channel through a barrier reef, usually with an outward flow of water

passage—an inside passage between an island and a barrier reef

patrilineal—a system of tracing descent through the father's familial line

pebai—a traditional Yapese community meetinghouse

pelagic—relating to the open sea, away from land

Polynesia—divided into Western Polynesia (Tonga and Samoa) and Eastern Polynesia (Tahiti-Polynesia, Cook Islands, Hawaii, Easter Island, and New Zealand)

purse seiner—a tuna fishing boat which encircles fish by using a net that is drawn up like a purse

Quonset hut—a prefabricated, semicircular, metal shelter popular during WW II

rai—Yapese stone money

rain shadow—the dry side of a mountain, sheltered from the windward side

reef—a coral ridge near the ocean surface

sakau—on Pohnpei, a mildly narcotic drink made from the root of the pepper plant; called *kava* in Polynesia

sashimi—edible raw fish; called *poisson cru* in French

scuba—self-contained underwater breathing apparatus

sennit—braided coconut-fiber rope

shareboat charter—a yacht tour for individuals or couples who join a small group on a fixed itinerary

shoal—a shallow sandbar or mud bank

shoulder season—a travel period between high/peak and low/off-peak

SPARTECA—South Pacific Regional Trade and Economic Cooperation Agreement; an agreement which allows certain manufactured goods from Pacific countries duty-free entry to Australia and New Zealand

subduction—the action of one tectonic plate wedging under another

subsidence—geological sinking or settling

tangantangan—a thick brush found in the Mariana Islands

taro—a starchy, elephant-eared tuber *(Colocasia esculenta)*, a staple food of the Pacific islanders

thu—a Yapese male loincloth

toddy—The spathe of a coconut tree is bent to a horizontal position and tightly bound before it begins to flower. The end of the spathe is then split and the sap drips down a twig or leaf into a bottle. Fresh or fermented, toddy *(tuba)* makes an excellent drink.

trade wind—a steady wind blowing toward the equator from either northeast or southeast, depending on the season

trench—an ocean depth marking the point where one tectonic plate wedges under another

tridacna clam—eaten everywhere in the Pacific, its size varies between 10 cm and one meter

tropical storm—a cyclonic storm with winds of 35 to 64 knots

tsunami—a fast-moving wave caused by an undersea earthquake

TTPI—Trust Territory of the Pacific Islands

udoud—Belauan traditional money

vigia—a mark on a nautical chart indicating a dangerous rock or shoal

windward—the point or side on which the wind blows, as opposed to leeward

wunbey—a Yapese stone platform

yam—the starchy, tuberous root of a climbing plant

zories—a Japanese term still used in Micronesia for rubber shower sandals, thongs, flip-flops

ALTERNATIVE PLACE NAMES

Abariringa—Kanton
Babeldaop—Babelthuap
Babelthuap—Babeldaop
Banaba—Ocean Island
Belau—Palau
Bokaak—Taongi
Canton—Kanton
Canton—Abariringa
Christmas—Kiritimati
Chuuk—Truk
Dublon—Tonoas
Ellice Islands—Tuvalu
Emwar—Losap
Enenkio—Wake
Enewetak—Eniwetok
Eniwetok—Enewetak
Fanning—Teraina
Gardner—Nikumaroro
Gilbert Islands—Tungaru
Gilberts—Kiribati
Houk—Pulusuk
Hull—Orana
Jabat—Jabwot
Jabwot—Jabat
Kanton—Canton
Kiribati—Gilberts
Kiritimati—Christmas
Kosrae—Kusaie
Kusaie—Kosrae
Losap—Emwar
Manra—Sydney

Moen—Weno
Mokil—Mwoakilloa
Mwoakilloa—Mokil
Ngatik—Sapwuahfik
Nikumaroro—Gardner
Ocean—Banaba
Onoun—Ulul
Orana—Hull
Palau—Belau
Phoenix—Rawaki
Pis—Pisemwar
Pisemwar—Pis
Pohnpei—Ponape
Ponape—Pohnpei
Pulusuk—Houk
Rawaki—Phoenix
Sapwuahfik—Ngatik
Sydney—Manra
Tabuaeran—Washington
Taongi—Bokaak
Teraina—Fanning
Tonoas—Dublon
Truk—Chuuk
Tungaru—Gilbert Islands
Tuvalu—Ellice Islands
Ulul—Onoun
Waab—Yap
Wake—Enenkio
Washington—Tabuaeran
Weno—Moen
Yap—Waab

INDEX

Page numbers in **boldface** indicate the primary reference; numbers in *italics* indicate
information in captions, illustrations, charts, or maps

A

Abaiang Atoll: 295-297, *295*
Abemama Atoll: 298-299, *298*
accommodations: 41-42; *see
also specific place*
African snail: 202
Agana (Guam): 225-226, *212*
agriculture: 16, 19, 25, 69, 114,
176, 280
Agrihan I.: 3, 252
AIDS: *see* diseases
Aieie Museum (Majuro): 76-77
Ailinglaplap Atoll: 86
ailments: 46-47; prickly heat 46;
airlines: *see specific airline;*
transportation
Air Micronesia: *53;* Chuuk 142;
Guam 222; Kosrae 109;
Kwajalein 88; Marshall Islands
74; Northern Marianas 240;
Pohnpei 128; Rota 259; Tinian
255; Yap 162
Air Marshall Islands: 61, 74-75;
Kirbati 286
Air Nauru: Chuuk 142; Guam
222; Kirbati 286; Kosrae 109;
Nauru 268; Pohnpei 128; Yap
162
Air Tungaru: 61; Bariki 295;
Kirbati 286-287
Alamagan: 252
American Possessions:
309-319; Baker 318-319;
Howland 317-318; Jarvis 319;
Johnston 312-314, *313;*
Kingman 314-315; Midway
310, *310;* Palmyra 315-317,
316; Wake 310-312, *311*
Anatahan I.: 253
Andersen Air Force Base
(Guam): 205, 228
Andesite Line, the: 4
Angaur I.: 196-199, *197*
angelfish: 12
Anibare Bay (Nauru): 272
Ant Atoll: 130-131
Apra Harbor (Guam): 226, 229

Arakabesan I.: 184
Arno Atoll: 83, *83*
arts and crafts: 39-40; *see also
specific place*
Asuncion I.: 253
atolls: 4, 5-6
Australia: 1, 17-18, 36

B

Babeldaop (Belau): 3, **191-193**
Bairiki: *292*
Baker I.: 318-319
Baker, Michael: 318
Balos, Senator Ataji: 92
Banaba Atoll: 3, **300-303;** *301*
Banzai Cliff (Saipan): 243
barracudas: 12, 14, 47, 160
bats: 202
Battle of the Coral Sea: *see*
Coral Sea, Battle of
Battle of the Leyte Gulf: *see*
Leyte Gulf, Battle of
Battle of Midway: *see* Midway,
Battle of
Battle of the Philippine Sea: *see*
Philippine Sea, Battle of
Battle of Tarawa: *see* Tarawa,
Battle of
bauxite: see minerals
Bechiyal (Maap): 157
Belau, Republic of (Palau): 3, 4,
24, **167-199,** *192, 198;*
accommodations 178- 179;
arts and crafts 178; climate
168; economy 176-177; fauna
168-169; government 176;
history 169-176; holidays and
events 178; information 179;
Koror 181-190, *182;* land
167-168; other islands
191-199; people 177-178;
transportation 179-180; visas
179
Belau National Museum: 181,
188
Beru Atoll: 300
betel nuts: 154

Betio I.: 289, *290*
bicycling: 63; *see also specific
place*
Bikenibeu: *294*
Bikini Atoll: 70, **90-91**
Bins, Bedor: 173
biointoxication: 47
Bird Island Lookout (Saipan): 243
birds: 202
Black Coral I.: 120
black pearls: 84
blacktip reef shark: *14*
Bloody Nose Ridge (Peleliu):
194-195
Blue Grotto (Saipan): 243
Blue Hole (Guam): 229
blue sharks: 36
boas: 15
Bonriki Airport: 287
Boo, Prince Lee: 169
breadfruit: 40, *41,* 42, 96, 114,
280, 305
Britain: 1, 17, 276
Brooks, Capt. N.C.: 310
Brum, Joachim de: 85
Buada Lagoon (Nauru): 270
Bush, George: 88, 315
Butaritari I.: 297-298, *297*
butterflyfish: 12
Byron, John: 275

C

Cairo Declaration: 24
camping: 41-42; *see also
specific place*
cancer: *see* diseases
canoeing: 62
Capitol Hill (Saipan): 243
Caroline Islands: 2, 5, 9, 201
Caroline Pacific Air: 61; Chuuk
142; Pohnpei 129
car rentals: 62-63; *see also
specific place*
Catholicism: 85, 163, 169, 275,
280, 299
centipedes: 202
Cetti Bay Overlook (Guam): 226

Chamorros: 17, 38, 233, 237, 238; language 208-209
Charles II (Spain): 232
Chief Quipuha Statue (Guam): 226
cholera: *see* diseases
Christmas I.: 3, **305-308**, *306*
Chuuk (Truk): 3, 4, 24, **132-151,** *133, 148;* accommodations 139-140; crafts 134-135; economy 133-134; entertainment 140; Fefan 145; food 140; the Hall Islands 148; health 135; history 17, 132-133; Houk 150; information 142; the Mortlock Islands 148; Namonuito Atoll 150-151; people 134; Pulap Atoll 150; Puluwat 149-150; services 141; shopping 141; sights 135-139; sports and recreation 140-141; Tol 146-147; Tonoas 144-145; transportation 142-144
Chuuk Ethnographic Exhibition Center (Weno): 135
ciguatera: 47, 73, 316
climate: 9-10; Belau 168; Federated States of Micronesia 97; Guam 201; Kirbati 274; Marshall Islands 65-66; Nauru 260; Northern Marianas 232; Pohnpei 110-111
cobalt: *see* minerals
coconut: 42, 69, 96, 97, 118, 280, 316
College of the Marshall Islands: 71
Colonia (Yap) 155, *161*
colonialism: 17-19
Command Ridge (Nauru): 270
Community College of Micronesia: 33
Compact of Free Association: 98
cone shells: 15
conservation: 9
Continental Air Micronesia: *see* Air Micronesia
Conveyor Belt Theory: 4
Cook, James: 306
Coolidge, Calvin: 314
copra: 69, 70, 98, 165, 278; development of industry 19
coral reefs: 6-9, *7;* exploring a reef 8-9; types 8
Coral Sea, Battle of: 21-22

Cow Town (Saipan): 243
crocodiles: 15, 168
crown-of-thorns starfish: *6*

D
dance: 39-40, 154, 186, 282, 292, 299,
Darwin, Charles: 4
dengue fever: *see* diseases
Denson, Henry E.: 261
De Roburt, Hammer: 262, 263
diabetes: 264
diptheria: *see* diseases
diseases: 47; AIDS 47; biointoxication 47; cancer 46, 94, 306; cholera 47, 73, 135, 286; dengue fever 47, 286; diptheria 47; dysentery 169, 261; elephantiasis *45,* 73; hepatitis 286; leprosy 45; malaria 286; polio 261; radiation sickness 23, 94; tetanus 47, 286; tuberculosis 73; typhoid fever 47, 73, 286; yellow fever 47, 73
documents: 51
dolphins: 12, 36
Double Reef (Guam): 229
driftnets: 36
Dublon, Manuel: 144
D-U-D (Darrit-Uliga-Delap): 69, 76, *79*
dysentery: *see* diseases

E
Earhart, Amelia: 317
Earth Island Institute: 36
Eauripik I.: 164-165
Ebeye (Kwajalein): 88-89
economy: **31-37;** Belau 176-177; Chuuk 133-134; education 33; Federated States of Micronesia 98-99; fishing 33-36; Guam 206-207; Kiribati 278-280; manufacturing 36; Marshall Islands 69-70; Nauru 263; Northern Marianas 236-237; Pohnpei 112-114; tourism 36-37; welfare 32; Yap 153
education: 33
eels: 12, 15
Eisenhower, Dwight D.: 88
Ejit I.: 78
Elato Atoll: 166
elephantiasis: *see diseases*
Elizabeth II: 279

Ellis, Albert: 261
Emidj I.: 86
Enemanet I.: 78
Enewetak Atoll: 4, 91, *91*
Enipein Marine Park (Pohnpei): 118
Enola Gay: 234
Etten Atoll: 145, 147
Exclusive Economic Zones (EEZ): 33, *34,* 70, 98, 207, 274, 309

F
Fairo (Weno): 136
Fais I.: 164
Falealop I.: 164
Fanning Atoll: 305, *305*
Fanning, Edmund: 305
fauna: **11-15;** Belau 168-169; Guam 201-203; marinelife 12-15; Northern Marianas 232; Phoenix Islands 304; reptiles 15
Fearn, John: 261
Federated States of Micronesia: 37, **95-166,** *97;* accommodations 99; Chuuk 132-151, *133, 148;* climate 97; economy 98-99; food 99; government 97-98; holidays 99; Kosrae 101-110, *104;* land 96-97; money 100; people 99; Pohnpei 110-132, *113;* transportation 100; visas 100; Yap 151-166, *156*
Fefan I.: 145
fiestas: Northern Marianas 238-239
fire corrals: 8
fishing industry: **33-36,** 207, 278, 279
flora: **11-15;** Guam 201-203
food: 42; *see also specific place*
Ford, Gerald: 234
Fort San Jose (Guam): 228
Fort Santa Agueda (Guam): 226
Fort Soledad (Guam): 228
Forum Fisheries Agency: 34
Fowler, James M.: 314
Freedom Air: 61, 222; Northern Marianas 240; Tinian 255
FSM capitol complex (Pohnpei): 118

G
Gaan Point (Guam): 226
Gagil-Tomil I.: 157
Gambierdiscus toxicus: 47

geckos: 15
General's Cave (Tonoas): 145
Germany: 1, 17, 67, 86, 112,
  145, 169, 203, 233, 261; copra
  trade 19
Gibbons, Ibedul Yutaka M.: 172
Gilbert Islands: 2, 3, 5, 9
Gilbert, Thomas: 275
golf: *see specific place*
government: Belau 176;
  Federated States of
  Micronesia 97-98; Guam 206;
  Kiribati 278; Marshall Islands
  68-69; Nauru 263; Northern
  Marianas 235; Yap 152-153
greenhouse effect: 6
Greenpeace: 12, *92,* 93
Guam, Territory of: 3, 4, 25, 36,
  37, **200-229,** *227;*
  accommodations 209-216;
  Agana 225-226; camping
  216-217; climate 201;
  economy 206-208;
  entertainment 218; flora and
  fauna: 201-203; food 217-218;
  government 206; history
  203-205; holidays and events
  209; information 221; land
  201; language 208-209;
  military 205-206; people 208;
  scuba diving 228-229;
  services 220-221; shopping
  219-220; sights 225-229;
  sports and recreation 218-219;
  tourism 36; transportation
  221-224; visas 220; volunteers
  221
Guam Commonwealth Act
  (1987): 206
Guam Museum: 225
Guam Territorial Seashore Park:
  226
Guano Act (1856): 276, 317
Gun Beach (Guam): 228

H
Hall Islands: 148
Hall of the Magic Chickens
  (Tonoas): 145
Halsey, Admiral: 22
health: 45-48; ailments 46-47;
  diseases 47; sunburn 46; toxic
  fish 47; vaccinations 47
Helen Reef: 199
hepatitis: *see* diseases
history: **16-28;** Belau 169-176;
  Chuuk 132-133; colonialism

17-19; Guam 203-205;
  Japanese 19; Kiribati 275-278;
  Magellan 17; Marshall Islands
  66-68; the Micronesians 16;
  Nauru 260-263; Northern
  Marianas 232-234; Pohnpei
  111-112; postwar period 24-27;
  WWII 2-24; Yap 151-152
holidays: Marshall Islands 71-72;
  Northern Marianas 239
Houk Atoll: 150
Howland I.: 317-318
hurricanes: 164; *see also*
  typhoons

I
Ibobang (Babeldaop): 191
Ichimantong (Tonoas): 145
Inarajan (Guam): 228
information: 48; *see also specific
  place*
ironwood: 202

J
Jaluit I.: 86, *86*
Japan: 1, **19-24,** 34-35, 36, 37,
  42, 67, 69, 83, 86, 102, 112,
  164, 169, 204; 207, 233-234;
  WWII 20-24, *20*
Japanese Peace Park (Majuro):
  77
Jarvis I.: 319
jellyfish 8
Jesuits: 203
Johnston Atoll: 312-314, *313*
Jones Act: 206
Joy I.: 118-120

K
Kabua, Amata: 67, 69
Kanton I.: 303-304, *304*
Kapingamarangi Atoll: 5, 131-132
karaoke: 218
kayaking: 62
Kayangel Atoll: 193-194, *194*
K-B Bridge (Babeldaop): 191
Kennedy, John F.: 25, 26, 316
Kepirohi Falls (Madolenihmw):
  118
Kingman Reef: 314-315
Kiribati: 1, 6, **273-303,** *276, 296;*
  Abaiang 295-297, *295;*
  Abemama 298-299, *298;*
  accommodations 283-284;
  Banaba 300-303, *301;* Beru
  300; Butaritari 297-298, *297;*
  climate 274; conduct 282;

economy 278-280; food 284;
  government 278; health
  285-286; history 275-278;
  holidays 282; information 286;
  Kuria 298; land 273-274;
  language 281-282; Makin 298,
  297; Marakel 297; Nonouti
  299; Onotoa 300; people
  280-281; Tabiteuea 299, *300;*
  Tarawa 288-295, *288;*
  transportation 286-287; visas
  284-285
Klederman, Bernie: 173
Kolonia (Pohnpei): *115,* 116, 122
Korea: 19, 36
Koror (Belau): 181-190, *182;*
  accommodations 184-186;
  entertainment 186-187; food
  186; information 189; services
  188; shopping 188; sights
  181-184; sports and recreation
  187
Kosrae I.: 3, 5, 9, **101-110,** *104;*
  accommodations 107;
  entertainment 108; food
  107-108; history 101-102;
  information 109; people 102;
  services 109; shopping 109;
  sights 102-107; sports and
  recreation 108; transportation
  109-110
Kosrae Museum: 102
Kosrae Terminal and
  Stevedoring Company: 109
Kotzebue, Otto von: 67
Kuma (Butaritari): 297
Kuop Atoll: 147
Kupwuriso (Pohnpei): 117-118
Kuria I.: 298
Kwajalein Atoll: 3, 4, **86-88,** *87*
Kwajalein Missile Range: 69, 87

L
Lamotrek Atoll: 166
land: **2-10;** atolls 5-6; Belau
  167-168; climate 9-10;
  conservation 9; coral reefs
  6-9; Federated States of
  Micronesia 96-97; Guam 201;
  Kiribati 273-274; Marshall
  Islands 64-65; Nauru 260;
  Northern Marianas 230-231;
  tectonics 4; volcanism 4-5
language: 38-39; Guam
  208-209; Kiribati 281-282;
  Marshall Islands 71
Latte Stone Park (Guam): 225

latte stones: 203
Laulau Beach (Saipan): 244
lava lava skirts: 40, 135, 154
Law of the Sea: 33
League of Nations: 19, 67, 261
Legaspi, Miguel Lopez de: 203
Lelu (Kosrae): 102, *106;* ruins 102-103, *103*
Lelu Hill: 104
Le May, General Curtis: 23
leprosy: *see* diseases
Leyte Gulf, Battle of: 23
libraries: 76, 127, 142, 160, 189, 221
Liduduhniap Falls (Pohnpei): 117
Likiep Atoll: 85
Line Islands: 5, **305-308;** Christmas I. 305-308, *306;* Fanning I. 305, *305;* Washington I. 305
Location (Nauru): 269
Lutke, Fedor: 112

M

Maap I.: 157-158
MacArthur, Douglas A.: 22, 23, 24
Madolenihmw (Pohnpei): 118
Magellan, Ferdinand: 17, 203
mail: 43-44
Majuro: 4, **76-85,** *76;* accommodations 78-80; entertainment 80-81; food 80; health 82; information 82; services 81-82; shopping 81; sights 76-78; sports and recreation 81; transportation 82-83
Majuro Airport: 75
Majuro Bridge: 77
Makin I.: *297,* 298
Malakal I.: 181-184
malaria: *see* diseases
Malekeok (Babeldaop): 193
Malem (Kosrae): 104
Maloelap Atoll: 84, *84*
Managaha I.: 244
manganese: *see* minerals
mangrove swamps: 11, 96, 110
manufacturing: 36
Marakei Atoll: 297
Mariana Islands: 2, 3, 230-259, *231,* 232
Marianas Trench: 4, 201, *231*
marinelife: 12-15

Marshall Islands: 2, 3, 4, 5, 6, 9, 24, **64-94,** *66;* accommodations 72-73; arts and crafts 71; climate 65-66; economy 69-70; food 72-73; government 68-69; health 73; history 66-68; holidays 71-72; information 73-74; land 64-65; language 71; Majuro 76-85, *76;* money 73; people 70-71; the Ratak Chain 76-85; the Relik Chain 86-94; transportation 74-75; visas 73; what to take 74
Marshall, John: 67
Massacre Monument (Guam): 228
Maug I.: 253
Medorm (Babeldaop): 191
Merizo (Guam): 228
Micro Beach (Saipan): 241
Micronesia Institute: 29-30
Micronesian Occupational College: 33
Midway Atoll: 309, 310, *310;* Battle of 22, 310
Mieco Beach (Majuro): 77
Mili Atoll: 83-84
minerals: bauxite 19, 170; cobalt 70, 305; manganese 70, 279, 305, 315; phosphate 112, 164, 170, 197, 260, 261, 269, 278, 279, 300, 303, 305; platinum 70, 305, 315
missionaries: 39, 232, 275
mitmit: 154
Mogmog Atoll: 164
Mokil Atoll: 131
money: 43, 51
monitor lizard: 15
monsoons: 168; *see also* hurricanes; typhoons
moray eels: 47, 160
Mortlock Islands: 148
Mt. Finkol (Kosrae): 101, **105-107**
Mt. Lamlam (Guam): 201, 226
Mt. Mutunte (Kosrae): 105
Mt. Tapochau (Saipan): 244
Mt. Tenjo (Guam): 226
Mt. Tonachau (Weno): 136
Mt. Witipon (Weno): 136
Mwoakilloa: *see* Mokil
mythology: 38, 66, 111, 169, 298, 300

N

Nakagawa, Colonel: 195
Nama I.: 148
Namonuito Atoll: 5, 151-151
Nan Madol I.: *119,* 120-121
native Micronesians: 16; *see also* people
naturalist tours: 60
Nauru International Airport: 269
Nauru, Republic of: 3, 5, **260-272,** *265;* accommodations 266-267; climate 260; conduct 266; economy 263; entertainment 267; food 267; government 263; history 260-263; holidays and events 265; information 268; land 260; people 264-265; services 268; shopping 267-268; sights 269-272; transportation 268-269; visas 268
Nauruans: 264-265; *see also* people
Nekkeng (Babeldaop): 191
New Zealand: 19, 36, 93
Ngadolog Beach (Anguar): 198
Ngardmau (Babeldaop): 193
Ngardok Lake (Babeldaop): 193
Ngatik Atoll: 131
Ngatpang State Office (Babeldaop): 191
Ngchemiangel (Babeldaop): 191
Ngchesar (Babeldaop): 193
Ngermeit Swimming Hole: 196
Ngermid (Belau): 184
Ngirmang, Gabriela: 173
Nimitz, Chester W.: 22
Nitigeia (Majuro): 77
Nixon, Richard M.: 26
Nonouti Atoll: 299
Noonan, Fred: 317-318
Northern Marianas: 9, 24, **230-259;** climate 232; crafts 238; economy 236-237; fauna 232; fiestas 238-239; food 239; government 235; history 232-234; holidays 239; information 240; land 230-231; military 234; people 237-238; Rota 255-259, *256;* Saipan 241-251, *242, 245;* sporting events 239; Tinian 253-255, *242;* transportation 240-241; visas 239-240; waste dumping 234-235

North Field (Tinian): 254
nuclear issues: 25, 70, 90-91,
    313, 316; Belau 170-172;
    Bikini Atoll 70, 92; radiation
    sickness 23; Rongelap 93-93
Nukanap (Weno): 136
Nukuoro: *128*, 131

O

Obyan Beach (Saipan): 244
Oceania: *27*
Oceanic Society Expeditions: 60
O'Connell, James F.: 112
Office of Territorial and
    International Affairs: 29
O'Keefe, David: 152
Okinawa: 23
Okinawa Peach Memorial
    (Saipan): 241
Olikong, Santos: 172
Onari I.: 151
Ono: 151
Onotoa Atoll: 300
Orange Beach: 195
Oroluk Atoll: 131
Our Lady of Lourdes Shrine
    (Saipan): 244

P

Pacific Islands National Wildlife
    Refuge: 309
Pacific Missionary Air: 61;
    Chuuk 142; Pohnpei 128; Yap
    162
Pagan I.: 252
Pakin Atoll: 130
Palau Paradise Air: 61
Paleliu I.: 194-196
Palmyra Atoll: 5, *315-317*, *316*
Palpalap (Pohnpei): 117
pandanus: 96
papaya: 42, 280
Parem I.: 147
Partial Test Ban Treaty: 306
Paseo de Susana Park (Guam):
    226
Peace Corps: 26, 142
Peleliu I.: 194, *195*
people: **38-40;** arts and crafts
    39-40; Belau 177-178; Chuuk
    134; Guam 208-209; Kiribati
    280-281; language 38-39;
    Marshall Islands 70-71
Philippines: 38
Philippine Sea: 201; Battle of 22,
    233

Phoenix Islands: 303-308;
    Kanton 303-304, *304;* fauna
    304
phosphates: *see* minerals
Pingelap Atoll: 131
Pisaris I. : 151
platinum: *see* minerals
Plaza de Espana (Guam): 225
Pohndolap: 116-117
Pohnpei, State of: 3, 9, 24,
    110-132, *113;*
    accommodations 121-124; car
    rentals 129; climate 110-111;
    crafts 116; economy 112-114;
    entertainment 125; food
    124-125; history 111-112;
    outer islands 130-132; people
    114-116; *sakau* 125-126;
    sights 116-121; transportation
    128-130
Pohnpei Agricultural and Trade
    School: 33, 118
Pohnpei Airport: 128
polio: *see* diseases
polyps: 6, 8
Porakiet: 116
Portugal: 17, 169
postal codes: 44
Protestantism: 280
Pulap Atoll: 150
Pulo Anna I.: 199
Puluwat Atoll: 149-150, *150*
Pwisehn Malek (Pohnpei): 118

R

radiation sickness: *see* diseases
Rainbow I.: 120
Rainbow Warrior: 93, 94
Ralik Chain: 86-94; Ailinglaplap
    86; Bikini Atoll 90-91; Ebeye
    88-90; Enewetak Atoll 91-92,
    91; Jaluit 86, *86;* Kwajalein
    86-88, *87;* Rongelap Atoll
    92-94
Ralik-Ratak Democratic Party: 69
Ratak Chain: 76, **83-85;** Arno
    83, *83;* Likiep 85; Maloelap 84,
    84; Mili 83-84; Wotje 84
Reagan, Ronald: 68, 97
Rameliik, Haruo I.: 172, 174
religion: 39
reptiles: 15
ridley turtle: *15*
Ring of Fire: 4, 201
Rock Islands: 168
Rocky Point (Angaur): 198
Rongelap Atoll: 92-94

Rota I.: 4, 230, 255-259, *256;*
    accommodations 257-258;
    entertainment 258; food 258;
    information 259; services 258;
    sights 256-257; Songsong
    255-256, *257;* sports and
    recreation 258; transportation
    259

S

Saavedra, Alvaro de: 67
Sahwariap (Pohnpei): 118
Sahwartik (Pohnpei): 118
Saiki, Pat: 309
Saipan International Airport: 241
Saipan I.: 4, 37, 230, **241-251,**
    242, 245; accommodations
    244-248; entertainment 248-
    249; food 248; information
    250; services 249-250; sights
    241-244; sports and recreation
    249; transportation 250-251;
    tourism 36; volunteers 250
sakau: 125-126
Sakaibara: 311
Salii, Lazarus E.: 172, 174
San Antonio Bridge (Guam): 225
San Jose: *252,* 253-255
San Vitores, Diego Luis de: 203
Sansrik (Kosrae): 104
Sakurakai Memorial (Koror): 184
sashimi: 42
Satawal Atoll: 166
Satawan Atoll: 148
Savio, Peter: 317
School of the Pacific Islands: 30
scorpions: 202
scuba diving: *see specific place*
scuba tours: 58-60
sea anemones: 8
sea cucumbers: 14
sea fans: 8
seals: 36
sea turtles: 15, 36, 108, 160,
    202, 168
sea urchins: 14
Seila Bay lookout (Guam): 226
Settlement (Nauru): 271
Shark Grotto (Guam): 229
sharks: **12-14,** 202
shellfish: 47, 284
Shibasaki, Keiji: 289
skinks: 15
snakes: 15; brown tree snake
    202, 232
snorkeling: *see specific place*
Sokehs Mountain: 116-117

Sokehs Rock: 117
Songsong: *257*
Sonsorol I.: 199
Sorol Atoll: 166
South Pacific Commission: 29
South Pacific Forum Fisheries
    Agency: 29
South Pacific Memorial Park
    (Guam): 228
South Pacific Regional Trade
    and Economic Cooperation
    Agreement: 29, 36
Spain: 17, 38, 67, 169, 275
Spanish-American War: 19, 203
"Star Wars": 87
Stevenson, Robert Louis: 274,
    284, 298
stick charts: 66, 71, *72*
stinging ants: 202
stingrays: 12
stonefish: 14
Sugar King Park (Saipan): 241
Suicide Cliff: Saipan 243; Tinian
    254
sunburn: 46
surfing: Guam 201; *see also*
    specific place
surgeonfish: 47

T
Tabiteuea I.: 299, *300*
Tachogna Beach (Tinian): 254
Taga Beach (Tinian): 254
Taga House (Tinian): 253
Tagachang Beach Park (Guam):
    228
Tagereng Canal: 157
Taiwan: 36
Takaiuh (Madolenihmw): 118
Taleyfac Bridge (Guam): 226
Talofofo Falls Park (Guam): 228
Tamag, John: 157
Tamuning Airport: 221-222
tangan tangan brush: 202
Tapwanu masks: 134, *135*
Tarawa Atoll: 288-295, *288;*
    accommodations 291;
    entertainment 292-293; food
    292; information 294; services
    293-294; shopping 293; sights
    289-290; transportation
    294-295
Tarawa, Battle of: 277
taro: 42, 114, 165, 280, 305
Tarzan Falls (Guam): 228
te babai: 284
tectonics: 4

te karewe: 284
telephone system: 44
tetanus: *see* diseases
Thulle, Abba: 169
Tobi I.: 199
Tobolar Copra Processing Plant
    (Majuro): 77
Tol I.: 146-147, *146*
Tonoas I.: 144-145, *144*
tourism: 36-37, 98, 176, 207, 236
tours: 58-61; naturalist 60; other
    60-61; scuba 58-60; veterans 60
tradewinds: 10
transportation: 52-63; getting
    around 61-63; tours 58-61;
    see also specific place;
    specific transportation
tree snakes: 15; Guam 202;
    Saipan 232
tropical storms: *see* typhoons
tropicbird: 237
Truman, Harry S.: 24, 33
Trust Territory of the Pacific
    Islands: 1, 24, 68, 95, 234
tuberculosis: *see* diseases
tuna: 12, 34, 69, 98, 160
Tuna Treaty: 35
Tunnuk (Weno): 136
turtles: *see* sea turtles
typhoid fever: *see* diseases
typhoons: 10, 201, 97, 150, 166,
    232, 274; *see also* hurricanes

U
Udot I.: 147
Ulithi I.: 164, *164*
Umatac (Guam): 228
United Nations: 24, 28, 68
United States: 36; in Guam
    203-206; in Micronesia 25-30;
    in Northern Marianas 234;
    military presence: 24-25;
    whaling 17-18
University of Guam: 228
Uracas: 253
U.S. Naval Cemetery (Guam):
    226
Utirik I.: 92-94
Utwe (Kosrae): 104-105

V
vaccinations: 47
visas: 43; Belau 179; Kiribati
    284-285; Marshall Islands 73;
    Nauru 268; Northern Marianas
    239-240
volcanism: 3

W
Wake Atoll: 310-312, *311*
Wake, William: 310
Walung (Kosrae): 105
wapeepe: see stick charts
War in the Pacific National
    Historical Park (Guam): 226
Washington: 305
water snakes: 15
Weno I.: 135-143, *136, 138;*
    accommodations 139-140;
    entertainment 140; food 140;
    information 142; services 141;
    shopping 141; sights 135-139;
    sports and recreation 140-141;
    transportation 142-143
West Field Airport (Tinian): 255
whales: 12, *13*, 36
whaling: 17-18, 275
what to take: 48-51
Wichon Falls: 136
Wilkes, Charles: 275, 310
Wilson, Henry: 169
Woleai I.: 165, *165*
Won Pat International Airport:
    223
World War II: *21*, **20-24;** 67, 68,
    76, 84, 86, 102, 112, 116,
    132-133, 170, 204, 229, 241,
    262, 270, 276, 298, 302, 303,
    305, 310, 311,
Wotje Atoll: 84

X
Xavier High School (Weno):
    136-137
Y
Yamamoto, Isoroku: 22
yams: 42
Yap, State of: 4, 24, 36,
    151-166, *156;*
    accommodations 158-159;
    crafts 154; economy 153;
    entertainment 159-160; events
    154; food 159-160;
    government 152-153; history
    151-152; information 160-161;
    outer islands 163-166; people
    153-154; services 160;
    shopping 160; sights 155-158;
    sports and recreation 160;
    transportation 161-163;
Yekula Falls (Kosrae): 104
yellow fever: *see* diseases

THE METRIC SYSTEM

1 inch = 2.54 centimeters (cm)
1 foot = .304 meters (m)
1 mile = 1.6093 kilometers (km)
1 km = .6214 miles
1 fathom = 1.8288 m
1 chain = 20.1168 m
1 furlong = 201.168 m
1 acre = .4047 hectares (ha)
1 sq km = 100 ha
1 sq mile = 2.59 sq km
1 ounce = 28.35 grams
1 pound = .4536 kilograms (kg)
1 short ton = .90718 metric ton
1 short ton = 2000 pounds
1 long ton = 1.016 metric tons
1 long ton = 2240 pounds
1 metric ton = 1000 kg
1 quart = .94635 liters
1 US gallon = 3.7854 liters
1 Imperial gallon = 4.5459 liters
1 nautical mile = 1.852 km

To compute centigrade temperatures, subtract 32 from Fahrenheit and divide by 1.8. To go the other way, multiply centigrade by 1.8 and add 32.

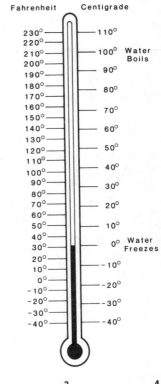

ABOUT THE AUTHOR

A quarter-century ago, David Stanley's right thumb carried him out of Toronto, Canada, and onto a journey which has so far wound through 138 countries, including a three-year trip from Tokyo to Kabul. His travel guidebooks to the South Pacific, Micronesia, Alaska, and Eastern Europe opened those areas to budget travelers for the first time.

During the late 1960s David got involved in Mexican culture by spending a year in several small towns near Guanajuato. Later he studied at the universities of Barcelona and Florence before settling down to get an honors degree (with distinction) in Spanish literature from the University of Guelph, Canada.

In 1978 Stanley linked up with future publisher Bill Dalton and together they wrote the first edition of *South Pacific Handbook* (now in its fifth edition). Since then Stanley has gone on to write additional definitive guides for Moon Publications, including *Fiji Islands Handbook, Micronesia Handbook, Tahiti-Polynesia Handbook,* and *Alaska-Yukon Handbook.* His books informed a generation of budget travelers.

From his base in Amsterdam Stanley makes frequent research trips to the areas covered in his guides, jammed between journeys to the 83 countries and territories world-

David Stanley atop Kosrae's Mt. Finkol

wide he still hasn't visited. To maintain his independence Stanley does not accept subsidized travel arrangements or "freebies" from any source. A card-carrying member of the National Writers Union, in travel writing David Stanley has found a perfect outlet for his restless wanderlust.

Moon Handbooks—The Ideal Traveling Companions

Open a Moon Handbook and you're opening your eyes and heart to the world. Thoughtful, sensitive, and provocative, Moon Handbooks encourage an intimate understanding of a region, from its culture and history to essential practicalities. Fun to read and packed with valuable information on accommodations, dining, recreation, plus indispensable travel tips, detailed maps, charts, illustrations, photos, glossaries, and indexes, Moon Handbooks are ideal traveling companions: informative, entertaining, and highly practical.

To locate the bookstore nearest you that carries Moon Travel Handbooks or to order directly from Moon Publications, call: (800) 345-5473, Monday-Friday, 9 a.m.-5 p.m. PST

The Pacific/Asia Series

BALI HANDBOOK by Bill Dalton
Detailed travel information on the most famous island in the world. 12 color pages, 29 b/w photos, 68 illustrations, 42 maps, 7 charts, glossary, booklist, index. 428 pages.   **$12.95**

BANGKOK HANDBOOK by Michael Buckley
Your tour guide through this exotic and dynamic city reveals the affordable and accessible possibilities. Thai phrasebook, 16 color pages, 55 b/w photos, 30 maps, 19 illustrations, 9 charts, booklist, index. 214 pages.   **$10.95**

BLUEPRINT FOR PARADISE: How to Live on a Tropic Island by Ross Norgrove
This one-of-a-kind guide has everything you need to know about moving to and living comfortably on a tropical island. 8 color pages, 40 b/w photos, 3 maps, 14 charts, appendices, index. 212 pages.   **$14.95**

FIJI ISLANDS HANDBOOK by David Stanley
The first and still the best source of information on travel around this 322-island archipelago. 8 color pages, 35 b/w photos, 78 illustrations, 26 maps, 3 charts, Fijian glossary, booklist, index. 198 pages. **$8.95**

INDONESIA HANDBOOK by Bill Dalton
This one-volume encyclopedia explores island by island the many facets of this sprawling, kaleidoscopic island nation. 30 b/w photos, 143 illustrations, 250 maps, 17 charts, booklist, extensive Indonesian vocabulary, index. 1,000 pages. **$19.95**

MICRONESIA HANDBOOK:
Guide to the Caroline, Gilbert, Mariana, and Marshall Islands by David Stanley
Micronesia Handbook guides you on a real Pacific adventure all your own. 8 color pages, 77 b/w photos, 68 illustrations, 69 maps, 18 tables and charts, index. 300 pages. **$11.95**

NEW ZEALAND HANDBOOK by Jane King
Introduces you to the people, places, history, and culture of this extraordinary land. 8 color pages, 99 b/w photos, 146 illustrations, 82 maps, booklist, index. 546 pages. **$14.95**

OUTBACK AUSTRALIA HANDBOOK by Marael Johnson
Australia is an endlessly fascinating, vast land, and *Outback Australia Handbook* explores the cities and towns, sheep stations, and wilderness areas of the Northern Territory, Western, and South Australia. Full of travel tips and cultural information for adventuring, relaxing, or just getting away from it all. 8 color pages, 39 b/w photos, 63 illustrations, 51 maps, booklist, index. 355 pages. **$15.95**

PHILIPPINES HANDBOOK by Peter Harper and Evelyn Peplow
Crammed with detailed information, *Philippines Handbook* equips the escapist, hedonist, or business traveler with thorough coverage of the Philippines's colorful history, landscapes, and culture. 8 color pages, 2 b/w photos, 60 illustrations, 93 maps, 30 charts, index. 587 pages. **$12.95**

SOUTHEAST ASIA HANDBOOK by Carl Parkes
Helps the enlightened traveler discover the real Southeast Asia. 16 color pages, 75 b/w photos, 11 illustrations, 169 maps, 140 charts, vocabulary and suggested reading, index. 873 pages. **$16.95**

SOUTH KOREA HANDBOOK by Robert Nilsen
Whether you're visiting on business or searching for adventure, *South Korea Handbook* is an invaluable companion. 8 color pages, 78 b/w photos, 93 illustrations, 109 maps, 10 charts, Korean glossary with useful notes on speaking and reading the language, booklist, index. 548 pages. **$14.95**

SOUTH PACIFIC HANDBOOK by David Stanley
The original comprehensive guide to the 16 territories in the South Pacific. 20 color pages, 195 b/w photos, 121 illustrations, 35 charts, 138 maps, booklist, glossary, index. 740 pages. **$15.95**

TAHITI-POLYNESIA HANDBOOK by David Stanley
All five French-Polynesian archipelagoes are covered in this comprehensive guide by Oceania's best-known travel writer. 12 color pages, 45 b/w photos, 64 illustrations, 33 maps, 7 charts, booklist, glossary, index. 235 pages. **$11.95**

THAILAND HANDBOOK by Carl Parkes
Presents the richest source of information on travel in Thailand. Color and b/w photos, illustrations, maps, charts, booklist, glossary, index. 600 pages **$16.95**

TIBET HANDBOOK by Victor Chan
This remarkable book is both a comprehensive trekking guide and a pilgrimage guide that draws on Tibetan literature and religious history. Color and b/w photos, illustrations, maps, charts, booklist, glossary, index. 1,200 pages. **$24.95**

The Hawaiian Series

BIG ISLAND OF HAWAII HANDBOOK by J.D. Bisignani
An entertaining yet informative text packed with insider tips on accommodations, dining, sports and outdoor activities, natural attractions, and must-see sights. 12 color pages, 72 b/w photos, 73 illustrations, 22 maps, 5 charts, booklist, glossary, index. 347 pages. **$11.95**

HAWAII HANDBOOK by J.D. Bisignani
Winner of the 1989 Hawaii Visitors Bureau's Best Guide Book Award and the Grand Award for Excellence in Travel Journalism, this guide takes you beyond the glitz and high-priced hype and leads you to a genuine Hawaiian experience. 12 color pages, 86 b/w photos, 132 illustrations, 86 maps, 44 graphs and charts, Hawaiian and pidgin glossaries, appendix, booklist, index. 879 pages. **$15.95**

KAUAI HANDBOOK by J.D. Bisignani
Kauai Handbook is the perfect antidote to the workaday world. 8 color pages, 36 b/w photos, 48 illustrations, 19 maps, 10 tables and charts, Hawaiian and pidgin glossaries, booklist, index. 236 pages. **$9.95**

MAUI HANDBOOK: Including Molokai and Lanai by J.D. Bisignani
"No fool-'round" advice on accommodations, eateries, and recreation, plus a comprehensive introduction to island ways, geography, and history. 8 color pages, 60 b/w photos, 72 illustrations, 34 maps, 19 charts, booklist, glossary, index. 350 pages. **$11.95**

OAHU HANDBOOK by J.D. Bisignani
A handy guide to Honolulu, renowned surfing beaches, and Oahu's countless other diversions. 12 color pages, 93 b/w photos, 67 illustrations, 18 maps, 8 charts, booklist, glossary, index. 354 pages. **$11.95**

The Americas Series

ALASKA-YUKON HANDBOOK by Deke Castleman and Don Pitcher
Get the inside story, with plenty of well-seasoned advice to help you cover more miles on less money. 8 color pages, 26 b/w photos, 95 illustrations, 92 maps, 10 charts, booklist, glossary, index. 384 pages. **$13.95**

ARIZONA TRAVELER'S HANDBOOK by Bill Weir
This meticulously researched guide contains everything necessary to make Arizona accessible and enjoyable. 8 color pages, 194 b/w photos, 74 illustrations, 53 maps, 6 charts, booklist, index. 505 pages. **$14.95**

BAJA HANDBOOK by Joe Cummings
A comprehensive guide with all the travel information and background on the land, history, and culture of this untamed thousand-mile-long peninsula. 8 color pages, 40 b/w photos, 28 illustratiqns, 41 maps, 29 charts, booklist, index. 356 pages. **$13.95**

BELIZE HANDBOOK by Chicki Mallan
Complete with detailed maps, practical information, and an overview of the area's flamboyant history, culture, and geographical features, *Belize Handbook* is the only comprehensive guide of its kind to this spectacular region. 8 color pages, 65 b/w photos, 43 illustrations, 25 maps, 30 charts, booklist, index. 212 pages. **$11.95**

BRITISH COLUMBIA HANDBOOK by Jane King
With an emphasis on outdoor adventures, this guide covers mainland British Columbia, Vancouver Island, the Queen Charlotte Islands, and the Canadian Rockies. 8 color pages, 56 b/w photos, 45 illustrations, 66 maps, 4 charts, booklist, index. 381 pages. **$13.95**

CANCUN HANDBOOK and Mexico's Caribbean Coast by Chicki Mallan
Covers the city's luxury scene as well as more modest attractions, plus many side trips to unspoiled beaches and Mayan ruins. 12 color pages, 76 b/w photos, 25 illustrations, 24 maps, 12 charts, Spanish glossary, booklist, index. 257 pages. **$10.95**

CATALINA ISLAND HANDBOOK: A Guide to California's Channel Islands
by Chicki Mallan
A complete guide to these remarkable islands, from the windy solitude of the Channel Islands National Marine Sanctuary to bustling Avalon. 8 color pages, 105 b/w photos, 65 illustrations, 40 maps, 32 charts, booklist, index. 245 pages. **$10.95**

COLORADO HANDBOOK by Stephen Metzger
Essential details to the all-season possibilities in Colorado fill this guide. Practical travel tips combine with recreation—skiing, nightlife, and wilderness exploration—plus entertaining essays. 8 color pages, 92 b/w photos, 15 illustrations, 57 maps, 10 charts, booklist, index. 422 pages. **$15.95**

IDAHO HANDBOOK by Bill Loftus
A year-round guide to everything in this outdoor wonderland, from whitewater adventures to rural hideaways. 8 color pages, 35 b/w photos, 21 illustrations, 42 maps, booklist, index. 275 pages. **$12.95**

JAMAICA HANDBOOK by Karl Luntta
From the sun and surf of Montego Bay and Ocho Rios to the cool slopes of the Blue Mountains, author Karl Luntta offers island-seekers a perceptive, personal view of Jamaica. 8 color pages, 21 b/w photos, 35 illustrations, 16 maps, 7 charts, booklist, glossary, index. 213 pages. **$12.95**

MONTANA HANDBOOK by W.C. McRae and Judy Jewell
The wild West is yours with this extensive guide to the Treasure State, complete with travel practicalities, history, and lively essays on Montana life. 8 color pages, 62 b/w photos, 43 illustrations, 49 maps, 10 charts, booklist, index. 393 pages. **$13.95**

NEVADA HANDBOOK by Deke Castleman
Nevada Handbook puts the Silver State into perspective and makes it manageable and affordable. 34 b/w photos, 43 illustrations, 37 maps, 17 charts, booklist, index. 400 pages. **$12.95**

NEW MEXICO HANDBOOK by Stephen Metzger
A close-up and complete look at every aspect of this wondrous state. 8 color pages, 85 b/w photos, 63 illustrations, 50 maps, 10 charts, booklist, index. 375 pages. **$13.95**

NORTHERN CALIFORNIA HANDBOOK by Kim Weir
An outstanding companion for imaginative travel in the territory north of the Tehachapis. 12 color pages, 200 b/w photos, 54 maps, 36 illustrations, booklist, index. 759 pages. **$16.95**

OREGON HANDBOOK by Stuart Warren and Ted Long Ishikawa
Brimming with travel practicalities and insider views on Oregon's history, culture, arts, and activities. 8 color pages, 113 b/w photos, 26 illustrations, 28 maps, 20 charts, booklist, index. 422 pages. **$12.95**

TEXAS HANDBOOK by Joe Cummings
Seasoned travel writer Joe Cummings brings an insider's perspective to his home state. 8 color pages, 79 b/w photos, 60 maps, 45 illustrations, 18 charts, booklist, index. 483 pages. **$13.95**

UTAH HANDBOOK by Bill Weir
Weir gives you all the carefully researched facts and background to make your visit a success. 8 color pages, 102 b/w photos, 61 illustrations, 30 maps, 9 charts, booklist, index. 452 pages. **$12.95**

WASHINGTON HANDBOOK by Dianne J. Boulerice Lyons and Archie Satterfield
Covers sights, shopping, services, transportation, and outdoor recreation, with complete listings for restaurants and accommodations. 8 color pages, 92 b/w photos, 24 illustrations, 81 maps, 8 charts, booklist, index. 433 pages. **$13.95**

WYOMING HANDBOOK by Don Pitcher
All you need to know to open the doors to this wide and wild state. 16 color pages, 30 b/w photos, 42 illustrations, 64 maps, 19 charts, booklist, index. 427 pages. **$12.95**

YUCATAN HANDBOOK by Chicki Mallan
All the information you'll need to guide you into every corner of this exotic land. 8 color pages, 154 b/w photos, 55 illustrations, 57 maps, 70 charts, appendix, booklist, Mayan and Spanish glossaries, index. 391 pages. **$12.95**

The International Series

EGYPT HANDBOOK by Kathy Hansen
An invaluable resource for intelligent travel in Egypt. 8 color pages, 20 b/w photos, 150 illustrations, 80 detailed maps and plans to museums and archaeological sites, Arabic glossary, booklist, index. 510 pages. **$14.95**

MOSCOW-LENINGRAD HANDBOOK by Masha Nordbye

Provides the visitor with an extensive introduction to the history, culture, and people of these two great cities, as well as practical information on where to stay, eat, and shop. 8 color pages, 36 b/w photos, 20 illustrations, 16 maps, 9 charts, booklist, index. 205 pages. **$12.95**

NEPAL HANDBOOK by Kerry Moran

Whether you're planning a week in Kathmandu or months out on the trail, *Nepal Handbook* will take you into the heart of this Himalayan jewel. 16 color pages, 76 b/w photos, 45 illustrations, 46 maps, 9 charts, booklist, glossary, index. 378 pages. **$12.95**

NEPALI AAMA by Broughton Coburn

A delightful photo-journey into the life of a Gurung tribeswoman of Central Nepal. Having lived with Aama (translated, "mother") for two years, first as an outsider and later as an adopted member of the family, Coburn presents an intimate glimpse into a culture alive with humor, folklore, religion, and ancient rituals. 67 b/w photos. 165 pages. **$13.95**

PAKISTAN HANDBOOK by Isobel Shaw

For armchair travelers and trekkers alike, the most detailed and authoritative guide to Pakistan ever published. 28 color pages, 86 maps, appendices, Urdu glossary, booklist, index. 478 pages. **$15.95**

Moonbelts

Made of heavy-duty Cordura nylon, the Moonbelt offers maximum protection for your money and important papers. This all-weather pouch slips under your shirt or waistband, rendering it virtually undetectable and inaccessible to pickpockets. One-inch-wide nylon webbing, heavy-duty zipper, one-inch quick release buckle. Accommodates traveler's checks, passport, cash, photos. Size 5 x 9 inches. Black. **$8.95**

Travel Matters

Travel Matters is a biannual newsletter for travelers, containing book reviews, practical travel news, articles, and humorous essays. For a free copy, call Moon Publications toll-free at (800) 345-5473.

**New travel handbooks may be available that are not on this list.
To find out more about current or upcoming titles,
call us toll-free at (800) 345-5473.**

IMPORTANT ORDERING INFORMATION

FOR FASTER SERVICE: Call to locate the bookstore nearest you that carries Moon Travel Handbooks or order directly from Moon Publications:
   (800) 345-5473 · **Monday-Friday** · **9 a.m.-5 p.m. PST** · **fax (916) 345-6751**

PRICES: All prices are subject to change. We always ship the most current edition. We will let you know if there is a price increase on the book you ordered.

SHIPPING & HANDLING OPTIONS:
   1) Domestic UPS or USPS first class (allow 10 working days for delivery):
      $3.50 for the first item, 50 cents for each additional item.

Exceptions:
   · **Moonbelt** shipping is $1.50 for one, 50 cents for each additional belt.
   · Add $2.00 for same-day handling.
   2) UPS 2nd Day Air or Printed Airmail requires a special quote.
   3) International Surface Bookrate (8-12 weeks delivery):
      $3.00 for the first item, $1.00 for each additional item. Note: Moon Publications cannot guarantee international surface bookrate shipping.

FOREIGN ORDERS: All orders which originate outside the U.S.A. must be paid for with either an International Money Order or a check in U.S. currency drawn on a major U.S. bank based in the U.S.A.

TELEPHONE ORDERS: We accept Visa or MasterCard payments. Minimum order is US $15.00. Call in your order: 1 (800) 345-5473. 9 a.m.-5 p.m. Pacific Standard Time.

WHERE TO BUY THIS BOOK

Bookstores and Libraries:
Moon Publications Handbooks are sold worldwide. Please write our sales manager for a list of wholesalers and distributors in your area that stock our travel handbooks.

Travelers:
We would like to have Moon Publications Handbooks available throughout the world. Please ask your bookstore to write or call us for ordering information. If your bookstore will not order our guides for you, please write or call for a free catalog.

MOON PUBLICATIONS INC.
722 WALL STREET
CHICO, CA 95928 U.S.A.
tel: (800) 345-5473
fax: (916) 345-6751

ORDER FORM

Be sure to call (800) 345-5473 for current prices and editions or for the name of the bookstore nearest you that carries Moon Travel Handbooks · 9 a.m.-5 p.m. PST
(See important ordering information on preceding page)

Name:_____Date:_____

Street:_____

City:_____Daytime Phone:_____

State or Country:_____Zip Code:_____

Quantity	Title	Price

	Taxable Total	
Sales Tax (7.25%) for California Residents		
Shipping & Handling		
TOTAL		

Ship: ☐ 1st class   ☐ UPS (no P.O. Boxes)   ☐ International Surface

Ship to: ☐ address above   ☐ other_____

_____

_____

Make checks payable to:
Moon Publications Inc., 722 Wall Street, Chico, California 95928 U.S.A.
We Accept Visa and MasterCard
To Order: Call in your Visa or MasterCard number, or send a written order with your Visa or MasterCard number and expiration date clearly written.

Card Number: ☐ **Visa**   ☐ **MasterCard**

☐☐☐☐ ☐☐☐☐ ☐☐☐☐ ☐☐☐☐

Exact Name on Card: ☐ same as above   expiration date:_____

☐ other_____

signature_____

3-80-8